Lecture Notes in Computer Science

Lecture Notes in Artificial Intelligence 16708

Founding Editor

Jörg Siekmann

Series Editors

The series Lecture Notes in Artificial Intelligence (LNAI) was established in 1988 as a topical subseries of LNCS devoted to artificial intelligence.

The series publishes state-of-the-art research results at a high level. As with the LNCS mother series, the mission of the series is to serve the international R & D community by providing an invaluable service, mainly focused on the publication of conference and workshop proceedings and postproceedings.

Wen-Chin Li · Anastasios Plioutsias
Editors

Engineering Psychology and Cognitive Ergonomics

23rd International Conference, EPCE 2026
Held as Part of the 28th HCI International Conference, HCII 2026
Montreal, QC, Canada, July 26–31, 2026
Proceedings, Part II

Editors
Wen-Chin Li
Cranfield University
Cranfield, UK

Anastasios Plioutsias
Coventry University
Coventry, UK

ISSN 0302-9743 ISSN 1611-3349 (electronic)
Lecture Notes in Computer Science
ISSN 2945-9133 ISSN 2945-9141 (electronic)
Lecture Notes in Artificial Intelligence
ISBN 978-3-032-29458-6 ISBN 978-3-032-29459-3 (eBook)
https://doi.org/10.1007/978-3-032-29459-3

LNCS Sublibrary: SL7 – Artificial Intelligence

This Springer imprint is published by the registered company Springer Nature Switzerland AG
The registered company address is: Gewerbestrasse 11, 6330 Cham, Switzerland

Foreword

The HCI International (HCII) conference was founded in 1984 by Gavriel Salvendy (Purdue University, USA, Tsinghua University, China, and University of Central Florida, USA) with the first event of the series, "1st USA-Japan Conference on Human-Computer Interaction" held in Honolulu, Hawaii, USA, 18–20 August. Since then, HCI International has been held jointly with several Thematic Areas and Affiliated Conferences, with each one under the auspices of a distinguished international Program Board and under one management and one registration. Twenty-eight HCI International Conferences have been organized so far (every two years until 2013, and annually thereafter).

Since its establishment, the HCII conference has become a hub for presenting groundbreaking research and novel ideas and a forum for collaboration for people from all over the world. Over the years, this conference has served as a platform for scholars, researchers, industry experts, and students to exchange ideas, connect, and address challenges in the ever-evolving HCI field. The conference has evolved, adapting to new technologies and emerging trends, while staying committed to its core mission of advancing knowledge and driving change.

The 28th International Conference on Human-Computer Interaction, HCI International 2026 (HCII 2026), was held during 26–31 July 2026 as an 'on-site' conference at the Montreal Convention Centre, in Montreal, Canada, with the additional option for 'on-line' participation. It incorporated the 21 thematic areas and affiliated conferences listed below.

A total of 7435 individuals from academia, research institutes, industry, and government agencies from 94 countries submitted contributions. 1463 papers and 360 posters (as short research papers) are included in the volumes of the proceedings published just before the start of the conference, presented further below. The contributions thoroughly cover the entire field of human-computer interaction, highlight the evolving role of computers in diverse contexts, and demonstrate how HCI research is shaping and improving user experiences across a wide range of domains, influencing technological progress and its effective integration into various sectors of everyday life.

The HCII conference also offers the option of presenting 'Late Breaking Work', both for papers and posters, with the corresponding proceedings volumes published after the conference. Full papers will be included in the 'HCII 2026 - Late Breaking Papers' volumes of the proceedings to be published in the Springer LNCS series, while 'Poster Extended Abstracts' will be included as short research papers in the 'HCII 2026 - Late Breaking Posters' volumes to be published in the Springer CCIS series.

I would like to thank the Program Board Chairs and the members of the Program Boards of all thematic areas and affiliated conferences for their contribution towards the high scientific quality and overall success of the HCI International 2026 conference. Their manifold support, including paper reviews (via a single-blind review process, with a minimum of two reviews per submission) and session organization, and their willingness to act as goodwill ambassadors for the conference is most highly appreciated.

This conference would not have been possible without the continuous and unwavering support and advice of Gavriel Salvendy, founder, General Chair Emeritus, and Scientific Advisor. For his outstanding efforts, I would like to express my sincere appreciation to Abbas Moallem, Communications Chair and Editor of HCI International News.

July 2026 Constantine Stephanidis

HCI International 2026 Thematic Areas and Affiliated Conferences

- HCI: Human-Computer Interaction Thematic Area
- HIMI: Human Interface and the Management of Information Thematic Area
- EPCE: 23rd International Conference on Engineering Psychology and Cognitive Ergonomics
- AC: 20th International Conference on Augmenting Cognition in the AI-Accelerated Era
- UAHCI: 20th International Conference on Universal Access in Human-Computer Interaction
- CCD: 18th International Conference on Cross-Cultural Design
- SCSM: 18th International Conference on Social Computing and Social Media
- VAMR: 18th International Conference on Virtual, Augmented and Mixed Reality
- DHM: 17th International Conference on Digital Human Modeling & Applications in Health, Safety, Ergonomics & Risk Management
- DUXU: 15th International Conference on Design, User Experience and Usability
- C&C: 14th International Conference on Culture and Computing
- DAPI: 14th International Conference on Distributed, Ambient and Pervasive Interactions
- HCIBGO: 13th International Conference on HCI in Business, Government and Organizations
- LCT: 13th International Conference on Learning and Collaboration Technologies
- ITAP: 12th International Conference on Human Aspects of IT for the Aged Population
- AIS: 8th International Conference on Adaptive Instructional Systems
- HCI-CPT: 8th International Conference on HCI for Cybersecurity, Privacy and Trust
- HCI-Games: 8th International Conference on HCI in Games
- MobiTAS: 8th International Conference on HCI in Mobility, Transport and Automotive Systems
- AI-HCI: 7th International Conference on Artificial Intelligence in HCI
- MOBILE: 7th International Conference on Human-Centered Design, Operation and Evaluation of Mobile Communications

List of Conference Proceedings Volumes Appearing Before the Conference

1. LNCS 16701, Human-Computer Interaction (Part I), edited by Masaaki Kurosu and Ayako Hashizume
2. LNCS 16702, Human-Computer Interaction (Part II), edited by Masaaki Kurosu and Ayako Hashizume
3. LNCS 16703, Human-Computer Interaction (Part III), edited by Masaaki Kurosu and Ayako Hashizume
4. LNCS 16704, Human-Computer Interaction (Part IV), edited by Masaaki Kurosu and Ayako Hashizume
5. LNCS 16705, Human Interface and the Management of Information (Part I), edited by Hirohiko Mori and Yumi Asahi
6. LNCS 16706, Human Interface and the Management of Information (Part II), edited by Hirohiko Mori and Yumi Asahi
7. LNAI 16707, Engineering Psychology and Cognitive Ergonomics (Part I), edited by Wen-Chin Li and Anastasios Plioutsias
8. LNAI 16708, Engineering Psychology and Cognitive Ergonomics (Part II), edited by Wen-Chin Li and Anastasios Plioutsias
9. LNAI 16709, Augmenting Cognition in the AI-Accelerated Era, edited by Dylan D. Schmorrow and Cali M. Fidopiastis
10. LNCS 16710, Universal Access in Human-Computer Interaction (Part I), edited by Margherita Antona and Constantine Stephanidis
11. LNCS 16711, Universal Access in Human-Computer Interaction (Part II), edited by Margherita Antona and Constantine Stephanidis
12. LNCS 16712, Cross-Cultural Design (Part I), edited by Pei-Luen Patrick Rau
13. LNCS 16713, Cross-Cultural Design (Part II), edited by Pei-Luen Patrick Rau
14. LNCS 16714, Cross-Cultural Design (Part III), edited by Pei-Luen Patrick Rau
15. LNCS 16715, Social Computing and Social Media (Part I), edited by Adela Coman and Simona Vasilache
16. LNCS 16716, Social Computing and Social Media (Part II), edited by Adela Coman and Simona Vasilache
17. LNCS 16717, Virtual, Augmented and Mixed Reality (Part I), edited by Jessie Y.C. Chen and Gino Fragomeni
18. LNCS 16718, Virtual, Augmented and Mixed Reality (Part II), edited by Jessie Y.C. Chen and Gino Fragomeni
19. LNCS 16719, Digital Human Modeling and Applications in Health, Safety, Ergonomics and Risk Management (Part I), edited by Vincent G. Duffy
20. LNCS 16720, Digital Human Modeling and Applications in Health, Safety, Ergonomics and Risk Management (Part II), edited by Vincent G. Duffy
21. LNCS 16721, Design, User Experience, and Usability (Part I), edited by Martin Schrepp

22. LNCS 16722, Design, User Experience, and Usability (Part II), edited by Martin Schrepp
23. LNCS 16723, Design, User Experience, and Usability (Part III), edited by Martin Schrepp
24. LNCS 16724, Design, User Experience, and Usability (Part IV), edited by Martin Schrepp
25. LNCS 16725, Culture and Computing (Part I), edited by Matthias Rauterberg
26. LNCS 16726, Culture and Computing (Part II), edited by Matthias Rauterberg
27. LNCS 16727, Distributed, Ambient and Pervasive Interactions (Part I), edited by Norbert A. Streitz and Shin'ichi Konomi
28. LNCS 16728, Distributed, Ambient and Pervasive Interactions (Part II), edited by Norbert A. Streitz and Shin'ichi Konomi
29. LNCS 16729, HCI in Business, Government and Organizations (Part I), edited by Fiona Fui-Hoon Nah and Keng Leng Siau
30. LNCS 16730, HCI in Business, Government and Organizations (Part II), edited by Fiona Fui-Hoon Nah and Keng Leng Siau
31. LNCS 16731, Learning and Collaboration Technologies (Part I), edited by Brian K. Smith and Marcela Borge
32. LNCS 16732, Learning and Collaboration Technologies (Part II), edited by Brian K. Smith and Marcela Borge
33. LNCS 16733, Learning and Collaboration Technologies (Part III), edited by Brian K. Smith and Marcela Borge
34. LNCS 16734, Human Aspects of IT for the Aged Population (Part I), edited by Qin Gao and Jia Zhou
35. LNCS 16735, Human Aspects of IT for the Aged Population (Part II), edited by Qin Gao and Jia Zhou
36. LNCS 16736, Human Aspects of IT for the Aged Population (Part III), edited by Qin Gao and Jia Zhou
37. LNCS 16737, Adaptive Instructional Systems, edited by Robert A. Sottilare and Jessica Schwarz
38. LNCS 16738, HCI for Cybersecurity, Privacy and Trust, edited by Abbas Moallem
39. LNCS 16739, HCI in Games (Part I), edited by Xiaowen Fang
40. LNCS 16740, HCI in Games (Part II), edited by Xiaowen Fang
41. LNCS 16741, HCI in Mobility, Transport and Automotive Systems (Part I), edited by Heidi Krömker
42. LNCS 16742, HCI in Mobility, Transport and Automotive Systems (Part II), edited by Heidi Krömker
43. LNAI 16743, Artificial Intelligence in HCI (Part I), edited by Helmut Degen and Stavroula Ntoa
44. LNAI 16744, Artificial Intelligence in HCI (Part II), edited by Helmut Degen and Stavroula Ntoa
45. LNAI 16745, Artificial Intelligence in HCI (Part III), edited by Helmut Degen and Stavroula Ntoa
46. LNAI 16746, Artificial Intelligence in HCI (Part IV), edited by Helmut Degen and Stavroula Ntoa

47. LNCS 16747, Human-Centered Design, Operation and Evaluation of Mobile Communications, edited by June Wei and George Margetis
48. CCIS 3047, HCI International 2026 Posters (Part I), edited by Constantine Stephanidis, George Margetis, Stavroula Ntoa, Margherita Antona and Gavriel Salvendy
49. CCIS 3048, HCI International 2026 Posters (Part II), edited by Constantine Stephanidis, George Margetis, Stavroula Ntoa, Margherita Antona and Gavriel Salvendy
50. CCIS 3049, HCI International 2026 Posters (Part III), edited by Constantine Stephanidis, George Margetis, Stavroula Ntoa, Margherita Antona and Gavriel Salvendy
51. CCIS 3050, HCI International 2026 Posters (Part IV), edited by Constantine Stephanidis, George Margetis, Stavroula Ntoa, Margherita Antona and Gavriel Salvendy
52. CCIS 3051, HCI International 2026 Posters (Part V), edited by Constantine Stephanidis, George Margetis, Stavroula Ntoa, Margherita Antona and Gavriel Salvendy
53. CCIS 3052, HCI International 2026 Posters (Part VI), edited by Constantine Stephanidis, George Margetis, Stavroula Ntoa, Margherita Antona and Gavriel Salvendy

https://2026.hci.international/proceedings

Preface

The 23rd International Conference on Engineering Psychology and Cognitive Ergonomics (EPCE 2026) was an affiliated conference of the HCI International Conference. The first EPCE conference was held in Stratford-upon-Avon, UK in 1996, and since 2001 EPCE has been an integral part of the HCI International conference series. Over the last 27 years, over 1,000 papers have been presented at this conference, which attracts a worldwide audience of scientists and human factors practitioners. The engineering psychology submissions describe advances in applied cognitive psychology that underpin the theory, measurement and methodologies behind the development of human-machine systems. Cognitive ergonomics describes advances in the design and development of user interfaces. Originally, these disciplines were driven by the requirements of high-risk, high-performance industries where safety was paramount, however the importance of good human factors is now understood by everyone, in order to not only increase safety, but also enhance performance, productivity and revenues.

Two volumes of the HCII 2026 proceedings are dedicated to this year's edition of the EPCE conference focusing on topics related to:

- Engineering Psychology and Cognitive Ergonomics (Part I): Interaction and Cognition; Risk, Safety and Decision-Making; Cognition at Work
- Engineering Psychology and Cognitive Ergonomics (Part II): Cognition in Driving; Cognition in Aviation

The papers in these volumes were accepted for publication after a minimum of two single-blind reviews from the members of the EPCE Program Board or, in some cases, from members of the Program Boards of other affiliated conferences. We would like to thank all of them for their invaluable contributions, support and efforts.

July 2026

Wen-Chin Li
Anastasios Plioutsias

23rd International Conference on Engineering Psychology and Cognitive Ergonomics (EPCE 2026)

Program Board Chairs: **Wen-Chin Li,** *Cranfield University, UK*, and **Anastasios Plioutsias,** *Coventry University, UK*

- James Blundell, *Cranfield University, UK*
- Mickaël Causse, *ISAE-SUPAERO, France*
- Wesley Tsz-Kin Chan, *Human Factor Asia, Hong Kong, P.R. China*
- Raj De, *Babcock International, UK*
- Maik Friedrich, *German Aerospace Center, Germany*
- Hannes Griebel, *CGI, UK*
- Min-Chih Hsieh, *Chung Yuan Christian University, Taiwan*
- Nektarios Karanikas, *QUT, Australia*
- Hannu Karvonen, *VTT Technical Research Centre of Finland Ltd., Finland*
- John Lin, *National Taiwan Normal University, Taiwan*
- Ting-Ting Lu, *Civil Aviation University of China, P.R. China*
- Chientsung Lu, *Southern Illinois University, USA*
- Pete McCarthy, *Cathay Pacific Airways, UK*
- Brett Molesworth, *UNSW Sydney, Australia*
- Miwa Nakanishi, *Keio University, Japan*
- Kam K. H. Ng, *The Hong Kong Polytechnic University, Hong Kong, P.R. China*
- Ewa Niechwiej-Szwedo, *University of Waterloo, Canada*
- Ibrahim Sarikaya, *Turkish Airlines, Turkey*
- Jens Schiefele, *Technical University Darmstadt, Germany*
- Axel Schulte, *University of the Bundeswehr Munich, Germany*
- Dujuan Sevillian, *NTSB, USA*
- Lauren Thomas, *Federal Aviation Administration, USA*
- Sebastien Tremblay, *Laval University, Canada*
- Lei Wang, *Civil Aviation University of China, P.R. China*
- Carl Westin, *Linköping University, Sweden*
- Jingyu Zhang, *Chinese Academy of Sciences, P.R. China*
- Frank Zinn, *German Aerospace Center (DLR), Germany*

The full list with the Program Board Chairs and the members of the Program Boards of all thematic areas and affiliated conferences of HCII 2026 is available online at:

http://www.hci.international/board-members-2026.php

HCI International 2027 Conference

The 29th International Conference on Human-Computer Interaction, HCI International 2027, will be held jointly with the affiliated conferences at the Estrel Hotel and Congress Center, in Berlin, Germany, 25–30 July 2027. It will cover a broad spectrum of themes related to Human-Computer Interaction, including theoretical issues, methods, tools, processes, and case studies in HCI design, as well as novel interaction techniques, interfaces, and applications. The proceedings will be published by Springer (part of Springer Nature) in a multi-volume set. More information will become available on the conference website: https://2027.hci.international/.

General Chair
Constantine Stephanidis
University of Crete and ICS-FORTH
Heraklion, Crete, Greece
Email: general_chair@2027.hci.international

https://2027.hci.international/

Contents

Cognition in Driving

A Driving Assistant HUD Design to Mitigate the Risk of Blind Spot in Cross-Border Driving

Yuanyuan Bu, Kam K. H. Ng(✉), Peter H. F. Ng, and Xin Yuan

The Hong Kong Polytechnic University, Hung Hom, Hong Kong SAR
kam.kh.ng@polyu.edu.hk

Abstract. With the increasing demand for international mobility, cross-boundary transportation has become more frequent, especially in regions where vehicles are allowed to operate across jurisdictions with different traffic regulations. A representative case is Hong Kong vehicles entering mainland China, where right-hand drive (RHD) vehicles must operate under left-hand traffic (LHT) conditions. This mismatch in driving position and traffic layout may enlarge blind-spot regions and increase collision risks during critical maneuvers. Although previous studies have reported that differences between LHD and RHD configurations can lead to increased blind spots and delayed reaction times, limited research has provided empirical risk assessments and practical mitigation strategies specifically for cross-boundary driving. To address blind-spot-related hazards in cross-boundary transportation, this study designed three representative high-risk driving scenarios—overtaking, intersection turning, and U-turning—based on typical blind-spot conflict mechanisms. A visual-guidance Head-Up Display (HUD) warning system was developed to provide intuitive blind-spot risk information and time-to-collision (TTC) feedback, aiming to improve drivers' situational awareness and safety performance. Six experienced Hong Kong drivers (with more than three years of driving experience) participated in a controlled driving simulation experiment. A Tobii eye tracker was used to record drivers' visual behaviors under two conditions: baseline driving (without HUD) and assisted driving (with HUD). The proposed HUD consisted of a flashing triangular warning icon combined with a dynamic TTC bar. The warning was triggered when TTC dropped below 30 s and was displayed at different windshield locations depending on the relative position of the blind-spot hazard. Eye-tracking analysis focused on scanpath patterns and fixation distributions, while TTC was used as a micro-level indicator of collision risk and driving safety.

The experimental results revealed clear improvements in driving safety and visual attention allocation when the HUD warning system was activated. Across all three scenarios, drivers in the baseline condition exhibited more scattered fixation distributions and longer scanpaths, indicating increased cognitive workload and extensive visual searching behaviors to compensate for blind-spot uncertainty. In contrast, under the HUD condition, gaze patterns became more centralized and goal-directed, with fixations more concentrated on the forward roadway and HUD projection region, suggesting that the visual guidance effectively reduced unnecessary searching and supported faster hazard awareness. TTC results further demonstrated that the HUD condition consistently produced higher mean TTC values compared to the baseline condition, indicating that drivers initiated braking

W. -C. Li and A. Plioutsias (Eds.): HCII 2026, LNAI 16708, pp. 3–16, 2026.
https://doi.org/10.1007/978-3-032-29459-3_1

or steering adjustments earlier and maintained a larger temporal safety margin before conflict events. The most pronounced TTC improvement was observed in the U-turn scenario, where A-pillar occlusion caused the highest baseline risk. Overall, the findings confirm that the proposed graphical HUD warning system can significantly enhance driver perception and response efficiency in blind-spot-related cross-boundary driving scenarios.

Keywords: cross-boundary driving · HUD design · driving simulation

1 Introduction

1.1 Blind-Spot in Cross-Boundary Driving

With the rapid growth of international mobility, cross-boundary driving has become increasingly common, particularly in regions where vehicles are permitted to operate across jurisdictions with different traffic regulations. A typical example is Hong Kong vehicles operating in mainland China, where right-hand drive (RHD) vehicles are required to drive under left-hand traffic (LHT) conditions [1]. This mismatch between vehicle configuration and traffic environment fundamentally alters the driver's field of view and enlarges blind-spot areas, especially on the overtaking side [2]. Empirical and policy-oriented studies have consistently shown that "wrong-hand drive" vehicles are associated with a significantly higher accident risk, largely due to impaired visibility and delayed hazard perception during critical maneuvers [3]. The problem is particularly severe during lateral interactions with surrounding vehicles, where drivers must rely heavily on mirrors or head movements to compensate for asymmetric blind spots [4]. In cross-border contexts, drivers are often required to adapt rapidly to unfamiliar visual-spatial layouts, increasing cognitive workload and prolonging perception–decision–response times [5]. Despite the well-documented macro-level safety risks of wrong-hand drive vehicles, relatively few studies have examined micro-level behavioral mechanisms or mitigation strategies tailored to cross-boundary driving scenarios.

In cross-boundary driving, typical high-risk blind-spot scenarios can be summarized into three major types as the Fig. 1 shows. First, during turning maneuvers (especially left turns), the left-side A-pillar blind zone can occlude pedestrians, cyclists, or approaching vehicles, leading to delayed hazard detection and unsafe gap acceptance [6]. Second, during overtaking maneuvers, the driver must continuously monitor vehicles approaching from the rear and adjacent lanes; however, the asymmetric blind spot caused by RHD vehicles in LHT environments can significantly reduce visibility on the overtaking side [2], increasing the likelihood of misjudging relative speed and time-to-collision (TTC), thus leading to unsafe lane changes or side-impact conflicts. Third, during U-turn maneuvers, the front-right A-pillar obstruction becomes critical, as vehicles, motorcycles, or pedestrians approaching from the forward-right direction may be temporarily hidden by the A-pillar structure, resulting in delayed perception and hazardous decision-making. Overall, these three scenarios highlight that blind-spot risks in cross-boundary driving are not limited to mirror-related rear zones but also include structural occlusions and maneuver-induced visibility constraints, which require targeted warning and visual guidance strategies [7].

Fig. 1. Three Common Blind Spots for RHD Driver views.

1.2 Driving Assistance Method Related to Blind Spot Detection

Driving assistance methods related to blind-spot detection have increasingly shifted from simple mirror-based warning systems toward quantitative risk assessment of invisible areas. Recent research proposes that blind spots should be treated as "shadow regions" created by occlusions from vehicles, buildings, trees, or roadside obstacles, where potential hazards may exist despite being unobservable to the driver or onboard sensors [8]. To address this issue, Lu et al. proposed the Uncertainty Shadow Safety (USS) framework, which combines static road information from high-definition maps with real-time perception data to model the geometry of blind areas and estimate the probability of different road users (e.g., cars, trucks, pedestrians, and cyclists) being present in these regions [9]. By incorporating uncertainty modeling, distance-based weighting, and abnormal motion cues from surrounding vehicles, USS generates a quantitative risk value that can be used to trigger early warnings or emergency interventions. The system is designed to cooperate with Advanced Driver-Assistance Systems (ADAS) by enabling proactive braking in critical situations, while in non-ADAS vehicles it can provide visual or auditory alerts to support safer driver decision-making in occlusion-prone scenarios such as intersections, ghost-probe events, and highway overtaking [10].

This uncertainty-based modeling approach can be further extended to the design of practical driving assistance systems, particularly in cross-boundary driving environments where blind-spot risks are amplified by mismatched vehicle configurations and traffic flow patterns. By transforming invisible areas into measurable risk indicators, such models can serve as a decision-support layer that determines when and where blind-spot hazards are likely to emerge. In real-world implementation, the quantified blind-spot risk values can be integrated with micro-level safety indicators such as TTC thresholds [11], enabling the system to generate timely and adaptive warnings. These warnings can be delivered through multimodal interfaces, including auditory alerts, visual icons, or HUD guidance, to inform drivers about the location and urgency of hidden threats without requiring excessive mirror-checking behavior. Such an integrated warning strategy has strong potential to enhance situational awareness, shorten driver reaction time, and ultimately improve safety performance in high-risk cross-border driving scenarios.

1.3 Visual Guidance Driving Assistance System - Head-Up Display

Head-Up Displays (HUDs) are widely recognized as an effective visual-guidance driving assistance system because they project safety-critical information directly into the driver's forward field of view, reducing gaze shifts between the road and traditional head-down displays [12]. This capability supports faster hazard recognition and decision-making, especially in time-critical situations. Recent studies emphasize that HUDs improve drivers' situational awareness by enabling a more balanced visual attention distribution between the road scene and the displayed information, and AR-based HUD designs further enhance this benefit by overlaying graphical cues onto the real driving environment, making risk information more intuitive and easier to interpret in real time [13].

To ensure that HUD warnings truly assist rather than distract drivers, HUD design must follow strict visual guideline principles. Betancur et al. summarized that HUD content should remain within the driver's line of sight and approximately within 10° of eccentricity, because information outside this range may require head movement and reduce usability [14]. They also highlighted that warning stimuli must be recognizable within very short exposure times, and the driver's road-to-HUD glance duration should ideally remain below 2 s to avoid increased accident risk. In addition, factors such as virtual image distance, luminance, size, color choice, and clutter level strongly influence recognition performance and reaction time, indicating that HUD design must integrate both quantitative optical constraints and human perceptual limitations.

In blind-spot detection and warning applications, HUDs provide a particularly valuable advantage because blind-spot hazards are often "invisible but imminent," requiring drivers to respond before direct visual confirmation is possible. Research on invisible-area modeling (e.g., USS shadow risk assessment) suggests that blind-spot danger can be quantified and translated into driver-assistance outputs, where HUDs serve as an ideal interface to present blind-zone location and urgency through visual icons, highlighted risk regions, or multimodal cues [8]. Such systems can cooperate with ADAS by triggering emergency braking when risk is extreme or provide visual/auditory alerts in vehicles without advanced automation, enabling drivers to slow down, increase attention, or avoid unsafe maneuvers such as overtaking and lane changes [15]. Therefore, HUD-based visual guidance represents a promising and human-centered approach for blind-spot risk mitigation, particularly in cross-boundary driving scenarios where perception limitations and mismatched scanning habits may significantly increase crash likelihood.

In summary, designing a blind-spot risk-warning HUD is essential for cross-boundary driving safety, as it can transform invisible hazards into intuitive visual guidance and TTC-based alerts, thereby reducing drivers' cognitive workload, improving situational awareness, and enabling earlier evasive actions in high-risk maneuvers such as turning, overtaking, and U-turning.

2 Methodology

2.1 Experiment Design

We employed driving simulation methods to investigate whether an auxiliary HUD design utilizing TTC values and warning symbols as blind spot alerts can help reduce collision risks and enhance driving safety [16]. The driving experiment was set in the SCANeRstudio_2023 (AviSimulation, France) in a Windows system host as the Fig. 2 shows. The 6 subjects were asked to sit in front of a simulated driving display consisting of three 20-inch screens, each with a resolution of 1980 × 1080, and an angle of 165 degrees between two screens. Driving control using the Logic G923 steering wheel. A total of six subjects participated in the experiment. Each subject was required to drive to across three designed scenarios with and without the HUD assistant.

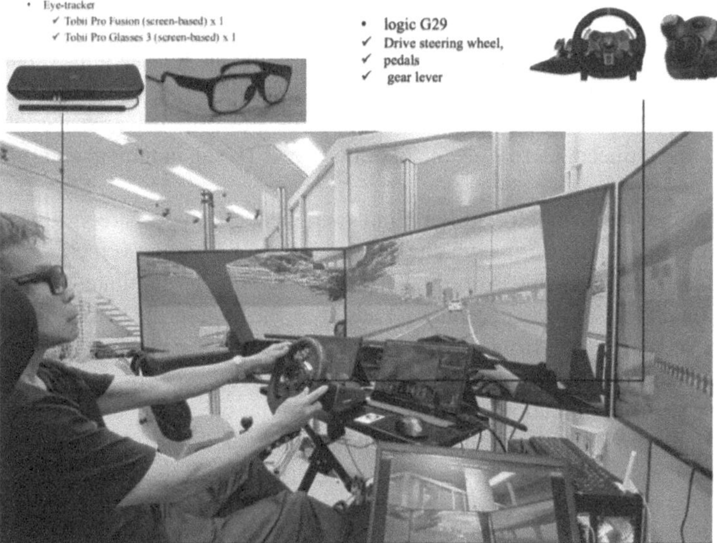

Fig. 2. The driving simulation experiment set up.

For the driver participants, they were asked to honk the car when seeing the oncoming vehicle in Scenario a, the left-coming vehicle in Scenario b, the right-coming vehicle in Scenario c. The reaction time was recorded to analysis the performance. The position of the ego vehicle and the distance to next vehicle and was calculated by the script in SCANeRstudio_2023. Participants were asked to drive continuously along a route containing four scenes. Each time they passed a fixed scene starting point, a time marker was triggered to record the start time of the scene. When they saw vehicle 2 in the scene that might cause a scrape or collision, participants were required to immediately press the Honk button on the Logitech G923 steering wheel as shown in Fig. 2. The script recorded the reaction time from the start of the scene to the pressing of the button. Eye movement data can reflect cognitive load, fatigue levels, and situational awareness while driving [17]. Additionally, participants were required to wear the Tobii Glass 3 eye tracker to record and analyze eye movement data.

2.2 Scenario Design

Based on the three typical blind-spot conflict scenarios identified in cross-boundary driving, we designed three representative simulation scenarios to reproduce hazardous situations that may lead to scrape events or near-collision conflicts under RHD driving in LHT conditions. The scenario layouts were constructed to highlight the differences in drivers' effective field of view caused by the asymmetric driving position and structural occlusions, as illustrated in Fig. 3. The blue shaded region indicates the approximate forward visibility area of RHD drivers. The width of each individual lane is set at 5.4 m [18].

The designed scenarios include:

(a) Overtaking scenario with asymmetric rear-side blind spot: the ego vehicle is instructed to overtake a slower vehicle ahead, while an approaching vehicle in the adjacent lane or rear region enters the critical blind zone. Due to the mismatch between RHD seating position and LHT traffic flow, the driver's overtaking-side visibility is reduced, increasing the likelihood of TTC misjudgment and side-impact conflict.
(b) Turning scenario with left A-pillar blind spot: the ego vehicle is required to perform a left-turn maneuver, during which pedestrians or approaching vehicles are partially occluded by the left-side A-pillar. This scenario aims to simulate delayed hazard detection and unsafe gap acceptance caused by the structural obstruction.
(c) U-turn scenario with front-right A-pillar occlusion: the ego vehicle performs a U-turn maneuver, while another vehicle or vulnerable road user approaches from the forward-right direction. The front-right A-pillar creates a temporary occlusion, which may prevent drivers from perceiving the hazard until the final stage of the maneuver, resulting in delayed braking or steering response.

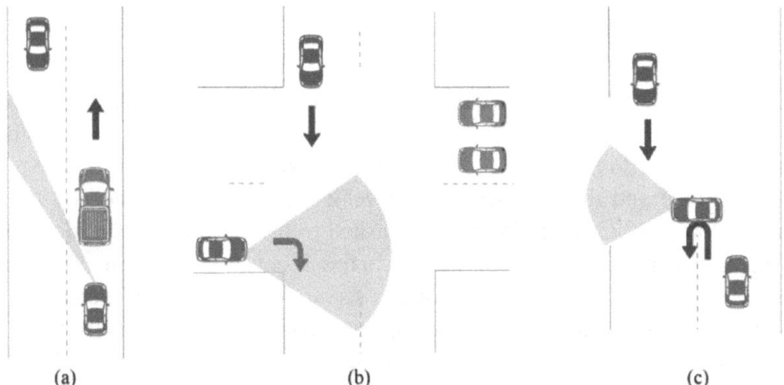

Fig. 3. Bird-view of four driving scenarios, where the ego vehicle is blue (a) Overtaking scenario with asymmetric rear-side blind spot (b) Turning scenario with left A-pillar blind spot (c) U-turn scenario with front-right A-pillar occlusion. (Color figure online)

2.3 HUD Assistant Design

Based on the three typical blind-spot conflict scenarios (Asymmetric blind spot during overtaking, Left A-pillar occlusion during turning, and Front-right A-pillar occlusion during U-turning), a unified HUD-based warning scheme was designed to provide intuitive and timely risk guidance [14]. The proposed HUD interface consists of two main components: a flashing triangular warning icon and a TTC-based vertical bar indicator. The triangular icon is used to attract the driver's attention and indicate the presence of a potential blind-spot hazard, while the TTC bar provides continuous quantitative information regarding collision urgency. When the estimated TTC value falls below 40 s, the triangular warning icon is triggered and starts flashing to emphasize the increasing risk level. Meanwhile, the TTC bar dynamically decreases according to the real-time TTC value, with the visualization range normalized from 0 s to 40 s, allowing drivers to intuitively perceive the temporal margin before a potential collision. This integrated graphical design enables drivers to quickly recognize both the existence of blind-spot threats and their urgency, supporting earlier braking or steering responses in cross-boundary driving scenarios.

According to the relative position of potential hazards, the HUD warning was designed to appear at different locations on the windshield to maintain spatial consistency between the warning cue and the risk direction. In the overtaking scenario shown in Fig. 4, the risk vehicle mainly approaches from the left-rear blind spot; therefore, the flashing warning triangle and TTC bar were projected on the lower-left of the medium area.

Fig. 4. HUD for asymmetric blind spot during overtaking.

In the left-turn scenario shown in Fig. 5 hazards are typically occluded by the left A-pillar and may emerge from the front-left conflict zone, thus the HUD was positioned near the left-front area of the windshield to guide attention toward the A-pillar occlusion boundary.

Fig. 5. HUD for left A-pillar occlusion during turning right.

In the U-turn scenario shown in Fig. 6, the major risk originates from the front-right direction and may be temporarily hidden by the front-right A-pillar, so the HUD warning was displayed on the right-front area of the windshield to provide intuitive visual guidance. Overall, this layout follows a risk-direction matching principle, ensuring that warning cues are presented in a location consistent with the hazard source, thereby reducing visual search effort and supporting faster driver responses.

Fig. 6. HUD for front-right A-pillar occlusion during U-turning.

3 Data Analysis

3.1 The Eye-Tracking Data Analysis

Eye-tracking data was analyzed using the Tobii Lab 2023 program (Tobii, Sweden). The Tobii I-VT (attention) algorithm was used to filter the raw eye-tracking data, and then the time of interests' method was used to divide the four scenarios into three events. The scanpath and fixation heatmaps calculated by the gaze point was used for Comparison. The virtual dataset consists of 6 video clips. Each clip is with 180 s in length and has a 60 Hz sampling rate. These clips are 3 scenarios for both with HUD and without HUD, which contain 25920 frames in total for driving tasks.

3.2 The Objective Risk Analysis Based on TTC

Time to collision (TTC) has been extensively studied by many scholars and is now the commonly used micro-indicator for evaluating the driving safety. According to the definition of TTC [19], a larger TTC provides drivers with more time to avoid a collision, thereby reducing the probability of a traffic collision. Conversely, a smaller TTC is more likely to result in a collision risk. Building on the classic TTC model, a two-dimensional TTC theoretical model, more suitable for complex environments, is proposed to analyze vehicle conflicts at intersections. The formula for calculating the two-dimensional TTC is

$$\frac{\sqrt{(O_i - O_j)^T (O_i - O_j)} - 0.5L_i - 0.5L_j}{\frac{1}{\sqrt{(O_i - O_j)^T (O_i - O_j)}} (O_i - O_j)^T (V_i - V_j)} \tag{1}$$

As shown in the formula, O_i and O_j are the position vectors of the centroids of vehicle A and vehicle B, V_i and V_j are the vector velocities of the vehicles, and L_i and L_j are the lengths of vehicle A and B. In this experiment, vehicle i in the TTC we calculated is ego vehicle 1, and vehicle j is the red vehicle.

4 Result

4.1 The Eye-Tracking Data

In the overtaking scenario shown in Fig. 7, drivers in the Without HUD condition exhibited a relatively dispersed scanpath pattern, with gaze points frequently shifting between the forward roadway and peripheral areas. The fixation clusters appear widely distributed across the central region and the upper-left area, indicating that drivers relied more heavily on active visual searching and mirror-related scanning to monitor the asymmetric blind spot during overtaking. This scattered gaze behavior suggests a higher cognitive workload, as drivers needed to repeatedly verify surrounding traffic conditions and estimate potential collision risk without direct guidance.In contrast, the With HUD condition shows a more structured gaze distribution. Fixations are more concentrated around the central forward driving region and the HUD projection area, with fewer unnecessary gaze transitions toward peripheral zones. The scanpath becomes shorter and more goal-directed, indicating that the HUD warning effectively guided the driver's attention to critical information. This suggests that the graphical warning (flashing triangle) combined with TTC bar reduced the need for extensive blind-spot searching and supported quicker risk interpretation during overtaking maneuvers. Overall, the overtaking results imply that the HUD system improved drivers' attention efficiency by reducing excessive visual exploration and enabling more stable forward monitoring while still maintaining awareness of blind-spot hazards.

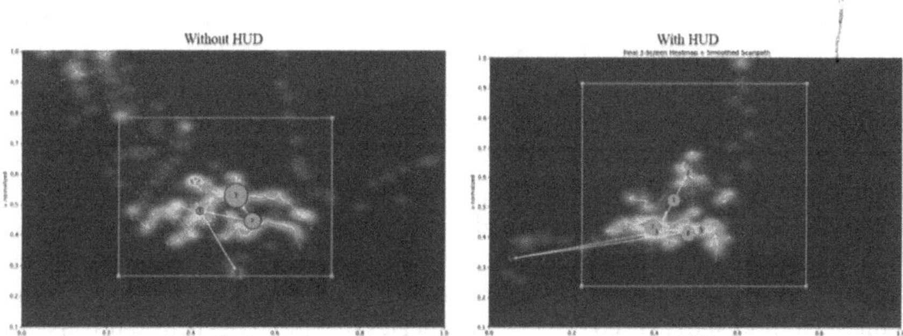

Fig. 7. Scanpath and gaze fixation in overtaking scenario.

The intersection scenario produced the most complex visual scanning behavior as shown in Fig. 8. Under the Without HUD condition, drivers demonstrated a wide scanning range with frequent fixation shifts across the intersection environment. Heatmap density was distributed across a large portion of the forward scene, suggesting that drivers attempted to actively search for hidden vehicles or cross-traffic threats behind occluding objects. The scanpath also shows multiple long saccades, reflecting a high demand for situational assessment and hazard prediction in the intersection conflict zone. When the HUD was enabled (With HUD), fixation points became significantly more concentrated in the central area and around the HUD warning location. Although the overall scanning remained relatively active (as intersections naturally require broad attention), the scanpath appears more organized and less random compared to the baseline condition, indicates that the HUD provided a salient visual anchor, helping drivers prioritize attention toward the most critical conflict direction rather than distributing gaze equally across all possible risk regions. These results suggest that in complex intersection environments, the HUD does not eliminate the need for broad scanning, but it improves attention allocation by reinforcing the risk-relevant region, thereby reducing uncertainty-driven visual searching.

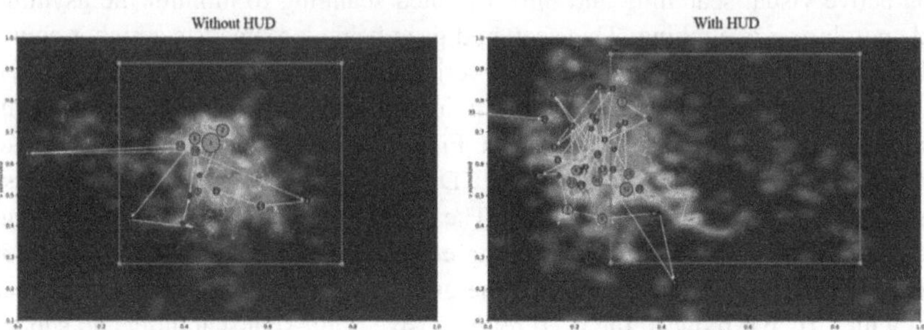

Fig. 8. Scanpath and gaze fixation in intersection scenario.

In the U-turn scenario as shown in Fig. 9, the Without HUD condition shows a highly extended scanpath with long diagonal gaze movements across the scene. Fixation clusters are spread between the forward roadway and peripheral regions, reflecting drivers' need to repeatedly check for potential hazards approaching from the front-right direction, which is partially occluded by the A-pillar. This pattern indicates increased visual workload, since U-turning requires continuous monitoring of multiple directions and may cause temporary loss of awareness due to structural occlusion. With the HUD warning activated (With HUD), fixation points shift upward and become more concentrated toward the HUD display region and the forward-right conflict area. The scanpath pattern becomes more centralized, suggesting that drivers relied more on HUD cues to interpret risk and guide their gaze toward the occluded direction. Compared with the baseline condition, the reduced dispersion indicates that the HUD helped drivers detect the potential threat earlier and reduced the need for repeated exploratory gaze shifts. The U-turn scenario demonstrates that HUD guidance is particularly beneficial under A-pillar occlusion conditions, as it compensates for structural visibility limitations by directing attention toward the most critical blind region.

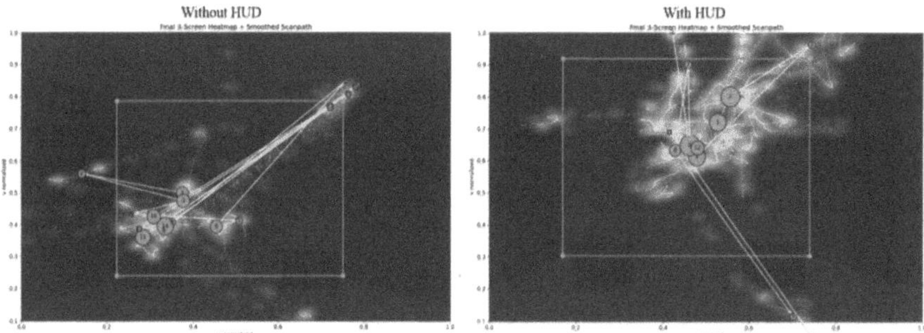

Fig. 9. Scanpath and gaze fixation in i U-turning Scenario.

Across all three scenarios, the eye-tracking results consistently demonstrate that the proposed HUD system improved visual attention efficiency. Without HUD, drivers tended to exhibit scattered fixation distributions and longer scanpaths, indicating greater reliance on active searching strategies to compensate for blind-spot uncertainty. With HUD, gaze behavior became more concentrated and goal-oriented, with fixations shifting toward the HUD projection area and the forward driving region. This suggests that the HUD warning system successfully served as a visual guidance mechanism, reducing the driver's cognitive effort in monitoring blind zones while maintaining attention on the roadway.

In summary, the scanpath and fixation heatmaps provide evidence that the graphical HUD warning design effectively optimized drivers' gaze allocation in blind-spot conflict scenarios, supporting faster hazard perception and more stable driving attention patterns.

4.2 The TTC Data

In the overtaking scenario, TTC values decreased rapidly as the ego vehicle approached the hazard vehicle, indicating an increasing collision risk near the overtaking decision point as shown in Fig. 10. Compared with the baseline condition, the With HUD condition showed consistently higher TTC values during the critical pre-event interval, suggesting that drivers maintained a larger temporal safety margin when HUD warnings were available. This indicates that the HUD system encouraged earlier risk perception and more conservative overtaking behavior, such as earlier braking or delayed lane-change initiation, thereby reducing the probability of near-collision conflicts. In the intersection scenario, TTC remained relatively stable and did not show a steep decline trend, reflecting that driver tended to adjust their speed earlier when approaching the intersection. Notably, the With HUD condition produced slightly higher TTC values across most time intervals, and the difference became more evident around the event time. This suggests that the HUD warning improved drivers' awareness of potential hidden threats from occluded cross-traffic, leading to earlier deceleration and safer gap acceptance when entering the intersection conflict zone.

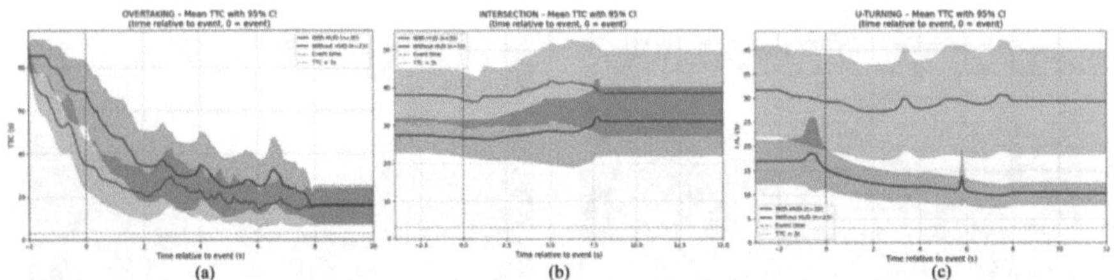

Fig. 10. TTC Variation Curves Across Three Scenarios (a) Overtaking scenario with asymmetric rear-side blind spot (b) Turning scenario with left A-pillar blind spot (c) U-turn scenario with front-right A-pillar occlusion.

The U-turn scenario demonstrated the most pronounced TTC difference between conditions. Under the Without HUD condition, TTC values stayed at a relatively low level, indicating a smaller safety margin and a higher risk of conflict caused by the front-right A-pillar occlusion. In contrast, the With HUD condition showed a significantly higher TTC curve throughout the entire event window, indicating that drivers reacted earlier and maintained safer distances when executing the U-turn maneuver. This implies that the HUD warning system was particularly effective in compensating for A-pillar-induced visibility limitations by providing timely risk cues before the hazard became directly visible.

5 Conclusion

Overall, the experimental results consistently demonstrate that the proposed blind-spot warning HUD can effectively improve driving safety and visual attention efficiency in cross-boundary driving conditions, particularly for RHD drivers operating under LHT environments. Eye-tracking analysis across the overtaking, intersection, and U-turn scenarios showed that, without HUD assistance, drivers exhibited scattered fixation distributions and longer scanpaths, indicating increased cognitive workload and extensive visual searching behaviors to compensate for asymmetric blind spots and A-pillar occlusions. In contrast, when the HUD was activated, drivers' gaze patterns became more centralized and goal-directed, with fixations more frequently concentrated in the forward roadway and HUD projection regions, suggesting that the graphical warning interface successfully guided visual attention and reduced unnecessary mirror-checking effort. TTC results further supported these findings by showing consistently higher TTC values under the HUD condition, indicating that drivers initiated evasive actions earlier and maintained a larger temporal safety margin before conflict events. These outcomes align with prior research emphasizing that HUD-based visual guidance can shorten the perception–decision–response chain by presenting critical information within the driver's forward field of view, thereby reducing gaze diversion and improving hazard recognition efficiency.

Acknowledgments. The research is supported by Department of Aeronautical and Aviation Engineering, The Hong Kong Polytechnic University, Hong Kong SAR (RNFT). The research is also supported by the Smart Traffic Fund (PSRI/85/2403/RA) sponsored by the Hong Kong Productivity Council. This study has been granted human ethics approval from the PolyU Institutional Review Board of The Hong Kong Polytechnic University (HSEARS20250124003).

Disclosure of Interests. The authors have no competing interests to declare that are relevant to the content of this article.

References

1. Zhang, G., Zhong, Q., Tan, Y., Yang, Q.: Risky behavior analysis for cross-border drivers: a logit model and qualitative comparative analysis of odds of fault and injury vulnerability in Guangdong, Hong Kong and Macau. J. Safety Res. **82**, 417–429 (2022). https://doi.org/10.1016/j.jsr.2022.07.009
2. Lewis, P., Shaw, D.M., Wild, U., Erren, T.C.: (Side) effects of the rule of the road and neurophysiology on traffic safety: a hypothesis. Environ. Res. **183**, 109246 (2020). https://doi.org/10.1016/j.envres.2020.109246
3. Roesel, F.: The causal effect of wrong-hand drive vehicles on road safety. Econ. Transp. **11–12**, 15–22 (2017). https://doi.org/10.1016/j.ecotra.2017.10.002
4. Unravelling situational awareness of multi-tasking pedestrians through average gaze fixation durations: An accelerated failure time modelling approach. https://pdf.sciencedirectassets.com/271664/1-s2.0-S0001457524X00159/1-s2.0-
5. Cooper, P.J., Meckle, W., Nasvadi, G.: The safety of vehicles imported from right-hand-drive vehicle configuration countries when operated in a left-hand-drive vehicle environment. Accid. Anal. Prev. **41**, 108–114 (2009). https://doi.org/10.1016/j.aap.2008.10.004
6. Narksri, P., Takeuchi, E., Ninomiya, Y., Takeda, K.: Crossing blind intersections from a full stop using estimated visibility of approaching vehicles. In: 2019 IEEE Intelligent Transportation Systems Conference (ITSC). pp. 2427–2434. IEEE, Auckland, New Zealand (2019). https://doi.org/10.1109/ITSC.2019.8917323
7. Ringhand, M., Siebke, C., Bäumler, M., Petzoldt, T.: Approaching intersections: gaze behavior of drivers depending on traffic, intersection type, driving maneuver, and secondary task involvement. Transport. Res. F: Traffic Psychol. Behav. **91**, 116–135 (2022). https://doi.org/10.1016/j.trf.2022.09.010
8. Saito, Y., Sugaya, F., Inoue, S., Raksincharoensak, P., Inoue, H.: A context-aware driver model for determining recommended speed in blind intersection situations. Accid. Anal. Prev. **163**, 106447 (2021). https://doi.org/10.1016/j.aap.2021.106447
9. Lu, J., et al.: A quantitative blind area risks assessment method for safe driving assistance. J. Syst. Architect. **150**, 103121 (2024). https://doi.org/10.1016/j.sysarc.2024.103121
10. Ra, M., Jung, H.G., Suhr, J.K., Kim, W.-Y.: Part-based vehicle detection in side-rectilinear images for blind-spot detection. Expert Syst. Appl. **101**, 116–128 (2018). https://doi.org/10.1016/j.eswa.2018.02.005
11. Fu, Q., Zhao, X., Chen, C., Ren, W.: How predictive-forward-collision-warning reduces the collision risk of leading vehicle driver. Accid. Anal. Prev. **211**, 107891 (2025). https://doi.org/10.1016/j.aap.2024.107891
12. Yuan, X., et al.: Exploring the human-centric interaction paradigm: augmented reality-assisted head-up display design for collaborative human-machine interface in cockpit. Adv. Eng. Inform. **62**, 102656 (2024). https://doi.org/10.1016/j.aei.2024.102656
13. Shi, J., et al.: Effects of various in-vehicle human–machine interfaces on drivers' takeover performance and gaze pattern in conditionally automated vehicles. Int. J. Hum Comput Stud. **192**, 103362 (2024). https://doi.org/10.1016/j.ijhcs.2024.103362

14. Betancur, J.A., Vargas, H., Sanchez, C., Merienne, F.: Visual guidelines integration for automotive head-up displays interfaces. Int. J. Interact. Des. Manuf. (2024). https://doi.org/10.1007/s12008-024-01877-0
15. Li, J., et al.: Lane changing maneuver prediction by using driver's spatio-temporal gaze attention inputs for naturalistic driving. Adv. Eng. Inform. **61**, 102529 (2024). https://doi.org/10.1016/j.aei.2024.102529
16. Chen, T., Sze, N.N., Bai, L.: Safety of professional drivers in an ageing society – a driving simulator study. Transport. Res. F: Traffic Psychol. Behav. **67**, 101–112 (2019). https://doi.org/10.1016/j.trf.2019.10.006
17. Ju, Y., Ye, S., Chen, T., Xing, G., Chen, F.: How do drivers manage speed at tunnel entrances? Insights from uncorrelated grouped random parameters duration models for model invalidation and performance recovery times. Anal. Meth. Accid. Res. **45**, 100371 (2025). https://doi.org/10.1016/j.amar.2025.100371
18. Chen, T., Sze, N.N., Chen, S., Labi, S.: Urban road space allocation incorporating the safety and construction cost impacts of lane and footpath widths. J. Safety Res. **75**, 222–232 (2020). https://doi.org/10.1016/j.jsr.2020.09.014
19. Tian, C., Zhang, C., Han, T., Chen, Y., Zhang, J., Feng, Y.: Evaluating the impacts of in-vehicle warnings at roundabouts with drivers' performance and eye movement data. Transport. Res. Part F: Traffic Psychol. Behav. **115**, 103348 (2025). https://doi.org/10.1016/j.trf.2025.103348

The Role of Transparency in Takeover Information for Trust Calibration in Automated Driving Systems

Xinze Liu, Lingyun Wan, and Yan Ge(✉)

State Key Laboratory of Cognitive Science and Mental Health, Institute of Psychology, Chinese Academy of Sciences, Beijing 100101, China
gey@psych.ac.cn

Abstract. Trust and trust calibration play a critical role in human decision-making and interaction quality when interacting with automated systems. The present study investigates the effects of system reliability, urgency, and transparency of takeover prompts on drivers' takeover decisions and trust calibration, with a particular focus on whether and under what conditions transparency can promote appropriate trust and trust calibration. A mixed experimental design was employed with 2 (system reliability: 70% vs. 100%) × 2 (transparency: low vs. high) × 2 (urgency: low vs. high). Dependent measures included trust-related indicators (overall trust and takeover rate), trust calibration indicators (takeover rate deviation and trust calibration deviation), usability-related indicators (understandability, satisfaction, perceived usefulness, and intention to use), as well as dynamic trust. Questionnaire data were collected from 61 valid participants. The results revealed significant main effects of transparency across all dependent measures. High transparency significantly increased drivers' trust, improved trust calibration, and enhanced subjective user experience. In addition, significant interaction effects were observed between transparency and both reliability and urgency. Specifically, high transparency primarily improved trust calibration under conditions of full system reliability (100%) and low urgency. Overall, the findings indicate that highly transparent takeover prompt designs are beneficial for automated driving use and user experience. This study provides practical implications for the design of information content in automated driving displays.

Keywords: Transparency · Automated Driving Takeover · Trust Calibration

1 Introduction

In human-automation interaction, trust has long been regarded as a critical factor because it directly influences the use of automated systems, particularly human intervention decisions in uncertain or hazardous environments (Hancock et al. 2011; Park et al. 2008). Trust in automation has been defined as "the attitude that an agent will help achieve an individual's goals in a situation characterized by uncertainty and vulnerability" (Lee & See 2004). As reflected in this definition, automated systems are rarely perfect, and

W. -C. Li and A. Plioutsias (Eds.): HCII 2026, LNAI 16708, pp. 17–32, 2026.
https://doi.org/10.1007/978-3-032-29459-3_2

a key challenge lies in calibrating operators' trust to the system's actual reliability. Inappropriate levels of trust may lead to adverse consequences: overtrust can result in misuse and overreliance, whereas undertrust may lead to disuse, both of which undermine the value of automation (Chen & Barnes 2014; Hancock et al. 2011; Lee & See 2004; Parasuraman & Riley 1997).

Appropriate trust requires that users understand both the strengths and limitations of the system (Chen & Barnes 2014). Such understanding forms the foundation of effective human-automation collaboration. When users possess knowledge of how an automated system operates, including its behaviors, capability boundaries, and particularly the conditions under which it is prone to error, they are more likely to use the system appropriately. From the human perspective, understanding refers to the operator's knowledge of the system's purpose and form, its functions, and its associated state structures—namely, the operator's mental model—which is constructed through interface information, observed system behavior, and instructions (Seppelt 2009; Seppelt & Lee 2015). From the system perspective, supporting the formation of accurate mental models requires a higher level of transparency. Increased transparency has been shown to facilitate trust calibration (Chen & Barnes 2014) and to promote shared awareness and intent between humans and machines (Lyons & Havig 2014). Chen et al. (2014) defined automation transparency as "the degree to which an interface supports operators in understanding the purpose, performance, processes, and future behaviors of an automated system" and proposed the Situation Awareness-based Agent Transparency (SAT) model. This model organizes system information into three levels: Level 1 conveys the automation's current actions and plans; Level 2 supports understanding of why the automation is acting as it is, including its reasoning processes; and Level 3 provides projections of future system states and outcomes. Naturally, operators' informational needs vary across systems, tasks, and environments, and the content, type, format, quantity, and organization of system-provided information should be adaptively designed (Doshi-Velez & Kim 2017; Seppelt 2009; Seppelt & Lee 2015). For example, when automation fails or behaves erroneously, information regarding its limitations and the actions required from human operators may become particularly critical (Lyons & Havig 2014; Seppelt 2009).

In recent years, growing attention has been devoted to the role of system transparency in shaping human trust and performance in automated systems. Research in various decision-support domains—such as aircraft identification, robotic supervision, and threat detection—has shown that increased transparency can improve operator task performance, enhance trust calibration (Mercado et al. 2016; Seong & Bisantz 2008), and support the dynamic development of trust over time (Yang et al. 2017), often without imposing excessive cognitive demands (Mercado et al. 2016). However, these benefits are not universal. Some studies suggest that operators' perceptions and performance may be more strongly influenced by system reliability than by transparency, depending on task characteristics and contextual demands (Wright et al. 2019).

Within the automated driving domain, prior work has emphasized the importance of informing drivers about automation behavior, particularly in takeover and conflict intervention scenarios following automation failures, to support accurate understanding of system capabilities and limitations (Seppelt 2009; Seppelt & Lee 2015; Victor et al.

2018). For instance, Seppelt (2009) proposed feedback designs grounded in discrepancies between drivers' mental models and system models, demonstrating that continuous audiovisual feedback can facilitate trust and reliance calibration. Nevertheless, most studies in this area have focused on the presence or absence of explanatory information, rather than systematically manipulating and comparing different levels of system transparency.

Only a small number of studies have explicitly examined how transparency influences trust development during automated driving failures and takeover situations. Kraus et al. (2020) found that trust typically declines following system failures and recovers during subsequent error-free interactions, and that higher transparency provided prior to interaction can mitigate trust degradation. However, in their study, driving context, failure modes, and explanatory content were held constant, leaving open questions regarding how transparency interacts with varying situational urgency and system reliability. As a result, the joint effects of transparency, reliability, and situational factors on drivers' trust, trust calibration, and takeover behavior in automated driving remain insufficiently understood.

Given that takeover behavior represents a critical form of human-automation interaction in automated driving, and that trust strongly influences whether and how drivers respond to system prompts, understanding the determinants of trust and trust calibration in takeover scenarios is of particular importance. Meta-analytic evidence indicates that system performance factors, especially reliability, exert the strongest influence on trust and should therefore be considered a primary driver (Hancock et al. 2011). Accordingly, the present study included system reliability as a key independent variable, examining drivers' trust and trust calibration of takeover requests under different reliability levels. In addition, prior research suggests that transparency can enhance trust and trust calibration, although its effects vary across automation types and task environments. Driving, however, takes place in highly dynamic and complex road environments, where events of varying urgency may substantially shape drivers' takeover decisions. Therefore, the present study simultaneously considers transparency and situation urgency, and investigates how reliability, transparency, and urgency jointly influence drivers' trust, trust calibration, and usability evaluations in automated driving takeover scenarios.

2 Method

2.1 Participants

Eighty drivers who had held a valid driver's license for at least one year and reported driving regularly were recruited to complete the questionnaire. Participants who provided inattentive responses or exhibited excessively long completion times were excluded from the analysis. The final sample consisted of 61 participants, including 37 males and 24 females, with ages ranging from 20 to 51 years ($M = 26.61$, $SD = 6.92$).

2.2 Experimental Design

A questionnaire-based study was conducted using a 2 (system reliability: 70% vs. 100%) $\times$ 2 (transparency: low vs. high) $\times$ 2 (urgency: low vs. high) mixed experimental design.

System reliability was treated as a between-subjects factor, whereas transparency and urgency were manipulated as within-subjects factors. The two reliability levels were selected based on prior research (Mercado et al. 2016; Wright et al. 2019) and were operationalized by varying the proportion of correct system takeover alerts. Transparency was manipulated following the Situation Awareness-based Transparency (SAT) model. In the low-transparency condition, only a takeover request was presented, corresponding to Level 1 information related to system goals and intentions. In the high-transparency condition, additional explanations for why a takeover was required were provided, corresponding to Level 2 information related to the system's reasoning processes. Urgency was manipulated using two levels of warning alerts, each associated with distinct takeover scenarios. Ten takeover scenarios were chosen for each urgency level. Compared with low-urgency scenarios, high-urgency scenarios involved a higher level of risk and more severe potential accident consequences.

Dependent variables were categorized into three groups: trust-related indicators, calibration-related indicators, and usability-related indicators. Trust-related indicators included takeover rate, defined as the proportion of trials in which participants chose to take over control; momentary trust, defined as participants' trust in the takeover system assessed on each trial; and overall trust, defined as participants' aggregated trust in the takeover system under each experimental condition.

Calibration-related indicators included trust calibration deviation, defined as the absolute difference between participants' percentage-based trust ratings and the actual system reliability level, as well as takeover rate deviation, defined as the absolute difference between participants' takeover rate and the corresponding system reliability level. Usability-related indicators included perceived understandability, satisfaction, perceived usefulness, and intention to use. Control variables included prior experience with automated driving systems, acceptance of automation, and personality traits.

2.3 Materials

Takeover Scenarios. A total of 20 takeover scenarios were developed in this study. High-urgency scenarios included situations such as a vehicle suddenly entering the intersection, an accident occurring ahead, a motorcycle suddenly crossing the roadway, vehicle skidding or loss of stability, and the presence of a road obstacle at a short distance ahead. Low-urgency scenarios included situations such as a nearby vehicle changing lanes, approaching a highway exit, negotiating a sharp curve, encountering a slow-moving vehicle ahead, approaching a railway junction, and the presence of a road obstacle at a relatively long distance.

In each trial, takeover scenarios were presented using a combination of a textual description, a roadway scene image, and an in-vehicle display interface image. The instructional text read: "*You are driving an automated vehicle on an urban road when you suddenly hear a beeping alert. The current traffic situation and the information shown on the in-vehicle display are illustrated below.*" The image materials showed the corresponding roadway context and the in-vehicle central display. Example stimuli are shown in Fig. 1.

Takeover Information Prompts. The takeover information was presented on the in-vehicle central display shown in the stimulus images. The content of the takeover prompts varied across transparency conditions. In the low-transparency condition, the display presented only a takeover request without further explanation. In the high-transparency condition, the display additionally provided explanations for the system's takeover recommendation, such as "*a red vehicle is cutting in ahead" or "a pedestrian is crossing the roadway ahead.*" Urgency was further conveyed through differences in both message description and color. In the low-urgency condition, the takeover prompt displayed on the in-vehicle central display read "*Takeover recommended*" and was presented in black (see Fig. 1C). In the high-urgency condition, the prompt read "*Take over immediately*" and was presented in red (see Fig. 1D).

Variable Measurement Materials. Trust-related measures included takeover rate, momentary trust, and overall trust. Takeover decisions and momentary trust were assessed after each trial. Following the presentation of a takeover scenario, participants were asked, "Would you take over control?", to which they responded by selecting "yes" or "no." Participants then rated their momentary trust in the automated driving system on a scale from 0 to 100, indicating how much they trusted the system at that moment. Overall trust was assessed after each block using the Trust in Automation (TIA) scale developed by Jian et al. (2000), which consists of 12 items. In addition, to compute trust calibration indicator, participants were additionally asked to rate their trust in each block on a 0–100 scale.

Usability-related evaluations of the automated driving takeover system were measured using 7-point Likert scales. Perceived understandability was assessed using four items, with internal consistency coefficients exceeding 0.80 across all experimental conditions. Satisfaction, perceived usefulness, and intention to use were each measured using a single item.

Control variables were also assessed. Prior experience with automated driving was measured using two items, including whether participants had previously used automated driving functions and which specific functions they had used. Acceptance of automated driving systems was measured using the Autonomous Vehicle Acceptability Scale (AVAS; Qu et al. 2019), which comprises four dimensions—benefits in situations, benefits in usefulness, system concern, and concern scenarios—and includes a total of 18 items. Personality traits were assessed using the 10-item version of the Big Five Inventory (BFI-10; Li 2013).

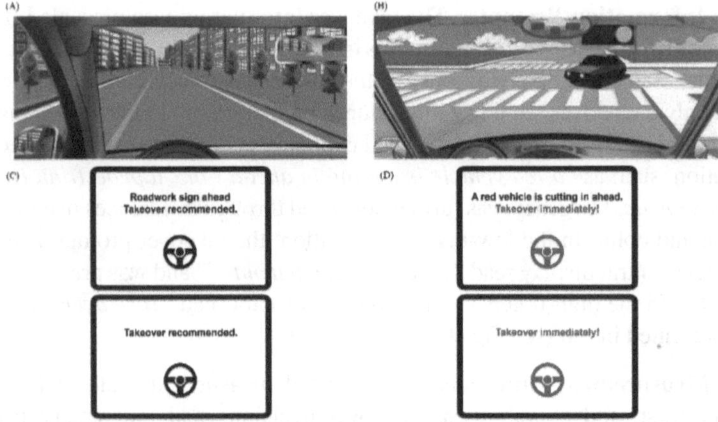

Fig. 1. Schematic illustration of the experimental materials. Panels A and B show roadway scene images under low- and high-urgency conditions, respectively. Panels C and D present in-vehicle display images under low- and high-urgency conditions, respectively, with the upper icons representing high-transparency displays and the lower icons representing low-transparency displays. All textual information in the experimental materials was presented in Chinese.

2.4 Procedure

The online questionnaire was administered via the Sojump platform and consisted of three parts: assessment of control variables, presentation of takeover scenario conditions with trust measurements, and collection of demographic information.

The first part assessed control variables, including prior experience with automated driving systems, acceptance of automation, and personality traits. In the second part, participants were presented with the experimental takeover scenarios and trust measures. After receiving an introduction to the automated driving system in the instructions, participants were randomly assigned to one of two system reliability conditions (70% or 100%). Within each reliability condition, participants were exposed to four experimental blocks in a 2 (transparency: low vs. high) × 2 (urgency: low vs. high) within-subjects design. Each block consisted of 10 trials. In the 70% reliability condition, trials 2, 5, and 8 within each block were false-alarm trials, in which no takeover was actually required based on the roadway scene, but the system incorrectly issued a takeover alert. In contrast, in the 100% reliability condition, all takeover alerts were correct and appropriate across trials. The order of urgency conditions was counterbalanced across participants. Within each urgency condition, the low-transparency block was always presented before the high-transparency block. For each experimental condition, the order of the 10 trials featuring different takeover scenarios was balanced using two pseudo-randomized sequences.

In each trial, participants were presented with a textual scenario description, a roadway scene image depicting the current traffic context, and an in-vehicle display image presenting the takeover prompt. Participants were instructed to use the textual and visual information to comprehend the driving situation, decide whether to take over control, and rate their momentary trust in the system on a percentage scale, enabling the assessment of dynamic changes in trust across trials (Yang et al. 2017). After completing all 10 trials within each block, participants evaluated their overall trust and percentage-based trust in the automated driving system and provided usability-related ratings for that block. After all four blocks had been completed, participants proceeded to the third part of the questionnaire, which collected demographic information, including age, gender, and driving experience. Upon completion of the questionnaire, participants were compensated for their time.

3 Results

3.1 Descriptive Statistics Across System Reliability Conditions

First, independent-samples *t*-tests were conducted to compare participants' prior experience with automated driving, acceptance of automated driving systems, and personality traits between the 70% and 100% reliability conditions. The results revealed no significant differences across any of these measures (see Table 1), indicating that the two groups were comparable in terms of baseline characteristics. Next, descriptive statistics were computed separately for the 70% and 100% reliability conditions for the three categories of dependent variables examined in this study—trust-related indicators, calibration-related indicators, and usability-related indicators. The detailed results are presented in Table 2.

Table 1. Descriptive statistics of control variables across system reliability conditions

Variables	Reliability 70% *M* (*SD*)	Reliability100% *M* (*SD*)	*t*	*p*
Prior experience with ADS	1.79 (2.13)	1.29 (1.38)	1.14	0.29
Acceptance of automation				
Benefits in situations	3.74 (1.11)	4.06 (1.20)	1.19	0.28
Benefits in usefulness	3.53 (1.01)	3.46 (0.99)	0.07	0.80
System concern	3.77 (0.88)	3.99 (0.91)	0.90	0.35
Concern scenarios	4.53 (0.96)	4.55 (0.86)	0.01	0.92
Personality traits				
Extraversion	3.94 (1.20)	3.77 (1.08)	0.34	0.56
Agreeableness	4.36 (0.83)	4.50 (1.00)	0.34	0.56
Conscientiousness	4.38 (0.98)	4.09 (1.21)	1.07	0.31
Neuroticism	4.24 (1.02)	4.11 (0.89)	0.30	0.59
Openness	4.24 (0.94)	4.23 (1.05)	0.002	0.97

Table 2. Descriptive statistics of dependent variables across experimental conditions.

Dependent variables	Reliability 70% *M* (*SD*)				Reliability 100% *M* (*SD*)			
	Low-U	Low-U	High-U	High-U	Low-U	Low-U	High-U	High-U
	Low-T	High-T	Low-T	High-T	Low-T	High-T	Low-T	High-T
Trust-related indicators								
Takeover rate	0.70 (0.27)	0.79 (0.25)	0.85 (0.17)	0.85 (0.18)	0.69 (0.35)	0.79 (0.35)	0.84 (0.25)	0.90 (0.22)
Overall trust	54.61 (12.37)	58.30 (11.22)	54.27 (11.07)	57.48 (10.05)	53.79 (10.13)	57.89 (10.08)	54.64 (8.76)	58.79 (9.16)
Calibration-related indicators								
Takeover rate deviation	0.22 (0.15)	0.23 (0.13)	0.20 (0.10)	0.21 (0.11)	0.31 (0.35)	0.21 (0.35)	0.16 (0.25)	0.10 (0.22)
Trust calibration deviation	18.21 (15.59)	14.48 (10.76)	19.00 (18.50)	19.15 (12.61)	43.32 (24.61)	26.64 (18.02)	38.50 (23.58)	29.29 (21.61)
Usability-related indicators								
Perceived understandability	5.11 (0.81)	5.61 (0.91)	5.13 (0.92)	5.61 (0.79)	4.98 (1.28)	5.60 (0.89)	5.35 (0.93)	5.81 (0.80)
Satisfaction	4.97 (1.24)	5.45 (1.03)	4.97 (1.16)	5.39 (0.93)	4.61 (1.52)	5.32 (1.31)	5.00 (1.41)	5.43 (1.40)
Perceived usefulness	5.21 (1.36)	5.42 (1.15)	5.24 (1.28)	5.61 (1.00)	4.96 (1.23)	5.21 (1.26)	5.43 (0.88)	5.46 (1.04)
Intention to use	5.12 (1.39)	5.61 (1.48)	5.30 (1.49)	5.52 (1.15)	5.00 (1.36)	5.36 (1.22)	5.11 (1.32)	5.43 (1.29)

Note. *U* denotes urgency, with Low-U indicating the low-urgency condition and High-U indicating the high-urgency condition; *T* denotes transparency, with Low-T indicating the low-transparency condition and High-T indicating the high-transparency condition

3.2 Effects of System Reliability, Urgency, and Transparency on Trust-Related Indicators

A series of 2 (system reliability: 70% vs. 100%) × 2 (urgency: low vs. high) × 2 (transparency: low vs. high) mixed-design analyses of variance (ANOVAs) were conducted in R for each dependent variable. This section focuses on trust-related indicators, including overall trust measured by the Trust in Automation (TIA) scale and takeover rate.

The ANOVA results for overall trust revealed a significant main effect of transparency, $F = 24.184$, $p < .001$, $\eta^2 = 0.291$. Specifically, participants reported significantly higher overall trust in the high-transparency condition ($M = 58.117$, $SD = 1.224$) than in the low-transparency condition ($M = 54.327$, $SD = 1.281$). No other main effects or interaction effects reached statistical significance.

For takeover rate, the ANOVA revealed a significant main effect of urgency, $F = 11.126$, $p = .001$, $\eta^2 = 0.159$, with a higher takeover rate observed under high-urgency conditions ($M = 0.861$, $SD = 0.025$) than under low-urgency conditions ($M = 0.741$, $SD = 0.037$). A significant main effect of transparency was also found, $F = 6.199$, $p = .016$, $\eta^2 = 0.095$, indicating that takeover rates were higher in the high-transparency condition ($M = 0.834$, $SD = 0.029$) than in the low-transparency condition ($M = 0.769$, $SD = 0.031$). In addition, a significant interaction between urgency and transparency was observed for takeover rate, $F = 4.770$, $p = .033$, $\eta^2 = 0.075$. As illustrated in Fig. 2, under low-urgency conditions, participants exhibited a higher takeover rate in the high-transparency condition than in the low-transparency condition. In contrast, under high-urgency conditions, the effect of transparency on takeover rate was not statistically significant.

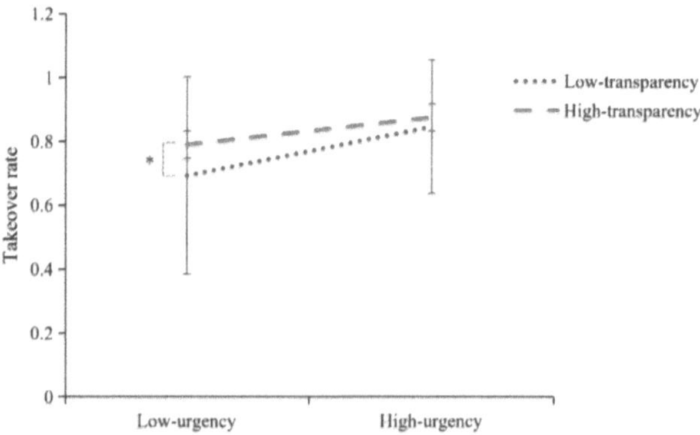

Fig. 2. Interaction effects of urgency and transparency on takeover rate.

3.3 Effects of System Reliability, Urgency, and Transparency on Calibration-Related Indicators and Usability-Related Indicators

Three-factor mixed-design ANOVAs were conducted to examine the effects of system reliability, urgency, and transparency on calibration-related indicators. Takeover rate deviation was calculated as the absolute difference between the observed takeover rate and the actual system reliability level. The analysis revealed a significant main effect of urgency on takeover rate deviation, $F = 11.126$, $p = .001$, $\eta^2 = 0.159$. Specifically, takeover rate deviation was significantly lower under high-urgency conditions ($M = 0.167$, $SD = 0.021$) than under low-urgency conditions ($M = 0.245$, $SD = 0.031$). A significant main effect of transparency was also observed, $F = 6.199$, $p = .016$, $\eta^2 = 0.095$, indicating that takeover rate deviation was lower in the high-transparency condition ($M = 0.188$, $SD = 0.024$) than in the low-transparency condition ($M = 0.225$, $SD = 0.026$). In addition, a significant interaction between urgency and system reliability was found, $F = 5.554$, $p = .022$, $\eta^2 = 0.086$, as well as a significant interaction between transparency and system reliability, $F = 8.973$, $p = .004$, $\eta^2 = 0.132$. As illustrated in Fig. 3A, when system reliability was 100%, takeover rate deviation was significantly lower under high-urgency conditions ($M = 0.130$, $SD = 0.031$) than under low-urgency conditions (M = 0.262, SD = 0.046). Similarly, as shown in Fig. 3B, takeover rate deviation was significantly lower in the high-transparency condition (M = 0.155, SD = 0.036) compared to the low-transparency condition (M = 0.237, SD = 0.038). However, under the 70% reliability condition, neither urgency nor transparency had a significant effect on takeover rate deviation.

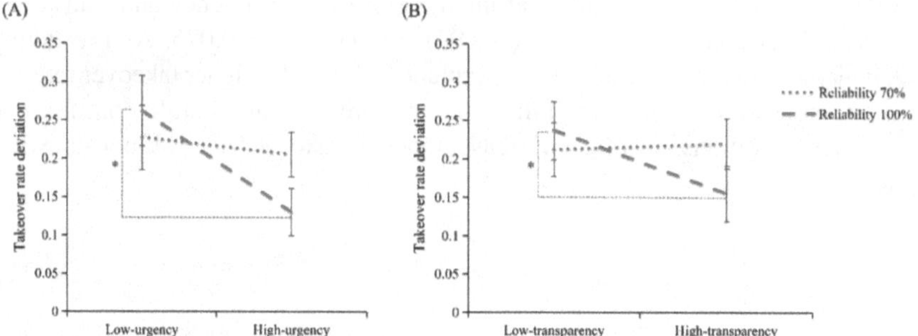

Fig. 3. Interaction effects of system reliability with urgency and transparency on takeover rate deviation. Panel A illustrates the interaction between system reliability and urgency, while Panel B illustrates the interaction between system reliability and transparency.

Trust calibration deviation was calculated as the absolute difference between participants' percentage-based trust ratings, reported after each experimental condition, and the actual system reliability level. A mixed-design ANOVA with trust calibration deviation as the dependent variable revealed a significant main effect of transparency, $F = 14.429$, $p < .001$, $\eta^2 = 0.199$. Specifically, trust calibration deviation was significantly lower under high-transparency conditions (M = 22.391, SD = 1.936) than under low-transparency conditions (M = 29.758, SD = 2.402). A significant main effect of system reliability was also observed, $F = 18.253$, $p < .001$, $\eta^2 = 0.236$, indicating that trust calibration deviation was significantly lower in the 70% reliability condition (M = 17.712, SD = 2.652) than in the 100% reliability condition (M = 34.438, SD = 2.879).

In addition, a significant interaction between transparency and system reliability was found, $F = 8.390$, $p = .005$, $\eta^2 = 0.125$, as well as a significant interaction between transparency and urgency, $F = 6.682$, $p = .012$, $\eta^2 = 0.102$. As illustrated in Fig. 4A, under the 100% reliability condition, trust calibration deviation was significantly lower in the high-transparency condition (M = 27.964, SD = 2.848) than in the low-transparency condition (M = 40.911, SD = 3.534), whereas no significant difference was observed between transparency conditions under the 70% reliability condition. Moreover, as shown in Fig. 4B, within the high-transparency condition, trust calibration deviation was significantly lower under low-urgency scenarios (M = 20.564, SD = 1.868) than under high-urgency scenarios (M = 24.219, SD = 2.225). In contrast, no significant difference between urgency levels was observed under the low-transparency condition.

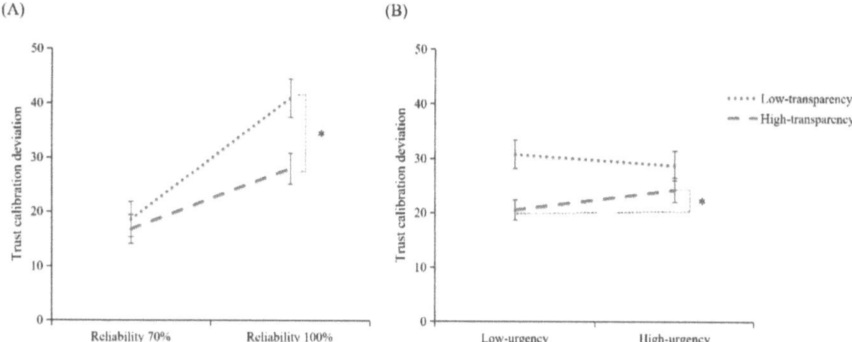

Fig. 4. Interaction effects of transparency with system reliability and urgency on trust calibration deviation. Panel A illustrates the interaction between transparency and system reliability, while Panel B illustrates the interaction between transparency and urgency.

Finally, three-way analyses of variance were conducted on the usability-related indicators. Significant main effects of transparency were observed for perceived understandability, satisfaction, and intention to use (all *ps* $< .001$). As illustrated in Fig. 5, compared with the low-transparency condition, participants reported higher perceived understandability, greater satisfaction, and stronger intention to use the automated driving system under the high-transparency condition. No significant main effects or interaction effects were found for perceived usefulness.

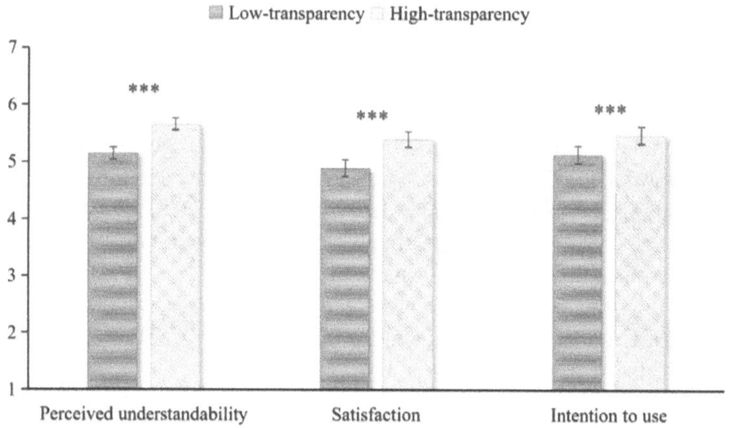

Fig. 5. Main effects of transparency on usability-related indicators.

3.4 Dynamic Trust Analysis

Changes in momentary trust across trials under different combinations of urgency and transparency are shown in Figs. 6A and 6B for the 70% and 100% reliability conditions, respectively. By comparison, larger fluctuations in momentary trust were observed when false-alarm trials occurred (i.e., Trials 2, 5, and 8 in the 70% reliability condition).

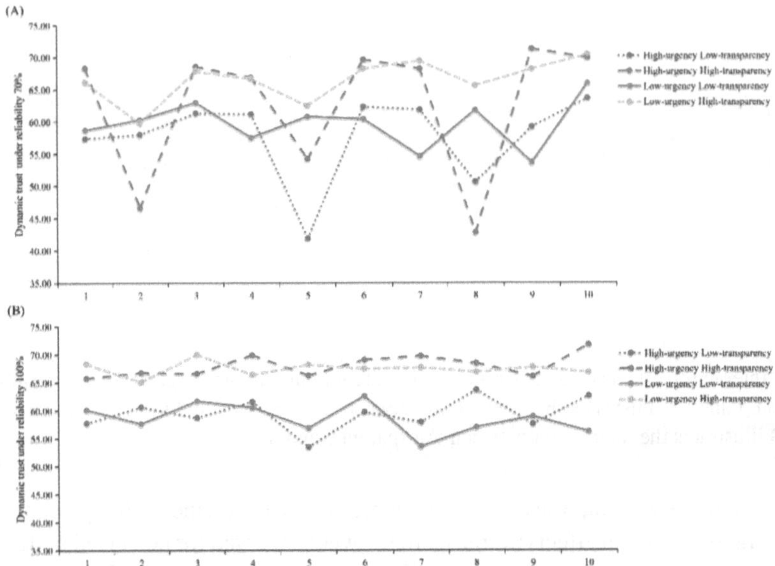

Fig. 6. Dynamic trust trajectories across experimental conditions under different levels of system reliability. Panel A shows the 70% reliability condition, and Panel B shows the 100% reliability condition.

To further examine the dynamic effects of false alarms on trust, changes in momentary trust were analyzed in greater detail. Trust decline was calculated as the difference in trust ratings between a false-alarm trial and the immediately preceding trial, whereas trust recovery was calculated as the difference between the trial immediately following a false alarm and the false-alarm trial. These values were averaged across the three false-alarm occurrences in each experimental condition. Two-way repeated-measures ANOVAs were then conducted on both trust decline and trust recovery, with urgency (low vs. high) and transparency (low vs. high) as within-subjects factors. For trust decline, significant main effects were found for transparency ($F = 13.327, p < .001, \eta^2 = 0.294$) and urgency ($F = 14.039, p < .001, \eta^2 = 0.305$). Specifically, trust decreased more sharply following system false alarms under the high-transparency condition ($M = -12.364, SD = 3.672$) than under the low-transparency condition ($M = -2.995, SD = 3.082$). Similarly, trust decline was greater under high-urgency alerts ($M = -14.960, SD = 4.640$) than under low-urgency alerts ($M = -0.399, SD = 2.391$).

A similar pattern was observed for trust recovery. Significant main effects of transparency ($F = 10.522, p = .003, \eta^2 = 0.247$) and urgency ($F = 12.719, p = .001, \eta^2 = 0.284$) were found. Trust rebounded more strongly following subsequent correct alerts under the high-transparency condition ($M = 13.697, SD = 2.984$) than under the low-transparency condition ($M = 4.429, SD = 2.765$). Likewise, trust recovery was greater under high-urgency alerts ($M = 16.364, SD = 4.231$) than under low-urgency alerts ($M = 1.763, SD = 1.717$).

4 Discussion

This study investigated how system reliability, urgency, and transparency jointly influence drivers' trust, trust calibration, and usability evaluations in takeover scenarios. Overall, the results indicate that drivers' takeover behavior was primarily shaped by situational urgency and the transparency of takeover prompts, whereas drivers' overall trust was more closely associated with system transparency. Consistent with prior research, drivers were more likely to take over control in high-urgency situations, where time pressure and risk salience are heightened. Previous studies have similarly shown that road environment characteristics (Agrawal et al. 2017; Jamson et al. 2013), the predictability of takeover events (Dogan et al. 2017), and the available time budget for takeover (Beukel & Van der Voort 2013; Gold et al. 2013) play critical roles in takeover performance. Under urgent conditions, reduced response time likely motivates drivers to intervene more readily to mitigate potential accidents.

Beyond urgency effects, the present study further demonstrated that providing explanations for takeover requests significantly enhanced drivers' trust and increased their likelihood of taking over control, supporting evidence that higher levels of system transparency improve operator performance and trust (Mercado et al. 2016). Notably, the impact of transparency on takeover behavior was most pronounced in low-urgency scenarios, in which potential hazards are less salient and may be difficult for drivers to detect. In such contexts, low-transparency prompts may fail to justify the necessity of a takeover, leading drivers to perceive the request as unwarranted and respond with lower trust and reduced engagement. In contrast, high-transparency prompts offer explanatory information that helps drivers identify safety-relevant cues, thereby supporting more appropriate takeover decisions even when situational urgency is low.

In contrast to transparency, system reliability did not exhibit a significant main effect on overall trust ratings, which remained at approximately 55 on the 0–100 scale under both the 70% and 100% reliability conditions. This pattern suggests that drivers' trust judgments were not determined solely by whether takeover alerts were correct or incorrect. Rather, drivers may have formed a more conservative assessment of the automated driving system's ability to independently handle complex road events, resulting in relatively stable trust evaluations across reliability conditions. However, analyses of calibration-related indicators revealed that urgency, transparency, and system reliability jointly influenced how accurately drivers calibrated their trust and takeover behavior. Transparency consistently showed significant main effects on both takeover rate deviation and trust calibration deviation, highlighting the importance of cognitive feedback in supporting trust calibration in automated decision-support systems (Seong & Bisantz 2008). Interaction analyses further indicated that the benefits of high transparency were most pronounced under conditions of high system reliability and low urgency. Even when system reliability reached 100%, drivers' baseline trust and takeover rates remained relatively low; nevertheless, transparent explanations appeared to compensate for this limitation by improving drivers' understanding of the system's rationale, thereby enhancing trust calibration. In low-urgency situations, where risks are less immediately apparent, transparency may therefore play a particularly critical role in drawing attention to latent hazards and supporting well-calibrated trust. In addition, a significant interaction between system reliability and urgency was observed for takeover rate deviation. Specifically, under high-reliability conditions, drivers exhibited greater takeover deviation in low-urgency scenarios. One possible explanation is that high system reliability not only increases drivers' trust in the system's ability to issue appropriate takeover requests but also strengthens their confidence in the system's automated driving capability. As a result, in low-urgency contexts, drivers may expect the system to handle the situation autonomously and are therefore less inclined to intervene, leading to reduced manual takeovers and increased takeover deviation.

Regarding usability-related indicators, significant main effects of transparency were observed for perceived understandability, satisfaction, and intention to use. Compared with low-transparency conditions, high-transparency prompts enhanced drivers' understanding of the automated driving system, increased satisfaction with the system, and strengthened their willingness to continue using it. These findings suggest that providing explicit explanations for takeover requests benefits users' comprehension and subjective evaluation of the system across both high- and low-urgency scenarios. This is consistent with previous research in other automated systems: Seong and Bisantz (2008) demonstrated that cognitive feedback supports operators' understanding of automated decision-support systems, while Mercado et al. (2016) found that perceived system usability increases with higher transparency levels. Collectively, these results indicate that high-transparency interfaces can simultaneously improve drivers' trust, trust calibration, and subjective experience, highlighting the broader value of explanatory information in automated driving systems.

In terms of dynamic trust, the present study revealed that when the system issued false takeover alerts—scenarios in which a takeover was unnecessary—providing explanations for the alert caused a pronounced immediate drop in trust. However, when subsequent alerts were accurate, trust rebounded more strongly. This rapid trust recovery aligns with findings by Kraus et al. (2020). Yet, whereas their study suggested that high transparency can mitigate trust loss during system failures, our results indicate the opposite in the context of false alerts: highly transparent explanations made the system's erroneous judgment more salient, leading to greater immediate trust degradation. This discrepancy may stem from differences in experimental context and transparency design. In Kraus et al. (2020), high transparency involved prior explanations of system failures and corresponding response strategies, which helped users form expectations and develop confidence in coping with system errors. In contrast, in the current study, false-alert scenarios made the system's error explicit, amplifying trust loss. Nonetheless, given that trust quickly recovered once correct information was provided, and that high transparency showed consistent benefits across interactions, providing explanatory information for takeover prompts remains advantageous. Beyond transparency, the urgency level of false alerts also influenced dynamic trust. Consistent with Yang et al. (2017), high-urgency alerts during false takeover scenarios induced larger trust reductions, likely because elevated warning levels magnify the perceived mismatch between system indication and actual road conditions. Moreover, no clear trend of incremental trust gain across successive trials was observed, even under conditions without system errors. This may be attributed, in part, to the limited number of trials, which constrains the observation of long-term trust calibration, and to the relative independence of each trial scenario, which emphasizes immediate situational judgment over cumulative interaction experience.

5 Conclusion

This study investigated the joint effects of system reliability, urgency, and transparency on drivers' trust, trust calibration, and usability in automated driving takeover scenarios. Results indicate that transparency consistently enhances drivers' understanding, satisfaction, and willingness to take over, while facilitating more accurate trust calibration, particularly under high reliability and low-urgency conditions. Takeover behavior is primarily influenced by situation urgency, with high-urgency scenarios prompting more frequent takeovers. Although system reliability had limited impact on overall trust, false alerts affected dynamic trust, with high-transparency prompts amplifying immediate trust reductions but supporting faster recovery when subsequent alerts were accurate. These findings highlight the importance of transparent, informative takeover prompts in improving trust, calibration, and user experience, offering critical guidance for designing safer and more effective human-automation interactions in automated driving systems.

Acknowledgments. This study was supported by the National Natural Science Foundation of China (Grant Nos. 32471132, 32071066).

Disclosure of Interests. The authors have no competing interests to declare that are relevant to the content of this article.

References

Agrawal, R., Wright, T.J., Samuel, S., Zilberstein, S., Fisher, D.L.: Effects of a change in environment on the minimum time to situation awareness in transfer of control scenarios. Transport. Res. Record J. Transport. Res. Board **2663**, 126–133 (2017)

Beukel, A.P.V.D., Voort, M.C.V.D.: The influence of time-criticality on Situation Awareness when retrieving human control after automated driving. In: International IEEE Conference on Intelligent Transportation Systems (2013)

Chen, J.Y., Barnes, M.J.: Human–agent teaming for multirobot control: a review of human factors issues. IEEE Trans. Hum.-Mach. Syst. **44**(1), 13–29 (2014)

Chen, J.Y., Procci, K., Boyce, M., Wright, J., Garcia, A., Barnes, M.: Situation awareness-based agent transparency. Army research laboratory. ARL-TR-6905 (2014)

Dogan, E., Rahal, M.C., Deborne, R., Delhomme, P., Kemeny, A., Perrin, J.: Transition of control in a partially automated vehicle: Effects of anticipation and non-driving-related task involvement. Transp. Res. Part F: Psychol. Behav. **46**, 205–215 (2017)

Doshi-Velez, F., Kim, B.: Towards a rigorous science of interpretable machine learning (2017). https://arxiv.org/abs/1702.08608v2

Gold, C., Dambock, D., Lorenz, L., Bengler, K.: "Take over!" How long does it take to get the driver back into the loop? Proc. Hum. Factors Ergon. Soc. Annual Meet. **57**(1), 1938–1942 (2013)

Hancock, P.A., Billings, D.R., Schaefer, K.E., Chen, J.Y., De Visser, E.J., Parasuraman, R.: A meta-analysis of factors affecting trust in human-robot interaction. Hum. Factors **53**(5), 517–527 (2011)

Jamson, A.H., Merat, N., Carsten, O.M.J., Lai, F.C.H.: Behavioural changes in drivers experiencing highly-automated vehicle control in varying traffic conditions. Transp. Res. Part C **30**(5), 116–125 (2013)

Jian, J.Y., Bisantz, A.M., Drury, C.G.: Foundations for an empirically determined scale of trust in automated systems. Int. J. Cogn. Ergon. **4**(1), 53–71 (2000)

Kraus, J., Scholz, D., Stiegemeier, D., Baumann, M.: The more you know: trust dynamics and calibration in highly automated driving and the effects of take-overs, system malfunction, and system transparency. Hum. Factors **62**(5), 718–736 (2020)

Lee, J.D., See, K.A.: Trust in automation: Designing for appropriate reliance. Hum. Factors **46**(1), 50–80 (2004)

Li, J.: Psychometric properties of ten-item personality inventory in China. Chin. J. Health Psychol. **21**(11), 1688–1692 (2013)

Lyons, J.B., Havig, P.R.: Transparency in a human-machine context: approaches for fostering shared awareness/intent. In: Shumaker, R., Lackey, S. (eds.) Virtual, Augmented and Mixed Reality. Designing and Developing Virtual and Augmented Environments. VAMR 2014. LNCS, vol. 8525. Springer, Cham (2014). https://doi.org/10.1007/978-3-319-07458-0_18

Mercado, J.E., Rupp, M.A., Chen, J.Y., Barnes, M.J., Barber, D., Procci, K.: Intelligent agent transparency in human–agent teaming for Multi-UxV management. Hum. Factors **58**(3), 401–415 (2016)

Parasuraman, R., Riley, V.: Humans and automation: use, misuse, disuse, abuse. Hum. Factors **39**(2), 230–253 (1997)

Park, E., Jenkins, Q., Jiang, X.: Measuring trust of human operators in new generation rescue robots. In: Proceedings of the JFPS International Symposium on Fluid Power, vol. 2008, pp. 489−492. The Japan Fluid Power System Society

Qu, W., Xu, J., Ge, Y., Sun, X., Zhang, K.: Development and validation of a questionnaire to assess public receptivity toward autonomous vehicles and its relation with the traffic safety climate in China. Accid. Anal. Prev. **128**, 78–86 (2019)

Seong, Y., Bisantz, A.M.: The impact of cognitive feedback on judgment performance and trust with decision aids. Int. J. Ind. Ergon. **38**(7–8), 608–625 (2008)

Seppelt, B.D.: Supporting operator reliance on automation through continuous feedback (doctoral dissertation). University of Iowa (2009)

Seppelt, B.D., Lee, J.D.: Modeling driver response to imperfect vehicle control automation. Procedia Manufac. **3**, 2621–2628 (2015)

Victor, T.W., Tivesten, E., Gustavsson, P., Johansson, J., Sangberg, F., Ljung Aust, M.: Automation expectation mismatch: incorrect prediction despite eyes on threat and hands on wheel. Hum. Factors **60**(8), 1095–1116 (2018)

Wright, J.L., Chen, J.Y., Lakhmani, S.G.: Agent transparency and reliability in human–robot interaction: the influence on user confidence and perceived reliability. IEEE Trans. Hum.-Mach. Syst. **50**(3), 254–263 (2019)

Yang, X.J., Unhelkar, V.V., Li, K., Shah, J.A.: Evaluating effects of user experience and system transparency on trust in automation. In: 12th ACM/IEEE International Conference on Human-Robot Interaction 2017 (HRI), pp. 408−416. IEEE (2017)

The Impact of Information Density on Driving Performance: A Comparative Study of Central Control and Instrument Cluster Displays

Zihao Liu[1,2], Xiaoyu Wang[1,2], Xiao Wang[3], and Liang Zhang[1,2](✉)

[1] State Key Laboratory of Cognitive Science and Mental Health, Institute of Psychology, Chinese Academy of Sciences, Beijing, China
zhangl@psych.ac.cn
[2] Department of Psychology, University of Chinese Academy of Sciences, Beijing, China
[3] Beijing Xiaoshi Technology Co., Ltd., Beijing, China

Abstract. Intelligent driving assistance systems deliver extensive data via in-vehicle interfaces; however, high information density can elevate cognitive demands and compromise safety. This research conducts two sequential simulator experiments to compare the differential impact of various in-vehicle displays on driver distraction. Experiment 1 focused on the Central Control Display (CCD), while Experiment 2 examined the Instrument Cluster Display (ICD), systematically exploring how information density affects driving performance and perceived workload. A Fuzzy Comprehensive Evaluation model synthesizing objective and subjective metrics was employed to quantify the distinct patterns of performance degradation under increasing informational load. The findings reveal that although high information density impairs performance for both displays, the underlying patterns differ fundamentally: the visual search accuracy on the CCD is highly sensitive to dense information, whereas increasing density on the ICD primarily delays information processing speed. These divergences indicate that differentiated design strategies are necessary for different display types when formulating human-machine interface guidelines. The conclusions advocate for a design philosophy that balances information provision with attentional resources, offering key insights for developing safety-centric adaptive in-vehicle information systems.

Keywords: Information Density · Instrument Cluster Display · Central Control Display · Driving Safety

1 Introduction

1.1 Study Background

Digital in-vehicle information systems (IVIS) have become the central carrier for presenting navigation, driving status, infotainment, and advanced driver-assistance functions in modern cars. These systems can improve comfort and situation awareness, but they also introduce additional visual and cognitive demands that compete with the primary task of

W. -C. Li and A. Plioutsias (Eds.): HCII 2026, LNAI 16708, pp. 33–44, 2026.
https://doi.org/10.1007/978-3-032-29459-3_3

vehicle control. Naturalistic and simulator studies have shown that demanding IVIS interactions increase driver workload and impair their performance [1]. As more functions are consolidated onto multi-function displays, a key ergonomics challenge is to determine how much information can be placed on each IVIS screen before safety-relevant performance begins to deteriorate.

Information density is defined as the amount of task-relevant information presented per unit visual area and time. Research on traffic signs and roadside information has demonstrated that dense visual layouts increase drivers' visual working-memory load, lengthen reaction times, and lead to more errors when interpreting sign content [2]. From the perspective of multiple resource theory, concentrating many visual elements in a limited field of view is likely to overload visual–spatial resources and central processing, particularly when drivers must divide attention between the roadway and a concurrent visual task [3]. However, acceptable levels of information density are unlikely to be universal: thresholds may depend on display location, the type of information presented, and the cost of moving gaze on and off the road.

Within the vehicle, the central control display (CCD) and the instrument cluster display (ICD) are now both visually rich interfaces that support frequent driver interactions. A substantial body of work has examined visual complexity in such interfaces, typically in terms of perceived visual complexity ratings and their relationship to glance behavior, search efficiency, and user preference [4–6]. For instrument clusters and dashboards, objective image-based metrics have been proposed to approximate visual complexity from feature-level properties such as element count, grouping, and spatial organization, and machine-learning models have been used to predict complexity ratings from these metrics [6, 7]. These approaches provide practical tools for evaluating static layouts and for screening alternative designs. Nevertheless, most studies treat the interface as a single category, use static screenshots rather than interactive driving tasks, and rarely ask whether increases in information density have different functional consequences for different in-vehicle displays.

Mental-workload research further suggests that subjective ratings (e.g., NASA-TLX) and task performance capture complementary facets of demand and should be interpreted jointly [2, 8]. Yet there is a lack of studies that integrate subjective workload and objective driving measures to compare how CCDs and ICDs behave when information density is systematically varied during active driving.

1.2 The Current Study

The present research addresses this gap by conducting two driving-simulator experiments that manipulate information density on the CCD and ICD, respectively. We combine measures of driving performance and secondary-task performance with a fuzzy comprehensive evaluation of workload to derive overall indices of driver state under different density conditions. This approach allows us to identify display-specific patterns of performance degradation and to derive differentiated design implications for safety-centric adaptive in-vehicle information systems.

2 Methods

2.1 Participants

Thirty-two drivers (Age from 19 to 41 years, $M = 28.34$ $SD = 6.40$ years) participated in the driving-simulator study.

2.2 Display Search Task

To assess drivers' awareness of visual information presented on the in-vehicle display, we employed a change-detection task, widely used in attention and driving safety research to measure visual awareness and change-detection performance [9]. While driving, participants were required to monitor the in-vehicle display and perform a concurrent display search task. On each trial, two images were presented sequentially on the display. Participants were instructed to (1) indicate whether the two images were identical or different and, when a change was detected, (2) verbally report the specific element that had changed (Fig. 1).

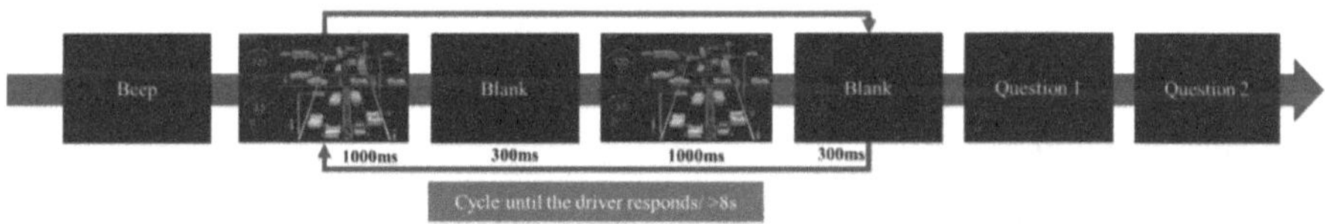

Fig. 1. One trail in change-detection task

In Experiment 1, the change-detection task was presented on the central control display (CCD), whereas in Experiment 2 the same task was presented on the instrument cluster display (ICD). This manipulation allowed us to compare how information presented on different in-vehicle display locations affected drivers' ability to detect and localize visual changes under comparable driving conditions. In present study, we set 6 sorts of CCD materials with different information density (6, 12, 18, 24, 30, 36 items, displayed in a 15.6 pad, 1920 * 1080) and 5 sorts of ICD materials with different information density (4, 8, 12, 16, 20 items, displayed in a 10.5 pad, 1280 * 480) (Fig. 2).

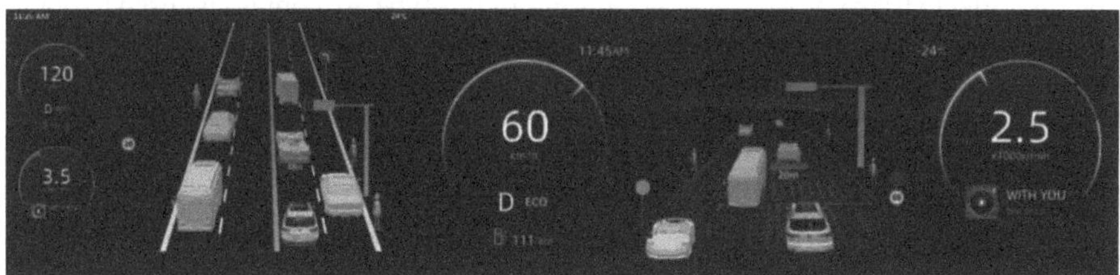

Fig. 2. The CCD (left) and ICD (right) Materials (12 items in each demo)

2.3 Driving Task

Throughout the experiment, participants performed a concurrent, continuous driving task. They were instructed to maintain a constant speed of 60 km/h while keeping the vehicle in the center of the lane. In addition, participants were told to respond promptly to traffic signals: whenever a red traffic light appeared, they were required to apply the brakes immediately. Thus, drivers had to regulate speed and respond to signal changes while simultaneously carrying out the display-based change-detection task (Fig. 3).

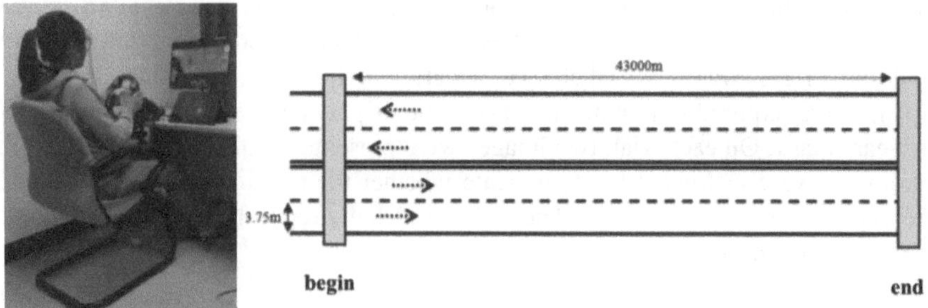

Fig. 3. The Driving Task. Participants engaging task (left) and simulated road in task (right).

2.4 Measurements

Driving Performance. Driving performance data were recorded by the STISIM driving simulator (STISIM Drive, Systems Technology Inc., Hawthorne, CA, USA). The system continuously logged standard kinematic and control variables at the simulator's default sampling rate, including vehicle speed, lateral lane position, and brake pedal status. From these signals we derived indices of safety-relevant performance such as mean speed, speed variability, lane-position variability, brake reaction time to red-light onset, and the proportion of missed or excessively delayed braking responses.

Subjective Visual Analogue Scales. Participants completed four visual analogue scales (VAS; 0–100) to capture more specific aspects of their subjective experience after driving. On each VAS, 0 represented "not at all" and 100 represented "extremely." The four probes assessed (1) perceived interference of the display task with driving (distraction), (2) perceived workload or burden, (3) perceived task difficulty, and (4) emotional state (negative affect/strain). Visual analogue ratings of this type are commonly used to obtain sensitive, continuous measures of perceived workload and affect in driving studies [7]. Higher scores indicated greater perceived interference, workload, difficulty, or more negative emotional experience.

2.5 Data Analysis

Data Processing and Statistical Analysis. Objective driving data were preprocessed using custom scripts written in Python 3.7.8. For each participant and trial, we extracted indices such as brake reaction time to red-light onset, lateral lane-deviation measures (e.g., proportion of time outside the lane center tolerance), and braking accuracy (proportion of appropriate braking responses). The derived variables were then exported for subsequent statistical analysis. Group-level analyses were conducted using IBM SPSS Statistics 23.0. For each experiment, one-way ANOVA was performed with information-density level (in CCD or ICD) as experimental factors, examining their effects on driving-performance indices and subjective measures.

Fuzzy Comprehensive Evaluation of Information Density Effects. To compare how information density influences driving performance for the Central Control Display (CCD, Experiment 1) and Instrument Cluster Display (ICD, Experiment 2), we adopted a fuzzy comprehensive evaluation (FCE) framework that aggregates objective and subjective indices into a single score for each display–density condition [10, 11]. The indicator system was designed to reflect both behavioral disruption and experienced workload. It comprised (a) objective driving and secondary-task metrics (brake reaction time, brake correctness, lateral lane deviation, secondary-task reaction time and item-wise accuracy) and (b) subjective ratings of perceived difficulty, mental workload, perceived interference, and emotional state. Indicator weights were determined by combining a data-driven "objective" component with an expert-based "subjective" component. For objective weights, we assumed that indicators whose normalized scores fluctuate more across density levels carry more information about the effect of informational load [12]. For indicator i, the sample mean and standard deviation across m conditions are:

$$\overline{r}_i = \frac{1}{m}\sum_{j=1}^{m} r_{ij}, \quad s_i = \sqrt{\frac{1}{m-1}\sum_{j=1}^{m}\left(r_{ij} - \overline{r}_i\right)^2}$$

The variance $v_i = s_i^2$ is taken as the objective information content, and objective weights are obtained by normalizing v_i:

$$w_i^{(\mathrm{obj})} = \frac{v_i}{\sum_{k=1}^{n} v_k}, \quad i = 1, \ldots, n$$

Thus, indicators that show stronger degradation with increasing information density (e.g., CCD visual search accuracy, ICD secondary-task reaction time) receive higher objective weights, whereas density-insensitive indicators contribute less. Variance-based schemes are widely used as transparent objective weighting methods in multi-criteria evaluation [12]. To capture theoretical priorities (e.g., safety-critical braking vs. secondary-task performance), we derived subjective weights with the Analytic Hierarchy Process (AHP) [13]. The hierarchy contained three levels: overall safety/usability (goal), first-level criteria (driving performance, secondary-task performance, subjective workload/affect), and second-level indicators. More than five experts in human factors, traffic safety and HMI design provided pairwise importance judgments using the 1–9 Saaty scale [13]. For each level, the resulting judgment matrix A yielded a principal eigenvector w, which was normalized and checked for consistency (CR < 0.10) to obtain subjective weights $w_i^{(subj)}$. Combining objective and subjective components, intermediate factors were computed:

$$u_i = w_i^{(\mathrm{obj})} \cdot w_i^{(\mathrm{subj})}$$

Then normalized to give final composite weights:

$$w_i = \frac{u_i}{\sum_{k=1}^{n} u_k}, \quad i = 1, \ldots, n$$

This multiplicative fusion of objective and subjective weights is consistent with previous work that integrates data-driven and expert knowledge in fuzzy evaluation models [14]. Given the comprehensive weight vector w = $(w_1 \ldots w_n)$ and the membership matrix *R*, the fuzzy synthetic score for information-density condition j was computed as:

$$S_j = \sum_{i=1}^{n} w_i r_{ij}$$

Because larger r_{ij} denote worse outcomes, lower S_j values indicate better overall safety and usability. Applying the same procedure separately to CCD and ICD yielded fuzzy score profiles across information-density levels for each display.

3 Results

3.1 One-Way AVNOVA Result

For the CCD display-search task, a one-way repeated-measures ANOVA with information density (6, 12, 18, 24, 30, 36 elements) as the within-subject factor revealed a significant main effect on search reaction time. As information density increased, drivers took progressively longer to complete the change-detection judgments, with mean reaction times rising monotonically across density levels. Accuracy showed the opposite pattern: overall, the proportion of correct judgments decreased as more elements were presented on the CCD. Pairwise comparisons indicated two pronounced drops in performance. The first significant decline in accuracy occurred between 6 and 12 elements, and a second significant decline occurred between 24 and 30 elements. When the number of elements exceeded 24, drivers' detection accuracy fell below 75%, indicating that high information density on the CCD substantially impairs their ability to correctly detect changes (Fig. 4).

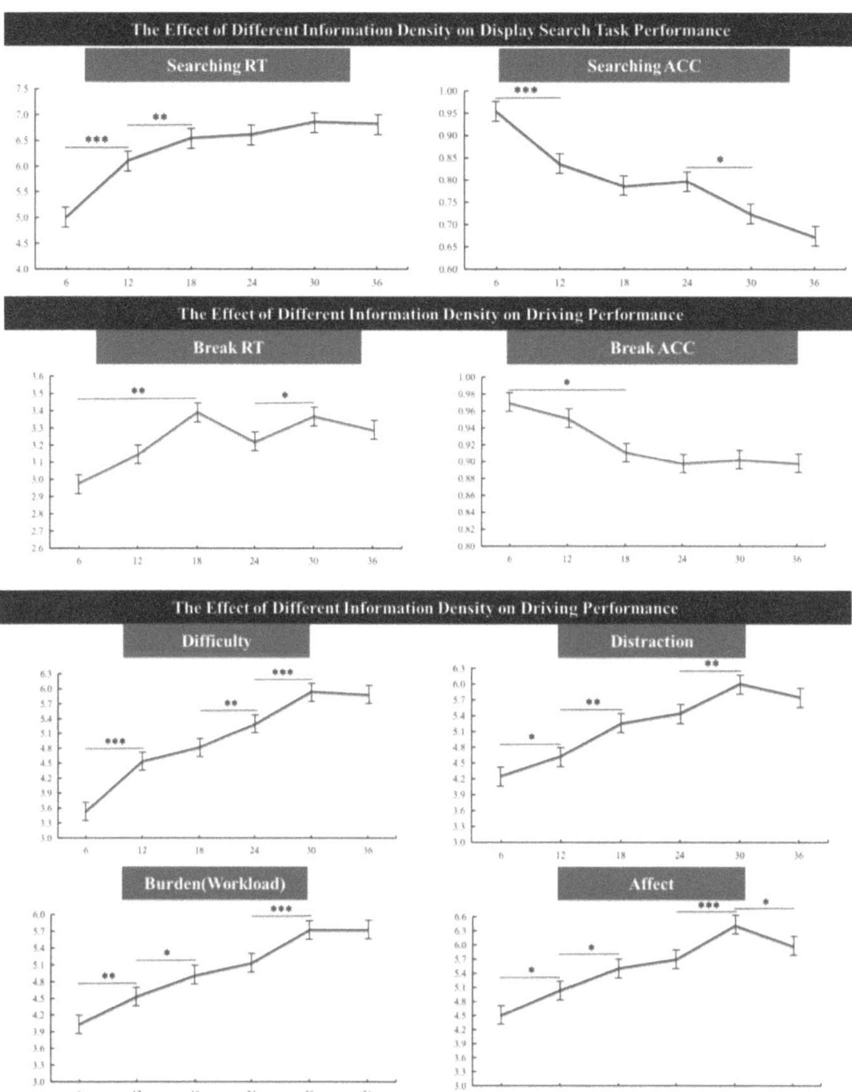

Fig. 4. The result of one-way ANOVA in different CCD information density situations *** $p < 0.001$, ** $p < 0.01$, * $p < 0.05$

For the ICD display-search task, a one-way repeated-measures ANOVA with information density (4, 8, 12, 16, 20 elements) as the within-subject factor revealed a significant main effect on search reaction time. As the amount of information presented on the instrument cluster increased, drivers' reaction times in the change-detection task rose steadily across density levels. Accuracy showed the opposite trend. The proportion of correct judgments decreased as information density increased, with pairwise comparisons indicating significant drops in accuracy from the lowest to the higher density conditions. These findings indicate that higher information density on the ICD not only slows drivers' visual search but also reduces their ability to correctly detect and identify the required information.

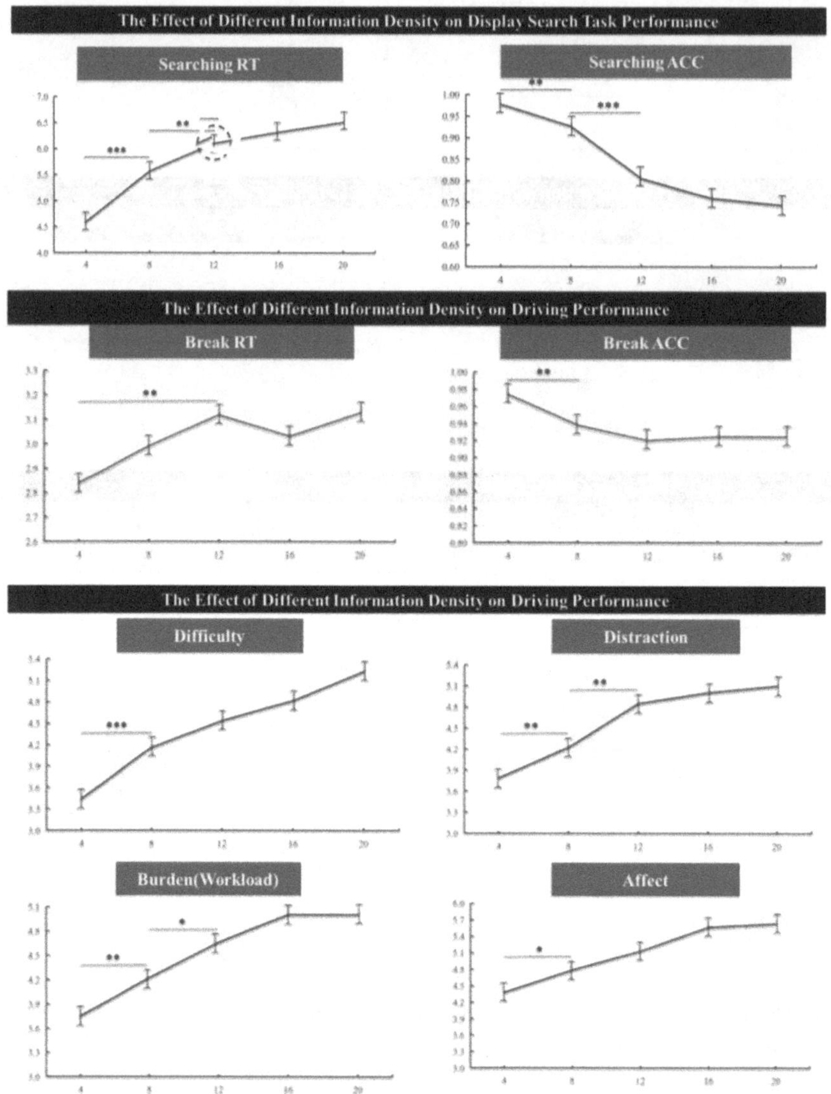

Fig. 5. The result of one-way ANOVA in different CCD information density situations *** $p < 0.001$, ** $p < 0.01$, * $p < 0.05$

3.2 Fuzzy Comprehensive Evaluation Result

For the CCD, the fuzzy comprehensive evaluation model yielded a single composite index Z for each information-density condition (6, 12, 18, 24, 30, 36 elements), defined as a weighted combination of standardized indicators (e.g., brake reaction time, braking accuracy, display-search accuracy, lateral deviation, and the subjective ratings of distraction, workload, difficulty and affect). Higher values of Z correspond to better overall driving performance and lower subjective strain.

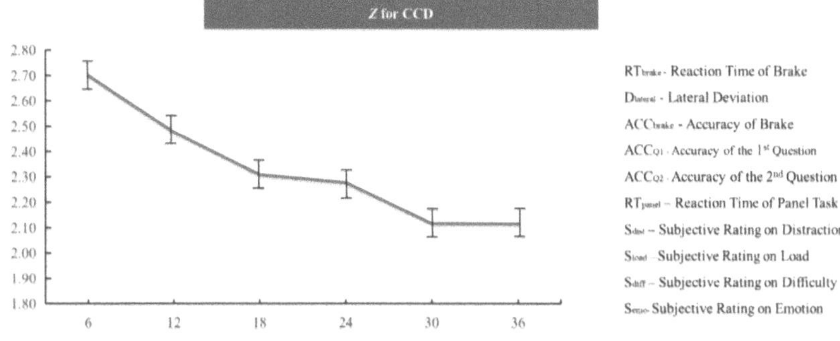

$$Z = 0.872RT_{brake} + 0.616ACC_{Q2} + 0.586ACC_{brake} + 0.550ACC_{Q1} + 0.545S_{dist} + 0.473S_{load} + 0.373S_{diff} + 0.332D_{lateral} + 0.229RT_{panel} + 0.197 \times S_{emo}$$

Fig. 6. The result of fuzzy comprehensive evaluation for CCD.

As shown in Fig. 5, the composite index decreased markedly as information density on the CCD increased. The steepest decline occurred between 6 and 18 elements, after which the curve began to flatten. Around 24 elements, the composite score reached a relatively low and stable level, and further increases to 30 and 36 elements produced only small additional changes. Taken together with the single-measure analyses, these results indicate that increasing CCD information density progressively deteriorates the overall safety-related state of the driver, and that densities above about 24 elements are associated with a sustained degradation in comprehensive performance.

For the ICD, the fuzzy comprehensive evaluation model similarly produced a single composite index Z for each information-density condition (4, 8, 12, 16, 20 elements), defined as a weighted combination of the standardized driving-performance and subjective measures (e.g., instrument-panel search accuracy, brake reaction time and accuracy, lateral deviation, and ratings of distraction, workload, difficulty, and affect). Higher values of Z indicate better overall performance and lower subjective strain (Fig. 7).

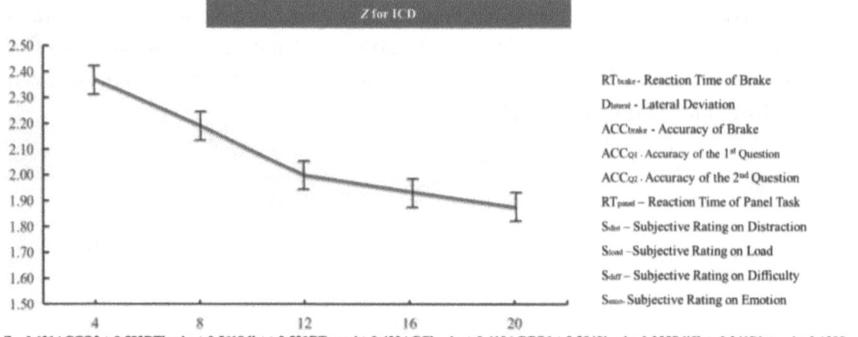

Fig. 7. The result of fuzzy comprehensive evaluation for ICD.

As shown in Fig. 6, the composite index decreased monotonically as information density on the ICD increased. The decline was relatively steep between 4 and 12 elements, after which the curve became flatter and additional increases to 16 and 20 elements yielded only modest further reductions in the composite score. Taken together, the ICD model suggests that increasing information density on the instrument cluster progressively degrades the overall driving–display performance state, with most of the deterioration occurring within the lower to medium density range.

4 Discussion

The present study examined how graded information density on two common in-vehicle displays—the central control display (CCD) and the instrument cluster display (ICD)—affects drivers' visual search, driving performance, and subjective experience. Across both experiments, increasing the number of on-screen elements systematically lengthened search times, impaired change-detection and braking performance, and elevated ratings of difficulty, distraction, workload and negative affect, confirming that information density is a major source of IVIS-related distraction [1, 2].

For the CCD, search reaction time increased monotonically with information density, whereas search accuracy showed two pronounced drops: a first decline between 6 and 12 elements and a second decline once more than 24 elements were displayed. Beyond 24 elements, change-detection accuracy fell below 75% and the fuzzy composite index stabilized at a low level. This pattern suggests that drivers initially compensate for added information by extending search and increasing gaze shifts between the forward view and the off-axis CCD, but this compensatory strategy breaks down at higher densities, when longer off-road glances would jeopardise lane keeping and hazard detection [15, 16]. High-density CCD layouts therefore primarily harm the quality of visual search.

For the ICD, information density also produced longer search times and lower accuracy, but the composite index declined more smoothly, with most degradation occurring between 4 and 12 elements and smaller losses at higher densities. Because the ICD lies close to the forward line of sight, eye movements are shorter and the spatial cost of glances is reduced, which may encourage drivers to spend slightly more time inspecting dense ICD layouts [17, 20]. Nevertheless, the monotonic decreases in accuracy and composite scores show that even near-roadway displays become problematic when visual layouts are crowded, overloading visual–spatial resources and working memory [2, 3].

These findings refine the notion of visual complexity in IVIS research [5, 6]. Rather than treating complexity as a single static property, our results demonstrate that the same nominal number of elements has different functional consequences depending on display location and associated search patterns. For the tested 15.6-inch CCD, densities above roughly 24 elements push drivers into an error-prone regime; for the 10.5-inch ICD, most deterioration already occurs from low to medium density. The fuzzy comprehensive evaluation, which integrates objective performance and subjective workload, further illustrates the value of multi-criteria assessment methods in identifying density levels at which additional information brings diminishing benefits but substantial safety costs [18]. Future work should validate these density–performance functions across different screen geometries, automation levels and task types, and relate them to existing glance-based safety criteria [15, 16, 19].

5 Conclusion

This study provides converging evidence that information density on in-vehicle displays is a key determinant of driver distraction and degraded performance. For both the CCD and ICD, adding more on-screen elements led to slower visual search, poorer change-detection and braking performance, and higher subjective workload. However, the pattern of degradation differed by display type: high-density CCD layouts produced step-like drops in accuracy and a low-performance plateau beyond about 24 elements, whereas ICD layouts showed a smoother, primarily time-based deterioration with most losses between 4 and 12 elements. From the human-car interaction perspective, our results argue for conservative limits on simultaneous information elements during manual driving and for display-specific strategies that priorities essential content within the driver's limited visual and cognitive resources. Practically, designers of safety-critical IVIS should avoid densely populated layouts, use progressive disclosure and context-adaptive displays for non-urgent information, and consider deferring detailed assistance information to phases of higher automation or low driving demand.

Acknowledgments. This study was funded by the National Natural Science Foundation of China (Grant No. T2192932).

Disclosure of Interests. The authors have no competing interests to declare that are relevant to the content of this article.

References

1. Strayer, D.L., Cooper, J.M., Goethe, R.M., McCarty, M.M., Getty, D.J., Biondi, F.: Assessing the visual and cognitive demands of in-vehicle information systems. Cogn. Res. Princ. Implic. **4**, 18 (2019)

2. Du, J., Ren, G., Liu, W., Li, H.: How is the visual working memory load of driver influenced by information density of traffic signs? Transp. Res. Part F Traffic Psychol. Behav. **86**, 65–83 (2022)
3. Wickens, C.D.: Multiple resources and mental workload. Hum. Factors **50**(3), 449–455 (2008)
4. Lee, S.C., Hwangbo, H., Ji, Y.G.: Perceived visual complexity of in-vehicle information display and its effects on glance behavior and preferences. Int. J. Hum.-Comput. Interact. **32**, 654–664 (2016)
5. Yoon, S.H., Lim, J., Ji, Y.G.: Assessment model for perceived visual complexity of automotive instrument cluster. Appl. Ergon. **46**, 76–83 (2015)
6. Lee, S.C., Ji, Y.G.: Effects of visual complexity of in-vehicle information display on drivers' visual search and driving performance. Appl. Ergon. **75**, 124–131 (2019)
7. Bai, H., et al.: Objective metrics for assessing visual complexity of vehicle dashboards: a machine-learning based study. In: Krömker, H. (ed.) HCI in Mobility, Transport, and Automotive Systems. HCII 2023, LNCS, vol. 14049, pp. 103–113. Springer, Cham (2023)
8. Hart, S.G.: NASA-Task Load Index (NASA-TLX); 20 years later. In: Proceedings of the Human Factors and Ergonomics Society Annual Meeting, vol. 50, pp. 904–908. HFES, Santa Monica (2006)
9. Rensink, R.A., O'Regan, J.K., Clark, J.J.: To see or not to see: the need for attention to perceive changes in scenes. Psychol. Sci. **8**(5), 368–373 (1997)
10. Chen, J., Wang, X., Cheng, Z., Gao, Y., Tremont, P.J.: Evaluation of the optimal quantity of in-vehicle information icons using a fuzzy synthetic evaluation model in a driving simulator. Accid. Anal. Prev. **176**, 106813 (2022)
11. Zhou, R., Li, Y., Li, H., et al.: Using a fuzzy comprehensive evaluation method to assess the usability of human–machine interfaces. J. Adv. Transp. **2017**, 5314802 (2017)
12. Diakoulaki, D., Mavrotas, G., Papayannakis, L.: Determining objective weights in multiple criteria problems: the CRITIC method. Comput. Oper. Res. **22**(7), 763–770 (1995)
13. Saaty, T.L.: The Analytic Hierarchy Process: Planning, Priority Setting, Resource Allocation. McGraw–Hill, New York (1980)
14. Liu, Z.W., Wei, H., Zhang, X., et al.: Research on comprehensive evaluation method of smart distribution network planning based on subjective and objective weighting approaches. Front. Energy Res. **10**, 975462 (2022)
15. Horrey, W.J., Wickens, C.D.: In-vehicle glance duration: distributions, tails, and a model of crash risk. Transp. Res. Rec. **2018**, 22–28 (2007)
16. Victor, T., Harbluk, J.L., Engström, J.A.: Sensitivity of eye-movement measures to in-vehicle task difficulty. Transp. Res. Part F Traffic Psychol. Behav. **8**(2), 167–190 (2005)
17. Konstantopoulos, P., Chapman, P., Crundall, D.: Driver's visual attention as a function of driving experience and visibility. Accid. Anal. Prev. **42**(3), 827–834 (2010)
18. Chen, S.J., Hwang, C.L.: Fuzzy Multiple Attribute Decision Making: Methods and Applications. Springer, Berlin (1992)
19. ISO 15007: Road vehicles—measurement and analysis of driver visual behaviour with respect to transport information and control systems. International Organization for Standardization, Geneva (2020)
20. Liu, Z., Liu, Z., Chen, T., Zhang, L.: A vehicle dashboard dataset towards visual complexity design. In: Praetorius, G., Mallam, S., Sharma, A., Ziakkas, D., Patriarca, R. (eds.) Advances in Human Factors of Transportation. AHFE 2025 International Conference, AHFE Open Access, vol. 186, AHFE International, USA (2025). https://doi.org/10.54941/ahfe1006519

Impact of Control Outcome Discrepancies Between Drivers and Driver Assistance Systems on Trust in the System

An Experimental Study Using a Driving Simulator

Yuki Mekata(✉), Mitsuharu Ogiya, and Hideki Katagiri

Kanagawa University, 3-27-1 Rokkakubashi Kanagawa-ku, Yokohama-shi, Kanagawa, Japan
yuki-mekata@kanagawa-u.ac.jp

Abstract. Calibrated trust in a driver assistance system is needed to ensure safe operation and proper system utilization. A previous study on trust dynamics revealed that discrepancies between driver expectations and system support outcomes affect trust in the system, whereas the level of discrepancy at which trust changes is unclear. This study aims to clarify the level of discrepancies between driver behavior and system assistance that affects trust in the system. Fifteen participants drove on straight roads using a driving simulator. The experiment involved cases of both manual braking and automatic braking. Trust in the system was evaluated under automatic braking in which the stopping-distance-gap deviation between the system and the driver was varied from −50% to 50%. The experimental results suggest that a system–driver deviation range of −30% to 20% could serve as a reference for the personal adaptation of driver assistance systems considering calibrated trust in the system. Although differences in braking distance may also affect trust in the system, the above findings about the acceptable range of discrepancies can serve as benchmarks for calibrating trust.

Keywords: personal adaptation · trust calibration · driving simulator

1 Introduction

1.1 Background

The development of driver assistance systems has advanced in recent years. According to the Society of Automotive Engineers' [1] automation levels, levels 3 and below of driving automation require drivers to remain involved in driving. The role of drivers while driving remains crucial, and they must properly recognize the system's limitations and capabilities for safe operation. Since both overtrust and undertrust can compromise safety [2], calibrated trust in the system is important for proper utilization.

In many driver assistance systems, the driver is warned or the system intervenes when the system detects a hazardous event based on criteria preset by manufacturers. Mismatches between the driver and the system's operating criteria may lead to negative

W. -C. Li and A. Plioutsias (Eds.): HCII 2026, LNAI 16708, pp. 45–56, 2026.
https://doi.org/10.1007/978-3-032-29459-3_4

behavioral changes, such as undertrust in the assistance, misunderstanding of system function or operation, or overtrust and dependence [3, 4]. A previous study on trust dynamics stated that the impact of changes in trust is significant, depending on the desirability of the final outcome [5]. In addition, a study on a forward collision warning system in automobiles found that driver trust is undermined when the warning timing does not align with driver expectations [6]. Although these results suggest that discrepancies between driver expectations and system support outcomes affect trust in the system, the level of discrepancy at which trust changes remains unclear.

Driver assistance systems are increasingly incorporating functions allowing drivers to adjust the system's behavior [7]. However, such driver-initiated adjustments may lead to bias toward overtrust [8]. Previous studies on personal adaptation in driver assistance systems have examined adaptation based on driving data acquired from each individual [9–11]. These studies indicated that the use of parameters adjusted to the individual effectively reduces false-alarm rates and improves system acceptance. However, the effect of personal adaptation on trust and perceived safety has not been sufficiently discussed. Therefore, these systems also carry the risk of inducing overtrust. With knowledge about the influence of discrepancies on trust in the system, the adaptation of systems to driver characteristics will realize systems that can appropriately calibrate trust levels.

1.2 Purpose

This study aims to quantify the range of discrepancy between driver behavior and system assistance that affects trust in the system. Quantitatively analyzing the effect of discrepancies will help realize appropriate systems from the perspective of trust calibration.

Specifically, through simulation experiments, we collected driving data on straight roads for two cases: (i) the driver manually controls braking and (ii) the automatic braking system (a driver assistance system) activates. In the latter case, the experiment was conducted under different deviations between the actual and driver-desired stopping distance gaps. The effect of system–driver discrepancies on trust in the system was investigated by recording and analyzing driving behavior data and trust scores.

2 Method

2.1 Experimental Outline

With the stopping distance gap during automatic braking as the outcome, data on changes in outcomes and trust in the driver assistance system were obtained through a simulation experiment. The experiment consisted of two phases, where the system's control was changed based on data concerning each driver's control. In Phase 1, the system was operated by the participant. In Phase 2, it was operated by the driver assistance system. Based on the data acquired in Phase 1, we identified reference values for each driver. By varying the magnitude of deviation of actual values from these reference values, we configured the system's control behavior for Phase 2.

2.2 Experimental Participants

The experiment involved 15 participants with driver's licenses (mean age 27.1, SD = 10.9). Each participant practiced driving on a simulator and became familiar with the controls before undertaking the task.

This study was implemented after obtaining written consent from the participants and was conducted after the review and approval of the Ethics Review Committee for Research Involving Human Subjects at Kanagawa University.

2.3 Experimental System

The driving simulator used in the experiment was built in Unity and controlled the vehicle via a steering wheel and pedals. Figure 1 shows an image of the experimental system and environment.

Fig. 1. Experimental scenery.

A 65-inch monitor (TH-65CQ1J, Panasonic Corp.) was used as the main display and positioned to provide a 60° horizontal field of view. Additionally, two 21.5-inch monitors (P2219H, Dell Technologies Inc.) and one 13.3-inch monitor (LCD-013-1080P, Broadwatch Inc.) were used as presenting mirrors; their placement, configured to match the mirrors' positions within the simulator, is shown in Fig. 2. A speedometer was displayed at the bottom of the screen, presenting a forward view and allowing the participant to confirm the vehicle's speed while driving.

The steering wheel and accelerator/brake pedals (PRO Racing Wheel and PRO Racing Pedals, Logitech International S.A.) were mounted on a wheel stand (AP2 Racing Wheel Stand, DELE Co., Ltd.) and positioned directly in front of the participant. The steering wheel angles and pedal positions were then adjusted to allow for comfortable control.

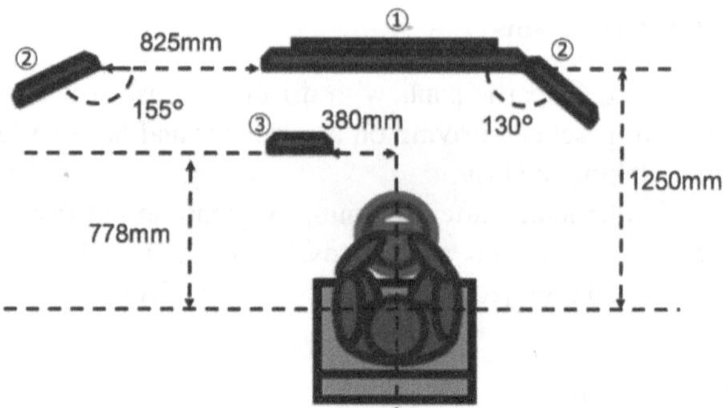

Fig. 2. Arrangement of displays.

2.4 Experimental Task

Driving Scene. On the driving simulator, we conducted a task where the participant decelerated and stopped their vehicle in response to a stationary preceding vehicle (Fig. 3). The experiment was conducted on a straight road with a single lane in each direction and a posted speed limit of 60 km/h. Driving was performed under left-hand traffic conditions, which are standard for Japanese drivers.

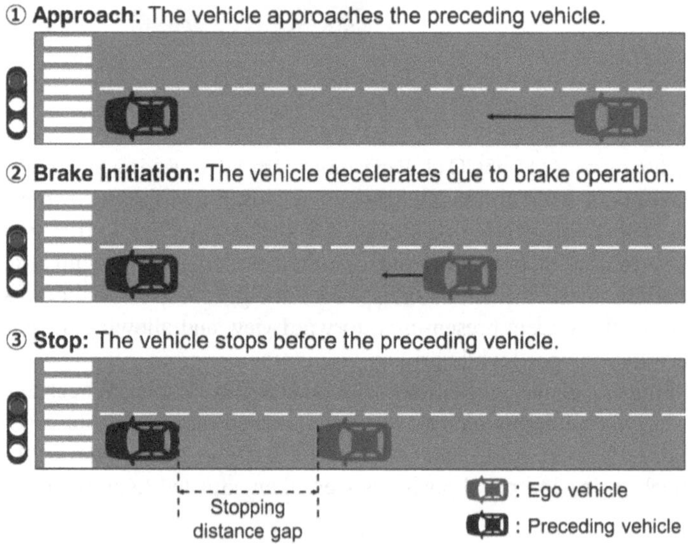

Fig. 3. Experimental task on the simulator. Driving on a straight road, the ego vehicle approaches a stationary preceding vehicle and stops.

This study focuses on the stopping distance gap at the moment the ego vehicle comes to a complete stop. The stopping distance gap is the distance between the rear end of the preceding vehicle and the front end of the ego vehicle when the ego vehicle's speed reaches 0 km/h.

Phase 1: Participant Control. In Phase 1, the ego vehicle was operated by the participant. The task was initiated while the vehicle was in motion, and the driving process, from initiation to the stopping of the vehicle. After completing each task, the participant evaluated their stop response, whether it was successful or a failure (because it was too early or too late).

One task consumed approximately 30 s. The task was repeated 30 times, and the overall time needed to complete Phase 1 was about 30 min.

Phase 2: Driver Assistance System Control. In Phase 2, the ego vehicle was operated by the driver assistance system. The system both maintained speed and decelerated via braking. In Phase 2, the vehicle repeatedly started and stopped, with one task consisting of three stops. Based on the experimental conditions (indicating stopping distance gap; Sect. 2.5), the task was repeated 11 times, under varying conditions across repetitions.

Except for the stopping distance gap, the system's control behavior was identical each time. Specifically, it traveled at 60 km/h during the approach. The braking distance, or the distance traveled from the moment of brake initiation until the vehicle came to a stop, was set to 26.8 m. When the brakes were initiated, a mark was displayed on the instrument panel on the screen, allowing the participants to confirm brake activation.

One task consumed about 4 min, and the overall time needed to complete Phase 2 was approximately 60 min.

2.5 Experimental Conditions

The stopping distance gap during Phase 2 was defined as an experimental condition, determined based on the data acquired in Phase 1.

First, among the 30 tasks in Phase 1, only those that were evaluated as "well" were selected. The average stopping distance gap was calculated as shown in Eq. (1).

$$\overline{g} = \frac{1}{|W|} \sum\nolimits_{i \in W} g_i, \tag{1}$$

where g_i is the stopping distance gap for task i and W is the set of tasks with positive assessments.

With $\overline{g}$ as the reference value, 11 conditions were defined by varying the deviation rate δ_k, or the discrepancy between the actual stopping distance gap and the gap desired by the driver, from -50% to 50% in 10% increments. The stopping distance gap for each condition is given by Eq. (2).

$$g_k = \overline{g}(1 + \delta_k/100) \tag{2}$$

A positive (negative) δ_k meant the stopping distance gap was greater (smaller) than the reference value, which was set per driver.

As described above, the braking distance was kept constant at 26.8 m across all conditions. For each condition k, deceleration was initiated when the distance to the preceding vehicle reached $g_k + 26.8$ m, and the vehicle came to a complete stop while maintaining a stopping distance gap of g_k.

2.6 Measurements and Metrics

Measurement of Driving and Monitoring Behaviors. Along with the pedal and steering wheel control inputs, the position coordinates and speeds of both the ego and preceding vehicles were recorded at 20 Hz during Phase 1 to analyze the driving behavior characteristics of each participant. In the experiment, the simulator had two pedals: an accelerator pedal and a brake pedal. The pedal control input was acquired as a continuous value ranging from -1 to 1, with a negative (positive) value indicating brake (accelerator) control.

The timing of each participant's brake initiation was detected based on a criterion established by confirming detection accuracy in preliminary experiments. This criterion was the time when the pedal input first turned negative before the ego vehicle came to a stop. The timing of the ego vehicle's stopping was the point at which its velocity reached zero. Based on the vehicle's coordinates at these points, the braking distance and the stopping distance gap were calculated.

In both phases, the participant's gaze point was measured using an eye-tracking device (EMR-10, NAC Image Technology Inc.) to capture and analyze behavioral changes caused by the deviation conditions. Each participant wore a visor-type measurement device, and head movement was not restricted during the experiment. The gaze points of both eyes were measured at 60 Hz. The experimental screen was divided into areas for the preceding vehicle, an instrument panel (the speedometer and the brake activation indicator), the mirrors (left, right, and rear), and other forward areas (traffic signals, vehicles in the opposite lane, etc.). The time spent by the gaze point in each area for the time interval from 5 s before deceleration began until the vehicle came to a stop was calculated.

Measurement of Trust in the System. The Scale of Trust in Automated Systems [12], which consists of 12 items on a 7-point scale, was used to measure trust in the system. The item responses yield a score reflecting the level of trust in the automated system. The 12-item Japanese translation was used in this study. After completing each task in Phase 2, the participants answered the 12 items regarding the driver assistance system they had just used. Some reversed items were considered, and the average value of these items was used as the trust score.

3 Results

3.1 Changes in Trust Score Based on Deviation

We compared the average trust scores obtained using the Scale of Trust in Automated Systems across conditions. The absolute value of the trust score varies depending on the respondent's level of trust in the automated system. Here, we standardized the trust scores by subtracting the mean score within each participant from each condition's score to analyze how they changed across conditions.

Figure 4 shows the average and standard deviation of the standardized trust score under each condition. One-way ANOVA results revealed a significant main effect of the deviation condition on the standardized trust score, F (10, 154) $= 4.70, p < 0.001$,

$\eta^2 = 0.23$, indicating a large effect. Multiple-comparison tests, performed using Tukey's Honestly Significant Difference test, showed significant differences (Fig. 4).

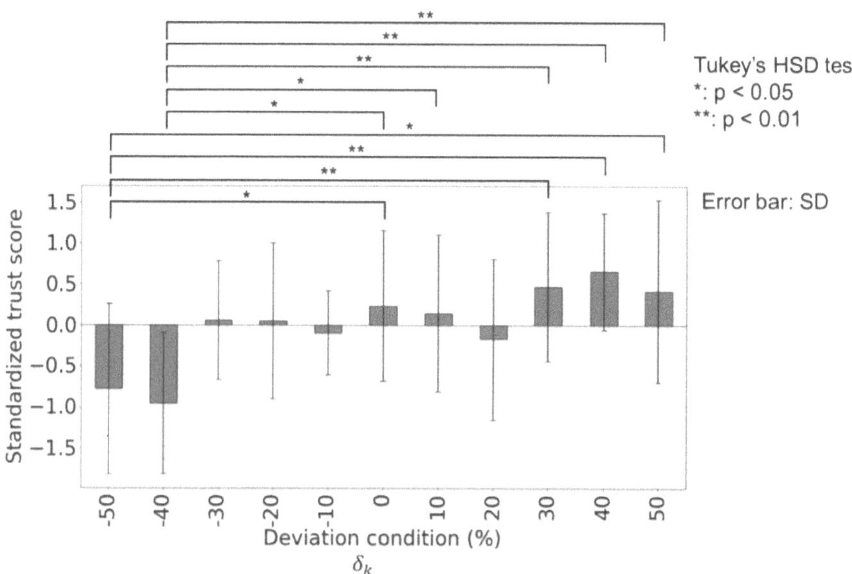

Fig. 4. Averages and standard deviations of standardized trust scores under varying conditions, along with results of multiple-comparison test.

The scores tended to be smaller (larger) when the deviation was negative (positive) (Fig. 4). Furthermore, the decrease in the average standardized trust score was greatest between deviations of −30% and −40%, after the deviation value was reduced from 0%. The increase in the average standardized trust score was greatest between deviations of 20% and 30%, when the deviation value was induced from 0%. The multiple-comparison test results showed significant differences in scores between deviations of below −40% and above 30%. Therefore, larger changes in the standardized trust scores occurred under these conditions.

3.2 Differences in Trust Score Between Participants

We analyze differences in trust scores between the participants based on driving behavior. In the experiment, the stopping distance gap varied according to operation outcome, whereas the braking distance was identical across individuals. Therefore, the participant characteristics regarding the braking process were not considered.

The effect of deviations in braking distance on trust scores was analyzed by calculating the average braking distance in Phase 1 for each participant through the procedure used for the stopping distance gap. The maximum average braking distance was 52.2 m, and the minimum was 14.2 m. In the experiment, the deviation in braking distance ranged from −50% to 90%.

Figure 5 shows the average and standard deviation of the trust score for each participant, ordered by the average braking distance. The participants were divided into two groups: those whose average braking distances were shorter than that of the Phase 2 system (positive deviation) and those whose distances were longer (negative deviation). A comparison of average trust scores between the two groups revealed a significant statistical difference (Welch's t-test: $t(7.4) = 2.48, p < 0.05$), with the participants exhibiting shorter average braking distances showing higher trust scores.

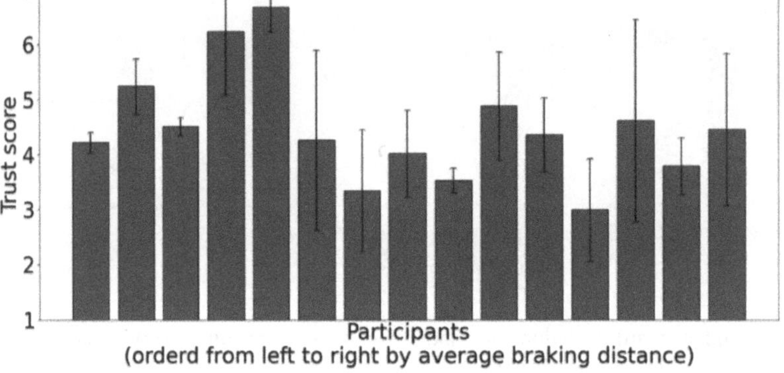

Fig. 5. Averages and standard deviations of trust score for each participant, grouped by the average braking distance.

Within the group exhibiting shorter braking distances, participants with lower average trust scores tended to show smaller within-participant variability. The group with shorter braking distances showed significantly higher minimum trust scores (Welch's t-test: $t(7.9) = 2.90, p < 0.05$).

Thus, the participants in this group exhibited higher overall trust scores, tending to maintain trust scores above a lower bound.

3.3 Changes in Behavior Based on Deviation

Driver monitoring behaviors may be affected by changes in the stopping distance gap. To investigate changes in monitoring behavior under different deviation conditions, we compared the total times spent by the gaze on various subjects in the three stop sections within the period from 5 s before deceleration began until the vehicle came to a stop.

Figure 6 shows the gaze-area proportions of two participants. We selected participants with low data-loss rates in the eye-tracking measurements from each of the two groups shown in Fig. 5. Participant A had a shorter braking distance than the system (fourth from the left in Fig. 5), whereas participant B had a longer braking distance than the system (third from the right in Fig. 5). Based on the results in Sect. 3.1, the deviation conditions were divided into three categories: −50% to −40%, − 30% to 20%, and 30%

to 50%. The gaze-area proportions were calculated based on the average gaze time in each area within each category.

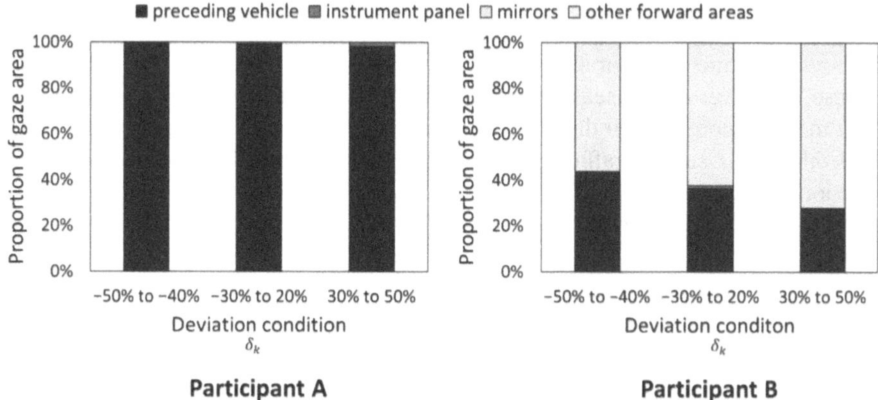

Fig. 6. Proportion of gaze area for two participants across deviation conditions.

Both participants focused their gaze on the preceding vehicle or other forward areas. During the target time interval (5 s before deceleration began), gaze in other areas was minimal. Participant A, who had a short braking distance, showed small variation across deviation conditions, tending to focus on the preceding vehicle. The gaze of Participant B, who had a long braking distance, toward the preceding vehicle increased as the deviation changed from positive to negative.

4 Discussion

4.1 Effect of Discrepancies Between Driver Behavior and System Assistance on Trust in the System

The changes in the standardized trust scores suggest that within a stopping-distance-gap deviation range of −30% to 20% between the driver and the system, trust is unlikely to change considerably. Therefore, trust changes do not show a linear response to deviations, with trust in the system remaining stable within a certain range and changing markedly beyond specific boundaries. This range may be an acceptable range, in which the driver does not perceive the system outcome as inappropriate.

Deviations of −40% or less mean the vehicle stops with a gap shorter than the driver's desired stopping distance gap. Thus, the safety margin of the system is smaller than that of the driver, who likely perceives the situation as dangerous driving. This behavior may be interpreted as risky, compromising trust in the system. Conversely, deviations of 30% or more mean the vehicle stops with a gap longer than the driver's desired stopping distance gap. This scenario provides a more conservative margin than the driver expects, which may increase trust in the system.

For a participant with a negative deviation in braking distance, the proportion of time spent looking at the preceding vehicle tended to change according to the stopping-distance-gap deviation. Specifically, the time spent looking at the preceding vehicle increased when the stopping-distance-gap deviation was negative. When braking is initiated later in cases where the control performs braking in a more forceful manner than that of drivers, the gaze duration at the preceding vehicle increases. This is possibly because the driver feels uneasy about whether the system is operating properly and needs to focus more on their distance from the preceding vehicle, leaving no capacity to check other areas, such as traffic signals. The fluctuations in standardized trust scores and behavioral changes of the participants in Fig. 6 are not contradictory. Thus, whether or not behavioral changes occur in response to these deviations may also influence changes in trust.

Humans are sensitive to failures in automated systems, and trust in the system declines when system failures accumulate [13]. Hence, the above findings can serve as a benchmark for calibrating discrepancies. In such benchmarking, a −30% deviation can be regarded as the lower threshold for failure in system settings, i.e., outcomes must not fall below this level. Aside from meeting this requirement, outcomes should be kept within a range not exceeding a 20% deviation to avoid overtrust.

4.2 Factors Affecting Changes in Trust Score

The trust scores of the participants suggest that the braking distance deviation influences the trust score and its susceptibility to decline. When the system's braking distance is greater than the driver's desired braking distance, the control performs gentler braking than the driver. In such cases, even with changes in the stopping distance gap, the trust score becomes less likely to drop below a certain level. This is because the effect of the control outcome is mitigated when the braking process is more cautious than the driver.

A participant with a shorter braking distance tends to look more at the preceding vehicle. When braking is applied more gently than by the participants, active monitoring may not occur. This may be because of a developing mindset in which control can be entrusted to the system. A positive deviation in braking distance may increase trust in the system, potentially leading to overtrust.

In this study, we varied the stopping distance gap as a control outcome, whereas changes in braking distance during the braking process may similarly affect trust in the system. Therefore, deviations should be considered comprehensively across multiple perspectives in practical application.

5 Conclusion

Through driving simulator experiments, we examined how discrepancies between driver behavior and the control outcomes of a driver assistance system influence trust in the system. The results demonstrated that trust in the system does not change linearly with the magnitude of system–driver deviation. Trust remains stable within a stopping-distance-gap deviation range of −30% to 20% between the driver and the system, and changes markedly beyond this range. This range can serve as a practical reference for personal adaptation aimed at trust calibration.

In addition to control outcomes, individual differences in braking distance affect the overall level of trust and its susceptibility to decline, indicating that braking behavior also affects trust dynamics. The monitoring behaviors of drivers under system control can also be affected by the stopping distance gap and the braking distance. Therefore, effective personalization of driver assistance systems should consider both outcome-based deviations and process-level characteristics to maintain appropriately calibrated trust in the system.

However, this study used a simulator experiment to conduct investigations based on driving in a limited scene. Therefore, the benchmark may not be immediately applicable to diverse systems. Based on the benchmark values identified in this study, further investigation will realize systems that adapt to individuals while maintaining appropriate levels of trust in the system.

Acknowledgments. This study was granted by JSPS KAKENHI (Grant No. JP24K17477).

Disclosure of Interests. The authors have no competing interests to declare that are relevant to the content of this article.

References

1. SAE International. Taxonomy and definitions for terms related to driving automation systems for on-road motor vehicles, SAE Standard J3016_202104 (2021)
2. Walker, F., Forster, Y., et al.: Trust in automated vehicles: constructs, psychological processes, and assessment. Front. Psychol. **14**, 1279271 (2023)
3. Masuda, T., Haga, S.: Models of driving behavior and accident prevention (education for reliability and quality engineering). J. Reliabil. Eng. Assoc. Japan **31**(3), 223–228 (2009)
4. Ishibashi, M., Miura, Y.: Application of driver's characteristic to human factor study in driver support system: a case of ergonomic evaluation in Hiroshima DSSS field operational test. IATSS Rev. **36**(1), 33–41 (2011)
5. Yang, X.J., Schemanske, C., Searle, C.: Toward quantifying trust dynamics: how people adjust their trust after moment-to-moment interaction with automation. Hum. Factors **65**(5), 862–878 (2023)
6. Abe, G., Richardson, J.: The effect of alarm timing on driver behaviour: an investigation of differences in driver trust and response to alarms according to alarm timing. Transport. Res. F: Traffic Psychol. Behav. **7**(4–5), 307–322 (2004)
7. Ford Motor Company: How do I adjust the pre-collision assist alert sensitivity in my Ford? https://www.ford.com/support/how-tos/ford-technology/driver-assist-features/how-do-i-adjust-pre-collision-assist-alert-sensitivity/. Accessed 25 Jan 2026
8. Lucas, G.M., Becerik-Gerber, B., Roll, S.C.: Calibrating workers' trust in intelligent automated systems. Patterns **5**(9), 101045 (2024)
9. Lefèvre, S., Carvalho, A., et al.: A learning-based framework for velocity control in autonomous driving. IEEE Trans. Autom. Sci. Eng. **13**(1), 32–42 (2016)
10. Wang, J., Yu, C., et al.: A forward collision warning algorithm with adaptation to driver behaviors. IEEE Trans. Intell. Transp. Syst. **17**(4), 1157–1167 (2016)
11. Tian, H., Wei, C., et al.: Personalized lane change planning and control by imitation learning from drivers. IEEE Trans. Industr. Electron. **70**(4), 3995–4006 (2023)

12. Jian, J.Y., Bisantz, A.M., Drury, C.G.: Foundations for an empirically determined scale of trust in automated systems. Int. J. Cogn. Ergon. **4**(1), 53–71 (2000)
13. Centeio Jorge, C., Bouman, N.H., et al.: Exploring the effect of automation failure on the human's trustworthiness in human-agent teamwork. Front. Robo. AI **10**, 1143723 (2023)

Peripheral Interaction Design in Autonomous Vehicles: Suitability Evaluation and Design Principles

Ruisi Shi[1,2] and Jingyu Zhang[1,2](✉)

[1] State Key Laboratory of Cognitive Science and Mental Health, Institute of Psychology, Chinese Academy of Sciences, Beijing, China
zhangjingyu@psych.ac.cn

[2] Department of Psychology, University of Chinese Academy of Sciences, Beijing, China

Abstract. With the rapid advancements in autonomous driving technology, human-machine co-driving has become an increasingly dominant paradigm. Traditional visual alert systems often require users to maintain focused attention through central field of vision, which not only interferes with non-driving-related activities (NDRAs) but also increases cognitive load. While existing peripheral interaction strategies have demonstrated potential in enhancing situational awareness during driving, challenges persist in assessing the suitability of the presented information. This study aims to develop a comprehensive evaluation framework for the suitability of peripheral interactions in autonomous driving scenarios. Insights were gathered through expert interviews from multidisciplinary domains, including autonomous driving applications, peripheral interaction research, and industrial design. These insights informed the identification of information types and design elements optimized for peripheral interaction. The study uses hierarchical linear regression to evaluate peripheral visual displays across five key dimensions: non-interference, simplicity, dynamic adaptability, symbolization, and coverage area. The findings also recommend design elements such as optimal and avoided display positions, content orientation, contrast, color usage and display methods. This research establishes a suitability evaluation framework, providing actionable insights and practical guidance for designing peripheral interaction systems in autonomous driving environments.

Keywords: Peripheral interaction · Autonomous Vehicle · Evaluation

1 Introduction

1.1 Autonomous Driving Era and Peripheral Interaction

With the rapid development of autonomous driving technology, the division of roles between humans and machines is undergoing significant transformation. In the era of autonomous driving, the driver's role is gradually shifting from traditional operational tasks to a more flexible state, allowing them to perform various non-driving-related tasks

W. -C. Li and A. Plioutsias (Eds.): HCII 2026, LNAI 16708, pp. 57–68, 2026.
https://doi.org/10.1007/978-3-032-29459-3_5

(NDRTs) inside the vehicle, such as using a phone, watching videos, or making calls [1]. Against this backdrop, human-machine shared control has emerged as a central focus in the field of autonomous driving, with takeover requests being a critical component for its realization.

While autonomous driving liberates humans from operational tasks, it also introduces the challenge of increased cognitive load. The original intent of autonomous driving was to free drivers' hands, enabling them to plan and enjoy their travel more freely, thereby alleviating the cognitive demands of driving. However, as the level of automation increases, so does the likelihood of drivers engaging in other NDRTs. This engagement significantly reduces their attention to the road environment [2]. According to the attention resource allocation theory, when drivers allocate more attention to other tasks, fewer cognitive resources are available for driving, leading to diminished situational awareness [3]. When the system detects potential dangers and issues a takeover request, drivers must possess the capability to supervise and assist the driving process, responding promptly to emergencies. However, distracted drivers often lack awareness of the current environment and the surrounding vehicle dynamics, resulting in inadequate situational awareness. This deficiency can lead to delayed or incorrect takeover decisions, potentially causing traffic accidents.

Traditional visual cue systems typically require users to consciously focus on them through their central vision to be effective. Additionally, these systems may interfere with non-driving-related activities (NDRAs) and are therefore often perceived as disruptive or intrusive, potentially impacting users' cognitive abilities and skills [4]. A good tool is an invisible tool. The tool does not intrude on your consciousness; people focus on the task, not the tool. There is an increase in awareness that this cognitive overload is potentially problematic and that future technologies should become "calm", "ambient" and "peripheral" [5, 6]. Peripheral interaction refers to interacting with physical or digital objects that sit outside the user's primary focus. Its value lies in conveying information unobtrusively.

To address these issues, many researchers have proposed the use of peripheral visual cues in recent years, such as ambient light cues, to optimize user experience. These peripheral light cue systems aim to reduce the need for direct attention, thereby minimizing interference with cognitive resources and skills [7]. Peripheral interaction, as an important tool for enhancing drivers' perceptual abilities and situational awareness, has shown potential for efficient information delivery and reduced cognitive load.

The multiple resource theory [8] provides theoretical support for this design. This theory assumes that human cognition consists of multiple limited resources, which are categorized by dimensions such as processing stages, coding methods, modalities, and visual channels. When two concurrent tasks compete for the same resources, interference occurs, leading to a significant decline in task performance compared to single-task conditions. Relevant computational models based on this theory have been widely applied in the driving domain [9]. Supported by this theory, peripheral visual cue systems can effectively alleviate the burden on central vision by leveraging peripheral vision, thereby optimizing the way information is conveyed.

1.2 Current Research on Peripheral Interaction

Peripheral vision and central vision exhibit significant differences in function and perception. Cones are primarily concentrated in the central retina and responsible for perceiving details and color information. In contrast, rods are distributed mainly in the peripheral retina, functioning effectively in low-light conditions with high light sensitivity, and are primarily responsible for detecting brightness and contrast changes [10]. Central vision is typically used to process fine, static information such as text, whereas peripheral vision is better suited for perceiving motion, shapes, and other dynamic information [11].

In the field of driving, researchers have proposed two functional modes of vision: the focal mode and the ambient mode [12, 13]. The focal mode primarily relies on central vision and is used to identify target objects on the road or other detailed information of interest. In contrast, the ambient mode depends on peripheral vision, which is responsible for perceiving motion and direction, supporting visual proprioception, and guiding actions in driving tasks [14].

Existing peripheral interaction methods have made considerable progress in enhancing the driving experience and improving the efficiency of information delivery. For example, some studies have developed LED light strips to display environmental information. These light patterns can indicate safe distances and speeds, providing intuitive visual feedback for real-time environmental awareness [15]. Further research has applied these systems to display vehicle operational states [16]. Additionally, color and positional information have been incorporated into interaction designs to improve drivers' perception of environmental changes [17]. Another approach involves the use of bubble motion as a physical metaphor, which provides drivers with stronger interactive feedback through dynamic visual effects [18]. Moreover, a 360-degree ambient light system has been developed to display object information through surrounding light displays, indicating situations such as conditions on both sides of the vehicle or blind spot attention areas [19].

Previous studies have explored various types and formats of information to present data in the driver's peripheral vision, aiming to enhance situational awareness. However, determining which types of information can be presented in a highly efficient manner with low cognitive load and without requiring focused attention remains an area that warrants further investigation. Additionally, the scientific evaluation of the suitability of such information is a critical challenge.

1.3 The Present Study

The present study focuses on constructing a suitability evaluation framework for peripheral interaction. It aims to identify the core dimensions and standards for evaluating the suitability of peripheral interaction in autonomous driving contexts. The study plans to collect insights from experts through interviews, integrating multidisciplinary perspectives, including those from autonomous driving applications, foundational vision research on peripheral interaction, and industrial design. Based on these expert opinions, the study will extract the core types of information and design elements suitable for peripheral interaction. Using a suitability scoring method, the study seeks to provide quantitative guidance for selecting and designing information.

The goal of this research is to develop a systematic suitability evaluation framework to establish clear evaluation standards for peripheral interaction. This framework will not only offer scientific guidance for the selection and design of peripheral interaction information but also address the existing gaps in suitability evaluation in autonomous driving.

2 Method

2.1 Participants

A total of 31 experts participated in this interview study, including 6 males and 25 females, with an average age of 26.03 years (SD = 2.27 years). Among them, 15 participants held a doctoral degree or higher, and 16 participants held a master's degree. Twenty-nine of the participants (93.6%) had a driver's license, with an average driving experience of 3.83 years and an average total driving distance of 13,200 km. The professional expertise of the interviewed experts spanned multiple domains, including traffic safety, cognitive psychology, peripheral interaction, autonomous driving, and industrial design.

2.2 Procedure

Prior to the formal interviews, a pilot study will be conducted with a subset of experts to refine the interview outline and process based on their feedback. This step ensures that the interview not only focuses on the research objectives but also comprehensively collects relevant information.

In the formal interviews, each invited expert will participate for 30 to 45 min in a semi-structured format. The interview conducted in a quiet, disturbance-free environment. Before participation, all experts received an information sheet outlining the study purpose, interview procedures and provided informed consent. The interview outline covers the following key areas:

The interview will begin with an introduction to its purpose and objectives. The primary goal is to identify the key types of information that need to be continuously communicated during autonomous driving and explore how to convey this information in a way that minimizes cognitive load and avoids occupying the driver's primary visual field. Experts are encouraged to discuss how peripheral visual information systems can be used effectively for this purpose and provide practical design recommendations.

Step 1 Identifying Key Information and Scenarios: The interview will start by addressing the question, "What critical information should be prioritized in autonomous driving?" Experts will be asked to identify the most important scenarios in autonomous driving and the specific information that needs to be monitored and addressed within these scenarios.

Step 2 Exploring the Suitability of Peripheral Visual Systems: The concepts and characteristics of central and peripheral vision will be briefly introduced. Experts will then assist in identifying information types suitable for display through peripheral interaction systems and propose relevant design standards and principles. Specifically, experts will be asked, "If information could be conveyed in a less demanding, low-load manner without requiring focused attention, what types of information would be most suitable for peripheral visual communication, and what design requirements or principles should such information meet?" Based on a combination of literature analysis and expert feedback, we aim to develop a comprehensive list of information suitable for peripheral interaction systems and their associated design principles. Experts will then evaluate the appropriateness of these information types and principles using a 10-point Likert scale.

Step 3 Designing Peripheral Interaction Systems: Following the identification of key information types, the experts will be guided to explore how peripheral interaction systems can be designed to achieve efficient and minimally intrusive outcomes. The discussion will focus on critical design elements, such as display positions, content dynamics, contrast levels, and visual forms.

3 Results

After concluding the interviews with 31 experts, we conducted a thorough coding and analysis of the data, focusing on key information content, peripheral visual design elements, and proposed design solutions. The resulting transcripts were analyzed using a structured coding scheme developed iteratively by the research team. The findings provide valuable insights for the development of peripheral visual prompt systems in autonomous driving, including suitable information for peripheral presentation, critical design elements and recommendations, as well as criteria for evaluating design suitability.

3.1 Suitability Evaluation Methods for Peripheral Interaction

Through a systematic review of the literature and the synthesis of expert opinions, this study identified 12 types of information suitable for transmission through peripheral vision during driving. To evaluate the suitability of peripheral interaction, five core assessment criteria were derived based on the characteristics of peripheral vision and the critical feedback provided by experts: Non-interference, Simplicity, Dynamic change, Symbolization, and Coverage area.

To further investigate the relationship between peripheral interaction suitability and these evaluation dimensions, each expert rated the suitability of peripheral interaction for various scenarios as well as its performance across the five dimensions. All scores were standardized into Z-scores and ranked in descending order of peripheral interaction suitability (See Fig. 1).

The results of the correlation analysis between peripheral interaction suitability and the evaluation criteria indicate significant positive correlations across all dimensions. Notably, suitability showed the strongest correlations with non-interference ($r = 0.487$, $p < .001$) and simplicity ($r = 0.448, p < .001$). Additionally, significant correlations were observed between suitability and dynamic change ($r = 0.390, p < .001$), symbolization ($r = 0.402, p < .001$), and coverage area ($r = 0.270, p < .001$) (See Table 1).

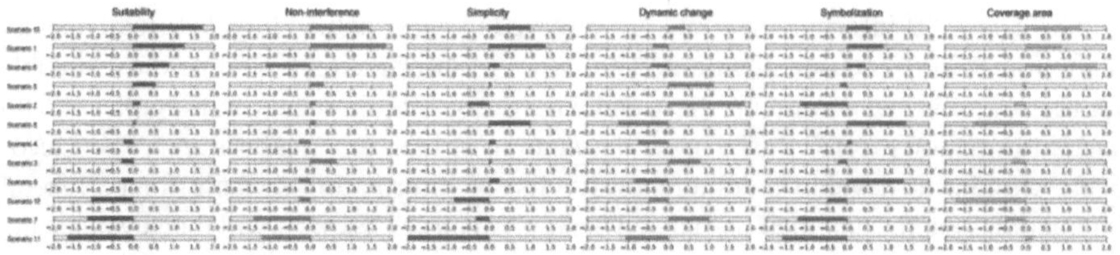

Fig. 1. Suitability Ratings and Evaluation Dimension Scores (Standardized Z-Scores)

Table 1. Pearson Correlations Between Suitability and Predictor Variables

	Suitability	Dynamic	Simplicity	Symbolization	Coverage area
Suitability					
Dynamic	0.390***				
Simplicity	0.448***	0.159**			
Symbolization	0.402***	0.114*	0.555***		
Coverage area	0.270***	0.242***	0.123*	0.043	
Non-interference	0.487***	0.213***	0.137**	0.185***	0.198***

Figure 2 illustrates the trends in peripheral interaction suitability across different evaluation criteria. The shaded areas represent confidence intervals (standard error, SE). The results reveal distinct variations in suitability values under different evaluation criteria.

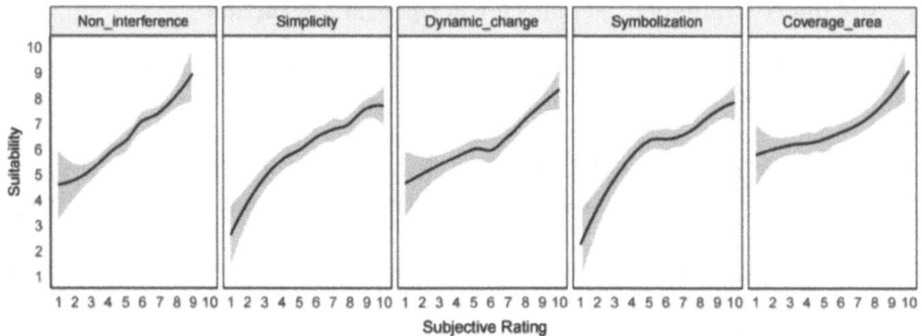

Fig. 2. Relationships Between Suitability and Predictor Variables. *Notes:* Each panel represents the relationship between suitability and one predictor variable (Non-Interference, Simplicity, Dynamic Change, Symbolization and Coverage Area)

The multicollinearity diagnostic results indicate that all predictor variables have variance inflation factors (VIF) below 1.5, which is significantly lower than commonly accepted thresholds, suggesting low multicollinearity among the variables. Additionally, all tolerance values exceed 0.65, confirming the absence of significant multicollinearity in the regression model and supporting the independence of predictor variables. Consequently, hierarchical linear regression analysis was employed.

Given the data structure, which involves individual evaluations across multiple tasks, a hierarchical linear regression model was used, treating participants as a second-level variable. The model estimates the proportion of variance explained by fixed effects as well as the combined contribution of fixed and random effects.

The hierarchical linear regression results for peripheral interaction suitability are presented (See Table 2). A stepwise regression approach was adopted to construct Models 1 to 5, incrementally including the predictors: non-interference, simplicity, dynamic change, symbolization, and coverage area. The results show that Model 5 achieves the best fit, with a fixed effect R^2 of 0.476 and a combined fixed and random effects R^2 of 0.529. Additionally, Model 5 exhibits lower AIC and BIC values compared to Models 1 to 4, confirming it as the optimal model. To assess whether the increases in R^2 between models were statistically meaningful, we compared the five nested models using likelihood-ratio tests between adjacent pairs: Model 2 vs Model 1 ($\chi^2 = 99.81$, $p < .001$), Model 3 vs Model 2 ($\chi^2 = 65.92$, $p < .001$), Model 4 vs Model 3 ($\chi^2 = 40.30$, $p < .001$), and Model 5 vs Model 4 ($\chi^2 = 17.54$, $p < .001$).

Table 2. Results of hierarchical linear regression for Suitability in peripheral interaction

	Model 1	Model 2	Model 3	Model 4	Model 5
Non-interference	0.56(.05)***	0.51(.05)***	0.46(.05)***	0.44(.05)***	0.42(.05)***
Simplicity		.37(.04)***	0.35(.04)***	0.27(.05)***	0.26(.05)***
Dynamic change			0.25(.04)***	0.24(.04)***	0.22(.04)***
Symbolization				0.16(.05)**	0.16(.05)**
Coverage area					0.11(.04)**
R^2 *(Marginal)*	0.23	0.375	0.447	0.464	0.476
R^2 *(Conditional)*	0.35	0.433	0.505	0.518	0.529

Notes: Standardized regression coefficients and standard errors are reported (** $p < .01$; *** $p < .001$)

For the key predictors in Model 5, all standardized regression coefficients reached significant levels, specifically: non-interference ($\beta = 0.36$, $p < .001$), simplicity ($\beta = 0.26, p < .001$), dynamic change ($\beta = 0.24$, $p < .001$), symbolization ($\beta = 0.15, p < .01$), and coverage area ($\beta = 0.11$, $p < .01$). These five factors were found to have a highly significant impact on peripheral interaction suitability. According to Cohen's criteria [20], an ICC of $1\% \leq$ ICC $< 5.9\%$ indicates low intra-class correlation (ICC), while an ICC $\geq 5.9\%$ warrants consideration of between-group variance through hierarchical modeling. In this study, an intercept-only null model without predictors was constructed to estimate ICC at both within- and between-individual levels. The ICC value of 16.03% for the dependent variable (suitability evaluation) indicates that a significant proportion of variance exists at the between-individual level, supporting the necessity of multilevel analysis.

Non-interference played a pivotal role in enhancing peripheral interaction suitability, while the simplicity of information presentation was also identified as a critical factor. Furthermore, the significant effect of dynamic change suggests that presenting information through dynamic variations can substantially improve the level of peripheral interaction suitability. Similarly, the significance of the coefficients for symbolization and coverage area indicates that symbolic design and adequate coverage area contribute positively to the suitability of peripheral interaction.

Given that Model 5 demonstrated the best goodness of fit, it was selected as the basis for constructing the regression equation for peripheral interaction suitability.

Level 1: Task Level

$y_{ij} = \beta_{0j} + \beta_{1j} \times$ Non-interference $+ \beta_{2j} \times$ Simplicity $+ \beta_{3j} \times$ Dynamic change $+ \beta_{4j} \times$ Symbolization $+ \beta_{5j} \times$ Coverage area $+ e_{ij}$(y_{ij} is the peripheral suitability rating of the i_{th} task for the j_{th} participant, β_{0j} is the regression coefficients for the j_{th} participant).

Level 2: Subject Level

$\beta_{0j} = \gamma_{00} + u_{0j}$.

$\beta_{1j} = \gamma_{10}, \beta_{2j} = \gamma_{20}, \beta_{3j} = \gamma_{30}, \beta_{4j} = \gamma_{40}, \beta_{5j} = \gamma_{50}$ (γ_{00} is the fixed effect coefficients, u_{0j} is the random effect for the j_{th} participant).

Overall Model

$Y_{ij} = \gamma_{00} + \gamma_{10} \times$ Non-interference $+ \gamma_{20} \times$ Simplicity $+ \gamma_{30} \times$ Dynamic change $+ \gamma_{40} \times$ Symbolization $+ \gamma_{50} \times$ Coverage area $+ u_{0j} + e_{ij}$ (γ_{00} is the overall intercept, γ_{10} is the fixed effect coefficients, u_{0j} is the random effects between participants, e_{ij} is the residual.)

Then, we obtained the regression equation for peripheral interaction suitability:

Suitability (For peripheral system) $= -0.511 + 0.419 \times$ Non-interference $+ 0.265 \times$ Simplicity $+ 0.220 \times$ Dynamic change $+ 0.164 \times$ Symbolization $+ 0.115 \times$ Coverage area $+ uj + eij$.

3.2 Key Scenarios and Design Principles

The interview results identified several key scenarios in autonomous driving, with the most frequently mentioned being sudden vehicle behaviors (e.g., lane changes), which require individuals to quickly recognize and respond to unexpected actions in dynamic environments (mentioned 16 times). Other high-frequency scenarios include road construction (mentioned 10 times) and low-visibility weather conditions (mentioned 9 times). Additionally, experts highlighted complex traffic situations (e.g., emergency vehicles or accidents, mentioned 9 times), highway scenarios (mentioned 8 times), pedestrians and vehicles in blind spots (mentioned 8 times), and mountainous or challenging road conditions (mentioned 6 times). Regarding key information content, experts primarily focused on three categories: distance keeping (mentioned 9 times), speed assessment (mentioned 7 times), and lane keeping (mentioned 2 times). The interviews focused on design elements such as display position, content dynamics, contrast levels, display shapes, color usage, and display methods. Experts were consulted for design recommendations regarding these elements, and the suggestions were systematically categorized and organized. The frequency and proportion of mentions for each recommendation were statistically analyzed (See Table 3).

Table 3. Design Factors in Peripheral Displays

Category	Design Suggestions	Count (Percentage)
Display Positions (Recommended)	Edges or outside of the car window	11 (32.35%)
	Below the windshield	10 (29.41%)
	Near both sides of the steering wheel	6 (17.65%)
	Near the central control screen	5 (14.71%)
	Near both sides of the seat	2 (5.88%)
Display Positions (Avoided)	Near the rearview mirror	8 (25.81%)
	Too close to the edge (e.g., outside 60 degrees)	8 (25.81%)
Content Direction	Aligned direction (e.g., right side displayed on the right)	20 (64.52%)
	Follow mapping relationships	11 (35.48%)
Content Contrast	Moderate contrast	15 (41.67%)
	Based on information importance	10 (27.78%)
	High contrast	9 (25.00%)
	Consider individual differences	2 (5.56%)
Display Shapes	Geometric shapes	16 (50.00%)
	Vehicle's shape (high fidelity)	7 (21.88%)
	Representative features	6 (18.75%)
	Icon-based forms	3 (9.38%)
Color Usage	No need for color	20 (64.52%)
	Color needed only in emergencies	6 (19.35%)
	Color required	5 (16.13%)
Display Methods (Equipment)	Peripheral screen	7 (36.84%)
	Multimodal	5 (26.32%)
	Light cues	5 (26.32%)
	AR (Augmented Reality)	2 (10.53%)
	Avoid: Wearable devices	11 (35.48%)

Firstly, regarding the display position within the peripheral vision, 31 experts proposed both recommended and avoided positions. Experts recommended placing displays at the edges and lower sections of the windows (mentioned 11 times), followed by below the windshield (mentioned 10 times). Additionally, positions near the sides of the steering wheel and around the central console screen were also mentioned. Conversely, experts frequently highlighted the need to avoid placing displays in areas that are too far to the sides, such as beyond a 60-degree range (mentioned 8 times), and near the rearview mirror (mentioned 8 times).

Furthermore, experts emphasized that display content should align with the vehicle's position (mentioned 20 times), such as displaying information about a vehicle on the right side of the screen if the vehicle is on the right, and that information should adhere to mapping principles (mentioned 11 times).

Regarding the contrast of display content, most experts suggested using moderate contrast (mentioned 15 times) or adjusting contrast based on the importance of the information. Some experts also proposed employing higher contrast and considering individual differences (mentioned 2 times).

Regarding display shapes, experts expressed varying opinions. The most frequently mentioned approach (16 mentions) was to use simple geometric shapes, while others advocated for accurately reflecting the vehicle's shape (mentioned 7 times) or extracting representative features for display (mentioned 6 times).

In terms of color usage, most experts believed that no color was necessary (mentioned 20 times), while some recommended using color only in emergencies (mentioned 6 times), and a few suggested adopting colors for general use (mentioned 5 times).

Lastly, experts mentioned multiple display methods (Equipment), including peripheral screens, multi-modality, and light prompts, while 11 experts explicitly stated that wearable devices should be avoided.

4 Discussion

The results of this study provide significant theoretical and practical insights for the design and evaluation of peripheral interaction systems in human-machine co-driving scenarios. By systematically analyzing five key dimensions, non-interference, simplicity, dynamic adaptability, symbolization, and coverage area, this study establishes a comprehensive suitability evaluation framework. Hierarchical linear regression (HLM) analysis was employed to provide robust data support for assessing the adaptability of peripheral interaction systems in real driving environments. Design recommendations, such as optimal display positions and contrast usage, offer concrete guidance for bridging theory and practice, contributing to the application of peripheral interaction technologies in the specific design of autonomous driving systems.

Future research could build on this study to explore the impact of individual differences [21] on the suitability of peripheral interaction or examine the long-term effects of such systems on driving behavior. By establishing a systematic evaluation framework, the findings of this study provide theoretical support and optimization directions for the design of peripheral interaction in future autonomous driving systems. The limitation of this study concerns its exclusive reliance on expert judgement. Although experts offer structured and domain-informed evaluations, their perceptions may not fully reflect how everyday drivers interpret peripheral cues during real-world autonomous driving.

5 Conclusion

This study, grounded in the current state of peripheral interaction technology within autonomous driving contexts, focuses on developing a scientific evaluation framework to address the critical issue of assessing information suitability for peripheral visual displays in autonomous driving. By conducting expert interviews to gather insights from multidisciplinary domains, including autonomous driving applications, peripheral interaction research, and industrial design, the study identifies core dimensions and design elements suitable for peripheral interaction. The study systematically evaluates performance across five key dimensions and offers design recommendations covering optimal and avoided display positions, contrast, display formats, providing theoretical support and quantitative tools for future peripheral interaction designs.

Acknowledgments. This study was supported by Natural Science Foundation of China (T2192932).

Disclosure of Interests. The authors declare no competing interests.

References

1. Cunningham, M.L., Regan, M.A.: Driver distraction and inattention in the realm of automated driving. IET Intel. Transport Syst. **12**(6), 407–413 (2018)
2. Merlhiot, G., Bueno, M.: How drowsiness and distraction can interfere with take-over performance: a systematic and meta-analysis review. Accid. Anal. Prev. **170**, 106536 (2022)
3. Endsley, M.R.: Toward a theory of situation awareness in dynamic systems. Hum. Factors **37**(1), 32–64 (1995)
4. Diels, C., Bos, J.E.: Great expectations: On the design of predictive motion cues to alleviate carsickness. In: Proceedings of the International Conference on Human-Computer Interaction, pp. 240–251 (2021)
5. Bakker, S., Hoven, E., Eggen, B.: Peripheral interaction: characteristics and considerations. Pers. Ubiquit. Comput. **19**(1), 239–254 (2015)
6. McCullough, M.: Ambient Commons: Attention in the Age of Embodied Information. MIT Press, Cambridge, Massachusetts (2013)
7. Müller, H., Fortmann, J., Pielot, M., Hesselmann, T., Poppinga, B., Heuten, W., et al.: Ambix: designing ambient light information displays. In: Proceedings of Designing Interactive Lighting Workshop at DIS (2012)
8. Wickens, C.D.: Multiple resources and mental workload. Hum. Factors **50**(3), 449–455 (2008)
9. Horrey, W.J., Wickens, J.D.: Multiple resource modeling of task interference in vehicle control, hazard awareness, and in-vehicle task performance. In: Driving Assessment Conference, vol. 2, University of Iowa, p. 2003 (2003)
10. Hunzelmann, N., Spillmann, L.: Movement adaptation in the peripheral retina. Vision. Res. **24**(12), 1765–1769 (1984)
11. Vater, C., Wolfe, B., Rosenholtz, R.: Peripheral vision in real-world tasks: a systematic review. Psychon. Bull. Rev. **29**(5), 1531–1557 (2022)
12. Bridgeman, B.: Complementary cognitive and motor image processing. In: Obrecht, G., Stark, L.W. (eds.) Presbyopia Research: From Molecular Biology to Visual Adaptation, pp. 189–198. Springer, Boston, MA (1991)

13. Trevarthen, C.B.: Two mechanisms of vision in primates. Psychol. Forsch. **31**(4), 299–337 (1968)
14. Leibowitz, H.W., Owens, D.A.: Nighttime driving accidents and selective visual degradation. Science (New York, NY) **197**(4302), 422–424 (1977)
15. Laquai, F., Chowanetz, F., Rigoll, G.: A large-scale LED array to support anticipatory driving. In: 2011 IEEE International Conference on Systems, Man, and Cybernetics, pp. 2087–2092. IEEE (2011)
16. Bohrmann, D., Bruder, A., Bengler, K.: Effects of dynamic visual stimuli on the development of carsickness in real driving. IEEE Trans. Intell. Transp. Syst. **23**(5), 4833–4842 (2022)
17. Marberger, C., Schulz, M., Alt, P., Teicht, M., Engeln, A.: Non-driving related task engagement in highly automated vehicles: How to mitigate emerging motion sickness? In: Proceedings of the International Conference on Driver Distraction and Inattention (DDI) (2022)
18. Meschtscherjakov, A., Strumegger, S., Trösterer, S.: Bubble margin: motion sickness prevention while reading on smartphones in vehicles. In: Human-Computer Interaction – INTERACT 2019, pp. 660–677 (2019)
19. Pfromm, M., Cieler, S., Bruder, R.: Driver assistance via optical information with spatial reference. In: 16th International IEEE Conference on Intelligent Transportation Systems (ITSC 2013), pp. 2006–2011. IEEE (2013)
20. Cohen, J.: Statistical Power Analysis for the Behavioral Sciences, 2nd edn. Routledge, New York (1988)
21. Huurneman, B., Cox, R.F., Vlaskamp, B.N., Boonstra, F.N.: Crowded visual search in children with normal vision and children with visual impairment. Vision. Res. **96**, 65–74 (2014)

Driving Strategies of Railway Drivers Practicing Energy-Efficient Operation Considering Signal Aspects

Tamaki Ueda[1(✉)], Daisuke Suzuki[1], Kazuma Matsui[1], Chizuru Nakagawa[1], Tomoyuki Ogawa[1], Hiroyuki Sako[2], and Yuta Yamamoto[2]

[1] Railway Technical Research Institute, Kokubunji Tokyo 185-8540, Japan
ueda.tamaki.61@rtri.or.jp
[2] Kyushu Railway Company, Fukuoka 812-0011, Japan

Abstract. The present study aimed to identify energy-efficient train driving strategies for avoiding signal-induced deceleration by analyzing operational log data from a limited express train. Data were collected from global navigation satellite system–equipped tablets carried by drivers. Analysis focused on a single segment between two scheduled stops on the same limited express line. Drivers were categorized into two groups: 5 members of the railway company's energy-efficient driving promotion team ("member group") and 74 other drivers ("general group"). A chi-square test showed that the member group exhibited a significantly lower incidence of signal-induced deceleration. At the intermediate passing station, the member group maintained a significantly larger headway, despite no significant difference at the departure station ($p < 0.05$). Further, a two-way analysis of variance revealed that avoiding signal-induced deceleration was associated with lower estimated energy consumption and shorter travel times. We also compared typical runs with similar departure conditions but differing in the occurrence of signal-induced deceleration. This comparison identified an energy-efficient driving technique: maintaining headway from the preceding train by incorporating coasting in the middle section.

Keywords: Energy-efficient train operation · GNSS data analysis · Train driving strategies

1 Introduction

In addition to enhancing the energy efficiency of rolling stock and infrastructure, improving driving techniques can reduce train energy consumption. Trains primarily require energy during acceleration, which typically occurs when accelerating to high speeds, such as after departure from stations, or when recovering from signal-induced deceleration. Therefore, energy-efficient operations must account for both situations.

Several studies have explored energy-efficient driving strategies, particularly under high-speed conditions. Kuwahara et al. (2015) reported an ecodriving assistant system designed to reduce acceleration and extend coasting time, thereby reducing total energy

W. -C. Li and A. Plioutsias (Eds.): HCII 2026, LNAI 16708, pp. 69–79, 2026.
https://doi.org/10.1007/978-3-032-29459-3_6

consumption [1], and Koizumi et al. (2018) conducted a field study on commuter trains to analyze ecodriving advisory systems [2]. In this study, an ecodriving advisory system recommending operations such as reducing the speed before braking reduced energy consumption by 9.4%. Similarly, our previous study analyzed the relation between driving speed and energy consumption without signal-induced deceleration. Train speed before braking onset was lower in low-energy consumption runs [3].

The present study focused on analyzing the energy loss associated with signal-induced deceleration. In railway systems, signal aspects are regulated to maintain safe headways. When a preceding train occupies a block section, the following one is shown a “caution” (with a speed restriction) or “stop” signal. When a train decelerates due to restrictive signal aspects, the subsequent acceleration requires increased energy consumption. Therefore, minimizing signal-induced deceleration is an effective strategy for energy-efficient railway operation. Train drivers could use driving strategies to avoid signal-induced deceleration. Coleman et al. (2009) analyzed a policy called “green wave,” which lets trains wait at stations to avoid speed profile modifications in open corridors using a detailed optimization model [4]. Using optimization models and computational experiments on two Dutch dispatching areas, these researchers demonstrated that this policy can reduce acceleration and deceleration, achieving energy savings of 7%–13%. In addition, Albrecht et al. (2015, 2018) investigated energy-efficient driving strategies for two trains traveling on the same track under safe separation constraints [5, 6]. Focusing on level and nonlevel track scenarios, they applied numerical optimization to derive optimal speed profiles that minimize total energy consumption while satisfying prescribed section clearance times. These studies reported that to prevent deceleration between stations and improve energy efficiency, the following trains must reduce speed in the early section to maintain headway, whereas preceding trains must increase speed early to reach the next station sooner. Despite this evidence, analyses using real-world operational data have not been conducted so far.

Here, we assumed that driving strategies would be reflected in the train’s running patterns. Accordingly, we analyzed operational log data from a limited express train line to identify how such behaviors manifest in actual service. Thus, the present study aimed to identify the driving strategies employed by train drivers to avoid signal-induced deceleration.

2 Methods

2.1 Data for Analysis

Data were collected over one year from global navigation satellite system (GNSS)-equipped tablets carried by drivers, to a total of 331 runs. The analysis focused on a single segment between two scheduled stops (Station A–Station K, passing through Stations B–J without stopping) of the same limited express train line (i.e., the target express train). The scheduled travel time from departure at Station A to arrival at Station K was 13 min 45 s. The preceding train was a local service overtaken by the target express train line at Station I.

The 331 runs were divided into two categories: with and without signal influence. Figure 1 shows examples of speed profiles that are affected and unaffected by signal aspects. Runs were considered signal-induced when train speed dropped to <60 km/h (B) in Fig. 1 or for a deceleration of >20 km/h over 1 km post (C) in Fig. 1.

In this study, we used the estimated energy consumption calculated from the GNSS data because direct measurements were not feasible. Using position and speed information from the GNSS data, the energy consumption required for acceleration and deceleration was estimated based on driving theory [7], considering factors such as vehicle running resistance and track gradient.

The target train was operated by 79 drivers working at the same workplace. These drivers were categorized into two groups: five members of the railway company's energy-efficient driving promotion team ("member group") and 74 others ("general group"). Age and years of driving experience are summarized in Table 1. The age of the member group ranged from 25 to 48 years (mean = 35.6 years, SD = 9.6 years), and their years of experience from 3 to 24 years (mean = 10.6 years, SD = 9.1 years). In the general group, the age ranged from 24 to 67 years (mean = 45.7 years, SD = 13.2 years), and the years of experience from 2 to 40 years (mean = 19.3 years, SD = 11.6 years). During the analysis period, a single driver could operate the target train multiple times.

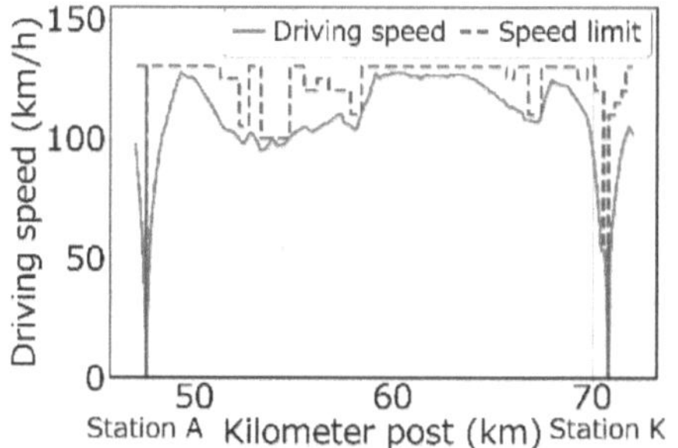

(A) Unaffected by signal aspects

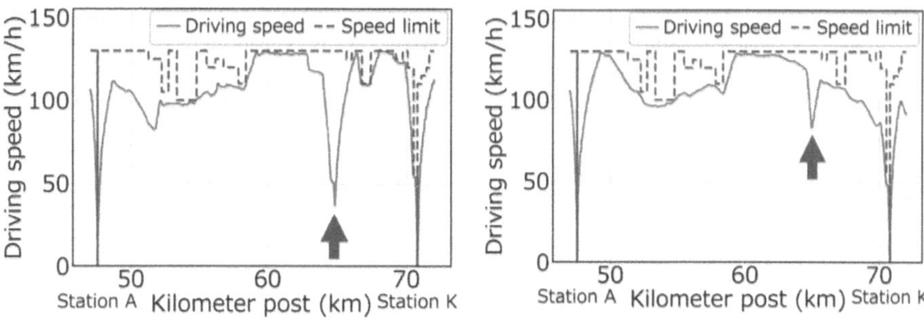

(B) Train speed dropped below 60 km/h

(C) Deceleration exceeding 20 km/h over 1 km post

Fig. 1. Examples of speed profiles.

Table 1. Drivers' age and years of experience.

		All drivers (79 drivers)	Member group (5 drivers)	General group (74 drivers)
Age (years old)	Range	24–67	25–48	24–67
	Average	45.0	35.6	45.7
	Standard deviation	13.2	9.6	13.2
Years of experience (years)	Range	2–40	3–24	2–40
	Average	18.7	10.6	19.3
	Standard deviation	11.6	9.1	11.6

2.2 Analysis Method

First, to clarify differences in susceptibility to the presence of signal-induced deceleration (i.e., signal influence) among drivers, the proportions of runs involving signal-induced deceleration were compared between groups using a chi-square test.

Next, headway was defined as the difference in kilometer post (distance markers along the railway) between the target train and the preceding one when the target train departs from a given station. Figure 2 shows how to calculate the headway to the preceding train at Stations A (HW_A) and F (HW_F). Welch's *t*-tests were used to compare differences in driving conditions between groups by analyzing headway at the departure station (Station A) and an intermediate passing station (Station F). The effect size—a standardized measure independent of sample size—was calculated using Cohen's d index (*d*). Effect sizes of 0.2, 0.5, and 0.8 were considered small, medium, and large, respectively.

Further, a two-way analysis of variance (ANOVA) was conducted to evaluate the effects of driver group and signal influence on estimated energy consumption and travel time. For ANOVA, effect sizes were quantified using partial eta squared (η^2), with values of 0.01, 0.06, and 0.14 considered small, medium, and large effects, respectively. The significance level was set at 5%.

Additionally, a typical example of data pairs with comparable operational conditions in terms of headway, but differing signal influence was used to identify the specific driving techniques used to avoid deceleration caused by signal aspects.

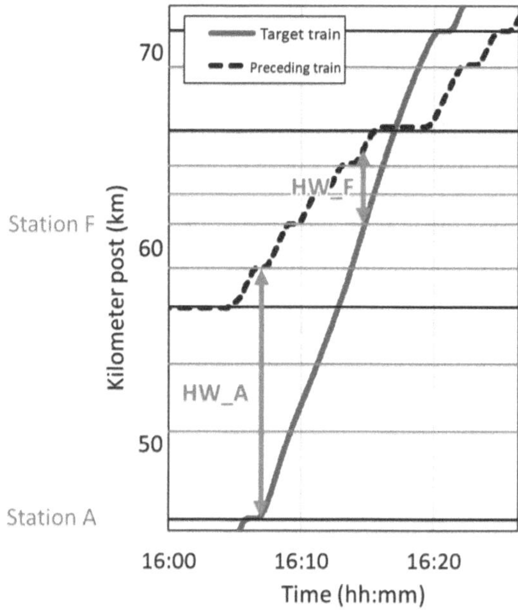

Fig. 2. Method for calculating the headway.

3 Results

3.1 Incidence of Signal-Induced Deceleration

Table 2 presents the case of occurrence of signal-induced deceleration for both driver groups. In the member group, seven runs involved signal-induced deceleration and 25 did not, resulting in a proportion of 21.88% for the former. In the general group, 132 runs involved signal-induced deceleration and 167 did not, yielding a proportion of 44.15% for the former.

A chi-square test showed a significantly lower incidence of signal-induced deceleration in the member group than in the general group [χ^2 (1) = 5.89, $p < 0.05$] (21.88% vs. 44.15%).

Table 2. Number of runs involving signal-induced deceleration.

	Runs involving signal-induced deceleration	Runs without signal-induced deceleration	Proportions of runs involving signal-induced deceleration (%)
Member group	7	25	21.88
General group	132	167	44.15

3.2 Headway to the Preceding Train

Figure 3 shows box-and-whisker plots of the headway to the preceding train at Stations A and F. The boxes represent the interquartile range. Data points lying beyond 1.5 times the interquartile range above or below the quartiles were defined as outliers. The whiskers indicate the maximum and minimum values of the data, excluding outliers. The cross mark represents the mean value.

According to the *t*-test results, the mean headway to the preceding train at Station A ([1] in Fig. 3) was 12.46 km for the member group and 12.30 km for the general group, indicating no significant difference, with a small effect size [t (298) = 0.77, $p = 0.44$, $d = 0.15$]. In contrast, at Station F ([2] in Fig. 3), the mean headway was 3.95 and 3.69 km, respectively, with the member group maintaining a significantly longer headway, with a small/medium effect size [t (41.1) = 2.24, $p < 0.05$, $d = 0.33$].

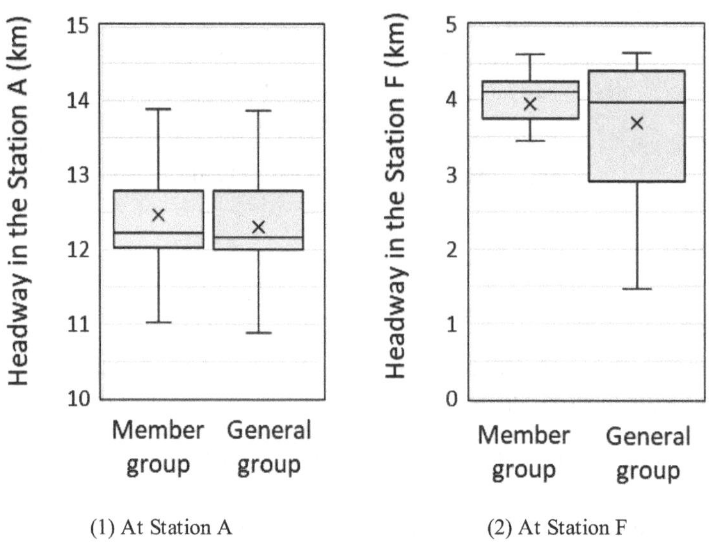

(1) At Station A (2) At Station F

Fig. 3. Headway from the preceding train.

3.3 Effects of Signal-Induced Deceleration on Energy Consumption and Travel Time

Figure 4 shows box-and-whisker plots of estimated energy consumption. A two-way ANOVA with estimated energy consumption as the dependent variable showed a significant main effect of signal [F (1,279) = 1.42, $p < 0.05$], with a large effect size ($\eta^2 = 0.14$). Conversely, the main effect of the driver group was not significant [F (1,279) = 1.42, $p = 0.23$], and the effect size very small ($\eta^2 = 0.01$). The interaction between these two factors was not significant [F (1,279) = 0.51, $p = 0.48$], with a very small effect size ($\eta^2 = 0.0016$).

Figure 5 shows box-and-whisker plots of travel time per group. Another two-way ANOVA with travel time as dependent variable indicated a significant main effect of signal [F (1,279) = 155, $p < 0.05$], with a large effect size ($\eta^2 = 0.35$), but not of the driver group [F (1,279) = 0.00, $p = 0.99$], which had a very small effect size ($\eta^2 = 0.0046$). As in the previous ANOVA, the interaction between the two factors was also not significant [F (1,279) = 0.038, $p = 0.85$], with a very small effect size ($\eta^2 = 0.000087$).

Figure 6 shows the relation between travel time and estimated energy consumption. The horizontal axis represents travel time, and the vertical axis represents estimated energy consumption. As shown in Fig. 6, runs in the general group involving signal-induced deceleration tended to exhibit longer travel times and higher estimated energy consumption. In contrast, runs in the member group without signal-induced deceleration were concentrated within the scheduled travel time and associated with lower estimated energy consumption.

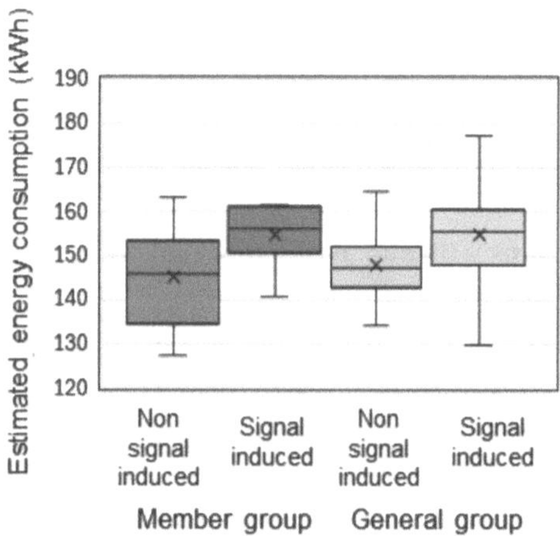

Fig. 4. Box-and-whisker plots of estimated energy consumption.

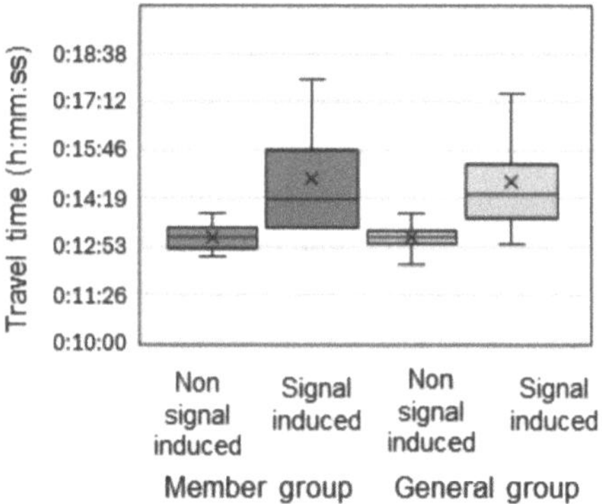

Fig. 5. Box-and-whisker plots of travel time.

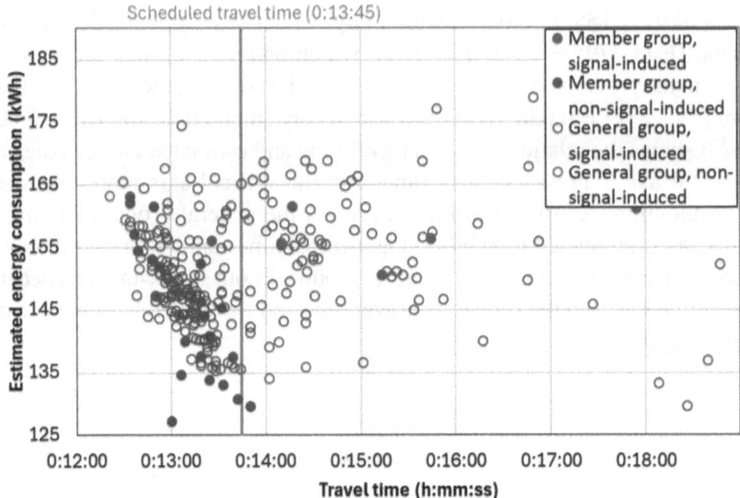

Fig. 6. Relation between travel time and estimated energy consumption.

3.4 Comparison of Runs with and Without Signal-Induced Deceleration

A typical example of runs with similar conditions at departure from Station A but differing in the occurrence of signal-induced deceleration was analyzed; the signal-induced run belonged to the general group and the non-signal-induced run to the member group.

Figure 7 shows a comparison of speed profiles. In the run with signal-induced deceleration, a sharp deceleration was observed near Station I, suggesting a signal effect. Conversely, no abrupt deceleration was observed within the target section in the run without signal-induced deceleration. In the latter case, coasting was observed in the middle section near Station E.

Table 3 shows other conditions in this comparison. The headway to the preceding train at the time of departure from Station A was 12.03 km for both signal-induced and non-signal-induced runs. At Station F, the headway to the preceding train was 3.16 km for the run with signal-induced deceleration and 3.82 km for the non-signal-induced run, with longer headway without signal-induced deceleration. The travel time from Station A to K was 13 min 59 s for the run with signal-induced deceleration and 13 min 5 s for the other, indicating a shorter travel time in the absence of signal-induced deceleration. The estimated energy consumption was 163.5 kWh for the former and 147.8 kWh for the latter, indicating lower energy consumption in the absence of signal-induced deceleration.

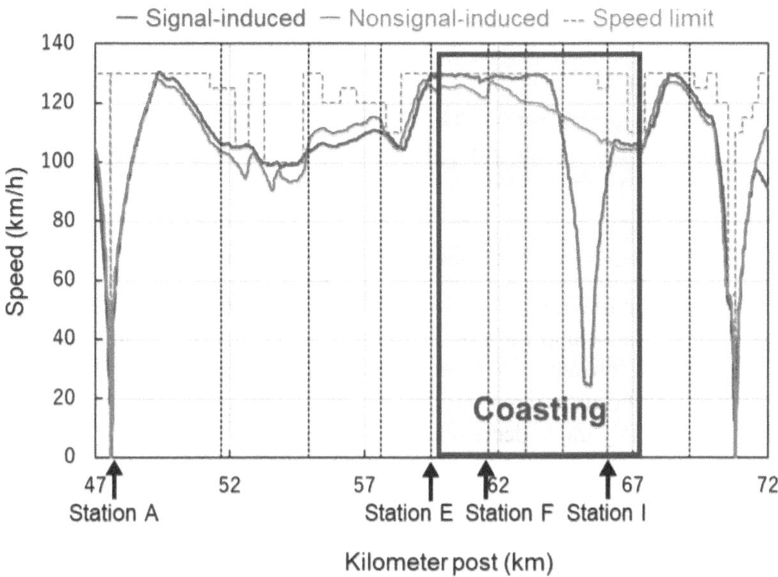

Fig. 7. Comparison of two example runs.

Table 3. Other conditions in the comparison.

		Signal-induced (General group)	Non-signal-induced (Member group)
Headway (km)	At Station A	12.03	12.03
	At Station F	3.16	3.82
Travel time (h:mm:ss)	Station A–Station F	0:13:59	0:13:05
Estimated energy consumption (kWh)		163.5	147.8
Departure delay at Station A (h:mm:ss)		0:00:59	0:00:25

4 Discussion

4.1 Signal Impact on Energy Consumption and Travel Time

The results indicate that in the member group, there was a smaller likelihood of signal-induced deceleration. Furthermore, avoiding such deceleration was associated with lower estimated energy consumption and shorter travel time. These findings align with previous research showing that minimizing deceleration and subsequent acceleration between stations reduces energy consumption [4]. Based on the results of the ANOVA tests for estimated energy consumption and travel time, signal, but not driver group, was identified as a significant factor associated with longer travel time and increased energy consumption. Therefore, reducing the likelihood of signal-induced deceleration can be an effective approach for decreasing energy consumption. From an operational perspective, these findings suggest that energy-efficient operation should be considered not only in terms of individual driving techniques, such as coasting before braking, but also in terms of strategies decreasing exposure to signal-induced deceleration. Driving practices that maintain sufficient headway and mitigate unnecessary deceleration may contribute to a more stable and energy-efficient operation.

4.2 Driving Strategies to Avoid Signal-Induced Deceleration

In this study, we identified an energy- and time-saving driving technique: maintaining headway from the preceding train by incorporating coasting in the middle section, as indicated by the longer headway at Station F in runs without signal-induced deceleration, and the lack of significant differences at the departure station. In contrast, earlier studies reported that following trains decreased speed in the early section [5, 6]. Deceleration in the early section increases the likelihood that the following train will be affected by signal aspects and forced to decelerate. In this study, however, the driver accelerated early and reduced speed midway, possibly to prevent subsequent trains from slowing down. Further, the driver may have been aware of locations where signals frequently cause deceleration and adjusted their speed accordingly.

4.3 Limitations and Future Work

Based on actual operational log data, this study identified a driving strategy that decreases the likelihood of signal-induced deceleration. A limitation of this study is that drivers' intentions were not directly examined. It remains unclear whether drivers consciously employed the technique identified in this study. Therefore, future work should include interviews with drivers to clarify their intentions and decision-making during operation.

Another limitation concerns the control of conditions relating to the preceding train. Despite selecting runs with similar headway conditions for comparison, the operational conditions were not strictly identical. As a result, applying the identified driving technique does not necessarily guarantee avoiding signal-induced deceleration. To address this issue, future studies should experimentally investigate driving strategies for avoiding signal-induced deceleration by reproducing headway conditions using a driving simulator.

Finally, the general group may have included drivers conscious of energy-efficient operations. In future work, drivers will be classified into groups based on their actual energy consumption reports, with further analyses focusing on signal-induced deceleration.

Based on the energy-efficient driving technique identified in this study for reducing signal-induced deceleration, a driving advisory system will be developed as future work.

5 Conclusion

The present study aimed to identify train driving strategies for avoiding energy losses associated with signal-induced deceleration by analyzing GNSS-based operational log data from a limited express train line.

The proportion of runs involving signal-induced deceleration was significantly lower for the member group (21.88%) than for the general group (44.15%). Furthermore, the effects of signals, not drivers, on estimated energy consumption and travel time were found to be significant. In other words, signal-induced deceleration resulted in longer travel times and higher energy consumption.

Comparing runs under similar operational conditions showed that drivers with a lower proportion of runs involving signal-induced deceleration tended to avoid deceleration by incorporating coasting in the middle section, which helped maintain headway from the preceding train.

Disclosure of Interests. The authors have no competing interests to declare that are relevant to the content of this article.

References

1. Kuwahara, R., Aoki, T., Kamo, Y.: Eco-driving trial runs in European railway environment and energy. In: Proceedings of International Symposium on Speed-up and Service Technology for Railway and Maglev Systems, 1E15-1 (2015)
2. Koizumi, Y., et al.: Four months field evaluation and the refinement of energy-efficient driver advisory system toward commercial operation. In: Proceedings of the 1st International Railway Symposium Aachen 2017, pp. 116–131 (2018)
3. Ueda, T., et al.: Analysis of energy-efficient operation characteristics of express trains using global navigation satellite system data. Appl. Hum. Fact. Ergon. **199**, 2055–2060 (2025)
4. Corman, F., et al.: Evaluation of green wave policy in real-time railway traffic management. Transport. Res. Part C: Emerg. Technol. **17**(6), 607–616 (2009)
5. Albrecht, R., et al.: Energy-efficient train control: the two-train separation problem on level track. J. Rail Transport Plan. Manage. **5**(3), 163–182 (2015)
6. Albrecht, R., et al.: The two-train separation problem on non-level track—driving strategies that minimize total required tractive energy subject to prescribed section clearance times. Transport. Res. Part B: Methodol. **111**, 135–167 (2018)
7. Hansen, I.A., Pachl, J. (eds.): Railway Timetabling & Operations. 2nd revised and extended edn. DVV Media Group GmbH I Eurailpress, Hamburg (2014)

Attention-Salient Object Consistency: A Quantitative Assessment Method for Drivers' Situation Awareness

Shuaishuai Wang, Rongbin Yao, Shanxin Huang, and Zhen Wang(✉)

Guangxi University Key Laboratory of Intelligent Networking and Scenario System, School of Information and Communication, Guilin University of Electronic Technology, Guilin 541004, China
wang57@mails.guet.edu.cn, wangzhen@guet.edu.cn

Abstract. Intelligent driving assistance has become a primary focus of contemporary automotive research. To address the "out-of-the-loop" phenomenon prevalent in Level 2 and Level 3 human-machine co-driving, and to overcome the inability of traditional monitoring systems to detect "inattentional blindness," this paper proposes a quantitative assessment method for driver Situation Awareness (SA) based on attention-salient object consistency. The method constructs a dual-stream collaborative architecture integrating environmental analysis with gaze tracking. On the environmental stream, the Tramba model—a Mamba architecture optimized for traffic scenes—is employed to extract salient objects, combining horizon geometry constraints with a lightweight semantic validation mechanism to precisely localize objective salient objects. On the driver stream, a self-supervised gaze estimation network based on geometric consistency constraints leverages road scene priors to enhance tracking accuracy in uncontrolled environments. For evaluation, a spatiotemporal mapping model calculates cumulative visual attention metrics via sliding time windows, while introducing an Attention-Salient Object Weighted Intersection over Union (IoU) to dynamically quantify perceptual consistency. Experiments on the Look Both Ways (LBW) dataset demonstrate that this method effectively characterizes the alignment between the driver's perceptual focus and objective salient objects. By integrating effective perception thresholds derived from cognitive psychology, this research achieves a "cognitive-level" evaluation of driver SA capabilities, providing novel theoretical foundations and technical approaches for addressing takeover safety challenges during human-machine co-driving.

Keywords: situation awareness · driver monitoring system · attention-Salient Object consistency · Human-machine co-driving

1 Introduction

The global automotive industry is currently undergoing profound restructuring centered on "intelligence" and "connectivity." Intelligent connected vehicles are accelerating their evolution from simple transportation tools into intelligent mobile terminals possessing

W. -C. Li and A. Plioutsias (Eds.): HCII 2026, LNAI 16708, pp. 80–96, 2026.
https://doi.org/10.1007/978-3-032-29459-3_7

"human-like" perception and interaction capabilities. With the proliferation of high-computing-power chips and the integration of large AI models into vehicles, the human-machine interaction paradigm within the smart cockpit [1] is shifting from physical buttons towards multimodal natural interactions such as voice, gaze, and gestures. However, given the short-term challenges of large-scale deployment for fully autonomous driving (Level 5), the industry will remain in a transitional phase of "human-machine co-driving" between Levels 2 and 3 for the next five years.

During this phase, the driver's role undergoes a fundamental shift [2], evolving from the vehicle's direct operator to the system's supervisor. This passive role transformation readily induces an "out-of-the-loop" effect, significantly diminishing the driver's situation awareness (SA). When the autonomous driving system (ADS) encounters failures or confronts edge cases, drivers often struggle to execute high-quality takeovers instantaneously. Statistics confirm that distracted driving remains the foremost threat to road safety. According to the US National Highway Traffic Safety Administration (NHTSA), 3,275 lives were lost in distracted driving incidents in 2023, with visual distractions (such as operating touchscreens or viewing mobile phones) being the primary cause. In Level 3 takeover scenarios, even two seconds of visual distraction can exponentially increase collision with salient objects.

Faced with these challenges, existing driver monitoring systems (DMS) reveal significant limitations. Traditional DMS primarily rely on facial features (such as closed eyes or yawning) for fatigue detection, failing to effectively assess whether the driver is genuinely attentive to environmental salient objects. Consequently, this approach struggles to address the cognitive failure of "seeing but not perceiving." To address this, this research proposes an "Attention-Salient Object Consistency" based quantitative assessment method for situation awareness. This approach extends beyond mere driver state monitoring to establish a spatiotemporal mapping model between the driver's visual focus and the objective distribution of salient objects. By quantifying the "perception" and "understanding" tiers within Endsley's model [3], this research aims to identify deviations between attention and perception of salient objects. This enables the development of a new generation of "cognitive-level" active safety warning strategies. This technological advancement holds significant scientific and engineering value for addressing safety challenges during human-machine co-driving phases and reducing traffic accident rates.

2 Related Work

Quantitative assessment of driver situation awareness (SA) spans multiple interdisciplinary fields, including environmental perception, gaze tracking, and cognitive modeling. Current SA evaluation is evolving from single metrics toward multidimensional systems. This chapter synthesizes recent research advances across three dimensions: traffic scenario salient object characterization, driver gaze estimation, and SA assessment methodologies.

Objectively accurate environmental salient object assessment serves as the ground truth for validating driver SA. Traditional salient object detection (SOD) methods, relying heavily on high-contrast features, often fail when encountering "visually weak yet safety-critical" salient objects such as pedestrians at night. Addressing this semantic gap,

Qiu et al. [4] developed the Tramba model for traffic scenes, building upon the Mamba linear sequence modeling theory proposed by Gu et al. [5]. This model employs a Dual-Frequency Visual State Space (DFVSS) module to achieve robust detection of minute salient objects under complex lighting conditions, overcoming the efficiency bottlenecks of traditional CNNs and Transformers in long sequence modeling.

Regarding salient object quantification at the physical level, researchers have introduced "field theory" to describe the continuous saliency distribution of road environments. The early Driving Safety Field theory proposed by Joo et al. [6] laid the foundation for this direction. Building upon this, Zuo et al. [7] and Li et al. [8] further refined the model. By mapping road geometric constraints and the kinetic energy of moving vehicles into a continuous potential energy field, they successfully quantified road environment saliency dynamically. This approach of converting discrete traffic elements into continuous saliency distributions provides a mathematical basis for calculating whether a driver's attention falls within a "high-potential saliency zone."

Establishing the spatial correlation between driver gaze and environmental salient objects depends on the accuracy of gaze point estimation. However, as revealed by the ETH-XGaze dataset [9], extreme head postures and complex lighting conditions within vehicles pose consistent technical challenges. To address gaze regression in uncontrolled environments, Cheng et al. [10] constructed the large-scale IVGaze dataset and proposed a dual-stream Transformer-based estimation network, significantly enhancing the robustness of in-vehicle gaze tracking.

To further address temporal jitter and spatial depth ambiguity in gaze signals, Hu et al. [11] introduced the Frame-to-Frame Fine-grained Attention (FIFA) mechanism, effectively smoothing sequential gaze signals. Meanwhile, Kawana et al. [12] proposed the GA3CE model, which achieves precise projection of gaze vectors from a 2D plane to 3D physical space by encoding 3D scene context. These methods enable the consistent calculation of "gaze-salient object consistency" within a unified 3D world coordinate system.

With the proliferation of Level 3 human-machine co-driving, SA assessment is evolving from single eye-tracking metrics towards multimodal cognitive fusion. The "Look-But-Fail-To-See" (LBFS) phenomenon, first proposed by Herslund et al. [13], demonstrates that mere fixation does not equate to effective cognitive processing. Addressing this issue, Lim et al. [14] demonstrated that incorporating electroencephalogram (EEG) signals significantly distinguishes effective SA establishment from LBFS failures. However, the intrusive nature of contact sensors limits their application. Consequently, Xie and Guo [15] developed the video-based, non-contact CogMamba model, which employs state-space modeling to estimate physiological load in real-time, offering a novel non-contact solution for multimodal fusion.

Moreover, semantic-level evaluation is gaining increasing attention. With the rise of large language models in autonomous driving [16], Zhou et al. [17] attempted to apply large vision-language models (LVLMs) to attention prediction, seeking to explain from a causal logic perspective "why the driver looked here." However, existing LVLM methods incur substantial computational overhead and lack refined temporal metrics for determining whether fixation duration reaches cognitive processing thresholds, rendering them unsuitable for real-time safety monitoring requirements.

In summary, while existing research has made significant progress in individual submodules, a systematic evaluation framework that balances computational real-time performance, geometric precision, and cognitive mechanisms remains elusive. Mainstream approaches often compartmentalize the objective environmental field from the subjective attention field, neglecting the minimal processing cycle required for human visual cognition. In light of this, this paper proposes a dual-stream evaluation method based on the Tramba perception model and dynamic geometric constraints. This aims to achieve a dual-loop assessment of the driver's situation awareness capability at both the "cognitive level" and "physical level" by constructing an Intersection-over-Union (IoU) based metric for Attention-Salient Object Consistency.

3 Method

To address the challenge of quantifying the effectiveness of driver situation awareness in complex dynamic environments, this chapter proposes a dual-stream collaborative assessment framework integrating environmental and attentional streams. This framework aims to quantify the driver's ability to acquire and cognitively process salient object information by achieving spatiotemporal alignment between objective environmental salient object distributions and subjective driver attentional distributions. As illustrated in Fig. 1, the assessment system comprises three core modules:

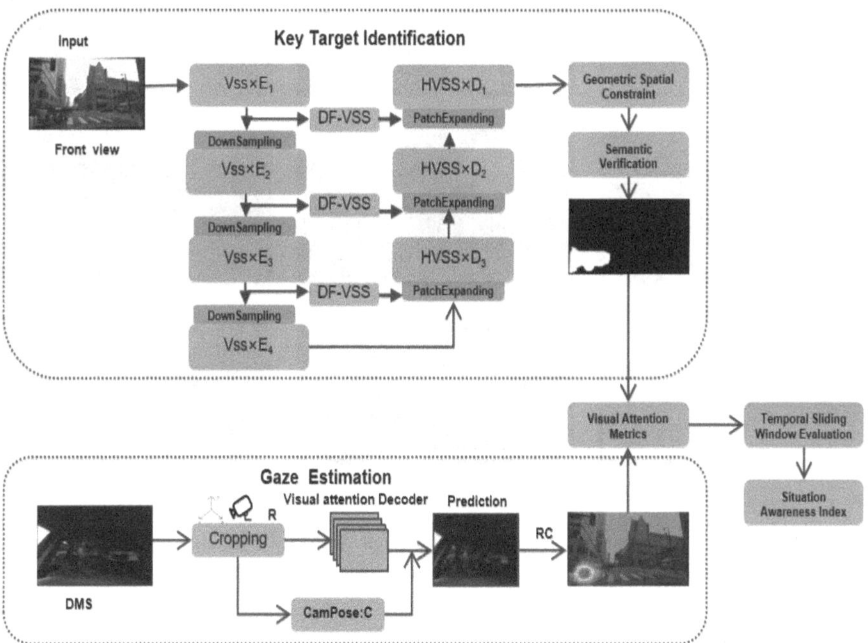

Fig. 1. Situation Awareness System Framework.

Scene Salient Object Identification Module: Extracts environmental information to locate and filter salient objects (e.g., vehicles, pedestrians) with significant impact on driving safety, establishing objective saliency zones.

Gaze Point Estimation Module: Analyzes the driver's line of sight, calculates 3D gaze vectors through facial feature and geometric mapping, and constructs a subjective "attention field."

Situation Awareness Capability Assessment Module: Aligns the aforementioned two information streams across spatiotemporal dimensions. It spatially calculates the consistency between gaze distribution and saliency distribution, while temporally employing a sliding window to smooth cognitive fluctuations, ultimately generating a dynamic situation awareness (SA) index.

3.1 Scene Salient Object Identification Module

Given that existing salient object detection (SOD) models struggle to identify dim yet safety-critical salient objects (e.g., pedestrians at night) based solely on luminance priors, this research addresses the inconsistency between "visual saliency" and "safety importance." By incorporating geometric spatial constraints and a semantic confidence mechanism, an enhanced traffic scene saliency model is constructed (Fig. 2).

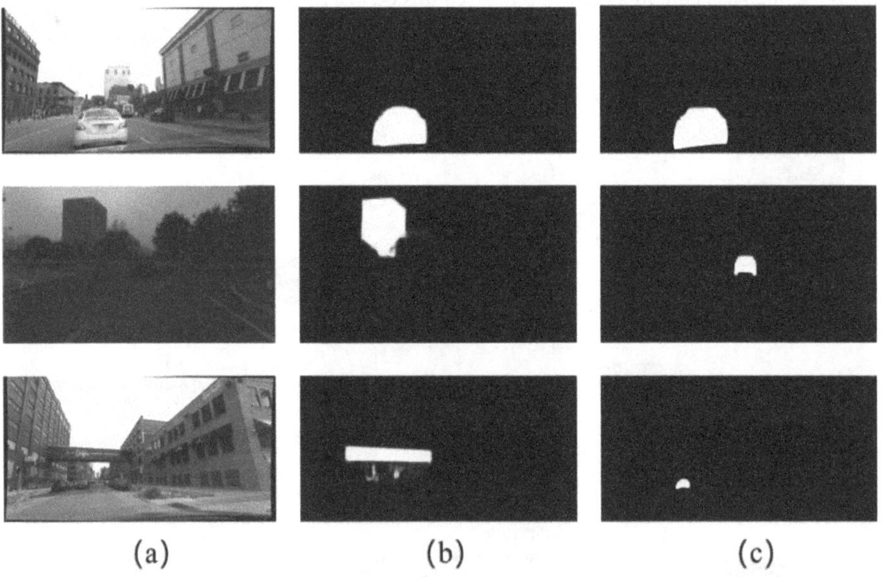

Fig. 2. Performance Comparison Between Traditional Saliency Models and Traffic Saliency Models (a) Original images; (b) Traditional saliency models; (c) Traffic saliency models.

This study employs the Tramba model, specifically designed for traffic scenarios, to perform Traffic Salient Object Detection (TSOD). By incorporating the VMamba architecture, the model leverages its linear complexity advantage to process high-resolution driving video streams. The core innovation lies in its Dual-Frequency Visual State Space

(DFVSS) module. Through a frequency-domain decoupling strategy—modeling global road structures with low-frequency components while enhancing local object details with high-frequency components—it significantly boosts the model's perceptual robustness under low-illumination and adverse weather conditions, ensuring initial recall rates for potential salient objects. While Tramba effectively addresses false negatives, its raw output M may still contain high-contrast yet non-safety-critical background artifacts such as roadside billboards or tree textures. To address this, this study introduces a post-processing filtering mechanism for secondary screening of the potential salient object set$\{R_1,R_2,...,R_N\}$. To suppress non-safety-related false detections, we define a comprehensive confidence score S_{final} for each candidate region R_i. This score is jointly determined by three components: saliency prior, geometric spatial constraints, and semantic confidence.

First, considering the perspective projection characteristics of the forward-facing vehicle camera, this study constructs a horizon geometric constraint model. Due to pitch motion during vehicle movement, fixed image region segmentation struggles to adapt to dynamically changing road scenes. Therefore, using camera intrinsic parameters calibrated during image acquisition and real-time pose information, the effective field-of-view boundaries for each frame are dynamically calculated. A spatial constraint function is constructed to implement soft suppression of spurious salient objects violating planar road geometry distribution—such as street lamps suspended above the horizon, birds in flight, or hood reflections at the image bottom. Let the height of the input image be H, and the vertical coordinate of the centroid of the i-th candidate region R_i be $y_{c,i}$. The geometric constraint score $F_{geo}(i)$ is defined as follows:

$$F_{geo}(i) = \begin{cases} \exp\left(-\frac{(y_{sky}-y_{c,i})^2}{2\sigma^2}\right), & if\ y_{c,i} < y_{sky} \\ 1, & if\ y_{sky} \le y_{c,i} \le y_{\text{hood}} \\ \exp\left(-\frac{(y_{c,i}-y_{\text{hood}})^2}{2\sigma^2}\right), & if\ y_{c,i} > y_{hood} \end{cases} \quad (1)$$

By jointly solving the vehicle-attitude-based horizon threshold y_{sky} and the body-occlusion threshold $y_{\text{h}ood}$, and introducing a Gaussian smoothing coefficient σ, we constructed a flexible geometric constraint model that adapts to driving vibrations while robustly eliminating background interference.

Second, concerning the semantic attributes of candidate regions, a lightweight classification network (ResNet-18) is employed for secondary verification. By feeding the cropped region R_i into the classification network, the semantic confidence score $C_{sem}(R_i)$, indicating the probability of belonging to traffic participants (vehicles, pedestrians, cyclists, etc.), is computed. This effectively filters out non-salient objects such as roadside vegetation and architectural textures.

Finally, through dual geometric and semantic constraints, the composite score for the i-th candidate salient object is computed using a multiplicative fusion strategy (serving as a "one-vote veto" mechanism):

$$S_{final}(i) = S_{sal}(i)^{\gamma_1} \cdot F_{geo}(i)^{\gamma_2} \cdot C_{sem}(i)^{\gamma_3} \quad (2)$$

Where γ represents the hyperparameter for balancing weights. This mechanism ensures that only targets satisfying visual saliency, spatial validity, and semantic matching are retained, providing a high-precision salient object map M_{risk} for subsequent consistency assessment.

3.2 Gaze Point Estimation Module

This module aims to precisely map the driver's gaze from 2D image space to 3D physical space, thereby establishing a unified analysis benchmark linking driving behavior and environmental salient objects. The process comprises two core stages: appearance-based gaze vector regression and gaze-scene geometric intersection (Fig. 3).

Fig. 3. Driver Gaze Estimation

First, at the gaze resolution level, to accommodate complex head posture variations within the confined vehicle interior, we employ ResNet-50 as the feature extraction backbone network. This network is pre-trained on a large-scale multi-view facial dataset, learning facial appearance features I_{g} to regress a normalized 3D gaze direction vector $g \in \mathrm{S}^2$.

Second, to project the head-centered gaze vector into the world coordinate system [18], a rigid transformation relationship must be established between the driver coordinate system and the road environment coordinate system. We employ the COLMAP algorithm to jointly calibrate the relative pose matrices [R|t] of the facial camera and scene camera, establishing a unified spatial reference frame. Meanwhile, a dense depth map D(x) of the road scene is obtained via stereo matching algorithms. Combining the scene camera's intrinsic parameters K with a pinhole camera model, image pixels are back-projected into 3D space to reconstruct the physical scene point cloud Xscene.

Finally, driver eye centers (e) are located in 3D space via facial key point detection. By integrating the calibrated matrix and gaze direction (g), a line of sight is constructed, and its intersection with the reconstructed 3D road scene surface (X_{scene}) is calculated.

This intersection point represents the driver's actual gaze landing point in the physical world, providing geometrically consistent spatial coordinates for subsequent salient object association.

3.3 Situation Awareness Capability Assessment Module

Given the driver's limited visual resources, the core of situation awareness lies in "focusing on the correct salient object at the correct time." This section first constructs a multi-dimensional visual attention metric, then combines it with the salient object distribution to propose a situation awareness index based on spatiotemporal consistency [19].

For a single target region z_i, the following two fundamental dimensional metrics are defined:

1. Cumulative Gaze Duration on Salient Objects

Cumulative gaze duration denotes the total gaze duration directed by the driver towards a specific target region z_i within a given time window T, reflecting the driver's overall attention allocation [20] to that region.

$$T_{cum}(z_i) = \sum_{k=1}^{n} d_k \tag{3}$$

In the formula, z_i denotes the i-th target region; n represents the total number of times the driver gazed at this region within the time window; and d_k indicates the duration of the k-th gaze at this region. To eliminate the influence of time window length and enable cross-scenario comparisons, the cumulative gaze time proportion is introduced:

$$P_{time}(z_i) = \frac{T_{cum}(z_i)}{T} \tag{4}$$

where $P_{time}(z_i) \in [0, 1]$. A higher value indicates greater visual resource allocation to the z_i

2. Proportion of Fixations

This metric quantifies the relative frequency with which the driver's gaze falls upon a salient object area. Specifically, it denotes the proportion of total gaze occurrences directed at the salient object zi within the time window T:

$$P_{freq}(z_i) = \frac{N(z_i)}{N_{total}} \tag{5}$$

In the equation, N_{total} denotes the total number of gaze points generated by the driver within the time window; and $N(z_i)$ represents the number of gazes falling upon the salient object z_i. A higher value of $P_{freq}(z_i)$ indicates a greater frequency of the driver's visual access to that salient object, reflecting heightened visual search interest.

3. Multidimensional Feature Extraction of Visual Attention

Given the limitations of single-dimensional representation, this study concurrently extracts metrics from temporal and frequency dimensions to comprehensively describe the driver's attentional state: Temporal metrics (e.g., P_{time}) fail to capture the dynamic frequency of gaze shifts. For instance, prolonged fixation duration resulting from fatigue-induced gaze retention does not necessarily indicate effective cognitive engagement. Conversely, frequency-based metrics (P_{freq}) reflect search activity but fail to indicate gaze depth or information extraction efficiency (e.g., frequent brief saccades may indicate distracted attention). To comprehensively quantify the validity of visual attention, this study constructs a geometric mean-based composite attention intensity metric $S(z_i)$, achieving complementary constraints between temporal and frequency dimensions through non-linear coupling:

$$S(z_i) = \sqrt{P_{time}(z_i)P_{freq}(z_i)} \tag{6}$$

This fusion logic achieves adaptive assessment of attentional states through non-linear coupling.

4. Visual Attention Modelling

As driving constitutes a highly dynamic, time-varying system, drivers' attentional levels exhibit significant non-stationary fluctuations influenced by the evolving driving environment. Furthermore, human visual cognition exhibits "temporal dependency," wherein current attentional states often represent the continuation and accumulation of past cognitive behaviors. Relying solely on cross-sectional assessments within a single temporal window fails to eliminate transient noise interference and thus cannot accurately reflect drivers' true attentional levels [21].

To overcome these limitations, smooth short-term fluctuations, and quantify visual attention characteristics over extended time sequences, this chapter proposes a comprehensive quantification model based on a Sliding Time Window (STW). This model sets a base window length of T and a sliding step size of Δt, constructing an evaluation sequence comprising n consecutive sub-windows along the time series. For the k-th time window ($k = 1, 2, \ldots$ n), its start and end times are t_{k} and $t_{\mathrm{k}} + T$, respectively. The driver's local visual attention level within this window towards the region z_{j} is denoted as $S_k(z_j)$.

Given the decaying nature of visual attention's memory effect over time, the contribution of observations from different historical moments to the current state requires dynamic adjustment. This study employs a linear weighting strategy, assigning higher weights to time windows closer to the present moment to emphasize the dominant role of recent behavior. The temporal composite visual attention quantification formula $S_{comp}(z_j)$ for region z_j is defined as follows:

$$S_{comp}(z_j) = \sum_{k=1}^{n} \omega_k \cdot S_k(z_j) \tag{7}$$

where ω_k denotes the weight coefficient for the k th time window. To satisfy the linear growth trend where weights increase with proximity to the present moment while ensuring weight normalization ($\sum \omega_k = 1$)), the calculation formula for ω_k is constructed as follows:

$$\omega_k = \frac{2k}{n(n+1)} \tag{8}$$

Here, k denotes the temporal index of the time window (where k indicates proximity to the current time), and n represents the total number of sliding time windows. This weighting mechanism preserves the smoothing effect of historical attention states while ensuring high sensitivity to current attention features.

5. Consistency Modelling

The aforementioned "comprehensive visual attention quantification" (S_{comp}) primarily evaluates driver attention intensity from a temporal dimension, yet fails to address the accuracy of attention targeting [22]. Should a driver maintain prolonged, high-intensity fixation on non-salient areas (e.g., roadside advertisements), their situation awareness of salient objects remains deficient despite elevated attention intensity. To address this, we propose an evaluation method grounded in attention-salient object spatial consistency. This approach constructs a dynamic situation awareness index by calculating the spatial match between the driver's "visual attention distribution" and "scene- salient objects ", integrated with the aforementioned "comprehensive attention quantification value" (S_{comp}).

To enable spatial alignment between gaze and scene salient objects, a self-supervised geometric mapping algorithm first projects the driver's gaze vector from 3D space onto the 2D forward-view image plane, yielding the fixation point's pixel coordinates $P_{gaze} = (x_g, y_g)$.Considering the foveal nature of human vision, where clear perception is concentrated within a small area around the fixation point, this study generates a visual attention map (M_{att}) centered on the fixation point, following a 2D Gaussian distribution:

$$M_{att}(x, y) = \exp\left(-\frac{(x-x_g)^2+(y-y_g)^2}{2\sigma^2}\right) \quad (9)$$

where (x, y) denotes the image pixel coordinates; and σ represents the standard deviation, whose value corresponds to the effective coverage range of the driver's foveal field of view (typically the pixel radius corresponding to a 2°–5° field of view). This distribution characterizes the driver's current spatial information acquisition range within the scene.

The salient object map M_{risk} generated by the aforementioned salient object recognition module represents the objectively distributed salient objects within the scene. To quantify the alignment between the driver's subjective attention and objective salient objects, the Weighted Intersection over Union (IoU) is calculated between the two, defined as the spatial consistency coefficient (C_{cons}):

$$C_{cons} = \frac{\sum_{x,y} min(M_{att}(x,y), M_{risk}(x,y))}{\sum_{x,y} max(M_{att}(x,y), M_{risk}(x,y))} \quad (10)$$

Where $C_{cons} \in [0,1]$. A value closer to 1 indicates a high degree of overlap between the driver's visual attention field and the scene's salient object distribution, signifying that the driver has accurately captured salient object information.

6. Construction of the Situation Awareness (SA) Index

A standalone consistency coefficient reflects only spatial overlap, failing to capture the depth of cognitive processing [22]. True effective situation awareness requires coupling spatial accuracy with temporal attentional intensity. Therefore, the integrated visual attention metric S_{comp} and spatial consistency coefficient C_{cons} are fused to construct the dynamic Situation Awareness Index (SA):

$$SA = C_{cons} \times S_{comp} \quad (11)$$

The physical significance of this formula lies in the fact that when C_{cons} is low (looking in the wrong place), regardless of fixation duration, the *SA* value is suppressed and deemed perceptual misalignment;

When C_{cons} is high but S_{comp} is low (glancing over without establishing cognition), the *SA* value remains low, indicating insufficient perception; Only when both metrics are high does the system determine the driver possesses effective situation awareness. Based on this, a perception failure threshold τ is established. When salient objects exist in the scene and $SA < \tau$, the system identifies a cognitive failure regarding salient objects and triggers a graded warning.

4 Experiments

4.1 Dataset and Model Selection

For gaze estimation, this study employs the Look Both Ways (LBW) dataset for experimentation, primarily due to its unique advantages in quantifying driver situation awareness. Unlike traditional single-view or simulator datasets, LBW provides synchronously calibrated driver RGB-D facial video, stereoscopic road scene video, and high-precision 3D gaze ground truth captured by wearable eye trackers. This multimodal data configuration enables the construction of precise geometric mappings from driver gaze to the 3D road space, thereby facilitating accurate analysis of the consistency between driver gaze behavior and salient objects within the road scene. Furthermore, the dataset encompasses approximately 6.8 h of real-world driving data from 28 drivers across diverse road types (urban, rural) and complex weather conditions (rain, snow, dusk), demonstrating exceptional ecological validity. This facilitates the validation of the proposed situation awareness assessment model's robustness and generalization capabilities in uncontrolled real-world scenarios.

The foreground saliency detection algorithm employs the Tramba model. Given the frequent inconsistency between "visual saliency" and "salient object relevance" in driving scenarios, this study adopts the Tramba model, which is specifically engineered for traffic environments. The rationale for selecting this model primarily lies in its two core mechanisms optimized for driving conditions:

- Enhanced Perceptual Capabilities: Tramba, built upon the Vmamba architecture, innovatively incorporates a Dual-Frequency Visual State Space module. This module decouples visual features via Discrete Cosine Transform (DCT), employing a sliding window mechanism to capture high-frequency texture details while utilizing hollow scanning to model low-frequency global structures. This design enables the model to accurately segment traffic elements with blurred edges even under adverse weather conditions such as rain, snow, fog, and nighttime driving.
- Integration of Driver Attention Priors: Addressing the distribution characteristics of visual attention during driving tasks, Tramba proposes the Helix-SS2D (Helical Selective Scanning in 2D) mechanism. Unlike traditional line-by-line scanning, Helix-SS2D simulates the driver's "center-priority" gaze habit, performing spiral-shaped feature aggregation from the image center outward. This mechanism effectively injects driver attention priors into the model, ensuring it prioritizes responses

to salient objects in the central field of view. Experiments demonstrate that Tramba exhibits significant superiority over existing CNN and Transformer baseline models on the large-scale traffic saliency dataset TSOD10K, particularly displaying enhanced robustness when processing minute objects and complex background distractions. Consequently, this model provides precise, semantically coherent foreground object inputs for the situation awareness assessment in this study.

4.2 Determining the Situation Awareness Threshold

To translate continuously varying attention scores into discrete Situation Awareness (*SA*) states, establishing a reasonable classification threshold (τ) is necessary. For this salient parameter, this study adopts a heuristic setting strategy grounded in cognitive mechanisms. By leveraging the "first principles" of cognitive psychology, this strategy theoretically derives a threshold that distinguishes "unconscious saccades" from "effective perception," defining the physiological lower bound of human visual cognition.

According to classical theories of eye-tracking and cognitive chronometry, human visual information acquisition alternates between rapid "saccades" and brief "fixations." During saccades, the visual system exhibits "saccadic suppression," wherein the cerebral cortex suspends the decoding of external information. Only during stable fixation phases can the complete visual cognitive cycle—from retinal imaging to semantic comprehension—be accomplished.

Traffic psychology research indicates that for a driver to complete a single cycle of higher-order cognitive processing—encompassing salient object detection, recognition, and salient object assessment—in a dynamic scene, the minimum effective fixation duration ($T_{cog\text{-}min}$) typically requires 250–300 ms. Any visual dwell time significantly shorter than this is generally regarded as unconscious gaze drift or mechanical saccadic movement, insufficient for establishing effective situation awareness.

Under the sliding observation window $T_{win} = 1.0$ s defined in this model, to ensure the physiologically meaningful "effective perception" state in model outputs (i.e., encompassing at least one complete cognitive cycle), we define the lower bound of the temporal duty cycle for effective perception, τ_{min}, as follows:

$$\tau_{min} \geq \frac{T_{cog-min}}{T_{win}} = \frac{300ms}{1000ms} = 0.30 \tag{12}$$

Where τ_{min} represents the minimum fixation duration required to support higher-order cognitive processing (conservatively set at 300ms). Combining this with the previously defined $SA = C_{cons} \times S_{comp}$, assuming the driver's gaze has accurately landed within the salient object zone (i.e., spatial consistency $C_{cons} \approx 1$), the value of *SA* is entirely determined by the cumulative temporal investment. Consequently, $\tau = 0.30$ constitutes the salient threshold distinguishing "physical seeing (physiological optical process)" from "cognitive perception (neuropsychological process)". When $SA < 0.30$, even if the gaze passes over the salient object, the system classifies it as an invalid scan.

5 Results and Discussion

5.1 Salient Object Detection Results

To validate the effectiveness of the proposed improved model for extracting salient objects in traffic scenarios, comprehensive comparative experiments were conducted between the enhanced detection model and the benchmark Tramba model on a proprietary traffic driving dataset. These experiments aimed to evaluate the model's detection accuracy for salient objects (e.g., vehicles and pedestrians) in complex driving environments, alongside its suppression capability for background distractions (e.g., roadside vegetation and billboards).

To intuitively demonstrate the improved model's superiority in precise salient object extraction, three typical challenging driving scenarios were selected for visual comparison, as illustrated in Fig. 4:

Scenario 1: Near-field Background Interference. As depicted in the first row of Fig. 4, high-contrast tree textures and commercial billboards are present on the right-hand side of the road. The baseline Tramba model, constrained by its reliance on purely visual saliency, erroneously identifies the brightly lit billboard as a salient object due to its high visual prominence. In contrast, the enhanced saliency model incorporates geometric spatial constraints and semantic filtering mechanisms, retaining only the vehicle targets on the road surface. This demonstrates exceptional safety-oriented semantic selectivity.

Scenario 2: Multi-object Selection at Signalized Intersections. As depicted in the second row, vehicles operate within the complex environment of a traffic light-controlled intersection. Straight-ahead vehicles are present on the left-hand side of the frame, while vehicles are entering from the right-hand junction. In this scenario, the baseline model typically applies indiscriminate saliency annotations to all dynamic objects within the field of view. Conversely, the enhanced saliency model demonstrates superior scene-selective attention: it effectively suppresses signals from distant oncoming vehicles on the left while allocating high saliency to vehicles on the right that pose greater potential interaction salient objects. This selective retention proves that the improved model not only "sees" salient objects but also distinguishes their potential object relevance based on spatial location.

Scenario 3: Distant Background Distractions. The third row depicts a typical driving scene with complex background infrastructure, featuring a distant bridge structure. As bridges typically possess prominent edge contours and geometric structures, the baseline Tramba model is susceptible to being misled by purely visual features, erroneously labeling it as a salient region. However, the focus for driving safety should remain on dynamic traffic participants in the foreground. Experimental results demonstrate the enhanced model's exceptional semantic filtering capability: it successfully disregards the visually prominent yet driving-irrelevant bridge structure in the distance while accurately retaining the salient vehicle object in the foreground on the left. This outcome validates the model's ability to effectively distinguish between "background environmental textures" and "foreground salient objects," ensuring attention resources are not diverted by non-salient infrastructure.

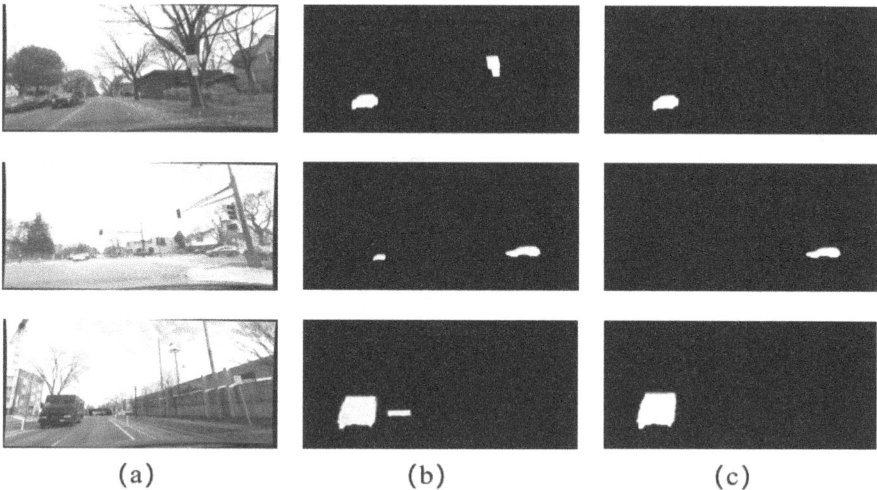

Fig. 4. Salient object detection results. (a) Original images; (b) Results of the baseline Tramba model; (c) Results of the proposed enhanced model.

5.2 Case Study: Analysis of Typical Scenarios

To validate the effectiveness of this approach in complex traffic environments, a representative urban intersection scenario was selected for detailed analysis. The experimental setup involved the ego-vehicle remaining stationary at a red light at the junction. The environmental background includes complex traffic signals, road markings, and stationary vehicles in the distance. In this sequence, a large truck emerges from the front-right of the ego-vehicle and initiates a left-turn maneuver, traversing the ego-vehicle's forward field of view diagonally from the right to the lower-left. This salient object exhibits characteristics of substantial size, a non-linear trajectory, and potential interaction importance, rendering it a high-priority salient hazard within the current scenario.

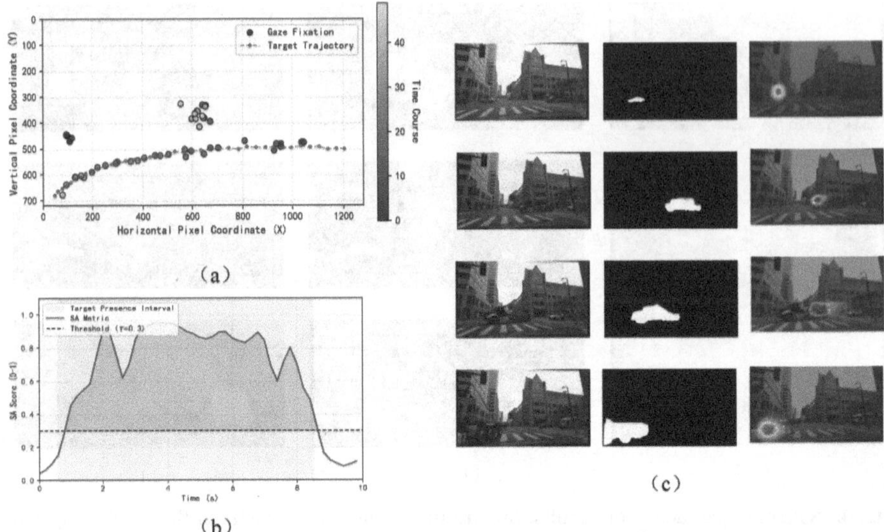

Fig. 5. Scenario Perception Results

Figure 5c illustrates the visual processing outcome of the proposed method. Despite complex background distractions such as traffic lights and road markings, the saliency detection network accurately suppressed background noise, identifying the left-turning truck ahead as the salient object. Simultaneously, the gaze point estimation precisely aligned with the truck's spatial region, indicating that the driver had visually locked onto this salient object at that moment.

Figure 5a illustrates the spatiotemporal distribution of the driver's gaze points relative to the target trajectory on the 2D image plane throughout the experimental process. The red dashed line represents the actual movement trajectory of the truck. Colored scatter points represent the driver's discrete gaze points, with color coding reflecting temporal evolution from cool tones (purple) to warm tones (yellow). Spatially, the vast majority of colored gaze points tightly cluster around the red target trajectory, forming a distinct "trajectory-following" pattern. This indicates that the driver's gaze maintained continuous tracking of the salient object as it crossed the field of view. Notably, a small number of outlier gaze points appear below the trajectory and in the central visual field. These represent genuine intermittent rapid sweeps of the road ahead while tracking the truck, rather than detection errors, confirming safe driving behavior.

Figure 5b translates these spatiotemporal behaviors into a quantified Situation Awareness (SA) metric curve, revealing the driver's actual cognitive state evolution. The yellow background area indicates the time interval during which the salient object was present and constituted a risk. The red solid line represents the real-time SA score curve calculated by the proposed algorithm, while the blue dashed line denotes the theoretically derived effective perception threshold ($\tau = 0.30$). Analysis reveals that following the salient object's initial appearance (the starting point of the yellow region), the SA curve does not rise vertically but exhibits a cognitive delay of approximately 400 ms. This accurately reflects the physiological reaction time required for the driver to detect the target and establish attention. During the subsequent tracking phase, the main body of the SA curve remains at a high level above 0.8. Notably, several distinct dips in the curve precisely correspond to the moments of gaze disengagement recorded in Fig. 5a. This demonstrates the algorithm's excellent dynamic sensitivity, capable of acutely detecting brief attention interruptions caused by distraction or saccadic eye movements. The red-shaded area demonstrates that throughout the majority of the salient period, the SA score consistently exceeded the threshold of τ. This quantitatively confirms that the driver successfully established effective and continuous situation awareness during this left-turning truck scenario, thereby validating the reliability of the assessment results obtained through the methodology presented herein.

6 Conclusion and Outlook

This study proposes a dual-stream collaborative assessment framework to explore its application in objectively quantifying driver Situation Awareness (SA). By analyzing the spatiotemporal coupling mechanism between environmental salient objects and driver attention allocation, it reveals the deep-seated distinction between "unconscious scanning" and "effective cognitive perception," emphasizing the core value of fusing spatial consistency and temporal attention intensity in breaking through traditional single-metric assessment frameworks. These strategies not only mitigate the uncertainty in cognitive state estimation but also provide a new perspective for understanding the coupling of physiological vision and psychological cognition, thus advancing the multidimensional analysis of driver behavior and providing a solid theoretical foundation for intelligent safety intervention systems.

However, as a data-driven approach reliant on specific training scenarios, the current model still has limitations. While it demonstrates high accuracy in standard conditions, its effectiveness in maintaining robustness under extreme environmental conditions—such as severe weather or low-light night-time driving—remains insufficient due to the constraints of dataset diversity. Future research could further integrate lightweight model optimization and multi-modal sensor fusion to encourage deeper system adaptability in complex real-world scenarios. By introducing diverse adverse weather datasets and conducting closed-loop validation, we can construct a more resilient human-machine co-pilot safety loop, thereby progressing the field from "state monitoring" to "proactive intervention."

References

1. Gao, F., et al.: Intelligent cockpits for connected vehicles: taxonomy, architecture, interaction technologies, and future directions. Sensors **24.16**, 5172 (2024)
2. Razak, S.F.A., et al.: Physiological-based driver monitoring systems: a scoping review. Civil Eng. J. **8.12**, 3952–3967 (2022)
3. Endsley, M.R.: From here to autonomy: lessons learned from human–automation research. Hum. Factors **59**(1), 5–27 (2017)
4. Qiu, Y., et al.: Salient Object Detection in Traffic Scenes through the TSOD10K Dataset. arXiv preprint arXiv:2503.16910 (2025)

5. Gu, A., Dao, T.: Mamba: linear-time sequence modeling with selective state spaces. arXiv preprint arXiv:2312.00752(2023)
6. Joo, Y.-J., et al.: A generalised driving risk assessment on high-speed motorways using field theory. Anal. Meth. Accid. Res. **40**, 100303 (2023)
7. Zuo, D., et al.: Composite safety potential field for highway driving risk assessment. Accid. Anal. Prevent. **220**, 108080 (2025)
8. Li, H., Zheng, X., Xiangyang, X.: Improved method of driving safety field modelling by considering the abnormal transfer of energy between vehicles. IEEE Access **13**, 43190–43200 (2025)
9. Zhang, X., et al.: Eth-xgaze: a large scale dataset for gaze estimation under extreme head pose and gaze variation. In: European Conference on Computer Vision. Springer International Publishing, Cham (2020)
10. Cheng, Y., et al.: What do you see in vehicle? Comprehensive vision solution for in-vehicle gaze estimation. In: Proceedings of the IEEE/CVF Conference on Computer Vision and Pattern Recognition (2024)
11. Hu, D., Cui, M., Huang, K.: FIFA: fine-grained inter-frame attention for driver's video gaze estimation. In: Proceedings of the Computer Vision and Pattern Recognition Conference (2025)
12. Kawana, Y., et al.: GA3CE: unconstrained 3d gaze estimation with gaze-aware 3D context encoding. In: Proceedings of the Computer Vision and Pattern Recognition Conference (2025)
13. Herslund, M.-B., Jørgensen, N.O.: Looked-but-failed-to-see-errors in traffic. Accid. Anal. Prev. **35**(6), 885–891 (2003)
14. Lim, C., et al.: Multimodal prediction of situation awareness during automated driving: a gaze and EEG-based approach. Ergonomics, 1–30 (2025)
15. Xie, Y., Guo, B.: CogMamba: multi-task driver cognitive load and physiological non-contact estimation with multimodal facial features. Sensors **25**(18), 5620 (2025)
16. Li, Y., et al.: Large language models for human-like autonomous driving: a survey. In: 2024 IEEE 27th International Conference on Intelligent Transportation Systems (ITSC). IEEE (2024)
17. Zhou, Y., et al.: Where, what, why: towards explainable driver attention prediction. arXiv preprint arXiv:2506.23088 (2025)
18. Kasahara, I., Stent, S., Park, H.S.: Look both ways: Self-supervising driver gaze estimation and road scene saliency. In: European Conference on Computer Vision. Springer Nature Switzerland, Cham (2022)
19. Chamberlain, L.: Eye tracking methodology; theory and practice. J. Cetacean Res. Manag. **10**(2), 217–220 (2007)
20. Underwood, G., et al.: Visual search while driving: skill and awareness during inspection of the scene. Transport. Res. Part F: Traffic Psychol. Behav. **5.2**, 87–97 (2002)
21. Dong, Y., et al.: Driver inattention monitoring system for intelligent vehicles: a review. IEEE Trans. Intell. Transport. Syst. **12.2**,596–614 (2010)
22. Zhou, Y., et al.: Behaviour-aware knowledge-embedded model for driver attention prediction. IEEE Trans. Circ. Syst. Video Technol. (2025)

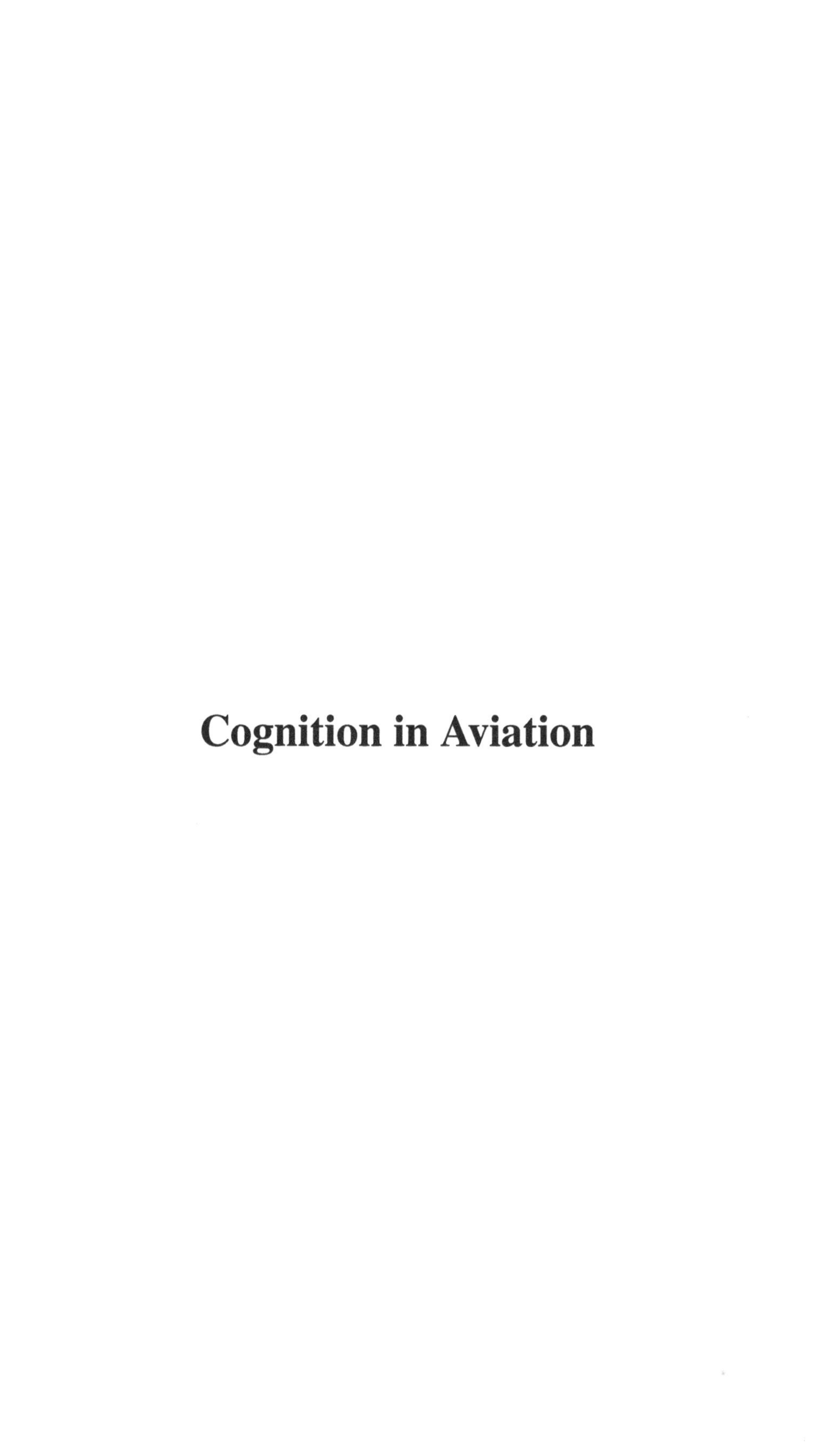

Cognition in Aviation

Human-Computer Interaction Work Load Assessment: Cockpit Use Case

Oriol Bracons Escarré(✉), Alfons Borràs Brell, Jordi Manzano Puigredon, and Miquel Ángel Piera Eroles

Department of Telecommunications and Systems Engineering, Autonomous University of Barcelona (UAB), Barcelona, Spain
oriol.bracons@uab.cat

Abstract. Modern flight decks increasingly rely on advanced automation and digital communication systems, which can introduce additional cognitive demands on pilots, particularly under abnormal and time-critical situations. Understanding how task interruptions, information modality, and timing affect pilot workload remains a key challenge for Human Machine Interface design. This paper explores a socio-technical methodological framework for assessing pilot workload by integrating Functional Resonance Analysis Method task modeling, eye-tracking metrics, and qualitative workload questionnaires.

The proposed approach is explored through a Formation Flight use case, focusing on the split maneuver under scheduled and abnormal conditions. FRAM models are used to represent task sequencing, concurrency, and interruptions, while synchronized eye-tracking data provide time-resolved physiological indicators of cognitive workload. Qualitative questionnaires complement the analysis by capturing pilot's perceived workload and situational awareness.

Results show that abnormal split scenarios introduce task interruptions and pending memory items that increase task execution times and cognitive demand, as captured by the FRAM models. Eye-tracking data reveal pupil size peaks aligned with critical interaction events, such as message reception and maneuver initiation, supporting the temporal validity of the modeled workload dynamics. While subjective assessments reflect increased workload at a global level, the combined methodology enables identification of when and why workload peaks appear.

Keywords: Eye-Tracking · Formation Flights · Workload · Human Performance

1 Introduction

The ongoing modernization of aviation has significantly changed pilot competency requirements, operational protocols, and aircraft instrumentation. Modern aircraft integrate advanced technologies, higher degrees of automation, and enhanced support systems to optimize operations. The pilot's role within the

W. -C. Li and A. Plioutsias (Eds.): HCII 2026, LNAI 16708, pp. 99–116, 2026.
https://doi.org/10.1007/978-3-032-29459-3_8

cockpit has evolved primarily into one of monitoring and supervising the proper functioning of the aircraft's systems and automated processes. At the same time, the growing connectivity between air and ground environments is progressively replacing traditional voice communication with a more digitalized flight deck supported by data-driven and automated forms of exchange. As a result, pilots are increasingly required to manage complex cognitive processes under time pressure, where monitoring, decision-making, and action execution must coexist.

Therefore, it is essential to examine how pilots allocate their cognitive resources within the cockpit and to identify which perceptual variables (visual and auditory) effectively enhance pilot situational awareness, since excessive or poorly timed information can degrade Human Performance (HP). In safety-critical systems such as a human flying an aircraft, pilot real-time decision-making coexists with psycho-motor skill actions, which can overload the pilot's cognitive capacity. New supporting services providing extra elaborated information to lessen the cognitive workload can have an adverse effect, as supporting services must capture human attention through visual or auditory channels while the pilot is attending ongoing tasks.

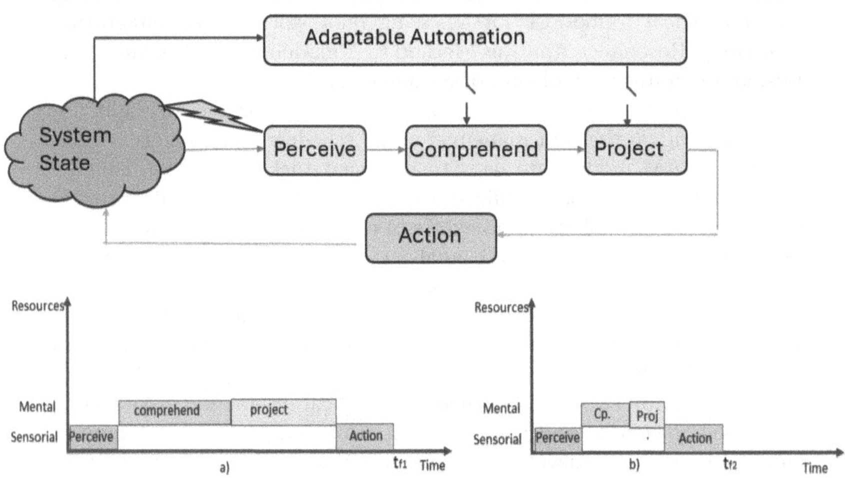

Fig. 1. Cognitive Tasks Description.

In the upper part of Fig. 1, the three-level model of Situational Awareness is represented [1], describing the cognitive tasks a human operator performs to take an action in the system. The perception of information from the system and the environment is performed through sensory cognitive channels. Most digitized systems provide the human operator with visual variables displayed on specific interfaces, coexisting with auditory information. Comprehension of the current situation and the projection of future states are mental activities that allow the human operator to decide whether an action is required when future system behavior does not adhere to target objectives.

Part (a) of Fig. 1 represents the temporal sequence of sensory perception, mental thinking (comprehension and projection), and action performed by a human operator without receiving any support. Part (b) represents the same sequence but with reduced mental processing times, achievable through adaptable automation.

Machine assistance can result in an un-opportunistic interruption when the human operator must postpone a critical task to analyze newly perceived information and prioritize the next task to attend. The interleaving of cognitive tasks each time a supporting service interrupts the human operator introduces small delays in concurrent tasks, increases mental workload, and negatively impacts HP.

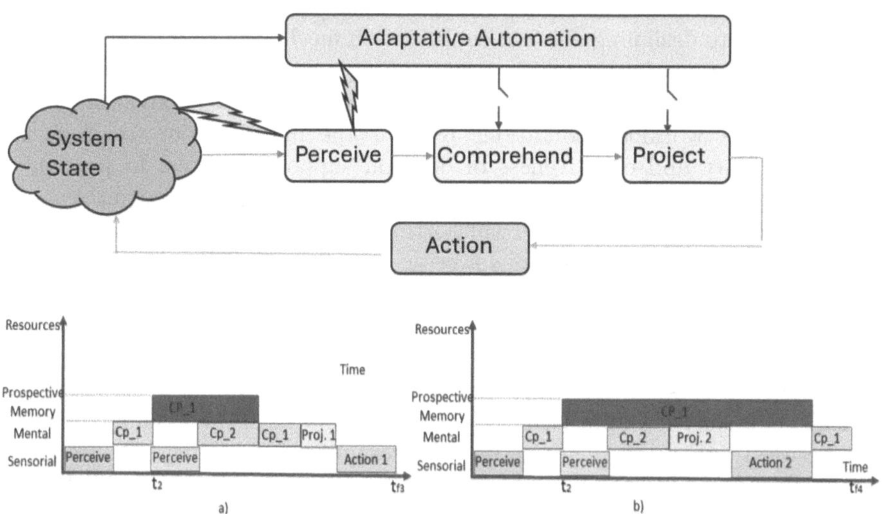

Fig. 2. Cognitive Tasks Description.

In the upper part of Fig. 2, two types of interrupting events are represented. A context-aware interruption arises from the system, such as a visual alarm or an auditory signal, while the other corresponds to elaborated information generated by a computer supporting service. Regardless of the information provided, both signals must capture the attention of the human operator through sensory channels, potentially while the operator is engaged in a demanding cognitive process such as decision-making.

The effects of a computer service capturing human attention during comprehension of monitored information at time t2 are illustrated in Fig. 1. The comprehension task (CP1) is postponed when the computer service captures the perception of the human operator, who then evaluates the interruption through a new comprehension task (CP2) and decides whether to resume the postponed task. In both scenarios, a prospective memory item is created, corresponding to a background "remember to remember" mental activity. An increase of up to 40% in mental task execution time has been reported when such a background activity is ongoing [2].

In operational applications of adaptable automation, the human operator must take decisions under time pressure while available data exceed the limits of human understanding. Adaptable automation support is usually provided on demand, requiring anticipatory trained behavior to predict when support will be needed. However, adaptive automation can cause undesirable reactive human behavior when supporting information appears as an interrupting event, potentially leading to a startling response [3] and even to a momentary "human out of the loop" condition.

Although several modeling formalisms have been reported in the scientific literature to describe human-computer assistance [4], they fall short in practice when it comes to designing efficient coordination mechanisms between computer supporting services and human decision-making processes in highly demanding operational contexts. Uncertainty regarding human cognitive behavioral dynamics under peak workload conditions remains the main barrier to predicting the acceptability and effectiveness of decision support systems. In particular, determining the appropriate time window and the appropriate cognitive channel (visual or auditory) to deliver supporting information to a human operator attending concurrent tasks remains a critical challenge for the design of future human-computer interfaces.

Therefore, a new modeling methodology is required to better describe interface mechanisms that enhance HP within a real-time human-machine teaming framework. Despite the availability of several socio-technical modeling formalisms, relatively few approaches support the analysis of the dynamic relationship between human cognitive status and computer supporting services under high workload conditions. To address this gap, this paper proposes an extension of the socio-technical FRAM modeling formalism combined with a simulation framework to analyze human workload and the impact of perceptual information channels in highly demanding operational contexts.

2 Related Work

The evaluation of workload, both in aeronautics and in multiple disciplines, has a wide field of study, as its applicability can be very useful in different aspects. In the aeronautical domain, the The Single European Sky ATM Research (SESAR) [5] Master Plan [6] highlights the importance of considering different Levels of Automation (LoA) to design new solutions that effectively improve different KPI's while reducing the workload of ATCos and pilots. In this context, concepts such as adaptable automation, where the operator decides how and when to use the automation, but also, adaptive automation, where the system dynamically adjusts the level of support, would benefit from the use of socio-technological models to ensure better balance between human-machine interaction, enhancing performance and reducing cognitive demand.

Different methodologies allow the evaluation of workload, both at a quantitative and qualitative level. At a qualitative level, there are various questionnaires to assess, the WL, situational awareness, trust in system or performance, among others.

Some studies use the NASA-TLX questionnaire [8,9] to evaluate workload in different tasks. Based on various questions with rating-scale responses, it is possible to estimate the level of WL perceived by the individual under study. Other studies compare different questionnaires by considering the differences in their design and focus [10]. On the other hand, the Solutions for Human Automation Partnerships in European ATM (SHAPE) project by Eurocontrol deals with multiple issues raised by the increasing automation in European Air Traffic Management (ATM). Presenting multiple questionnaires to assess not only workload, but also situational awareness, trust in the system, or teamwork among others, for Air Traffic Controllers (ATCo) have been reported in [11]. Although the results may be subjective to individual perception and biases, they are one of the most widespread methods for evaluating WL and show good results [12].

Modeling formalisms such as FRAM [13] provides an excellent baseline to define the interdependencies among cognitive actions and technological supporting tools. The FRAM formalism supports both a qualitative and a quantitative analysis of HP. Some studies have used FRAM to assess risk situations [14], or to describe pilot tasks in different situations [15].

At a quantitative level, different data gathering technologies, supports the evaluation of a subject's workload. Based on the collection of data from an electroencephalogram (EEG) and measuring variations in the signals, it is possible to establish the level of workload [16]. However, when applied to very demanding systems such as in a flight deck, the EEG data shows variable delays with respect to contextual inputs [17]. On the other hand, the use of eye tracking can, through data on the pupil, movement, or blinking, among others, allow the evaluation of WL at real time [18] [19]. Furthermore, unlike the EEG, the eye tracking data gathering also allows the study of scanning patterns and gaze direction, which is an asset in the design of procedures to react to unpredicted events, while it can be also used as a support tool for pilot training [20,21], or ATC monitoring [22].

3 Formation Flights

SESAR [5] is a European Union initiative aimed at modernizing and harmonizing Air Traffic Management (ATM). The Gain Environmental Efficiency by Saving Energy (GEESE) [23] project is one such example, focusing on analyzing the industrialization of Formation Flight (FF) procedures in the Atlantic airspace and assessing their feasibility within continental airspace from a comprehensive perspective. FF are divided into five phases:

- Rendez-vous: Aircraft proceed to their meeting point, within a request time of arrival to do the operation.

- Catch-up: Maneuver where the aircraft pair closes the longitudinal gap while still separated vertically.
- Join-up: Maneuver where the aircraft pair closes the lateral and vertical gap once leader-follower.
- Formation Keeping: This is the flight phase where both aircraft are correctly positioned and can start benefiting from fuel savings.
- Split: The split point marks the end of the formation segment, at which both aircraft split and proceed to their final destination.

All of these phases require the design of new supporting tools and specific procedures to ensure optimal operation. The use of simulations with Eye-Tracking and FRAM models has been employed to identify the critical points of the procedure and thus guide its design, taking into account the pilot's needs. While theoretical models provide insight into HP [24] under varying workloads, very demanding scenarios such as FF, in which task must be coordinated among different actors and must be performed under tight time-outs, requires new simulation frameworks

4 Methodology

This paper describes a methodological approach to evaluate Work Load of pilots through a Formation Flight use case that integrates quantitative eye-tracking data with qualitative questionnaires data to validate FRAM WL models.

4.1 Cockpit Subsystems Components

See Fig. 3.

- Side Stick (Side-st): This control device allows the pilot to issue pitch and roll commands to the flight control computers, while manual flight.
- Primary Flight Display and Navigation Display (PFD-ND): This subsystem presents essential flight and aircraft information to the pilot as heading, speed, altitude, flight plan progress or surrounding traffic.
- Electronic Flight Instrument System (EFIS): This subsystem allows the pilot to configure barometric settings, choose navigation display modes or select PFD-ND display modes.
- Flight Control Unit (FCU): This subsystem enables the pilot to select and adjust parameters to adjust guidance modes, vertical speed, heading, Speed, altitude and other related settings from autopilot.
- Electronic Centralized Aircraft Monitoring (ECAM): This subsystem consists of two displays. The upper display shows engine and fuel data, flap and slat positions, and system warnings, while lower display provides flight data along with system status and alert messages.
- Thrust (Thr): This subsystem allows the pilot flying to manage engine thrust settings, such as IDLE, CLIMB, and TOGA.
- Multipurpose Control and Display Unit (MCDU): This subsystem is used to create and manage the flight plan, aircraft systems, and CPDLC messages. CPDLC messages will appear on the upper screen.

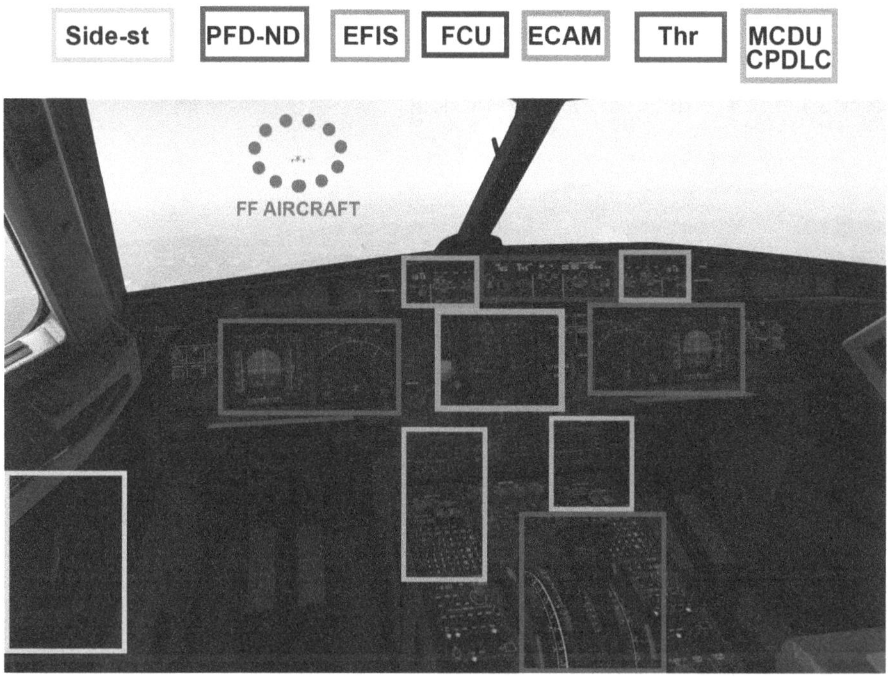

Fig. 3. Cockpit Subsystems Components Airbus A320.

4.2 Flight Simulator

The simulation is carried out using the X-Plane 12 flight simulator. The simulator has been enhanced with the capacity of Controller-pilot datalink communications (CPDLC) messages to authorize the start of the maneuvers. All flight data and pilot inputs in the aircraft has been collected, e.g., modification of flight level, speed increase in the autopilot.

4.3 Eye-Tracking

For the extraction of pupil data, Pupil Labs glasses [7] are used. These allow the generation and extraction of real-time data and video of multiple eye variables, such as blinking, pupil size, and fixations. To obtain data with the highest possible reliability, prior to the simulations, pupil data is recorded for a 5 min in a calm environment with relaxed music without any external inputs, to capture the baseline reference values of the subject before performing each flight simulation. External factors such as light or noise are controlled by isolating the subject in a room, ensuring the same amount of external light and no noise, thereby minimizing the potential impact of external factors on pupil data. All the simulations are preformed at the same day, sequentially, with the same subject.

4.4 FRAM

Each FF procedure requires a different FRAM to be developed, thus, allows the description of the different tasks to be done.

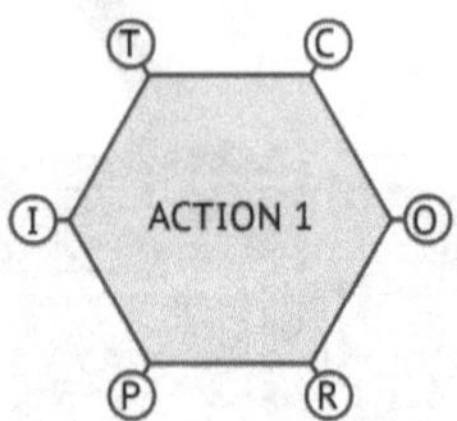

Fig. 4. FRAM Task.

Figure 4 shows an action as it can be represented in a FRAM model. A cognitive action performed by a human operator can be defined in FRAM using 6 interfaces with the operational context:

- Time (T): Available time to perform the action.
- Control (C): An action, requires supervision, regulation or motorization of the function.
- Output (O): Result produced by the action.
- Resource (R): Resource is needed to be consumed or used by the action.
- (P): State variables that must be satisfied before the action.
- Input (I): Is what activates the action, external, human or machine can trigger the action.

A FRAM model is made up of multiple actions, which constitute the entirety of the system or procedure described. The actions can occur sequentially or in parallel, as long as the necessary requirements are met. By using a FRAM model and the times recorded in the simulation, it is possible to observe when the actions overlap, postponed, delayed or missed due to time-out deadlines, and provide an estimation of the impact on the human cognitive WL.

4.5 Questionnaires

For this study, different questionnaires were used, depending on the use case requirements. The combination of these questionnaires enables cross-validation of the results, allowing for stronger conclusions.

4.6 Data Gathering

All data corresponding to the simulation and pilot's eye will be gathered during all simulation. Eye tracking device provides a dataset with all information. For action count and flight data, it will be saved via Xplane 12 data recorder.

5 Use Case

The simulated scenario used in this paper corresponds to the Split phase of a FF, from pilot flying of follower aircraft under three different situations:

1. Scenario 1 - Schedule Split: Pilot receives a CPDLC message instruction to perform lateral split maneuver in 4 min. After that time, pilot initiate split and report when finished. No abnormal situation is simulated in this scenario. As illustrated in Fig. 5, the flight crew initiates the sequence by an ATC communication related to anticipation of split operations. The Pilot Monitoring receives and reads the message, while confirmations are exchanged to ensure shared understanding. The crew then acknowledges the request through standard ROGER callouts. The sequence concludes once the message transmission is completed and closed.

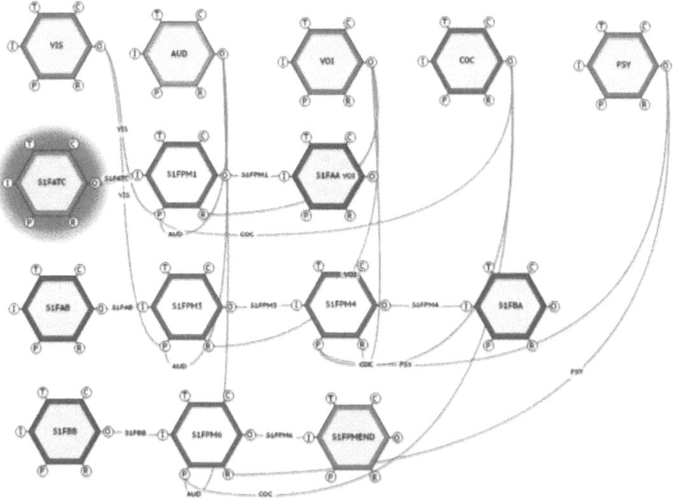

Fig. 5. FRAM Scenario 1 - Schedule Split.

2. Scenario 2 - Auditory: Pilot will receive an auditory message from Air Traffic Controller to perform an immediate lateral split maneuver due to an abnormal situation. Pilot report when finishing maneuver.
   According to Fig. 6, the crew is operating non-normal condition Split phase. The sequence starts with an auditory ATC message "Split" x3, followed by a formal non-normal callout. Heading actions and FMA cross-checks are performed to maintain trajectory awareness. The process ends with confirmation and radio communication to external agents.
3. Scenario 3 - Auditory + Visual: Pilot will receive a CPDLC message on the cockpit, this kind of messages triggers an auditory sound and visual light flash on a button inside the cockpit. CPDLC message requires the pilot to

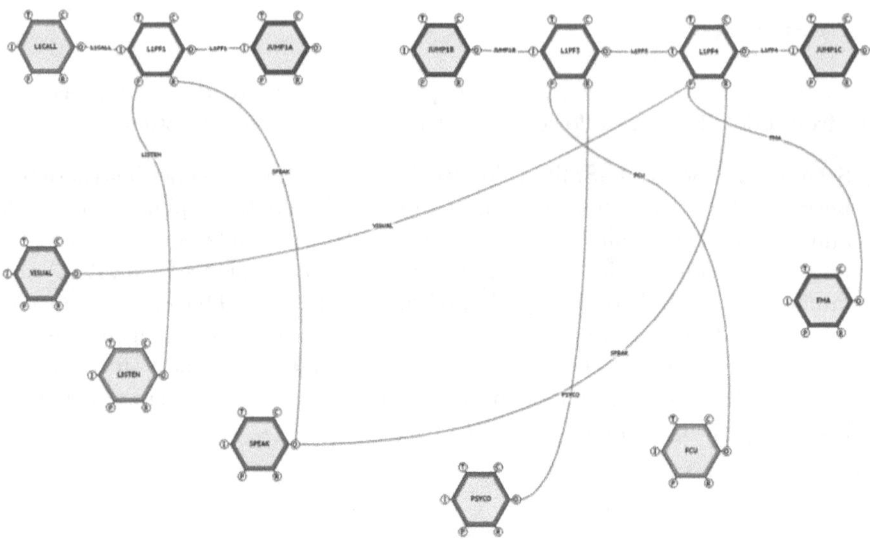

Fig. 6. FRAM Scenario 2 - Auditory.

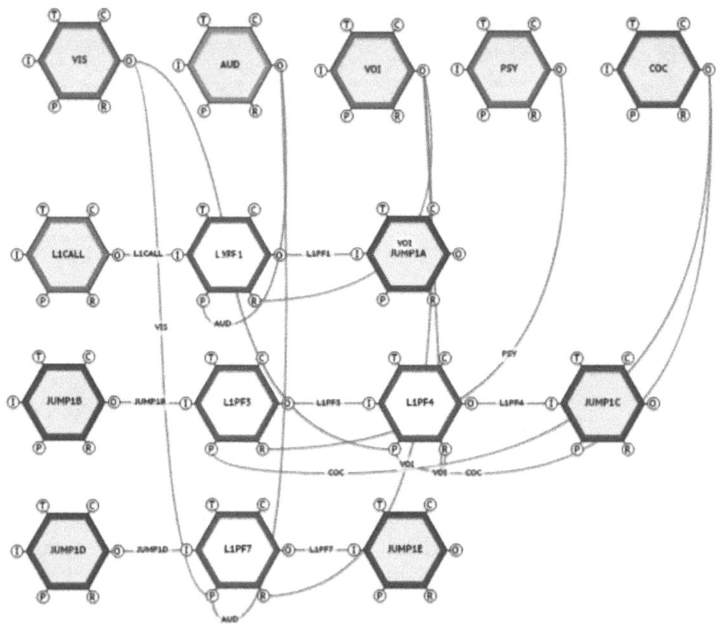

Fig. 7. FRAM Scenario 3 - Auditory + Visual.

perform an immediate lateral split maneuver due to an abnormal situation. However, pilot must read the message first and follow the standard procedure of a CPDLC message reception. Pilot report when finishing maneuver.

As shown in Fig. 7, the crew is operating non-normal condition Split phase. After receiving CPDLC split request message, Pilot performs callouts, and starts performing split. The confirmation and WILCO response ensure closed-loop CPDLC communication. The sequence is finalized once the emergency message exchange and split maneuver is completed.

Fig. 8. Pilot and Simulator with eye-tracking.

Figure 8 shows the simulation facilities. A laboratory was adapted for use in simulations, equipped with a flight simulation setup in which a synchronization mechanism has been implemented to allow Formation Flight vortex use. Data collection is carried out simultaneously on the computer, which records both flight data and pilot inputs, while the eye-tracking glasses capture ocular data, as illustrated in Fig. 8. The simulator is also adapted to receive CPDLC messages remotely from another computer, which are then displayed to the pilot on the MCDU.

The study involved two pilots with different experience levels to exercise the proposed socio-technical methodology under realistic and time-critical operational conditions. The study focuses on the validation of the methodological framework, assessing its ability to integrate FRAM-based task modeling with synchronized eye-tracking data and qualitative workload measures, rather than on the statistical characterization of pilot performance.

6 Results

6.1 FRAM

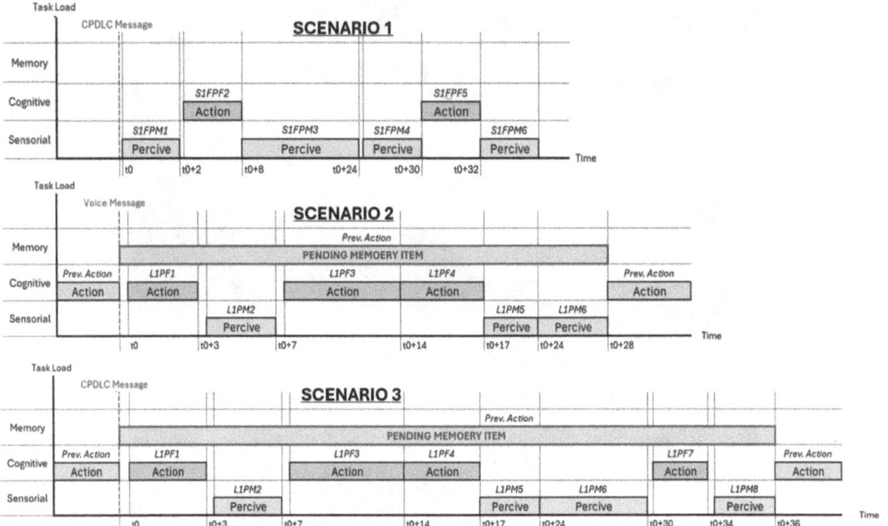

Fig. 9. FRAM Results

Figure 9 presents the results of the modeled FRAM tasks for each scenario, together with the real-time data collected during the simulation to perform the split tasks. Scenario 1 shows the task results for a scheduled split; since the tasks are planned in advance, they are executed within the corresponding time frame, and the pilot has no pending memory items.

In Scenarios 2 and 3, the pilot presents a memory item, when an abnormal message is received, the task that the pilot is currently performing becomes pending, as the split requires task prioritization. This pending memory item increases the execution time of each task required to carry out the split. Once the split is completed, the previous task can be resumed. It can be observed that Scenario 3, which is performed through CPDLC messages, requires a greater number of tasks and more time to be completed. Some actions take a few seconds to be initiated, as the pilot needs time to interpret the message and begin executing the corresponding procedural task.

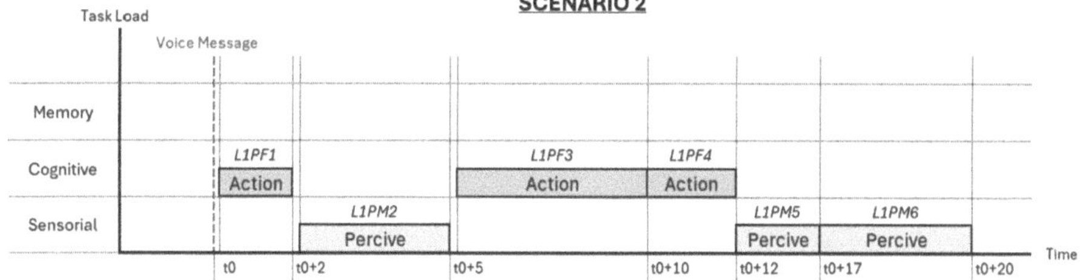

Fig. 10. FRAM Results Scenario 2 without Pending Memory Item.

Figure 10 shows the results for Scenario 2 when no pending memory item is present. It can be observed that the execution time of the actions is shorter, resulting in a more concise procedure while maintaining the same set of actions.

6.2 Eye Tracking Data

When comparing eye data with action count gathered from flight simulator, two different correlations are found. Pupil size Fixation count, an average of $R = 0.2$ is found for Pupil size and fixation count with an average of $R = 0.29$. Rather than serving as predictive indicators, these correlations are interpreted as complementary evidence supporting the temporal alignment between physiological responses and task-related events identified in the FRAM models. In particular, peaks in pupil size consistently coincide with task interruptions, message reception, and maneuver initiation, suggesting that eye-tracking metrics provide meaningful time-resolved insights into cognitive workload fluctuations that are not captured by global subjective assessments.

Figure 11 illustrates pupil size variations throughout the entire simulation. The red vertical line indicates the reception of a message. In Scenario 1, two markers are displayed: the first red line corresponds to the reception of the schedule split message, while the second marker indicates the initiation of the split maneuver. Pilot 1 exhibits greater sensitivity in pupil size responses, characterized by continuous fluctuations and clearly defined peaks associated with message reception and maneuver initiation across all three scenarios. In contrast, Pilot 2, who represents a more experienced pilot, shows lower variability in pupil size measurements. Nevertheless, when an abnormal message is received, a significant increase in pupil size is observed, with pronounced peaks in Scenarios 2 and 3. In Scenario 1, following the reception of the schedule message, pupil size decreases during the waiting period until the scheduled time elapses. Once the scheduled time is reached, pupil size increases again.

6.3 Questionnaires

Figure 12 show the average results of both pilots for the questionnaires. The higher the result, the higher the result the higher the workload perception

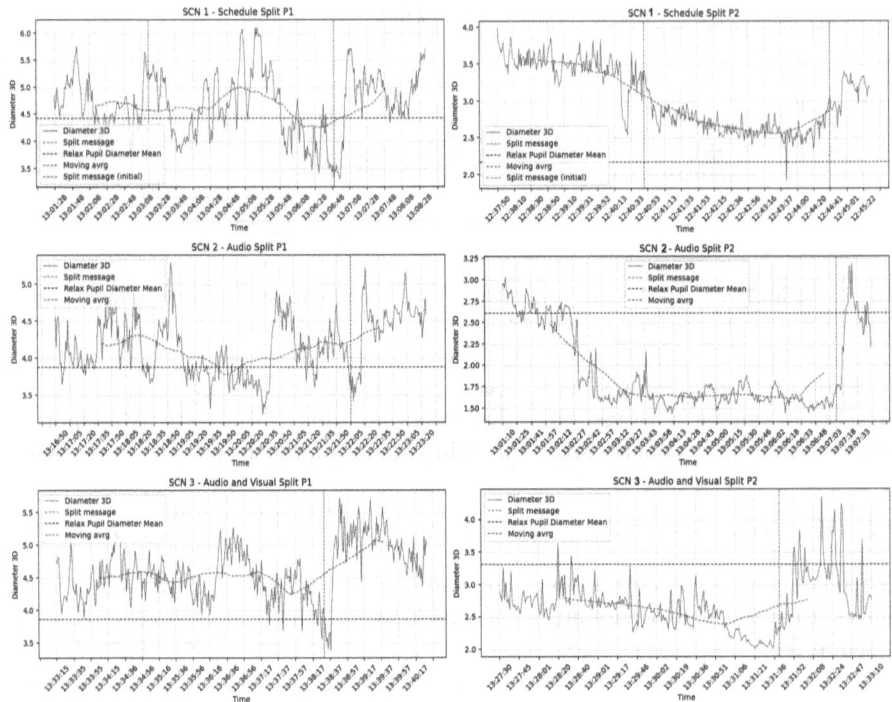

Fig. 11. Novice Pilot (P1) and Expert Pilot (P2) Pupil Size During Simulations.

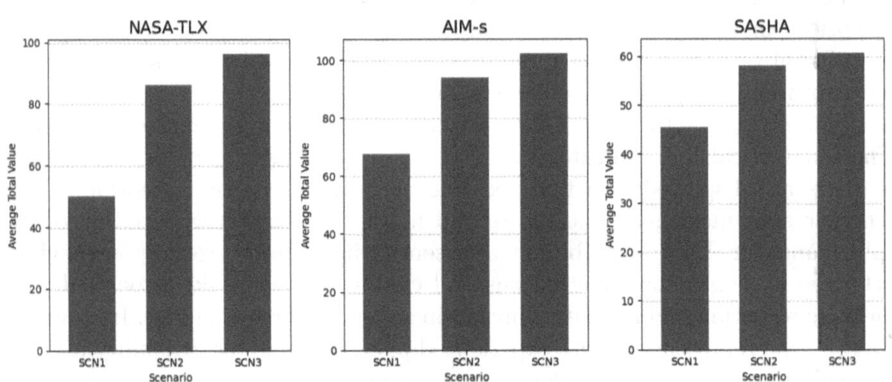

Fig. 12. Questionnaire results.

from the pilots, for NASA and AIM-s results. For SASHA questionnaire, higher results, show lower situational awareness perception. Results show that there is a negative impact on workload and situational awareness when unexpected situations as an abnormal situation simulated on this study.

7 Discussion

The results obtained from the combined use of FRAM modeling, eye-tracking metrics, and workload questionnaires highlight several relevant implications for the design of Human-Machine Interfaces in highly automated flight decks, particularly under abnormal operational conditions.

Quantitative workload assessments confirm that unexpected split instructions significantly increase cognitive demand and negatively affect situational awareness. However, these quantitative questionnaires provide only a global, retrospective perception of workload and do not reveal when workload peaks occur or which interaction events trigger them. From an HMI perspective, this limitation highlights the need for complementary design approaches capable of capturing temporal and contextual variations in human-machine interaction, particularly during time-critical events.

The FRAM-based analysis contributes to temporal understanding by explicitly modeling how task sequencing, concurrency, and interruptions affect pilot cognitive workload by using real time data. In the scheduled split scenario, tasks are anticipated and executed within their allocated time windows, resulting in a smooth procedural flow without pending memory items. In contrast, both abnormal scenarios introduce an interrupt-driven task reorganization, generating a pending memory item when the pilot must suspend an ongoing task to prioritize the split maneuver. This aligns with previous findings on prospective memory and cognitive overhead, where the need to "remember to remember" a postponed task leads to increased execution times and mental workload. The FRAM results show that this effect is particularly pronounced in Scenario 3, where CPDLC-based communication imposes additional procedural steps, such as message interpretation and acknowledgment, before action execution can begin. These findings support the argument that additional information or automation does not necessarily reduce workload if it is delivered through interruptive mechanisms that compete for the same cognitive resources.

Eye-tracking data complements the FRAM analysis by offering objective, time-resolved indicators of pilot cognitive state during interaction with the cockpit interface. Peaks in pupil size observed at message reception and maneuver initiation coincide with critical interaction points identified in the FRAM model. The higher variability observed in the novice pilot suggests increased sensitivity to cockpit interface and information presentation, whereas the expert pilot exhibits more stable responses, reflecting more calm interaction strategies. Nevertheless, both pilots show significant pupil size increase in abnormal scenarios, indicating that current interface designs may not sufficiently mitigate workload under time pressure, regardless of experience level.

When comparing auditory-only and combined auditory and visual interruptions, the results indicate that multimodal notifications do not automatically lead to better performance or reduced workload. In Scenario 3, the combination of an auditory alert with a visually demanding CPDLC message increases task duration and cognitive load, as evidenced by both FRAM execution times and pupil size responses. This supports the notion introduced in the literature that poorly timed information can degrade human performance, even when intended as decision support. From an HMI view, this finding emphasizes the importance of not only selecting appropriate perceptual channels but also aligning information delivery with the pilot's cognitive state and ongoing task demands.

The integration of FRAM modeling with eye-tracking and subjective workload assessments demonstrates the value of a multi-layered evaluation framework for human-machine teaming. While questionnaires capture perceived workload outcomes, FRAM reveals the structural causes of workload escalation, and eye-tracking provides quantitative evidence of when and how HP is affected. These results support the need for adaptive interface strategies that regulate not only the content but also the timing and modality of information delivery, particularly in highly dynamic and safety-critical operations such as Formation Flight.

8 Conclusions

This paper presents a multimodal socio-technical approach for evaluating pilot workload in abnormal Formation Flight scenarios. By combining FRAM modeling, eye-tracking data, and qualitative workload questionnaires, the study provides complementary qualitative and quantitative insights into how pilots interact with cockpit systems under abnormal conditions, using a Formation Flight use case.

Results show that unexpected and abnormal split instructions significantly increase pilot workload and reduce situational awareness compared to scheduled operations. While questionnaires capture this effect at a global level, FRAM modeling reveals the underlying cognitive mechanisms, particularly task interruptions, re-prioritization, and pending memory items that extend task execution times under time pressure. Eye-tracking results provide objective, time-resolved indicators of workload, with pupil size peaks consistently associated with critical interaction events identified in the FRAM models. Although expert pilots show more stable responses, both novice and expert pilots experience increased pupil size peaks during abnormal scenarios.

From an HMI perspective, the findings indicate that interruptions and multimodal information delivery, such as CPDLC messages combined with auditory alerts, may increase cognitive demand when introduced during time-critical tasks. This highlights the need for adaptive interface designs that consider the pilot's cognitive state, task context, and timing of information presentation.

References

1. Endsley, M.R.: Toward a theory of situation awareness in dynamic systems. Human Factors **37**(1) 32–64 (1995). https://doi.org/10.1518/001872095779049543
2. Piera, M.A., Munoz, J.L., Gil, D., Martin, G., Manzano, J.: A Socio- technical simulation model for the design of the future single pilot cockpit: an opportunity to improve pilot performance. IEEE Access **10**, 22330–22343 (2022). https://doi.org/10.1109/access.2022.3153490

3. Rivera, J., Talone, A.B., Boesser, C.T., Jentsch, F., Yeh, M.: Startle and surprise on the flight deck: Similarities, differences, and prevalence. In: Proceeding of the Human Factors and Ergonomics Society Annual Meeting (2014). https://doi.org/10.1177/1541931214581219
4. Inga, J., et al.: Human-machine symbiosis: A multivariate perspective for physically coupled human-machine systems. Int. J. Human-Comput. Stud. **170** (2023)
5. Bolić, T., Ravenhill, P.: SESAR: the past, present, and future of european air traffic management research. Engineering **7**(4), 448–451. Elsevier BV (2021). https://doi.org/10.1016/j.eng.2020.08.023
6. SESAR Joint Undertaking. European ATM Master Plan 2025 edition. Publications Office of the European Union (2024). https://www.sesarju.eu/sites/default/files/documents/reports/SESAR%20Master%20Plan%202025.pdf
7. Kassner, M., Patera, W., Bulling, A.: Pupil: An Open Source Platform for Pervasive Eye Tracking and Mobile Gaze-based Interaction. arXiv (2014). https://doi.org/10.48550/ARXIV.1405.0006
8. Hoonakker, P., et al.: Measuring workload of ICU nurses with a questionnaire survey: the NASA Task Load Index (TLX). IIE Trans. Healthc. Syst. Eng. **1**(2), 131–143 (2011). https://doi.org/10.1080/19488300.2011.609524
9. Zhang, Y., Zheng, H., Duan, Y., Meng, L., Zhang, L.: An integrated approach to subjective measuring commercial aviation pilot workload. In 2015 IEEE 10th Conference on Industrial Electronics and Applications (ICIEA), pp. 1093–1098. 2015 IEEE 10th Conference on Industrial Electronics and Applications (ICIEA). IEEE (2015). https://doi.org/10.1109/iciea.2015.7334270
10. Finomore, V.S., et al.: Measuring the workload of sustained attention: further evaluation of the multiple reources questionnaire. Proc. Human Factors Ergonomics Soc. Ann. Meet. **52**(18), 1209–1213 (2008). https://doi.org/10.1177/154193120805201812
11. Dehn, D.M.: Assessing the Impact of Automation on the Air Traffic Controller: The SHAPE Questionnaires. Air Traffic Control Q. **16**(2), 127–146 (2008). https://doi.org/10.2514/atcq.16.2.127
12. Said, S., et al.: Validation of the Raw National Aeronautics and Space Administration task load index (NASA-TLX) questionnaire to assess perceived workload in patient monitoring tasks: pooled analysis study using mixed models. J. Med. Internet Res. **22**(9), e19472 (2020). https://doi.org/10.2196/19472
13. Tian, W., Caponecchia, C.: Using the functional resonance analysis method (FRAM) in aviation safety: a systematic review. J. Adv. Transp. **2020**, 1–14 (2020). https://doi.org/10.1155/2020/8898903
14. de Carvalho, P.V.R.: The use of functional resonance analysis method (FRAM) in a mid-air collision to understand some characteristics of the air traffic management system resilience. Reliab. Eng. Syst. Safety **96**(11), 1482–1498 (2011). https://doi.org/10.1016/j.ress.2011.05.009
15. Piera, M. A., Munoz, J. L., Gil, D., Martin, G., Manzano, J.: A socio-technical simulation model for the design of the future single pilot cockpit: an opportunity to improve pilot performance. IEEE Access **10**, 22330–22343 (2022). https://doi.org/10.1109/access.2022.3153490
16. Rabbi, A.F., Zony, A., de Leon, P., Fazel-Rezai, R.: Mental workload and task engagement evaluation based on changes in electroencephalogram. Biomed. Eng. Lett. **2**(3), 139–146 (2012). https://doi.org/10.1007/s13534-012-0065-8
17. Hernández-Sabaté, A., Yauri, J., Folch, P., Piera, M.À., Gil, D.: Recognition of the Mental Workloads of Pilots in the Cockpit Using EEG Signals. Appl. Sci. **12**(5), 2298 (2022). https://doi.org/10.3390/app12052298

18. Tolvanen, O., Elomaa, A.-P., Itkonen, M., Vrzakova, H., Bednarik, R., Huotarinen, A.: Eye-tracking indicators of workload in surgery: a systematic review. J. Invest. Surg. **35**(6), 1340–1349 (2022). https://doi.org/10.1080/08941939.2021.2025282
19. Schulz, C.M., et al.: Eye tracking for assessment of workload: a pilot study in an anaesthesia simulator environment. Br. J. Anaesth. **106**(1), 44–50 (2011). https://doi.org/10.1093/bja/aeq307
20. Hämäläinen, R., et al.: Using eye tracking to support professional learning in vision-intensive professions: a case of aviation pilots. Edu. Inf. Technol. **29**(18), 24803–24833 (2024). https://doi.org/10.1007/s10639-024-12814-9
21. Knabl-Schmitz, P., Cameron, M., Wilson, K., Mulhall, M., Da Cruz, J., Robinson, A., Dahlstrom, N.: Eye-Tracking. Aviation Psychol. Appl. Human Factors **13**(1), 47–57 (2023). https://doi.org/10.1027/2192-0923/a000240
22. Wee, H.J., Lye, S.W., Pinheiro, J.-P.: Real Time Eye Tracking Interface for Visual Monitoring of Radar Controllers. In: AIAA Modeling and Simulation Technologies Conference. AIAA Modeling and Simulation Technologies Conference. American Institute of Aeronautics and Astronautics (2017). https://doi.org/10.2514/6.2017-1317
23. Gain Environmental Efficiency by Saving Energy (GEESE). Funded by European Union's HORIZON.2.5 - Climate, Energy and Mobility, Grant Agreement No 101114611. Duration 2023 - 2026 (2023). Retrieved from https://doi.org/10.3030/101114611
24. Bommer, S.C., Fendley, M.: A theoretical framework for evaluating mental workload resources in human systems design for manufacturing operations. Int. J. Ind. Ergonomics **63**, 7–17 (2018). https://doi.org/10.1016/j.ergon.2016.10.007

Which Direction Am I Banking? A Comparison of Moving-Horizon, Moving-Aircraft, and Realistic Attitude Indicators Using Performance and Eye-Tracking Measures

Mickaël Causse(✉) and Baptiste Capel

Fédération ENAC ISAE-SUPAERO ONERA, Université de Toulouse, Toulouse, France
Mickael.Causse@isae-supaero.fr

Abstract. Roll reversal errors occur when pilots unintentionally command a roll in the direction opposite to that intended, as a result of misinterpreting attitude information. Such errors have contributed to several aviation accidents, underscoring the need for intuitive attitude indicators that minimize cognitive load and confusion. This research compares two established formats, the moving-horizon (inside-out) and moving-aircraft (outside-in) attitude indicators, and evaluates the effect of a novel, more realistic aircraft symbol designed to enhance figure–ground segregation. A laboratory experiment was conducted with 17 participants, including pilots and non-pilots, using a 2 × 2 design manipulating attitude indicator format (moving-horizon vs moving-aircraft) and aircraft symbol (standard vs realistic). Participants performed a wing-leveling task at various bank angles while reaction times and roll reversal errors were recorded. Eye-tracking data were collected from a subset of participants to assess visual attention allocation. In addition, a preliminary flight-simulator experiment was conducted with two pilots to obtain subjective evaluations under realistic flight conditions. The results confirmed previous findings from the literature: the moving-aircraft format yielded faster reaction times (130 ms shorter) and fewer roll reversal errors (2.94% lower) than the moving-horizon format. Importantly, our realistic aircraft symbol significantly improved performance across both formats, with particularly strong benefits for the moving-horizon indicator. In this format, the realistic aircraft symbol produced faster reaction times (0.60 s vs. 0.72 s) and a lower percentage of roll reversal errors (1.71% vs. 5.39%) compared with the standard aircraft symbol. Eye-tracking analyses revealed more focused gaze patterns with the realistic aircraft symbol, suggesting more intuitive interpretation of banking information. Subjective evaluation in the flight simulator session confirmed that the moving-aircraft format used with the realistic aircraft symbol was the most preferred attitude indicator design. Overall, the findings confirm the superiority of the moving-aircraft format and indicate that enhancing aircraft symbol realism may represent a simple and effective means of improving attitude indicator readability.

Keywords: Attitude indicator · Roll reversal error · Moving-aircraft · Moving-horizon · Realistic aircraft symbol · Eye tracking

W. -C. Li and A. Plioutsias (Eds.): HCII 2026, LNAI 16708, pp. 117–129, 2026.
https://doi.org/10.1007/978-3-032-29459-3_9

1 Introduction

1.1 Current Attitude Indicator Design

Historically, maintaining control of an aircraft's trajectory and orientation has been a core responsibility of pilots. Although automation now performs these functions most of the time, pilots must still be able to regain manual control, sometimes in non-routine or emergency situations. These manual maneuvers can become particularly challenging during episodes of spatial disorientation, in which the pilot suffer from false sensations and perception of aircraft motions [1] and is unable to accurately perceive the aircraft's attitude relative to the ground. This insidious phenomenon accounts for 7.4% of general aviation fatal accidents, and 94% of such events are fatal [2]. In commercial aviation, spatial disorientation accounts for 16% of mishaps during initial climb and up to 21% during go-around maneuvers [3]. Spatial disorientation can arise from reliance on unreliable sensory cues (e.g., the somatogravic illusion), conflicts between these cues and the attitude display, or stress that impairs instrument interpretation. To mitigate this risk, attitude indicators must be intuitive, minimizing cognitive load and confusion, and preventing errors such as roll reversal during recovery maneuvers. Instruments that present aircraft attitude in a manner consistent with pilot expectations, and that require minimal mental transformation, can be critical for timely recovery in disorienting conditions. This underscores the importance of evaluating and optimizing attitude-indicator design to further enhance flight safety.

The current standard for presenting aircraft attitude information is the moving-horizon format (see Fig. 1), also known as the inside-out or Western format. This format is certified by aviation authorities (e.g., the FAA) and has been ubiquitous in Western civil and military aviation for decades. In this configuration, the aircraft symbol remains fixed at the center while the artificial horizon line tilts in the opposite direction of the aircraft's roll. This means that when the aircraft banks left, the horizon line on the instrument rotates to the right, and vice versa. This behavior replicates the view a pilot would have of the real horizon from the cockpit, following the principle of pictorial realism [4]. Indeed, the attitude indicator presents information in a manner analogous to viewing a pictorial representation of the world through a forward-facing port hole [5]. However, this format requires pilots to correctly interpret a moving background horizon that shifts in the opposite direction of both the pilot's control inputs and the aircraft's actual bank. This inversion demands additional training and cognitive effort, especially in abnormal or high-stress situations.

In contrast, in the moving-aircraft format (see Fig. 1), also referred to as the outside-in or Soviet format, the artificial horizon line remains fixed while the aircraft symbol moves to represent the aircraft's actual attitude. A real left bank is therefore depicted by the aircraft symbol banking to the left against a stationary, level horizon line. This format is based on the so-called principle of the moving part [5], stating that "the moving element on a display should correspond with the element that moves in the pilot's mental model, or mental representation of the aircraft", and should move in the same direction as that mental representation [6]. Pitch is typically displayed in a similar manner to the Western format.

Despite its intuitive nature, the moving-aircraft format has remained a minority solution outside Soviet-influenced aviation, likely due to institutional inertia in training practices and the retraining burden for pilots accustomed to the Western display. In addition, the widespread adoption of head-up displays, with their moving horizon superimposed on the external world, makes it now difficult to introduce a moving-aircraft format into the cockpit [7].

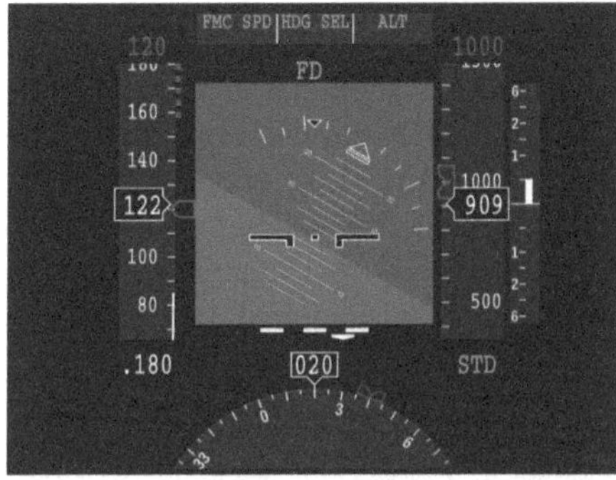

Moving-horizon (Western format) Moving-aircraft (Soviet format)

Fig. 1. Left: Illustration of a moving-horizon attitude indicator. In this example, the actual aircraft is banking to the left, while the horizon line moves in the opposite direction of the aircraft's bank. The aircraft is represented by a fixed aicraft symbol (also called the aircraft miniature). Right: Illustration of a moving-aircraft attitude indicator. In this example, the actual aircraft is also banking to the left, the artificial horizon line remains fixed, and the aircraft symbol moves in the same direction as the actual aircraft's bank.

1.2 The Western Format and Roll Reversal Errors

Despite its broad prevalence, the moving-horizon format has known weaknesses [8]. Studies and incident reports have shown that pilots may confuse the moving horizon line with the aircraft symbol and attempt to "level the horizon line" rather than the airplane, resulting in roll reversal errors that further worsen the bank. Such errors have been documented at rates of up to 7.2% in actual flight [9]. Historically, several studies have found the moving-aircraft format to be more intuitive for tasks such as trajectory tracking and unusual-attitude recovery, including shorter roll-input times [10] and less directional error [11] compared with the moving-horizon format. It should be noted that some studies, such as Müller et al. [8], found no performance differences between the two formats in specific situations, such as tracking tasks. However, in the same study the moving-aircraft format was still found to be superior for performing progressive attitude changes.

The moving-aircraft format provides a strong control–display compatibility [12, 13] with a straightforward relationship between the direction of the movement at the controls and the anticipated effect in terms of a change indicated in the display. With this format, a leftward control input causes a corresponding rotation of the moving element (the aircraft symbol) in the display. To correct a bank, the pilot simply "flies" the symbolic aircraft back to level with the horizon. There is no inversion between the visual cue and the required control input: if the aircraft symbol is tilted, the pilot instinctively levels it by tilting it back, which directly corresponds to the appropriate control action. With the moving-horizon format, this relationship is reversed.

Another possible effect that might contribute to the ambiguity of the moving-horizon format is the figure–ground reversal issue [14, 15]. Typically, when an element moves against a stationary environment, it is interpreted as the figure. In the case of the attitude indicator, however, the horizon line, though intended to mimic the outside view from the cockpit, does not display the usual properties of a background. It is neither placed visually far behind the aircraft symbol nor presented as a large, stable surface. Instead, it appears as a relatively small, mobile feature embedded within a large and essentially stable instrument panel. This configuration easily provokes a figure–ground reversal, with the horizon being seen as the moving figure and the panel as the background. Johnson and Roscoe [14] noted that both novice and experienced pilots may easily misinterpret the horizon as the moving part that is being manipulated by their control input, which then leads to exact reversed control responses compared to what is required, (see Fig. 2).

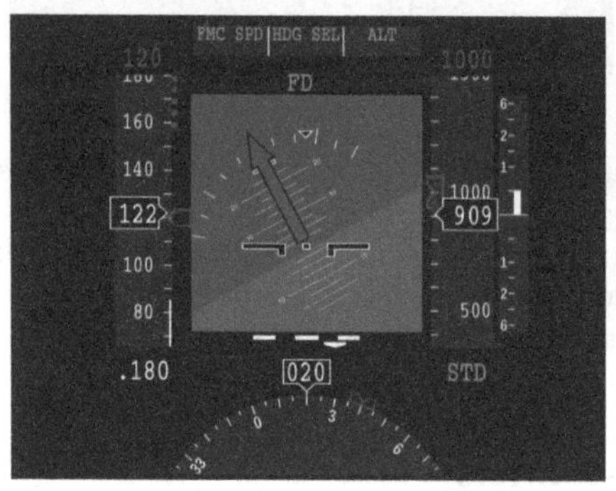

Moving-horizon (Western format)   Moving-aircraft (Soviet format)

Fig. 2. This illustration shows how a right turn on a moving-horizon indicator (left) can resemble a left turn displayed on a moving-aircraft indicator (right). A pilot may instinctively attempt to control the horizon line on the moving-horizon format, treating the background (horizon line) as the aircraft. Specifically, in this situation, the pilot may attempt to level the horizon by applying a rightward control input, which leads to a roll reversal error.

In order to limit such issues with the moving-horizon, previous studies have attempted to improve the attitude indicator appearance, such as that of Van Droogenbroeck et al. [16], which added subtle perspective ground lines intended to clarify attitude representation. Although pilots appreciated the added cues, the results were somehow mixed. Another promising avenue would be to refine the aircraft symbol within the attitude indicator to reduce the risk of confusion with the horizon line, which is the central objective of the present study.

1.3 Variant with Realistic Aircraft Symbol

We propose in this study to use a more realistic aircraft symbol in the attitude indicator to improve the understanding of the banking direction. In this variant, the classical aircraft symbol is replaced with a more detailed, realistic model of aircraft miniature. The rationale is to strengthen figure–ground segregation, lessening the confusion between the aircraft symbol and the horizon line, thereby improving the instrument's overall interpretability and reducing the risk to try to control the horizon line instead of the aircraft. However, increased realism comes with potential trade-offs. A larger or more detailed aircraft symbol could clutter the display by obscuring parts of the artificial horizon or pitch markings behind it, and it might distract the pilot's attention. There is a balance to be struck between visual richness and instrument readability.

1.4 Objective and Hypotheses

This study re-examines performance differences between moving-horizon and moving-aircraft attitude indicators in a static task in which participants were required to indicate as quickly as possible the correct direction to level the wings. Consistent with findings from numerous previous studies, we hypothesized that the moving-aircraft display would yield faster reaction times and greater accuracy. In addition, we evaluated a novel realistic aircraft symbol integrated into the attitude indicator, designed to be more intuitive than the standard aircraft symbol currently used in airliners, with the aim of improving figure–ground segregation and reducing the risk that pilots attempt to control the horizon rather than the aircraft. Eye tracking was employed to visualize fixation density across the four attitude indicator designs, with particular emphasis on assessing the effect of the proposed realistic aircraft symbol. Finally, a subjective evaluation of the possible advantages of this realistic aircraft symbol was conducted in flight simulator.

2 Method

2.1 Laboratory Experiment

Seventeen participants took part in the laboratory experiment. All had experience with flight simulators, and eight had flight experience as private pilots. All participants were familiar with the moving-horizon indicator, and none had prior experience with the moving-aircraft attitude indicator. We used a 2 × 2 experimental design to compare the moving-horizon and moving-aircraft formats, as well as the standard aircraft symbol versus our new "realistic" aircraft symbol (see Fig. 3). Participants were shown the four attitude indicators designs with different bank angles (15°, 30°, 45°, or 60°, each left or right, each stimulus repeated 3 times, for a total of 96 trials during the experiment) for 2.5 s, followed by a 1-s black screen, and were instructed to press a specific key as quickly as possible to level the wings in the correct direction. A training was performed with a few examples of each attitude indicator design before the actual experiment. The main performance measures were reaction times (from stimulus onset to the first keypress) and roll reversal errors (incorrect initial direction). Eye-tracking data were collected for eight participants, including five with flight experience. Heatmaps were generated to assess gaze dispersion across the four designs and to identify which features of the attitude indicators attracted the greatest number of fixations.

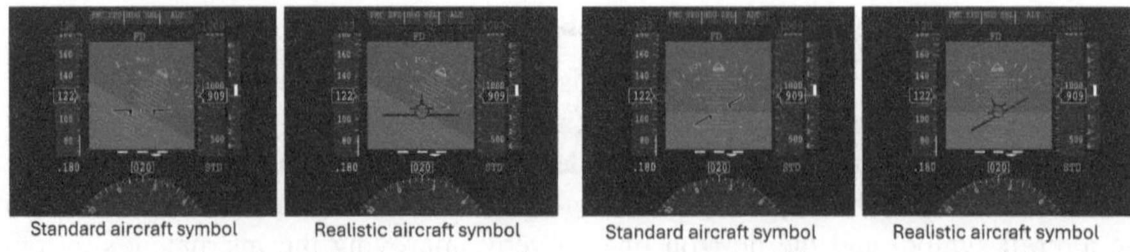

Fig. 3. The four attitude indicator designs that were tested during the laboratory and flight simulator experiments.

2.2 Flight Simulator Experiment

Two participants (a private pilot and a novice experienced only with flight simulator) took part in the second experiment that was conducted in an Airbus A300 flight simulator, see Fig. 4. The four attitude indicator designs have been implemented in the flight simulator.

Fig. 4. Illustration of the flight simulator experiment. The realistic aircraft symbol is visible in the primary flight display.

Each participant completed a series of maneuvers under zero-visibility conditions, including a 180° turn, stall recovery, steep turns, and a disorientation–recovery task. In the latter, participants were instructed to close their eyes, then reopen them and immediately return the aircraft to wings-level flight. The objective was to assess subjective preferences among the four attitude indicator designs using a satisfaction questionnaire based on five criteria, including ease of use, aesthetics, interpretation time, and confidence, see Fig. 5. Beyond preference assessment, the experiment also aimed to evaluate the attitude indicators in a realistic flight context with increased workload.

criteria	Western standard miniature	Western realistic miniature	Russian standard miniature	Russian realistic miniature
The easiest design to understand	□	□	□	□
The most aesthetic and visually pleasant	□	□	□	□
The least time-consuming to interpret (lowest mental workload)	□	□	□	□
The one that inspires me the most confidence in a critical situation	□	□	□	□
Overall, the one I prefer among these four designs	□	□	□	□

Fig. 5. The questionnaire used to evaluate the four attitude indicator designs. Participants were asked to select one or two preferred designs for each criterion.

3 Results

3.1 Laboratory Experiment

Reaction Times. The results confirmed that the moving-aircraft format produced significantly faster reaction times than the moving-horizon format (F(1,16) = 9.02, $p =$ .008, $\eta_p^2 = .36$). With the standard aircraft symbol, average reaction time was 0.59 s for the moving-aircraft compared with 0.72 s for the moving-horizon format, representing a 130 ms advantage, see Table 1 and Fig. 6.

Moreover, our new realistic aircraft symbol was associated with significantly faster reaction times than the standard aircraft symbol across both artificial horizon formats (F(1,16) = 13.41, $p = .002$, $\eta_p^2 = .45$), see Fig. 6. For example, with the moving-horizon format, the realistic aircraft symbol yielded an average reaction time of 0.60 s, whereas reaction time was 0.72 s with the standard aircraft symbol (LSD, $p = .014$), a difference of 120 ms, see Fig. 6 and Table 1. The difference between the two symbols was also significant with the moving-aircraft format (LSD, $p = .016$). The interaction term was not significant ($p = .423$).

Table 1. Average reactions times for the tested attitude indicator designs.

Attitude indicator design	Reaction times (s)
Moving-horizon format (both aircraft symbols averaged)	0.66 s
Moving-aircraft format (both aircraft symbols averaged)	0.55 s
Standard aircraft symbol (both attitude indicator formats averaged)	0.66 s
Realistic aircraft symbol (both attitude indicator formats averaged)	0.55 s
Moving-horizon format with standard aircraft symbol	0.72 s
Moving-horizon format with realistic aircraft symbol	0.60 s
Moving-aircraft format with standard aircraft symbol	0.59 s
Moving-aircraft format with realistic aircraft symbol	0.51 s

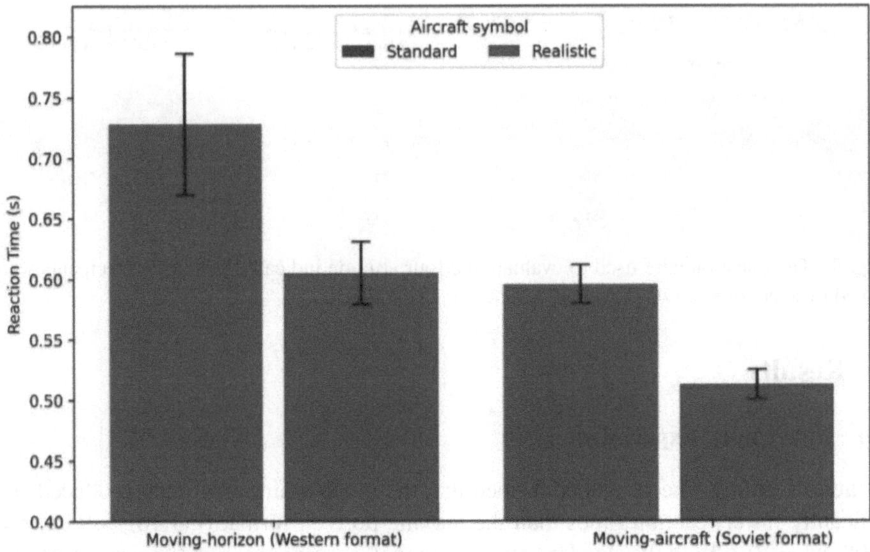

Fig. 6. Reaction times according to the attitude indicator format and aircraft symbol. Bars represent the standard error of the mean (SEM).

Roll Reversal Errors. The interaction between attitude indicator format and aircraft symbol type was significant ($F(1,16) = 4.68, p = .045, \eta_p^2 = .23$), with a lower number of roll reversal errors with the moving-aircraft (2.45%) vs moving-horizon (5.39%) when using the standard aircraft symbol (LSD, $p = .046$). Moreover, roll reversal errors were lower with the realistic (1.71%) vs standard (5.39%) aircraft symbol when using the moving-horizon attitude indicator (LSD, $p = .016$), see Fig. 7 and Table 2. Differences between the two attitude indicator formats were not significant when using the realistic aircraft symbol (LSD, $p = 0.38$). Main effects of attitude indicator format ($p = .39$) and aircraft symbol type ($p = .102$) were not significant.

Table 2. Roll reversal errors for the tested attitude indicator designs.

Attitude indicator design	Roll reversal errors (%)
Moving-horizon (both aircraft symbols)	3.55%
Moving-aircraft (both aircraft symbols)	2.69%
Standard aircraft symbol (both attitude indicator formats)	3.92%
Realistic aircraft symbol (both attitude indicator formats)	2.32%
Moving-horizon with standard aircraft symbol	5.39%
Moving-horizon with realistic aircraft symbol	1.71%
Moving-aircraft with standard aircraft symbol	2.45%
Moving-aircraft with realistic aircraft symbol	2.94%

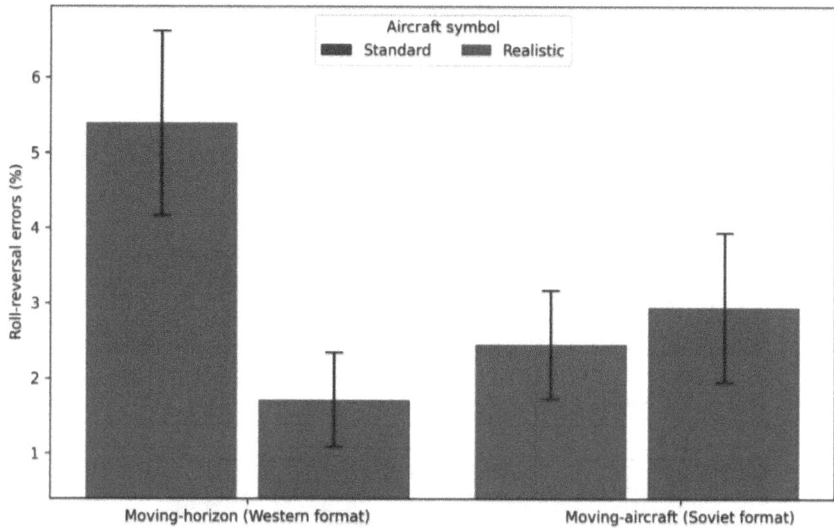

Fig. 7. Roll reversal errors according to the attitude indicator format and aircraft symbol. Bars represent the standard error of the mean (SEM).

Eye-Tracking Data. The eye-tracking heat maps revealed differences in visual behavior between the two aircraft symbols. For 75% of participants (6 out of 8), gaze dispersion was noticeably higher when using the standard aircraft symbol, with attention distributed between the aircraft symbol and the roll scale. This pattern suggests that participants searched for additional visual cues, such as the roll scale. In contrast, when using our realistic aircraft symbol, gaze was more focused on the center of the attitude indicator (i.e., on the aircraft symbol itself). This more concentrated visual attention likely contributed to the observed faster reaction times and lower error rates. Figure 8 shows an example from one participant.

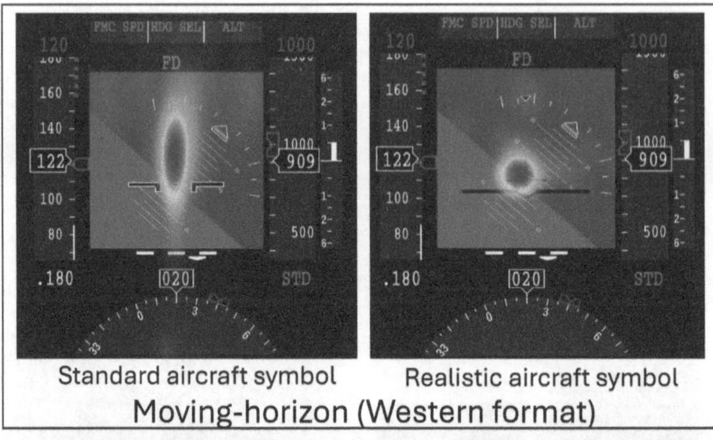

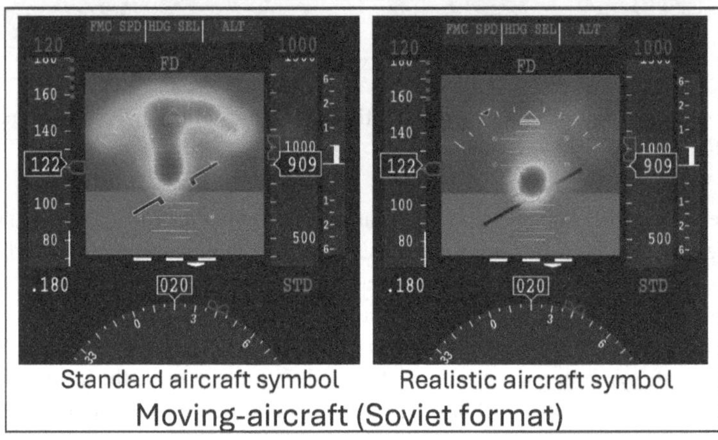

Fig. 8. Illustration of the gaze distribution for standard (left) and realistic (right) aircraft symbol in a moving-horizon (top) and moving-aircraft (bottom) formats during the laboratory task. With the standard aircraft symbol, gaze was more diffused, in particular toward the roll scale on the top.

Flight Simulator Experiment. After the simulator session, both participants selected the moving-aircraft format combined with the realistic aircraft symbol as their preferred format across all five questions.

4 Discussion

In this study, we re-examined the usability differences between the moving-horizon attitude indicator, traditionally used in Western countries, and the moving-aircraft attitude indicator, historically implemented in aircraft manufactured in the Soviet Union. We also proposed a different aircraft symbol within the attitude indicator, in order to enhance figure–ground segregation, a widely acknowledged weakness of the moving-horizon display. Specifically, we hypothesized that a more realistic aircraft symbol would reduce figure–ground confusion sometimes experienced by pilots, which may lead them to fly the horizon line by mistake [14]. In addition, we incorporated an eye-tracking analysis to compare visual fixations across the four tested attitude indicator designs. To our knowledge, only one prior study has compared moving-horizon and moving-aircraft attitude indicator with eye tracking [17].

Participants viewed static images of the four tested attitude indicators at various banking angles and were instructed to indicate the correct direction to level the wings as quickly as possible. Our results confirmed older and more recent studies showing that the moving-aircraft format produces significantly faster reaction times and fewer roll reversal errors than the moving-horizon [15, e.g., 18]. For instance, in our study, when used with the standard aircraft symbol (i.e., the type of symbol implemented in airliners), the moving-aircraft attitude indicator required 0.59 s to level the wings, compared with 0.72 s for the moving-horizon indicator, a difference of 130 ms. Roll reversal errors were also lower with the moving-aircraft (2.45%) vs moving-horizon (5.39%), still with the standard aircraft symbol.

Importantly, our realistic aircraft symbol simultaneously improved objective performance, perceptual effort, and subjective preferences with both attitude indicator formats. In the laboratory experiment, our new realistic aircraft symbol allowed reduced reaction times across both artificial horizon formats. This effect was significant with the moving-horizon format, where our realistic aircraft symbol yielded average reaction times of 0.60 s vs 0.72 s with the standard aircraft symbol, a difference of 120 ms. Overall, the greatest difference in reaction times was observed between the moving-aircraft format with the realistic aircraft symbol (0.51 s) and the moving-horizon format with the standard aircraft symbol (0.72 s).

Eye-tracking data revealed that, with the realistic aircraft symbol, visual attention was directed toward the symbol itself for most of the participants. This focused allocation of gaze on the aircraft symbol may reflect a more intuitive understanding of the banking direction and may have contributed to the observed lower reaction times and roll reversal errors (i.e., vs the standard symbol). On the contrary, for the majority of the participants, when using the standard aircraft symbol, participants often needed to use additional visual cues, such as the roll scale, on the upper part of the attitude indicator. This kind of focused attention on the upper part of the screen has also been found by Arinicheva et al. [17] in some of their participants. This result might reflect sub-optimal visual strategies and deserve to be further explored in a future study. Finally, the questionnaire filled by two pilots after the flight simulator experiment revealed that their favorite attitude indicator design was the moving-aircraft with the realistic aircraft symbol. This latter result provides additional support for the efficiency of this design under ecologically valid conditions.

5 Conclusion

We confirmed in a static wing-leveling task that the moving-aircraft format (also referred to as outside-in) enables faster response times and greater accuracy than the moving-horizon format, in line with previous research. We also found that our realistic aircraft symbol improved response time and accuracy, especially with the classical moving-horizon. The combination of the moving-aircraft format and the realistic aircraft symbol was the participants' preferred choice during the flight simulator session. While a full transition to a totally new attitude indicator design may be challenging, due to international standards, the possible danger of switching format and habits, [7], and the compatibility between head-up displays and moving-horizon, coming back to moving-aircraft format would be very difficult. However, integrating a more realistic aircraft symbol may provide a simple and immediately beneficial improvement for operational safety by reducing potential confusion between the horizon line and the aircraft symbol during banking maneuvers, particularly in degraded conditions such as spatial disorientation or following a startle reflex [19, 20]. Further studies with larger samples and more varied operational conditions will help to validate these promising findings.

Acknowledgments. The authors would like to thank Patrice Labedan and Guillaume Garrouse for their valuable technical support in the implementation and setup of the experimental environment within the PEGASE simulator.

References

1. Benson, A.J., Stott J.: Spatial disorientation in flight. Ernsting's aviation medicine, pp. 433–458 (2006)
2. Baumgartner, H.M., Sigmon, J., Ciesielski, A., Lewis, R.J.: Spatial Disorientation in Fatal General Aviation Accidents (2003–2021). United States. Department of Transportation. Federal Aviation Administration (2025)
3. Newman, R.L., Rupert, A.H.: The magnitude of the spatial disorientation problem in transport airplanes. Aerospace Med. Hum. Perform. **91**, 65–70 (2020)
4. Geiselman, E.E., Osgood, R.K., Biers, D.W.: A comparison of three aircraft attitude display symbology structures (1993)
5. Roscoe, S.N.: Airborne displays for flight and navigation. Hum. Factors **10**, 321–332 (1968)
6. Wickens, C.: Aviation displays. In: Tsang, P., Vidulich, M. (eds.) Principles and practice of aviation psychology. Erlbaum, Mahwah, NJ (2002)
7. Pongratz, H., Vaic, H., Reinecke, M., Ercoline, W., Cohen, D.: Outside-in vs. inside-out: flight problems caused by different flight attitude indicators. SAFE J. **29**, 7–11 (1999)
8. Müller, S., Korff, C., Manzey, D.: Moving-horizon versus moving-aircraft: effectiveness of competing attitude indicator formats on recoveries from discrete and continuous attitude changes. J. Exp. Psychol. Appl. **27**, 102 (2021)
9. Hasbrook, A.H., Rasmussen, P.G.: In-flight performance of civilian pilots using moving-aircraft and moving-horizon attitude indicators (1973)
10. Self, B.P., Breun, M., Feldt, B., Perry, C., Ercoline, W.R.: Assessment of pilot performance using a moving horizon (inside-out), a moving aircraft (outside-in), and an arc-segmented attitude reference display (2003)
11. Janczyk, M., Yamaguchi, M., Proctor, R.W., Pfister, R.: Response-effect compatibility with complex actions: the case of wheel rotations. Atten. Percept. Psychophys. **77**, 930–940 (2015)
12. Janczyk, M., Pfister, R., Crognale, M.A., Kunde, W.: Effective rotations: action effects determine the interplay of mental and manual rotations. J. Exp. Psychol. Gen. **141**, 489 (2012)
13. Singer, G., Dekker, S.: The effect of the roll index (sky pointer) on roll reversal errors. Hum. Factors Aerospace Safety **2**, 33–43 (2002)
14. Johnson, S.L., Roscoe, S.N.: What moves, the airplane or the world? Hum. Factors **14**, 107–129 (1972)

15. Müller, S., Sadovitch, V., Manzey, D.: Attitude indicator design in primary flight display: revisiting an old issue with current technology. Int. J. Aerospace Psychol. **28**, 46–61 (2018)
16. Van Droogenbroeck, C., Landman, A., Stroosma, O., Van Paassen, M.R., Mulder, M.: Improving bank angle representation of the attitude indicator using monocular visual depth cues. Transport. Res. Procedia **88**, 97–103 (2025)
17. Arinicheva, O., Lebedeva, N., Malishevskii, A., Arefyev, R.: Attitude indicators in bank angle determination: a study of errors. In: Gorbachev, O.A., Gao, X., Li, B. (eds.) Proceedings of 10th International Conference on Recent Advances in Civil Aviation, pp. 281–289. Springer Nature Singapore, Singapore (2023)
18. Browne, R.: Figure and ground in a two dimensional display. J. Appl. Psychol. **38**, 462 (1954)
19. Causse, M., et al.: Cognitive incapacitation in aviation: a narrative review. Theoretical Issues in Ergonomics Science, pp. 1–19 (2025)
20. Deniel, J., Dupuy, M., Duchevet, A., Matton, N., Imbert, J.-P., Causse, M.: An in-depth examination of mental incapacitation and startle reflex: a flight simulator study. In: Harris, D., Li, WC. (eds.) Engineering Psychology and Cognitive Ergonomics. HCII 2023. LNCS, vol. 14018. Springer, Cham (2023). https://doi.org/10.1007/978-3-031-35389-5_4

Near-Infrared Functional Characteristics of Flight Trainees and Instructors in Night Training Scenarios

Nongtian Chen(✉), Linlin Li, Hao Yuan, and Ting Ma

Civil Aviation Flight, University of China, Chengdu 641400, Sichuan, China
chennongtian@hotmail.com

Abstract. The complex environment of night flights poses unique challenges to flight training safety. During night flight training, pilots must not only master general flight techniques but also overcome the intricate factors associated with nighttime navigation. These distinctive challenges test not only pilots' technical skills but also place high demands on their psychological and physiological states. This study analyzes and empirically investigates the cognitive behavioral differences between flight trainees and instructors during night flight training. Using functional near-infrared spectroscopy, it explores the modulating effects of night flight environments and flight experience on pilots' cognitive neural activity, revealing dynamic patterns of activation in the prefrontal and parietal lobes during night flight training scenarios, as well as behavioral strategy differences among individuals with varying levels of flight experience. The analysis of operational behaviors in night flight training between trainees and instructors found that instructors exhibited significantly superior brain activation patterns in cognitive neural processes related to night flight compared to trainees, particularly in the frontal lobe regions. Instructors demonstrated greater adaptability in cognitive neural performance to task difficulty changes, showing more flexible resource allocation capabilities. Flight experience also influences the coordinated processing across the entire frontal lobe and the frontoparietal network. The findings provide references for enhancing pilots' night flight adaptability and improving night flight safety management systems.

Keywords: Near-infrared functional · night training scenarios · flight trainees · instructors · flight safety

1 Introduction

Nighttime aircraft operations, as a crucial component ensuring the efficient operation of aviation networks, have garnered close attention from airlines and research institutions. While nighttime operations play an irreplaceable role in enhancing flight operational efficiency and meeting passenger demands, they also pose additional challenges to flight safety. Compared to daytime flights, nighttime operations are characterized by low visibility, increased visual illusions for pilots, and potential physiological reactions such as

W. -C. Li and A. Plioutsias (Eds.): HCII 2026, LNAI 16708, pp. 130–147, 2026.
https://doi.org/10.1007/978-3-032-29459-3_10

fatigue and drowsiness, all of which may elevate the risk of unsafe events during flight. The complex environment of nighttime operations presents unique challenges to novice pilots. During nighttime flight training, pilots must not only master general aviation skills but also overcome the difficulties posed by nighttime operations. These unique challenges not only test pilots' technical abilities but also impose high demands on their psychological and physiological states. Approach and landing, as a complex and dangerous aspect of flight missions, are influenced by factors such as pilot quality, aircraft status, weather conditions, and lighting. During this process, pilots must maintain high vigilance while executing precise maneuvers on the aircraft, significantly increasing their cognitive load and work pressure. Consequently, the probability of flight accidents caused by human error factors rises sharply.

In terms of scholarly research, Wang Lei et al. [1] explored the applicability of fNIRS technology in measuring mental workload in pilots by designing and implementing simulated flight missions under low visibility conditions. They found that after the emergence of low visibility conditions, the concentration of oxyhemoglobin increased and the concentration of deoxyhemoglobin decreased, while heart rate and heart rate variability indicators did not show corresponding changes, indicating that fNIRS technology exhibits sensitivity in reflecting mental workload. Gao Lina and Wang Changyuan [2] employed a visual perception state detection method based on an implicit semi-Markov model to explore the patterns of visual fixation changes in flight cadets under different flight tasks, and uncovered the scanning strategies of fixation rules under different situations. The proposed model can detect the visual perception state of flight cadets in real time, achieving an accuracy rate of 93.55%, which is 13.55% higher than that of the hidden Markov model. Liu Yu et al. [3] systematically reviewed relevant research on the application of fNIRS technology in aviation psychology, and proposed directional suggestions for applying fNIRS technology to pilot selection and training, as well as crew resource management, in order to promote the application of fNIRS in aviation psychology research. Yu Guoming et al. [4] studied human-machine collaborative decision-making methods and intervention training strategies based on cognitive scenarios under emergency conditions for pilots, and proposed a more dynamic, targeted, and adaptable human-machine collaborative decision-making scheme for complex nonlinear emergency scenarios. Duan Ya et al. [5] addressed the risk of pilot fatigue in air combat missions by constructing an equivalent experimental task scenario to induce fatigue, collecting real-time electrocardiogram (ECG) and blood oxygen data from pilots, and using support vector machines to construct a comprehensive fatigue state identification model, providing technical support for real-time monitoring of pilot fatigue status. Regarding the detection of key points in pilots under complex lighting conditions, Sun Ruishan et al. [6] recorded the visual fixation data of subjects in a flight simulator environment and applied Markov chain mathematical methods to analyze the transition probabilities of attention states within various visual regions. Li et al. [7] used multimodal physiological monitoring technology (ECG, electromyography, skin conductance, etc.) to analyze the impact of pilot behavior on physiological indicators and proposed new ideas for optimizing human-machine interaction systems. Kawaguchi et al. [8] measured the activity of the dorsolateral prefrontal cortex (DLPFC) in pilots using fNIRS technology and found that long-term training affects brain activity patterns, providing a noninvasive method for evaluating the abilities of aging pilots. Yuan et al. [9] combined fNIRS and machine learning to discover that pilots' turning behavior is correlated with the activity in Brodmann areas 17, 18, and 46, providing a physiological basis for improved training. Causse et al. [10] recorded pilots' brain activity under stress using fNIRS and found that cognitive load and stress activate the executive control network, necessitating optimization of human-machine function allocation. Zhang et al. [11] analyzed pilots' brain activity during equipment malfunctions through large-sample experiments and found a high correlation between cognitive load and activity in specific brain regions, providing a reference for emergency training.

Overall, research on night flight training is increasingly focusing on monitoring and evaluating pilots' cognitive psychological states, actively exploring the application of advanced technological means in night flight training, and covering various aspects such as pilot selection and training, human-machine coordination, and risk-taking behaviors, striving to comprehensively enhance pilots' night flight adaptability and flight safety levels. This study employs multimodal neuroimaging technology to deeply explore the brain cognitive mechanisms of night flying, promoting the transformation process of night flight training from experiential to scientific, and from standardized to personalized.

2 Method

2.1 Experimental Principles

The principle of control in experiments: There may be multiple unrelated variables that can affect the experiment, so it is necessary to eliminate all irrelevant variables according to the experiment. The purpose of setting up a control group is to highlight the effect of the treatment being tested. Therefore, except for the parts to be compared, the other non-treatment parts that need to be referenced should be consistent across all groups.

The principle of repeatability in experiments: Various experiments require a large amount of experimental data to make the results obtained from the experiments convincing. The principle of repeatability in experiments refers to conducting multiple experiments under the same experimental conditions, repeatedly obtaining multiple sets of data, and thereby improving the universality and authenticity of experimental conclusions. To achieve the principle of repeatability, it should be ensured that the experimental conclusions can be reflected in the data results, and the same experiment can be repeated by different subjects. Even for a single subject, sufficient data should be obtained before corresponding processing is carried out.

The principle of single variable in experiment: For different variables in the experiment, it is necessary to ensure that the experimental variables and results are one-to-one corresponding. This approach can simplify the processing of experimental results, while also making the experimental results more accurate and the experimental scheme more reliable.

2.2 Participants

The experiment recruited 23 healthy pilot volunteers, aged between 22 and 26. All participants reported no history of using psychotropic drugs and no visual, auditory, language, or cognitive impairments before the experiment. Among them, there were 18 flight cadets and 5 flight instructors. Due to experimental requirements, 2 left-handed subjects were excluded to eliminate the potential influence of handedness differences on the experimental results. The actual available participants included 16 cadets and 5 instructors.

The participants were divided into two groups: the flight instructor group and the flight student group. The flight instructor group comprised 5 senior pilots engaged in night flight instruction, with an average flight time exceeding 1500 h. The flight student group included 16 enrolled flight students, with an average flight time of approximately 200 h. The two groups were matched in demographic variables such as age and gender to control for the influence of irrelevant variables.

All experimental procedures adhered to the Declaration of Helsinki and were approved by the relevant ethics committee. Each participant signed an informed consent form prior to the experiment.

2.3 Materials

The experiment utilizes the Brite23 near-infrared spectrometer, manufactured by Artinis, to collect data on changes in blood oxygen levels in the prefrontal brain region. This device is equipped with 23 measurement channels, each consisting of a pair of transmitting and receiving probes, with a source-probe spacing of 3 cm. The transmitting probes emit near-infrared light at two wavelengths (760 nm and 850 nm), while the receiving probes record the attenuation of these photons after passing through the head tissue.

Before the experiment, the subjects wore specially designed hats, with 23 optodes (photoelectric sensors) distributed on the forehead area according to the International 10–20 System for positioning, as shown in Fig. 1. During the experiment, continuous data on changes in light density were collected at a frequency of 50 Hz.

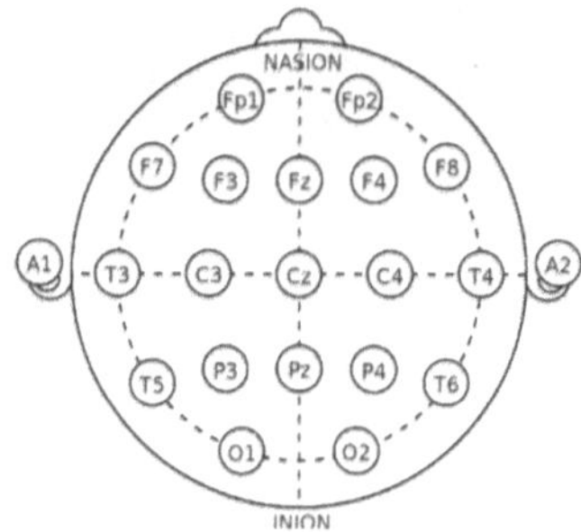

Fig. 1. System positioning of EEG and fNIRS electrode locations

The specific channels correspond to the prefrontal lobe region. According to the standards of the 10–20 system, the channel distribution of the Brite23 near-infrared spectrometer is as follows:

Anterior lateral cortex: Channels 1, 2, 3, 4, 5, 6, 7 in the left prefrontal lobe (near F3); Channels 17, 18, 19, 20, 21 in the right prefrontal lobe (near F4).

Medial prefrontal cortex: central prefrontal (near Fz) channels 8, 9, 10.

The experimental image of the near-infrared spectrometer is shown in Fig. 2.

Fig. 2. Experimental diagram of Artinis' Brite23 near-infrared spectrometer

2.4 Experimental Design and Procedure

The experiment was conducted in a flight simulator, utilizing the SR20–05 flight simulation training device manufactured by ALSIM. This device holds a certificate of conformity for flight simulation training equipment issued by the Flight Standards Department of the Civil Aviation Administration of China. The simulated aircraft experimental environment is depicted in Fig. 3.

Fig. 3. Simulated aircraft experimental environment

The subjects completed flight missions of three difficulty levels, respectively:

Task 1: Visibility is normal, with no crosswind influence.

Task 2: 15-knot crosswind in the 020 direction, with level 1 turbulence.

Task 3: 15-knot crosswind from direction 020, level 1 turbulence, glide slope failure.

Each task lasted for 2 min, requiring the subjects to complete the landing maneuver as smoothly and accurately as possible. The tasks were conducted under both daytime and nighttime lighting conditions. Each subject completed a total of 6 experiments, calculated as 2 (daytime/nighttime) $\times$ 3 (task difficulty). The presentation order of tasks and lighting conditions was balanced among the subjects.

During the flight mission, the near-infrared brain functional imaging system continuously records the concentration changes of HbO2 (oxyhemoglobin) and HbR in the prefrontal cortex. Simultaneously, flight operation data such as joystick and pedal inputs, as well as the subject's gaze data, are collected for behavioral analysis.

3 Results

3.1 Data Preprocessing and Analysis

The fNIRS data from the experiment underwent data preprocessing before analysis, which mainly involved the following steps:

1. Baseline correction method

Since fNIRS measures the relative change in blood oxygen concentration, a reference baseline needs to be selected to correct the raw signal. There are several common practices:

① Baseline correction for task blocks: The average value of a certain period (e.g., 1 min) before the start of each task block (such as takeoff, landing, etc.) is taken as the baseline. The data at all time points within that task block are then subtracted from this baseline value. This method assumes that the task blocks are independent of each other and is suitable for discrete experimental designs.
② Whole-segment baseline correction: Using the average value from a period before the start of the entire experimental process (such as a resting state) as the baseline, subtract this baseline value from the data at all time points. This method assumes that the entire experimental process is continuous and is suitable for continuous task designs.
③ Sliding baseline correction: The average value of a certain time window (such as 10 s) before each time point is taken as the baseline, and the data at that time point is subtracted from this baseline value. This method can dynamically track the slow drift of the signal and is suitable for long-duration complex tasks.

In this experiment, considering the continuity and complexity of the flight mission, an improved baseline correction method based on task blocks was adopted. Specifically, the average value of the first minute before the start of each flight block (cruise, descent, landing) was taken as the baseline for that block, and the data of all sampling points within the block were subtracted from this baseline value. This approach not only considers the differences between flight phases but also preserves the continuity within the block. At the same time, the 1-min baseline time window can better balance signal stability and sensitivity. The corrected signal reflects the dynamic changes in blood oxygen concentration relative to the quiet state before the start of the block, which can better reflect the immediate effect of cognitive load.

2. Divide the baseline time period into periods

Period refers to the division of continuous fNIRS signals into several time segments of interest based on research objectives, with each time segment representing a relatively stable cognitive processing state. The length of a period can be flexibly set according to task characteristics and research questions, generally ranging from seconds to minutes. Reasonable period division can improve the temporal resolution and specificity of fNIRS signal analysis.

In this experiment, a two-level period division strategy was adopted:

The first level is a rough division based on flight blocks. Each flight mission is divided into five blocks: takeoff, climb, cruise, descent, and landing, with each block lasting 3 to 5 min. This division primarily takes into account the operational process and cognitive stages of the flight mission.

The second level involves a fine-grained division based on key events. Within each flight block, further subdivisions are made into several 30- to 60-s periods based on changes in flight parameters such as altitude, speed, and throttle. Each period represents a relatively stable flight state or cognitive processing stage. For example, within the landing block, key periods such as glide, go-around, and hover can be identified based on the descent rate and throttle changes.

By employing this two-tier period division, the macrostructure of the flight mission is taken into account, while also considering the micro-changes in cognitive state. This provides a suitable time unit for subsequent statistical modeling of fNIRS signals.

3. Remove low-frequency drift and high-frequency noise using band-pass filtering

Firstly, the fNIRS signal is processed using a bandpass filter with a frequency range of 0.02 Hz to 0.3 Hz. The purpose of this step is to remove low-frequency physiological noise (such as drift caused by blood pressure fluctuations, body temperature regulation, etc.) and high-frequency noise (such as heartbeat, breathing, etc.) from the signal. Here, a 6th-order Butterworth filter is used, with the transfer function being:

$$H(z) = \frac{b_0 + b_1 z^{-1} + \cdots + b_n z^{-n}}{a_0 + a_1 z^{-1} + \cdots + a_n z^{-n}} \tag{1}$$

In this context, b_i and a_i represent filter coefficients, n denotes the filter order, and z signifies the complex frequency domain variable. The Butterworth filter is characterized by its maximally flat passband and monotonic transition band, effectively preserving signal components within the frequency range of interest.

4. Remove head motion artifacts using the TDDR algorithm

Head movement is a common artifact in fNIRS signals, manifesting as abrupt changes in the signal and baseline drift. Traditional correction methods, such as the accelerometer method and short-channel regression method, have limitations in practical applications. This study adopts the novel Temporal Derivative Distribution Repair (TDDR) algorithm.

The mathematical principle of the TDDR algorithm is as follows: Let x_t be the fNIRS signal at time t, and its time derivative is:

$$y_t = x_t - x_{t-1} \tag{2}$$

Under normal circumstances, the derivative follows a Gaussian distribution with a mean of 0. However, the derivative values caused by head movement-induced artifacts are usually abnormally large, deviating from the normal distribution. The TDDR algorithm achieves the purpose of correcting artifacts by adaptively pruning these abnormal derivative values and reintegrating the signal. The specific steps include:

① Perform adaptive thresholding y_t with a threshold value of "\lambda" on the derivative sequence to obtain the trimmed derivative y_t':

$$y'(t) = \begin{cases} y(t), \ if\,|y(t)| \leq \lambda \\ sign(y(t))\lambda, \ if\,|y(t)| > \lambda \end{cases} \tag{3}$$

② Restore the signal through cumulative summation: $\mathrm{x't} = \mathrm{x}_1 + \sum \mathrm{i} = 2^{\mathrm{t}}\mathrm{y'i}$
③ Optimize the threshold λ to minimize the sum of squared residuals between the reduced signal x' and the original signal x:

$$\lambda^* = \arg\ min\ \lambda \sum \mathrm{t} = 1^N (x_\mathrm{t} - x_t')^2 \tag{4}$$

Where N represents the signal length. The aforementioned process is achieved through iterative optimization.

5. Extract task-related brain activation using Generalized Linear Model (GLM)

GLM is a commonly used statistical analysis method in the field of fNIRS. Its basic assumption is that the measured fNIRS signal can be represented as a linear combination of multiple explanatory variables, plus an error term:

$$y(t) = \beta_0 + \beta_1 x_1(t) + \beta_2 x_2(t) + \cdots + \beta_n x_n(t) + \varepsilon(t) \tag{5}$$

Among them, β_i represents the weight coefficient to be estimated, $x_i(t)$ reflecting the contribution of each explanatory variable to the fNIRS signal. It can be the convolution of the task boxcar function and the hemodynamic response function (HRF), or other covariates such as head movement and drift.

GLM estimation employs the least squares method, which involves finding a set of parameters β that minimize the sum of squared residuals:

$$\hat{\beta} = arg\ \min_{\beta} \sum_{t=1}^{N} (y(t) - \sum_{i=1}^{N} \beta_i x_i(t))^2 \tag{6}$$

The estimated values $\hat{\beta}$ represent the contribution weights of each explanatory variable. The task-related values β reflect the activation level of the brain region for a specific task.

The GLM design matrix of this experiment encompasses factors such as difficulty, lighting, flight experience, and their corresponding interaction terms. By estimating the β values of each factor and conducting statistical inference (such as t-test), we can investigate the differences in brain activation patterns under different experimental conditions.

3.2 HbO Index Data Analysis

1. Flight mission

In the flight workload experiment designed and conducted in this paper, regarding the HbO index, at 60 s after the experiment began, during the aircraft's approach phase, by comparing flight task data under three different levels of workload, the comparison results showed that as the workload increased, the HbO concentration in the blood also increased. At 60 s before the end of the experiment, during the aircraft's landing phase, by comparing flight task data under three different levels of workload, the comparison results showed that as the workload increased, the HbO concentration in the blood first increased, and finally, when the workload became too high, the value began to decrease again.

The results indicate that as the workload increases, the concentration of HbO in the blood also increases. When the workload becomes too heavy and exceeds a certain threshold, this value becomes unstable, and the measured data for most subjects tend to decrease.

2. Lighting conditions

At 60 s after the experiment began, during the aircraft's approach phase, by comparing data between daytime (where performing flight missions can be considered to have a lower workload than at night) and nighttime, the comparison results indicated that as the workload increased, the concentration of HbO in the blood also increased. At 60 s before the end of the experiment, during the aircraft's landing phase, by comparing data between daytime (where performing flight missions can be considered to have a lower workload than at night) and nighttime, the comparison results again showed that as the workload increased, the concentration of HbO in the blood also increased.

The result significantly indicates that there is a clear positive correlation between the concentration of HbO in the blood and the workload.

3. Flight experience

At 60 s after the experiment began, during the aircraft approach phase, by comparing the data of student X and instructor (instructor performing flight tasks can be considered to have a lower workload than student performing flight tasks), the average difference in HbO concentration values in their blood was small, making it difficult to draw significant conclusions about the relationship between workload and HbO concentration. At 60 s before the end of the experiment, during the aircraft landing phase, by comparing the data of student X and instructor (instructor performing flight tasks can be considered to have a lower workload than student performing flight tasks), the average difference in HbO concentration in their blood was also small, making it similarly difficult to draw significant conclusions about the relationship between workload and HbO concentration.

The reason for this phenomenon may be attributed to the fact that the pilot trainees had undergone longer flight hours of simulator training, and the instructor trainees had been engaged in prolonged simulated flight operations in the recent period. Consequently, both the pilot trainees and the instructor trainees exhibited similar proficiency in operating the driving simulator during the experiment designed and conducted in this paper, leading to minimal differences in the analysis results.

3.3 HbR Index Data Analysis

1. Flight mission

Regarding the HbR index, at 60 s after the experiment began, during the aircraft's approach phase, by comparing data from flight missions with three different levels of workload, the comparison results indicated that as workload increased, the HbR concentration in the blood decreased. At 60 s before the end of the experiment, during the aircraft's landing phase, by comparing data from flight missions with three different levels of workload, the comparison results showed that as workload increased, the HbR concentration in the blood first decreased, and then when the workload became too high, the value began to increase again, but the overall change was not significant.

The results indicate that as the workload increases, the concentration of HbR in the blood decreases accordingly. When the workload exceeds a certain threshold, the value becomes unstable, and the measured data for most subjects tend to increase.

2. Lighting conditions

At 60 s after the experiment began, during the aircraft's approach phase, by comparing data between daytime (where flight missions can be considered to have a lower workload compared to those conducted at night) and nighttime, the comparison results indicated that as the workload increased, the concentration of HbR in the blood decreased. At 60 s before the end of the experiment, during the aircraft's landing phase, by comparing data between daytime (where flight missions can be considered to have a lower workload compared to those conducted at night) and nighttime, the comparison results showed that as the workload increased, the concentration of HbR in the blood also decreased, but the overall change was not significant.

The results indicate that there may be a negative correlation between the concentration of HbR in the blood and workload.

3. Flight experience

Sixty seconds after the experiment began, during the aircraft's approach phase, by comparing the data of Cadet X with that of the instructor (whose workload during flight missions can be considered less than that of a cadet), the comparison results indicated that as the workload increased, the concentration of HbR in the blood decreased. Sixty seconds before the end of the experiment, during the aircraft's landing phase, by comparing the data of Cadet X with that of the instructor (whose workload during flight missions can be considered less than that of a cadet), the comparison results showed that as the workload decreased, the concentration of HbR in the blood increased, but the overall change was not significant.

The results indicate that there may be a negative correlation between the concentration of HbR in the blood and workload.

4 Discussion

4.1 Differences in Brain Function Between Night Navigation and Daytime Training

Through meticulous statistical analysis of fNIRS data, the experiment uncovered significant differences in brain function among pilots under night flight and daytime training conditions. The comparison of HbR concentration levels under daytime and nighttime conditions is illustrated in Fig. 4.

Fig. 4. Comparison of HbR concentration levels under daytime and nighttime conditions

Firstly, the results of repeated measures analysis of variance indicated a significant interaction effect between lighting conditions (night/day) and the channels 1, 2, 17, and 18 of the prefrontal, parietal, and temporal lobes in terms of HbO2 and HbR responses [HbO2: $F(1, 16) = 12.35$, $P < 0.001$; HbR: $F(1, 16) = 8.74$, $P < 0.01$]. Further post-hoc tests revealed that under nighttime conditions, pilots exhibited significantly higher activation in the prefrontal and parietal lobes (increased HbO2 and decreased HbR) compared to daytime conditions ($P < 0.05$), while there was no significant difference in temporal lobe activation. This suggests that the nighttime environment imposes higher demands on pilots' cognitive control and sensorimotor integration abilities, leading to a greater allocation of neural resources to the fronto-parietal network.

Secondly, functional connectivity analysis revealed distinct patterns of brain region coordination under nighttime and daytime conditions. The results of the non-parametric permutation test indicated that under nighttime conditions, the functional connectivity within the prefrontal-parietal network and its connection with the occipital lobe significantly increased ($P < 0.05$, FDR corrected), while the prefrontal-temporal connectivity decreased. This alteration in connectivity patterns suggests that the nighttime environment may induce a reorganization of brain networks centered on sensory and perceptual processing, facilitating greater reliance on somatosensory and auditory information to complete flight tasks in the absence of visual cues.

Furthermore, the results of time-frequency domain analysis indicate that lighting conditions modulate the frequency domain characteristics of pilots' brain activity. Specifically, under nighttime conditions, the energy of HbO2 response in the prefrontal and parietal lobes in the 0.01–0.1 Hz frequency band is significantly higher than that under daytime conditions ($P < 0.05$), while the energy in the 0.1–1 Hz frequency band is significantly reduced. This suggests that the nighttime environment may cause pilots to focus more of their attention and cognitive resources on slow rhythms, reducing their reliance on fast rhythms. This change in frequency domain characteristics may reflect the decreased arousal level and adjusted cognitive strategies induced by nighttime flying.

Finally, the analysis revealed that flight experience plays a crucial role in regulating the effects of lighting. The results of the mixed design analysis of variance indicated that under nighttime flight conditions, flight instructors exhibited significantly lower prefrontal activation compared to flight cadets ($P < 0.05$), and this between-group difference was not significant during daytime conditions. Furthermore, the instructor group demonstrated stronger prefrontal-parietal connectivity under nighttime flight conditions ($P < 0.05$), while the cadet group exhibited more extensive prefrontal-temporal connectivity. This suggests that extensive nighttime flight experience may assist pilots in developing more effective cognitive resource allocation strategies, reducing reliance on prefrontal control, and making greater use of sensory processing automation to adapt to nighttime flight environments.

4.2 The Brain Activity Patterns During Nighttime Aviation Special Situation Handling

The changes in HbO2 levels during various special situation handling tasks are shown in Fig. 5. Through detailed analysis of the fNIRS data, some interesting brain activity patterns were discovered during nighttime special situation handling.

Firstly, it was observed that as the complexity of specific situations increased, the activation levels of the prefrontal and parietal regions of pilots exhibited a significant upward trend. Specifically, under high-risk situations such as complex runways and system failures, the HbO2 concentration in regions such as the dorsolateral prefrontal lobe, orbitofrontal lobe, and inferior parietal lobule was significantly higher than that in medium-risk situations such as meteorological changes ("$P < 0.05$"). This suggests that the fronto-parietal network allocates more cognitive resources when dealing with complex situations, potentially reflecting stronger demands for decision-making, planning, and sensorimotor integration.

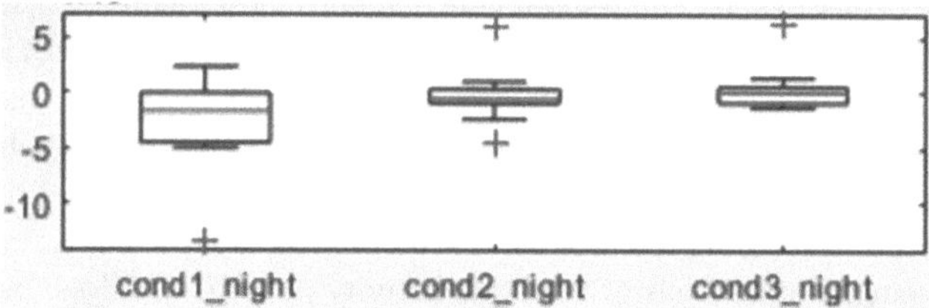

Fig. 5. Changes in HbO2 levels during various tasks involving special handling during night flight

Secondly, it was found that flight experience plays a significant role in regulating brain activity related to specific situations. For the instructor group, the increase in frontal lobe activation levels with the increasing difficulty of specific situations was significantly less than that of the trainee group ("$P < 0.05$"). This indicates that extensive flight experience may help instructors allocate cognitive resources more calmly when facing complex specific situations, reducing excessive activation of the prefrontal lobe.

In addition, it was observed that the instructor group exhibited stronger consistency in activation in the parietal lobe region, while the parietal lobe activation in the trainee group varied more significantly across different specific situations, which may reflect the shaping effect of flight experience on perceptual-motor strategies.

Furthermore, brain region correlation analysis revealed some interesting dynamic collaborative patterns. Under medium-risk scenarios such as meteorological changes, pilots exhibited significant enhancement of intra-frontal lobe coordination, manifested as increased functional connectivity between the dorsolateral prefrontal lobe and regions such as the anterior cingulate gyrus and orbitofrontal gyrus ($P < 0.05$). However, under high-risk scenarios such as complex runways and system failures, significant enhancement of fronto-parietal coordination was observed, manifested as increased functional connectivity between the dorsolateral prefrontal lobe, orbitofrontal gyrus, and inferior parietal lobule ("$P < 0.05$"). This shift in dynamic collaborative patterns may reflect a phased adjustment of cognitive strategies from medium to high-risk scenarios, namely, a transition from frontal lobe-centered decision-making evaluation to fronto-parietal network-centered action implementation. The brain blood oxygen index data acquisition and β value topography are shown in Fig. 6.

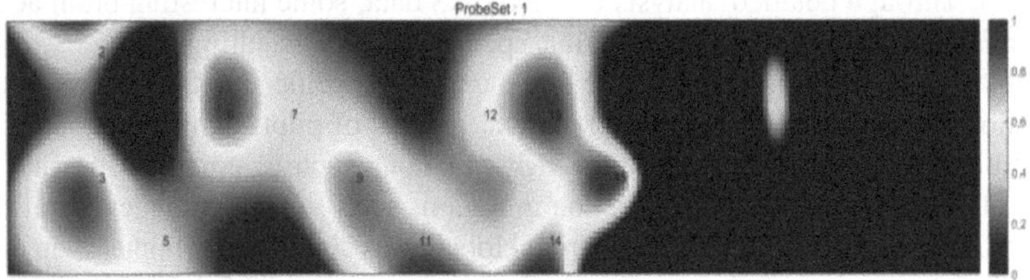

Fig. 6. Data acquisition of cerebral blood oxygen indicators and β value topography

Finally, we preliminarily explored the relationship between pilots' subjective stress levels and objective brain activity. It was found that for the instructor group, their subjective stress scores showed a significant negative correlation with the activation levels of the dorsolateral prefrontal cortex and orbitofrontal cortex ("r" = "-0.45, $P < 0.05$"), while there was no such correlation in the trainee group. This indicates that flight experience may endow instructors with a stronger sense of subjective controllability, thereby regulating the impact of stress response on cognitive function. This provides a new perspective for understanding the protective effect of flight experience.

Through systematic analysis of the brain activity patterns of pilots during the handling of special situations during night flights, dynamic brain adaptation rules under the modulation of factors such as cognitive load and flight experience have been discovered. As the severity of special situations increases, human brain activity also changes. Under high-pressure special situations, human brain load increases significantly, and the concentration of oxygenated hemoglobin increases significantly. The activation levels of different regions are synergistically enhanced. This not only expands the understanding of the brain mechanism of pilots' emergency response capabilities but also provides important basis for optimizing special situation risk assessment and emergency training.

4.3 Comparison of Brain Functional Activities Between Trainees and Instructors

Through repeated measures analysis of variance on experimental data, it was found that flight experience (trainees vs. instructors) exhibited a significant moderating effect on both local brain region activation and overall brain network coordination.

Within 60 s after the task began, the HbR levels in the instructor group in channels 14, 17, 20, and 21 were significantly lower than those in the trainee group ($P < 0.05$), indicating stronger activation in these areas among instructors. These areas are primarily located in the dorsolateral prefrontal cortex, which is closely related to advanced cognitive functions such as working memory and decision-making. At the beginning of the task, compared to instructors, flight trainees exhibited stronger activation in the lateral prefrontal cortex and higher HbR levels. In these same areas, the average HbO2 levels of instructors were lower than those of trainees, reflecting that in the same task, more experienced pilots experience a lower workload compared to less experienced ones. The comparison of HbR concentrations between trainees and instructors is shown in Fig. 7 below.

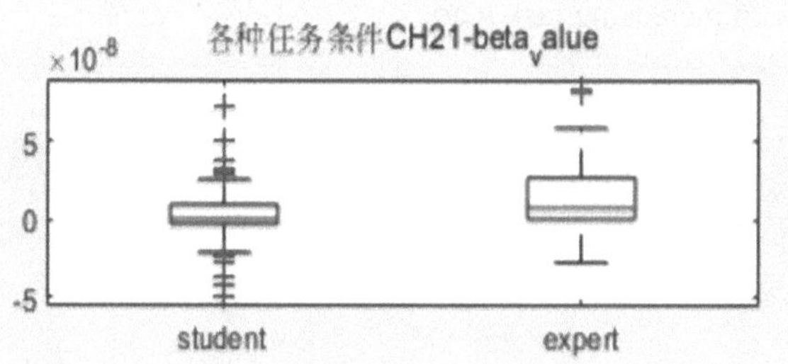

Fig. 7. Comparison of HbR concentrations between students and faculty members

The screenshots of HbO2 concentration under various task conditions are shown in Fig. 8. Analyzing the β-level changes of HbO2 within 60 s of the start of the task, under night flight conditions, there is an interactive effect between the instructor and trainee groups under different flight task difficulties. In channel 18, there is a significant difference in the level of HbR change ($P < 0.05$), with the trainee group exhibiting a higher level of HbO2 change compared to the instructor group. The HbO2 changes in other channels are not significant, indicating that under night flight conditions, flight experience has a more pronounced effect on frontal lobe activation in specific regions during the early stages of the task, and the experience effect reduces the workload of pilots. Combined with the conclusion of analyzing the level of HbR change, under night flight conditions, there is an experience effect that leads to lower brain load for instructors when dealing with the same task, and they have better coordination and adaptability compared to flight trainees.

Within 60 s before the end of the task, the difference between the instructor group and the trainee group was mainly reflected in the HbR level in the channel 20 area ($P < 0.05$), indicating that under nighttime conditions, the influence of flight experience on frontal lobe activation in the later stages of the task may be limited. Analyzing and comparing the changes in HbO2 levels, the interaction effect between the trainee-instructor group and task level was not significant, and the interaction effect decreased compared to 60 s before the start of the task.

In the simple effect analysis of nighttime flight scenarios, the difficulty level of flight tasks plays a significant role in regulating brain activation. Under the same nighttime conditions but different task difficulty levels, the HbR levels in channels 10, 17, and 19 of the instructor group exhibited a trend where the greater the task load, the lower the HbR change level ($P < 0.05$). The change level of HbO2 β was more pronounced, with significant effects observed in channels 3, 5, 6, 7, 8, 17, 18, 19, and 21 during tasks 1 and 3. The HbO2 level during task 3 was significantly higher than that during flight tasks 2 and 1. In the trainee group, differences between task conditions were observed in channel 2 ($P < 0.05$), with HbO2 concentration during task 3 being significantly higher than that during task 2. Both the student group and instructor group experiments indicated that under nighttime flight conditions, an increase in task difficulty leads to a certain degree of increase in hemoglobin content and decrease in deoxygenated concentration, reflecting the activation of closely related areas of human brain cognitive activity, primarily in the dorsolateral prefrontal cortex and orbitofrontal cortex regions, which are enhanced to varying degrees with increasing task load.

Fig. 8. Screenshot of HbO2 concentration under various task conditions

Further simple effect analysis revealed significant differences ($P < 0.05$) in the responses of multiple brain regions (channels 10, 17, 19) to task difficulty within the instructor group, with task 1 performing better than task 3. However, within the trainee group, only channel 2 showed a significant effect of task difficulty (task 2 performing better than task 3). This indicates that the brain activity of instructors is more sensitive to changes in cognitive load, exhibiting stronger neural plasticity.

Correlation analysis at the brain network level reveals extensive coordination within the frontal lobe and between the frontal and parietal lobes in pilots. In the instructor group, this coordinated activity involves multiple brain regions such as the dorsolateral prefrontal lobe, orbitofrontal lobe, dorsal anterior cingulate gyrus, and inferior parietal lobule. In contrast, the brain region coordination in the trainee group is more limited and less influenced by task conditions than that in the instructor group. This implies that flight experience may optimize the allocation and integration of cognitive resources by enhancing functional connectivity between key brain regions.

4.4 Analysis of Key Brain Region Activity During Night Navigation Training

In addition to examining the modulation effects of flight experience and task difficulty conditions on overall brain activation, we also focused on analyzing several key brain regions closely related to flight cognitive activities, including the dorsolateral prefrontal cortex (corresponding to channels 14, 16, 17, 19, 20), orbitofrontal cortex (corresponding to channels 1, 2, 3, 9, 10), and parietal cortex (corresponding to channels 12, 13) are shown in Fig. 9.

The dorsolateral prefrontal cortex (DLPFC) plays a pivotal role in multiple cognitive domains, including working memory, executive control, and decision-making. Experimental results indicate that during task execution, the level of HbR in the DLPFC exhibits a significant decrease overall ($P < 0.05$), suggesting significant activation of this region, particularly evident in the instructor group. Furthermore, a notable enhancement in functional connectivity between the DLPFC and the orbitofrontal cortex, as well as the parietal cortex, was observed ($P < 0.05$), with this enhancement being most prominent during high-load flight for instructors. This suggests that night flight tasks require the collaborative engagement of the fronto-parietal network to support the online processing of complex information. Flight experience may enhance task performance by strengthening this network collaboration.

The orbitofrontal cortex is associated with functions such as emotional regulation, risk decision-making, and self-monitoring. During nighttime flights and when task difficulty increases, the decrease in HbR in the orbitofrontal cortex is attenuated ($P < 0.05$), suggesting that the activation of this region may be inhibited. This may reflect the greater uncertainty and stress levels in the nighttime aviation environment. Additionally, it was observed that the functional connectivity between the orbitofrontal cortex and the amygdala region was stronger in the instructor group than in the trainee group ($P < 0.05$). Considering the role of the amygdala in emotional arousal and motivation maintenance, this may suggest that instructors are better able to regulate stress responses related to nighttime aviation and maintain task engagement. This difference may stem from adaptive changes brought about by long-term flight practice.

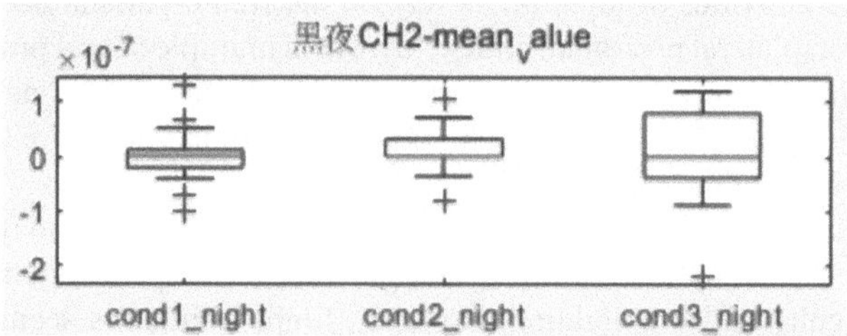

Fig. 9. Screenshot comparing HbO2 concentrations for various tasks in a nighttime environment

The parietal region is inextricably linked with spatial attention and sensorimotor integration. During challenging night navigation tasks (such as Task 3), a significant decrease in parietal HbR was observed in the instructor group ($P < 0.05$), whereas no such trend was seen in the trainee group. This suggests that, when faced with high-load tasks, instructors are able to more effectively mobilize the parietal region to participate in visual-spatial information processing and motor coordination. Furthermore, the instructor group exhibited stronger parietal-frontal coordination during challenging night navigation tasks ($P < 0.05$), particularly in the functional connectivity between the parietal region and the DLPFC, which may reflect a more flexible attention resource allocation strategy in complex flight situations.

5 Conclusion

By comparing the brain functional activities of trainees and instructors, the following conclusions can be drawn:

1. Flight instructors exhibit significantly superior brain activation patterns compared to trainees during cognitive neuroprocessing related to night flying, particularly in the frontal lobe region. This advantage may be closely related to their extensive flight experience and proficient cognitive skills.
2. Lighting conditions are an important factor in regulating pilots' cognitive processing. Daylight environments may be conducive to leveraging the advantages of flight experience, while nighttime environments have a certain "balancing" effect on the brain activity of both instructors and students. This may be related to factors such as reduced visual cues at night, making pilots more reliant on instrument readings.
3. The cognitive neural performance of instructors is more adaptable to changes in task difficulty, demonstrating a more flexible resource allocation ability. This may be attributed to their extensive flight practice, which enables them to optimize cognitive strategies from a top-down perspective.
4. Flight experience also affects the collaborative processing of the entire frontal lobe and even the fronto-parietal network. The brain region coordination in the instructor group is generally stronger than that in the trainee group, which may reflect their more effective information integration and resource allocation abilities in complex tasks.

The analysis of key brain region activity during night approach and landing training can lead to the following conclusions:

1. The cognitive activities of night pilots rely on the fronto-parietal network centered around the dorsolateral prefrontal cortex, involving multiple neural processes such as working memory, executive function, and attentional control. This network exhibits stronger activation levels and internal coordination under conditions of rich flight experience and daytime visual conditions.
2. The orbitofrontal cortex, as a key hub for emotional regulation, may experience a certain degree of inhibition during night flight missions, especially under conditions of high difficulty and low lighting. However, flight instructors seem to be able to

better cope with task pressure by strengthening the functional connectivity of the orbitofrontal-limbic system. This may be attributed to long-term adaptive training.

3. The parietal lobe plays a crucial role in the perceptual-motor integration related to night flying, which is particularly evident under instructor-led and high-load conditions. Its coordination with the frontal lobe may be an important manifestation of how flight experience optimizes the allocation of cognitive resources.

References

1. Wang, L., Zhang, Z., Tan, W., Gao, S., Hong, R., Sun, Y.: Application of fNIRS technology in measuring pilots' mental workload. Comprehen. Transport. **46**(02), 91–100 (2024)
2. Gao, L., Wang, C.: Research on visual perception state detection algorithm for flight cadets. J. Xi'an Univ. Technol. **44**(01), 1–10+133 (2024)
3. Yu, Liu, Pan, Y., Li, M., Li, C., Wang, X., You, X.: Application and prospects of near-infrared spectroscopy in aviation psychology research. Psychol. Sci. **46**(06), 1518–1528 (2023)
4. Yu, G., et al.: Evaluating the effectiveness of human-machine collaboration and trust in cognitive overload scenarios: a case study of cognitive scenarios for pilots in emergency conditions. Acad. Explor. **10**, 84–94 (2023)
5. Duan, Y., Feng, Y., Peng, R., Cai, Y., Feng, X.: Research on real-time fatigue monitoring model for flight operators. J. Flight Mech. **42**(02), 68–74 (2024)
6. Sun, R., Wang, Z.: Visual characteristics of pilots in a flight simulator environment. J. Beihang Univ. **39**(7), 897–901 (2013)
7. Li, Y., Li, K., Wang, S., et al.: Pilot behavior recognition based on multi-modality fusion technology using physiological characteristics. Biosensors **12**(6), 404 (2022)
8. Kawaguchi, K., Nikai, Y., Yomota, S., et al.: Effects of age and flight experience on prefrontal cortex activity in airline pilots: an fNIRS study. Heliyon **10**(9) (2024)
9. Yuan, J., Ke, X., Zhang, C., et al.: Recognition of different turning behaviors of pilots based on flight simulator and fNIRS data. IEEE Access **12**, 32881–32893 (2024)
10. Causse, M., Mouratille, D., Rouillard, Y., et al.: How a pilot's brain copes with stress and mental load? Insights from the executive control network. Behav. Brain Res. **456**, 114698 (2024)
11. Zhang, C., Yuan, J., Jiao, Y., et al.: Variation of pilots' mental workload under emergency flight conditions induced by different equipment failures: a flight simulator study. Transp. Res. Rec. **2678**(4), 365–377 (2024)

Research on the Mechanism of the Impact of Physical Exercise on Psychological Resilience of Flight Trainees in Different Phases of Flight Training

Jiuxia Guo[1](✉), Jiale Liu[1], Guoxuan He[2], and Yi Yang[3]

[1] Air Traffic Management College, CAFUC, Sichuan 618307, Guanghan, China
didiyes@163.com
[2] Flight Technology College, CAFUC, Sichuan 618307, Guanghan, China
[3] Strategic Development Department, Xinjiang ATMB, CAAC, Xinjiang, Urumqi 830016, China

Abstract. Under high-intensity training and high-pressure operational environments, flight trainees are prone to increased emotional fluctuations, limited attention distribution, and diminished decision-making capabilities. These deficiencies in psychological resilience can be further amplified during critical mission phases, posing potential threats to flight operations and aviation safety. To address these issues, this paper proposes a semi-quantitative assessment method for the psychological resilience of flight trainees. By classifying different training types and designing a survey, this study evaluates psychological resilience levels and introduces physical activity interventions based on the assessment results. First, a psychological resilience indicator system covering various training stages was established. Then, a survey was conducted among 334 flight trainees using the Physical Activity Rating Scale (PARS-3) and the Sports psychological resilience Questionnaire (SMTQ). Finally, Spearman rank correlation analysis was applied for data processing. Results indicate that the intensity, duration, and frequency of physical activity are significantly and positively correlated with the psychological resilience of flight trainees. Regression analysis reveals that for every unit increase in the scores of exercise intensity, duration, and frequency, the total psychological resilience score improves by 3.365, 3.408, and 3.940, respectively ($p < 0.001$). Furthermore, one-way Analysis of Variance (ANOVA) results show that as the training stages progress from theory learning and private pilot training to commercial pilot training, the intensity, duration, frequency, and total volume of physical activity among flight trainees show a gradual upward trend. Similarly, the scores of each dimension and the total score of psychological resilience also increase significantly ($p < 0.001$). These findings suggest that increasing participation in physical activity significantly enhances the psychological resilience of flight trainees, and significant differences exist across various training stages. Therefore, it is recommended that pilot training institutions develop stage-specific and differentiated physical education curricula and psychological resilience cultivation programs based on the characteristics of different training stages to systematically improve the comprehensive quality and flight safety of flight trainees.

W. -C. Li and A. Plioutsias (Eds.): HCII 2026, LNAI 16708, pp. 148–164, 2026.
https://doi.org/10.1007/978-3-032-29459-3_11

Keywords: Flight trainees · psychological resilience · Physical activity · Training stages

1 Introduction

With the rapid expansion of the civil aviation industry, balancing "scale" and "quality" in pilot cultivation is critical. Flight training involves high workloads and escalating difficulty across different training stages, severely testing the psychological resilience of flight trainees. As a vital psychological trait for stability under pressure, psychological resilience directly affects training efficacy and safety. While insufficient toughness leads to emotional dysregulation and increased operational risks, high psychological resilience ensures sustained cognitive focus. Physical activity is a recognized non-pharmacological intervention to alleviate stress. For flight trainees, systematic exercise acts as a psychological buffer, enhancing regulatory capacity. By integrating aviation psychology and physical education, this study explores how physical activity intervenes in the psychological resilience of flight trainees to optimize curricula and fortify flight safety.

Accumulating evidence on physical activity interventions for flight trainees has shifted toward optimizing training content and evaluating psychological outcomes. Aerobic and mind–body exercises, particularly Tai Chi, have been shown to significantly enhance mood and mitigate training-related stress [1]. Physical activity contributes to emotional stability through the mediating roles of perceived social support and self-efficacy [2], while also improving stress tolerance, psychological resilience, and reducing burnout symptoms [3, 4]. Furthermore, regular exercise engagement promotes subjective well-being via the sequential mediating effects of psychological resilience and self-control [5–9]. Neuroscientific research confirmed that the integration of professional flight training with structured physical exercise facilitates synergistic development in both cognitive and psychological domains [10]. Despite these advancements, three critical research gaps persist: (1) the absence of longitudinal, stage-specific comparisons across the Theory–Private–Commercial training trajectory; (2) insufficient investigation into the interactive effects of exercise intensity, duration, and frequency on psychological resilience; and (3) limited application of empirical findings into standardized, implementable physical education curricula within flight training institutions.

Parallel research on psychological resilience among flight trainees identifies academic pressure, professional demands, and cumulative stress as core influencing factors [11], particularly salient during emergency decision-making and role transitions [12, 13]. High psychological resilience is closely associated with preserved cognitive functioning, enhanced task performance [14], and superior emergency response capabilities [15]. Consequently, resilience has been formally integrated into pilot competency evaluation frameworks [16], with research revealing its role in motivation and mental health [17–19]. However, existing literature lacks longitudinal depictions across training stages and quantitative, actionable exercise intervention strategies. Therefore, this study analyzes flight trainees at various stages to examine the independent and synergistic effects of exercise loads on psychological resilience. By constructing stage-specific strategies, this research provides empirical evidence for a cultivation system tailored to the Chinese context, promoting the integration of "research-training-safety".

Psychological resilience has been widely applied in various interdisciplinary fields with fruitful achievements. Based on its assessment approaches, this study classifies training types, uses a questionnaire to assess flight trainees' psychological resilience, and adopts physical activity interventions for targeted improvement during training stages. Based on existing theoretical frameworks and flight training practices, this study proposes the following hypotheses:

H1: The intensity, duration, and frequency of physical activity have a significant positive predictive effect on the psychological resilience of flight trainees.

H2: As the training stages advance (Theory-Private-Commercial), the promotion mechanism and performance levels of physical activity on psychological resilience exhibit significant stage-specific differences and evolutionary characteristics.

2 Research Methods

2.1 Participants and Sampling

Sample Source and Stage Grouping. This study employed stratified sampling to select enrolled flight trainees at different cultivation stages from a flight college. Based on the training task differences outlined in the flight trainee syllabus, the sample was divided into three training stage: Theory Learning Stage (TLS), Private Pilot License (PPL) Stage, and Commercial Pilot License (CPL) Stage.

Descriptive Statistics of the Sample. A total of 334 valid questionnaires were recovered. Table 1 shows the sample composition: 114 participants in the Theory Stage (34.1%), 108 in the Private Pilot Training Stage (32.3%), and 112 in the Commercial Pilot Training Stage (33.5%).

Table 1. Descriptive Statistics of the Training Phase.

		Number	Percentage	Valid Percentage	Cumulative Percentage
Valid	TLS	114	34.1	34.1	34.1
	PPL	108	32.3	32.3	66.5
	CPL	112	33.5	33.5	100.0
	Total	334	100.0	100.0	

2.2 Instruments and Measurement

A comprehensive questionnaire served as the data collection tool, comprising demographic information, the PARS-3 scale, and the SMTQ scale (see Fig. 1 for the questionnaire framework).

Fig. 1. Framework of the questionnaire.

Physical Activity Rating Scale (PARS-3) and its Reliability. The Physical Activity Rating Scale (PARS-3), revised by Liang (1994), is a standardized tool for measuring exercise behavior based on exercise load theory. It quantifies abstract physical behavior across three dimensions: intensity, duration, and frequency (each scored 1–5). Intensity reflects physiological load; duration influences metabolic systems and willpower; and frequency relates to physiological adaptation and self-efficacy. The total score, ranging from 1 to 100, is calculated by the product of these three dimensions, objectively representing the total volume of physical activity through their interaction.

Given the high-pressure and high-skill nature of flight training, PARS-3 allows for an objective assessment of flight trainees' exercise involvement across various training stages. This provides a precise quantitative basis for exploring the mechanisms linking exercise behavior to psychological resilience. To ensure research quality, a reliability test was conducted on PARS-3 prior to formal statistical analysis to verify the consistency and stability of the measurement results [20].

Sports Mental Toughness Questionnaire (SMTQ) and its Validity. The Sports Mental Toughness Questionnaire (SMTQ), developed by Sheard et al. (2009), is a standardized instrument designed to assess the psychological advantages of maintaining firmness, focus, and confidence under pressure. Research indicates that individuals with high psychological resilience perceive stress as a challenge and demonstrate superior self-efficacy and performance. The scale consists of 14 items across three dimensions: Confidence (belief in one's abilities), Constancy (persistence toward goals), and Control (regulation of emotions and behavior).

SMTQ utilizes a 5-point Likert scale. To mitigate response bias, items 2, 4, 7, 8, 9, and 10 are reverse-scored, requiring score inversion during data processing to ensure dimensional consistency. Given the high-risk and high-load nature of flight training, the application of SMTQ allows for an objective assessment of flight trainees' psychological profiles. This provides a scientific basis for personalized psychological interventions and optimized training management. Prior to formal analysis, a reliability test was conducted on the SMTQ to ensure the instrument's consistency and validity.

Control Variables. To enhance the internal validity of the research findings, the first section of the questionnaire measured and controlled for non-core variables that could potentially confound the results:

Training Stage Based on the questionnaire options, trainees were classified into three levels, TLS, PPLand CPL Stage. This classification serves as the foundation for exploring the phase-specific evolution of psychological resilience.

Demographic Indicators: Background information, including gender, age, and educational attainment, was collected at the beginning of the questionnaire. These indicators provide supporting data for sample distribution characteristics and were observed as constants during the statistical analysis.

2.3 Data Collection and Processing

Procedures and Quality Control. The study was organized through a secondary college of a flight institution, with data collected via electronic questionnaires. To ensure research integrity, the following quality control measures were strictly implemented:

(1) Pre-set Scoring Rules: According to the questionnaire design (see Appendix A, Part III), scores for the six reverse-coded items in the SMTQ (Items 2, 4, 7, 8, 9, and 10) were transformed (i.e., $1 \rightarrow 5, 2 \rightarrow 4, 3 \rightarrow 3, 4 \rightarrow 2, 5 \rightarrow 1$) to maintain consistency in the direction of the total score calculation.
(2) Exclusion of Invalid Samples: Questionnaires were excluded through a background monitoring system if the completion time was less than 100 s, if answers showed obvious patterned regularity, or if significant logical contradictions were found in the reverse-coded items. Ultimately, 334 valid samples were obtained, with an effective recovery rate of 95.4%.

Common Method Variance (CMV) Test. Since all variables in this study were obtained through self-reports, there was a potential risk of Common Method Variance (CMV). In addition to procedural controls-such as reverse scoring and maintaining anonymity-Harman's single-factor test was conducted prior to formal analysis. The results indicated that the data were not significantly affected by CMV, satisfying academic statistical requirements.

2.4 Data Analysis Strategy

Statistical software was employed to perform in-depth data mining. One-way ANOVA was used to test for differences across training stages [21], Spearman correlation was utilized to explore associations between variables [22], and a multiple linear regression model was constructed to verify predictive mechanisms.

Descriptive Statistics and ANOVA. Descriptive statistics were used to outline the mean and dispersion characteristics of physical activity and psychological resilience among flight trainees. Subsequently, using the training stage as the grouping variable, a One-way ANOVA was conducted to compare score differences across the TLS, PPLS, and CPLS. For variables with homogeneity of variance, the LSD method was used for post-hoc multiple comparisons; for variables with heterogeneous variance, Tamhane's T2 test was applied to ensure the robustness of statistical inferences.

Correlation Analysis. Given the characteristics of the variables, Spearman's rank correlation analysis was selected to examine the monotonic association strength between exercise parameters (intensity, duration, frequency) and the sub-dimensions of psychological resilience (confidence, constancy, control) and the total score. This step aimed to verify significant linear or non-linear positive associations, laying the logical foundation for the regression model.

Spearman's Rank Correlation Coefficient. Spearman's rank correlation is a non-parametric measure of the strength and direction of monotonic association between two variables. Unlike Pearson's correlation, it does not require normality or linearity; instead, it operates on the ranked values of the data. The coefficient r_s is calculated as:

$$r_s = 1 - \frac{6\sum d_i^2}{n(n^2-1)} \tag{1}$$

where d_i is the difference between the ranks of the i-th observation on the two variables, and n is the sample size. When tied ranks exist, a corrected formula based on the Pearson correlation coefficient applied to the ranks is used:

$$r_s = \frac{\sum(R_x-\overline{R_x})(R_y-\overline{R_y})}{\sqrt{\sum(R_x-\overline{R_x})^2\sum(R_y-\overline{R_y})^2}} \tag{2}$$

where R_x and R_y are the ranks of variables X and Y, respectively, and $\overline{R}_x$, $\overline{R}_y$ are the mean ranks.

In this study, Spearman's rank correlation was particularly suitable because the PARS-3 and SMTQ data are ordinal in nature and do not strictly follow normal distributions. The method robustly captures both linear and non-linear monotonic relationships, providing reliable estimates of the associations between exercise intensity, duration, frequency, and the dimensions of psychological resilience.

Hierarchical Regression Analysis. Multiple linear regression was employed to explore the main effect mechanism of physical activity on psychological resilience. The model used the total psychological resilience score as the dependent variable, with the three elements of exercise participation as predictors. The contribution of each exercise factor to the enhancement of flight trainees' psychological quality was quantified through regression coefficients (B) and significance levels (p-values).

3 Research Results

3.1 Common Method Variance, Reliability, and Descriptive Statistics

Before exploring variable relationships, this study examined the data's reliability and distributional characteristics.

CMV and Reliability Testing. Cronbach's alpha (Cronbach's α)was used as the primary indicator for reliability testing ($0 < \alpha < 1$), where $\alpha > 0.7$ indicates good scale reliability. As shown in Table 2, the α coefficient for the PARS-3 was 0.892, and the α for the SMTQ reached 0.939. Both results are significantly higher than the 0.7 threshold, demonstrating that the measurement tools exhibited excellent stability in this survey and that the results are authentic and reliable for subsequent analysis. Furthermore, both procedural and statistical tests confirmed that no serious common method variance exists in this study.

Table 2. Reliability Test of the Scale.

Scale Name	Cronbach's α	Number of Item
PARS-3 Scale	0.892	3
SMTQ Scale	0.939	14

Descriptive Statistical Results. To gain a comprehensive understanding of the current state of physical activity participation among flight trainees, this study first conducted descriptive statistics for each dimension and the total score of the PARS-3. Through the analysis of means and standard deviations, the overall characteristics of this group regarding exercise load, duration, and regularity were identified. The specific statistical data are presented in Table 3:

Table 3. Descriptive Statistics of Physical Activity.

	Minimum	Maximum	Mean (SE)	SD
Exe. Intensity	1	5	2.93(0.077)	1.409
Exe. Duration	1	5	2.87(0.080)	1.457
Exe. Freq	1	5	2.84(0.077)	1.415
Activity Level	0	100	27.10(1.737)	31.737

Note: Abbreviations: Exe. = Exercise; Freq. = Frequency. Sample size $N = 334$ for all variables

As shown in Table 3, the descriptive statistics of the PARS-3 reveal the quantitative characteristics of physical activity among flight trainees:

1. Exercise Intensity: Dominated by moderate load with individual variations. The mean score for exercise intensity was 2.925 (SD = 1.409), indicating that most trainees opt for moderate-intensity exercise. This level of intensity effectively alleviates physical and mental stress while avoiding the negative impacts of excessive fatigue or sports injuries on flight training.
2. Exercise Duration: Characterized by fragmentation and volatility. The mean score for exercise duration was 2.865 (SD = 1.457). This reflects that, constrained by

intensive flight training schedules, the duration of single exercise sessions varies among trainees. The fragmentation of leisure time leads to significant fluctuations in sustained exercise duration.

3. Exercise Frequency and Total Volume: Wide distribution with polarized participation levels. The mean score for exercise frequency was 2.841 (SD = 1.415), showing substantial differences in weekly exercise frequency among trainees. Integrating the three dimensions, the mean total physical activity score was 27.102 (SD = 31.737), with scores widely distributed across the 0–100 range. This suggests that the degree of physical participation is influenced by factors such as personal preference, time management, and training-induced fatigue, resulting in significant non-uniformity. This variance in participation levels likely leads to varying degrees of impact on psychological resilience.

As shown in Table 4, a statistical analysis of the 14 items and various dimensions of the SMTQ provides a precise profile of the psychological characteristics among flight trainees.

1. At the item level, mean scores are concentrated in the 2.9–3.2 range with standard deviations between 1.4 and 1.6, reflecting an overall convergence in performance alongside notable individual differences. For example, Item 1 (psychological adaptation) and Item 2 (emotional stability, positively coded) yielded mean scores of 3.060 and 3.114, respectively. These results indicate that while some trainees can rapidly adapt to high-pressure tasks, others experience significant anxiety in practical training environments, highlighting a critical need for enhanced psychological regulation.
2. Regarding specific dimensions, the scores reveal divergent confidence, relatively low constancy, and moderate control. The Confidence dimension (Mean = 15.147, SD = 5.712) shows high dispersion, suggesting a polarization in trainees' self-efficacy regarding their flight capabilities. The Constancy dimension yielded a relatively low mean of 9.135, indicating that the willpower required to navigate training setbacks still needs refinement, as some individuals exhibit a tendency to withdraw. Meanwhile, the Control dimension (Mean = 18.479) reflects an acceptable level of foundational mastery over behaviors and emotions, though the precision of this control in complex flight environments remains to be optimized.
3. In terms of overall levels, the data demonstrate significant heterogeneity in psychological resilience. The mean total score is 42.760 (SD = 15.667), with a broad distribution spanning from 15 to 68 points. This disparity suggests that while high-resilience trainees are capable of maintaining stable performance under pressure, those with low resilience are at a higher risk of psychological imbalance during high-pressure flight missions. Such variations in psychological resilience directly impact overall training efficiency and safety margins.

3.2 Phase-Specific Difference Analysis of Variables

Comparison of Physical Activity Participation Levels Across Training Stages. The physical activity participation levels across different training stages were compared using one-way ANOVA, as shown in Table 5.

Table 4. Descriptive Statistics of the SMTQ Scale.

	N	Min	Max	Mean (SE)	SD
Item 1	334	1	5	3.06(0.080)	1.463
Item 2	334	1	5	3.11(0.083)	1.514
Item 3	334	1	5	2.96(0.077)	1.410
Item 4	334	1	5	3.11(0.084)	1.544
Item 5	334	1	5	3.05(0.082)	1.504
Item 6	334	1	5	2.98(0.085)	1.546
Item 7	334	1	5	3.12(0.082)	1.503
Item 8	334	1	5	3.07(0.082)	1.491
Item 9	334	1	5	3.11(0.083)	1.518
Item 10	334	1	5	2.96(0.084)	1.526
Item 11	334	1	5	2.99(0.083)	1.520
Item 12	334	1	5	3.06(0.082)	1.492
Item 13	334	1	5	3.10(0.080)	1.456
Item 14	334	1	5	3.08(0.080)	1.470
Conf	334	5	25	15.15(0.313)	5.712
Const	334	3	15	9.13(0.202)	3.695
Ctrl.	334	6	30	18.48(0.400)	7.310
Total Score	334	15	68	42.76(0.857)	15.667

Note: Abbreviations: Conf. = Confidence; Const. = Constancy; Ctrl. = Control. For scoring consistency, Items 2, 4, 7, 8, 9, and 10 were reverse-coded (transformed)

As illustrated in Table 5 and Fig. 2, significant differences exist across all physical activity indicators among flight trainees at different training stages:

1. Exercise intensity exhibits a stepwise increase. ANOVA results ($F = 86.037$, $p < 0.001$) indicate that intensity rises significantly as training progresses. The mean score increased from 1.96 ± 1.08 at the TLS to 2.88 ± 1.24 at the PPLS, reaching 3.96 ± 1.13 at the CPLS. This reflects that as training complexity grows, trainees proactively pursue higher physical loads to meet the rigorous demands of the CPLS.
2. Exercise duration shows significant prolongation. One-way ANOVA confirms that the training stage has a significant impact on exercise duration ($F = 90.958$, $p <$

Table 5. Summary Table of One-Way Analysis of Variance.

Variable	TLS	PPL	CPL	*F*	Levene's Test
Exe. Intensity	1.96 ± 1.08	2.88 ± 1.24	3.96 ± 1.13	86.037	0.116
Exe. Duration	1.79 ± 1.03	2.94 ± 1.28	3.89 ± 1.20	90.958	0.072
Exe. Freq	1.78 ± 0.94	2.78 ± 1.23	3.98 ± 1.08	115.82	0.001**
Activity Level	6.01 ± 14.20	22.42 ± 25.17	53.09 ± 32.35	103.08	< 0.001**
Conf	10.16 ± 3.85	15.33 ± 4.71	20.04 ± 3.40	171.39	0.001**
Const	6.11 ± 2.47	9.24 ± 3.24	12.11 ± 2.52	133.6	0.002**
Contrl	12.09 ± 4.17	18.62 ± 6.40	24.85 ± 4.50	177.24	< 0.001**
Total Score	28.36 ± 8.95	43.19 ± 12.92	57.00 ± 8.73	217.01	< 0.001**

Notes:
Training Stage: TLS = Theory Learning Stage = 1; PPL = Private Pilot License Stage = 2; CPL = Commercial Pilot License Stage = 3.
Data Presentation: Data in the table are presented as M ± SD. Exercise level is an ordinal categorical variable.
ANOVA and Post Hoc Comparisons: The main effect of one-way analysis of variance (ANOVA) was significant for all items. Post hoc pairwise comparisons revealed consistent between-group differences for all variables: CPL stage > PPL stage > TLS stage, with all comparisons significant at $p < 0.05$.
Homogeneity of Variance Correction: ** indicates a significant Levene's test ($p < 0.05$), suggesting heterogeneity of variance. For items with significant Levene's test results, *F*-test statistics were derived from Welch's correction, and post hoc comparisons were based on Tamhane's T2 test.

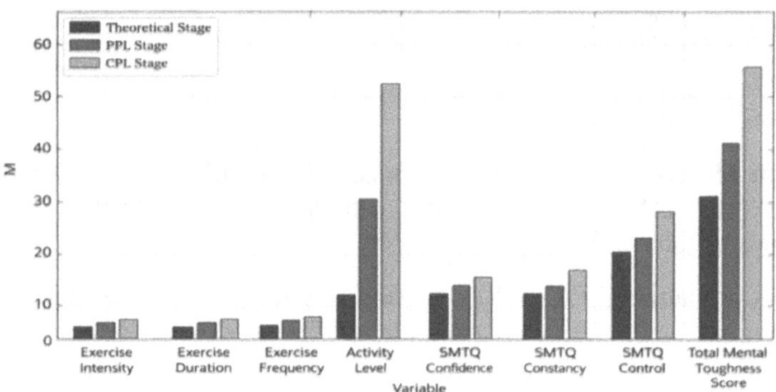

Fig. 2. Bar Chart of One-Way ANOVA.

0.001). The average duration per session rose from 1.79 ± 1.03 during the TLS to 3.8 ± 1.20 by the CPLS.

3. Synergistic leap-forward in exercise frequency and total volume. Exercise frequency differed significantly across stages ($F = 115.824, p < 0.001$). Since the Levene's test indicated heterogeneity of variance ($p = 0.001$), Tamhane's T2 test was employed for post-hoc multiple comparisons. Results show that mean frequency grew from 1.78 ± 0.94 at the TLS to 3.98 ± 1.08 at the CPLS, following a significant stepwise distribution of CPLS > PPLS > TLS ($p < 0.05$).
4. Total physical activity volume grows significantly driven by multidimensional factors. Driven by the combined effects of intensity, duration, and frequency, the total physical activity score showed highly significant differences ($F = 103.077, p < 0.001$). Confirmed by Tamhane's T2 test, the total volume escalated dramatically from 6.01 ± 14.20 at the TLS to 53.09 ± 32.35 at the CPLS.

Comparison of Psychological Resilience Levels Across Training Stages. Analysis of Table 5 reveals that psychological resilience levels strengthen significantly as training progresses ($p < 0.001$):

1. Dimensional Comparison. The SMTQ sub-dimensions Confidence, Constancy, and Control, all display a monotonic increasing trend. Trainees in the CPLS scored highest across all dimensions. This likely stems from the fact that after long-term technical refinement, trainees gradually adapt to high-pressure flight tempos, establishing professional self-confidence, tempering their willpower, and enhancing their psychological management of complex environments.
2. Overall Level Analysis. The total psychological resilience score showed highly significant differences across the three stages ($F = 217.008, p < 0.001$). These results confirm a clear divergence in psychological resilience levels among flight trainees at different stages, following a pattern of continuous reinforcement throughout the training process.

Flight trainees' physical activity and psychological resilience exhibit a synergistic promotion across training stages, with the superior performance in the CPLS validating the role of long-term training in psychological development and providing a scientific basis for stage-specific interventions.

3.3 Correlation Analysis Results

Correlation Matrix of Variables. Spearman correlation analysis was conducted to examine the relationships among variables, with the results presented in Table 6.

As shown in Table 6 and Fig. 3:

1. Internal Correlation of PARS-3 Dimensions: exercise intensity is highly correlated with duration ($r = 0.751$) and frequency ($r = 0.730, P < 0.001$), reflecting synergistic exercise behavior among flight trainees. Intensity serves as the core determinant of total workload, showing the strongest correlation with the activity level ($r = 0.856$).
2. Driving Effects of Physical Activity on psychological resilience: Correlation analysis reveals that all physical activity indicators are significantly positively correlated with psychological resilience ($P < 0.001$). High intensity is closely linked to confidence and willpower; duration has the most pronounced impact on confidence ($r = 0.770$); and frequency is vital for enhancing psychological control ($r = 0.766$).

3. Overall Promotion Effect of Total Activity Level: The total activity level shows the most significant correlation with all psychological resilience dimensions and the total score ($r = 0.767$ to 0.853). Spearman correlation analysis confirms that as cumulative activity increases, trainees' willpower, sense of control, and self-efficacy improve significantly. These findings provide a theoretical basis for flight colleges to design targeted physical curricula for optimizing psychological resilience.

Table 6. Results of the correlation analysis.

		Exe. Intensity	Exe. Duration	Exe. Freq	Activity Level	Conf	Cons	Contrl	Total Score
Rho	Exe Intensity	1.000	0.751 **	0.730**	0.856**	0.761 **	0.718**	0.754**	0.797 **
	Exe. Duration	0.751 **	1.000	0.714**	0.953**	0.770 **	0.719**	0.744**	0.796 **
	Exe. Freq	0.730 **	0.714 **	1.000	0.840**	0.752 **	0.710**	0.766**	0.801 **
	Activity Level	0.856 **	0.953 **	0.840**	1.000	0.817 **	0.767**	0.802**	0.853 **
	Conf	0.761 **	0.770 **	0.752**	0.817**	1.000	0.766**	0.824**	0.934 **
	Const	0.718 **	0.719 **	0.710**	0.767**	0.766 **	1.000	0.800**	0.891 **
	Contrl	0.754 **	0.744 **	0.766**	0.802**	0.824 **	0.800**	1.000	0.952 **
	Total Score	0.797 **	0.796 **	0.801**	0.853**	0.934 **	0.891**	0.952**	1.000

Note: Correlation is significant at the 0.01 level (2-tailed). All 2-tailed significance values are 0.000 and not shown in the table. $N = 334$ for all variables

3.4 Hypothesis Testing Results

Main Effect Test of Physical Activity on psychological resilience (Validation of H1). A multiple linear regression model was constructed with the total psychological resilience score as the dependent variable and exercise intensity, duration, and frequency as the independent variables. As shown in Table 7, the model demonstrates good fit, and the overall regression equation is statistically highly significant. The model constant is 11.959 ($SE = 0.983, t = 12.171, p < 0.05$), indicating a significant intercept. The detailed analysis is as follows:

1. Exercise intensity has a significant positive predictive effect on psychological resilience ($B = 3.365$, $SE = 0.476$, $\beta = 0.303$, $t = 7.076$, $p < 0.05$). This indicates that, while controlling for exercise duration and frequency, for every one-unit

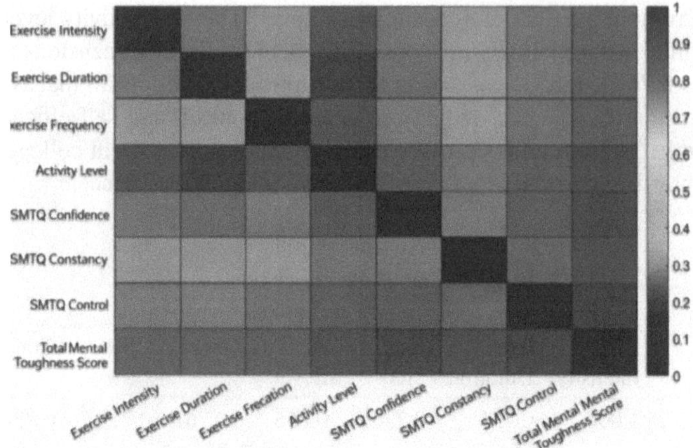

Fig. 3. Heatmap of the correlation analysis.

increase in intensity, the total psychological resilience score increases by an average of 3.365 units.

2. Exercise duration shows a stable and significant positive influence ($B = 3.408$, $SE = 0.452$, $\beta = 0.317$, $t = 7.539$, $p < 0.05$). After controlling for other variables, every one-unit increase in exercise duration results in an average increase of 3.408 units in the total psychological resilience score.
3. Exercise frequency is the most influential positive predictor ($B = 3.940$, $SE = 0.450$, $\beta = 0.356$, $t = 8.755$, $p < 0.05$). This means that for every one-point increase in exercise frequency, the total psychological resilience score increases by an average of 3.940 units, making it the most prominent contributor among the three dimensions.

In summary, all three dimensions of physical activity have a significant positive impact on flight trainees' psychological resilience, supporting Hypothesis H1. Higher exercise intensity improves stress resistance, longer exercise duration facilitates stress relief, and regular exercise frequency fosters stable psychological adjustment.

Table 7. Summary Table of Multiple Linear Regression.

Model	$B(SE)$	β	t	95.0% Confidence Interval for B	
				Lower Bound	Upper Bound
(Constant)	11.959(0.983)		12.171	10.026	13.892
Exe. Intensity	3.365(0.476)	0.303	7.076	2.430	4.301
Exe. Duration	3.408(0.452)	0.317	7.539	2.519	4.297
Exe. Frequency	3.940(0.450)	0.356	8.755	3.054	4.825

Note: Dependent Variable = Total psychological resilience Score. Standardized Coefficients (B) are reported. All 2-tailed significance values are 0.000 and not shown in the table. $N = 334$

Testing the Moderating Effect of Training Stages (Validation of H2). This study integrates the results of the variance analysis from Sect.2.2 with the regression mechanism outlined in Sect.2.4 to conduct a comprehensive evaluation

1. Evolution of the Influence Path: Based on ANOVA and regression analyses, the progression of flight trainees from the Theory to Commercial stage is marked by a synchronized increase in total physical activity (from 6.01 ± 14.20 to 53.09 ± 32.35) and psychological resilience. This trend suggests that as training stages shift the physiological and psychological load environment, physical activity consistently functions as a stable psychological "buffer."
2. Deepening Mechanism: Upon reaching the Commercial stage, increased flight pressure prompts a behavioral shift toward higher frequency and intensity in exercise. This stage-specific transition aligns with the high correlation ($r = 0.853$) observed in psychological resilience scores, reflecting a significant evolutionary mechanism of exercise-induced resilience across different cultivation phases.
3. Hypothesis Validation: Empirical results demonstrate a high degree of congruence between the progression of training stages and the enhancement path of psychological resilience. The distinct patterns of physical and mental regulation across stages provide preliminary support for research hypothesis H2.

4 Research Recommendations

4.1 Optimizing the Physical Training Curriculum System

Given the significant positive role of physical activity in enhancing psychological resilience, optimizing the curriculum is essential. The following four strategies are proposed:

1. Developing Stage-Specific and Differentiated Curricula: Tailor programs to specific training stages. The TLS focuses on foundational fitness and cognitive fatigue relief; the PPLS emphasizes environmental adaptation and coordination; and the CPLS targets high-pressure resilience through extreme challenges and mindfulness. This ensures precise alignment between exercise and psychological needs.
2. Quantifying Exercise Parameters to Strengthen Defense Mechanisms: Given that frequency is the strongest predictor of psychological resilience, a minimum of 3–4 physical activity sessions per week is recommended. For trainees with lower resilience, the frequency-first and moderate-intensity approach should be adopted to establish a stable psychological defense system.
3. Diversifying Exercise Modalities and Enhancing Faculty Intervention: Integrate team sports and challenging activities to cultivate resilience. Strengthen instructors' mental health expertise to form an integrated teaching, identification, and intervention system for flight trainees.

4.2 Enhancing the Psychological Resilience Management Mechanism

A full-chain management system from precise assessment to classified intervention should be established:

1. Multidimensional Assessment: Integrate psychological scales with physiological monitoring (e.g., Heart Rate Variability, HRV) and behavioral observations to create psychological resilience profiles. Implement layered interventions: advanced regulation techniques for high-resilience trainees and Cognitive Behavioral Therapy (CBT) for those with lower scores.
2. Teaching-Training Integration: Incorporate psychological coping strategies into flight cases and set challenging goals in physical training (e.g., obstacle courses) to cultivate persistence.
3. Social Support Networks: Establish home-school cooperation and professional social resources to broaden the paths for resilience development.

4.3 Strengthening Long-Term Health Consciousness Cultivation

Transforming short-term behavioral interventions into long-term professional qualities requires the continuous influence of a health culture and the motivation provided by evaluation mechanisms.

1. Systematic Health Education: Offer courses in exercise physiology and nutrition to reinforce the core concept that "physical and mental health ensures flight safety." Use wearable technology and apps for visualizing health data.
2. Comprehensive Health Culture: Create an environment of health through Health Flight Months and Mental Health Weeks, utilizing mutual aid groups to supervise and encourage healthy lifestyles.
3. Long-term Evaluation Mechanisms: Integrate health consciousness and psychological resilience into the comprehensive evaluation system for graduation and awards.

5 Conclusions and Prospects

The study on the relationship between physical activity and psychological resilience among flight trainees concludes:

1. Significant Influence: Physical activity has a clear positive impact on psychological resilience, both of which increase as trainees progress through their training stages.
2. Variable Correlation: Intensity, duration, and frequency are all closely linked to resilience, with frequency being the most significant predictor.
3. Phase Differences: Distinct differences exist across the TLS, PPLS, and CPLS, necessitating stage-specific physical and psychological training programs.
4. Practical Significance: This study provides an empirical foundation for optimizing flight trainee cultivation systems, offering significant value for enhancing comprehensive cadet quality, ensuring flight safety, and advancing the civil aviation industry. However, several limitations warrant consideration: the sample representativeness is limited by its relatively small scale and singular source, which may affect the generalizability of the findings; the cross-sectional design precludes the determination of causal relationships and the differential effects of specific exercise types; and the exclusion of certain variables, such as personality traits and family support, may have influenced the results. Future research should focus on constructing multidisciplinary

theoretical models to elucidate the physiological, psychological, and social mechanisms underlying the impact of exercise on psychological resilience. Additionally, efforts should be directed toward developing personalized intervention programs tailored to individual characteristics and training stages-potentially incorporating VR technology for situational training as well as conducting international comparative studies and establishing longitudinal databases to evaluate the sustained efficacy of exercise interventions and support continuous systemic refinement.

Acknowledgments. This research was funded by the Project Specification of National Key Research and Development Program (grant number 2024YFB2605201), and the Civil Aviation Education Talent Project (grant numbers MHJY2025002, MHJY2025003).

Disclosure of Interests. The authors have no competing interests to declare that are relevant to the content of this article.

References

1. Chen, Y., Meng, Y., Yi, X., et al.: The effect of Tai Chi Chuan on the mood and mental health of civil aviation flight cadets. J. Aerosp. Med. Med. Eng. **33**(5), 427–431 (2020)
2. Zhao, Y., Huang, L., Li, Y.: The influence of physical exercise on the emotional stability of flight cadets: the chain mediating role of perceived social support and self-efficacy. Chin. J. Health Psychol. **31**(3), 446–451 (2023)
3. Liang, K., Du, T.: Research on the influence of sports activities on college students' psychological toughness. In: China Bandy Association (ed.) Proceedings of the First China Smart Sports Science Conference in 2025, vol. 1, pp. 202–205. Chengdu University of Information Technology, Chengdu (2025)
4. Wang, J., Liu, J., Nian, Q.: The influence of physical exercise on college students' healthy lifestyle: the mediating effects of psychological resilience and exercise self-efficacy. In: Chinese Society of Sport Science (ed.): Abstract Collection of the 13th National Sports Science Conference –Sports Psychology Branch, p. 1416. Northeast Normal University, Changchun (2023)
5. Liu, W., Li, Z., Zhao, H.: Analyzing the effect of physical exercise on subjective well-being of university students using the chain mediation model. Sci. Rep. **15**(1), 18913 (2025)
6. Qiu, W., Wang, X., Cui, H., et al.: The impact of physical exercise on college students' physical self-efficacy: the mediating role of psychological resilience. Behav. Sci. **15**(4), 541 (2025)
7. Yu, H., Li, X., Yu, X., et al.: How physical exercise enhances life satisfaction in Chinese senior college students: mediating roles of self-efficacy and resilience. Front. Psychol. **16**, 1515101 (2025)
8. Cao, L., Ao, X., Zheng, Z., et al.: Exploring the impact of physical exercise on mental health among female college students: the chain mediating role of coping styles and psychological resilience. Front. Psychol. **15**, 1466327 (2024)
9. Li, X., Cui, L., Shen, Q., et al.: Relationship between Chinese college students' attitude to physical exercise and psychological capital: the mediating effects of self-control and gender. Front. Public Health **12**, 1443489 (2024)
10. Wang, L., Yang, C., Yan, D., et al.: The effects of flight training on flying cadets' brain structure. PLoS ONE **20**(2), e0313148 (2025)

11. Li, S.: A study on the mental health status and influencing factors of pilots. J. Civ. Aviat. **3**(2), 50–53 (2019)
12. Su, X.: A study on pilots' psychological resilience in response to accidents and frights. J. Civ. Aviat. **8**(Suppl. 1), 92–93 (2024)
13. Li, C.: Theoretical construction and protective mechanism of psychological resilience in civil aviation pilots. Ph.D. thesis, Shaanxi Normal University (2021)
14. Zhang, M., Liao, J., Peng, K., et al.: The impact of psychological tension and psychological resilience on pilots' job performance: a case study of general aviation pilots. J. Shanghai Univ. (Soc. Sci. Edn.) **34**(2), 134–140 (2017)
15. Qiu, R., Wang, X., Yang, M., et al.: The relationship between category characteristics of flight cadets' special situation handling ability and psychological qualities: based on latent profile analysis. Psychology Monthly **18**(10), 17–19 (2023)
16. Chen, F., Han, S.: The influence of social support and psychological resilience on pilots' safety behavior. J. Saf. Environ. **18**(6), 2252–2256 (2018)
17. Zheng, Y., Ezarina, Z., Md, N., et al.: Resilience, dispositional hope, and psychological well-being among college students: a systematic review. Open Psychol. J. **17** (2024)
18. Guo, J.: The dual impact of physical exercise on university students' mental health: the chain mediating effects of mindfulness and psychological resilience. Front. Psychol. **16**, 1545370 (2025)
19. Yu, C., Zeng, Z., Xue, A., et al.: The effect of exercise motivation on college students' self-efficacy: the mediating roles of leisure satisfaction and mental toughness. Front. Psychol. **15**, 1465138 (2024)
20. Chai, H.: Research on reliability and validity testing methods in questionnaire design. World Sci. Tech. R & D **32**(4), 548–550 (2010)
21. Yang, X.: A brief analysis of variance analysis method: one-way ANOVA. Exp. Sci. Technol. **11**(1), 41–43 (2013)
22. Fan, R., Meng, D., Xu, D.: Research progress on statistical correlation analysis methods. Math. Model. Appl. **3**(1), 1–12 (2014)

How Multi-sector Planning Shapes Shared Situation Awareness Among Air Traffic Controllers: A Team-Level Eye-Tracking Evaluation

Zhimin Li[1], Meng-Hsueh Hsieh[1,2], Mercedes Premalatha Ramesh[1], Imen Dhief[1], Mengtao Lyu[3], and Mir Feroskhan[1,2](✉)

[1] Air Traffic Management Research Institute, Nanyang Technological University, Singapore 637460, Singapore
mir.feroskhan@ntu.edu.sg
[2] School of Mechanical and Aerospace Engineering, Nanyang Technological University, Singapore 639798, Singapore
[3] Georgia Institute of Technology, Atlanta, GA 30332, USA

Abstract. Air traffic control (ATC) systems worldwide are increasingly adopting Multi-Sector Planning (MSP) to address staffing shortages. While prior studies have examined MSP's effects on individual workload and situation awareness, how MSP reshapes shared situation awareness within controller teams remains poorly understood. Existing evaluations also rely largely on post-hoc questionnaires, leaving limited objective, process-level evidence on team communication and visual attention during joint airspace management. To address this gap, we conducted a high-fidelity ATC simulation comparing MSP with a baseline configuration, integrating synchronized communication analysis and eye-trackingâĂŞbased attention measures. In the baseline condition, each sector was managed by a dedicated planningâĂŞtactical controller (PCâĂŞTC) pair, whereas under MSP, one PC supervised two sectors with separate TCs, emphasizing cross-sector coordination. Each one-hour scenario included routine operations and an embedded abnormal-weather event to examine shared situation awareness under increased complexity. Results indicate that MSP increases PCs' workload and is associated with systematic changes in visual attention and communication. PCs under MSP show more frequent visual sampling, broader spatial attention allocation, and elevated sustained cognitive engagement, whereas TCs exhibit largely stable patterns across conditions. Communication demands are redistributed toward the planning role while overall coordination breakdowns remain infrequent. These findings provide objective, team-level evidence on how MSP reshapes shared attention and coordination, informing the design of role-sensitive support mechanisms for future multi-sector ATC operations.

Keywords: Multi-sector planning · Shared situation awareness · Team coordination · Eye-tracking · Air traffic control

Z. Li and M. Hsieh—Equal contribution.

W. -C. Li and A. Plioutsias (Eds.): HCII 2026, LNAI 16708, pp. 165–176, 2026.
https://doi.org/10.1007/978-3-032-29459-3_12

1 Introduction

Air traffic control (ATC) faces escalating challenges from increasing air traffic volumes amid staffing shortages and capacity constraints [9]. For example, 77% of U.S. ATC facilities are understaffed, exacerbating risks of delays [3]. To address this pressing need for greater efficiency without compromising safety, the aviation industry is actively developing evolving concepts of operations. Multi-sector planning (MSP) has emerged as a pivotal strategy in this endeavor, designed to optimize human resources by fundamentally restructuring controller roles [22]. The core of MSP involves consolidating the strategic planning responsibilities for two or more sectors under a single Planner Controller (PC), while Tactical Controller (TC) retains execution duties within their respective sectors. This architecture is anticipated to enhance strategic coherence and decision-making flow across sectors, thereby directly addressing the imperative of handling more traffic with constrained resources. However, MSP's consolidation may raise human factors issues. The PC, as a central node, bears an increased cognitive load from expanded responsibilities, which may compromise the PC's shared situation awareness with TC from a specific sector, undermining team coordination [8]. Therefore, recognizing MSP's operational implications is essential for ensuring its safe and effective implementation.

Existing research has extensively examined the effects of MSP on controller workload and situation awareness, yielding valuable insights into its cognitive demands and operational viability [12]. For instance, simulation-based evaluations of MSP concepts have investigated how MSP tools influence planning processes in en-route operations, suggesting potential shifts in workload distribution and operational practices [19]. However, most existing investigations focus on individual-level effects, leaving the team-level implications of MSP comparatively underexplored. Recent discussions highlight that MSP inherently modifies information dependencies among controllers and may influence the formation of shared situation awareness across team members, underscoring the need to consider cognitive dynamics beyond the individual [20].

Moreover, current evaluation methods of MSP remain dominated by post-hoc questionnaires, which are retrospective and lack the temporal resolution for capturing real-time fluctuations in cognitive states and underlying behavioral mechanisms [4]. Recent research has proposed objective approaches. For example, team communication can serve as quantitative indicators of shared situation awareness [2], while eye-tracking metrics, such as pupil diameter and fixation dispersion, provide additional markers of cognitive effort and visual attention allocation [16]. Yet, despite these advances, a significant gap remains in methods that integrate team communication and visual attention dynamics to capture the team-level cognitive effects of MSP.

This study addresses this gap by investigating how MSP influences shared situation awareness by examining team communication data and eye-trackingâĂŞbased indicators of visual attention. Using a within-subjects design in a high-fidelity ATC simulation, we assess how MSP alters real-time interaction dynamics and attention allocation among controllers across both routine operations and an embedded abnormal-weather event. This research establishes an empirical foundation for evaluating human factors in next-generation ATC systems. The findings inform the design of adaptive interfaces and coordination protocols that preserve team situation awareness and safety as air traffic management systems evolve toward higher levels of operational integration.

2 Related Work

Research on MSP has largely examined its implications for individual controller performance. Prior studies have explored how MSP affects workload, planning efficiency, cognitive demands, and individual situation awareness, demonstrating that consolidating sectors can substantially alter controllers' cognitive operating conditions [10]. These works have established MSP as a feasible strategy under staffing constraints while documenting its potential challenges for individual cognition. However, these investigations concentrate primarily on effects at the individual level and offer limited discussion of how MSP may influence collective cognitive processes in multi-sector operations.

Shared situation awareness enables team members to maintain compatible understandings of traffic evolution, sector priorities, and emerging risks, forming the basis for effective collaborative decision-making. The experiment of Endsley et al. revealed that situation awareness was enhanced through information sharing among the pilot and the en route air traffic controller [6]. Human factors and ATC research suggests that changes in task structure, such as those introduced by MSP, can alter communication patterns and information dependencies, thereby affecting how shared situation awareness is formed and maintained during operations.

Research on methods for assessing shared situation awareness provides further context for understanding the challenges of evaluating team cognition in ATC settings. Most existing MSP studies rely on post-hoc questionnaires, which capture subjective impressions but offer limited insight into the real-time cognitive processes that shape coordination [18,21]. Hauland measured both individual and team situation awareness through eye-movement data [7]. These studies provide approaches for evaluating shared situation awareness but have rarely been used to examine how MSP affects team interaction dynamics and attentional coordination during operational tasks. Communication behavior can quantify shared and complementary SA within teams, while eye-tracking metrics such as pupil diameter and fixation dispersion offer objective indicators of cognitive effort and visual attention distribution.

3 Methodology

3.1 Participants

Three experienced (operationally trained) air traffic controllers participated in this study. Participants ranged in age from 29 to 30 (Mean = 29.33, SD=0.47, average working years=1.67), reported normal or corrected-to-normal vision, and provided informed consent prior to the study. All procedures were approved by the Institutional Review Board of Nanyang Technological University (IRB-2025-166) and conducted at the Air Traffic Management Research Institute.

3.2 Apparatus

Eye-movement data were collected using the Gazepoint GP3 HD Professional eye tracker, which records binocular gaze data at 150 Hz sampling rate suitable for ATC cognition research [15]. Experimental scenarios were implemented using the AIR-Lion Simulator, ATMRI's in-house research platform developed for high-fidelity ATC behavioural experimentation. The system supports multi-sector configurations, real-time communication logging, and synchronized data acquisition of controller actions. Figure 1 shows the MSP experimental setup, in which one PC coordinated two sectors with one TC per sector. The baseline setup is not shown, as it corresponds to a standard single-sector configuration, while the MSP condition required system-level modifications to support MSP.

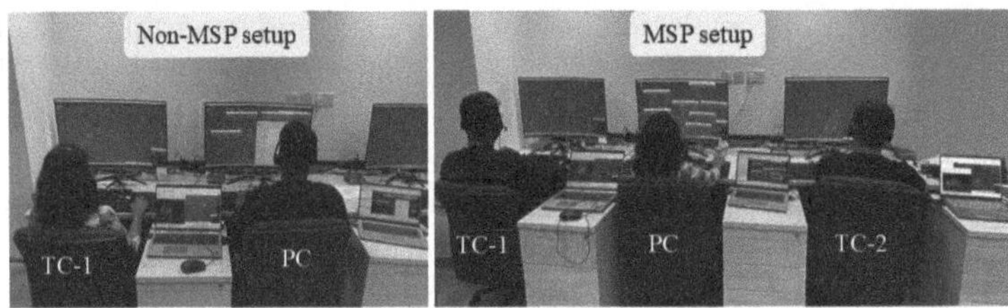

Fig. 1. Experimental setup under MSP condition. One PC was responsible for two sectors, with one TC assigned to each sector. All participants were equipped with a Gazepoint GP3 HD eye tracker and a radar-display monitor. In the baseline setup, one PC and one TC were assigned to a single sector.

3.3 Experimental Design

A within-subjects design was employed with two operational conditions: a non-MSP (baseline) setup and an MSP setup. Each participant first completed a briefing session that introduced the sector configurations, task objectives, and communication protocols, followed by a 30-minute practice scenario to gain familiarity with the interface and controls.

The experimental setup is shown in the Fig. 2. In the Baseline condition, one PC and one TC jointly managed a single sector. In the MSP condition, a single PC simultaneously supervised two adjacent sectors, each staffed with its own TC, thereby creating a contrast between single-sector and MSP configurations. The order of the two conditions was counterbalanced across participants to reduce potential learning effects. Across the experiment, three participants took

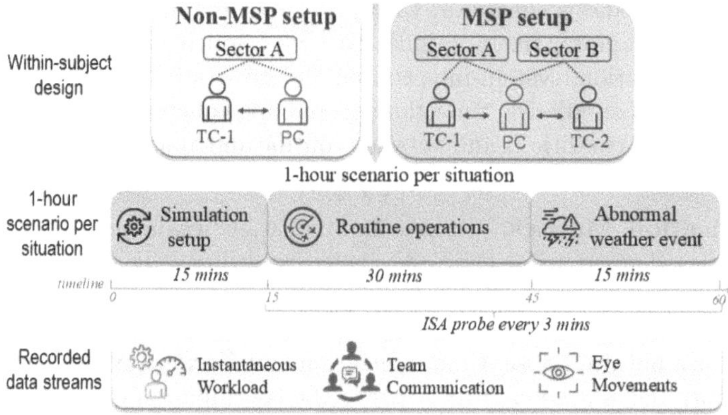

Fig. 2. Experimental setups. Note: PC, TC and ISA denote planning controller, tactical controller, and Instantaneous Self-Assessment.

turns serving as the PC, each contributing data under both the Baseline and MSP conditions. To further mitigate learning effects, each experimental session employed a different but equivalent traffic scenario: while the number of aircraft was held constant, aircraft appearance sequences, timing, and call signs varied across sessions.

Each experimental scenario lasted 60 min and consisted of three phases, including a 15-minute simulation setup, 30-minute routine traffic operations with stable traffic demand and moderate complexity, and a 15-minute abnormal-weather event introduced at a predefined time to increase complexity and coordination demands. Throughout each scenario, an Instantaneous Self-Assessment (ISA) probe appeared every 3 min [5]. Participants verbally reported their current workload levels in response to these prompts. During all runs, three synchronized data streams were recorded, including controller communication (audio and timestamps), system interaction logs, and eye-tracking data.

3.4 Data Analysis

Data Collection. To obtain behavioural indicators relevant to shared situation awareness, both controller communication and eye-movement behaviour were recorded throughout the experiment, as these modalities jointly reflect how teams maintain common ground and coordinate attention during dynamic ATC tasks [2,17]. All controller communication was audio-recorded, transcribed, and segmented into operationally meaningful utterances (e.g., traffic coordination, sector handover, weather-related information exchange), following established procedures in ATC communication analysis [11]. Eye-tracking data were collected continuously at 150 Hz and segmented into 3-minute windows aligned with the ISA probes. This windowing approach preserves fine-grained temporal variations in attentional dynamics that would otherwise be obscured by averaging over extended periods, and is consistent with prior work emphasising short-timescale sensitivity in oculomotor metrics under varying cognitive demands.

All communication, system-interaction, and eye-tracking data were synchronised using shared simulation timestamps, enabling coherent comparisons across Baseline and MSP conditions and between routine and abnormal-weather phases.

Communication Metrics. Team communication was analysed using event-based metrics derived from controller voice recordings. Following established practices in team communication and air traffic management research [1,23], a communication event was defined as a single speaker turn, bounded by a change of speaker or a natural pause. Communication metrics were extracted separately for each controller role to capture role-specific coordination characteristics.

Communication Duration. Communication duration was defined as the total accumulated time that each controller spent engaging in verbal communication during a scenario. Total communication duration has been widely used as an indicator of coordination load and communication demands in ATC and other high-reliability team settings [11]. For each experimental condition, communication duration was computed separately for each controller and then averaged across repeated experimental runs.

Clarification Requests. Clarification requests were counted whenever a controller explicitly asked for repetition, confirmation, or additional information, reflecting potential uncertainty or misalignment in shared understanding. Clarification behaviour has been commonly used as an indicator of coordination difficulty and shared situation awareness in team communication research [1].

Missed Communication. Missed communication referred to expected operational messages or coordination exchanges that were not delivered or acknowledged during the scenario. Missed or omitted communications have been identified as a key source of coordination breakdowns in air traffic control and other safety-critical domains [11].

Readback Errors. Readback errors were recorded when a controller's readback did not accurately reflect the content of the original instruction or coordination message. Readback accuracy has been extensively studied in aviation and ATC as a critical indicator of communication quality and operational safety [23].

Eye-Tracking Metrics. Eye-tracking metrics were extracted to characterize controllers' visual attention behavior from three complementary aspects: visual sampling and processing, sustained cognitive engagement, and spatial allocation of attention. The selected metrics are widely used to quantify how visual information is sampled, processed, and distributed under varying task demands [16]. All metrics were computed at the controller level and synchronized with the scenario timeline to enable comparisons across experimental conditions and task phases.

Table 1 summarizes the eye-tracking metrics and their definitions. Specifically, fixation count and average fixation duration were used to capture visual sampling frequency and focal processing depth, respectively [17]. Fixation dispersion and average scanpath length quantified the spatial distribution and extent of gaze behavior [13]. Sustained cognitive engagement was indexed using average pupil diameter, calculated as the deviation from a pre-experiment baseline, and average blink rate, defined as the number of blinks per minute [14]. All metrics were computed within consistent temporal windows aligned to the scenario timeline, allowing direct comparison between routine operations and the abnormal-weather phase.

Table 1. Eye-tracking metrics and their definitions.

Metrics	Definition
Fixation Count	The total number of fixations within a defined area or time window.
Average Fixation Duration	The mean length of time the eyes remain relatively stationary on a specific point of interest within a defined time window.
Fixation Dispersion	Root mean square of the distances from each fixation to the average fixation position.
Average Pupil Diameter	The average pupil diameter over a specified period, calculated as the deviation from a baseline measured prior to the experiment start.
Average Blink Rate	The number of blinks per minute.
Average Scanpath Length	The mean cumulative distance of gaze movements across successive fixations within a defined time window.

4 Results

4.1 Subjective Workload Assessment

Each participant completed 15 Instantaneous Self-Assessment (ISA) during the 45-minute scenario. As shown in Fig. 3, the PC in the MSP position exhibited higher ISA workload scores than the non-MSP condition in most of the measurements. For the PC, the average ISA levels for the non-MSP and MSP conditions were 3.51 and 4.18, respectively. For TC-1, the average ISA levels for the non-MSP and MSP conditions were 3.11 and 3.47, respectively. The ISA workload results for the MSP condition were higher than those for the non-MSP condition, showing that the planner controllers' workload increased when managing two sectors. In contrast, the ISA results for tactical planners showed less differences between the MSP and non-MSP conditions.

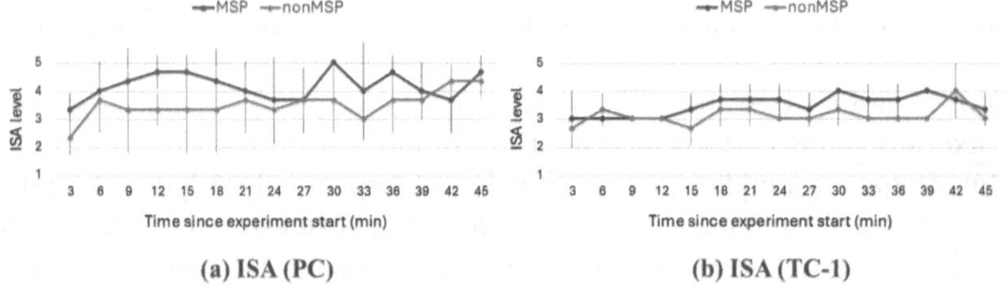

Fig. 3. Instantaneous Self-Assessment (ISA) results under MSP and non-MSP conditions. Different controller roles (PC and TC-1) are shown.

4.2 Visual Attention Dynamics Under MSP and Non-MSP

This section reports eye-tracking results comparing MSP and non-MSP conditions, focusing on differences in controllers' visual attention dynamics over time. Figure 4 presents eye movement-based measures reflecting visual sampling and processing, cognitive engagement, and visual attention allocation. In each subplot, curves represent the mean values across participants for different controller roles and conditions, with shaded bands indicating the corresponding standard deviation over time. For PCs, MSP is associated with higher fixation counts and shorter average fixation durations across time (Fig. 4a, c), indicating more frequent information sampling with reduced focal processing depth. In contrast, fixation count and fixation duration trajectories for TCs largely overlap between MSP and non-MSP (Fig. 4b, d), showing no consistent condition-related differences in visual sampling behavior.

Regarding sustained cognitive engagement, for PCs, pupil size under MSP remains smaller across the task (Fig. 4e, g), while blink rate shows a gradual increase over time, particularly in later phases (Fig. 4i), suggesting prolonged cognitive engagement accompanied by fatigue-related responses. Notably, this increase in blink rate becomes more pronounced during the final 15 min of the scenario, when an abnormal weather event was introduced, indicating elevated cognitive strain during the weather-affected phase. For TCs, both pupil size and blink rate exhibit largely comparable patterns between MSP and non-MSP throughout the scenario (Fig. 4f, h, j), including the weather-affected period, indicating limited MSP- or weather-related effects on sustained cognitive engagement at the tactical level.

As for visual attention allocation, for PCs, average scanpath length shows substantial overlap between MSP and non-MSP (Fig. 4k), whereas fixation dispersion is consistently higher under MSP (Fig. 4m), indicating less spatially concentrated gaze allocation. For TCs, MSP is similarly associated with higher fixation dispersion and average scanpath length with greater variability (Fig. 4l, n), with no clear additional modulation during the weather-affected phase. These results indicate that MSP primarily affects how visual attention is spatially distributed.

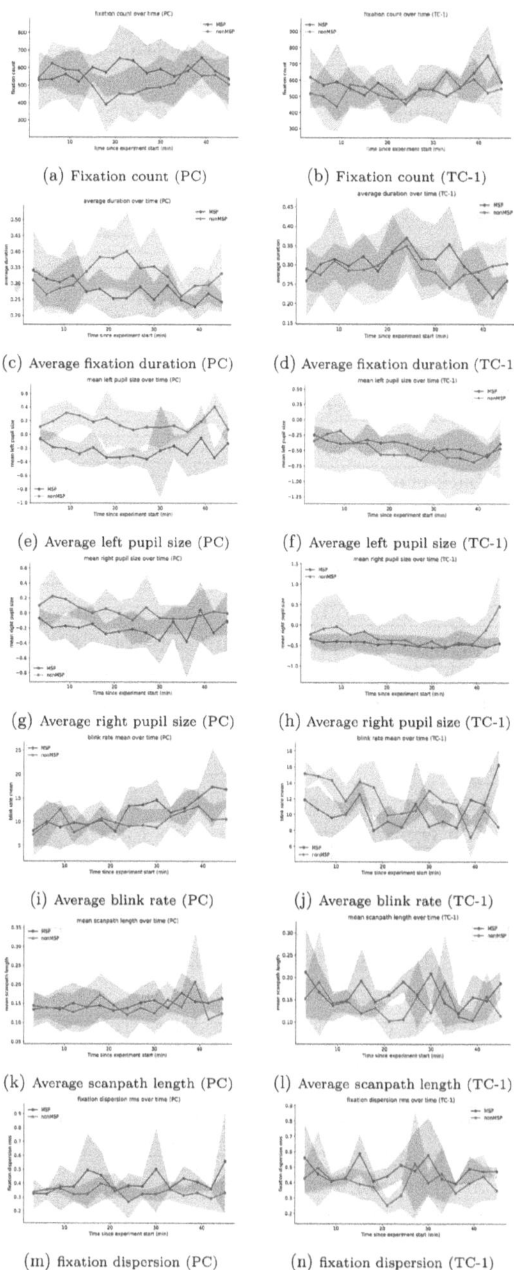

(a) Fixation count (PC) (b) Fixation count (TC-1)

(c) Average fixation duration (PC) (d) Average fixation duration (TC-1)

(e) Average left pupil size (PC) (f) Average left pupil size (TC-1)

(g) Average right pupil size (PC) (h) Average right pupil size (TC-1)

(i) Average blink rate (PC) (j) Average blink rate (TC-1)

(k) Average scanpath length (PC) (l) Average scanpath length (TC-1)

(m) fixation dispersion (PC) (n) fixation dispersion (TC-1)

Fig. 4. Eye-tracking results under MSP and non-MSP conditions. (a–n) represent different metrics and controller roles.

4.3 Team Coordination and Communication Performance

This section examines team coordination performance under the MSP and non-MSP conditions using communication-based metrics that capture coordination efficiency and communication breakdowns. Table 2 summarizes team communication characteristics under the non-MSP and MSP conditions, focusing on communication efficiency and coordination quality.

Table 2. Summary of team communication metrics under non-MSP and MSP conditions across controller roles.

Metrics	nonMSP		MSP		
	PC	TC-1	PC	TC-1	TC-2
Comm. duration (s)	339.37	519.96	883.79	316.27	189.5
Clarification request	5	5	7	2	4
Miss comm.	0	1	0	0	1
Readback error	0	0	0	0	2
Total	5	6	7	2	7

Under the non-MSP condition, communication exhibits relatively balanced patterns across roles, with comparable numbers of clarification requests and few coordination breakdowns. Communication duration is shorter for the PC and longer for the TC, reflecting the role-specific communication demands and a relatively stable distribution of shared understanding between planning and tactical functions.

In contrast, the MSP condition shows a clear redistribution of communication across team roles. The communication duration for the PC increases substantially relative to non-MSP, while the duration for individual TCs decreases, indicating that coordination becomes more centralized and sustained at the planning level across sectors. At the same time, clarification requests are unevenly distributed across roles, with higher counts observed for the PC and TC-2, whereas TC-1 exhibits fewer clarification requests. This pattern suggests more frequent alignment and verification processes under MSP, reflecting increased effort to establish and update shared situation awareness in a more complex coordination structure. Coordination breakdowns remain infrequent overall. However, under MSP, missed communications and readback errors are observed only at the TC level, while none are recorded for the PC. Therefore, these results indicate that MSP reshapes how shared situation awareness is constructed through communication, shifting coordination demands toward the planning role while maintaining overall communication reliability.

5 Conclusions

This study evaluates the effects of MSP by jointly examining workload, visual attention, and communication behaviors in controller teams. Results indicate that MSP increases PCs' workload and sustained cognitive engagement, accompanied by systematic shifts in visual attention toward more frequent sampling and broader spatial distribution, with effects becoming more evident under abnormal weather conditions. In contrast, TCs exhibit largely stable patterns, with MSP-related effects mainly reflected in spatial attention allocation. Overall, these findings indicate that MSP reshapes the mechanisms through which shared situation awareness is constructed and maintained, redistributing cognitive and coordination demands across roles and underscoring the need for attention-aware, role-sensitive support in future multi-sector ATC operations.

Several limitations should be noted. The limited availability of experienced controllers constrained the sample size, and the study focused on a single level of task complexity. Future work should examine multiple levels of task demand to assess the robustness of the findings.

Acknowledgments. This research is supported by the National Research Foundation, Singapore, and the Civil Aviation Authority of Singapore, under the Aviation Transformation Programme.

Disclosure of Interests. The authors have no competing interests to declare that are relevant to the content of this article.

References

1. Bowers, C.A., Jentsch, F., Salas, E., Braun, C.C.: Analyzing communication sequences for team training needs assessment. Hum. Factors **40**(4), 672–679 (1998)
2. Cain, A.A., Edwards, T., Schuster, D.: A quantitative measure for shared and complementary situation awareness. In: Proceedings of the Human Factors and Ergonomics Society Annual Meeting, vol. 60, pp. 1823–1827. SAGE Publications Sage CA, Los Angeles, CA (2016)
3. Cargo Forwarder: ATC staffing shortages vs growing aviation (2025). https://cargoforwarder.eu/2025/02/02/atc-staffing-shortages-vs-growing-aviation/. Accessed 22 Feb 2025
4. Dehn, D.M.: Assessing the impact of automation on the air traffic controller: the shape questionnaires. Air Traffic Control Q. **16**(2), 127–146 (2008)
5. Flumeri, D., et al.: On the use of cognitive neurometric indexes in aeronautic and air traffic management environments. In: International Workshop on Symbiotic Interaction, pp. 45–56. Springer (2015)
6. Endsley, M.R., Hansman, R.J., Farley, T.C.: Shared situation awareness in the flight deck-ATC system. IEEE Aerosp. Electron. Syst. Mag. **14**(8), 25–30 (1999)
7. Hauland, G.: Measuring individual and team situation awareness during planning tasks in training of en route air traffic control. Int. J. Aviat. Psychol. **18**(3), 290–304 (2008)
8. Herr, S., Teichmann, M., Poppe, M., Suarez, N.: The impact of multi sector planning and new working procedures on controller tasks. In: 24th Digital Avionics Systems Conference, vol. 1, pp. 3–B. IEEE (2005)
9. Hu, X., Pang, B., Feroskhan, M.: Airspace reconfiguration for urban air mobility: a spatial-temporal analysis of airspace availability within aerodrome. In: 2024 IEEE 27th International Conference on Intelligent Transportation Systems (ITSC), pp. 1296–1301. IEEE (2024)

10. Jia, Q., et al.: Space situational awareness systems: bridging traditional methods and artificial intelligence. Acta Astronaut. **228**, 321–330 (2025)
11. Kanki, B.G.: Communication and crew resource management. In: Crew resource management, pp. 103–137. Elsevier (2019)
12. Lee, P.U., Smith, N.M., Prevot, T., Homola, J.R.: Managing demand and capacity using multi-sector planning and flexible airspace: Human-in-the-loop evaluation of NextGen. Technical Report (2010)
13. Li, F., Lee, C.H., Chen, C.H., Khoo, L.P.: Hybrid data-driven vigilance model in traffic control center using eye-tracking data and context data. Adv. Eng. Inform. **42**, 100940 (2019)
14. Li, Z., Li, F.: Vigilant air traffic control: gaze-based recognition of detection failures to visual warnings. Adv. Human Factors Transp. **148**(148) (2024)
15. Li, Z., Li, F., Xu, G., Li, D.: Beyond the gaze: peripheral vision-aware visual detection failures recognition through LLM-based fixation coordinate-sensitive analysis. IEEE Trans. Intell. Transp. Syst. **99**, 1–20 (2025)
16. Li, Z., Li, R., Yuan, L., Cui, J., Li, F.: A benchmarking framework for eye-tracking-based vigilance prediction of vessel traffic controllers. Eng. Appl. Artif. Intell. **129**, 107660 (2024)
17. Mengtao, L., Fan, L., Gangyan, X., Su, H.: Leveraging eye-tracking technologies to promote aviation safety-a review of key aspects, challenges, and future perspectives. Saf. Sci. **168**, 106295 (2023)
18. Nguyen, T., Lim, C.P., Nguyen, N.D., Gordon-Brown, L., Nahavandi, S.: A review of situation awareness assessment approaches in aviation environments. IEEE Syst. J. **13**(3), 3590–3603 (2019)
19. Prevot, T., Mainini, M., Brasil, C.: Multi sector planning tools for trajectory-based operations. In: 10th AIAA Aviation Technology, Integration, and Operations (ATIO) Conference, p. 9375 (2010)
20. Svensson, Å., Ohlander, U., Lundberg, J.: Design implications for teamwork in ATC. Cogn. Technol. Work **22**(2), 409–426 (2020)
21. Taylor, R.M.: Situational Awareness Rating Technique (SART): the development of a tool for aircrew systems design. In: Situational awareness, pp. 111–128. Routledge (2017)
22. Williams, A., Rodgers, M.D., Mondoloni, S., Liang, D.: Improving ATC efficiency through an implementation of a multi sector planner position. In: Proceedings of the 7th USA/Europe Air Traffic Management Research and Development Seminar, pp. 2–5. Barcelona, Spain (2007)
23. Zhang, Y., Li, F., Man, S.S., Han, S.: Enhancing readback verification in ATCOs-pilot communication using audio-visual interaction: insights from fNIRS and eye-tracking. Int. J. Hum. Comput. Interact. 1–19 (2025). https://doi.org/10.1080/10447318.2025.2564270

The Investigation of the Captain's Neurophysiological Activation Patterns as Situational Awareness Loss During Single-Pilot Operations Through EEG

Qinbiao Li[1(✉)], Cho Yin Yiu[1,2], Xin Yuan[1], and Kam K. H. Ng[1]

[1] Human Factors and Ergonomics Laboratory, Department of Aeronautical and Aviation Engineering, The Hong Kong Polytechnic University, Hung Hom, Hong Kong SAR, China
qinbiao-leo.li@polyu.edu.hk

[2] Safety and Accident Investigation Centre, Cranfield University, Cranfield, Bedfordshire, UK

Abstract. Advances in cockpit automation have enabled the concept of single-pilot operations (SPO), proposed to alleviate pilot scarcity and reduce crew expenses while sustaining operational capacity. A major barrier to SPO adoption is maintaining situational awareness (SA), the cognitive ability to perceive, comprehend, and anticipate flight conditions, i.e., a leading factor in aviation incidents and is exacerbated in SPO due to the lack of a first-officer's support. This study aimed to identify neurophysiological patterns of SA loss during SPO using EEG. Twenty licensed airline pilots participated in a high-fidelity SPO simulation encompassing whole flight phases with embedded emergencies designed to induce SA fluctuations. Brain activity was recorded via a 32-channel EEG, while situational awareness was measured in real time using the validated Situational Present Assessment Method (SPAM). Twenty-three SPAM probes were administered at specific moments to minimize task interference. SPAM scores were categorized into high SA and low SA groups to label EEG data using unsupervised learning based on the reaction time. After EEG preprocessing and analysis, compared to high SA states, low SA was associated with significant PSD reductions in θ and α bands across frontal, parietal, temporal, and occipital lobes. Reductions in β and γ bands were confined to temporal and occipital regions. These findings provide objective, brain-based indicators of SA loss in SPO, addressing limitations of subjective measures and supporting SPO safety validation. The study integrated high-fidelity simulation, real-time EEG, and validated SA probing offers a replicable framework for future cognitive state research in complex aviation environments.

Keywords: Single-pilot operation · EEG · situational awareness · power spectrum density

1 Introduction

The ever-increasing pilot shortage and growing operating crew expenses are two of the civil aviation industry's significant obstacles to the long-term growth of air travel [1, 2]. With the ever-developing of cockpit automation and avionics technologies and organized

W. -C. Li and A. Plioutsias (Eds.): HCII 2026, LNAI 16708, pp. 177–187, 2026.
https://doi.org/10.1007/978-3-032-29459-3_13

aviation procedure, the concept of single-pilot operations (SPO) has been put up and promoted as a solution to these problems while upholding operating capacity and safety standards [3, 4]. SPO aims to decrease the flight crew from two to one, by leveraging sophisticated automated systems to complete functions that were traditionally completed by the first officer, thereby optimizing human resource allocation and cutting crew-related expenses significantly. As a transformative operational mode, SPO has attracted extensive attention from aviation authorities, aircraft manufacturers, and airlines, yet unresolved safety concerns hinder its commercialized implementation [5].

A key factor in determining flight safety is Situational Awareness (SA), which is described as the cognitive capacity to recognize important components in the operational environment, understand their significance, and predict future situations [6]. SA loss (or low SA) is a major contributing cause to aircraft accidents, accounting for a significant percentage of human-error-related events, which will be, definitely, magnificent in SPO [3]. Specifically, the lack of the first officer in SPO results in the crew members' mutual monitoring, cross-validation, and workload sharing being eliminated, increasing the cognitive load and task pressure. Under this context, it exacerbates the difficulty of maintaining SA, making SA loss or lower SA a primary barrier to the safe implementation of SPO. To the best of our knowledge, the single captain's SA investigation, recognition and comprehension in SPO domain are severely lacking.

Existing approaches for SA assessment mainly rely on subjective or task-target objective tools, such as the Situation Awareness Rating Technique (SART) [7] and the Situational Present Assessment Method (SPAM) [8]. While these methods have been validated for specific scenarios, they suffer from inherent limitations. Specifically, subjective assessment is susceptible to individual perception biases, memory decay, and response delays, and cannot provide real-time, objective insights into the dynamic changes of SA during flight operations, while task-target objective tool has the nature of interpreting operations, and case-by-case (weak generalization). Fortunately, with the advancement of neuro-ergonomics technology, neurophysiological measurement techniques, particularly EEG, offer a promising solution for objective SA monitoring [9]. EEG can capture real-time brain activity with high temporal resolution, enabling the identification of neurophysiological correlations of cognitive states involving SA status, which are not easily detectable by subjective and task-target objective measures.

Despite the potential of EEG in cognitive state assessment, few studies relating to EEG-based SA research in aviation, even when conducted in simulated laboratory environments, have specifically targeted SA performance in SPO scenarios or explored how captain's cognitive and neurophysiological patterns adapt when transitioning from DPO to SPO across different SA levels. As a result, the investigation into SA-related neurophysiological correlations unique to SA, and the comparison analysis on captain's SA-related brain activity patterns between DPO and DPO, specifically, how the removal of crew coordination, workload redistribution, and sole decision-making in SPO alter their neurophysiological responses underlying SA. This gap hinders a comprehensive understanding of SPO's cognitive impacts on captains and limits the development of targeted safety countermeasures for SPO implementation, which is urgent to be addressed and revealed.

To address the above-mentioned unrevealed problem, the present study aims to identify neurophysiological activation patterns associated with SA loss or lower SA in SPO utilizing EEG, while laying a foundation for subsequent DPO-SPO comparative analyses from neuro perspective. We conducted high-fidelity SPO simulations covering full flight phases, with embedded emergency scenarios to induce different levels of task loads and collected real-time EEG data from licensed airline captains. Combined with the validated SPAM for real-time SA measurement, this study intends to explore differences in EEG patterns between high and low SA states specifically in SPO, to identify brain wave bands and cortical regions correlated with SPO-specific SA loss, and to establish a baseline of captains' SA-related brain activity in SPO through the comparisons with their performance in DPO. The findings will fill the void of SPO-focused SA neurophysiological research and offer valuable insights into investigating DPO-SPO cognitive transitions in future civil aviation environments.

2 Methodology

2.1 Experiment Protocol

Since no dedicated cockpit for civil single-pilot operations current exists, the simulated experiment was conducted to simulate both dual-pilot operations and single-pilot operations scenarios using a fix-based Airbus 320 simulator (Fig. 1) configured for dual pilots. The experiment was carried out in the *Human Factors and Ergonomics Laboratory* at the *Hong Kong Polytechnic University*. Pseudo-support for onboard automation systems and ground stations was provided via off-board auxiliary support and configurations (e.g., software central control). Additionally, the corresponding *"Lockhead Marin Prepar 3D v5"* software and *"Instructor Operating Station"* were used to configure and present predefined flight scenarios through a 220-degree wide-angle display, ensuring an immersive flight operation experience.

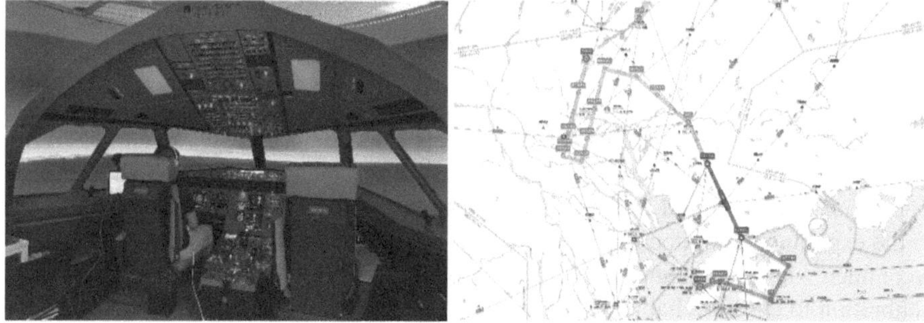

Fig. 1. The fix-based Airbus 320 simulator (Left) and flight route (Right) for flight simulation.

The simulated flight route departed from Hong Kong International Airport (ICAO code: VHHH), using Runway 07R, and arrived at Guangzhou Baiyun Airport (ICAO code: ZGGG), using Runway 02L, with an approximate flight duration of 50 min for an

Airbus 320 (Fig. 1). The simulated flight was assigned the callsign "HX123". A pseudo air traffic control officer (ATCO) was deployed to provide instructions to HX 123 (among other simulated flights) throughout all flight phases, involving taxiing from gate S45 to Runway 07R, take-off, departure, climb, cruise at 21,700 feet, descend, approach, and landing. Normal weather conditions were set for the simulation: general wind conditions were 020°/06 knots, broken clouds were incorporated between 16,500 and 21,500 feet, and visibility was 50,000 feet. To further increase the complexity of flight tasks, four in-flight events were inserted and triggered at different time points, which participants were required to resolve. These events included: (1) LANDING GEAR NOT UPLOCKED, (2) AIR DATA REFERENCE and AUTOPILOT FAILURE, (3) DUAL-ENGINE FLAME OUT, and (4) SINGLE-ENGINE FIRE. All events could be resolved in accordance with the guidance provided by the Electronic Centralized Aircraft Monitor (ECAM) procedures. The interval between each pair of events was sufficient for participants to calm down, ensuring no interference between consecutive events.

Participants were recruited in pairs with comparable flying experience, forming groups to complete the experiment collaboratively. In each session, the designated captain was responsible for pilot flying (PF) tasks, while the first officer undertook pilot monitoring (PM) duties. As noted earlier, off-side support was provided to simulate the remote collaboration mechanisms envisioned for future SPO. Each group completed four experimental sessions, each consisting of a one-way flight from VHHH to ZGGG, i.e., two sessions under SPO and the other two under dual-pilot operations (DPO), as detailed in Table 1.

Table 1. The task allocation of two participants in group x.

Group *x*	1st Participant	2nd Participant	Scenario
1st session	Captain		SPO
2nd session	Captain	First officer	DPO
3rd session	First officer	Captain	DPO
4th session		Captain	SPO

Prior to the experiment, all participants received a comprehensive briefing covering experimental requirements, mission objectives, flight plans, and simulated scenarios. They were then required to sign an informed consent form if they agreed to adhere to the experimental protocols. Subsequently, participants assigned to the captain's role were fitted with physiological measurement apparatus (Sect. 2.3) and completed system calibration to ensure reliable collection of physiological signals (i.e., EEG data). During each session, the captain was instructed to operate the aircraft in accordance with the flight plan and ATCO instructions, while completing additional assessment tasks at specified intervals (Sect. 2.4) to directly evaluate SA. A 15-min rest interval was allocated between consecutive sessions to mitigate mental drowsiness and fatigue, thereby maintaining consistent performance across all trials.

2.2 Participants

Twenty male pilots employed by Hong Kong-based airlines were recruited for the simulated flight experiment. Their average age was 35.6 ± 5.0 years, and their designated position, total flying hours, and qualified aircraft type are detailed in Table 2. Upon successful completion of the experiment, participants received a HK $2,000 supermarket vouchers as a token of gratitude for their efforts and time. The experiment was conducted in compliance with the ethical standards laid down in the 1975 Helsinki Declaration, and ethical approval was granted by the Institutional Review Board of The *Hong Kong Polytechnic University (No.: HSEARS20210318002).*

Table 2. Detailed information about the recruited pilots.

Position held	Age (years)*	Flying hours (hours)*	Aircraft types
Captain (N = 4)	41.75 ± 1.71	9625 ± 2286.74	Airbus 319/320/321330/350/Boeing 737
First officer (N = 12)	36 ± 2.95	4850 ± 833.94	Airbus 300/320/330/350
Second officer (N = 4)	25 ± 2.83	775 ± 689.81	Airbus 320/330/350/Boeing 777

"N' is the number of subjects
'' represents the mean ± standard deviation*

2.3 Apparatus

To record participants' neurophysiological activity throughout the flight experiment, a wireless saline-based EEG headset (EMOTIV Flex) was utilized to capture the captain's neurophysiological signals. The EMOTIV Flex features 32 saline electrodes, which are placed over the frontal (FRO), parietal (PAR), left temporal (LTEM), right temporal (RTEM), and occipital (OCC) lobes in accordance with the international 10-10 electrode placement system [10, 11]. EMOTIV Pro software was employed to provide auxiliary support and visually record cerebral activity in real time. Prior to the experiment, the EEG device was calibrated via its built-in calibration algorithms to ensure a good collection quality. Once calibration was completed and the experiment commenced, continuous EEG recording was initiated for the entire duration of each session.

2.4 Secondary Tasks for Direct SA Measurement

Although EEG was used to record neurophysiological data throughout the experiment, we still cannot determine which components of the EEG signals correspond to low SA and which related to high SA, due to the non-representational nature of raw EEG signals before label engineering, where labels will be derived from direct SA measurement outputs (will be used as proxy to first associate EEG data with corresponding SA states, so-called labelling). This limitation underscores the necessity of integrating real-time

SA assessments (e.g., SPAM probes, no need to freeze simulation) with EEG data to establish meaningful correlations between neural activity and SA states.

Secondary tasks were designed as a direct measurement tool to assess the captain's SA, based on the SPAM concept. Specifically, the captains were asked questions delivered via a tablet at predefined moments, and they were required to answer the designated questions as promptly as possible by relying on their memory or identifying relevant cues from the cockpit environments. A total of 23 secondary tasks (i.e., SA probes) were administered per session, triggered at distinct time points to minimize interference with primary flight tasks. Each SA probe consisted of a four-option multiple-choice question, with only one correct answer corresponding to the real-time flight context. An example is provided below:

***Q:** Which flight-stage will you enter after GG423?*
***A.** Downwind (correct answer)* ***B.** Base*
***C.** Final* ***D.** I don't know.*

The secondary tasks were presented to the captains via 'E-prime 3.0' software and a Microsoft Surface Pro touchable tablet. An audio prompt was issued when a task appeared, and the captain was instructed to respond as promptly as possible. The SA probe was displayed immediately following the audio prompt, and for each task, both response accuracy and reaction time were recorded. Two sets of SA probes with comparable difficulty were developed for SPO and DPO scenarios, respectively, to eliminate cross-scenario interference. Furthermore, EEG data streams were simultaneously marked each time a secondary task was triggered, enabling precise alignment between neural activity and SA assessment moments.

2.5 Data Analysis

Not all data recorded data throughout the experiment could be utilized, as SA states are dynamic. Only data aligned with the secondary tasks (SA probes) were considered valid, as these correlated directly with the measured SA. Consequently, the neurophysiological data (EEG) were extracted using the synchronous markers associated with the secondary tasks, resulting in a total of 920 segments, calculated as $20 subjects * 2 scenarios (SPO and DPO) * 23 secondary tasks$ per scenario. These segments were first labelled using SA metrics obtained from the secondary tasks. Based on our previous study, a leading time of up to 20 s is required for pilots to develop SA and comprehend cockpit situations. Therefore, the final neurophysiological dataset incorporated this 20-s lead time, which facilitated the analysis of fluctuations in neurophysiological patterns associated with SA changes.

SA Label Engineering Using Direct SA Measurement. The core assumption was that a captain who responded to questions correctly and more quickly exhibited a higher SA level. Specifically, the reaction time (from probe presentation to response submission) was used as the primary metric for SA assessment, with shorter reaction times indicating higher SA. All 920 data segments underwent labelling following preprocessing of SPAM probe outputs, conducted in the following steps: First, probes with no response were excluded, resulting in the removal of nine tasks (eight from SPO sessions). Segments corresponding to incorrect answer were directly categorized as low SA. Subsequently, to counteract individual differences in reaction time among participants, the absolute deviation (*Td*) of the normalized individual response variability, ensuring SA classification was not biased by inherent differences in reaction speed. Finally, K-means clustering was employed to group the pre-processed segments (since Td is continuous data) into two clusters (high SA and low SA) based on similarity theory. This unsupervised learning approach objectively partitioned the data using the normalized *Td* values, avoiding subjective bias in SA level delineation and enabling reliable labelling of EEG segments for subsequent neurophysiological pattern analysis.

EEG Data Pre-processing and Feature Extraction. First, artefacts were removed from the EEG signals to improve the signal-to-noise ratio (SNR). EEG data segments were extracted using synchronous markers, covering the 20-s lead time (from 20 s before marker onset to marker onset). The preprocessing pipeline, as established in our previous study [12], was applied to the raw time-series voltage signals, following these steps: (1) After selecting 32 channels, confirming channel locations, and applying a 1–45 Hz band-pass filter, each extracted EEG segment was divided into 2-s epochs; (2) Eye movement-induced artefacts were detected via Independent Component Analysis (ICA) and rejected. Eye movements exhibit stereotyped scalp topographies that ICA can effectively isolate. Figure 2 illustrates the typical power spectrum, scalp topographies, and time courses of eye blink and saccade components, with high/low power concentrated near the orbital regions; (3) For each channel, EEG epochs containing extreme values exceeding ±75 μV were replaced with the mean of adjacent normal epochs (within the activation threshold) to automatically eliminate other artefacts; (4) All pre-processed EEG data were re-referenced to the whole-brain average.

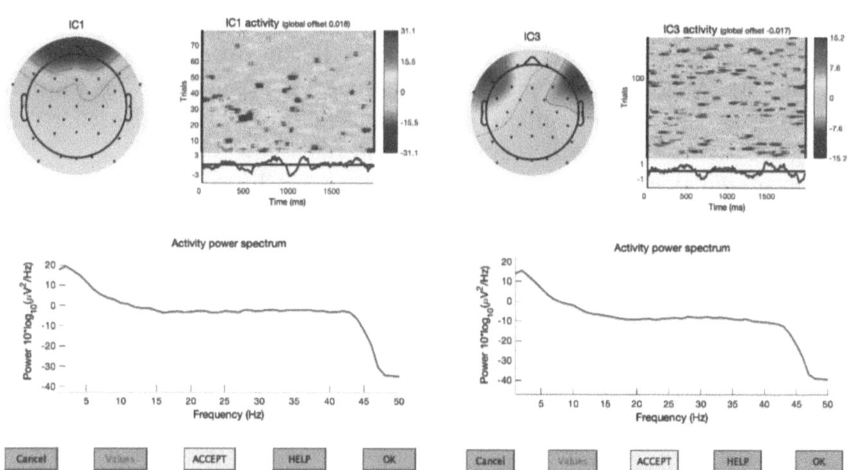

Fig. 2. The typical scalp topographies (upper left), activity power spectrum (upper right), and time course (below)for eye blink (Left) and eye glance (Right).

Power Spectral Density (PSD), a frequency-domain indicator, was extracted from the preprocessed EEG data. PSD values for the θ (4–8 Hz), α (8–12 Hz), β (13–30 Hz), and γ (30–45 Hz) bands across the FRO, PAR, LTEM, RTEM, and OCC regions were calculated using Fast Fourier Transform (FFT), as described in our previous study. Fluctuations in these bands are closely associated with cognitive processes and attentional states: for instance, increased β-band activity correlates with higher task complexity and logical reasoning. Given the highly similar signal characteristics of channels within the same brain region, channel signals were averaged per region (see [13] for detailed procedures). Prior to regional averaging, outliers in each channel's extracted features were replaced with the median using the Interquartile Range (IQR) method.

Neurophysiological Pattern Comparison Using Statistical Analysis. Based on the extracted PSD indicators from SPO and DPO samples (stratified by high and low SA), statistical methods were utilized to investigate whether significant increases or decreases in PSD indicators existed across three comparison groups: (1) high vs. low SA in SPO; (2) high SA in SPO vs. high SA in DPO; (3) low SA in SPO vs. low SA in DPO.

Prior to hypothesis testing, *IBM SPSS Statistic 23* software was used, and the Shapiro-Wilk test was employed to verify the normality of PSD data distributions (p-value > 0.05 means normality). For data that met the normality assumption, independent samples t-tests were used for between-group comparisons; for non-normally distributed data, Mann-Whitney U tests were applied. A p-value < 0.05 was considered statistically significant for all tests.

3 Results and Discussion

3.1 Labelling Results

Following pre-processing of SPAM probes, including the exclusion of segments with no responses or incorrect answers, a total of 758 valid samples were retrained across all experimental sessions, which were used for subsequent K-means clustering. Clustering was performed based on the within-subject absolute deviations (*Td*) of reaction times, yielding 658 segments categorized as high SA and 100 as low SA.

Manual validation was conducted to confirm the reliability of the K-means outputs, involving an examination of participants' response consistency and confidence, as well as comparative analysis of *Td* values across the clustered segments. When incorporating the segments with incorrect answers (previously labeled directly as low SA), the final SA classification resulted in 658 high SA segments and 253 low SA segments. Breaking down the final classification by operational scenario: there were 290 high SA samples and 162 low SA samples in SPO, while DPO yielded 368 high SA samples and 91 low SA samples. This scene-specific distribution aligns with the operational logic that dual-pilot support in DPO helps maintain higher SA levels, as reflected by the larger proportion of high SA samples compared to SPO. This distribution also reflects the relative rarity of low SA states in the simulated flight scenarios, which aligns with the operational reality that experienced pilots maintain effective SA under normal and moderately challenging conditions.

3.2 Neuropsychological Pattern Fluctuations

The Shapiro-Wilk test revealed that all extracted PSD features were non-normally distributed across both SPO and DPO sessions, and at both high and low SA levels. Consequently, the Mann-Whitney U test was employed to examine significant differences in PSD values between SPO and DPO, as well as between high and low SA states, across different EEG frequency bands, aimed at revealing fluctuations in neurophysiological patterns associated with SA and operational scenarios.

In the SPO context, comparisons between high and low SA states showed a significant increase in θ (4–8 Hz) and α (8–12 Hz) band power across all brain regions (all $p < 0.001$) in high SA relative to low SA. For the β (13–30 Hz) and γ (30–45 Hz) bands, significant increases in power were only observed in the LTEM, RTEM, and OCC lobes in high SA compared to low SA (all $p < 0.001$). The observed increases in θ and α band power in high SA relative to low SA within SPO align with well-established EEG band functions. θ band activity is closely linked to sustained attention, working memory integration, and cognitive control, critical processes for maintaining high SA in SPO, where the captain must independently perceive, comprehend, and anticipate flight conditions without first-officer support. α band enhancements, typically associated with focused attention and reduced distractibility, reflect the captain's ability to filter irrelevant cockpit stimuli and prioritize task-relevant information when SA is high. The region-specific increases in β and γ bands (temporal and occipital lobes) further support this interpretation: temporal lobes are involved in auditory information processing (e.g., ATCO instructions, ECAM alerts) and memory retrieval, while occipital lobes mediate visual information processing (e.g., cockpit displays, flight instruments). Together, these findings indicate that high SA in SPO is characterized by enhanced neural activity related to multi-sensory integration and focused attention, whereas low SA is associated with reduced engagement of these cognitive processes.

When comparing high SA states between SPO and DPO, PSD values for all EEG bands were higher in SPO than in DPO. Exceptions included non-significant increases in β and γ band power in the RTEM lobe ($p = 0.382$ and $p = 0.270$, , respectively) and β band power in the LTEM lobe ($p = 0.134$). Strongly significant increases (all $p < 0.001$) were observed in most brain regions, with moderately significant increases in β band power in the PAR lobe ($p = 0.014$) and LTEM lobe ($p = 0.005$), and γ band power in the PAR ($p = 0.018$). In contrast, an opposite pattern was observed when comparing low SA states between SPO and DPO: PSD values for all EEG bands were higher in DPO than in SPO. Specifically, significantly decreased power in SPO (relative to DPO) was observed for: θ band in the LTEM lobe ($p = 0.006$); α band in the FRO ($p = 0.002$), PAR ($p < 0.001$), LTEM ($p < 0.001$), and RTEM ($p = 0.001$) lobes; β band in the FRO ($p < 0.001$), LTEM ($p < 0.001$), RTEM ($p = 0.002$), and OCC ($p < 0.001$) lobes; and γ band in the FRO ($p < 0.001$), LTEM ($p < 0.001$), RTEM ($p = 0.001$), and OCC ($p < 0.001$) lobes.

The higher PSD values across most bands in high SA-SPO compared to high SA-DPO reflect the increased cognitive demand of maintaining SA in SPO. Even when SA is high, the absence of a first officer's support requires the captain to allocate more neural resources to attentional control, multi-sensory integration, and decision-making processes supported by β (alertness, task engagement) and γ (high-level cognitive integration) bands and modulated by θ and α bands (attention regulation). The non-significant increases in temporal lobe β / γ bands may reflect that auditory/visual information processing (e.g., monitoring ATCO instructions) is similarly demanding in high SA states across both scenarios, as these tasks are core to pilot responsibilities regardless of crew configuration.

The reversed pattern in low SA states (higher PSD in DPO than SPO) highlights the protective role of dual-pilot support in mitigating cognitive decline during SA loss. In DPO, even when SA is low, the first officer's monitoring and workload sharing provide a cognitive buffer, allowing the captain to maintain residual neural engagement in attention and information processing (evidenced by higher $\theta/\alpha/\beta/\gamma$ power). In contrast, SPO eliminates this buffer, leading to a steeper decline in neural activity related to SA when cognitive resources are depleted, consistent with the higher proportion of low SA samples in SPO (162 vs. 91 in DPO). The widespread reduction in PSD across frontal, temporal, parietal, and occipital lobes in low SA-SPO indicates a systemic decrease in cognitive engagement, which may contribute to the increased risk of flight errors in single-pilot configurations. Collectively, these cross-scenario comparisons confirm that SPO alters the neurophysiological correlations of SA, placing greater cognitive demands on captains even at high SA, and exacerbating cognitive decline when SA is lost.

4 Conclusion

This study investigated neurophysiological patterns associated with situational awareness (SA) in single-pilot operations (SPO) and dual-pilot operations (DPO) using EEG. Through high-fidelity simulation and K-means clustering of SA probe data, we identified distinct power spectral density (PSD) fluctuations across EEG frequency bands, with a specific focus on differences between high and low SA within SPO. Specifically, in SPO, high SA was characterized by significantly higher PSD values in θ and α bands across all brain regions, as well as increased β and γ band power in temporal and occipital lobes, compared θ to low SA. Cross-scenario comparisons further showed that maintaining high SA in SPO requires greater neural resource allocation than in DPO, while SPO exacerbates cognitive decline during SA loss (evidenced by lower PSD across most bands) compared to DPO, where dual-pilot support provides a protective cognitive buffer. These findings provide objective neurophysiological indicators for SA assessment in SPO, address the research gap of comparing captains' SA-related neural patterns between SPO and DPO, and offer practical insights for the safety validation and optimization of future single-pilot operational systems. Limitations include the single-aircraft simulator setting and male-only participants, which may limit the generalizability to broader aviation contexts.

Acknowledgments. The research is supported by the Department of Aeronautical and Aviation Engineering, The Hong Kong Polytechnic University, Hong Kong SAR. We also extend our gratitude to the Research Committee and the Department of Aeronautical and Aviation Engineering, The Hong Kong Polytechnic University, for support of the project (BDWV and ZGV4). This study has been granted human ethics approval from the PolyU Institutional Review Board of The Hong Kong Polytechnic University (IRB Reference Number: HSEARS20210318002).

Disclosure of Interests. The authors have no competing interests to declare that are relevant to the content of this article.

References

1. Geoff, M., Jeffrey, G.: After COVID-19, aviation faces a pilot shortage. Insights (2023). https://www.oliverwyman.com/our-expertise/insights/2021/mar/after-covid-19-aviation-faces-a-pilot-shortage.html
2. Karina, M.: Pilot shortage in 2023: Causes, impacted regions, and opportunities for aspiring pilots. Flight Training Blog 2023 2023/06/05. https://baatraining.com/blog/pilot-shortage-in-2023-causes-impacted-regions-and-opportunities-for-aspiring-pilots/
3. Liu, J., et al.: Cognitive pilot-aircraft interface for single-pilot operations. Knowl. Based Syst. **112**, 37–53 (2016)
4. Myers, P.L., Starr, A.W.: Single pilot operations in commercial cockpits: background, challenges, and options. J. Intell. Rob. Syst. **102**(1), 19 (2021)
5. Li, Q., et al.: Single-pilot operations in commercial flight: effects on neural activity and visual behaviour under abnormalities and emergencies. Chin. J. Aeronaut. **37**(8), 277–292 (2024)
6. Endsley, M.R.: Measurement of situation awareness in dynamic systems. Hum. Factors **37**(1), 65–84 (1995)
7. Valerie Jane, G.: Measures of situational awareness, in human performance and situation awareness measures, pp. 135–174 (2019)
8. Endsley, M.R.: A systematic review and meta-analysis of direct objective measures of situation awareness: a comparison of SAGAT and SPAM. Hum. Factors **63**(1), 124–150 (2019)
9. Kästle, J.L., et al.: Correlation between situational awareness and EEG signals. Neurocomputing **432**, 70–79 (2021)
10. Li, Q., et al.: Using EEG and eye-tracking as indicators to investigate situation awareness variation during flight monitoring in air traffic control system. J. Navigation, 1–22 (2025)
11. Yiu, C.Y., et al.: Keeping pilots in the loop: an explainable spatiotemporal EEG-driven deep learning framework for adaptive automation in cruising flight phase. IEEE Trans. Intell. Transport. Syst., 1–14 (2025)
12. Li, Q., et al.: Recognising situation awareness associated with different workloads using EEG and eye-tracking features in air traffic control tasks. Knowl.-Based Syst. **260**, 110179 (2023)
13. Li, Q., et al.: Securing air transportation safety through identifying pilot's risky VFR flying behaviours: an EEG-based neurophysiological modelling using machine learning algorithms. Reliab. Eng. Syst. Saf. **238**, 109449 (2023)

Pilot Debriefing with Immersive Retrospection for Post-flight Analysis and Cockpit Interface Design

Xue Ying Liu[1(✉)], Tomás Dorta[1], and Philippe Doyon-Poulin[2]

[1] Hybridlab, Université de Montréal, Montreal, Canada
{xue.ying.liu,tomas.dorta}@umontreal.com
[2] Polytechnique Montréal, Montreal, Canada
philippe.doyon-poulin@polymtl.ca

Abstract. During the design process, pilot debriefing after a flight helps identify cockpit usability issues, but rarely captures unspoken reflections. This exploratory study investigates whether immersive retrospection can stimulate pilots' memory and enrich post-flight analysis. Six certified pilots completed a stressful simulated flight and participated in debriefing sessions using either an immersive projection (n = 3) or a flat screen (n = 3). Results indicate that immersive retrospection appears to enhance richer non-verbal explanations and improve recall of interactions, ultimately leading to deeper understanding and more precise design recommendations. These findings suggest that immersive retrospection is a promising method for post-flight analysis and cockpit interface design.

Keywords: Immersive Retrospection · Debriefing · UX · HCI · Cockpit Design

1 Introduction

In the cockpit, pilots interact with numerous onboard interfaces. The complexity of tasks and systems can sometimes lead to interaction problems. To understand their causes and improve interface design, post-flight debriefing sessions, also referred to as retrospective sessions are generally conducted. These sessions allow pilots to verbalize their actions and identify the causes of the problems encountered, within a feedback-oriented framework [26].

User feedback constitutes a crucial stage in the design process [35]. Observing actual use and placing users in realistic situations make it possible to confront design intentions with real-world experience. However, users often find it difficult to precisely articulate the sources of their problems, as certain thoughts or reactions remain implicit. These unexpressed reflections can be elicited through retrospective methods supported by visual aids [13, 31].

Virtual reality (VR) enables researchers to immerse users in the task context during retrospection by means of immersive projections. This approach allowed Dorta et al. [13] to access the concealed cognition of designers. One of the methods employed

W. -C. Li and A. Plioutsias (Eds.): HCII 2026, LNAI 16708, pp. 188–203, 2026.
https://doi.org/10.1007/978-3-032-29459-3_14

was immersive retrospective interviewing, which helped participants relive the activity, recall their actions more accurately, and express previously hidden cognitive elements. Social VR, implemented without head-mounted displays (using systems such as Hyve-3D [14] or CAVE environments with shutter glasses [7]), provides a more natural shared experience and facilitates direct communication between participants and researchers.

The objective of this paper is to identify and understand pilots' unexpressed thoughts during interactions with a flight simulator interface under stressful conditions. To this end, we employed immersive retrospection in a headset free immersive display (Hyve-3D) and compared it with a non-immersive display (flat screen). These sessions, recorded in 360° video, allowed pilots to relive their activity and analyze their interactions in context. This exploratory study aims to determine whether immersion enhances pilots' ability to recall and explain the interaction problems encountered, in order to formulate design recommendations. While the simulated flight scenario resembles situations commonly used in pilot training, the objective of this study is not to evaluate training effectiveness, but to support a design-oriented analysis of cockpit interfaces through immersive retrospective debriefing.

2 Issues in Retrospection

According to Deppermann [11], retrospection is an interactive process that makes it possible to revisit past actions in order to clarify their meaning within an interactional sequence. It relies on linguistic practices such as repetition, reformulation, and correction, which help identify key moments marked by errors, misunderstandings, or emotional reactions (stress, hesitation, etc.). By analyzing these moments, retrospection contributes to the maintenance of intersubjectivity, understood as a level of shared understanding considered sufficient to allow the action to continue. Acting in accordance with the context therefore implies retrospection, namely taking previous events in the interaction into account [11]. Although retrospection helps clarify misunderstandings and restore intersubjectivity, it remains highly dependent on the immediate context, which may limit its effectiveness when dealing with older or implicit events. Moreover, as the interaction progresses, participants are often encouraged to integrate markers of understanding implicitly in order not to slow down the action. While effective for pinpointing critical moments and understanding decision-making, retrospection demands heightened vigilance to avoid overlooking crucial information in situations requiring precision.

2.1 Existing Techniques for Retrospection

The *think-aloud* method is based on participants verbalizing their thoughts while performing a task. Frequently used in usability testing, it makes it possible to capture conscious cognitive processes in real time [22]. When combined with video recordings, it offers a dual perspective, namely verbalizations and physical interactions with the system, which makes it a valuable tool for designing user-centered interfaces. Vanden Haak et al. [33] confirm the richness of the data obtained, which is particularly well suited to complex or cognitively demanding environments. This method reveals usability issues, specific difficulties encountered, the information mobilized, and action strategies. However, it also presents limitations. First, verbalization may interfere with task execution, especially in cognitively demanding contexts. In complex tasks such as piloting, it can lead to cognitive overload that may affect performance [15]. Second, it is limited to the contents of working memory, thereby excluding implicit or automatic processes [16]. These processes can nevertheless be partially explored through retrospective interviews.

Karapanos et al. [23] propose the iScale tool, a retrospective method structured through questionnaires that enables the reconstruction of user experience by means of temporal curves. This approach facilitates the identification of critical events and allows large-scale longitudinal analysis. However, it remains sensitive to memory biases and tends to favor salient events at the expense of contextual details. Hansen [20] uses video combined with eye-tracking recordings to analyze interactions in computer-based tasks. This method allows participants to comment on their actions while viewing their visual fixations, which facilitates the identification of strategies and critical issues. Video provides precise temporal cues, thereby limiting memory biases. However, some fixations may be involuntary. Huang & Stolterman [21] introduce temporal retrospection through visual tools such as UXCurve, which allow events to be marked over time and their perceived impact to be evaluated. This method supports a structured reconstruction of experiences, although it is also subject to memory biases and variability in temporal reference points.

Boubée [5] proposes an approach based on self-confrontation with a video recording, in which participants comment on their actions while watching themselves. This process confronts participants with their own perceptions and promotes in-depth reflection [28]. Visual support facilitates recall and the expression of elements that remained implicit during the activity. Boubée [5] emphasizes that participants rely heavily on images to verbalize their reflections, which enhances reflexivity. However, visual support does not allow participants to fully re-enter the initial situation. This may reduce the precision of recalls and limit access to contextual details of the interactions.

2.2 Immersion in Retrospection

Immersion constitutes a key variable for improving the quality of retrospection. Krokos et al. [25] showed that participants remember elements more effectively in an immersive environment than on a flat screen. In their study, participants were asked to memorize and then reposition images within a virtual space presented through two devices, a flat screen and a VR headset. The results indicate that immersion significantly enhances attention and memory, suggesting strong potential for enriching retrospective interviews.

Beaudry-Marchand et al. [3] demonstrated that an immersive environment, closely aligned with the lived experience, facilitates recall by visually and auditorily stimulating participants' memories and generating a strong sense of presence. This sense of presence promotes the activation of precise memories related to past tasks. According to Dorta et al. [13], headset-free immersive retrospection allows participants to focus more on self-observation, thereby facilitating the verbal and gestural expression of internal discourse during the co-design activity in the presence of the researcher. This method thus provides more accurate access to feelings and thoughts, enabling the analysis of internal changes and the identification of sources underlying fluctuations in experience.

Immersion also proves useful for detecting interaction problems, as shown by Beaudry-Marchand et al. [3] in a museum context, where the collected reflections were translated into design recommendations. While this method has its advantages, it's time-consuming. It begins with an immersive self-assessment focused on the perceived optimal experience related to Flow [8], followed by a retrospective interview with the researcher. This second stage allows for a deeper exploration of the reflections emerging from self-assessment of the experience, but it extends the overall duration of the process.

3 Pilot Debriefing with Immersive Retrospection

Debriefing plays a central role in improving pilots' skills and preventing errors in aviation [9]. It consists of a critical review of individual and collective performance, aimed at understanding errors, identifying areas for improvement, and reinforcing good practices [24]. This process is particularly relevant in complex environments such as in a flight deck, where pilots interact with multiple systems and interface elements under demanding conditions.

Within this context, retrospection is used as a structured method for analyzing pilots' actions and decisions after a flight or a simulation. As highlighted in recommendations for cockpit certification [12, 17, 27], retrospection makes it possible to assess the effectiveness of systems and the information provided to pilots, with the objective of reducing human error. When combined with video recording, retrospection facilitates the identification of critical moments, namely situations characterized by high cognitive load, stress, or misinterpretation of interface information, which may affect performance [19, 34]. Such video-assisted debriefing is already common in aviation training contexts. Our contribution is to examine whether a headset-free immersive display of the recorded flight (Hyve-3D), compared to a conventional flat-screen review, changes what pilots can articulate during retrospection, specifically regarding previously unspoken elements and design-relevant interface issues.

3.1 Improving Cockpit Testing and Design

User testing directly influences the design of cockpit interfaces by revealing specific issues such as excessive cognitive load or ergonomic shortcomings in displays and controls. An effective interface must promote human–machine compatibility by facilitating readability, information organization, and alert management [34], thereby reducing errors related to attention, interpretation, or manipulation.

It is essential to identify interaction errors from the earliest stages of design [6]. For example, modifying the dimensions of a button made it possible to correct its inappropriate use in a commercial aircraft [10]. Through a questionnaire, experienced pilots were able to report frequent errors that are rarely documented because they do not lead to major consequences. Similarly, Fala & Marais [18] show that the type of display influences risk perception, with pilots perceiving low-risk situations more clearly when information is presented graphically rather than alphanumerically.

Debriefing enables pilots to articulate their experiences from memory and to explain the difficulties encountered during flight [30], with the aim of improving existing interfaces [2]. It supports the identification of interaction errors, contributing to the design of more intuitive systems [12]. However, some thoughts remain only briefly expressed, as details may be forgotten or distorted due to memory biases [30]. To address these limitations, technologies such as onboard cameras in simulators provide objective visual feedback on crew performance [1]. This setup allows pilots to review their actions with precision, thereby facilitating the explanation of interaction errors and supporting subsequent interface analysis. Interface analysis also relies on combined methods that integrate analytical and experimental approaches. Inspection methods, including heuristic reviews and cognitive task analyses, assess system ergonomics by detecting inconsistencies and ambiguities [29].

Rigorous interpretation is required to ensure designs that are aligned with pilots' needs. Key design challenges include managing cognitive load, ensuring the effectiveness of alert systems in demanding situations, and providing clear information about the aircraft's state [19]. Immersive retrospection enables the formulation of concrete improvements by fully integrating human factors into the design of contemporary cockpits. However, few studies have explored immersive retrospection in this field, particularly for accessing implicit elements such as unexpressed thoughts or subtle errors that are difficult to observe. This gap is especially evident in debriefing practices, where current tools, although useful, struggle to fully stimulate memory. The integration of immersive approaches offers a promising perspective, as recreating a realistic environment may facilitate both the recall of critical events and the expression of internal reflections.

4 Methodology

This exploratory study investigated the potential of immersive retrospection to provide more nuanced access to pilots' unspoken thoughts. It also aims to identify critical interaction moments more effectively than in a non-immersive setting. This paper seeks to verify whether immersion improves pilots' memory and enriches their feedback on interfaces, based on the assumption that immersion can strengthen presence and recall of lived experiences. Through immersive and non-immersive retrospection conducted after a stressful simulated flight scenario, namely a *go-around due to bird strike*, the study examined interaction problems and pilots' unexpressed thoughts.

The results were analyzed according to the richness of the feedback and the ability to identify critical moments, with the objective of contributing to cockpit design by formulating recommendations. To this end, participants were exposed to two types of displays: immersive (Hyve-3D) and non-immersive (flat screen).

4.1 Participants

Six pilots qualified for instrument flight participated in the study, all men aged between 23 and 60 years. All participants were accustomed to flying solo, in accordance with the planned flight scenario. Before participating, they signed an informed consent form approved by our university's ethics committee and received compensation for their time.

4.2 Equipment and Retrospection Environments

A collaborating company provided a single-seat simulator connected to X-Plane 11. The selected aircraft model, the Avanti P180, offered the best compatibility with the available equipment. Five screens of varying sizes composed the visual interface, and the FS-FlightControl application made it possible to trigger specific events, such as bird strikes, without interrupting the simulation.

The absence of a co-pilot required the adoption of the think-aloud method to compensate for the lack of verbal interaction and to access spontaneous thoughts related to interface problems. A pretest confirmed that this method encouraged participants to focus on interaction-related issues rather than on providing general technical details.

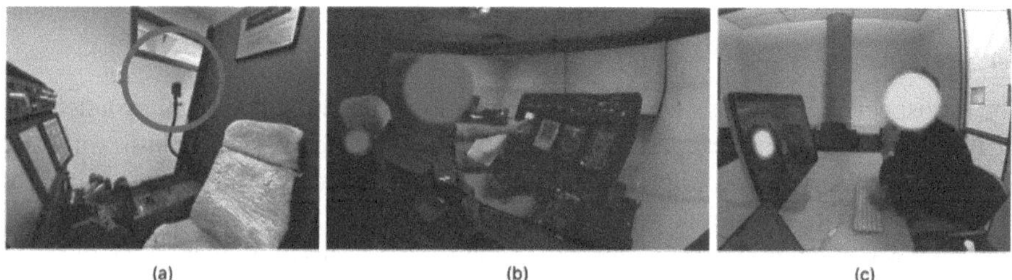

Fig. 1. (a) Positioning of the 360° camera in the simulator. (b) Immersive display (Hyve-3D). (c) Non-immersive display.

A 360° camera (GoPro Max), positioned at shoulder height, recorded the flight session (Fig. 1-a). The recording was subsequently viewed during a retrospective interview using one of two display configurations:

- Immersive: non-stereoscopic projection on a semi-spherical screen (±210°), presented the scene life-size. This setup made it possible to recreate the moment of the flight activity and to support natural communication with the researcher (Fig. 1-b).
- Non-immersive: full-screen playback on a 24-inch flat monitor with a 90° field of view, using a standard perspective (Fig. 1-c).

The camera was intended to reproduce the pilot's point of view with coherent realism, thereby facilitating the evocation of memories and interaction details during the interviews.

4.3 Experimental Procedure

The flight mission consisted of an RNAV (area navigation) approach to runway 32 at Ottawa International Airport (CYOW). The pilots' objective was to land the aircraft by following standard procedures applicable to real-world flight and to comply with any instructions provided when relevant. No air traffic control was present to issue landing clearances, thereby allowing pilots to decide autonomously when to land.

The exercise began with a five-minute standard landing phase under clear weather conditions, allowing pilots to familiarize themselves with the simulator. Once ready, they restarted the simulation from the same position, this time under foggy conditions. At an altitude of 500 feet, they were required to perform a go-around. One minute later, a bird strike was simulated, resulting in a failure of the left engine. The pilots then continued the landing under these critical conditions. The simulation lasted approximately 20 min.

Following the simulator session, participants took part in a retrospective interview while viewing the recording using one of two display conditions, immersive or non-immersive. Three pilots viewed the video in an immersive display, while the other three viewed it on a non-immersive display. Each participant reviewed the entire flight with the researcher. When a problematic moment was identified, the participant paused the video to explain their reflections and the difficulties encountered. This procedure made it possible to reveal interaction problems that were not expressed during the simulation, despite concurrent verbalization. The retrospective interviews lasted in average 47 min, resulting in 4.6 h of recordings; excerpts were selectively transcribed for analysis.

4.4 Data Analysis

The retrospective interviews were recorded in both audio and video to allow a detailed analysis of pilots' speech and gestures. Coding was conducted using the Atlas.ti software. Each topic addressed by a pilot was assigned a specific code, based on the amount of time devoted to it. When a new topic emerged, a new code was created, until content saturation was reached. The codes were then analyzed in terms of frequency and duration to assess whether the type of display influenced the externalization of thoughts that had remained unexpressed during the simulation.

The analysis aimed to compare newly emerging information during the interviews with that obtained in flight through think-aloud. The analysis focused on several dimensions, including *gestures*; *the richness of verbalized information*; the severity of the identified *problems*; and the *explanations and recommendations* proposed for interface design. *Problem severity* was coded by the researcher: *Major* issues were those to significantly hinder situation assessment or decision-making during abnormal situations. *Moderate* issues referred to problems that could increase workload or lead to minor errors in interaction. *Minor* issues were problems with limited operational impact, but which could detract from interface clarity or usability.

The *gestures* produced by participants during the retrospective session were divided into three categories [32]: *pointing gestures* toward an element in the video (indicating the instrument concerned); *concrete gestures* representing visible objects or actions, (drawing a shape); and *abstract gestures* expressing ideas or concepts (acceleration).

5 Results

Although the scenario was identical for all participants, behaviors, reactions, and flight durations varied across pilots. During the retrospective interviews, participants frequently paused the video to add explanations that had not been mentioned during the simulation, often accompanied by gestures. In the immersive display, pilots used both their finger and the laptop cursor to point at elements, with 216 occurrences compared to 175 in the non-immersive condition. They also produced three times as many abstract gestures in the immersive condition (Fig. 2 left). Gestures in immersion were broader and more expressive, involving both arms and hands, whereas in the non-immersive condition they were more restrained and primarily limited to finger movements (Fig. 2 right).

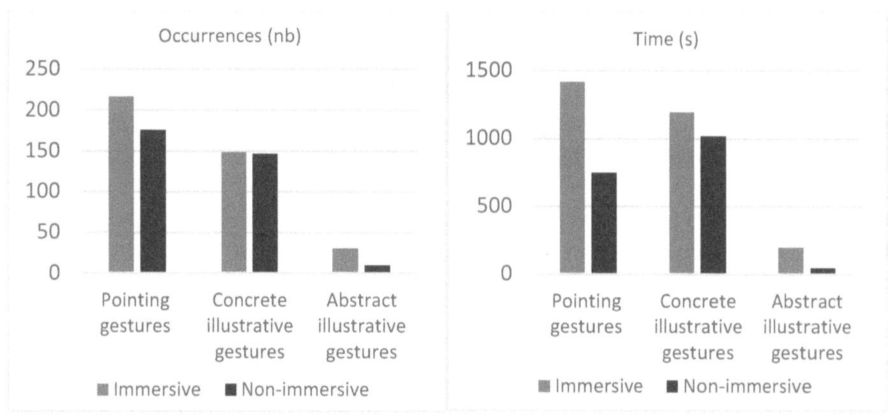

Fig. 2. Comparison of gesture occurrences (left) and gesture duration in seconds (right) across the different display conditions.

In terms of verbal content, eleven categories were defined based on the coding of the interviews (Table 1).

Table 1. Descriptions of the verbal content categories.

- "I remember" (**IR**)	The pilot explicitly uses such expressions to evoke a specific memory during the interview
- Self-criticism (**SC**)	The pilot criticizes an action or decision made during the activity
- Simulator/aircraft comparison (**S/AC**)	The pilot compares general knowledge or experience between the simulator and the real aircraft
- Piloting knowledge (**PK**)	The pilot explains the manipulations and underlying logic required to fly an aircraft
- Explaining the problem (**EP**)	The pilot justifies why an identified element was unclear or why it was judged to be incorrect
- Familiarity with the simulator (**FS**)	The pilot expresses a lack of familiarity with the simulator used
- Identifying a problem (**IP**)	The pilot reports an unclear, unexpected, or problematic element encountered during the simulation
- Does not recall the experience (**DNRE**)	The pilot expresses uncertainty regarding their memories or what they recall at that specific moment
- Unspoken elements (**UE**)	The pilot provides additional explanations about an action or thought that was briefly mentioned during the simulation through think-aloud but not initially developed
- Proposing solutions (**PS**)	The pilot suggests ideas or solutions to improve the design
- Recalling the activity (**RA**)	The pilot recalls their actions and thoughts during the simulation

The unspoken elements (UE) and recalling the activity (RA) categories showed a clear advantage in immersion, both in terms of the number of occurrences and the duration of interventions (Fig. 3, top). Pilot P2, for instance, explicitly used the expression "I remember" (IR) highlighting more precise access to personal memories, a phenomenon that was not observed among pilots in the non-immersive condition. By contrast, the category identifying a problem (IP) exhibited fewer differences between the two conditions. Immersion led to a higher number of occurrences (Fig. 3, top), whereas pilots in the non-immersive condition devoted more time to this category (Fig. 3, bottom), which suggests slightly longer and extended verbalizations.

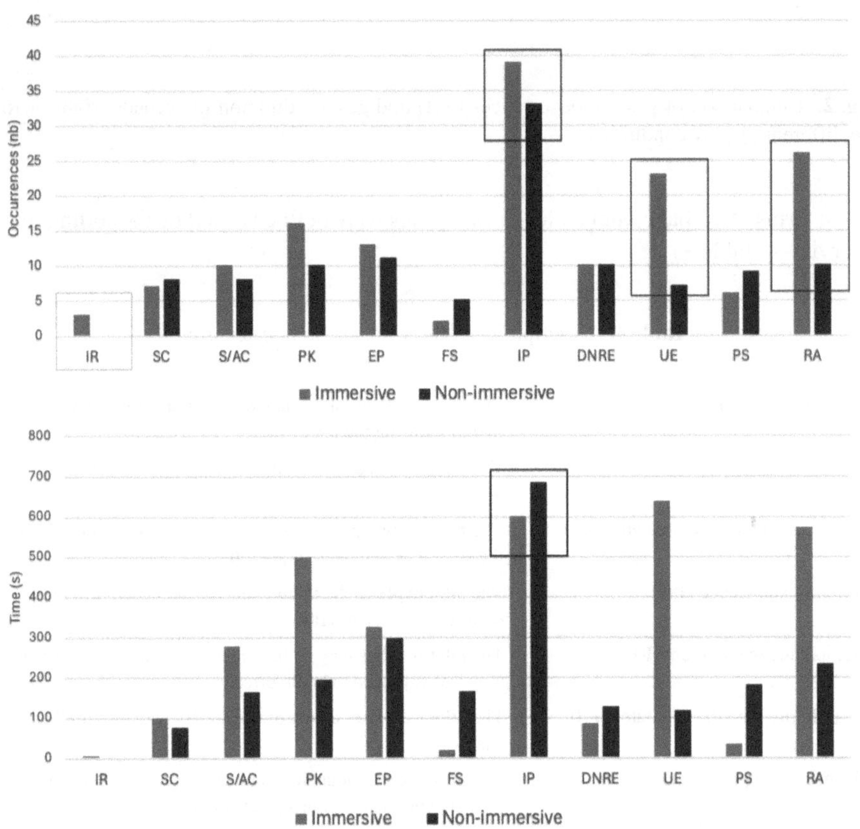

Fig. 3. Comparison of the number of occurrences (top) and the duration in seconds (bottom) of the different retrospection content categories across immersive and non-immersive displays.

5.1 Unspoken Elements

In the immersive condition, 43% of the 23 occurrences of unspoken elements (UE) were related to piloting knowledge (PK). The remaining occurrences were distributed across the following categories: recalling the activity (RA) and explaining the problem (EP) each account for 22%, identifying a problem (IP) 9%, and self-criticism (SC) 4%. This distribution can be explained by the effect of immersion, which recreated a visually and auditorily rich environment that stimulated contextual memory and promoted more precise recall of the knowledge applied during the activity. In addition, the enhanced sense of presence in immersion appeared to encourage pilots to explore more deeply the links between their actions and their knowledge.

By contrast, the seven UE occurrences in the non-immersive condition were more evenly distributed. Categories for identifying a problem (IP) and self-criticism (SC) each accounted for 29%, while familiarity with the simulator (FS), recalling the activity (RA), and explaining the problem (EP) each represented 14%. This uniform distribution may be explained by the lack of realistic stimulation, which limited pilots' ability to fully project themselves into the situation and lead to reflection that were less focused on a specific type of content.

When comparing the data side by side, a major difference emerged in the categories recalling the activity (RA) and explaining the problem (EP) (Fig. 4). The immersive display promoted a fivefold increase in the externalization of thoughts that were not expressed during the activity, as well as more detailed explanations of the problems encountered (Fig. 4). For example, pilot P1 faced an engine failure issue related to the ambiguity of the propeller indicator. During the flight, he explained to the researcher: "*In principle, my left engine is dead, so it should turn by itself to the right*". However, during the retrospective interview, he provided additional details about what he had described in flight: "*The needle came back toward zero. At that point, I thought I had power on the left, and then I really had none on the right. It is the opposite*".

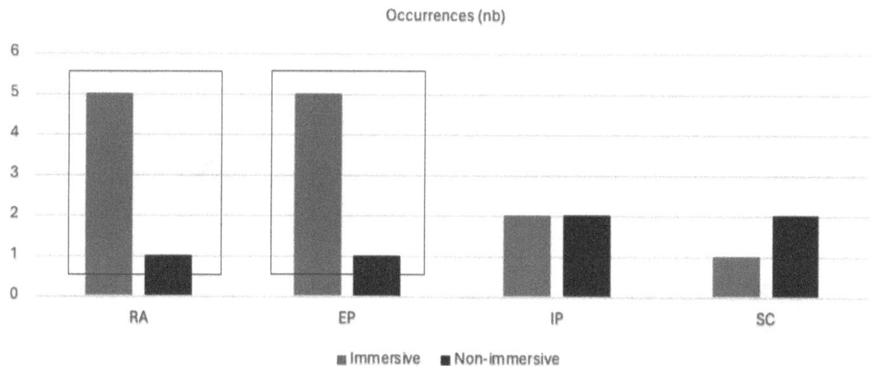

Fig. 4. Comparison of the occurrences of "unspoken elements" during the retrospective interview between immersive and non-immersive displays.

These previously unexpressed thoughts make it possible to precisely locate the difficulties encountered by pilots. Through the immersive display, deeper access to pilots' reflections on the problem was achieved, revealing specific details related to interaction issues and interface ambiguities. The non-immersive condition yielded less detailed content that was more evenly distributed, highlighting the impact of the immersive condition on the richness of user feedback.

5.2 Interaction Problems

In total, 32 specific problems were identified during the retrospective interviews, including 27 related to the interface and 5 related to technical failures of the simulator (see Fig. 5). Their distribution by display condition shows that 14 problems were identified exclusively in the immersive condition, 9 exclusively in the non-immersive condition, and 9 in both conditions. In immersion, the problems mainly concerned information overload and visual elements that were poorly suited to interaction. In the non-immersive condition, pilots primarily mentioned issues related to readability and clarity. The problems common to both conditions related to fundamental design weaknesses. Among the difficulties most frequently reported were the following:

- Unexpected placement of information, forcing pilots to divert their attention to locate it (Major).
- Dispersed distribution of elements across screens, requiring extensive visual scanning (Major).
- Text that was too small and inappropriate color choices, making certain information difficult to read (Moderate).
- Critical absences or imprecisions, such as the slip indicator or the engine power needle, which dropped to zero while remaining in the green zone, thereby generating confusion (Major).
- Lack of clear feedback during certain failures, for example activation of the main alarm without a warning message, which disoriented several pilots in critical situations (Major).

These findings informed a set of design recommendations, which are illustrated through a before-and-after interface comparison presented in Sect. 7.

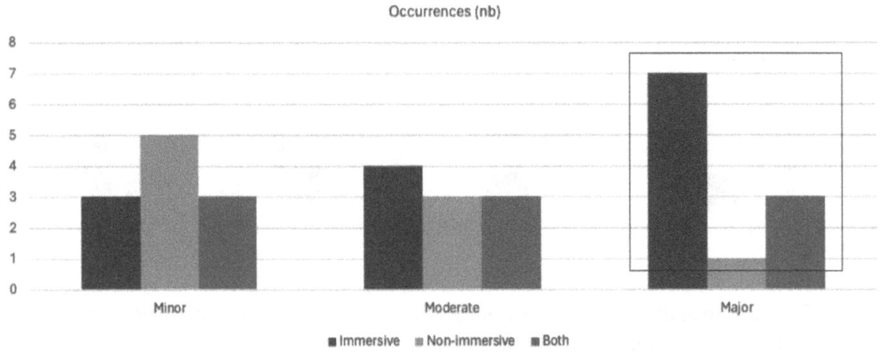

Fig. 5. Occurrences and Classification of problems according to their importance.

The problems were classified into three levels of importance. The total number of problems identified was comparable across the two conditions, with 23 in immersion and 18 in non-immersion. However, the severity of the problems differed. Pilots in the immersive condition reported 10 major problems (7 immersive + 3 both), compared with only 4 in the non-immersive condition (1 non-immersive + 3 both) (Fig. 5). These results indicate that the immersive environment facilitates the identification of more critical issues. Nevertheless, both conditions revealed significant limitations of the tested interfaces, notably cognitive overload, information readability, and the lack of clear feedback.

6 Discussion

The results indicate that the use of an immersive display during the retrospective interview seems to have a notable impact on the expression of thoughts that were not verbalized during the activity. In the immersive condition, pilots expressed a greater number of unspoken elements (UE) and activity-related memories (AR), both in terms of frequency and duration. This richer verbal output suggests enhanced stimulation of contextual memory, supported by the immersive display, which visually and auditorily reproduces the flight context. Immersed pilots tended to evoke more precise memories and to provide more detailed explanations. Immersion thus appears to strengthen their ability to recall and analyze experienced interactions by facilitating the reactivation of the cognitive processes engaged during the task.

However, while immersion promotes richer verbalization, it does not necessarily lead to the identification of a greater number of problems. The total number of detected problems remains similar across the two conditions. The difference lies instead in the importance of the problems identified, with pilots in the immersive condition reporting a higher number of issues considered to be major. This suggests that immersion encourages deeper reflection and greater awareness of critical interface-related challenges.

This phenomenon may be explained by the contextual fidelity of the immersive display, which encourages pilots to mobilize cognitive strategies closer to those used in real activity. By feeling present in the simulated situation, pilots are prompted to analyze their interactions with cockpit instruments more precisely and to identify shortcomings in the support provided by the interface. As a result, the immersive display used for retrospection appears to be a powerful means of enriching the analysis of complex situations, strengthening risk management, and improving the identification of design shortcomings in cockpit systems.

7 Design Recommendations

Following the review of the identified interaction problems, a series of ergonomic adjustments were proposed to improve the clarity and relevance of the displayed information (Fig. 6).

A. Merging the primary flight display and navigation display: The lateral deviation indicator (localizer) and vertical deviation indicator (glideslope) were relocated to the primary flight display. This consolidation brings essential navigation information together in a single location, thereby reducing the need for visual scanning across multiple screens and decreasing the risk of confusion.
B. Addition of the slip and skid indicator: This element was missing in the original version (before), yet it is critical for accurate flight control, particularly in situations involving engine failure.

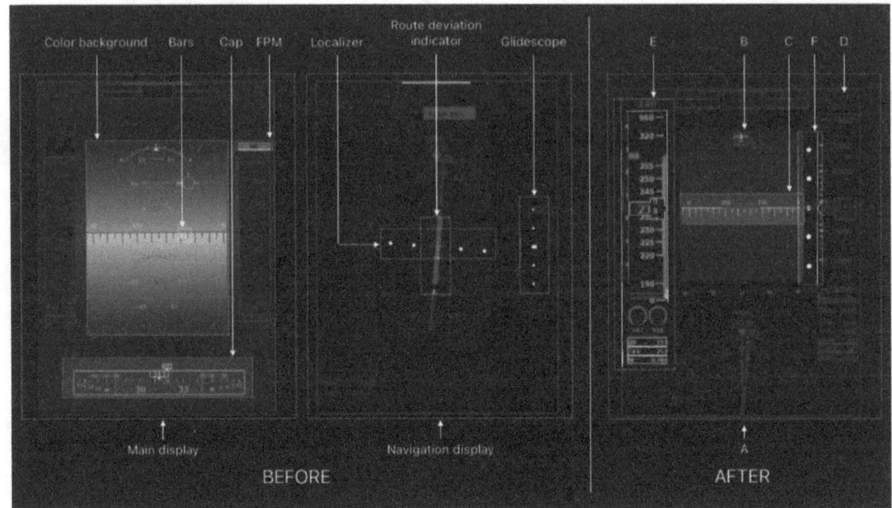

Fig. 6. Recommended modifications to the primary flight display.

C. Simplification of the heading display: The heading display in the original interface distracted pilots' attention due to the density of information presented. Simplifying it through a top-down representation aims to refocus attention on essential information.
D. Changing the background color to black: This modification increases contrast with white text, making information easier to read, especially under low-light conditions.
E. Increasing font size: This improvement reduces the visual effort required to read information, thereby enabling faster and more intuitive decision making.
F. Modifying the colors of the vertical deviation indicator (glideslope): The use of lighter and more contrasting colors improves the differentiation of critical indications, thereby reducing potential errors related to visual misinterpretation.

8 Limitations

This study is subject to two main limitations: the number of pilots was small to include statistical analysis, since recruiting pilots certified for instrument flight proved to be a major challenge. Nevertheless, the results of this exploratory study provide an initial indication of the influence of different display conditions during retrospection on the verbalization of unexpressed thoughts. Second, technical issues with the simulator affected the study. Difficulties with the alarm management system complicated the diagnosis of an engine failure for one participant. In addition, a slight visual lag between the instruments and the visual feedback, as well as high simulator sensitivity, may have influenced the behavior of some pilots.

9 Conclusion

This paper examined the effectiveness of immersive retrospection as an innovative method for identifying interaction problems in the cockpit. The objective was to gain a deeper understanding of pilots' experiences in complex and stressful situations to improve the design of cockpit interfaces. The results showed that the unspoken elements (UE) and recalling the activity (RA) categories exhibited a clear advantage under immersive conditions, both in terms of the number of occurrences and the duration of interventions.

These preliminary findings suggest that the immersive display used during retrospection seems to support a richer and more precise identification of interaction problems by revealing aspects that are overlooked when a non-immersive display is used for retrospective interviews. Pilots in the immersive condition reported a greater number of problems considered to be critical, particularly those related to display readability, clarity of feedback, and organization of essential information. This study also made it possible to formulate detailed design recommendations to address these issues.

This exploratory study provided directions for improving cockpit interfaces by relying on immersive retrospection approach that is more sensitive to recall processes and pilot experience. This approach may also have relevant applications beyond aviation, particularly in the design of interfaces for other interaction design domains. By enabling more direct access to users' unexpressed thoughts, immersive retrospection represents a valuable opportunity to design systems that are more intuitive and better aligned with operators' real needs.

Acknowledgments. The authors would like to thank Marinvent Corporation for providing access to the flight simulator, as well as the pilots who generously participated in the study. This research activity is funded by the Science and Engineering Research Council of Canada (NSERC) ALLRP 567177-21, the aviation research Consortium of Québec (CRIAQ) and the following industrial partners: Bombardier, CMC Electronics, Marinvent, Presagis and Thales.

References

1. Alkov, R.A.: Enhancing safety with aircrew coordination training: communication and coordination among crew members aid decision making in the cockpit. Ergon. Des. **2**(2), 13–18 (1994)
2. Banks, V.A., Plant, K.L., Stanton, N.A.: Development of a usability evaluation framework for the flight deck. In: Charles, R., Wilkinson, C. (eds.), Contemporary Ergonomics and Human Factors 2018. CIEHF, pp. 1–7 (2018)
3. Beaudry-Marchand, E., Han, X., Dorta, T.: Immersive retrospection by video- photogrammetry: UX assessment tool of interactions in museums, a case study. In: Fioravanti, A, (eds.), ShoCK! - Sharing Computational Knowledge! - Proceedings of the eCAADe conference-Volume 2, Sapienza University of Rome, Rome, Italy, 20–22 September 2017, pp. 729–738 (2017)
4. Billman, D.O., Mumaw, R.J., Feary, M.S.: Best practices for evaluating flight deck interfaces for transport category aircraft with particular relevance to issues of attention, awareness, and understanding CAST SE-210 Output 2 Report 6 of 6 (20200001615). NASA National Aeronautics and Space Administration (2019)
5. Boubée, N.: La méthode de l'autoconfrontation : une méthode bien adaptée à l'investigation de l'activité de recherche d'information ? Études de Commun. **35**(2), 47–60 (2010)
6. Chaparro, A., Miranda, A., Grubb, J.: Aviation displays: design for automation and new display formats. In: Human Factors in Aviation and Aerospace, pp. 351–371, Academic Press (2023)

7. Cruz-Neira, C., Sandin, D.J., DeFanti, T.A., Kenyon, R.V., Hart, J.C.: The CAVE: audio visual experience automatic virtual environment. Commun. ACM **35**(6), 64–72 (1992)
8. Csikszentmihalyi, M.: Creativity: Flow and the Psychology of Discovery and Invention. Harper Collins, New York (1997)
9. Dattel, A.R., Babin, A.K., Wang, H.: Human factors of flight training and simulation. In: Keebler, J.R., Lazzara, E.H., Wilson, K.A., Blickensderfer, E.L. (eds.) Human Factors in Aviation and Aerospace, pp. 217–255. Academic Press (2023)
10. Demagalski, J., et al.: Design Induced errors on the modern flight deck during approach and landing. In: Proceedings of the International Conference of Human Computer Interaction in Aeronautic. HCI-Aero, pp. 126–130 (2002)
11. Deppermann, A.: Retrospection and understanding in interaction. In: Deppermann, A., Günthner, S. (eds.) Temporality in Interaction, pp. 57–94. John Benjamins Publishing Company, Amsterdam (2015)
12. Dismukes, R.K., Smith, G.M.: Facilitation and Debriefing in Aviation Training and Operations. Routledge (2000)
13. Dorta, T., Beaudry-Marchand, E., Pierini, D.: Externalizing co-design cognition through immersive retrospection. In: Gero, J.S. (ed.), Design Computing and Cognition (DCC 2018). pp. 97–113, Springer, Cham (2018)
14. Dorta, T., Kinayoglu, G., Hoffmann, M.: Hyve-3D: a new embodied interface for immersive collaborative 3D sketching. In: SIGGRAPH 2014: ACM SIGGRAPH 2014 Studio, Article. 37, p. 1 (2014)
15. Earl, L., Mavin, T.J., Soo, K.: Demands on cognitive processing: implications for verbalisation in complex work environments. Cogn. Technol. Work **19**(1), 31–46 (2017)
16. Ericsson, K.A., Simon, H.A.: Verbal reports as data. Psychol. Rev. **87**(3), 215–251 (1980)
17. European union aviation safety agency: AMC 29.1302 at Amendment 9. EASA (2021)
18. Fala, N., Marais, K.: Cognitive biases in risk communication during post-flight debrief. Int. J. Aerosp. Psychol. **32**(4), 227–239 (2022)
19. Feary, M.S., Mumaw, R.J., Billman, D.O.: Summary of results from technologies for aircraft state awareness safety enhancement 210 output 2 (N19–0004920/XAB). NASA, Moffett Field, CA. Ames Research Center (2019)
20. Hansen, J.P.: The use of eye mark recordings to support verbal retrospection in software testing. Acta Physiol (Oxf.) **76**(1), 31–49 (1991)
21. Huang, C.C., Stolterman, E.: Temporal anchors in user experience research. In: Proceedings of the 2014 conference on Designing interactive systems (DIS 2014). ACM, pp. 271– 274 (2014)
22. Jaspers, M.W.M., Steen, T., Vanden Bos, C., Geenen, M.: The think aloud method: a guide to user interface design. Int. J. Med. Informatics **73**(11/12), 781–795 (2004)
23. Karapanos, E., Martens, J., Hassenzahl, M.: Reconstructing experiences with iScale. Int. J. Hum. Comput. Stud. **70**, 849–865 (2012)
24. Kikkawa, Y., Marvin, T.J.: A review of debriefing practices. Aviat. Psychol. Appl. Hum. Factors **7**(1), 42–54 (2017)
25. Krokos, E., Plaisant, C., Varshney, A.: Virtual memory palaces: immersion aids recall. Virtual Reality **23**, 1–15 (2019)
26. Lallemand, C., Gronier, G., Koenig, V.: User experience: a concept without consensus? Exploring practitioners' perspectives through an international survey. Comput. Hum. Behav. **43**, 35–48 (2015)
27. Mavin, T.J., Kikkawa, Y., Billett, S.: Key contributing factors to learning through debriefings: commercial aviation pilots' perspectives. Int. J. Train. Res. **16**(2), 122–144 (2018)
28. Mollo, V., Falzon, P.: Auto- and allo-confrontation as tools for reflective activities. Appl. Ergon. **35**(6), 531–540 (2004)

29. Mumaw, R.J., Haworth, L., Billman, D.: Evaluation issues for a flight deck interface CAST SE-210 Output 2 Report 4 of 6. NASA (2019)
30. Roth, W.-M., Jornet, A.: Situational awareness as an instructable and instructed matter in multi-media supported debriefing: a case study from aviation. Comput. Support. Cooperat. Work (CSCW) vol. 24, pp. 461–508, Springer Nature (2015)
31. Safin, S., Dorta, T., Pierini, D., Kinayoglu, G., Lesage, A.: Design flow 2.0, assessing experience during ideation with increased granularity: a proposed method. Des. Stud. **47**, 23–46 (2016)
32. Tellier, M., Guardiola, M., Bigi, B.: Types de gestes et utilisation de l'espace gestuel dans une description spatiale: méthodologie de l'annotation. In: Atelier DEGELS, 18e conférence annuelle Traitement Automatique des Langues Naturelles, pp. 45–56 (2011)
33. Vanden Haak, M., De Jong, M., Jan Schellens, P.: Retrospective vs. concurrent think-aloud protocols: testing the usability of an online library catalogue. Behav. Inf. Technol. **22**(5), 339–351 (2003)
34. Yeh, M., Swider, C., Jo, Y., Donovan, C.: Human factors considerations in the design and evaluation of flight deck displays and controls, version 2.0. (No. DOT-VNTSC-FAA-17–02). John A. Volpe National Transportation Systems Center (US) (2016)
35. Zimmerman, J., Stolterman, E., Forlizzi, J.: An analysis and critique of research through design: towards a formalization of a research approach. In: Proceedings of the 8th ACM. Conference on Designing Interactive Systems, pp. 310–319 (2010)

Towards Digital Assistance in Air Traffic Control: Supporting Pilot Request Management

Erik Gøsta Nilsson[1(✉)], Amela Karahasanović[1], Md Zia Uddin[1], Ophelia Prillard[1], Maria Emine Nylund[1], Aida Omerovic[1], Jiaxin Li[1], Jan Håvard Skjetne[1], Yannick Migliorini[2], Serge Pierre[2], Thomas Roques[2], Sylvain Martin[2], Bertille Somon[3], Samy Chikhi[3], Bruno Berberian[3], Efecan Yilmaz[4], and Anne-Marie Brouwer[4]

[1] SINTEF, Forskningsveien 1, 0373 Oslo, Norway
erik.g.nilsson@sintef.no
[2] DSNA – DTI, 1 rue du Dr Grynfogel, 31035 Toulouse CEDEX 1, France
[3] DTIS, ONERA, FR-13661 Salon Cedex Air, France
[4] DCC, Radboud University, Nijmegen, The Netherlands

Abstract. There are clear opportunities in exploiting artificial intelligence (AI) in air traffic control. One of the relevant areas where AI has a potential is in supporting air traffic controllers in their work, particularly in periods with high workload. A possible approach to providing such support is to have a digital assistant as part of the air traffic controllers (ATCOs) support tools. To investigate how such an assistant may be designed, we have developed the DIALOG system. This system supports ATCO when responding to pilot requests. An Intent Inferring System listens to the radio communication between ATCO and pilot, and based on pilot utterances, it identifies the request and collects the most important information needed by the ATCO to respond to the request. A Teammate Awareness Service measures physiological data from ATCOs and uses machine learning models to induce the ATCOs workload in an unobtrusive manner. A Teamwork Assistant uses information from the Teammate Awareness Service to determine which type of assistance to provide to the ATCO at any given time. When a pilot issues a request, the Teamwork Assistant presents information from the Intent Inferring System in a manner suiting the ATCO's current state. In this paper we present the different parts of the DIALOG system, focusing on the interplay between the Teamwork Assistant and the ATCO in the user interface of the ATCO. We also explain how the assistant was validated and discuss the main challenges and experiences faced while designing its user interface.

Keywords: Human-Centred AI · Human-AI interaction · Air Traffic Management

1 Introduction

Global air traffic is experiencing significant growth, with passenger numbers projected to exceed 12 billion by 2030 and reach 19.5 billion by 2042 [1]. This trend increases pressure on Air Traffic Management (ATM) systems, which must maintain high levels

W. -C. Li and A. Plioutsias (Eds.): HCII 2026, LNAI 16708, pp. 204–220, 2026.
https://doi.org/10.1007/978-3-032-29459-3_15

of safety and efficiency despite growing complexity. As traditional ATM approaches are reaching their limits, it becomes essential to develop innovative, scalable solutions. Artificial Intelligence (AI) has been recognized as a key enabler in transforming ATM operations [2]. However, the benefits of AI can only be achieved through effective human-AI collaboration, assuring trust, transparency, and shared situational awareness [3, 4].

The task of assisting pilots and managing their requests has been identified among the core cognitive processes that are performed by Air Traffic Controllers (ATCOs) [5]. This process is demanding for ATCOs, as pilot requests "have to be evaluated regarding the criteria of safety, own workload and workload of the adjacent controller" [5]. Consequently, controllers may deny pilots' optimization requests (e.g. requests for another level or direct routing) if their workload is too high. Assisting controllers in such situations could reduce environmental impact, improve safety and increase capacity.

This paper presents the design and implementation of an AI-infused system that supports en-route ATCOs in managing pilot requests. An en-route ATCO controls aircraft during their cruising phase at high altitudes.

We explore if and how an AI-infused system can provide valuable assistance to ATCOs by answering the following research questions:

1. How to assess ATCOs' workload and intention in real time in an unobtrusive manner?
2. How to infer ATCOs' goals and intent based on messages from pilots?
3. How to enable effective human-AI teaming based on Human-centric state and exectations?

To answer these questions, we applied an overall technology science process [6]. We envisaged a system that i) understands ATCOs' intent and goals, ii) assesses ATCOs' workload and attention, iii) either provides needed support or performs tasks autonomously.

The design and development of the system have been guided by the HCAI approach which augments the human role while ensuring transparency and trust. For this, ATCOs' expertise, feedbacks and insights about classical controlling environments have been gathered. Iterative design and evaluation of the system components have been done through standard methods such as interviews, workshops and focus groups, as well as novel methods for user involvement in the design of AI systems [8].

The structure of this paper is as follows. First, we present some relevant background information for our research. Then we briefly present the research method used in the work. The main content of the paper is a more detailed presentation of the three components in the DIALOG system, with a focus on the Teamwork Assistant responsible for the main part of human-AI interaction in the system. Then we present how the Teamwork Assistant has evolved as result of extensive validation activities. Finally, we discuss our results, focusing on design challenges for the Teamwork Assistant followed by a summary of the main conclusion and plans for future research.

2 Background

Research on human-AI interaction increasingly examines how artificial intelligence systems can be developed to support, rather than replace, human decision-makers. Human-Centric Artificial Intelligence (HCAI) frames AI as a technology that strengthens human capabilities while preserving accountability, transparency, and safety. Instead of positioning AI as an autonomous substitute for human expertise, HCAI promotes systems that enhance performance and maintain meaningful human oversight. Xu [7] and Shneiderman [8] argue that AI technologies should reinforce human agency and reliability. Reviews of the HCAI literature further identify key elements such as an augmentation-oriented purpose, alignment with socio-technical values, and development processes grounded in human-centred principles [9]. This perspective builds on established human-centred design standards, including ISO 9241-210 [10], while also recognizing AI as a novel design material characterized by adaptive, data-driven, and probabilistic behavior [11].

A critical aspect of HCAI concerns the distribution of authority between human operators and AI systems. The European Union Aviation Safety Agency (EASA) proposes three levels of AI applications: assistance to humans (Level 1), human–AI teaming (Level 2), and advanced automation (Level 3) [12]. These levels primarily differ in the degree of decision-making authority granted to AI systems. At Level 1, humans retain full authority; at Level 2, decision-making may be shared but remains under human supervision; and at Level 3, AI systems may execute decisions with limited human intervention. The concept of human–AI teaming aligns with research on human–autonomy teaming, which conceptualizes AI as an active partner in joint activities [13]. Effective teaming requires shared situational awareness, transparent communication of intent, and mechanisms for mutual monitoring. In air traffic control (ATC), situational awareness involves maintaining a comprehensive and forward-looking understanding of traffic conditions and operational constraints. Within such contexts, AI systems are expected to complement Air Traffic Control Officers (ATCOs) by dynamically adjusting task allocation based on operational and human factors [14].

To operationalize HCAI principles, several design methods and guidelines have been proposed. Persona-based approaches, originally introduced by Cooper [15], have been adapted to AI systems to capture attributes such as communicative style, system limitations, transparency, and trust dynamics [16]. In addition, structured guidelines for Human–AI interaction have been developed in industry. For example, Microsoft introduced a set of design recommendations addressing different phases of interaction, from initial onboarding to long-term use [17]. Complementary work on trustworthy AI emphasizes principles such as fairness, robustness, explainability, transparency, and accountability as essential for fostering user trust in AI-supported systems [18].

Despite these conceptual advancements, practical implementation presents ongoing challenges. Empirical studies show that organizations often face difficulties related to early end-user involvement, systematic value integration, and clear communication of AI capabilities and limitations [19]. Although Human–AI guidelines generally contribute positively to user experience, they may also create unintended effects, such as over-reliance on automated recommendations when explanations are perceived as authoritative [20]. In the aviation domain, digital teammate concepts illustrate how AI agents can collaborate with ATCOs through adaptive task allocation and shared control mechanisms [21]. Nevertheless, transforming high-level HCAI principles into context-sensitive and operational design practices remains a significant research challenge [22].

3 Digital Assistance for ATCOs in the DIALOG System

The system, named DIALOG - Deciphering Intents of Air traffic controllers, workLOad assessment and Gaze analysis) is presented in Fig. 1.

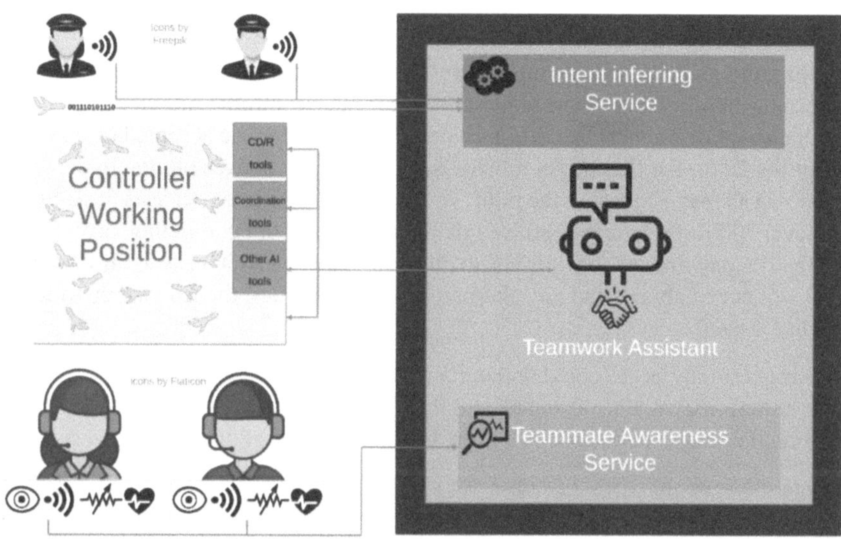

Fig. 1. DIALOG system

The system consists of the following components:

- An Intent Inferring Service that recognises the requests of the pilots and predicts ATCOs' future operational goals.
- A Teammate Awareness Service that provides information about ATCO's state based on their workload, attention and context data.
- A digital assistant, called Teamwork Assistant, that supports the ATCOs in performing their tasks.

In the following, we present these components in some more detail, focusing on the Teamwork Assistance.

3.1 The Intent Inferring Service

The Intent Inferring Service (IIS) recognizes the requests of the pilots and predicts ATCOs' future operational goals. It listens to the radio communication between pilots and ATCOs and uses an advanced speech recognition system called Scribe[1] to analyze the pilots' utterances. Some of these utterances are requests from the pilots to alter the aircraft's trajectory, such its altitude or heading. When attending to such requests, the IIS

[1] https://www.eurocontrol.int/sites/default/files/2024-04/20240430-flyai-forum-session-5-roques-carol.pdf.

uses procedures that are based on hierarchical task analyses (HTAs) describing standard procedures for how ATCOs handle different pilot requests.

For a given request, the IIS uses goals identified through HTAs to identify which information the ATCO needs for handling this type of request, as well as which operations the ATCO is likely to perform in response to the request. Examples of operations are "check compatibility with flow management", "check in-sector conflicts" and "check exit point capacity".

Furthermore, the IIS checks the feasibility and what the outcome of these operations will be at the point of time of the request, taking the current traffic situation into account. The conclusion of such checks is either that the request may be accepted or that it may not. For the latter, the IIS checks if there is a suitable alternative solution to the request that the ATCO may suggest to the pilot. For example, if the pilot requests to climb from flight level 300 to flight level 380, and there are one or more conflicting aircraft at this level, the IIS may find out that it is OK to climb to flight level 360 instead. In some cases, the IIS will not be able to find any alternative solutions. Thus, the IIS may provide three possible results:

1. The request may be accepted without any changes
2. The request may not be accepted, and there are no alternative solutions
3. The request may not be accepted as is, but there is at least one alternative solution

Regardless of the IIS's response to a request, it also provides the rationale that supports this response. The information provided in the rationale varies for different requests.

The current version of the DIALOG system supports three pilot requests:

R1: Directs, laterally changing the flight path towards a waypoint further along the route

R2: Level requests, vertically changing the flight path for a higher level, potentially to avoid turbulence

R3: Avoidance requests, laterally changing the flight path to avoid cumulonimbuses and thunderstorms on a heading

These requests were selected for their frequency and their expected high impact on safety and operational efficiency.

When the IIS has analysed one of the supported requests, the outcome is communicated to the Teamwork Assistant. Such messages contain all relevant details about the request and the results of IIS's assessment of the request. How the messages are handled by the Teamwork Assistant is described in Sect. 3.3.

3.2 The Teammate Awareness Service

The Teammate Awareness Service (TAS) provides information about ATCO's state based on their workload, attention and context data. This service supports the assessment of the ATCO's cognitive and attentional state by integrating information such as speech features, physiological indicators (e.g., heart rate variability and skin conductance), eye-movement measures, and system-interaction logs. By combining these inputs, the service can form an overall view of the controller's workload and attention allocation.

Machine-learning models are trained on annotated datasets to identify patterns—such as shifts in gaze behaviour, vocal characteristics, or physiological responses—that indicate changes in cognitive state. These models are trained to validate on separate datasets to ensure that they should perform reliably in new conditions. During operation, the service interprets the available inputs and provides estimates of how the controller is coping with current demands, offering insights that can support more informed task allocation and system-level decision making.

In the current version of the TAS, the following data sources are being used to assess the ATCOs' state and report their workload: electrocardiography (ECG) for heart rate and heart rate variability analysis, electrodermal activity (EDA) for sympathetic arousal measurement, voice recordings for extraction of acoustic and prosodic workload-related features, and video-based facial tracking. Building on these data sources, workload prediction relies on a multimodal sensing setup that captures complementary indicators of the ATCO's cognitive and physiological state. ECG is used to derive heart rate and heart rate variability metrics, while EDA measures changes in skin conductance associated with sympathetic nervous system activation. Voice recordings enable the extraction of acoustic and prosodic features, such as pitch, intensity, speech rate, and spectral characteristics, which reflect variations in cognitive effort and communication dynamics. Video-based facial tracking supports the monitoring of facial expressions, head pose, and gaze-related cues, contributing to the assessment of visual attention and affective state. Together, these modalities form a comprehensive and minimally intrusive framework for continuously monitoring workload in operational environments. Recent work demonstrates that multimodal physiological signals can be effectively fused to predict cognitive load with high classification accuracy, highlighting the value of combining complementary inputs for robust workload assessment [23].

To integrate the heterogeneous data streams, both early fusion and late fusion strategies are applied. In the early fusion approach, features extracted from the different modalities are temporally aligned, normalized, and concatenated into a unified feature vector before being provided to a single machine-learning model. This approach enables the model to learn cross-modal relationships directly at the feature level and to capture interactions between different types of signals. The late fusion approach involves training separate models for each modality and subsequently combining their predictions using ensemble techniques such as weighted averaging or meta-learning. Late fusion allows each model to specialize in modality-specific patterns while improving robustness in cases of partial data loss or degraded signal quality. Recent research has shown that advanced machine learning architectures using multimodal fusion can significantly improve human workload recognition performance across different operational domains, including air traffic control and driving scenarios [24]. By comparing these strategies, the system evaluates how different multimodal integration methods influence workload prediction performance and generalization across varying operational contexts.

The TAS combines data from these sources and leverages their accuracy to report the current induced workload to the Teamwork Assistant. Currently, these workload data are reported on two levels: high or low. Such messages contain the source of the induced workload as well as the accuracy. They are only sent if the accuracy is above a certain level.

When running the DIALOG system in our research, the reported workload data is supplemented with workload data reported by the ATCOs using the ISA scale[2]. The ISA values are reported at five levels (1–5), where 1 is very low and 5 is very high. Using ISA in addition to the induced workload values is partly done to assess the performance of the TAS and its data sources, and partly to have a fallback workload to use when the accuracy of the induced workload values is too low. The reported ISA values are also communicated to the Teamwork Assistant. Hence, the ISA tool is part of the TAS. How the messages from TAS (including the ISA values) are handled by the Teamwork Assistant is described in Sect. 3.3.

3.3 The Teamwork Assistant

The Teamwork Assistant (TA) is a digital assistant that supports ATCOs in performing their tasks. It receives information from the IIS and the TAS. The IIS provides information about requests from pilots, and suggestions for how these should be handled as described in Sect. 3.1. The TAS provides information about the current workload of the ATCO, as described in Sect. 3.2.

A main principle for the TA is that all its possible interventions are initiated by pilot requests. This means the TA does not have functionality for trying to find out if the ATCO needs help. Furthermore, the ATCO will not have functionality for asking explicitly for assistance.

The Controller Working Position. The user interface of the TA is integrated into the Controller Working Position (CWP). A CWP is the primary interface that an operational ATCO is using to obtain situational awareness through overview of the traffic in the sector controlled by the ATCO as well as its surroundings, like neighboring sectors and airspaces. Before going into details about the functionality and user interface of the TA, we give a brief description of the CWP that is used in the DIALOG system.

En-route ATCOs are assigned to a sector, i.e., the portion of the airspace (horizontally and vertically) in which the ATCO is managing the traffic. The ATCO must make sure that the aircraft in the sector are not in conflict with each other, and when they are leaving the sector, they must be safely handed over to the ATCO of the sector they are entering.

The central part of the CWP is the radar display, depicted in Fig. 2. It shows real-time geographical representation of all aircraft in 2D seen from above on a map. Each aircraft is represented by a symbol showing where on the map the aircraft is located and heading, as well as a flight label (see Fig. 3). The flight label provides essential information about the aircraft like callsign, speed, heading, altitude, as well as key information about its trajectory, e.g. next waypoint and sector. Both the location on the map and the information in the flight label are updated continuously.

In addition to showing key information about an aircraft, the flight label is also used to document changes that are agreed with the pilot, like changing heading or altitude. Unless it is hovered, a flight label shows only the most important information about the aircraft. When hovered, the label expands and additional information is shown. The

[2] https://skybrary.aero/articles/instantaneous-self-assessment-isa.

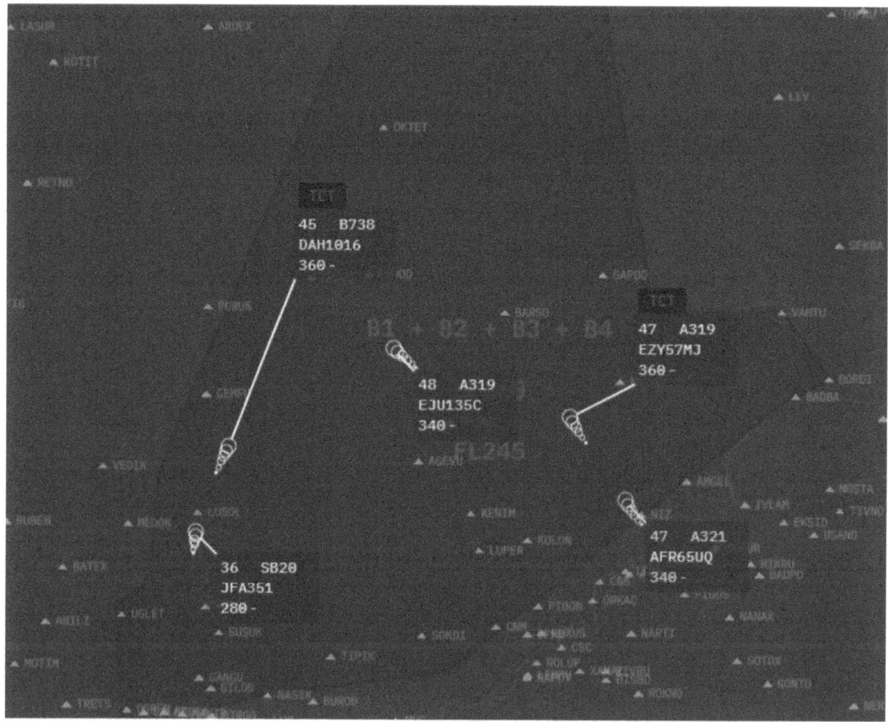

Fig. 2. Radar display in CWP.

Fig. 3. Flight label in compact (left) and expanded (right) variant.

ATCO may also show the trajectory of the aircraft, as well as how far the aircraft will reach within given time intervals.

The CWP is also equipped with tools supporting conflict detection and resolutions, to help in situations where the minimum separation between two aircraft may be breached. Some of the tools are automatically run in the background, while others are controlled by the ATCO.

Autonomy Profiles. An overarching idea of the TA is that it will provide different types of assistance depending on the workload and context of the ATCO. The current version of the TA has two different ways of providing assistance, denoted Autonomy Profile 1 and 2.

- Autonomy Profile 1 (AP1) is used when the ATCO workload is low, and the traffic complexity is not very high. When this profile is used, the TA informs the ATCO about which request has been identified, as well as key information that is relevant to assessing and responding to the request. The implementation of the response will be the sole responsibility of the ATCO. AP1 corresponds more or less to EASA's automation Level 2A.
- Autonomy Profile 2 (AP2) is used when the ATCO workload is high and/or the traffic complexity is high. When this profile is used, the TA provides the same information as in AP1, but in addition it presents an alternative solution if relevant and possible. Furthermore, it offers to take over some of the implementation of the response. AP2 corresponds more or less to EASA's automation Level 2B.

The details of the user interface of the TA when these two profiles are used are presented below in the Integration into the CWP section.

To determine which autonomy profile (AP) to use, the TA takes four types of information into consideration:

1. The task load (TL) of the ATCO, which is computed based on number of aircraft in the airspace, number of current and recent requests and number of conflicts.
2. The workload (WL) of the ATCO induced from physiological data obtained by the TAS including the accuracy of this value.
3. The ISA values reported by the ATCO, including a timestamp of when they were reported.
4. The urgency of the request. The urgency for R1 and R2 is always low, while the urgency of R3 (pilot wanting to avoid bad weather conditions) is always high.

- When determining the AP, a simple computation is done based on this information:

$AP = W1*WL + W2*ISA + W3*urgency + W4*TL.$[3]

W1 to W4 are weights (W1 to W3 are values between 0 and 1) for how much each of the four factors should contribute to the computation of AP.

- W1 is the accuracy of the induced workload value.
- W2 is computed based on time since the ISA value was reported. It is high when the ISA value is just reported and lower the longer it is since the value was reported.
- W3 is always 1. This increases the probability of using AP2 for R3
- W4 is 4-(W1 + W2 + W3). This means that the task load is most important when the accuracy is low, the ISA value is not current and the urgency is low.

If the computed AP value is above a certain threshold, AP2 is used, else AP1 is used.

Integration into the CWP. When the TA receives a message from the IIS about a pilot request that is supported, the TA first determines which AP profile to use. How the information in the message from the IIS is used depends on the AP profile. The main principles for this are:

[3] The actual formula used in the TA is more complex, resulting in a value between 0 and 1.

- In AP1, the TA provides information about which request is identified, whether the IIS recommends accepting it or not, and the reason for the recommendation. As it is the sole responsibility of the ATCO to implement the response, the TA only presents this information to the ATCO.
- In AP2, the TA's acts differently based on the three types of results the IIS may provide (described in Sect. 3.1). As in AP1 the TA always provides information about which request is identified, whether the IIS recommends accepting it or not, and the reason for the recommendation. If the request should not be accepted, but there is an alternative solution, this solution is presented. In addition, the TA offers functionality for supporting the implementation of the recommended response to the request.

The TA integrates into the CWP only through extending the flight label of the aircraft from which the request originates. This TA part of the flight label is located to the right of the standard flight label, adjacent to it. As the TA part of the flight label is slightly different in AP1 and AP2, we present them separately below.

TA part of the flight label in AP1. The TA part of the flight label used in AP1 comes in two variants.

Variant AP1.1. When the message about the request is received from the IIS, a small variant of the TA label is shown, as depicted in Fig. 4.

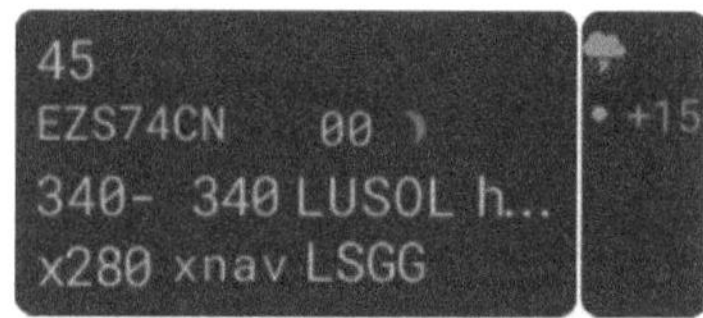

Fig. 4. Flight label with AP1.1 TA label to the right.

This variant contains an icon showing which request is identified, and a parameter showing the main content of the request (see Table 1). Besides the parameter, light is shown to indicate the recommended response, green suggesting accepting the request or red for suggesting rejecting the request.

Table 1. Parameters and icons used for the three supported requests.

Supported request	Parameter	Icon
R1 - Request to go directly to a waypoint	Waypoint name	
R2 - Request to change flight level	Flight level	FL↕
R3 - Weather avoidance request	Degrees to left or right	

Variant AP1.2. If the ATCO enters the TA label with the mouse pointer (hover), a large variant of the TA label is shown, as depicted in Fig. 5.

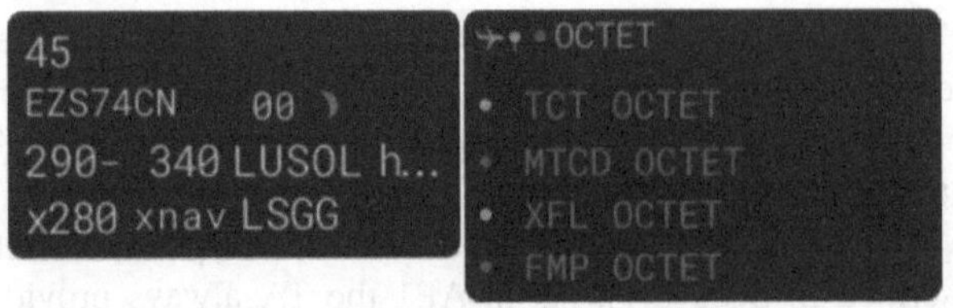

Fig. 5. Flight label with AP1.2 TA label to the right.

The top part is identical to Variant AP1.1, and below this the explanation of why the light is red or green is given (the rationale for the IIS suggestion). The explanation is a list of what has been checked by the IIS. The list contains abbreviations that are well known by ATCOs. Beside each list item there is a light (green or red) telling whether the check turned out OK or not. If there is a green light for the request, all the list items also have green lights. If one or more of the list items have a red light, the request also has a red light. If the request has a green light, this list will tell the ATCO what has been checked for the TA by the IIS, thus making the suggestion more trustworthy. If the request has a red light, this list will tell the status of each check, thus providing the ATCO an indication of which measures the ATCO may take to make the request acceptable. The TA does not provide any interaction with the TA label for AP1.

TA part of the flight label in AP2. The TA part of the flight label used in AP2 comes in three variants.

Variant AP2.1. When the message about the request is received from the IIS, a small variant of the TA label is shown, as depicted in Fig. 6. For a given request, this variant is identical to the small variant used in AP1 and explained above.

Fig. 6. Flight label with AP2.1 TA label to the right

Variant AP2.2. If the ATCO enters the TA label with the mouse pointer (hover), a slightly large variant of the TA label is shown, as depicted in Fig. 7.

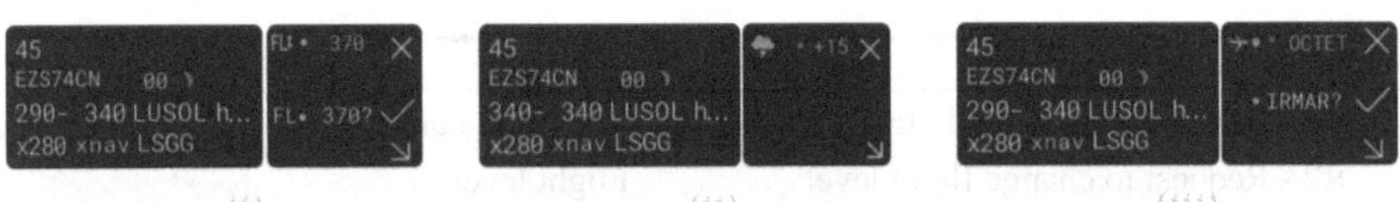

Fig. 7. Flight labels with AP2.2 TA label to the right for the three recommendations

The top part is identical to the small variant, and below this the suggested response is presented. As discussed above, there are three possible recommendations.

(i) If the recommendation is to accept the request (left part of Fig. 7), a green light is shown together with a conformation button for accepting the request. If the ATCO for some reason does not want to follow the recommendation, the ATCO must communicate the rejection to the pilot and may close the TA label.
(ii) If the recommendation is to reject the request and the IIS has no alternative suggestion (middle part of Fig. 7), a red light is shown. If the ATCO agrees to the suggested rejection, the ATCO must communicate the rejection to the pilot and may close the TA label.
(iii) If the recommendation is to reject the original request but the IIS has an alternative suggestion (right part of Fig. 7), a red light is shown for the requested value together with the suggested alternative value as well as a conformation button for using the alternative suggestion. If the ATCO does not agree to the alternative suggestion, the ATCO must either provide an alternative solution or communicate a rejection to the pilot and may close the TA label.

For all three types of recommendations, the ATCO may also expand the label further to get an explanation for the suggestion in the same way as in AP1 by clicking on the downright arrow. This will open variant AP2.3 of the label.

Variant AP2.3. If the ATCO clicks the downright arrow the TA label, the largest variant of the TA label is shown, as depicted in Fig. 8.

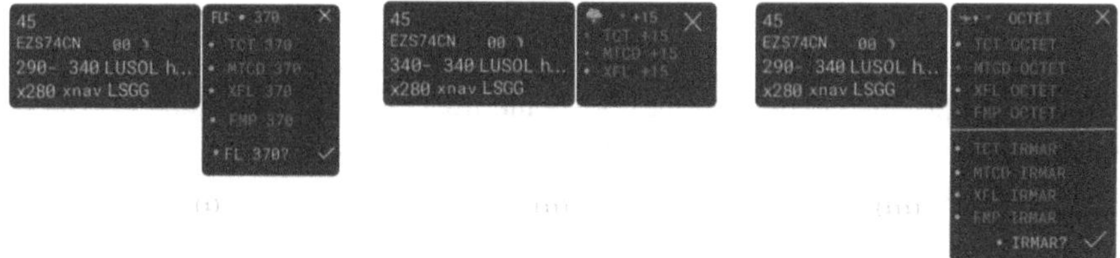

Fig. 8. Flight labels with AP2.3 TA label to the right for the three recommendations.

The top part is identical to the other two variants, and below this the explanation of why the light is red or green is given, as well as why the alternative suggestion will work. Also for this variant there are three possible recommendations.

(i) When the recommendation is to accept the request (left part of Fig. 8), the content of this variant is similar to Variant AP1.2, with the addition of a conformation button for accepting the recommendation.
(ii) When the recommendation is to reject the request and IIS has no alternative suggestion (middle part of Fig. 8), the content of this variant is similar to Variant AP1.2. If the ATCO agrees to the suggested rejection, the ATCO must communicate the rejection to the pilot and may close the TA label.
(iii) If the recommendation is to reject the original request but the IIS has an alternative suggestion (right part of Fig. 8), explanations are shown both for the original request and the alternative suggestion. In addition, there is a conformation button for using the alternative suggestion. If the ATCO does not agree to the alternative suggestion,

the ATCO must either provide an alternative solution or communicate a rejection to the pilot and may close the TA label.

If the ATCO agrees to a suggestion for accepting the request or using a suggested alternative (in both cases by clicking the confirmation button), the necessary value(s) will be automatically changed in the ordinary part of the flight label (e.g., the flight level value is updated). If the request is rejected, there is no need to change anything in the ordinary part of the flight label.

4 Validation of the Teamwork Assistant

The Teamwork Assistant presented in the previous section is the result of iterative, user-centered design and implementation work. To come to the current version of the TA, a number of validations have been conducted, with connected evolvement of the TA design and operation. All validations were conducted with a combination of domain experts in air traffic management, operational ATCOs and usability experts.

The earliest, low-fidelity prototypes of the TA design were to a large extent based on using a dialog/chat-bot window as the main user interface of the TA. The validation of this design concluded that this approach, despite being common in HCAI, does not fit well to the way ATCOs work.

Based on this validation, the next low- and medium-fidelity prototypes located the user interface of TA as an extension to the flight labels. This version supported different subsets of the HTAs for a request as a sequence of interactions between the TA and the ATCO. Validations of this design concluded that the design approach, particularly the TA label, was promising, but that the TA should treat each request in one instead of a sequence of interaction between the TA and the ATCO. This change would also fit better with how the IIS operates.

Based on these validations, higher fidelity prototypes were developed handling the requests as a unit in the user interface. In these, different levels of autonomy were also investigated. Validations of these designs were important for concluding on the two autonomy profiles used in the current implementation.

With the main user interface principles and autonomy profiles in place, high-fidelity protypes were developed ending up in the current implementation. Validations of these prototypes focused mainly on details in the user interface design and interaction, to ensure efficient and effective operation, and that the TA user interface fits the work and mindset of ATCOs. Planned validations of the current implementation are described in Sect. 6.

In a previous publication [25], we have assessed a previous version of the TA design towards design guidelines and patterns for HCAI including [17, 26, 27]. This assessment showed that the design follows most of the guidelines and patterns that are relevant given characteristics of the air traffic control domain.

5 Discussion

An important challenge when designing the DIALOG system in general, and the TA in particular is balancing automation and transparency. The main reason for having a TA is to assist and relieve the ATCO when the workload is high. As the ATCOs need to maintain situational awareness at all times, they need to be assisted in a way that does not reduce their situational awareness. In solutions where an assistant takes over too much work, it will need to inform the ATCO about all operations performed in an autonomous way. In such a situation there is a risk that the workload needed from the ATCO to be up to date on the assistant's operations turns out to be higher than the workload reduction from the automation.

One may argue that keeping a balanced workload over time by reducing it when it is at its highest is more important than the total workload in a longer period of time, and thus that it can be OK that there is not a net workload reduction. This argument is only partly valid in domains like air traffic control, which is characterized by high stakes and responsibility for the ATCO's work. The stakes and responsibilities give ATCOs mental barriers against giving up control. Furthermore, ATCOs must be able to handle emergency situations at any time. To do this, situational awareness is paramount, and handling such situations could usually not be delegated to an assistant.

Such considerations were among the reasons for ending up with the autonomy profiles used in the TA. During the work, designs were made for higher levels of automation (corresponding to EASA level 3A) where the TA should not only suggest responses to the pilot requests but also implement these automatically. As part of this, designs supporting effective communication of autonomous assistant operations were developed, like using shadow flight labels. An important reason for abandoning higher levels of automation is that responses to the requests must be communicated to the pilots. As long as this in most cases is done using radio communication, the ATCOs need to be in the loop more or less continuously. In future operations when data link to the aircraft is expected to be more common, the response problem will become less important.

At the other end of the workload scale, there have also been considerations about whether the TA should always be active when the supported requests are issued. It may be argued that when the task load and workload are low, and the request is not urgent, the ATCO will not need any assistance from an assistant. The main reasons for not having an autonomy profile 0 where the TA is not present in the CWP are (i) to keep the user interface consistent, and (ii) the fact that the TA label when not hovered is very compact and non-intrusive. This is supported by Klien et al. [28] who points of the importance of being predictable and having clear intentions. One can argue that it builds trust between human and AI when ATCO can explore, get used to and build a better mental model of how TA makes decisions during low workload. Getting familiar with using the TA also gives a lower threshold for using it when the workload is high. Furthermore, in most cases it is worse not to show the TA label when the ATCO may have benefit from it, than showing it when the ATCO will not have any benefit from it. It may also be argued that the TA label helps to draw the ATCO's attention to the aircraft issuing a request, and even that it is difficult to imagine situations where the TA label is not useful.

6 Conclusions and Future Work

This research advances knowledge in Human-Computer Interaction by providing novel design solutions for ATCO-AI collaboration. We presented the design and implementation of an AI-infused system assisting en route Air Traffic Controllers in managing pilot requests—an activity that is both cognitively demanding and tightly coupled with safety, workload, and coordination constraints. Our research contributes with insights into all the research questions presented in Sect. 1. To address RQ1, we have an operational prototype of the TAS predicting ATCOs' workload in an unobtrusive manner. To address RQ2, we have an operational prototype of the IIS that is able to identify pilot requests and provide the most important information needed by the ATCO to attend to these requests. To address RQ3, we have an operational prototype of the TA integrated into the experimental SIMADES CWP platform. It receives messages from IIS and TAS and uses the information in these messages to provide ATCO support that adapts to the ATCOs' task- and workload.

Promising features for monitoring ATCOs' attention and workload have been identified in try-outs and semi-realistic laboratory experiments. They include speech characteristics and responses in facial expression to auditory information. Based on the identified workload and attention, pilot requests and ATCOs' predicted actions, Teamwork Assistant assist the ATCO in two different manners denoted Autonomy Profiles. The dialogue between ATCOs and Teamwork Assistant is implemented as an integral part of ATCOs' CWP. The design was guided by the need to provide help and communicate it clearly without increasing ATCOs workload. Several solutions have been developed and thoroughly validated with domain experts and operational ATCO. These validations have caused both quite radical changes and more limited optimizations of the UI, including the interplay between ATCOs and TA. Although our validations so far have involved a limited number of ATCOs and domain experts, we believe that the proposed solutions are useful.

Future work includes the validation of the integrated solution in a one-week-long real-time simulation with a dozen of ATCOs from France and Germany. Other future work includes supporting more requests in the IIS, enhancing the TAS' non-obtrusive measurements of ATCOs' workload based on physiological data, particularly through combining data from different sensors and sources to obtain higher accuracy, and enhancing and expanding the TA. The latter will partly be done by using more advanced reasoning to determine the most appropriate autonomy profile, and partly by supporting autonomy profiles providing EASA level 3 automation.

Acknowledgements. The described work has been supported by the SESAR JU-funded project DIALOG (Deciphering Intents of Air traffic controllers, workLOad assessment and Gaze analysis) with Grant ID 101166886. This paper presents ongoing research.

References

1. Joint ACI World-ICAO Passenger Traffic Report, Trends, and Outlook | ACI World
2. SJU: Strategic research agenda, digital European sky, pp. 64–67. Publications Office of the European Union, Luxembourg (2020)
3. Ref footnote 2 - SJU: Strategic research agenda, digital european sky, pp. 64–67. Publications Office of the European Union, Luxembourg (2020)
4. The FLY AI report - demystifying and accelerating AI in aviation/ATM, European aviation artificial intelligence high level group (2020)

5. Kallus, W., Van Damme, D., Dittmann, A.: Integrated task and job analysis of air traffic controllers - phase 2: task analysis of en-route controllers, EUROCONTROL (1999)
6. Stølen, K.: Technology Research Explained, Springer (2022). https://doi.org/10.1007/978-3-031-25817-6
7. Xu, W.: Toward human-centered AI: a perspective from human-computer interaction. Interactions Magazine (2019)
8. Shneiderman, B.: Human-centered artificial intelligence: reliable, safe & trustworthy. Int. J. Hum. Comput. Interact. **36**(6), 495–504 (2020)
9. Schmager, S., Pappas, I.O., Vassilakopoulou, P.: Understanding human-centred AI: a review of its defining elements and a research agenda. Behav. Inf. Technol. (2025)
10. ISO: ISO 9241-210: Ergonomics of human–system interaction—Part 210: Human-centred design for interactive systems (2010)
11. Holmquist, L.E.: Intelligence on tap: artificial intelligence as a new design material. Interactions **24**(4), 28–33 (2017)
12. European union aviation safety agency: Concept paper: guidance for level 1 & level 2 machine learning applications (2024)
13. Lyons, J.B., Sycara, K., Lewis, M., Capiola, A.: Human–autonomy teaming: definitions, debates, and directions. Front. Psychol. **12** (2021)
14. Pham, D.-T., Ali, H., Fennedy, K., Hsieh, M.-H., Alam, S., Duong, V.: Human-AI hybrid paradigm for collaborative air traffic management systems. In: SESAR Innovation Days Proceedings (2024)
15. Cooper, A.: The Inmates are Running the Asylum. Sams Publishing, Indianapolis (2004)
16. Karahasanović, A., Følstad, A., Schittekat, P.: Putting a face on algorithms: Personas for modeling artificial intelligence. In: Degen, H., Ntoa, S. (eds.) AI-HCI 2021, LNCS, vol. 12797, pp. 229–240. Springer (2021). https://doi.org/10.1007/978-3-030-77772-2_15
17. Amershi, S., et al.: Guidelines for human-AI interaction. In: CHI 2019, pp. 1–13. ACM (2019)
18. Wickramasinghe, C.S., Marino, D.L., Grandio, J., Manic, M.: Trustworthy AI development guidelines for human system interaction. In: HSI 2020, pp. 130–136. IEEE (2020)
19. Hartikainen, M., Väänänen, K., Lehtiö, A., Ala-Luopa, S., Olsson, T.: Human-centered AI design in reality: a study of developer companies' practices. In: NordiCHI 2022, pp. 1–11. ACM (2022)
20. Li, T., Vorvoreanu, M., Debellis, D., Amershi, S.: Assessing human-AI interaction early through factorial surveys. ACM Trans. Comput.-Hum. Interact. **30**(5), 69 (2023)
21. Jameel, M., et al.: Enabling digital air traffic controller assistant through human-autonomy teaming design. In: DASC 2023, pp. 1–9. IEEE (2023)
22. Liao, Q.V., Gruen, D., Miller, S.: Questioning the AI: informing design practices for explainable AI user experiences. In: CHI 2020, pp. 1–15. ACM (2020)
23. Liu, Y., et al.: Cognitive load prediction from multimodal physiological signals using multiview learning. IEEE J. Biomed. Health Inform. **29**(5), 3282–3292 (2025)
24. Yu, X., Yang, H., Chen, C.-H.: Human operators' cognitive workload recognition with a dual attention-enabled multimodal fusion framework. Expert Syst. Appl. **280**, 127418 (2025)
25. Karahasanović, A., et al.::Human-centric AI in safety critical domains – air traffic management case. In: Human centric AI: harmonizing humans and technology. Misra, S., Traymbak, S., Chockalingam, S., Kjølerbakken, M., Braarud, P.Ø. (eds.) CRC Press, A Taylor & Francis Group (2026)

26. Shneiderman, B.: Human-Centered AI. Oxford University Press (2022)
27. Shneiderman, B., Plaisant, C., Cohen, M., Jacobs, S., Elmqvist, N., Diakopoulos, N.: Designing the User Interface: Strategies for Effective Human-Computer Interaction. Pearson (2017)
28. Klien, G., Woods, D.D., Bradshaw, J.M., Hoffman, R.R., Feltovich, P.J.: Ten challenges for making automation a "team player" in joint human-agent activity. IEEE Intell. Syst. **19**(6), 91–95 (2004)

Human-AI Decision Support for Sustainable Air Traffic Controller Workload: Forecast-Informed Bilevel-Optimized Task-Load Estimation

Mercedes Premalatha Ramesh[1,2], Mengtao Lyu[3], Imen Dhief[1], Zhimin Li[1], and Mir Feroskhan[1,2](✉)

[1] Air Traffic Management Research Institute, Singapore 637460, Singapore
mir.feroskhan@ntu.edu.sg
[2] School of Mechanical and Aerospace Engineering, Nanyang Technological University, Singapore 639798, Singapore
[3] Georgia Institute of Technology, Atlanta, GA 30332, USA

Abstract. Flight activity continues to grow, and international forecasts anticipate that global air traffic movements will more than double by mid-century . This sustained increase, combined with weather volatility and recurring staffing constraints, tightens day-to-day operating margins in air traffic control. In this context, supervisors must decide whether adjacent sectors should operate independently or be combined, when configuration changes are required, and how long such configurations should be maintained. These decisions are operationally constrained by letters of agreement, hand-off procedures, dwell-time policies, staffing limits, and flow-management measures. They are often made with limited predictive insight into how air traffic controller workload will evolve under traffic surges or disruptive conditions.

This paper addresses this gap by introducing a forecast-informed decision-support framework that integrates short-term task-load prediction with operationally constrained sector configuration planning. Calibrated quantile forecasts for single sectors and admissible pairs incorporate weather via effective monitoring values, then are reconciled into smooth trajectories and mapped to feasible configuration timelines using mixed-integer optimisation under dwell-time, compatibility, and switching constraints.

Retrospective evaluation using three years traffic data from Automatic Dependent Surveillance-Broadcast (ADS-B) shows that forecast-informed planning reduces expected overload minutes from 91 to 65 per three-hour horizon (approximately 29%). A pilot human-in-the-loop evaluation with three experienced air traffic controllers using 45-min traffic replays further confirms that estimated task-load aligns with simulation-computed workload.

Keywords: air traffic control · controller workload · decision support · workload forecasting · sector combining

W. -C. Li and A. Plioutsias (Eds.): HCII 2026, LNAI 16708, pp. 221–237, 2026.
https://doi.org/10.1007/978-3-032-29459-3_16

1 Introduction

International outlooks from the International Air Transport Association (IATA), the European Organisation for the Safety of Air Navigation (EUROCONTROL), the Federal Aviation Administration (FAA), and the International Civil Aviation Organization (ICAO) indicate sustained growth in flight activity over the coming decade and beyond [7,9,15,16]. For en route operations, this growth reduces operational slack because workload can rise quickly when demand interacts with convective weather, Special Use Airspace activation, or temporary route restrictions. Staffing constraints can further tighten the operating envelope and increase the importance of timely configuration decisions [32]. In day-to-day practice, supervisors therefore rely on *sector combining*, temporarily operating two adjacent sectors as a single position to match resources. Combining can preserve staffing for later peaks and consolidate coordination, but it also concentrates monitoring and interaction load. As conditions evolve, supervisors must decide when to keep sectors combined, when to split them, and how long to hold a configuration, while complying with Letters of Agreement, handoff procedures, minimum dwell-time policies, and local compatibility rules that constrain when switching is permitted.

A substantial body of prior research supports workload-aware capacity management in air traffic control. Analytical models and operational indices relate observable traffic and interaction features such as aircraft count, entries and exits, crossing flows, conflict opportunities, communications, and coordination events to controller workload and sector capacity limits [5,26,27,31,33]. More recent data-driven approaches infer overload risk from historical sector operations [10] and classify workload intensity using traffic indicators and expert labels [22,37], with complementary studies incorporating multimodal signals such as eye tracking and physiological measures [23,29]. Yet, despite these advances, near-term supervisory planning remains challenging, as most existing approaches provide either static snapshots or point predictions and do not translate short-horizon workload evolution into feasible, rule-compliant sector configuration timelines under operational constraints. As a result, supervisors often must infer configuration timing and trade-offs manually from current displays, with limited predictive support for anticipating workload escalation under traffic growth and weather volatility.

This paper addresses that integration gap with a forecast-informed, bilevel decision-support framework for sector combining and separating. Figure 1 shows the supervisory-level workflow. The system produces multi-horizon, quantile-based task-load forecasts for sectors and admissible pairs using XGBoost and a quantile-output TCN, and applies calibration so that prediction bands align with observed frequencies [11,18,34]. The outputs are designed to support supervisory judgement by making uncertainty, constraints, and trade-offs visible and discussable rather than automated away. The paper reports retrospective evaluation on multi-year data and includes a pilot human-in-the-loop validation with three air traffic controllers (ATCOs) using replayed traffic scenarios, with a larger study as the next step. Constraint-aware decision support under uncertainty has also

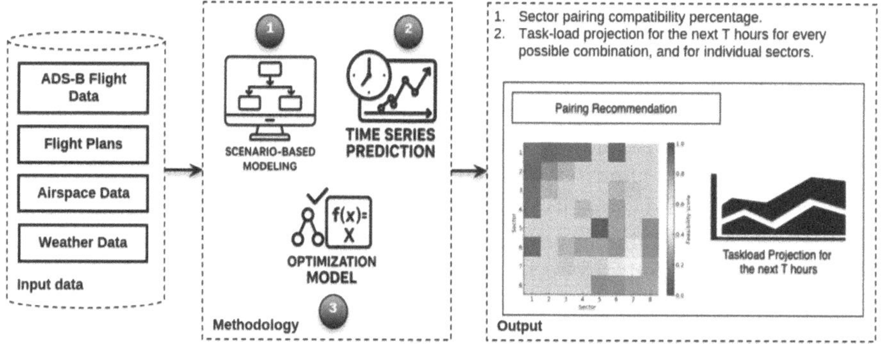

Fig. 1. High-level architecture of the forecast-informed decision-support framework.

been studied in other safety-critical cyber-physical systems, reinforcing the value of combining prediction with operational constraints and robustness considerations [19,36].

2 Related Work

Controller workload has long been studied because it is tightly coupled to safety margins, staffing, and capacity management. Early formulations relate traffic intensity and service processes to operator effort [31,33]. Operational practice subsequently adopted task-based indices that map observable traffic and interaction features, such as aircraft count and density, entries and exits, crossing flows, conflict opportunities, communications, and coordination events, into workload scores or monitoring values used for capacity decisions [5,26,27]. These indices remain valuable because they are interpretable and can be computed from operational data, but they are often applied as deterministic snapshots. As a result, they provide limited foresight into how workload evolves under uncertainty from demand fluctuations, convective weather, and airspace constraints. Surveys and science-mapping work highlight the continuing need for proactive support that helps maintain sustainable operations rather than reacting to exceedances [6,30,39].

Data-driven approaches increasingly predict workload and overload risk directly from historical operations. Sector overload states have been learned from past configurations [10], and AI-based methods classify workload intensity from traffic indicators and expert labels [22,37]. Parallel research explores multimodal indicators, including eye tracking and EEG-based measures, to infer cognitive workload [23,29], while simulation-based methodologies estimate event-level task-load at fine temporal resolution [38]. These efforts improve prediction, yet many outputs are still point estimates or discrete classes, and uncertainty is not always treated as a first-class requirement for operational decisions. Recent controller-focused eye-tracking studies further show that detection failures and workload-related inattentional blindness can be quantified from gaze behaviour, strengthening the case for objective workload validation alongside subjective measures [24,25].

Short-horizon probabilistic forecasting provides useful building blocks. XGBoost and Temporal Convolutional Networks are widely used for structured and temporal prediction [1,4], and quantile and conformal approaches support uncertainty quantification with reliable empirical coverage [11,18,34]. Sector combining and capacity management have also been studied as operational levers. Algorithmic approaches evaluate combining benefits and propose combining schemes under demand [2,21], optimisation and fast-time simulation support workload balancing objectives [35], and high-fidelity studies examine combining effects on task-load and feasibility [28]. Operational decision support tools and handbooks largely focus on flow management and conflict detection [8,14] and staffing guidance [32], but typically do not provide calibrated multi-horizon task-load forecasts for specific pairing options, nor do they translate uncertainty into transparent, rule-compliant configuration timelines.

In summary, prior work establishes strong foundations in workload measurement, prediction, and combining analysis, but an end-to-end supervisor-facing workflow remains uncommon. The present framework addresses this integration gap by coupling calibrated probabilistic forecasting for single and paired sectors with convex reconciliation and constraint-aware planning to produce feasible timelines and explainable decision-support views.

3 Data and Setting

We study upper-airspace en route operations in a de-identified ACC context where temporary sector combining is routinely used to align demand with available controller positions. The sectorization used in this study comprises 8 control sectors and 12 admissible sector pairs. Admissible pairs are defined by a compatibility mask reflecting operational feasibility (e.g., local combining practice and procedural constraints), and the planning layer enforces this mask directly. Decisions are evaluated on a 15-min grid, consistent with supervisory planning cadence and with the 15–180 min horizon used for forecasting and optimisation. The sector polygons used for mapping ADS-B trajectories and aggregating sector-level features on a 15-min grid is illustrated in Fig. 2.

Traffic Data. Traffic inputs consist of 3 years of historical ADS-B trajectories obtained from Flightradar24 under research use. ADS-B is a publicly broadcast surveillance signal, and Flightradar24 provides aggregated historical records suitable for trajectory reconstruction and sector-level feature extraction. No proprietary operational ATC data were used; inputs are derived exclusively from ADS-B records obtained via Flightradar24. After quality filtering (removing duplicate timestamps, invalid positions, and fragmented tracks) and restricting to upper-airspace operations above FL240, the dataset contains approximately 1.1–1.4 million flights intersecting the study area (depending on seasonal demand). Each trajectory is mapped to sector occupancy by intersecting state vectors with official sector polygons. Sector-level time series are then constructed on a uniform

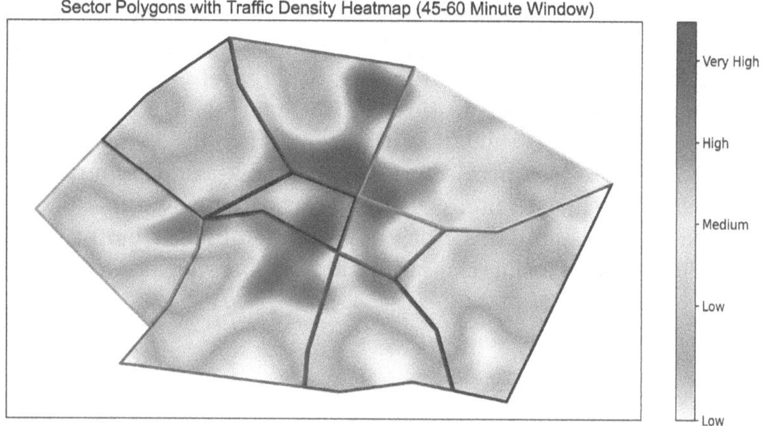

Fig. 2. Sector geometry (top view) and an example of ADS-B-derived traffic density used for feature construction.

15-min grid, including aircraft count, entries/exits, dwell-time summaries, and boundary-crossing proxies.

Over the three-year window, the 15-min grid yields 105,120 decision intervals. This produces 840,960 sector-interval records for single sectors (8 sectors × 105,120) and 1,261,440 pair-interval records for admissible pairs (12 pairs × 105,120), for a total of 2,102,400 entity-interval records used by the forecasting and planning layers.

Weather and Constraint Indicators. Weather and airspace-status conditions are encoded as sector-level indicators at the same 15-min cadence. Gridded meteorological fields (e.g., convective intensity proxies and wind-related features) are spatially aggregated over each sector footprint, and operational constraint flags capture periods in which airspace restrictions increase complexity (e.g., SUA activation or temporary restrictions). These signals serve two roles: (i) as forecasting covariates, and (ii) to derive an effective monitoring value that reduces the practical capacity reference under degraded conditions.

Task-load Index and Monitoring Values. Task-load labels are computed using a normalised index derived from demand and interaction proxies widely used in workload monitoring and modelling [5,26,27]. For each sector and 15-min interval, the index aggregates aircraft count, entry/exit rates, crossing-flow intensity, a conflict-density proxy from converging trajectory geometry, climb/descent activity, and coordination proxies based on boundary crossings. A baseline monitoring value is estimated per sector from historical distributions and operational capacity guidance, and then adjusted using weather/constraint indicators so exceedances reflect reduced practical capacity under degraded conditions [6,39]. For paired sectors, the index is computed over the union of polygons and includes an additive pairing overhead term to capture additional coordination and shared monitoring when two sectors are worked as one position.

Splits for Training and Evaluation. All learning is evaluated using chronological splits to avoid leakage: the first 24 months for training (70,080 intervals), the next 6 months for validation and calibration (17,520 intervals), and the final 6 months for held-out testing (17,520 intervals). In addition to offline testing, a small pilot HITL validation uses replayed traffic scenarios (Sect. 6) to compare estimated task-load trajectories against task-load computed from simulation logs at the same 15-min cadence. Transparent benchmarking practice in human-centered AI and dataset-driven evaluation further motivates publishing reproducible preprocessing and evaluation pipelines alongside model results [3,12].

4 Method

The method integrates short-horizon task-load forecasting with constraint-aware sector combining at a 15-min decision cadence, as summarised in Fig. 3. Every 15 min, the system constructs sector features and a task-load index, forecasts task-load for both single sectors and admissible pairs over a 3-h horizon, and produces a feasible configuration timeline that respects local operational rules. Compared with prior workload prediction or sector combining approaches, the proposed framework makes three design choices explicit: (i) paired-sector task-load is modelled directly with a coordination overhead term, (ii) calibrated predictive bands are reconciled into smooth, limit-aware trajectories suitable for optimisation, and (iii) a mixed-integer planner produces feasible timelines under one-cover, dwell-time, compatibility, and switching constraints. The proposed pipeline is outlined in Fig. 3: sector-level feature construction, calibrated quantile forecasting, convex reconciliation into smooth workload trajectories, and constraint-aware mixed-integer planning to produce feasible configuration timelines.

Entities and Targets. Let $\mathcal{S}$ be the set of sectors and $\mathcal{P}$ the admissible sector pairs (compatibility mask). We define $\mathcal{E} = \mathcal{S} \cup \mathcal{P}$ and discretise time into 15-min intervals indexed by t. The planning horizon uses $K = 12$ steps (180 min), indexed by $k \in \{1, \ldots, K\}$. For each entity $e \in \mathcal{E}$ we model task-load $y_{e,t}$ and an effective monitoring value $m_{e,t}$ representing an operational limit under prevailing conditions. Overload exceedance is

$$z_{e,t} = \max\{0,\, y_{e,t} - m_{e,t}\}. \tag{1}$$

For paired sectors, task-load is computed over the union of polygons and includes an additive pairing overhead to reflect increased coordination and shared monitoring.

Quantile Forecasting. Given features $\mathbf{x}_{e,t}$ (traffic counts/flows, boundary-crossing proxies, kinematic summaries, and weather/constraint indicators), we forecast conditional quantiles of task-load:

$$\hat{q}^{(\tau)}_{e,t+k} \approx Q_\tau(y_{e,t+k} \mid \mathbf{x}_{e,t}), \quad \tau \in \{0.1, 0.5, 0.9\}. \tag{2}$$

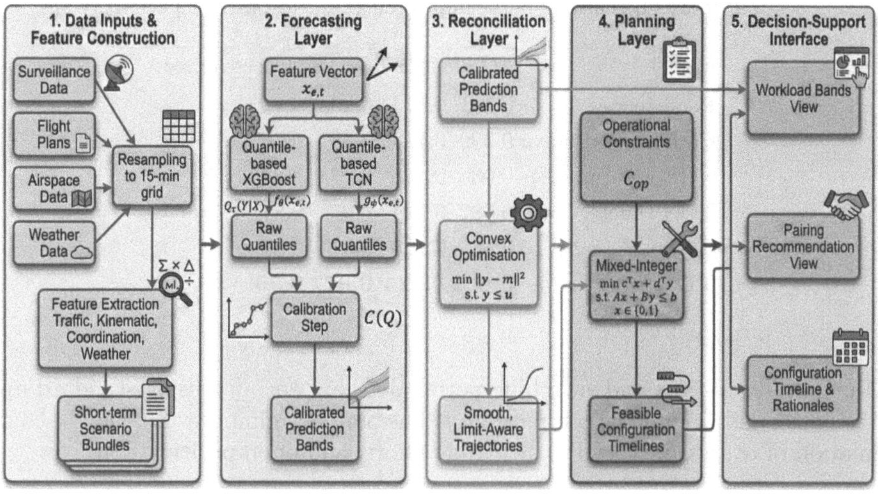

Fig. 3. Pipeline of the proposed framework.

We use (i) quantile XGBoost and (ii) a quantile-output TCN to capture structured and temporal dependencies [1,4,11,34]. Models are trained with chronological splits and tuned using pinball loss and interval diagnostics.

Calibration. To make prediction intervals decision-relevant, we apply post-hoc calibration on the validation period so that nominal coverage matches empirical coverage (overall and stratified by weather severity) [18]. Calibration yields bands that supervisors can interpret as reliable risk envelopes and that the planner can treat as conservative constraints.

Reconciliation. Stepwise forecasts can be noisy near the monitoring value. We compute a smooth decision-grade trajectory $\tilde{y}_{e,t+k}$ by solving a strictly convex quadratic program that stays close to the calibrated median while penalising sharp step-to-step changes, and remains bounded by a high-quantile risk envelope:

$$\min_{\tilde{y}} \sum_{k=1}^{K} \left(w_1 (\tilde{y}_{e,t+k} - \hat{q}_{e,t+k}^{(0.5)})^2 + w_2 (\tilde{y}_{e,t+k} - \tilde{y}_{e,t+k-1})^2 \right) \text{ s.t. } \tilde{y}_{e,t+k} \le \hat{q}_{e,t+k}^{(0.9)}. \quad (3)$$

We set $\tilde{y}_{e,t+0} = y_{e,t}$ for continuity.

Configuration Planning. Let $u_{s,k} \in \{0,1\}$ indicate sector s operates singly at step k, and $v_{p,k} \in \{0,1\}$ indicate pair p is active. One-cover constraints enforce a valid configuration:

$$u_{s,k} + \sum_{p \in \mathcal{P}: s \in p} v_{p,k} = 1 \qquad \forall s \in \mathcal{S}, \ \forall k. \quad (4)$$

Table 1. Forecasting performance on the held-out test period

Model	MAE	RMSE	CRPS	90% coverage
Persistence	0.121	0.174	0.104	–
Count-based linear	0.099	0.148	0.089	0.76
XGBoost (uncal.)	0.085	0.129	0.074	0.82
TCN (uncal.)	0.082	0.124	0.071	0.84
XGBoost (cal.)	0.085	0.129	0.075	0.89
TCN (cal.)	**0.082**	**0.124**	**0.072**	**0.90**

Minimum dwell-time and switching permissions are encoded using standard up-time logic, and $\mathcal{P}$ enforces compatibility. The planner minimises a weighted combination of overload exposure, switching effort, and open-position cost:

$$\min \sum_{k=1}^{K} \Big(\alpha \sum_{e \in \mathcal{E}} o_{e,k} + \beta \, \text{switch}_k + \gamma \, \text{pos}_k \Big), \tag{5}$$

where $o_{e,k} \geq \tilde{y}_{e,t+k} - m_{e,t+k}$ are overload slacks and pos_k counts active positions (each pair counts as one).

Decision-Support Views. Outputs include workload bands against monitoring values, a pairing recommendation summary, and a feasible configuration timeline with short rationales derived from compact feature attributions expressed in operational terms.

On a standard workstation, forecasting and optimisation are designed to execute within the 15-min decision cycle, supporting real-time supervisory use.

5 Results

We evaluate the framework on a held-out test period using a 15-min decision cadence and a 3-h look-ahead horizon ($K = 12$). We report (i) task-load forecasting quality for single sectors and admissible pairs, and (ii) decision-aligned outcomes when forecasts drive the mixed-integer configuration planner.

5.1 Forecasting Performance

We compare quantile XGBoost and quantile TCN against two baselines: persistence (last value) and a count-based linear model. Point accuracy uses MAE/RMSE of the median prediction; probabilistic quality uses CRPS and empirical coverage of the nominal 90% interval.

As indicated in Table 1, calibrated probabilistic forecasting achieves near-nominal 90% coverage while improving point accuracy over persistence and count-based baselines; among the evaluated models, the calibrated TCN provides the strongest overall trade-off in this setting.

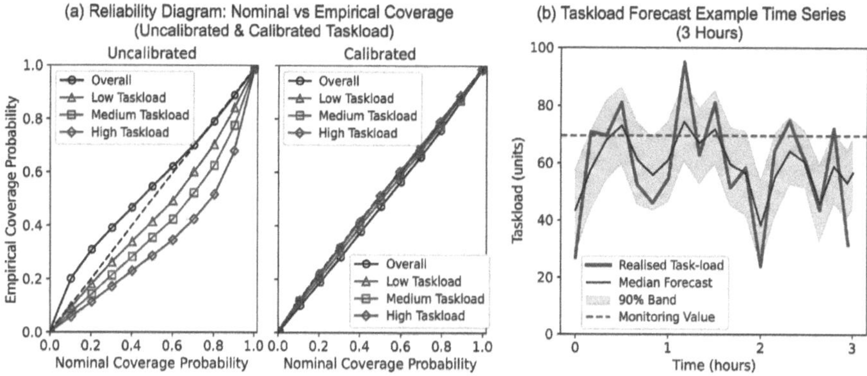

Fig. 4. Forecast reliability and an example 3-h task-load forecast.

Table 2. Decision-aligned outcomes per 3-h horizon

Policy	Overload (min)	Switches	Dwell compliance	Open positions
Persistence + threshold	91.0	2.4	0.94	6.1
Count-based rule	83.5	2.6	0.95	6.0
Planner (XGBoost, cal.)	67.2	1.9	0.98	6.4
Planner (TCN, cal.)	64.8	1.8	0.98	6.3

Coverage remains stable when stratified by task-load regime (Low, Medium, High), supporting the use of calibrated bands as an operational risk signal.

The effect of calibration is illustrated in Fig. 4: panel (a) highlights improved interval reliability after recalibration, while panel (b) provides a representative 3-h forecast in which realised task-load largely remains within the 90% band around the monitoring value.

5.2 Decision Outcomes with Configuration Planning

We compare the proposed planner-driven policy against (i) persistence with a threshold-triggered split and (ii) a count-based rule with basic dwell enforcement. All methods share the same compatibility mask; only the proposed method uses calibrated multi-horizon forecasts, reconciliation, and optimisation.

As indicated in Table 2, forecast-informed planning reduces overload exposure and configuration switching compared with baseline policies while maintaining high dwell compliance, reflecting more stable and feasible configuration timelines.

The case study in Fig. 5 illustrates how forecasted pressure relative to the monitoring value aligns with earlier and more stable configuration timing under dwell and compatibility constraints. The top plot shows calibrated forecast bands against the monitoring value, and the bottom plot shows the recommended single/paired state with switch markers under dwell and compatibility constraints.

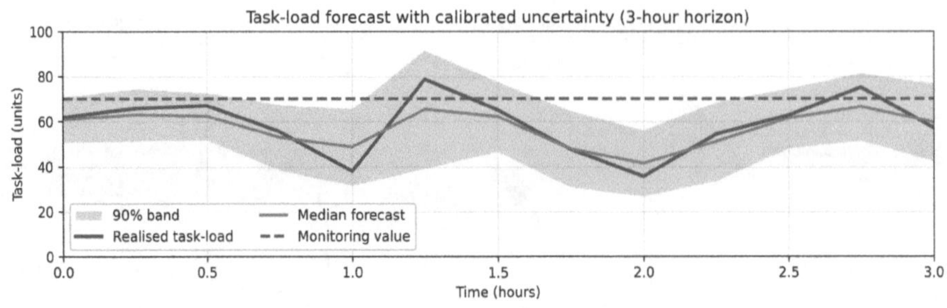

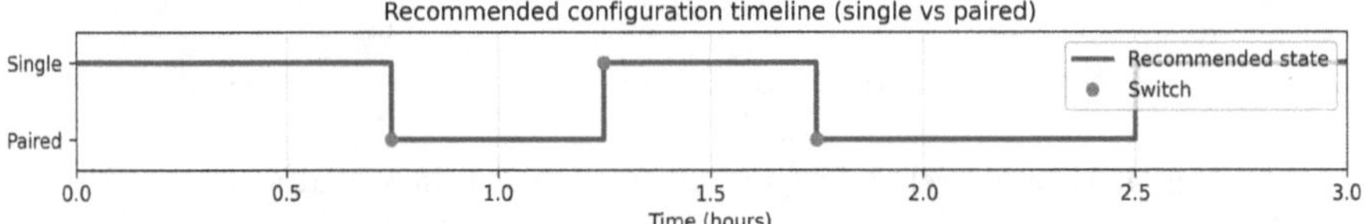

Fig. 5. Case study linking task-load forecasts to a configuration timeline.

Table 3. Ablation summary

Variant	Overload (min)	Switches
Full framework	64.8	1.8
w/o calibration	71.5	1.8
w/o reconciliation	66.2	2.1
w/o pairing overhead	69.8	1.7

5.3 Ablation

We ablate three components: (i) calibration, (ii) reconciliation, and (iii) pairing overhead. Removing calibration tends to under-estimate risk during adverse weather; removing reconciliation increases switching near the monitoring value; removing pairing overhead can over-select pairings in borderline conditions (Table 3).

6 Human-in-The-Loop Evaluation

Retrospective testing quantifies forecast reliability and decision-aligned outcomes, but it does not fully capture how controllers interpret uncertainty, coordinate around recommended timelines, or decide to accept or override advice under time pressure. To assess practical utility and human factors outcomes, a pilot human-in-the-loop (HITL) evaluation was conducted using simulated traffic replay from past scenarios. The goal was to examine whether the proposed decision-support views (workload bands, pairing recommendations, and a configuration timeline with short rationales) improve near-term foresight and configuration stability while preserving controller authority.

6.1 Participants and Experimental Setting

Three operationally experienced air traffic controllers (ATCOs) participated. All participants provided informed consent; the study followed institutional human-subjects/ethics requirements. Each ATCO completed one 45-min simulation session, resulting in three HITL experiments in total. The simulation used traffic replay based on a past scenario to reproduce realistic transitions in demand and complexity. Sector boundaries and admissible sector pairings matched the polygons and compatibility rules used in the offline analysis. The decision-support interface was presented as an advisory display alongside standard traffic and weather views, and it did not execute actions automatically. All sector combining and separating decisions remained with the ATCO.

6.2 Task and Procedure

During each 45-min session, the ATCO managed sector configuration decisions at a 15-min decision cadence. The interface displayed task-load bands for candidate single sectors and admissible pairs together with a recommended configuration timeline that respected one-cover, dwell-time, and compatibility constraints. ATCOs could accept, modify, or ignore the recommendations, and all configuration decisions remained under ATCO control. System logs captured (i) configuration decisions and their timing, (ii) recommendation acceptance or override events, and (iii) the underlying forecast and planning outputs shown at each decision step.

6.3 Measures

The evaluation focused on a compact set of objective and subjective measures suitable for a pilot study with a small sample size. Objective measures included: predicted overload exposure relative to monitoring values, number of configuration switches, dwell compliance, and time-to-action after major scenario transitions (for example, rising demand or increased weather impact). Subjective measures included perceived workload (NASA-TLX or a short supervisory variant) and brief usability and trust items aligned with ISO 9241-11 and standard trust scales [13,17,20]. Short debrief prompts were used to capture qualitative feedback on the clarity of workload bands, usefulness of the timeline, and whether rationales matched operational judgement. The use of attention-related validation signals is consistent with prior controller studies linking gaze patterns to warning-detection failures under elevated task-load [24].

6.4 HITL Validation Plot

To connect the HITL sessions to the forecasting claims, each session is visualised as a time-series comparison between estimated task-load and task-load computed from simulation logs. Figure 6 compares the median estimate and 90% interval against the computed task-load at a common cadence, with the

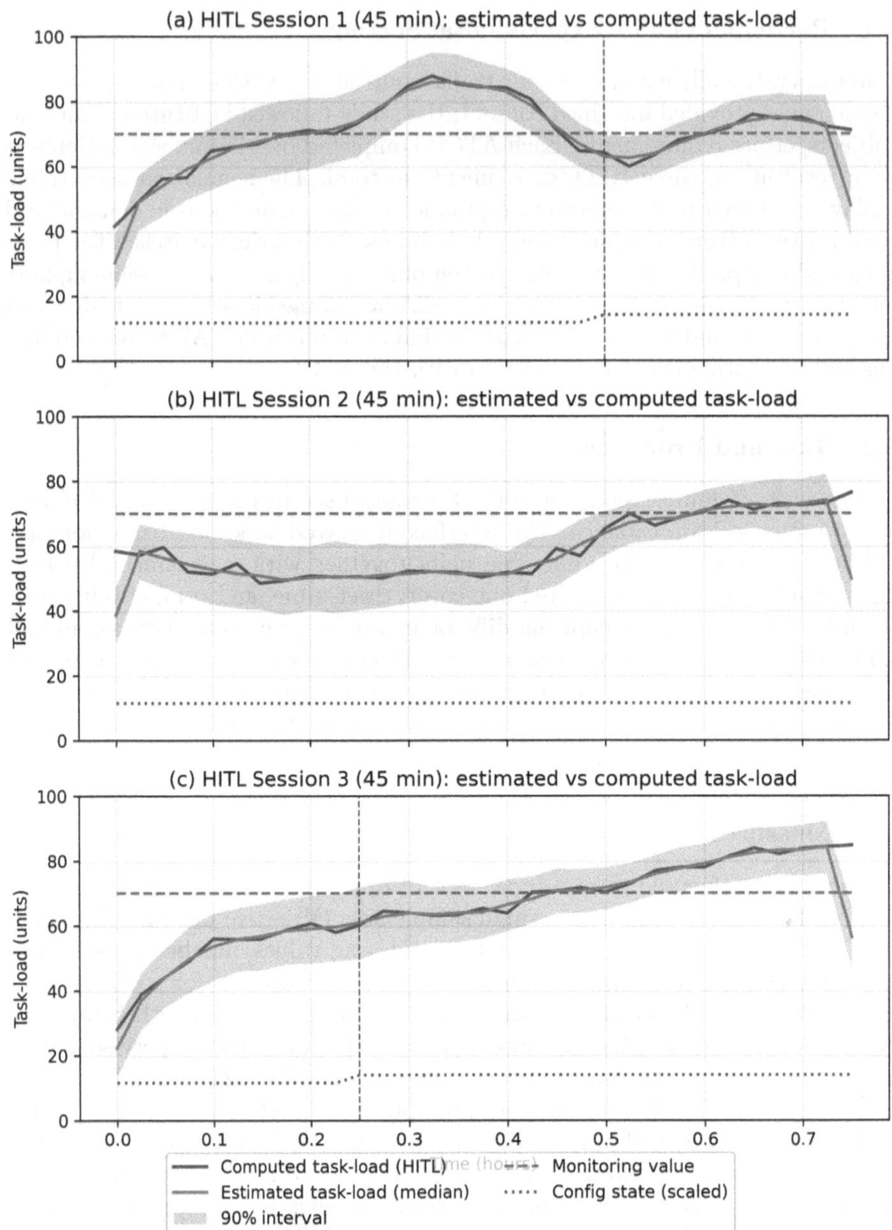

Fig. 6. Pilot HITL sessions: estimated vs. simulation-computed task-load.

monitoring value and configuration state overlaid to show how recommended combining/separating aligns with forecasted pressure.

Across the three HITL sessions, the estimated task-load closely tracks the simulation-computed task-load, and observed values largely remain within the 90% prediction interval. Configuration changes occur near sustained increases relative to the monitoring value rather than transient fluctuations, supporting the interpretability of the timeline recommendations. While the pilot is not intended for statistical inference, it provides face validity that the forecast-to-timeline pipeline produces actionable and explainable supervisory cues under replayed traffic dynamics.

6.5 Summary and Limitations

Across the three HITL experiments, the decision-support views enabled ATCOs to review near-term workload evolution and configuration feasibility in a single place, supporting earlier discussion of pressure points and configuration timing. Because this was a small-sample pilot, results are reported descriptively and are used primarily to validate workflow feasibility, interpretability, and face validity of the recommendations. A larger controlled study is the next step to quantify effects on decision quality, perceived workload, and trust with sufficient statistical power and a broader range of scenarios.

7 Discussion

This work targets a practical supervisory challenge: deciding when to combine or separate adjacent sectors under rapidly changing demand, weather, and operational constraints. Rather than treating workload as a static snapshot, the framework links calibrated short-horizon task-load forecasts for both single sectors and admissible pairs to a constraint-aware planning layer. This coupling is important operationally because it translates near-term risk into feasible timelines that already respect one-cover, dwell policies, and compatibility rules, instead of leaving supervisors to manually infer timing and feasibility from raw indicators.

From a human factors perspective, the framework is designed to support judgement rather than replace it. First, uncertainty is communicated explicitly through prediction bands, which helps supervisors reason about risk without relying on a single point estimate. Second, recommendations are presented as a timeline with concise rationales, which supports briefing and coordination by making the trade-offs visible and discussable. Third, operational rules are encoded directly in the planner, which improves transparency because the system can explain why certain pairings are infeasible or why a change is delayed to satisfy dwell constraints.

Methodologically, two design choices are central. Quantile-based forecasting provides a direct way to estimate near-term workload distributions using available surveillance-derived features, and calibration improves reliability of prediction bands so they can be treated as decision-relevant rather than purely illustrative. The convex reconciliation layer reduces oscillation near monitoring values, which improves interpretability and prevents the planning layer from reacting to noise. Together, these steps enable a planner that balances overload exposure, switching stability, and the staffing implications of opening additional positions.

Several limitations should be noted. The task-load index and monitoring values are derived from observable traffic and interaction proxies and may not capture all elements of cognitive or team workload, especially during rare events or atypical procedures. The evaluation is retrospective and therefore does not measure how supervisors attend to the bands, interpret rationales, or incorporate recommendations into team communication. Finally, optimisation weights reflect a reasonable trade-off between overload, switching, and open-position cost, but they may require tuning to local policy and staffing posture.

These limitations motivate extending the completed pilot HITL into a larger controlled evaluation. That study will test whether the decision-support views improve decision timing, reduce overload exposure, and support coordination without increasing perceived workload or reducing trust. The findings will also inform refinements to the workload index, the calibration strategy under adverse conditions, and the way rationales are phrased for supervisory use. More broadly, the results will clarify how calibrated forecasting and constraint-aware planning can be integrated as an advisory layer alongside existing ATC displays and procedures.

8 Conclusion

This paper presented a human-AI decision-support framework for sustainable ATCO workload management focused on sector combining and separating decisions. The approach predicts task-load 15 to 180 min ahead for both single sectors and admissible sector pairs using quantile-based models with calibrated uncertainty. A convex reconciliation step then yields smooth, limit-aware trajectories, and a mixed-integer planner selects feasible configuration timelines that respect one-cover, dwell-time, and compatibility constraints while balancing overload exposure, switching effort, and open-position cost. The resulting outputs are designed for supervisory use, combining workload bands against monitoring values with a configuration timeline and concise rationales.

Retrospective evaluation is structured to assess both forecasting reliability and decision-aligned outcomes, including overload duration, switching stability, and dwell compliance. A larger human-in-the-loop study is planned to quantify usability, perceived workload, and trust with sufficient statistical power. Overall, the work provides a transparent path for combining calibrated short-horizon forecasting with operationally realistic optimisation to support supervisory decision making in a safety-critical, high-variability environment.

Acknowledgments. This research is supported by the National Research Foundation, Singapore, and the Civil Aviation Authority of Singapore, under the Aviation Transformation Programme.

Disclosure of Interests. The authors have no competing interests to declare that are relevant to the content of this article.

References

1. Bai, S., Kolter, J.Z., Koltun, V.: An empirical evaluation of generic convolutional and recurrent networks for sequence modeling. In: International Conference on Learning Representations (ICLR) (2018)
2. Bloem, M., Gupta, P., Lai, C.F., Kopardekar, P.: Benefits assessment of algorithmically combining generic high altitude airspace sectors. 27th Congress of the International Council of the Aeronautical Sciences (2009)
3. Chakravarthi, B.R., et al.: Dravidianmultimodality: A dataset for multi-modal sentiment analysis in tamil and malayalam. arXiv:2106.04853 (2021). https://arxiv.org/abs/2106.04853
4. Chen, T., Guestrin, C.: Xgboost: A scalable tree boosting system. In: Proceedings of the 22nd ACM SIGKDD International Conference on Knowledge Discovery and Data Mining, pp. 785–794 (2016). https://doi.org/10.1145/2939672.2939785
5. Crutchfield, J., Rosenberg, C.: Predicting subjective workload ratings: A comparison and synthesis of operational and theoretical models. DOT/FAA/AM-07/6 Tech. Rep. FAA Office of Aerospace Medicine (2007)
6. Durso, F.T., Manning, C.A.: Air traffic control. Rev. Human Factors Ergonomics **3**(1), 195–244 (2008). https://doi.org/10.1518/155723408X342826
7. EUROCONTROL: Seven-year flight forecast 2025–2031 (2025). https://www.eurocontrol.int/publication/eurocontrol-forecast-2025-2031
8. Federal Aviation Administration: En route decision support tool (edst) description (2025). https://www.faa.gov/air_traffic/publications, Accessed 2025
9. Federal Aviation Administration: Faa aerospace forecast, fiscal years 2025–2045 (2025). https://www.faa.gov/data_research/aviation/aerospace_forecasts
10. Gianazza, D.: Learning air traffic controller workload from past sector operations. In: USA/Europe Air Traffic Management Research and Development Seminar (2017)
11. Guo, H.: Probabilistic load forecasting for integrated energy systems using quantile temporal convolutional networks. Energy Syst. (2024)
12. Hande, A., others, Thamburaj, K.P.: Hope speech detection in under-resourced kannada language. arXiv:2108.04616 (2021). https://arxiv.org/abs/2108.04616
13. Hart, S.G., Staveland, L.E.: Development of nasa-tlx (task load index): Results of empirical and theoretical research. Adv. Psychol. **52**, 139–183. Elsevier (1988). https://doi.org/10.1016/S0166-4115(08)62386-9
14. Herschler, D., et al.: Air Traffic Control Decision Support Tool Design and Implementation Handbook. Tech. rep, FAA Human Factors Division (2019)
15. International Air Transport Association: Global outlook for air transport (2025). https://www.iata.org/
16. International Civil Aviation Organization: Icao strategic plan 2026–2050 (2024). https://www.icao.int/
17. International Organization for Standardization: Iso 9241-11: Ergonomics of human-system interaction — part 11: Usability: Definitions and concepts (2018), International Standard
18. Jensen, V., Bianchi, F.M., Anfinsen, S.N.: Ensemble conformalized quantile regression for probabilistic time series forecasting, arXiv preprint arXiv:2202.08756 (2022)

19. Jia, Q., Xiao, J., Feroskhan, M.: Multitarget assignment under uncertain information through decision support systems. IEEE Trans. Industr. Inf. **20**(8), 10636–10646 (2024). https://doi.org/10.1109/TII.2024.3397392
20. Jian, J.Y., Bisantz, A.M., Drury, C.G.: Foundations for an empirically determined scale of trust in automated systems. Int. J. Cogn. Ergon. **4**(1), 53–71 (2000). https://doi.org/10.1207/S15327566IJCE0401_04
21. Kopardekar, P., Magyarits, S.: An algorithmic approach for airspace sector combining. In: USA/Europe Air Traffic Management Research and Development Seminar (2009)
22. Laskowski, J., et al.: Ai-based method of air traffic controller workload assessment. In: 2024 11th International Workshop on Metrology for AeroSpace (MetroAeroSpace), pp. 46–51 (2024). https://doi.org/10.1109/MetroAeroSpace61015.2024.10591524
23. Lemetti, A., Meyer, L., Peukert, M., Polishchuk, T., Schmidt, C., Wylde, H.A.: Eye in the sky: Predicting air traffic controller workload through eye-tracking based machine learning. In: IEEE/AIAA Digital Avionics Systems Conference (2024)
24. Li, Z., Li, F., Lyu, M.: Tracking the unseen and unaware: Deciphering controllers' detection failures to warnings through eye-tracking metrics. Int. J. Human–Comput. Inter. 1–20 (2025). https://doi.org/10.1080/10447318.2024.2448877
25. Li, Z., Li, Z., Li, F.: Visual attention analytics for individual perception differences and task load-induced inattentional blindness. In: Cross-Cultural Design. HCII 2023. Lecture Notes in Computer Science, pp. 71–83. Springer, Cham (2023). https://doi.org/10.1007/978-3-031-35939-2_6
26. Manning, C.A., Mills, S.H., Fox, C., Pfleiderer, E.M., Mogilka, H.J.: Using air traffic control taskload measures and communication events to predict subjective workload. Tech. Rep. DOT/FAA/AM-02/4, FAA Office of Aerospace Medicine (2002)
27. Oktal, H., Yaman, K.: A new approach to air traffic controller workload measurement and modelling. Aircraft Eng. Aerosp. Technol. **83**(1), 35–42 (2011). https://doi.org/10.1108/00022661111119900
28. Moreno, P., Zamarreño Suárez, F., Gómez Comendador, M., V.F.: Dynamic methodology for air traffic control sector combining. In: International Conference on Research in Air Transportation (2023)
29. Radüntz, T.: Eeg-based psychophysiological assessment of mental workload in air traffic control using the dfhm workload index. Front. Neurosci. (2020)
30. Roychoudhury, I., Spirkovska, L., O'Connor, M., Kulkarni, C.: Survey of methods to predict controller workload for real-time monitoring of airspace safety. Tech. Rep. NASA/TM-2018-219985, NASA Ames Research Center (2018)
31. Schmidt, D.K.: A queueing analysis of the air traffic controller's workload. IEEE Trans. Syst. Man Cybern. SMC. **8**(6), 492–498 (1978). https://doi.org/10.1109/TSMC.1978.4309962
32. Transportation Research Board: Air Traffic Controller Staffing in the En Route Domain. Special Report 301, National Academies Press (2010)
33. Tulga, M.K., Sheridan, T.B.: Dynamic decisions and workload in multitask supervisory control. IEEE Trans. Syst. Man Cybern. **10**(5), 217–232 (1980). https://doi.org/10.1109/TSMC.1980.4308343
34. Vasseur, C.: A comparison of quantile regression methods for probabilistic load forecasting. Int. J. Forecast. (2021)
35. Volf, P., Rollo, M.: Airspace sectorization optimization using fast-time simulation of air traffic controller's workload. In: Proceedings of the 12th USA/Europe ATM Seminar (2017)

36. Xiao, J., Feroskhan, M.: Cyber attack detection and isolation for a quadrotor UAV with modified sliding innovation sequences. IEEE Trans. Veh. Technol. **71**(7), 7202–7214 (2022). https://doi.org/10.1109/TVT.2022.3170725
37. Yu, X., Chen, C.H., Yang, H.: Cognitive workload quantification for air traffic controllers with ensemble semi-supervised learning. Adv. Eng. Inform. (2025)
38. Zamarreño Suárez, M., et al.: Methodology for determining the event-based taskload of an air traffic controller using real-time simulations. Aerospace **10**(2), 97 (2023). https://doi.org/10.3390/aerospace10020097
39. Zamarreño Suárez, M., et al.: Understanding the research on air traffic controller workload and its implications for safety: A science mapping-based analysis. Safety Sci. **176**, 106545 (2024). https://doi.org/10.1016/j.ssci.2024.106545

VERA: A Validation Environment for Researching ATC Interfaces and Tools

Justus Renkhoff(✉), Julian Böhm, Lennard Nöhren, and Mohsan Jameel

German Aerospace Center, Institute of Flight Guidance, Lilienthalplatz 7, 38108 Braunschweig, Germany
{justus.renkhoff,julian.boehm,lennard.noehren,mohsan.jameel}@dlr.de
https://www.dlr.de/en/fl

Abstract. While air traffic demand continues to grow, there is a shortage of air traffic controllers (ATCOs). Therefore, new operational concepts and assistance systems are being explored to maintain safety and improve efficiency. Their successful development requires close collaboration between researchers, developers, and domain experts to ensure a user-centred design.

Traditionally, the development and evaluation of such tools rely on high-fidelity air traffic simulation environments. Although these platforms provide realistic conditions, they require complex technical setups and in-person studies, making iterative, human-centred development slow and resource-intensive. As a result, a gap emerges between early-stage design ideas and large-scale validation of mature prototypes.

To address this challenge, this paper introduces a Validation Environment for Researching Air Traffic Control Interfaces and Tools (VERA). VERA is designed to enable rapid, remote, and easily configurable validation studies while preserving essential aspects of ATCO interaction and decision-making. It supports testing of interface protoypes, collection of behavioural data, and the development and assessment of systems based on artificial intelligence across different stages of system maturity. The paper presents the overall concept, core functionalities, an example application scenario, and outlines future extensions.

Keywords: Air Traffic Control · Human Factors · Validation

1 Introduction

EUROCONTROL forecasts continued growth in European IFR traffic over the coming years [3]. At the same time, air traffic management (ATM) is confronted with both emerging responsibilities, such as the implementation of climate-optimized flight planning, and a persistent shortage of air traffic controllers (ATCOs) [7,19]. To address these challenges, new concepts and tools are required to help mitigate staff shortages and support ATCOs in managing emerging operational demands. One example is the development of highly automated systems

W. -C. Li and A. Plioutsias (Eds.): HCII 2026, LNAI 16708, pp. 238–255, 2026.
https://doi.org/10.1007/978-3-032-29459-3_17

like a digital controller that can be assigned responsibility either for controlling entire aircraft or for performing specific tasks, such as conflict resolution [8,18]. The development and evaluation of such concepts and tools typically rely on human-in-the-loop (HITL) studies conducted in high-fidelity simulated controller working positions (CWPs). Major research institutions operate advanced air traffic control (ATC) simulators that enable realistic validations like the German Aerospace Center's (DLR) Air Traffic Management and Operations Simulator (ATMOS)[1], Tower and Apron simulator (ATS)[2] or NASA's Air Traffic Control Lab[3]. Such simulators are capable of closely approximating operational CWPs, allowing newly developed concepts and tools to be validated and their potential operational impact to be assessed. However, these systems are complex, require specialized personnel to operate, and incur substantial costs. In addition, they are typically stationary installations, meaning that participants must be physically present on site. Given the existing shortage of ATCOs, recruiting sufficient numbers of operational experts for frequent validation sessions is challenging. Consequently, studies in this domain often involve relatively small sample sizes. These constraints complicate user-centered design and development processes, which typically rely on iterative cycles of prototyping, testing, and refinement. In industry, however, such iterative and user-centered approaches have long been recognized as important for developing systems more efficiently, incorporating structural user feedback early, and identifying necessary changes before costly implementation. In the ATC domain, by contrast, these approaches are still comparatively uncommon [13]. Additionally, the high entry barrier associated with large-scale simulators also limits their accessibility for smaller projects. As a result, there is a need for simulation environments that can represent air traffic operations with sufficient realism, while deliberately avoiding the overhead of full operational fidelity. Such a simulation environment should emphasize ease of use, modification of components, support for remote validations, straightforward setup, and the possibility of integrating training environments for reinforcement learning applications. To address these needs, the Validation Environment for Researching ATC Interfaces and Tools (VERA) is introduced within this paper. This paper presents related work in Sect. 2, concept and core functionality of VERA in Sect. 3 as well as demonstrates its applicability through an example use case in which the platform is used to validate novel ATC support concepts and interaction designs in Sect. 4. Finally, in Sect. 5 the paper is concluded followed by the next steps in the development of VERA presented in Sect. 6.

[1] https://www.dlr.de/en/research-and-transfer/research-infrastructure/air-traffic-management-and-operations-simulator-atmos - accessed 12.02.2026.

[2] https://www.dlr.de/en/research-and-transfer/research-infrastructure/apron-and-tower-simulator-ats-en - accessed 12.02.2026.

[3] https://www.nasa.gov/ames/aviationsystems/air-traffic-control-lab/-accessed 12.02.2026.

2 Related Work

Existing simulation environments for ATC research differ substantially in their scope, fidelity, and intended use.

Commercial simulators such as the SimCWP[4] by Frequentis are designed as training environments for ATCOs. Consequently, they aim to realistically replicate operational CWPs and are not intended as platforms for validating novel concepts or experimental tools.

ATMOS and ATS are research-oriented simulators intended for the development and validation of new tools and operational concepts while still replicating a realistic CWP. To ensure flexibility, these and comparable simulators typically follow a highly modular architecture. In such setups, air traffic is generated by dedicated traffic simulation frameworks, such as NARSIM [20] or BlueSky [6], which provide realistic traffic behaviour, whereas the user interfaces and assistance tools can be exchanged or adapted depending on the specific use case or project. Despite their flexibility, these systems require specially trained personnel due to their complexity and are not easily deployable outside dedicated facilities.

Accordingly, there is a need for high-fidelity simulated CWPs that can be used by a broader community. An example for such a tool is the digital twin provided by NATS, which emphasizes realistic traffic representation and provides data sets and training environments ("gyms") for reinforcement learning applications [16]. Their goal is to make this project publicly available by April 2026. In contrast, other approaches deliberately reduce simulation fidelity in order to isolate specific aspects of ATCO behavior or system interaction. The "microworlds" developed at DLR, for example, simplify operational complexity in order to study individual problems in a controlled manner [4,9,15].

VERA is positioned between NAT's high-fidelity approach and DLR's "microworlds". Rather than maximizing operational realism or strongly abstracting the task, VERA emphasizes ease of use, adaptability, and rapid prototyping. VERA relies on a simplified traffic simulation preserving the look and feel of a CWP, while avoiding to rely on external traffic simulators to reduce complexity to focus on early validation of new concepts and interface concepts to allow continuous involvement of ATCOs without the overhead of large-scale simulation setups.

3 Concept, Design and Functionalities of VERA

VERA is implemented using the Godot 4 engine[5], which provides an integrated framework for real-time visualization, interaction handling, and user interface (UI) development. Godot's deterministic update loop and scene-based architecture enable precise control over timing, interaction events, and visualization

[4] https://www.frequentis.com/sites/default/files/pr/2021-10/20211021-FREQUENTIS-Orthogon-MicroNav-SimCWP_EN.pdf - accessed 16.02.2026.

[5] https://godotengine.org/ - accessed 05.03.2026.

layers, which is essential for HITL experiments and detailed interaction logging. In addition, its low deployment overhead facilitates the creation of different configurations and experimental setups and lowers the practical barriers to involving ATCOs without requiring access to large-scale simulators. Different versions can be easily exported as executable files for Windows and Linux, or even as web applications if the installed plugin and extensions allow it. This enables both mobile validation setups and fully remote studies, as no complicated installation is required and starting an exported validation setup is as simple as running a single executable or opening a website.

VERA is designed to focus on scenario for the upper-airspace. The environment provides a UI that displays the airspace, aircraft-related information and allows the issuance of typical clearances, such as heading, speed, flight level changes, or directs. By default, VERA includes, among others, a mid-term conflict detection tool and a distance measurement tool. Additional tools can be integrated into the environment to support the evaluation of new concepts and interaction designs. Furthermore, tools and systems based on artificial intelligence (AI) can be directly trained and tested within the environment. VERA provides by default an environment for training agents capable of resolving mid-term conflicts using reinforcement learning. All interactions with VERA and aircraft information are logged automatically and can be accessed for further analysis. These logs can, for instance, be used to train supervised learning models, to evaluate ATCO behavior or tool usage patterns and to replay scenarios. The overall concept and system architecture of VERA are illustrated in Fig. 1. At present, VERA only uses its own internal traffic simulation. In the future, an interface will be implemented to enable the use of data from external traffic simulations.

3.1 Configuring Airspaces and Scenarios

VERA allows for the flexible integration of different traffic scenarios across multiple airspaces. To this end, the project maintains separate directories for airspace definitions and scenario files. This separation supports a modular configuration of simulation setups and simplifies the management and adaptation of scenarios. Airspace files define the static structure of the controlled environment. The structure of these files is based on the airspace representation used in the Swedish Civil Air Traffic Control (SCAT) dataset [10], allowing such data to be reused with only minor modifications. Each airspace definition consists of a set of named waypoints and one or more sectors, where sectors are represented by polygonal volumes with specified minimum and maximum flight levels. This enables the modeling of adjacent upper-airspace sectors and their vertical boundaries in a compact and extensible format. Scenarios are defined independently of the airspace geometry and specify the dynamic elements of a simulation run. A scenario file references an airspace definition and describes one or more aircraft, including their callsigns, initial cruise altitudes, speeds and flight plans. This modular design allows scenarios to be easily modified, duplicated, or extended

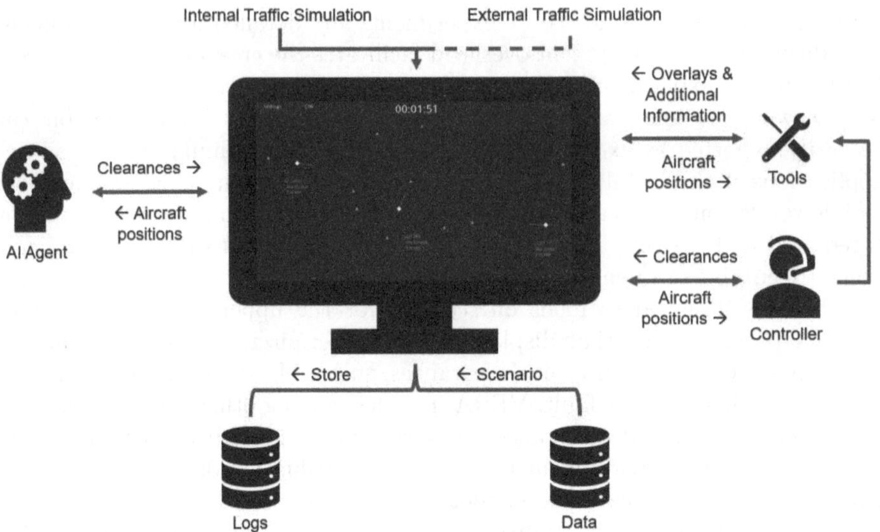

Fig. 1. Overview of VERA and its core components.

while relying on a consistent airspace definition. As a result, new traffic situations can be created efficiently without duplicating airspace information.

When starting VERA, the user is presented with a start screen that lists the scenarios available in the corresponding scenario directory and allows one of them to be selected for execution. Optionally, the start screen also provides access to a settings menu, for example to adjust the visual theme. Since this menu is implemented as a separate node in Godot, it can easily be shown or hidden depending on the experimental setup and the degree of freedom intended for the participant. The start screen is shown in Fig. 2.

To further support scenario creation, a dedicated scenario editor is currently under development. The editor is intended to provide a visual interface for defining and configuring traffic scenarios and will allow scenarios to be exported directly in the format required by VERA. This is expected to reduce manual configuration effort and lower the entry barrier for creating new experimental scenarios.

3.2 User Interface and Default Tools

The color scheme and layout of VERA are based on the results of the research project Envision [11]. In Envision, DLR and the project partners Frequentis Orthogon and the University of Osnabrück investigated how to improve the development cycle of controller working positions (CWPs) and how to modernize their design. For this purpose, a prototypical CWP was developed as a case study and evaluated by ATCOs in multiple validation studies [13]. Based on these studies, several key design principles for modern CWPs were derived,

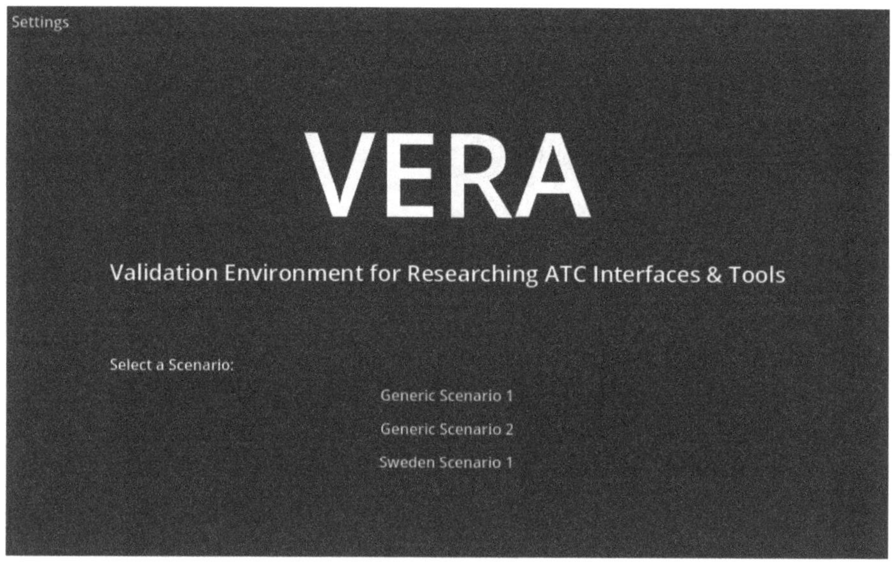

Fig. 2. The start screen of VERA allows the user to select a scenario. In addition, a button located in the top-left corner opens a settings menu that provides customization options, such as the selection of a color theme.

which form the basis for the design of VERA. One of these principles is to structure the layout of the user interfac in a simple and organized manner and use minimalistic shapes to make it more intuitive and less distracting. Another design principle is the right selection of colors. Most of the UI should use low contrast and muted colors to reduce distraction and improve legibility, while high contrast colors should only be used for elements that should grab the attention of the user, for example warnings [14]. The following sections describe the main interface elements of VERA and how these design principles are reflected in its implementation.

Scenario Interface. After a scenario has been selected, VERA loads the corresponding airspace configuration and scenario files described in Sect. 3.1. Subsequently, the scenario interface is initialized, presenting the participant with a radar-like display that emulates a CWP. The interface is shown in Fig. 3. It provides the ATCO with all information required to manage the traffic situation. Aircraft are displayed together with their labels, sector boundaries, waypoints, and flight trajectories. In addition, overlays such as flight plans and conflict indications can be displayed. A simulation time indicator is shown at the top of the screen to support temporal orientation during the run. To support orientation and consistent interaction, interface elements are spatially organized into dedicated functional regions around the radar view. By default, tools, such as conflict-related assistance functions, can be accessed via the tool area located

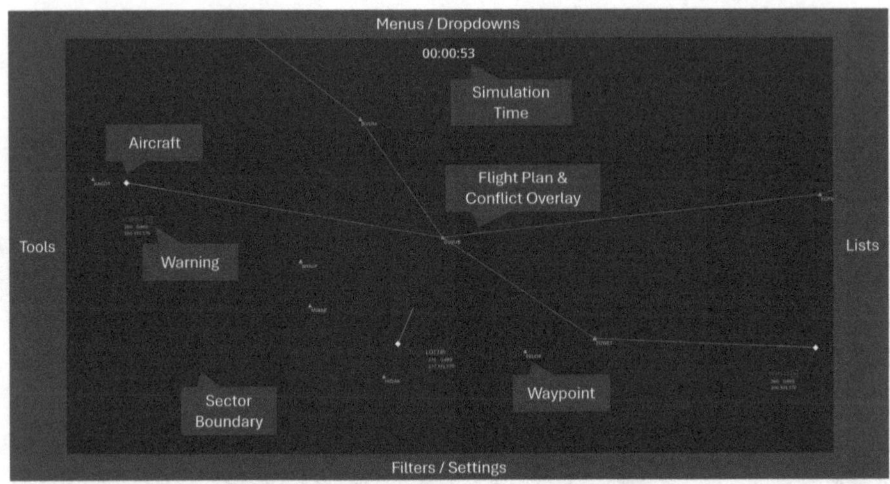

Fig. 3. Scenario Interface.

on the left side. Lists, providing additional information e.g. on actions taken by assistance tools [22], are on the right side, and filters and settings at the bottom of the screen, while additional menus are positioned at the top. This follows the recommendations from the Envision project. User interaction is supported through contextual menus that can be opened by right clicking on an aircraft's label and allow the issuance of typical clearances (e.g., heading, speed, flight level, and direct-to instructions). Overall, the interface aims to reproduce the core interaction principles of operational CWPs while following recommendations from the Envision project. Additionally, it should remaining flexible enough to integrate experimental tools as well as additional design and interface elements.

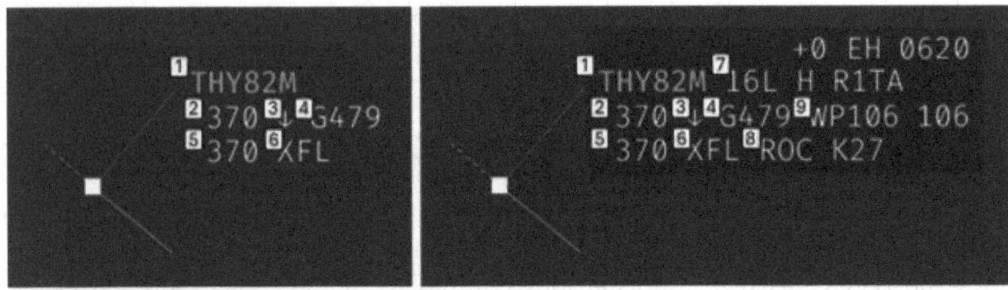

Fig. 4. Two examples for possible track label layouts. Left: minimal label with most important information. Right: enhanced label with additional information.

Label Design. One of the key components of a CWP is the aircraft track label. It contains important information for the flights and is the main interface for interactions with the flight in the CWP. Therefore, choosing a good layout and design of the track label is crucial for the usability of a CWP. Feedback from the Envision project shows that the most important information of flights always needs to be visible in the label without overloading it. As there are usually many labels on the radar display at the same time, too much information might distract the user or block other information. Furthermore, many users have different preferences which information should always be contained in the label and which information should only be shown on demand. Therefore, the contents of the track label in VERA are configurable and can be easily adapted via the Node-Structure of Godot to fit the needs of the user. The option to increase the size of the label on demand (e.g. by selecting the flight) to include additional information was also well received in the envision project, providing the user with a simple and quick way to acquire additional information for a flight without cluttering the user interface permanently. The right selection of colors and highlights also proved to be an important factor for the track label design, as this can be used to include additional information in the label without increasing its size. Nevertheless, to many colours might cause confusion. Finally, track label interactions were an important topic for the users in the past, as this is the simplest way to adapt the state of the flight. It should be possible to open menus to adapt the values in some of the fields of the track label simply by clicking them. The design and position of these menus needs to be chosen carefully to not obstruct other important information as well [14].

Figure 4 shows two examples for how a track label in VERA could look like, depending on the configuration. On the left is the default label provided without any further configuration, that only shows information that is absolutely necessary for ATCOs. The fields contain the following data: Callsign (1), actual flight level (2), climb/descend indicator (3), ground speed (4), cleared flight level (5) and exit flight level (6). Using Godot's node structure it is possible to configure and adjust the information to create custom track labels based on different needs. On the right of Fig. 4, is an example, showing a custom label, containing advanced information for the flight, like landing runway (7), rate of climb/descend (8), next waypoint (9) and more.

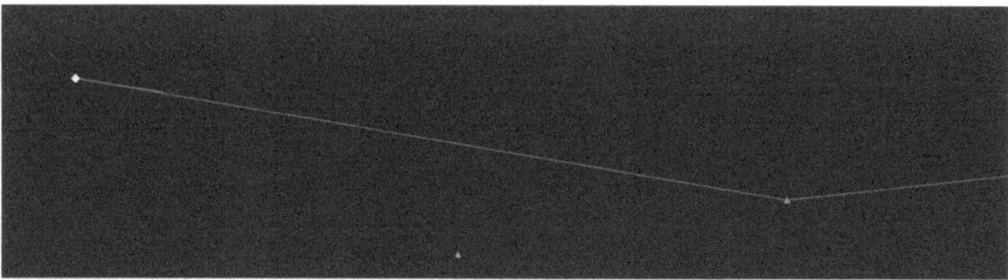

Fig. 5. An aircraft, displayed as a white diamond marker, with the flight-plan overlay and 5 NM indication enabled. The cyan polyline represents the planned route via the displayed waypoints, the circular ring marks the 5 NM reference distance.

Flight Plan Overlay. By right-clicking on an aircraft's track symbol, its corresponding flight plan is displayed as an overlay. In addition, a circular marker with a radius of 5 nautical miles is shown around the track symbol to provide a quick reference for separation assessment. An example of the flight plan overlay is illustrated in Fig. 5.

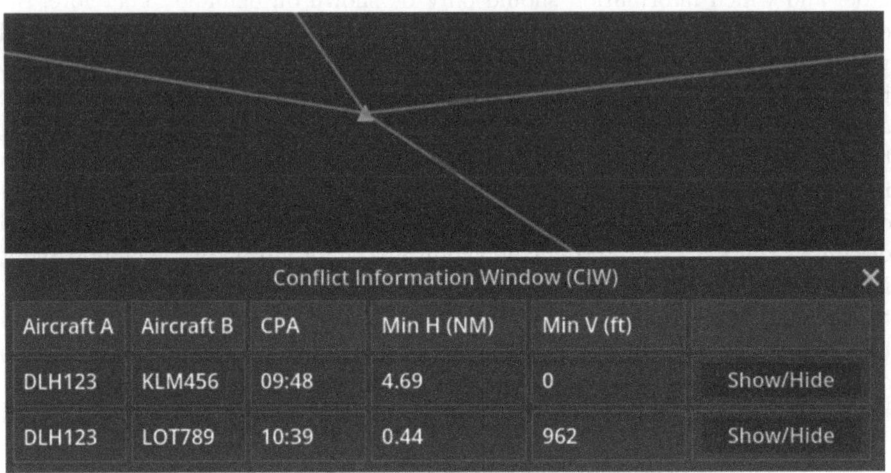

Fig. 6. Conflict detection overlay highlighting predicted separation infringements along aircraft trajectories or flight plans. Conflict-relevant segments are shown in red. Conflict Information Window (CIW) provides additional information.

Conflict Detection. The conflict detection tool comprises more than a simple visual overlay. It highlights the segments of the involved aircraft trajectories or flight plans in which the prescribed separation minima are violated. As illustrated in Fig. 6, conflict-relevant portions are marked in red along the otherwise cyan route lines. In addition, the tool provides a Conflict Information Window (CIW) that lists all currently detected conflicts together with y information for each case, including the involved aircraft pair, the calculated closest point of approach (CPA), the minimum horizontal separation in nautical miles, and the minimum vertical separation in feet. The CIW also allows individual conflict visualizations to be shown or hidden.

Minimal Distance Between Aircraft. Another important functionality is the measurement of distances, particularly the determination of the minimum separation between two aircraft. To support this, a tool was implemented that predicts based on the flight plan or trajectory when and at which position two aircraft will potentially be closest to each other. The overlay and interface of the tool are shown in Fig. 7.

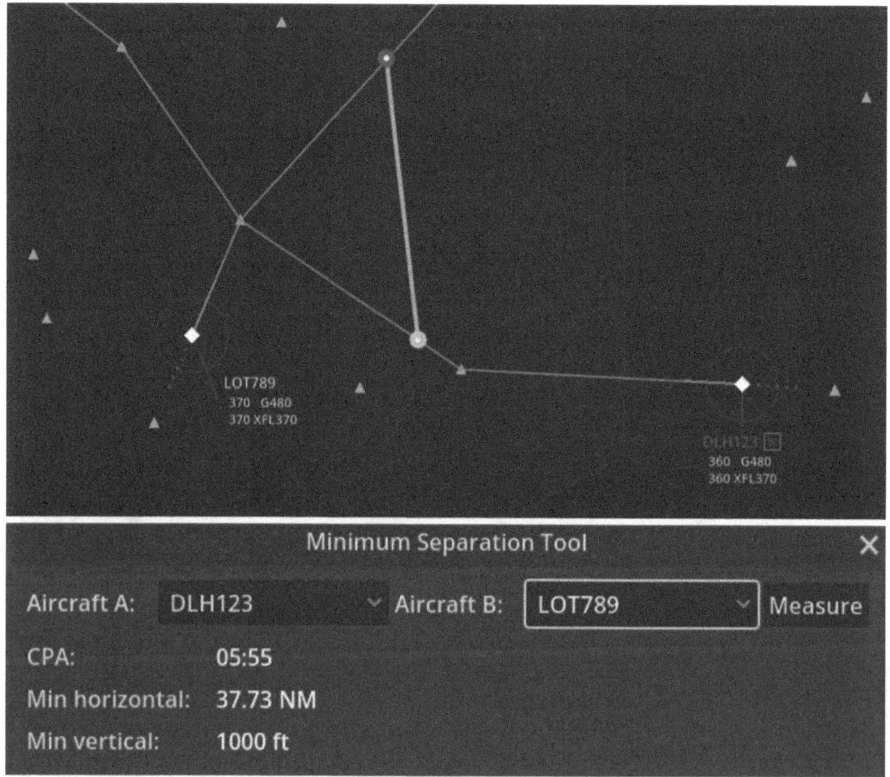

Fig. 7. A tool to measure the minimal distance between two aircraft and displays the result as an overlay.

Configure Simulation Rate. In some situations, it is useful to run a scenario faster or slower than real time. Therefore, the default tools in VERA include a simulation rate adjustment that allows scenarios to be executed either faster or slower than real time. The simulation rate can be modified dynamically during runtime. The corresponding interface is shown in Fig. 8.

Color Themes and Configuration Files. To support different preferences and experimental requirements, VERA provides a theme manager that controls the visual appearance of the interface. The system allows the selection of predefined default themes as well as the creation of custom themes. Themes are implemented using Godot resource files (`.tres`), which store color configurations for relevant interface elements such as sector lines, aircraft tracks, labels, connectors, and background colors. At runtime, the theme manager loads the selected configuration and applies to the interface. This enables rapid switching between standardized layouts. In addition, researchers can easily define new themes by creating or modifying `.tres` configuration files without changing the

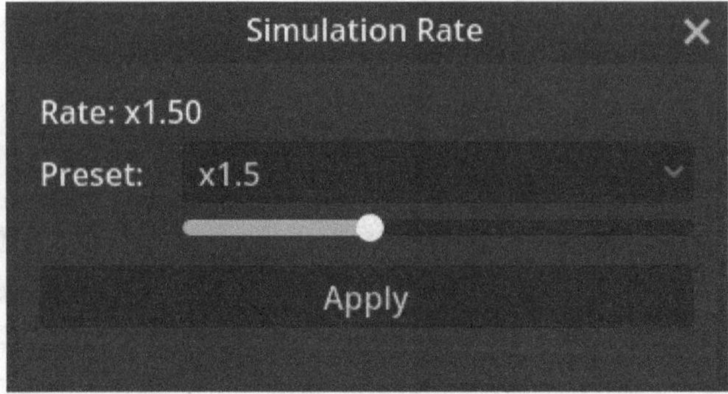

Fig. 8. The "Sim Rate" tool lets the user adjust the speed of the simulation.

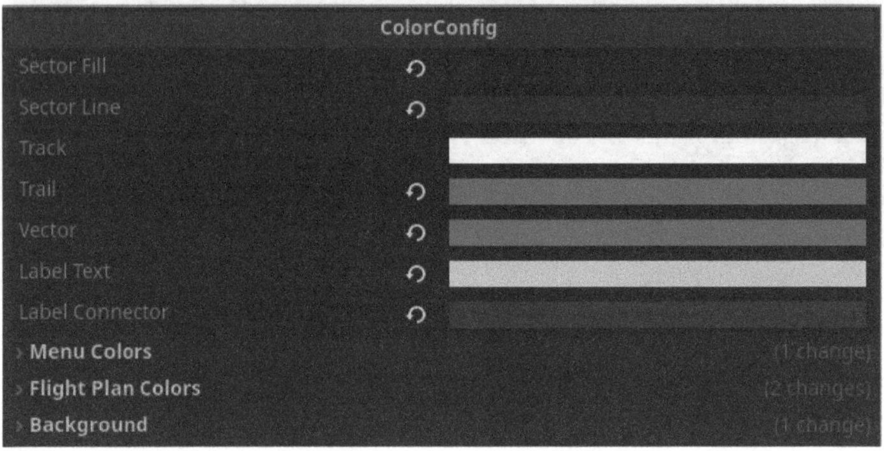

Fig. 9. The default color theme based on the colors from the CWP developed in the Envision project. The theme can be directly edited in Godot's UI.

source code. An example for one of these configurations can be seen in Fig. 9. A comparable configuration mechanism is also used to define additional visual parameters beyond colors. Separate resource configurations allow the adjustment of text sizes and the appearance of other interface elements, such as aircraft labels and related display properties. This makes it possible to adapt readability and information density to different study conditions or participant preferences. This approach allows the researchers to either enforce a fixed appearance for controlled studies or grant participants the possibility to adjust the visualization to their personal preferences.

Configuration of Tools. In Godot, both individual components and entire views or user interfaces, such as the radar display, can be implemented as scenes and stored in `.tscn` files. These scenes are organized as hierarchical node trees.

Depending on their intended function or representation, different node types can be used, each inheriting from a corresponding base class. Scripts can be attached to nodes to define their behavior and interaction logic. Furthermore, nodes can be enabled or disabled directly within the Godot editor. This is particularly advantageous for configuring validation environments, as interface elements, e.g. overlays or buttons for opening specific tools, can easily be shown or hidden depending on the requirements of a given study. When a node is selected in the Godot editor, all variables marked with `@export` in the associated script are exposed in the user interface. This enables selected properties to be configured directly within the editor without modifying the underlying code. Functionalities that cannot be conveniently enabled or disabled by hiding a node alone, can instead be activated or deactivated via dedicated interface elements, for example through a checkbox in the user interface. An example for this can be seen in Fig. 10.

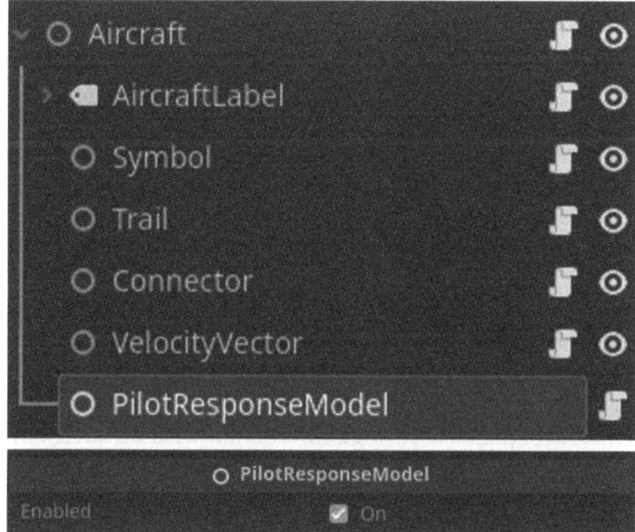

Fig. 10. The node tree of the aircraft scene. Selecting the "PilotResponseModel" node allows users to activate or deactivate it and to modify the script parameters directly in the Godot editor without having to access the code.

3.3 Simulation of Pseudo Pilots and Aircraft Behavior

In large-scale validation environments, such as DLR's ATMOS simulator, pseudo-pilots are typically required to realistically simulate the interaction between ATCO and pilot. However, for many research questions this level of realism is not necessary and introduces considerable additional effort. Therefore, some environments simulate pilot behavior instead of using actual pseudo-pilots [16]. Accordingly, to realistically model pilot responses in VERA, results from previous research were incorporated that analyzed typical pilot response and execution times for issued clearances [24]. These findings allow the system to approximate how long it takes pilots to acknowledge and implement clearances. In addition, aircraft motion must be simulated, including climb and descent behavior as well as aircraft dynamics during turns, acceleration, and deceleration. While such behavior can be modeled using EUROCONTROL's Base of Aircraft Data (BADA) [12], a different approach was chosen for VERA. Instead of relying on performance tables, aircraft behavior was derived from real operational data. Specifically, aircraft trajectories from the SCAT dataset [10] were analyzed, and the observed average behavior was reproduced in the simulation with added stochastic noise. This data-driven approach allows VERA to approximate realistic aircraft motion characteristics while avoiding the need for complex physics-based calculations, be dependent on external sources and licence agreements or traffic simulations like NARSIM [20] and BlueSky [6].

3.4 Logging

For the evaluation of ATCO behavior, the information listed in Table 1 is stored in `.jsonl` format. By default, the logs for each run are saved locally on the computer on which the experiment is conducted. Alternatively, the data can be transmitted to a WebSocket server. If the server is exposed to the internet via a public address, the data can be stored centrally for later analysis, thereby supporting remote validation studies.

3.5 Reinforcement Learning in VERA

Automation is becoming an increasingly important topic in air traffic management, particularly in the context of decision support and conflict resolution. Reinforcement learning represents a promising approach for such applications, as agents learn control policies through interaction with an environment by optimizing long-term reward signals. To support the development and evaluation of reinforcement learning-based approaches, VERA makes use of the Godot RL Agents plugin [1]. The plugin provides a straightforward integration of common reinforcement learning algorithms and enables the implementation of custom training environments directly within the Godot engine. Accordingly, VERA includes an integrated training environment designed to train and evaluate reinforcement learning agents for the use case it is currently being developed for, namely medium-term conflict resolution. The training environment generates randomized traffic scenarios in which at least two aircraft are placed on a conflict course. Within the environment the agent controls one aircraft and can apply different actions to resolve the conflict. Additionally, almost 170,000 flights from the SCAT [10] were analyzed for conflicts that were resolved by ATCOs, processed and converted into over 500 scenarios compatible with VERA [17]. These scenarios can be used to train mid-term conflict resolution or other important tasks. Similar scenarios can be implemented with little effort and seamlessly integrated into VERA, enabling agents to be trained directly within the simulation

Table 1. Overview of Logged Information

Category	Field	Description
Action	action.type	Type of ATCO instruction or system action (e.g., ASSUME, FL, SPEED, HEADING, DIRECT_TO).
	action.payload	Action-specific parameters, such as assigned flight level, speed, heading, climb rate, target waypoint, and previous values where applicable.
Aircraft State	aircraft.callsign	Unique aircraft identifier.
	aircraft.altitude_ft	Aircraft altitude at the time of the action (feet).
	aircraft.ground_speed_mps	Ground speed at the time of the action (m/s).
	aircraft.track_deg	Current ground track angle (degrees).
	aircraft.lat_deg, aircraft.lon_deg	Geographic position (latitude, longitude).
	aircraft.world_x, aircraft.world_y	Internal simulation coordinates used for visualization and spatial calculations.
Metadata	meta.sim_time_s	Simulation time at which the action occurred (seconds).
	meta.source	Originating system component or method that triggered the log entry.
	meta.next_wp	Next planned waypoint, if applicable.
	meta.route_follow_*	Flags indicating whether route following is enabled or disabled.
Temporal	sim_time_s	Simulation time duplicated at the top level for direct access.
	ts_unix_ms	Wall-clock timestamp in Unix time (milliseconds).

environment. This facilitates the development and testing of new reinforcement learning algorithms for ATC.

4 Example Use-Case: Development of Human-Conforming Conflict Resolution

One example that illustrates the usefulness of VERA is the development of human-conforming support for mid-term conflict resolution. In upper airspace, one of the main tasks of ATCOs is to ensure safe separation between aircraft. While current operational systems typically detect mid-term conflicts within a look-ahead horizon of approximately 20 min and provide corresponding warnings, they generally do not autonomously resolve these conflicts or provide concrete resolution proposals to controllers. As a result, the development of such support systems remains an active field of research [23].

A key challenge in this context is that conflict resolution support should not only be technically effective, but also align with controllers' established strategies, expectations, and working practices [18]. Developing such systems therefore requires more than the implementation of a suitable algorithm. Instead, it involves an iterative process that includes the analysis of human behaviour, the design and evaluation of suitable interaction concepts, and, depending on the selected approach, the training and integration of AI models. VERA is particularly useful in this context because it supports these different development steps within one flexible and easily deployable environment, therefore reducing the effort required for repeated evaluations with controllers.

Analysis of Human Behavior. A first step in the development of human-conforming conflict resolution support is to analyze how controllers currently resolve conflicts and which strategies they follow [5]. Such analyses require behavioural data from controllers interacting with representative traffic situations. However, due to the current shortage of ATCOs, it is often difficult to recruit sufficient participants. In addition, experiments with operational systems or larger simulation facilities typically require controllers to be invited on-site and supervised during the study, which creates substantial logistical overhead and high costs.

VERA simplifies this process by enabling remote and comparatively low-threshold data collection as described in Section. The system can be exported as a standalone executable, allowing controllers to run the simulation on their own systems without complex setup. The recorded interaction data can then be transmitted to the researchers via the internet for later analysis. This reduces organizational effort and cost, facilitates access to a larger number of participants, and enables behavioural data to be collected already in early phases of development.

Interaction Design and Tool Evaluation. Based on the insights obtained from behavioural analyses, the next step is to design and evaluate concepts that are aligned with controller strategies and needs. In this phase, VERA can be used to prototype and compare different forms of conflict resolution support. For example, it can be investigated whether conflicts should be resolved autonomously by the system or whether advisory-based support should be provided to the controller. Likewise, different design questions can be explored, such as whether advisories should remain valid only for a limited time and how such constraints should be communicated. And finally, which technical approach is the most suitable and deliverers the best results, e.g. supervised learning [5], reinforcement learning [21] or generic algorithms [2].

In addition, VERA allows the evaluation of alternative interface and tool concepts. Different conflict visualization methods, trajectory prediction displays, or separation monitoring tools can be implemented and compared across experimental conditions. Since the settings menu allows specific tools to be activated or deactivated for a given scenario design, different tool combinations can be tested systematically. This makes VERA particularly suitable for rapid iteration in early development stages, as different interface concepts and assistance mechanisms can be distributed to controllers, evaluated remotely, and refined based on their feedback before more resource-intensive HITL studies are conducted.

AI Development. Once relevant behavioural patterns and suitable interaction concepts have been identified, VERA can also support the development of AI-based conflict resolution components. In addition to human-centred design studies, the environment can therefore be used as a proof-of-concept platform for AI-based support functions. Using Godot RL Agents [1], reinforcement learning capabilities are integrated into the environment. With training scenarios included in VERA's default configuration (see Sect. 3.5), conflict resolution agents can be trained directly within the simulation environment.

The resulting models can be exported as `.onnx` files and deployed in operational VERA scenarios. This makes it possible to evaluate trained agents not only in simplified training settings, but also in more realistic traffic situations and, where required, in interaction with human controllers. In this way, VERA supports the transition from the analysis of human behaviour, to the design of suitable support concepts, and finally to the implementation and early evaluation of AI-based conflict resolution approaches.

5 Conclusion

This paper introduced VERA (Validation Environment for Researching ATC Interfaces and Tools), a simulation environment designed to support research on human–AI collaboration in ATC. While existing high-fidelity simulation platforms provide realistic operational environments, they often require significant infrastructure and operational effort, which can limit their suitability for early-stage interface prototyping and exploratory experimentation. VERA addresses this gap by providing a flexible research platform that enables rapid development and evaluation of novel tools and concepts.

The system provides a UI with a set of configurable overlays and tools. These components allow researchers to investigate how different types of decision support, automation behavior, and interaction mechanisms influence controller strategies, situation awareness, and coordination between humans and automated systems.

VERA supports iterative design and evaluation of future ATC support tools as it can be extended with additional functionalities, algorithms, or interfaces with comparatively low development effort.

6 Future Work

The development of a dedicated scenario editor is planned to simplify the creation and configuration of simulation scenarios. Furthermore, aircraft behavior could be modeled more realistically using BADA [12]. Alternatively, it is planned to integrate an interface to use the traffic simulation from BlueSky [6] or NARSIM [20] in case a higher fidelity is needed in the future. In addition, further tools will be integrated into the environment, including various functionalities for conflict resolution. The user interface will also be further refined and aligned with the design principles of the Envision project in order to improve usability and ensure visual and interactional consistency across related systems. Moreover, additional configuration options will be implemented to allow researchers to adapt both the environment and the interface more easily to their specific experimental needs. Finally, the long-term goal is to make the simulation environment available to the research community as an open-source tool. At present, the environment can be provided upon request.

Acknowledgments. The authors have no competing interests to declare that are relevant to the content of this article.

References

1. Beeching, E., Dibangoye, J., Simonin, O., Wolf, C.: Godot reinforcement learning agents. arXiv preprint arXiv:2112.03636 (2021). https://doi.org/10.48550/arXiv.2112.03636
2. Durand, N., Alliot, J.M., Noailles, J.: Automatic aircraft conflict resolution using genetic algorithms. In: Proceedings of the 1996 ACM symposium on Applied Computing, pp. 289–298 (1996). https://doi.org/10.1145/331119.331195
3. EUROCONTROL: Eurocontrol seven-year forecast 2025-2031. https://www.eurocontrol.int/sites/default/files/2025-02/eurocontrol-seven-year-forecast-2025-2031-february-2025.pdf (2025). Accessed 17 Sep 2025
4. Friedrich, M., Papenfuß, A., Jipp, M., Solf, L., Möhlenbrink, C.: Eine studie zur interferenz von arbeitsgedächtnisprozessen bei einer fluglotsenaufgabe. 9, Berliner Werkstatt Mensch-Maschine-Systeme Reflexionen und Visionen der Mensch-Maschine-Interaktion (2011)
5. Guleria, Y., Pham, D.T., Alam, S., Tran, P.N., Durand, N.: Towards conformal automation in air traffic control: Learning conflict resolution strategies through behavior cloning. Adv. Eng. Inform. **59**, 102273 (2024). https://doi.org/10.1016/j.aei.2023.102273
6. Hoekstra, J.M., Ellerbroek, J.: Bluesky atc simulator project: an open data and open source approach. In: Proceedings of the 7th International Conference on Research in Air Transportation, vol. 131, p. 132. FAA/Eurocontrol Washington, DC, USA (2016)
7. IFATCA: IFATCA EVP Europe on the European Staff Shortage - IFATCA — ifatca.org (2023). https://www.ifatca.org/2023/04/ifatca-evp-europe-on-the-european-staff-shortage/, Accessed 02 Feb 2024
8. Jameel, M., Tyburzy, L., Gerdes, I., Pick, A., Hunger, R., Christoffels, L.: Enabling digital air traffic controller assistant through human-autonomy teaming design. In: 2023 IEEE/AIAA 42nd Digital Avionics Systems Conference (DASC), pp. 1–9. (2023). https://doi.org/10.1109/DASC58513.2023.10311220
9. Möhlenbrink, C., Friedrich, M., Papenfuß, A.: Remotecenter: Eine mikrowelt zur analyse der mentalen repräsentation von zwei flughäfen während einer lotsentätigkeitsaufgabe. Tagungsband **8**, 6 (2009)

10. Nilsson, J., Unger, J.: Swedish civil air traffic control dataset. Data Brief **48**, 109240 (2023). https://doi.org/10.1016/j.dib.2023.109240
11. Nöhren, L.: Envision cwp documentation (2025)
12. Nuic, A., Poles, D., Mouillet, V.: Bada: an advanced aircraft performance model for present and future atm systems. Int. J. Adapt. Control Signal Process. **24**(10), 850–866 (2010). https://doi.org/10.1002/acs.1176
13. Nöhren, L., et al.: New approaches for the use of extended mock-ups for the development of air traffic controller working positions. Aerospace **12**(2) (2025). https://doi.org/10.3390/aerospace12020114, https://www.mdpi.com/2226-4310/12/2/114
14. Nöhren, L., et al.: Design and evaluation of a modern controller working position using high-fidelity mock-ups. In: 2025 AIAA DATC/IEEE 44th Digital Avionics Systems Conference (DASC), pp. 1–10 (2025). https://doi.org/10.1109/DASC66011.2025.11257389
15. Oberheid, H., Hasselberg, A., Söffker, D.: Know your options-analysing human decision making in dynamic task environments with state space methods. Human Centred Automation, pp. 285–300 (2011)
16. Pepper, N., et al.: A probabilistic digital twin of UK en route airspace. In: AIAA SCITECH 2026 Forum. American Institute of Aeronautics and Astronautics (2026). https://doi.org/10.2514/6.2026-1794
17. Renkhoff, J.: Identifying potential conflicts and corresponding resolutions in the upper airspace from historical air traffic data. DLRK 2025 (2025). https://doi.org/10.25967/650174
18. Renkhoff, J., Ternus, S., Guleria, Y.: A survey on personalized conflict resolution approaches in air traffic control. Aerospace **12**(9), 751 (2025). https://doi.org/10.3390/aerospace12090751
19. Simorgh, A., Soler, M.: Climate-optimized flight planning can effectively reduce the environmental footprint of aviation in Europe at low operational costs. Commun. Earth Environ. **6**(1), 66 (2025). https://doi.org/10.1038/s43247-025-02031-8
20. Ten Have, J.: The development of the nlr atc research simulator (narsim): Design philosophy and potential for atm research. Simul. Pract. Theory **1**(1), 31–39 (1993)
21. Tran, P.N., Pham, D.T., Goh, S.K., Alam, S., Duong, V.: An interactive conflict solver for learning air traffic conflict resolutions. J. Aerosp. Inf. Syst. **17**(6), 271–277 (2020). https://doi.org/10.2514/1.I010807
22. Tyburzy, L., Renkhoff, J., Jameel, M., Bruder, C.: User centered interface design for human autonomy teaming in air traffic control: A case study. In: International Conference on Human-Computer Interaction, pp. 219–236. Springer, Cham (2025). https://doi.org/10.1007/978-3-031-93721-7_16
23. Wang, Z., Pan, W., Li, H., Wang, X., Zuo, Q.: Review of deep reinforcement learning approaches for conflict resolution in air traffic control. Aerospace **9**(6), 294 (2022). https://doi.org/10.3390/aerospace9060294
24. Wüstenbecker, N., Renkhoff, J., Zeppenfeld, D., Jameel, M., Schier-Morgenthal, S.: Analysis and prediction of pilot response time to air traffic control clearances. CEAS Aeronaut. J. (2025). https://doi.org/10.1007/s13272-025-00848-9

Psychophysiological Response, User Experience and Performance in Routine and Emergency Flight Simulation Training Scenarios Using Multimodal Wearable Sensing

Anika Fairooz Shafi[1(✉)], John Edison Muñoz[1,2], and Shi Cao[1]

[1] Systems Design Engineering, University of Waterloo, Waterloo, ON N2L 3G1, Canada
{afshafi,john.munoz.hci,shi.cao}@uwaterloo.ca

[2] User Experience Design, Wilfred Laurier University, Brantford, ON N3T 2Y3, Canada

Abstract. Wearable sensors are continually extending the possibilities for physiological monitoring and physio-adaptive (biocybernetic) systems, with particularly relevant applications in pilot training. This study explored psychophysiological responses, performance and user experience of pilot trainees (n = 16) as they interacted with routine and high-stress flight simulation scenarios. Outcome measures include electrodermal activity (EDA), heart rate (HR) and heart rate variability (HRV) parameters, competency-based performance metrics and perceived user experience and stress. Sympathetic activation was observed, characterized by elevated HR and reduced HRV time-domain measures (Mean NN, RMSSD, and pNN50) alongside decreases in non-linear measures (SD1 and the SD1/SD2 ratio) across progressively more stressful conditions. Self-reported stress significantly differed across conditions, while EDA data showed notable individual variability. Performance, measured by mean application of procedure scores, was significantly affected. Results indicate initial evidence that the multimodal wearable physiological sensors employed in the study sensitively and consistently gauge changes in stress inducements. These findings have important implications for stress inoculation training, personalized instructor feedback and development of future biocybernetic training systems.

Keywords: Physiological Monitoring · Multimodal Psychophysiology · Wearable Sensors · Adaptive Simulation Training

1 Introduction

Physiological monitoring using wearable sensors allows for non-invasive, near real-time, objective and continuous quantification of psychophysiological states such as stress. Given how affordable and accessible wearables are becoming and advances in sensing technologies, we can now easily integrate psychophysiological responses into simulations. In the context of aviation, wearables have been utilized to investigate various factors such as arousal, gaze behavior, performance [1–8], while a smaller number of

W. -C. Li and A. Plioutsias (Eds.): HCII 2026, LNAI 16708, pp. 256–274, 2026.
https://doi.org/10.1007/978-3-032-29459-3_18

studies focussed on assessing stress [4–10]. There is a need for flight simulator studies to validate the use of unobtrusive sensing technologies for assessing pilot states [3] and reliably inducing stress during training and testing [11]. Moreover, systematic coupling of stress training with flight skill acquisition has shown to enhance performance in future stressful situations [12]. The few studies that have examined stress responses in pilot trainees using wearables have predominantly relied on a single modality [6–9]. Cacioppo [13] proposed a construct to describe the relationship between physiological measures and psychological states, such that if all psychological states constitute one domain and all physiological measures another, five general categories may represent the possible relationships: one-to-one, one-to-many, many-to-one, many-to-many and null. For instance, in a one-to-one relationship, a single psychological state corresponds unIEqely to a physiological measure, while in one-to-many, one psychological state is associated with multiple physiological measures. Considering the non-exclusive and complex nature of psychophysiological inference and validation, a multimodal approach is essential for characterizing stress responses and in designing and implementing adaptive training systems.

Early work by Kelley [14] explored the potential of adaptive flight simulation training "in which the problem, the stimulus, or the task is varied as a function of how well the trainee performs" (p. 547). They proposed five key elements of an adaptive trainer: the adaptive variable, measuring performance, adaptive logic, error standard and difficulty level and knowledge-of-results displays (informing the trainee of their progress). In the same year, Caro [15] described an army-wide system of aircraft simulators, Synthetic Flight Training System (SFTS), aimed at automating the flight instructor's function of problem selection to effectively challenge trainees. Moving from performance as the adaptive variable to psychophysiological metrics, physio-adaptive (biocybernetic) systems leverage psychophysiology to sense, analyze and respond to a user in real-time [16]. Palsson and Pope [17] proposed stress counter-response training based on the concepts of instrument functionality feedback and biocybernetic modulation, where a flight simulator changes its behavior according to a trainee's stress management skills. Other scholars have proposed systems that use a trainee's state to modify flight simulation exercise [18], training content and presentation [19]; and context-aware learning such that flight instructors and trainees know when mastery of a skill has been achieved [20].

There is a need for physio-adaptive systems that integrate states beyond mental workload or engagement [21]. Before a trainee's stress levels can be used to adapt training, research needs to explore which combinations of wearable sensors and metrics reliably and sensitively capture such psychophysiological state change, effectiveness of stress inducement scenarios and best ways and practices to collect and synchronize multimodal physiological data while maintaining signal quality. These are gaps that this current study seeks to address by studying psychophysiological response, performance and user experience in simulated routine and high-stress flight scenarios using multimodal wearable sensing.

2 Related Work

Psychophysiological measures have been utilized in a wide range of aviation environments. Electroencephalography (EEG) measures electrical activity of the brain and is a reliable tool to study and predict psychophysiological states in different task conditions [22]. Spontaneous brain activity can be characterized by oscillatory rhythms, which can be quantified using power spectral density (PSD) into different frequency bands, including delta (δ, 1–4 Hz), theta (θ, 4–8 Hz), alpha (α, 8–12 Hz), beta (β, 12–30 Hz), and gamma (γ, 30–100 Hz) and show certain relationships with stress. Another widely supported measure is the P300 event-related potential (ERP) (also referred to as 'evoked potential' and is the brain's response to an event or stimuli) [23]. Additionally, central to understanding stress responses are two branches of the autonomic nervous system: sympathetic and parasympathetic nervous systems. The sympathetic nervous system is responsible for mobilizing our body's response to threat or stressors, known as the "fight-or-flight" response. In contrast, the parasympathetic nervous system promotes relaxation and recovery or "the-rest-and-digest" response [24]. Of the autonomic measures, heart rate variability (HRV) is the variation in time interval between successive heartbeats (measured as RR intervals in an ECG), while Electrodermal Activity (EDA) is the electrical conductivity of the skin. HRV, a measure of autonomic balance [25] and EDA, a reliable quantifier of sympathetic arousal [26].

In commercial airline pilots, HRV has been used to explore the impact of maneuver difficulty on performance [4]. Liang et al. [27] tested stress induction with Tier Social Stress Test (TSST) in a sample of 42 pilots, all holding commercial pilot licenses. The authors utilized heart rate, State Anxiety Inventory and salivary cortisol concentrations. Additional research in drone, general aviation, military pilots and non-pilots leveraged HRV and EEG to explore stress responses. Wojciechowski et al. [10] sought to elucidate the impact of stress on a single drone pilot's sympathetic and parasympathetic activity in familiar and unfamiliar simulation environments. Wang et al. [28] reported that different flight simulation tasks successfully induced varying stress responses in a group of 20 university engineering students. In another study, researchers evaluated 11 fighter pilots' stress levels as they conducted high performance maneuvers in long-term training [5]. Bustamante-Sánchez et al. [29] analyzed the effect of night and instrument flights on cortical arousal, autonomic modulation, and stress perception. Causse and Dehais [30] demonstrated that compared to other flight segments, take-off and landing involve higher stress. Bruna et al. [31] assessed stress inducement in ultra light aircraft simulators using HRV and respiration measures. Lastly, Villafaina et al. [32] used both HRV and EEG band powers to study the psychophysiological responses of Spanish Air Force pilots to different simulated combat maneuvers.

Among pilot trainees, most of the studies used HRV and rarely employed EDA [8]. With a small sample size of 5 pilot trainees and 5 instructors, Lee [7] studied the role of flight experience, approach area and glide angle on stress and performance. Peng et al. [6] explored how urgency and familiarity impact stress and performance in pilot trainees during unexpected events. In another study, 9 aviator cadets and 6 instructors performed a series of tasks mirroring ground-based flight training allowing the authors to explore the utility of HRV time-domain, frequency-domain and non-linear parameters in stress response monitoring [33]. Regula et al. [9] in their study with beginner pilots with no flying experience examined how transitioning from analog to digital presentation of avionic data elicits enhanced stress responses in trainees. Overall, almost all prior studies relied on a single modality, leaving multimodal assessment in pilot trainees largely unexplored.

3 Method

The setup (see Fig. 1) was utilized to create a controlled environment where pilot trainees interacted with the ALSIM AL 250 flight simulator [34], while data on their physiological responses, user experience, performance, and self-reported levels of stress were collected.

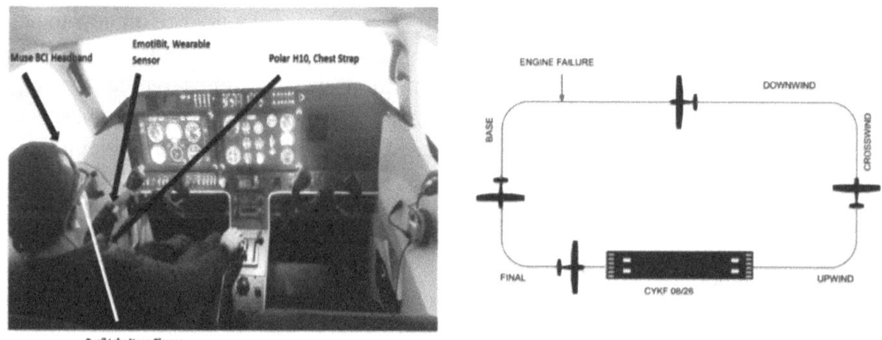

Fig. 1. The various physiological sensors employed in the study (left) and the standard left-hand circuit flown by the pilot trainees (right).

3.1 Participants

A total of sixteen pilot trainees (male: 11, female: 5; age range: 18–34 years, mean: 21.53 years) participated in the study. All participants had prior experience with simulation technology, and most belonged to a single university aviation program. Additionally, the majority already obtained their Private Pilot License (PPL) or Commercial Pilot License (CPL), along with various ratings, including, night, multi-engine and instrument flight ratings. The study was approved by the Research Ethics Board at the University of Waterloo (45409) and conducted in alignment with the principles outlined in the Declaration of Helsinki. All participants provided written informed consent prior to the start of the study. De-identified data was stored in a password-protected OneDrive folder.

3.2 Scenario

ALSIM AL 250 flight simulator was configured to replicate the aircraft dynamics of a single-engine Cessna 172. The simulation scenario employed weather settings reflecting

Ceiling and Visibility OK (CAVOK) conditions suitable for Visual Flight Rules (VFR) flight. Visibility was plus 6 statute miles with 110 at 10 kts wind, no clouds, altimeter setting: 29.92 ″Hg and a surface temperature of 15 °C. Pilot trainees were tasked with performing one taxi and three standard left hand circuits at the Region of Waterloo International Airport (CYKF) (Fig. 1, right). One of the three circuits simulated an emergency in the form of an engine failure. Order of circuit 2 and emergency were counterbalanced.

3.3 Procedure

Upon arrival, the participants filled out informed consent forms and completed a demographic questionnaire. Following this, they were equipped with wearable sensors, and a three-minute physiological baseline was recorded. Afterwards, a briefing took place where participants received information about the scenario and guidance on how to perform the tasks. Each participant's session was organized into five conditions: baseline, taxi, circuit 1, circuit 2, and emergency. The conditions were designed to reflect increasing task difficulty, ranging from baseline (lowest), taxi (second lowest) to emergency (highest). Circuit 1 and circuit 2 were anticipated to impose similar task difficulty. For each condition, a flight instructor seated next assessed performance. At the end of each condition, participants self-reported their stress. After the final condition, they completed a user experience questionnaire. Following which, sensors were removed and a brief debriefing held.

3.4 Outcome Measures

Data from 16 participants is reported here. While additional data types (electroencephalography, eye tracking, simulator-based performance metrics, and self-report of workload and situational awareness) were collected from a larger sample, analysis is ongoing.

Physiological Metrics

Cardiovascular. Cardiovascular responses were recorded using a Polar H10 chest strap. The sensor contains built-in proprietary algorithms specifically designed to filter and calculate ECG parameters essential for Heart Rate Variability (HRV) analysis. The polar streams data at 1 Hz and calculates RR Intervals with a unit of 1/1024s [35]. A python toolbox for neurophysiological signal processing, NeuroKit2 [36], was used to analyze the HRV data. Extracted HRV time-domain measures include standard deviation of NN intervals (SDNN), root mean square of successive RR interval differences (RMSSD) and percentage of successive RR intervals that differ by more than 50 ms (pNN50). Moreover, non-linear analysis was conducted to capture the complexity and fractal properties of variability in the cardiac signal that may be missed by linear time-and frequency-domain analysis [37].

Electrodermal Activity. Electrodermal activity (EDA) was recorded using the Emotibit wristband sensor. The sensor streams data wirelessly from over 16 bio signals over any Adafruit Feather-enabled protocol (Wi-Fi, Bluetooth, LoRA, etc.) at 15 Hz to a local computer connected to the same network [38]. EDA data preprocessing included noise removal using a low-pass Butterworth filter with a 0.3 Hz cutoff frequency, outlier removal and normalization. EDA data was decomposed into Skin conductance level (SCL) or tonic reflecting the overall arousal level during the session using a low-pass Butterworth filter with 0.05 Hz cutoff frequency.

Physiological Data Acquisition and Synchronization. Collection of multimodal physiological data and synchronizing them to conduct consolidated analysis is one of the biggest challenges in the field of psychophysiology and aviation training. A combination of third party and custom-built software clients was used to interface the various physiological sensors and stream the data using the lab streaming layer (LSL) communication protocol [39]. The Excite-O-Meter Devices[1] android application compatible with the chest strap sensor Polar H10 was used to send Heart Rate (HR) and Heart Rate Variability (HRV) data over LSL (see Fig. 2).

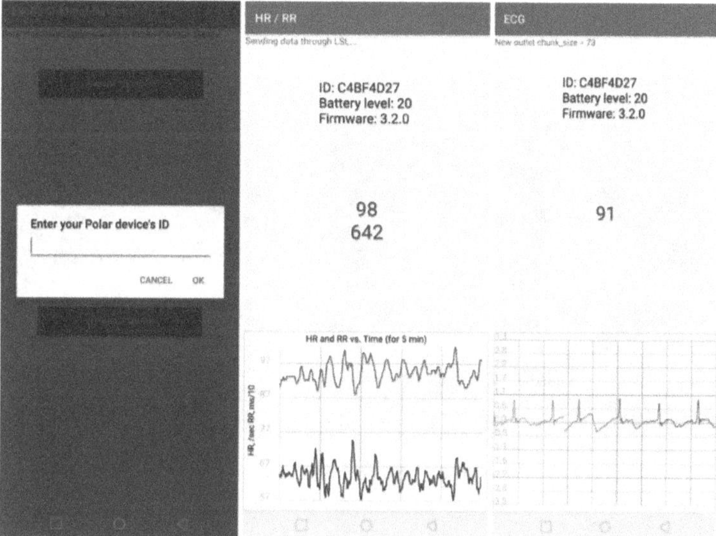

Fig. 2. Excite-O-Meter Devices android application.

The Emotibit Oscilloscope[2] (v1.11.4) was used to visualize and stream the various physiological metrics collected from the Emotibit device in real time via LSL (see Fig. 3).

The Pupil Labs Companion LSL Relay[3] was used to stream gaze and event data from the Neon Companion Device to LSL (see Fig. 4).

[1] https://github.com/luisqtr/exciteometer/blob/main/docs/2_SetupDevices.md
[2] https://github.com/EmotiBit/ofxEmotiBit/releases.
[3] https://pupil-invisible-lsl-relay.readthedocs.io/en/stable/index.html.

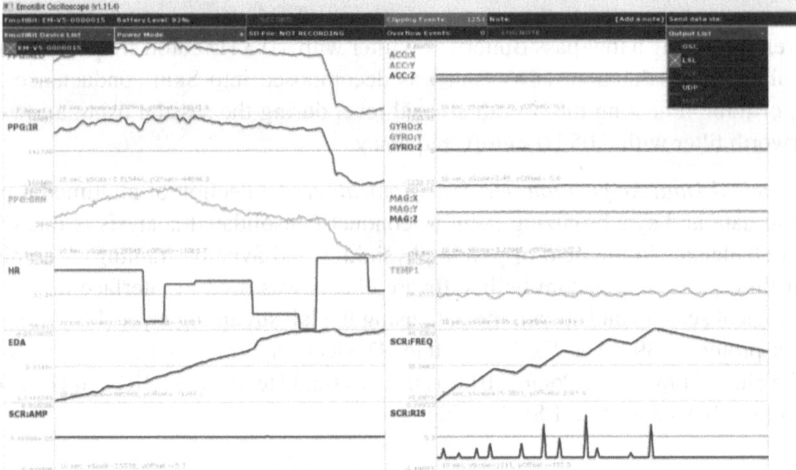

Fig. 3. Emotibit Oscilloscope Interface.

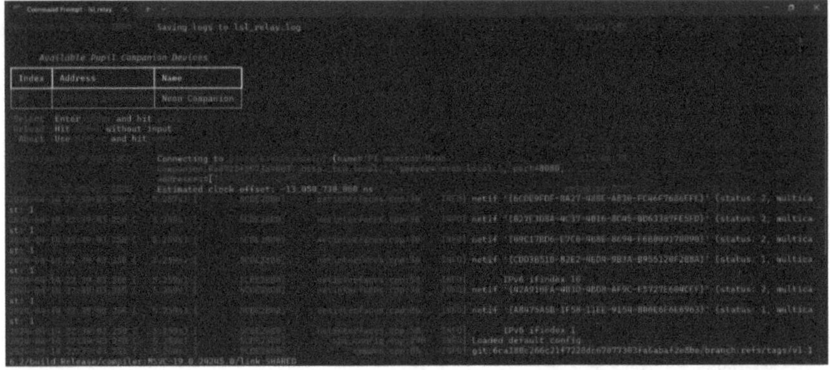

Fig. 4. LSL Relay for Neon.

The Petal Metrics desktop application[4] provides a Graphical User Interface (GUI) to connect to a Muse BCI headband and was used create an LSL outlet to stream the EEG data (see Fig. 5).

Lab Recorder[5], an LSL recording application, was used to subscribe and synchronize all the data samples being pushed to LSL and store the data in a single file in the Extensible Data Format (XDF).

Flight Instructor Assessment. A flight instructor seated next to the pilot trainees assessed their performance using a modified version of an assessment tool created by Moncion et al. [40]. Based on Transport Canada's 4-point marking scale and assessment methodology used by their examiners during Private Pilot License - Aeroplane (PPL

[4] https://petal.tech/.

[5] https://github.com/labstreaminglayer/App-LabRecorder.

Fig. 5. Petal Metrics GUI.

- A) flight test as well as ICAO Doc 9995, this tool allows for performance ratings across eight competencies. For this study, performance ratings across five competencies were calculated: Application of Procedures, Aircraft Flight Path Management – Manual, Problem Solving and Decision Making, Situational Awareness, and Workload Management. For each participant, the total score for each competency in each condition was first calculated and then converted to a mean score by dividing the total score by the number of items. These mean scores were then averaged across all participants to obtain a final mean for each competency in each condition.

User Experience and Stress. The Virtual Reality Neuroscience Questionnaire (VRNQ) was utilized to evaluate the quality of the flight simulation in two main aspects: user experience (UX) and VR-induced symptoms and effects (VRISE). Participants responded to five questions for each category using a 1 to 7 Likert scale with 1 representing extremely low immersion/absent VRISE and 7 extremely high immersion/intense VRISE [41]. We reverse-coded the VRISE portion of the VRNQ so 7 would be intense VRISE instead of 1. The VRNQ specifies cutoffs for sub-scores to determine adequate simulation quality. A minimum ≥ 25 and parsimonious ≥ 30 cutoff scores were applied to UX. We modified the cutoff for VRISE scores to maximum ≤ 15 and parsimonious ≤ 10. Participants also reported their perceived stress levels on a 0 to 10 Likert scale with 0 representing minimal and 10 maximum stress.

4 Data Analysis

All analyses were conducted in Python. Data normality was assessed using the Shapiro-Wilk test. Friedman tests were applied for non-normally distributed data followed by Wilcoxon-signed rank test with Bonferroni correction. Results were significant at a corrected α level $p < .005$ for physiological and $p < .008$ for performance and self-report data, respectively.

5 Results

5.1 Physiological Responses

Cardiovascular Responses: Stress Regulation. Cardiac regulation responses were quantified using HR and HRV parameters. Figure 6 shows a box plot illustrating the distribution of HR across the conditions. Friedman test revealed a significant effect of condition on HR, $\chi^2(4)$, 39.09, $p < .001$. Post-hoc Wilcoxon signed-rank tests showed HR increased significantly from baseline to all conditions: taxi ($Z = -3.41, p < .001$), circuit 1 ($Z = -3.35, p < .001$), circuit 2 ($Z = -3.35, p < .001$), and emergency ($Z = -3.41, p < .001$). Additionally, HR was significantly higher in emergency compared to taxi ($Z = -3.07, p < .001$), circuit 1 ($Z = -3.35, p < .001$) and circuit 2 ($Z = -3.24$, $p < .001$).

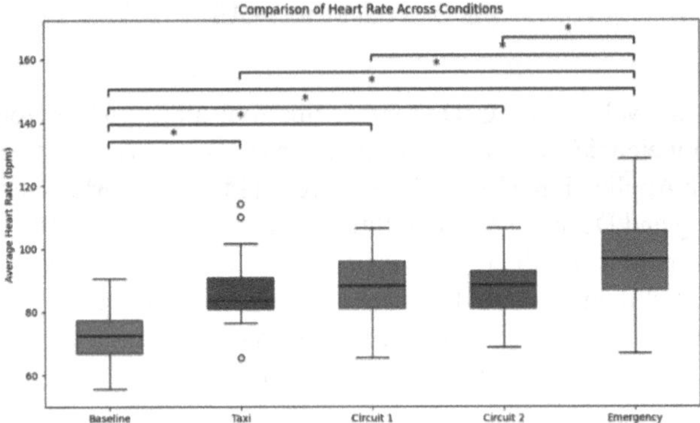

Fig. 6. Heart Rate boxplot across conditions. Asterisk (∗) denotes significant results following Wilcoxon tests.

Further HRV analysis involved computing time-domain metrics. The time-domain metrics were Mean NN, SDNN, RMSSD and pNN50. Freidman test revealed a significant effect of condition for all four metrics. Mean NN, $\chi^2(4) = 37.49, p < .001$; SDNN, $\chi^2(4) = 23.57, p < .001$; RMSSD, $\chi^2(4) = 33.97, p < .001$; and pNN50, $\chi^2(4) = 30.33$, $p < .001$. Post-hoc Wilcoxon signed-rank tests showed significant pairwise comparisons for each of the metrics. Significant reductions occurred in Mean NN (Fig. 7, top-left) from baseline to other conditions: taxi ($Z = -3.41$, $p < .001$), circuit 1 ($Z = -3.41$, $p < .001$), circuit 2 ($Z = -3.41$, $p < .001$), and emergency ($Z = -3.41, p < .001$). Additionally, differences between emergency and other conditions: taxi ($Z = -2.78, p = .003$), circuit 1($Z = -3.01, p = .001$), and circuit 2 ($Z = -3.18, p < .001$) were also significant. RMSSD values (Fig. 7, bottom-left) significantly declined from baseline to all conditions: taxi ($Z = -3.35$, $p < .001$), circuit 1 ($Z = -3.35, p < .001$), circuit 2 ($Z = -3.41, p < .001$), emergency ($Z = -3.41, p < .001$). A similar trend emerged for pNN50 (Fig. 7, bottom-right) from baseline to other conditions: taxi ($Z = -3.41, p < .001$), circuit 1 ($Z = -3.35, p < .001$), circuit 2 ($Z = -3.41, p < .001$) and emergency ($Z = -3.35, p < .001$). In contrast, differences in SDNN (Fig. 7, top-right) were significant only between baseline to circuit 1 ($Z = -3.41, p < .001$) and circuit 1 to emergency ($Z = -3.24, p < .001$).

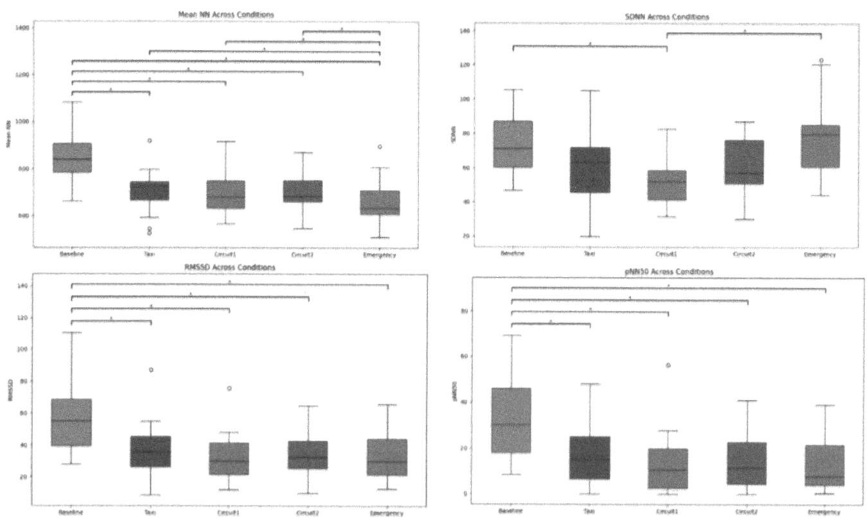

Fig. 7. Time-domain features of HRV across conditions: (Top-left) Mean NN, (top-right) SDNN, (bottom-left) RMSSD and (bottom-right) pNN50. Asterisk (∗) denotes significant results following Wilcoxon tests.

A Poincaré plot is a graphical means of visualizing and quantifying the evolution of dynamic systems, most represented on a cartesian coordinate space with x and y axes. In a Poincaré plot, consecutive RR intervals are plotted in pairs forming a time series (R-R1, R-R2) (R-R2,R-R3) (R-R3,R-R4).....(R-Rn-1,R-Rn). Successive points with equal values fall along the 45° diagonal, known as the line of identity, where y = x. SD1 is the standard deviation of points perpendicular to the line of identity while SD2 is the standard deviation of points along the line of identity. SD1 and SD2 can be used to draw an ellipse which summarizes the shape of the Poincaré plot. SD1 reflects short term heart rate variability dominated mainly by parasympathetic activity and SD2 reflects long term heart rate variability or both sympathetic and parasympathetic activity. The SD1/SD2 ratio is a measure of autonomic balance [37]. Figure 8 depicts visual patterns of the Poincaré plot that vary with stress. As seen in the Poincaré plot for Participant 003, the shape of the ellipse gets increasingly narrower and points cluster near the identity line from baseline to emergency. The length of the SD1 (blue vector) also decreases with increasing stress and is shortest for the emergency condition consistent with parasympathetic or vagal withdrawal and sympathetic dominance.

Statistical analysis of non-linear parameters revealed significant effect of condition: SD1, $\chi^2(4) = 33.97, p < .001$; SD2, $\chi^2(4) = 17.23, p = .002$; SD1/SD2, $\chi^2(4) = 26.29, p < .001$. SD1 (Fig. 9, top-left) showed a general downward trend from baseline to emergency with post-hoc Wilcoxon-signed rank test difference being significant from baseline to all conditions: taxi ($Z = -3.35, p < .001$), circuit 1 ($Z = -3.35, p < .001$), circuit 2 ($Z = -3.41, p < .001$) and emergency ($Z = -3.41, p < .001$. SD2 baseline

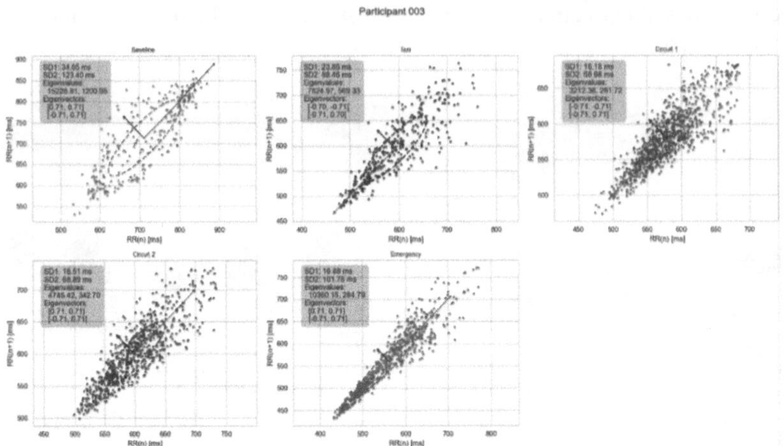

Fig. 8. Poincaré plot across conditions for Participant 003.

to circuit 1 ($Z = -3.12$, $p < .001$) and circuit 1 and emergency ($Z = -3.24$, $p < .001$) differences were significant (Fig. 9, top-right). SD1/SD2 ratio (Fig. 9, bottom-left) pairwise comparisons were significant for baseline to conditions: circuit 1 ($Z = -2.71$, $p = .004$), circuit 2 ($Z = -3.07$, $p = .001$), emergency ($Z = -3.41$, $p < .001$); taxi to emergency ($Z = -2.90$, $p = .002$), circuit 1 to emergency ($Z = -2.72$, $p = .004$) and circuit 2 to emergency ($Z = -2.84$, $p = .003$).

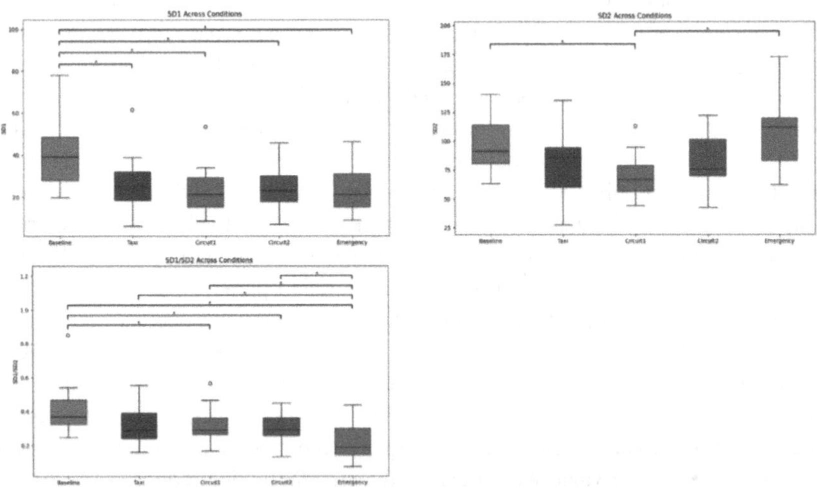

Fig. 9. Poincaré plot parameters analysis across conditions: SD1 (top-left), SD2 (top-right) and SD1/SD2 (bottom-left). Asterisk (∗) denotes significant results following Wilcoxon tests.

Electrodermal Activity: Physiological Arousal. EDA data was analyzed to infer physiological arousal levels. Due to technical challenges with the EmotiBit device, data from only eight participants was used for analysis. The line plot (see Fig. 10) displays EDA patterns for Participant 004 across conditions showing the raw signal (top-left), clean signal (top-right), and tonic decomposition (bottom). Higher arousal responses were observed during conditions other than baseline, with taxi responses higher than circuit 1 and emergency. Additionally, the emergency triggered a visible increase in arousal after the emergency onset.

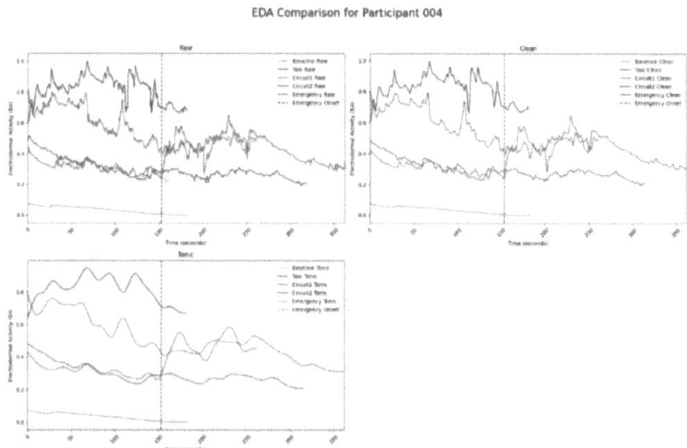

Fig. 10. EDA patterns for Participant 004 depicting baseline behavior and arousal responses to the scenario training in flight simulator.

The clean EDA signal was used for all analysis and visualilzation. The EDA heat map and radar plot below illustrate individual differences in arousal across conditions. Compared to the rest of the group, Participants 004 and 016 exhibited elevated responses in taxi, Participant 002 during circuit 2, and Participant 009 in emergency (Fig. 11, left). Taxi in general evoked moderate (e.g., Participant 001) to high responses in participants (e.g., Participants 004 and 016) (Fig. 11, right).

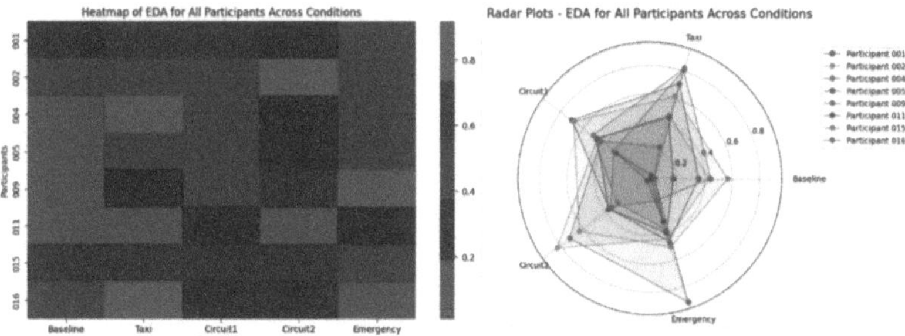

Fig. 11. EDA heat map (left) and radar plot (right) created to compare the arousal levels of participants across all conditions.

The emergency conditions were segmented into pre- and post-emergency for further comparison to see how arousal levels change during high-stress conditions (see Fig. 12). The upward trend in EDA from baseline to post-emergency indicates an increase in physiological arousal, reflecting enhanced sympathetic activation occurring during the post-emergency phase.

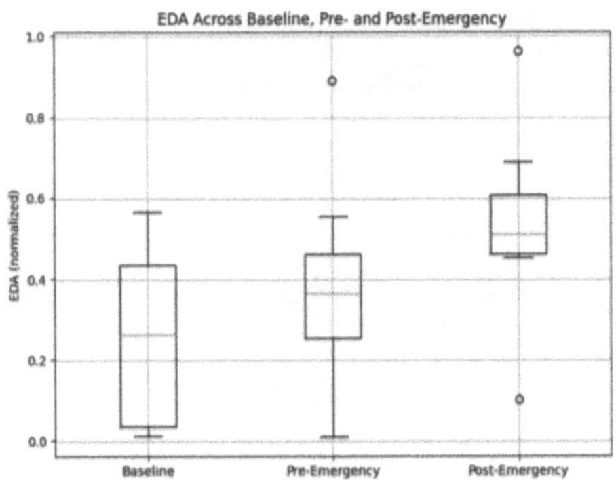

Fig. 12. Box plot comparing EDA across conditions (baseline, pre- and post-emergency)

5.2 Flight Instructor Assessment

The visualization on left (see Fig. 13) compares the mean performance scores for all five competencies. Scores for four of the five competencies did not significantly differ across conditions. However, statistical analysis revealed a significant effect of condition on mean application of procedure scores (Fig. 13, right), $\chi^2(3) = 23.38, p < .001$. Post-hoc Wilcoxon-signed rank found significant differences for taxi and circuit 1 ($Z = -2.73, p = 0.006$), taxi and circuit 2 ($Z = -3.12, p = 0.002$), circuit 1 and emergency ($Z = -2.98, p = 0.003$) and circuit 2 and emergency ($Z = -3.18, p = 0.001$) (see Fig. 13, right). The average application of procedure scores were taxi ($M = 3.44$, $SD = 0.35$), circuit 1 ($M = 3.84$, $SD = 0.24$), circuit 2 ($M = 3.91$, $SD = 0.20$) and emergency ($M = 3.11$, $SD = 0.71$) out of total possible score of 4. The lowest competency scores were for situational awareness with average score being taxi ($M = 2.88$, $SD = 0.72$), circuit 1 ($M = 3.25$, $SD = 0.68$), circuit 2 ($M = 3.56$, $SD = 0.63$) and emergency ($M = 3.00$, $SD = 0.55$).

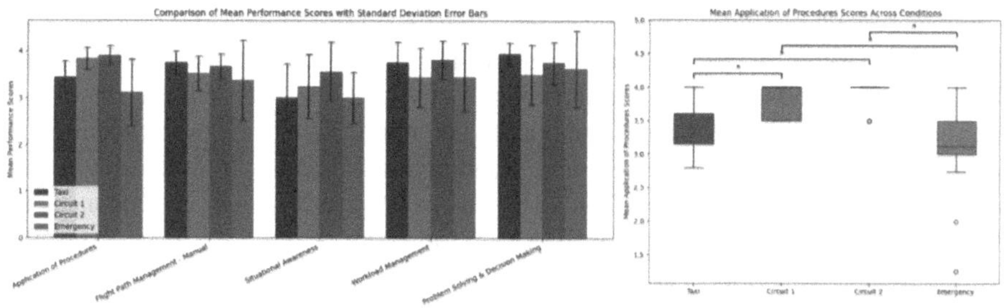

Fig. 13. Comparison of Mean Performance Scores with Standard Deviation Error Bars (left) and Mean Application of Procedures Scores Across Conditions (right). Asterisk (∗) denotes significant results following Wilcoxon tests.

5.3 Perceived User Experience and Stress

The visualization (Fig. 14, left) shows that the simulation met the minimum UX cutoff, with a median score of 27, whereas VRISE met the more stringent cutoff, with a median score of 6. Additionally, statistical analysis revealed a significant effect of condition on self-report of stress (see Fig. 14, right), $\chi^2(3) = 40.56, p < .001$. Post-hoc Wilcoxon-signed rank found significant difference for taxi and circuit 1 ($Z = -3.41, p = 0.001$), taxi and circuit 2 ($Z = -3.08, p = 0.002$), taxi and emergency ($Z = -3.52, p < .001$), circuit 1 and emergency ($Z = -3.52, p < .001$) and circuit 2 and emergency ($Z = -3.41, p = 0.001$).

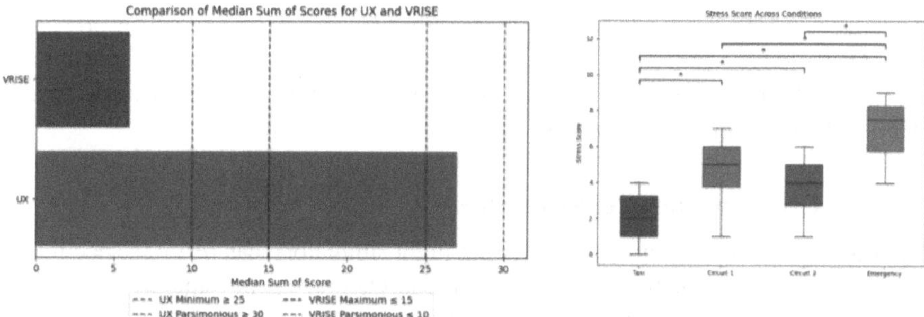

Fig. 14. Median Total Score for UX and VRISE (left) and Stress Score Across Conditions (right). Asterisk (∗) denotes significant results following Wilcoxon tests.

6 Discussion

6.1 Psychophysiological Responses and Autonomic Balance

Findings for HR and HRV time-domain measures (RMSSD, Mean NN and pNN50) are consistent with studies demonstrating that HR increases during high stress situations while time-domain measures generally decrease with increasing stress [4, 6, 10, 28, 29]. Non-linear analysis suggests an overall reduction in SD1 and a lower SD1/SD2 across conditions from baseline to emergency. Taken together, the findings offer support for the notion that participants experienced dynamic shifts in their "fight-and-flight" (sympathetic) and "rest-and-digest" (parasympathetic) activity [24] from baseline to emergency, with emergency eliciting the most pronounced autonomic imbalance. Additionally, contrary to our expectation, taxi and circuit 1 and taxi and circuit 2 differences were not significant. This likely reflects anticipatory stress related to upcoming task demand and performance evaluation. In terms of EDA, we could only use 56.25% of the data. With small sample sizes outliers can skew findings so we refrained from computing any statistical analysis. From the visualizations, however, the individual variability is evident. For some taxi had the highest EDA values, while for others emergency or circuit 1. Reinforcing these individual differences, studies have reported that not all participants demonstrate higher EDA values in stressful or emergency situations [1].

6.2 Performance

Consistent with findings of Cao et al. [4], Shao et al. [5], Peng et al. [6] and Lee [7], the results suggest that stress negatively impacts performance. For Emergency, flight instructors noted memory items not being completed, glide speed not maintained and radio calls not made given sufficient time. Failure to check instruments, brakes and aileron not being positioned into the wind during taxi. Additionally, taxi resulted in the second lowest mean application of procedure scores, consistent with HR findings. Furthermore, stress appears to impact certain competencies more than others. For instance, emergency application of procedure scores were significantly lower than other conditions while situational awareness had the lowest performance scores of all competencies across conditions, with worst performance in taxi followed by emergency. One explanation could be that competencies such as flight path management largely rely on procedural skills. On the other hand, stress has been shown to impair situational awareness through its effect on higher-order cognition processes in the form of working memory decline, attentional narrowing, among others [42].

6.3 User Experience and Perceived Stress

Exposure to virtual environments, including flight simulators, can result in specific side effects, known as simulator sickness, which can encompass physiological symptoms reflecting changes in cardiovascular, respiratory or temperature regulation functions [43]. UX and VRISE can modulate stress responses making it imperative to rule out their confounding effects. UX and VRISE scores meeting minimum and parsimonious cutoffs, respectively, suggest that the simulator induced quality immersion and realism without any significant VRISE impacting the experience. Additionally, perceived stress differed significantly across conditions except for circuit 1 and circuit 2, while physiological measures did not consistently align with this finding, suggesting a partial dissociation between subjective and psychophysiological stress responses.

6.4 Sensors and Signal Quality

The scenario and the sensor employed in the study are certainly challenging for data quality. Because of the long duration of recordings (often 30+ minutes), we encountered short circuits in the EDA for the final circuit in several participants. Given within-subject design, we had to exclude any participants who had missing data in one of the conditions. Other researchers have also commented on challenges with EDA. In one study using Emotibit, only 2 out of 10 participants' EDA was usable [44], and in another study using the Empatica E4, only 18 out of 30 participants' EDA could be included in the analysis [3]. Heart rate and heart rate variability data from the Polar H10 turned out to be extremely stable, with no data loss or quality issues. The eye tracker and aviation headset worn over the Muse BCI produced noisy but manageable signals.

6.5 Future Work

While still preliminary, this study lays the groundwork for integrating multimodal wearable physiological sensing into flight training. Understanding stress responses can help flight instructors assess which maneuvers or phases of a flight may be more stressful or challenging. This can support stress inoculation training and personalized instructor assessment and feedback. Physiological insights interfaced with biofeedback technologies may also aid in acquisition of important self-regulation and stress-management skills. A secondary objective of the study is to create a database with the collected physiological, system metrics and user experience data for the development of computational models to characterize, simulate and predict pilot trainees' psychophysiological states, addressing the current paucity of such datasets [45, 46]. This includes rule-based or machine-learning-based models to inform the design of adaptive training systems that modulate flight simulation difficulty (for instance, by injecting instrument failures or environmental variable modifications through the instructor station interface) using interpreted psychophysiological indices or state.

7 Conclusion

This preliminary, incremental work, is one of the few studies using multimodal, fully wearable sensors to quantify and characterize pilot trainees' stress responses across a wide variety of training conditions. Results indicate initial evidence that the multimodal wearable physiological sensors employed in the study sensitively and consistently gauges changes in stress inducements. HR and HRV time-domain and non-linear metrics varied significantly across conditions, whereas EDA showed a non-significant trend of increased stress post-emergency compared to pre-emergency. Performance and self-report of stress in general corroborated psychophysiological insights. User experience scores further confirm this and the fidelity of the simulator and minimum VRISE indicate stress responses were highly likely to be task-induced. Envisioning future implications, we anticipate psychophysiological responses associated with skills training in interactive simulator programs beneficially complementing conventional training and yielding valuable insights to designing biocybernetic training systems.

Acknowledgments. This study was partially funded by a Natural Sciences and Engineering Research Council of Canada Discovery Grant (RGPIN-2024-04808 to S.C.). The authors express gratitude to the pilot trainees, flight instructors, and Waterloo Institute for Sustainable Aeronautics Research Coordinator Raphael Repato.

Disclosure of Interests. The authors have no competing interests to declare that are relevant to the content of this article.

References

1. Guerrero, I., Vallès-Català, T.: Virtual reality flight simulation for pilot training: studying arousal levels during an emergency landing. In: INTED2023 Proceedings, pp. 2594–2599 (2023). https://doi.org/10.21125/inted.2023.0729
2. Vallès-Català, T., Guerrero, I.: Comparing arousal and workload during an emergency landing in a virtual reality and a conventional flight simulator. Int. J. Hum. -Comput. Interact. (2025). https://doi.org/10.1080/10447318.2025.2474464
3. Lutnyk, L., Rudi, D., Schinazi, V.R., Kiefer, P., Raubal, M.: The effect of flight phase on electrodermal activity and gaze behavior: a simulator study. Appl. Ergonom. **109**, 1 (2023). https://doi.org/10.1016/j.apergo.2023.103989
4. Cao, X., et al.: Heart rate variability and performance of commercial airline pilots during flight simulations. Int. J. Environ. Res. Public Health **16**(2), 237 (2019). https://doi.org/10.3390/ijerph16020237
5. Shao, S., Zhou, Q., Liu, Z.: A new assessment method of the pilot stress using ECG signals during complex special flight operation. IEEE Access **7**, 185360–185368 (2019). https://doi.org/10.1109/ACCESS.2019.2959626
6. Peng, X., Niu, Q., Liang, Y., Luo, Y., Lu, N., Li, X.: Effects of unexpected event urgency and flight scenario familiarity on pilot trainees performance and stress responses. Front. Physiol. **16**, 1599122 (2025). https://doi.org/10.3389/fphys.2025.1599122
7. Lee, K.: Effects of flight factors on pilot performance, workload, and stress at final approach to landing phase of flight. Electronic Theses and Dissertations, 2004–2019, 1628 (2010). https://stars.library.ucf.edu/etd/1628
8. Vallès-Català, T., Pedret, A., Ribes, D., Medina, D., Traveria, M.: Effects of stress on performance during highly demanding tasks in student pilots. Int. J. Aerospace Psychol. **31**(1), 43–55 (2021). https://doi.org/10.1080/24721840.2020.1841564
9. Regula, M., et al.: Study of heart rate as the main stress indicator in aircraft pilots. In: Proceedings of the 16th International Conference on Mechatronics – Mechatronika 2014, Brno, Czech Republic, pp. 639–643 (2014). https://doi.org/10.1109/MECHATRONIKA.2014.7018334
10. Wojciechowski, P., et al.: Evaluation of drone pilots' sympathetic and parasympathetic nervous system responses during simulated flight in familiar and unfamiliar environments. In: 2024 IEEE International Workshop on Technologies for Defense and Security (TechDefense), Naples, Italy, pp. 7–12 (2024). https://doi.org/10.1109/TechDefense63521.2024.10863445
11. Bruna, O., Levora, T., Holub, J.: Stress measurement and inducement in experiments with low-cost flight simulator for testing of General Aviation pilots. Commun. Comput. Inf. Sci., 218–223 (2017). https://doi.org/10.1007/978-3-319-58750-9_31
12. McClernon, C.K., McCauley, M.E., O'Connor, P.E., Warm, J.S.: Stress training improves performance during a stressful flight. Hum. Factors **53**(3), 207–218 (2011). https://doi.org/10.1177/0018720811405317
13. Cacioppo, J.T., Tassinary, L.G.: Psychophysiology and psychophysiological inference. In: Cacioppo, J.T., Tassinary, L.G. (eds.) Principles of Psychophysiology: Physical, Social, and Inferential Elements, pp. 3–33. Cambridge University Press, Cambridge (2000)
14. Kelley, C.R.: What is adaptive training? Hum. Factors **11**(6), 547–556 (1969). https://doi.org/10.1177/001872086901100602
15. Caro, P.W.: Adaptive training—an application to flight simulation. Hum. Factors **11**(6), 569–576 (1969). https://doi.org/10.1177/001872086901100605

16. Fairclough, S.H.: Fundamentals of physiological computing. Interact. Comput. **21**(1–2), 133–145 (2009). https://doi.org/10.1016/j.intcom.2008.10.011
17. Palsson, O.S., Pope, A.T.: Thermal biofeedback: clinical applications and potential for pilot stress counter-response training. In: AIAA Paper 99-3501 (1999)
18. Schmorrow, D.D.: Aviation training: a future avenue. Avionics Mag., October 2005
19. Vartak, A.A., Fidopiastis, C.M., Nicholson, D.M., Mikhael, W.B., Schmorrow, D.: Cognitive state estimation for adaptive learning systems using wearable physiological sensors. In: Biosignals, vol. 2, pp. 147–152 (2008)
20. Wilson, J.C., Nair, S., Scielzo, S., Larson, E.C.: Objective measures of cognitive load using deep multi-modal learning: a use-case in aviation. In: Proceedings of the ACM on Interactive, Mobile, Wearable and UbIEqitous Technologies, vol. 5, no. 1, pp. 1–35 (2021)
21. Rissler, R., Nadj, M., Li, M.X., Knierim, M.T., Maedche, A.: Got flow? In: Mandryk, R., Hancock, M. (eds.) Extended abstracts of the 2018 CHI Conference on Human Factors in Computing Systems, pp. 1–6. ACM, New York (2018)
22. Guo, Z., Pan, Y., Zhao, G., Cao, S., Zhang, J.: Detection of driver vigilance level using EEG signals and driving contexts. IEEE Trans. Reliab. **67**(1), 370–380 (2017). https://doi.org/10.1109/TR.2017.2778754
23. Sanei, S., Chambers, J.A.: EEG Signal Processing. John Wiley & Sons Ltd., Chichester (2007). https://doi.org/10.1002/9780470511923
24. Cacioppo, J.T., Tassinary, L.G., Berntson, G.G. (eds.): Handbook of Psychophysiology, 3rd ed. Cambridge University Press, Cambridge (2007). https://doi.org/10.1017/CBO9780511546396
25. Kim, H.G., Cheon, E.J., Bai, D.S., Lee, Y.H., Koo, B.H.: Stress and heart rate variability: a meta-analysis and review of the literature. Psychiatry Investig. **15**(3), 235–245 (2018). https://doi.org/10.30773/pi.2017.08.17
26. Ghiasi, S., Greco, A., Barbieri, R., et al.: Assessing autonomic function from electrodermal activity and heart rate variability during cold-pressor test and emotional challenge. Sci. Rep. **10**, 5406 (2020). https://doi.org/10.1038/s41598-020-62225-2
27. Liang, Y., et al.: Effect of acute stress on working memory in pilots: investigating the modulatory role of memory load. PLoS ONE **19**(1), e0288221 (2024). https://doi.org/10.1371/journal.pone.0288221
28. Wang, Y., Fan, X., Shao, S., Fu, C., Wang, Y.: Research on the psychological stress of pilots under complex flight interaction tasks. In: 2nd International Conference on Artificial Intelligence, Human-Computer Interaction and Robotics (AIHCIR), Tianjin, China, pp. 1–5 (2023). https://doi.org/10.1109/AIHCIR61661.2023.00007
29. Bustamante-Sánchez, Á., Clemente-Suárez, V.J.: Psychophysiological response in night and instrument helicopter flights. Ergonomics **63**(4), 399–406 (2020). https://doi.org/10.1080/00140139.2020.1718772
30. Causse, M., Dehais, F., Faaland, P., Cauchard, F.: An analysis of mental workload and psychological stress in pilots during actual flight using heart rate and subjective measurements (2012). In: 5th International Conference on Research in Air Transportation (ICRAT 2012), 22 May 2012 - 25 May 2012 (Berkeley, United States).
31. Bruna, O., Levora, T., Holub, J.: Assessment of ECG and respiration recordings from simulated emergency landings of ultra-light aircraft. Sci. Rep. **8**, 7232 (2018). https://doi.org/10.1038/s41598-018-25528-z
32. Villafaina, S., Fuentes-García, D.J.P., Gusi, N., Tornero-Aguilera, J.F., Clemente-Suárez, V.J.: Psychophysiological response of military pilots in different combat flight maneuvers in a flight simulator. Physiol. Behav. **238**, 113483 (2021). https://doi.org/10.1016/j.physbeh.2021.113483

33. Ruseva, B.K., Vezenkov, S.R., Tonchev, P.T., Mihaylov, I.I., Manolova, V.R., Radoyski, U.G.: Comparative analysis of heart rate variability in aviator cadets and instructors during ground training. Arch. Balk. Med. Union **60**(1), 21–31 (2025). https://doi.org/10.31688/ABMU.2025.60.1.02
34. ALSIM: AL250 Instructor Station Manual (2019)
35. Polar Electro Oy: Polar H10 Heart Rate Sensor. Polar. https://www.polar.com/ca-en/sensors/h10-heart-rate-sensor
36. Makowski, D., et al.: NeuroKit2: a Python toolbox for neurophysiological signal processing. Behav. Res. Methods **53**(4), 1689–1696 (2021). https://doi.org/10.3758/s13428-020-01516-y
37. Shaffer, F., Ginsberg, J.P.: An overview of heart rate variability metrics and norms. Front. Public Health **5**, 258 (2017). https://doi.org/10.3389/fpubh.2017.00258
38. Montgomery, S.M., Nair, N., Chen, P., Dikker, S.: Validating EmotiBit: an open-source multimodal sensor for capturing research-grade physiological signals from anywhere on the body. Measur. Sens. **32**, 101075 (2024). https://doi.org/10.1016/j.measen.2024.101075
39. Kothe, C., et al.: The lab streaming layer for synchronized multimodal recording. Imaging Neurosci. **3** (2025). https://doi.org/10.1162/IMAG.a.136
40. Moncion, B., Cao, S., Kearns, S.: Creating competency-based assessment grade sheets and a rubric for private pilot license training. Waterloo Institute for Sustainable Aeronautics, University of Waterloo, Report 2024-001 (2024)
41. Kourtesis, P., Collina, S., Doumas, L.A.A., MacPherson, S.E.: Validation of the virtual reality neuroscience questionnaire: maximum duration of immersive virtual reality sessions without the presence of pertinent adverse symptomatology (2021). https://doi.org/10.3389/fnhum.2019.00417
42. Matthews, G., Wohleber, R.W., Lin, J.: Stress, skilled performance, and expertise: overload and beyond. In: Ward, P., Schraagen, J.M., Gore, J., Roth, E. (eds.) The Oxford Handbook of Expertise, pp. 490–524. Oxford University Press, Oxford (2019). https://doi.org/10.1093/oxfordhb/9780198795872.013.22
43. Polak, E., Ślugaj, R., Gardzińska, A.: Postural control and psychophysical state following a flight simulator session in novice pilots. Front. Public Health **10**, 788612 (2022). https://doi.org/10.3389/fpubh.2022.788612
44. Muñoz, J.E., Lavoie, J.A., Pope, A.T.: Psychophysiological insights and user perspectives: enhancing police de-escalation skills through full-body VR training. Front. Psychol. **15**, 1390677 (2024). https://doi.org/10.3389/fpsyg.2024.1390677
45. Xu, R., et al.: An in-flight multimodal data collection method for assessing pilot cognitive states and performance in general aviation. MethodsX **15**, 103589 (2025). https://doi.org/10.1016/j.mex.2025.103589
46. Fettrow, T., et al.: Human contributions to safety data testbed flight simulation study: data methods, processing, and quality. Sci. Data **12**, 1247 (2025). https://doi.org/10.1038/s41597-025-05336-7

Towards a Speech-Based Resolution of In-Flight Abnormal Situations

Hélène Unrein[1(✉)], Elodie Bouzekri[2(✉)], Benoit Ouellette[3], and Jeremy R. Cooperstock[1]

[1] McGill University, Montréal, Canada
helene.unrein@mcgill.ca, jer@cim.mcgill.ca
[2] Univ Brest, Lab-STICC, CNRS, Brest, France
elodie.bouzekri@univ-brest.fr
[3] Bombardier, Montréal, Canada
benoit.ouellette@aero.bombardier.com

Abstract. This paper presents a remote study with ten airline pilots exploring speech-based interactions to resolve an abnormal situation using an Autonomous Voice Assistant for Checklists. The results show that although speech-based interactions are less usable and reliable than click-based interactions for starting the checklist and performing check actions, they increase both the pilots' capacity to divide attention, as well as their accuracy on a concurrent task, while preserving awareness of checklist completion. Even though pilots mostly preferred the familiar click-based interactions, they found speech-based interactions useful as a complement to classical interactions when not available or practicable in specific situations. From these results, we derived nine guidelines for the conception of speech-based interactions for an Autonomous Voice Assistant for Checklists. These guidelines should be further consolidated through studies in more realistic and controlled environments.

Keywords: User Research · Aviation · Speech-based interface

1 Introduction

Resolving alarms due to abnormal situations is a cumbersome task for pilots, even in normal settings, where the burden is shared with a co-pilot, each having a clearly defined role. They must stabilize the aircraft, identify and analyze the nature of the issue by consulting multiple cockpit indicators, agree on the diagnosis, and apply the correct checklist while continuing to fly the aircraft and manage communications with the ground and the rest of the flight crew [37]. However, some rare situations can impair the pilots' capacity to exchange efficiently or require a pilot to manage these situations by themselves without the assistance of a copilot. For example, in a complex multi-failure situation, each pilot may be too focused on their task to cross-check each recovery action. Furthermore, the copilot may become incapacitated, either as a result of illness,

W. -C. Li and A. Plioutsias (Eds.): HCII 2026, LNAI 16708, pp. 275–299, 2026.
https://doi.org/10.1007/978-3-032-29459-3_19

loss of consciousness, or injury. Under such conditions, the workload increases dramatically [7,26], as pilots must stabilize the aircraft, communicate the issue to the ground, and resolve the situation independently, following the guidance provided by existing checklists. Although such occurrences are rare today, supporting pilots by increasing awareness and the pilots' capacity to divide attention between a main (i.e., fly the aircraft) and a secondary task (i.e., resolve the checklist) is needed to enhance safety under these conditions.

To support pilots in such situations, we propose to explore a speech-based autonomous checklist resolution system. Speech-based interaction for checklist resolution is already integrated into military aircraft [17], light business jets or turboprops (e.g., Goose Co-Pilot [29]). These systems read the actions to pilots, and some can process voice commands. However, these systems do not meet the safety certification requirements for large commercial aircraft. In addition, none of them integrates an autonomous execution of the checklist action. The aviation industry has begun to establish guidelines for the design of highly automated systems (e.g., [14]). Especially, some researchers proposed concepts for single-pilot operation (SPO) that involve automation technology handling new tasks and changing the pilot's role (e.g., [27,30]). In such a context, researchers and industry practitioners have considered the potential benefits offered by natural language and speech-based interactions [11,14,17]. However, this research was limited to defining guidelines for an automated copilot [11] or enabling speech-based interaction to request information and enabling context-relevant notifications [17].

In this paper, we investigate the potential benefits and drawbacks of such speech-based interaction in the context of resolving alarms tied to aircraft system failures, where the pilot must work through Electronic Checklists (ECLs). For this purpose, we designed a speech-based version of the Electronic Checklist (ECL) of the Airbus 220 (A220) and simulated automatic execution of checklist actions, the Autonomous Voice Assistant for Checklists (AVAC). We tested this speech-based version against the baseline click-based version of a semi-autonomous ECL during an online study with airline pilots. Although the speech-based version was found to be less usable, it nevertheless increased awareness and accuracy of the main task, and through interviews with pilots, identified situations where speech-based interactions could increase safety. Based on these results, we derive guidelines for the design of speech-based interactions in future cockpits.

2 Related Work

To manage abnormal situations in the flight deck, speech has been used to convey alarms in military and civil aviation, support checklist completion in small aircraft, and facilitate communication with autonomous systems in single-pilot operations.

Conveying alarms through synthesized speech was studied in military aviation to enable quicker response time and better accuracy to emergencies [9].

Synthesized speech has become a standard in military aviation [3] and civil aviation [13] for conveying critical alarms to pilots. For example, the Ground Proximity Warning System produces a synthesized voice of "TERRAIN, TERRAIN" when the aircraft is too close to the ground.

Beyond alerting pilots to critical issues, speech-based interaction and introduction of autonomous agents to support pilots in their tasks were proposed for single-pilot operations. Künzel et al. [25] propose natural language interaction in a military helicopter to help pilots in Manned-Unmanned Teaming, where a high-level task is requested to an intelligent agent. Gosper et al. [20] conducted interviews with airline pilots during which they identified potential utility of speech assistants in the cockpit, such as retrieving information in time-critical situations, pilot monitoring, and single-pilot operations. Crew Assistant Military Aircraft (CAMA) [33] enables both touch and speech interaction for various commands, among them activating warning related actions. For general aviation, Digital Copilot [17] offers vocal notifications and speech interactions to request information on traffic, airports, weather, or the checklist. Conversational interface for checklist resolution was abandoned because recreational pilots found it "slow" and "burdensome" [18]. However, the authors did not provide details on the evaluation of this conversational system, which enabled checklist resolution with a vocal cognitive assistant.

In small aircraft, speech interaction systems are used for checklist management. The CMS-400 Digital Voice Checklist Management system (Redimec S.A., PDF brochure [36]) automates the reading of cockpit checklists using a digitised human voice. The system is only activated at the pilot's request and uses a dedicated command to move through items, skip steps, or navigate the checklist, but its use declined in favour of integrated glass cockpits and tablets. For light business aviation, the Goose CoPilot tablet application (MiraCheck website [29]) is marketed as a "hands-free co-pilot" capable of reading checklists and advancing through the sequence using voice commands. The pilot can either touch the screen or use speech commands to mark the item as completed. As such, these tools provide only slight automation of the checklist: they can check off completed items by comparing the checklist with real-time data, ignore items that are not applicable, uncheck an item if its status changes, or redirect the procedure to the previous item or to an abnormal procedure branch in the event of an item failure. Depending on the conditions, the systems can activate the appropriate checklist without prior intervention by the pilot, interrupt the normal checklist in the event of a critical emergency, or perform an automatic action, such as engaging the autopilot. Although these systems operate without speech interactions, comparable automation is implemented in the Electronic Centralized Aircraft Monitor on the A320/A350 ([23]) and in the Electronic Checklist (ECL) on the A220.

3 Investigating the Role of Autonomous Checklists in Civil Aviation

3.1 Autonomous Assistant for Checklist Design

In civil aviation, an autonomous checklist system would radically change current crew resource management. Beyond merely recommending actions, the system could automatically execute actions and monitor the checklist's progress, with pilot cross-checking actions performed by the system. In this context, our study explores airline pilots' views of speech-based checklist supervision and resolution.

To investigate the user experience and usability of Autonomous Voice Assistant for Checklists (AVAC), we endeavored to replicate the conversational dynamics prescribed between two crew members, modifying the existing interface to integrate similar two-way natural language interaction between the pilot and an autonomous system, and then conducted a within-subjects study with airline pilots using both AVAC (speech condition) and that of a baseline of standard click-based interaction (manual condition) (see Fig. 1). For speech recognition, we used the Google Cloud Speech API[1]. For speech synthesis, we used the Alloy voice provided by OpenAI [34]. This voice is described as neutral and balanced.

(a) Speech interface with checklist not started, assistant waiting for a voice command.

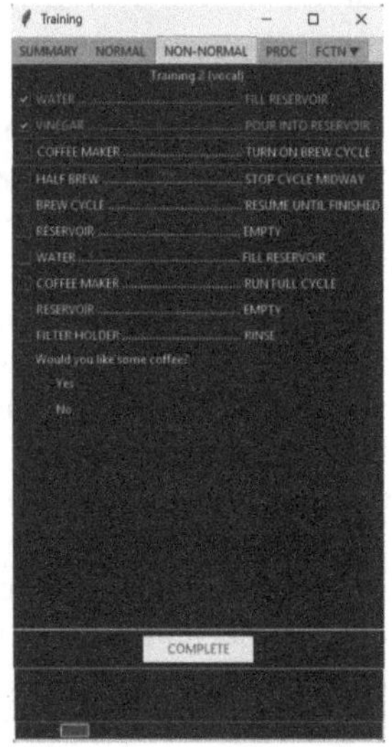

(b) Speech interface with a fictional checklist in progress, the assistant is processing a speech command

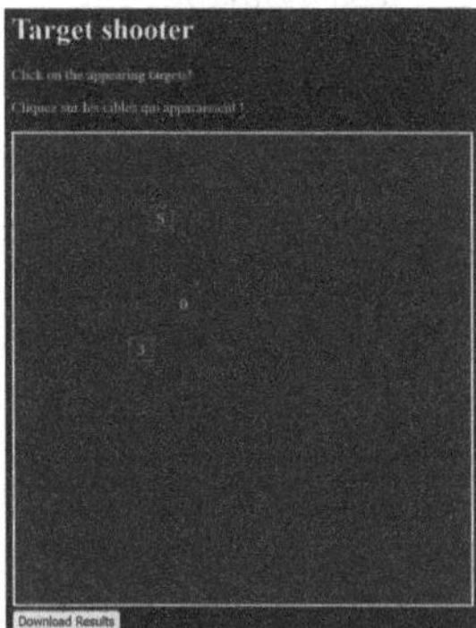

(c) The game played simultaneously with completing the checklist.

Fig. 1. The speech-based electronic checklist interface.

[1] Google Cloud Speech version 2.33.0.

3.2 Participants

We recruited ten pilots, mostly from Air France, with the others from Aviation Corporative, Transavia France, VistaJet, and Air Canada. All were French-speaking males, with a mean age of 46. Eight were captains, and the remaining two were first officers, having worked at this grade for an average of 9.3 years. Ethics approval was obtained from both McGill University (REB #25-07-006-01) and the University of Brest (REB #25061902). Each participant received an information sheet and a consent form, which they signed before proceeding with the study. The data from two participants were excluded because their equipment did not meet our requirements (see Sect. 7).

3.3 Protocol and Materials

This exploratory study was conducted remotely using Google Meet or Zoom. Participants were instructed to take part in the study in a quiet environment. Demographic information was collected, including piloting experience on different aircraft. Each session comprised three phases: training, test, and a semi-structured interview.

After a training phase during which participants practiced a fictitious checklist, both in a manual and speech condition, each pilot performed the experimental scenario with the two systems in counterbalanced order. The scenario simulated a left engine failure resolution after the pilot stabilized the flight. Participants requested that the autonomous system initiate the checklist, check the actions performed automatically, and then confirm checklist completion either by speech or by mouse click on the interface. Participants simultaneously performed a vigilance game that simulates multitasking in flight. Interactions were logged to measure game success rate and command failure rates.

After each scenario, participants completed the System Usability Scale (SUS) [6] to assess overall usability, as well as the User Experience Questionnaire+ (UEQ+), which included dimensions specifically related to voice interaction [24].

Each session concluded with a semi-structured interview (about 40 min). With participant consent, interviews were audio-video recorded, transcribed, and anonymized before any analysis; otherwise, notes were taken. This format was chosen to allow exploration of participants' perspectives while maintaining flexibility to capture unexpected insights. The interview guide included questions regarding perceptions and evaluations of interaction modalities, operational scenarios deemed appropriate or inappropriate for either manual or speech interaction, potential future adaptations and enhancements of the voice assistant interaction.

3.4 Thematic Analysis Procedure

Braun and Clark [5] highlight the diversity of pattern-based approaches and reject the idea of a single or "canonical" qualitative analysis method. In our case, two researchers conducted a hybrid deductive and inductive thematic analysis. We followed four stages: (1) familiarization with the data by two researchers, (2) coding in which both researchers coded the entire transcripts, (3) after sharing and discussing coding results one researcher applied and refined the unified codes to the transcript and (4) thematic consolidation of the predefined themes and categories on which the semi-structured interview questions are based from which new themes and categories were identified: those that emerged in at least two interviews were retained. During this last phase, iterative revisions reduced overlap and brought out coherent themes, enabling the two researchers to reach consensus. We used generic coding (e.g., [28, p. 119]), which is based on a priori-established themes but allows the discovery of unexpected themes. The interview recordings were converted into textual data using an open-source automatic speech recognition model: OpenAI's Whisper, downloaded locally onto researchers' computers.

4 Quantitave Results

In this section, we present results for checklist resolution performance (i.e., failed commands during the scenario), game performance (i.e., success in hitting targets), SUS, and UEQ+ scores. As recommended by Dragicevic [12], given our small sample size ($n = 10$), we report the mean values and their 95% bootstrap confidence intervals ($R = 5000$), and the effect size using Cohen's d, rather than relying on classical null-hypothesis significance testing.

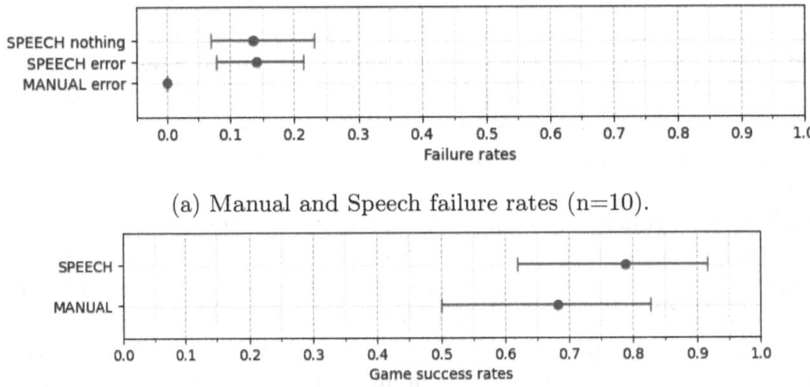

(a) Manual and Speech failure rates (n=10).

(b) Game success rates in manual and speech conditions (n=8).

Fig. 2. Performance results in manual and speech conditions.

Error rates in checklist resolution strongly increased in the speech condition over the manual condition (Cohen's $d = -2.34$, CI $[-3.66 - 1.39]$). Results are shown in Fig. 2a. We labeled 'SPEECH nothing' when the assistant briefly checked if the user spoke a command, but no words were registered. The mean per participant is 13.5%, CI [0.07, 0.23]. We labeled 'SPEECH error' when the assistant failed to recognize the speech command correctly, or the user triggered a command that failed in the current interaction context (e.g., the system waited for a "check", but the user read the line instead). The mean rate of failed commands per participant in the speech condition is 14.0%, CI [0.08, 0.21]. No errors were recorded with the manual version, meaning that each interaction correctly hit the checkbox line area.

For the game results, shown in Fig. 2b, participants made fewer errors in the speech condition (Cohen's $d = -0.43$, CI $[-1.16, 0.07]$). On average, the participants successfully hit targets 79% of the time, CI [0.62, 0.92], in the speech condition. On average, the participants successfully hit targets 68% of the time, CI [0.50, 0.83], in manual condition, suggesting a facilitated division of attention and improved accuracy on the secondary task when using vocal commands.

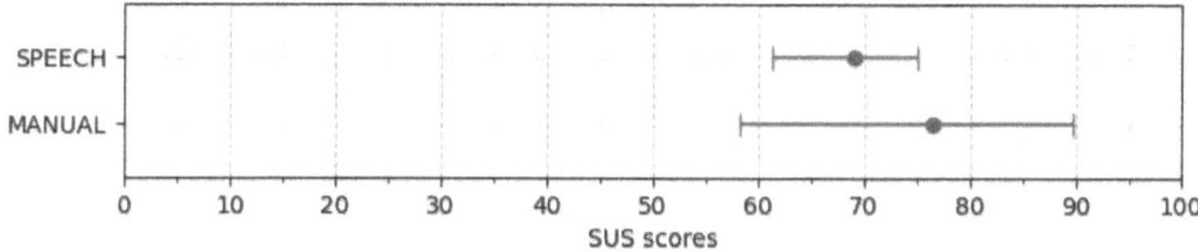

Fig. 3. F-SUS [21] scale means for manual and speech conditions ($n = 10$).

For the SUS scores, there was a mild preference for the manual version over the speech version (Cohen's $d = 0.37$, and CI $[-0.71, 2.71]$. Six out of the ten participants perceived the manual version as more usable than the speech version. The SUS score varies from one participant to another, with one participant considering the manual version as "the worst imaginable" [2] (SUS score of 20.00). Nevertheless, despite the higher failure rate experienced with the speech interface, the results of Fig. 3 indicate that the manual version (mean SUS score of 76.50, CI [58.25, 89.75]) was perceived, in general, as only slightly more usable than the speech version (mean SUS score of 69.00, CI [61.25, 75.00]).

With respect to user experience, participants strongly preferred the manual version over the speech version (Cohen's $d = 0.95$, CI [0.14, 1.93]). The overall mean UX score for the manual version was 1.55, CI [1.22, 1.86] and for the speech version was 0.87, CI [0.36, 1.35]. The manual version scored well for perspicuity ($m = 2.47$, CI [2.10, 2.75]), adaptability ($m = 2.35$, CI [2.02, 2.65]), and intuitive use ($m = 2.40$, CI [2.00, 2.70]), but not for novelty, whereas none of the UX dimensions evaluated for the speech version reached an excellent score (see Fig. 4 and Fig. 5).

We can point out scores obtained for the vocal response quality ($m = 1.65$, CI [1.02, 2.07]), the value ($m = 1.55$, CI [1.02, 2.12]), and intuitive use ($m = 1.28$, CI [0.67, 1.85]) of the speech interface. However, the value (Cohen's $d = 0.66$, CI [0.12, 1.43]) and intuitive use (Cohen's $d = 1.35$, CI [0.66, 2.51]) of the manual interface were preferred over the speech interface.

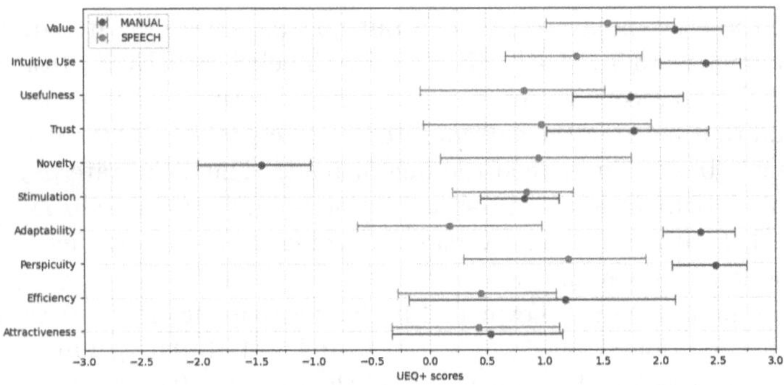

Fig. 4. UEQ+ scale means for manual and speech conditions (n = 10).

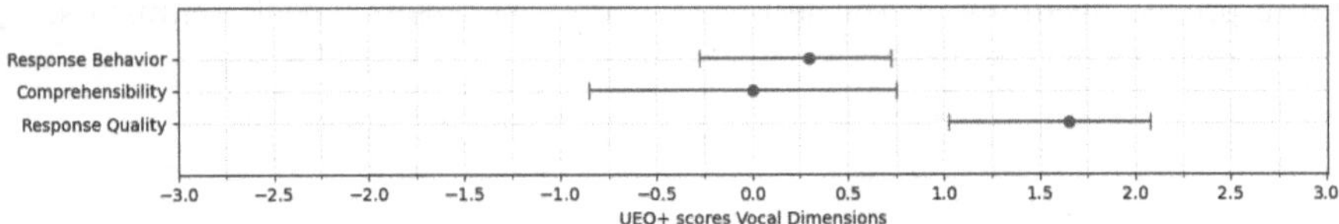

Fig. 5. UEQ+ scale means for response behavior, comprehensibility, and response quality in the speech condition.

5 Qualitative Results: Themes, Categories and Subcategories

The analysis of all interview transcripts resulted in the identification of 126 units of meaning associated with the predefined themes and new themes that emerged from the analysis. Each category is illustrated with verbatim examples to support the analysis. All participant quotes have been translated from French to English. Translations were conducted by the authors and aim to preserve the original meaning and nuance. The participant codes are indicated at the end of each verbatim transcript.

5.1 Theme 1: Perceived Performance and Attention Distribution

Six of the pilots expressed a preference for the manual version, while four others preferred the voice version. Four of the pilots described the speech version as "interesting", but two of these were among those who preferred the manual version. Some participants justified their low usability ratings by the lack of a real cockpit environment and the resulting inability to verify information before checking actions.

A total of 23 units of meaning relating to subjective experience were identified, and 77 occurrences were recorded, representing 19.5% of the interviewees' total discourse. These units were grouped into two categories, each corresponding to a condition described as follows.

Perception of the Manual Version: Reliability and Familiarity, but Limited Division of Attention- Three pilots considered visual feedback to be the most robust and reliable way to perceive and understand information, as it is familiar, predictable, persistent, and reassuring: "We know it works, there are no surprises. The expected behaviour is known and it delivers what is expected. That's pretty good. It works every time" (P9).

Six pilots stated that it corresponds to their habits and previous training and provides them with comfort and efficiency: "I preferred the one with the click. Probably because I'm more used to it. So naturally it's more comfortable for me" (P4).

Seven pilots reported that this task caused attention conflicts. The task required intense visual and manual attention, making it difficult to divide their attention between the checklist and the secondary task: "I struggled because I was trying to click on all the targets. They appeared quickly, and the problem is that conscious reading takes time. The whole time you're focusing on the checklist on the left-hand side, you completely lose track of the squares. So I missed quite a few" (P8).

Five pilots indicated that the manual interface was easy to use, "very simple" (P5), "very intuitive, and effective" (P2). Participants found this interface to be usable, immediate, and effective, allowing them to quickly validate each element thanks to clear visual feedback.

Perception of the Speech Version: Reliability Issues, but Improved Attention- Seven pilots reported problems with voice recognition reliability. The system did not always understand commands; "words were sometimes understood and sometimes not" (P9), forcing them to repeat or rephrase them. Six pilots are unfamiliar with voice command technology. They stated that they "do not use it very often" (P8), that this technology is new and not used much in everyday life.

Eight pilots stated that voice commands made it easier to perform the experimental task, particularly when checking the checklist : "I don't have to look at the visual feedback means that if I've heard my audio feedback. If we've heard the feedback, we can move on and just glance at the feedback, which is always a bonus. If we have any doubts, we can take a look" (P3).

Four pilots reported a simple learning process and "relatively orthodox operation, in line with industry standards" (P6), which makes the system "practical" (P8) and effective.

Eight pilots noted that using voice commands allowed them "to be faster" (P1), and "therefore 'save time" (P10).

Three pilots noted that the voice version is consistent with operational reality. It imitates teamwork, where one reads the items and the other confirms them, making the experience closer to actual practice in the cockpit : "Compared to my work as a pilot in two-person crews, I have found the same kind of teamwork that I am used to in my professional life" (P8).

5.2 Theme 2: Assistant Communication

The information provided by the assistant and the way in which it is communicated form the heart of the participants' discussion. A total of 34 units of meaning were identified, representing 97 occurrences, 24.6% of the total dialogue. These units of meaning fall into four categories described below.

Visibility

Lack of Vocal Feedback About the Status and Operation of the Voice Assistant: Eight pilots expressed the need to receive a vocal confirmation that the requested action was understood and in progress, or an aural signal indicating that the assistant is waiting for pilots' input. Furthermore, pilots would appreciate an explanation of the speech-command malfunction. These observations indicate that the visual feedback failed to support transparency and visibility regarding the status and actions of the assistant.
"What annoyed me was that I didn't know whether what I was saying was being taken into account or not" (P7); "A confirmation of my response has been taken into account. Each time, I had to change screens to check that the line had been validated and that we had changed lines. If I had had voice feedback, I might have been able to stay focused on my game" (P2).

Targeted Training: Five pilots underlined the need for training for both vocal interactions and the functionalities of the vocal assistant. They also insisted on the importance of being able to experiment with the system in order to directly assess the real dynamics of interactions.

"You need a little experience with a system to know its normal response time" (P3); "Training should be incorporated as soon as type certification is obtained, explaining to pilots whether they should use this tool and what words they should use" (P8).

Multimodality- Five pilots highlighted the importance of maintaining both vocal and visual modalities simultaneously. According to them, even when vocal communication is available, visual support remains indispensable.

"I think it provides double feedback. I think that's the main benefit. It's that you get both vocal and visual feedback" (P3).

Oral Communication

Phrasing Used by the Assistant: Six pilots commented on how the voice assistant reads items, reports results, and follows procedures. The aim is for the voice agent to behave in a manner consistent with a human co-pilot: compliance with Standard Operating Procedures, clarity, logical order, and adaptation to cultural preferences.

"You can't really stray from what the manufacturer's QAH says. That's what you have to say" (P6); "The AI should speak exactly like a co-pilot following their SOPs. A verification procedure for a certain step must be followed verbatim" (P10).

Naturalness of the Voice: Nine pilots commented on the naturalness of the voice assistant. The pilots are all satisfied with the naturalness of the voice. The level of intonation is considered satisfactory, but their perceptions vary: some pilots identified and appreciated it, while others did not perceive it and appreciated its absence. Three pilots noted the usefulness of slight functional intonations to distinguish between questions and statements, provided they remain discreet. A human-like voice is perceived as counterproductive, blurring the distinction between human and machine interactions. The pilots recommended a neutral, synthetic, and formal tone, promoting immediate understanding and safety in the cockpit.

"I was surprised, it was more natural than I expected. It was definitely a computer voice, but I can't say whether it was natural or not. I know it's not a natural human voice, but it wasn't robotic. It was still good" (P1).

Form of the Assistant- Six pilots were in favour of the voice assistant remaining an abstract and functional entity, without embodying a co-pilot or human presence. The assistant must reflect its role in the cockpit: its embodiment and interactions must remain consistent with its actual operational capabilities.

"If the tool is limited to this function, if it is simply a voice assistant used to perform simple tasks, it must remain somewhat abstract" (P9).

5.3 Theme 3: Role of the Assistant and Control Exercised by the Pilot

Pilots questioned the role that a synthetic assistant could play beyond simply executing checklists. A total of 16 meaning units relating to the role of the assistant were identified, representing 41 occurrences, or 10.4% of the total speech of the interviewees. These units of meaning are concentrated around four categories described below.

Human Authority over the Assistant- Six pilots highlighted the importance of their ultimate responsibility in the cockpit and the need for all actions initiated by the assistant to be under the direct control of the pilot, who retains the authority to start, pause, deactivate, or override the assistant at any time. The assistant facilitates the work without ever making decisions on the pilot's behalf.

"It's great that it only starts when I tell it to start. That's definitely something to keep" (P1). "Like any system, an autopilot or anything else, it's about being able to block or cancel it when it's no longer helping you" (P8).

Decision Support- Seven pilots proposed a decision support role for the assistant. This role includes the functions of the voice assistant, which helps guide, validate, and support the pilot in their decision-making, particularly in complex or critical situations. Decision support does not replace the pilot's judgment, but acts as a responsive and factual support.

"I really appreciated it. I was surprised in a reassuring way, when I heard 'I agree.' The system agreed and had the same analysis as me. It surprised me, but it reassured me a little at that moment" (P2).

Complementary Role- Seven pilots mentioned that the voice assistant could take on certain specific operational tasks to lighten the pilot's workload, without interfering in decision-making. Three pilots cited the example of the assistant managing functions such as CPDLC, simply to validate clearances or display relevant information, strictly following the pilot's instructions.

"We have to connect to CPDLC, maybe an AI that would say, "OK, we're going to arrive in oceanic airspace, here are the tasks to be done." Maybe that could be a good idea" (P5).

Supervision Tool- According to two pilots, the voice assistant can detect omissions or errors and alert the pilot to confirm or correct their actions, thereby improving situational awareness without replacing human decision-making.

"The same applies to Engine Runoff: the algorithm should be able to detect human error. For example, in the heat of the moment, if I mistakenly select the left engine when it is the right engine that is causing the problem, the system could inhibit the action based on the engine parameters" (P10).

5.4 Theme 4: Specific Cases of Assistant Use

This theme responds to comments from pilots on the specific conditions in which the assistant provides real added value, but also those in which its intervention does not meet the needs of pilots. A total of 21 meaning units related to this theme were identified, representing 31 occurrences, or 7.8% of the total discussion of the interviewees. These units of meaning were organized into six analytic categories, which are detailed below.

Inaccessibility of Visual Information: Two pilots identified the usefulness of a voice assistant when visual information is not readily available. For abnormal checklists, one pilot explained that he had no choice but to use the iPads placed under the side window and that vocal feedback could be useful when visual ergonomics are limited. In his opinion, in more modern cockpits, the visual presentation of checklists remains sufficiently clear, even if it could be improved. "We have no choice, we use the iPad. This is where voice feedback also makes sense, because if the visual ergonomics are not optimal, voice feedback is more interesting" (P3).

In another situation, a second pilot mentioned a case of smoke in the cockpit, where it becomes difficult to read the instruments. He pointed out that receiving voice instructions in this context could be an advantage, allowing pilots to focus on flying in severely degraded conditions.
"It's a case of smoke in the cockpit, you can't read the instruments. And that can be really interesting, because you're already struggling to fly the plane in an extremely difficult situation, so being able to give voice commands in an emergency is a real advantage. I can see a real benefit there" (P8).

Hands Occupied- Three pilots identified the voice assistant as useful when they manipulate an instrument. When the crew is alone, flying manually without autopilot, their hands are occupied, making it difficult to perform simultaneous actions such as checking checklists or manipulating controls. In a scenario where a crew member is incapacitated, voice control allows critical procedures to be followed without physically manipulating the instruments and, in particular, allows the co-pilot's side stick to be isolated or locked to prevent any unintentional interference with the control of the aircraft.

High Workload Situations- Five pilots indicated that the assistant would be useful in high-workload situations. For example, during a go-around or an engine failure, some actions are critical (e.g., retracting the landing gear). An automatic voice reminder could then be useful to ensure safety. During a water landing or emergency evacuation, speech recognition could allow the pilot to simultaneously execute commands and put on his life jacket. Two pilots reported that the voice assistant would be useful, particularly during takeoff and landing, which require maximum concentration and constant visual attention to the instruments and the outside environment. The voice assistant would allow them to receive critical information and manage procedures without taking their eyes off. Pilots noted that the voice assistant can improve the efficiency of their scanning and prevent distraction. Finally, in situations involving highly complex failures, pilots are not always able to perform a complete cross-check. The voice assistant could help by supervising checklist actions. All critical actions would be properly cross-checked, even under significant time pressure and cognitive load.
"In a situation where there are several pilots present, the workload can sometimes be so heavy that certain actions are not confirmed by the PF. The PM would supervise the result and could check the aircraft controls. In this case, I understand the value of having this agent" (P6).

Low Workload Situations- Five pilots considered the voice assistant useful in low workload situations. Pilots indicated that the voice assistant could be useful for routine checklists (e.g., pre-startup, pre-takeoff, or pre-landing checklists), as well as for non-critical or secondary procedures.

A pilot indicates that the assistant could also be useful for memory items or reminders, particularly during cruising or ETOPS (Extended-range Twin-engine

Operation Performance Standards) flights, where numerous secondary checks (e.g., weather conditions, landing distances, regulatory constraints) and other repetitive tasks are required. The voice assistant could guide the pilot, remind them of actions, check that they have been carried out correctly, and even help interpret certain complex information (e.g., landing performance depending on weather conditions), thereby reducing cognitive load and the risk of omission. "To cross the Atlantic, you will need to carry out a large number of checks. We check the weather, landing distances, snow conditions, to see which terrain we would choose and, above all, to see if we are within the regulatory framework. These additional tasks take up a lot of our time and are very energy-intensive. Perhaps AI could help us to decipher the conditions" (P5).

Unuseful in Low Workload Situations- Three pilots explained that critical moments mainly occur when the aircraft is close to the ground or during significant changes in status, such as leveling off. Outside of these sensitive phases, if the situation is stable, such as during cruise flights or long flights over the Atlantic, they prefer to maintain control over the timing of checklists, as they are capable of managing the controls themselves. They considered that automation and current procedures are sufficient and that a voice assistant is not necessary.

5.5 Theme 5: Technical Obstacles and Cockpit Audio Coordination

Pilots identify a set of issues that need to be resolved before they can truly appreciate the advantages and disadvantages of this system. A total of 19 units of meaning relating to problems to be resolved were identified, representing 62 occurrences, or 15.7% of the total discourse of the interviewees. These units of meaning are concentrated around two categories: Technical obstacles and Cockpit audio coordination. These two categories have been grouped together because, according to the pilots, they reflect problems that designers must resolve before the assistant's effectiveness can be fully evaluated in real conditions.

These categories are not discussed in detail in this section, as they are issues already well known in the literature. Noisy environments, the complexity of cross-cockpit communications, and interactions with other systems can impair speech recognition in the cockpit [18] and are sources of potential overload for pilots, who must simultaneously manage radio, alarms, and cabin communications [20]. The fluctuating cognitive load on the crew reinforces the importance of adapting the voice assistant to its cognitive availability [40]. Reliable word detection of cockpit communication could also help assess the trustworthiness of human-autonomy teams [38].

6 Discussion and Preliminary Design Guidelines

The speech condition led to more execution errors, whereas the manual condition was more efficient. On the other hand, performance on the game suggests better attention distribution with the speech modality, indicating a reduction in the visual-manual load. In terms of usability and UX, the manual interface is globally better evaluated, particularly in terms of "intuitive use", adaptability, and efficiency, although judgments vary among participants. The speech version, despite lower overall scores, reached good response quality and perceived value. Identified themes from the thematic analysis are consistent with these observations. From our results, we draw preliminary guidelines for the design of an autonomous speech-based checklist assistant.

6.1 Coordination with the Assistant

Perceived usability, UX, and interview results show the pilots' preference for the manual version of the interface. This preference seems to be explained by two factors. First, the pilots felt familiar with the manual interface, as they recognized the ECL interface of the A220. Second, no errors were made, resulting in perceived reliability, efficiency, and ease of use of the interface. These qualities are supported by an excellent SUS score and very good scores on the "intuitive use" and "adaptability" scales.

However, there are situations where pilots must focus all their attention on the instruments and the environment, preventing them from communicating or performing other tasks optimally. To address such situations, speech interactions offer an interesting alternative. Participants highlighted a notable increase in their awareness when using the interface with speech interactions, which was reflected in both the interviews and the game results, where more targets were clicked before disappearing. These results are consistent with the literature: speech appears to be an effective way of supporting information processing without prior learning, particularly when visual attention is focused on driving or the external environment (e.g., [8,16]). Accordingly, we propose that future cockpits should offer the option to use speech interaction in contexts where it can be beneficial (e.g., when high workload prevents optimal cross-checking, or when smoke is in the cabin). During a checklist resolution task, speech interaction could be an option, leaving the pilot free to use it when appropriate.

Guideline n°1 : Speech interaction may be best positioned as a complement rather than a replacement for manual interaction, particularly in situations where manual input becomes impractical or attentionally costly.

Pilots expressed a strong need to retain control over interactions and the sequence of actions. In addition, the participants valued a high controllability of the assistant. When evaluating the importance of UX dimensions, the interface's adaptability was praised. This need to control, initiate, and direct tasks was also repeated during the interviews. Pilots remaining the final authority in the cockpit and their capacity to intervene in autonomous functions are compliant with their role and responsibilities as defined by aviation regulation agencies [13,19].

Guideline n°2 : Interaction with the assistant should remain user-initiated and user-driven, allowing pilots to retain full authority over task execution and timing.

Even once these technical obstacles have been overcome, voice interaction requires careful coordination with other sound sources. The literature highlights the limitations of the audio channel, which can interfere with radio communications and crew members' exchange [39]. Participants repeatedly highlighted the complexity of the cockpit's auditory environment, already populated by radio communications, alarms, and crew interactions. Within this context, interaction with a voice assistant raises challenges related to interference, ambiguity, and cognitive load. In response to this concern, pilots emphasized the importance of clearly distinguishing communication addressed to the assistant from communication with other human interlocutors. We propose that a dedicated vocabulary could be designed for communication with the voice assistant.

Guideline n°3 : The use of a dedicated and clearly identifiable vocabulary for interacting with the assistant may help reduce ambiguity and unintended activations.

Finally, as expressed by pilots in theme 2, visual persistence is essential. Speech interactions must be supplemented with visual feedback to ensure the availability of critical information and task continuity, particularly during cognitive overload. In line with [18] and literature on multimodal interaction [35], we suggest that certain speech information must be displayed so that the pilot can inhibit auditory information in the event of auditory overload and return to the visual information at a time of their choosing.

Guideline n°4 : Speech interactions should be supplemented with visual feedback, without systematically displaying all verbal information in order to avoid overload. However, critical spoken information should always be displayed.

6.2 Transparency and Visibility of the Assistant

Theme 3 reveals potential roles for the voice assistant beyond the scope of checklist resolution. The feedback on the diagnosis of the left engine state ("I agree") caused mixed feelings among participants. Some received it positively, while others feared the potential bias this validation might introduce. Then, participants were generally not in favor of having a human-like conversation with the system and preferred using it as a tool that provides only factual, explainable information based on its sensor data. Pilots emphasized that the assistant should reflect its true functional scope and limitations, remaining clearly identifiable as a tool rather than a teammate.

Guideline n°5 : The assistant's form—whether in terms of its vocal characteristics or its potential embodiment in the interface—and behavior should remain consistent with its actual operational capabilities. Anthropomorphic cues could create unrealistic expectations.

Participants rejected forms of expressive interaction that could be perceived as emotionally intrusive, further emphasizing the need for transparency and controllability.

Guideline n°6 : Voice assistants in safety-critical domains should prioritize factual, concise, and transparent communication over expressive or conversational behavior. Intonations would only be used to distinguish between different types of sentences—questions, statements—to make it easier to understand what the system expects.

The work of Estes et al. [18] indicates that pilots prefer the assistant to read the items on the checklist at a steady pace. However, this communication can be enriched by aural cues of system transparency on its current status, plans, and future actions [10], such as whether a voice command is pending, being processed, validated, or failed. In situations where a voice command fails, pilots expressed a need to explain the cause. This information could be represented by indicators that are easily noticeable during a quick visual scan, without requiring sustained attention. It could also be conveyed audibly, integrated in an appropriate and coordinated manner within the crew, in order to preserve the main advantage of the assistant identified in theme 1: allowing the pilot to maintain visual attention on other critical tasks while remaining informed of the status of commands.

Guideline n°7 : Adding auditory information about the status of the system is a relevant option in order to keep pilots' attention on other operational tasks.

6.3 Acceptability

Errors occurred during the use of speech commands. In interviews, participants expressed frustration with the speech command accuracy of the prototype, as reflected in the lower usability and UX ratings. To meet safety requirements, speech recognition technology must reach a high level of reliability and accuracy to be considered for future cockpits.

The interviews revealed that environmental noise was identified as a major limiting factor for speech-based interaction, particularly in abnormal or degraded situations. Because there is a constant noise in the cockpit, vocal interactions should be robust to ambient noise to be considered in future cockpits as highlighted by [18].

Guideline n°8 : Robustness to ambient noise should be considered a prerequisite for trust in speech-based interaction; without it, pilots may revert to more familiar modalities and limit the operational use of the assistant.

As suggested in theme 4, the assistant provides maximum added value in situations where pilots can no longer rely on current interfaces, particularly in contexts involving high cognitive load. Conversely, in situations with low workload or where the visual interface is sufficient, its contribution is less significant. We suggest focusing the deployment of the assistant on those contexts with high operational value, where its benefits are most clear and immediately apparent to pilots.

Guideline n°9 : When developing voice assistants, priority should be given to use cases with high operational value, i.e., situations where traditional methods are limited, where hands are occupied, where visual attention is restricted or impaired (e.g., in the presence of smoke), and when high cognitive load prevents cross-checking of actions.

7 Limitations and Perspectives

We chose to conduct the study remotely in order to facilitate participation and offer greater scheduling flexibility. However, this configuration introduced certain limitations. Participants' equipment was not controlled: although we required a specific operating system (Windows), a microphone, headphones, and a webcam, no specific model was imposed. This heterogeneity led to variations in accuracy and latency in speech recognition, affecting the usability results of the speech version. In addition, internet connection interruptions and other technical issues disrupted the recording of game performance.

We intended to recruit twenty participants, but we were able to recruit ten. We faced the challenge of recruiting pilots, who are in high demand and rarely available. In addition, we received numerous refusals to participate due to the prototype's autonomous nature and the potential link between our study and SPO. SPO is seen by pilots as a threat to safety and the future of the pilot profession [1,15]. This suspicion may also be explained by a lack of systematic identification of human and autonomy roles, division of responsibility and authority in task sharing, in current SPO concepts [4,32], while addressing SPO's recognized limitations, such as deskilling in scientific literature (the interested reader can refer to [22,31]).

The study focused on a single scenario involving a left engine failure, without access to redundant cockpit information to validate the alarm or assess the effects of checklist actions. This limitation, combined with the small sample size, restricts the generalizability of the results.

For future research, it would be relevant to replicate the study in a controlled simulated environment and test more varied and realistic scenarios, incorporating different workloads, weather conditions, and noise levels. Such protocols would allow for a more accurate assessment of the effectiveness and reliability of speech interactions in diverse operational situations.

Voice is currently used as a means of recording and traceability, not as an operational command channel on aircraft systems. To date, no certified system allows automatic execution of voice commands for checklists, and no autonomous system directly executes critical actions, due to strict reliability, certification, and catastrophic risk management constraints. Thus, all critical actions remain performed and verified by both pilots to prevent any catastrophic operational consequences.

8 Conclusion

This study shows that integrating a natural language voice assistant into cockpit checklist management could facilitate multitasking and reduce visual cognitive load, while highlighting the need to maintain human control and manage audio channel saturation. These results highlight the potential of speech interactions with an autonomous checklist resolution agent to improve performance and safety, provided that technical reliability and appropriate training are in place. This exploratory study complements previous findings [18] and opens the way for future developments of integrated speech-based autonomous assistants capable of effectively supporting pilots, particularly in situations of high cognitive load.

Acknowledgments. This research activity is funded by the Science and Engineering Research Council of Canada (NSERC) ALLRP 567177-21, the aviation research Consortium of Québec (CRIAQ) and the following industrial partners: Bombardier, CMC Electronics, Marinvent, Presagis and Thales. The authors thank Abbas Raza and Maël Crenn-Durif for their contributions to the development of the prototype. The authors also want to express their gratitude to the pilots who participated in this study for their availability and the fruitful discussions.

A Appendix

A.1 Quantitative Results

See Figs. 6 and 7.

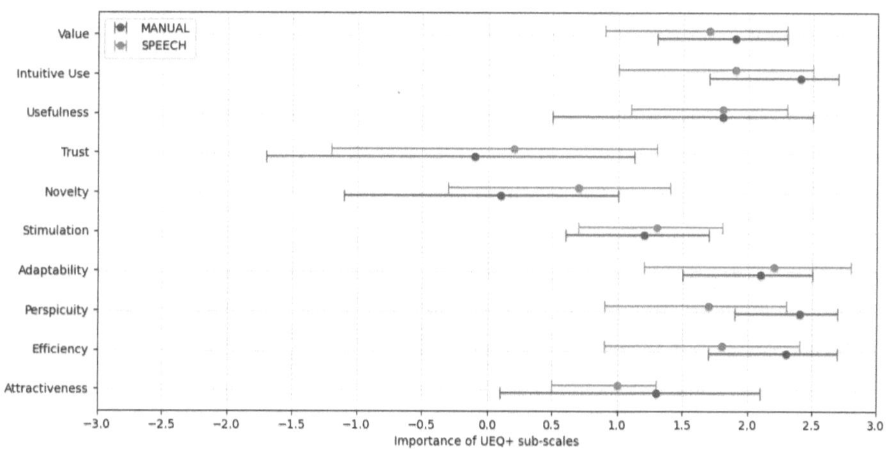

Fig. 6. UEQ+ importance ratings for each UEQ+ subscale for manual and speech conditions (n=10).

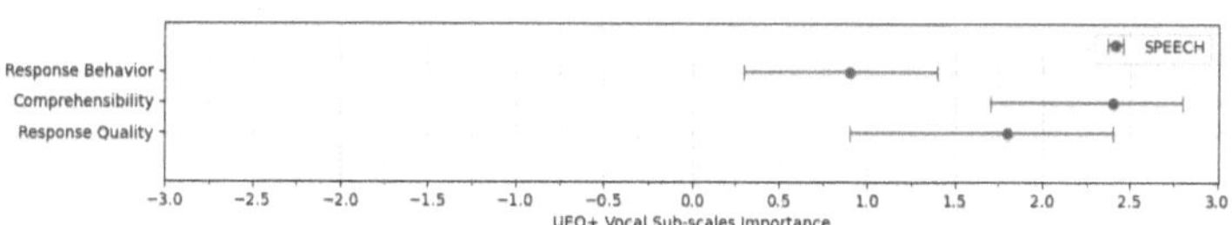

Fig. 7. UEQ+ importance ratings for vocal response behavior, comprehensibility, and response quality for speech condition.

A.2 Qualitative Results

See Tables 1, 2, 3, 4, 5 and 6.

Table 1. Number of occurrences in the category "Manual version" of Theme 1 "Comparison of feelings between the two modalities"

Category	Perception of the manual version : Reliability and familiarity, but limited division of attention			
Subcategory	Robustness	Familiar	Limited multitasking	Ease of use
P1	0	0	3	3
P2	0	3	0	0
P3	1	0	0	0
P4	0	1	1	1
P5	1	4	2	1
P6	0	2	1	1
P7	0	0	0	1
P8	0	0	1	3
P9	1	1	1	0
P10	0	1	2	1
Tot = 36	3	12	11	10

Table 2. Number of occurrences in the category "Speech version" of Theme 1 "Comparison of feelings between the two modalities"

Category	Perception of the speech version: Reliability issues, but interesting potential, particularly in terms of improved attention					
Sub-category	Unreliable	Unfamiliar	Easier multitasking	Fluidity	Efficiency	Two-pilot reality
P1	1	0	5	1	3	1
P2	0	1	1	0	0	1
P3	1	1	4	0	2	0
P4	3	2	1	0	0	0
P5	1	2	2	1	1	0
P6	2	0	0	1	0	0
P7	0	0	0	0	1	0
P8	1	1	1	1	2	3
P9	1	4	1	0	0	0
P10	0	0	1	0	1	0
Tot = 56	10	11	16	4	10	5

Table 3. Number of occurrences in the category "Technical obstacles" of Theme 2 "Technical obstacles and Coordination audio en cockpit"

Category	Technical obstacles		
Sub-category	Cockpit noise	Voice processing time	Word detection
P1	0	0	0
P2	0	0	0
P3	1	1	0
P4	0	0	1
P5	0	0	0
P6	2	2	0
P7	0	1	0
P8	3	0	0
P9	1	0	3
P10	0	0	0
Tot = 15	7	4	4

Table 4. Number of occurrences in the category "Cockpit audio coordination" of Theme 2 "Technical obstacles and Coordination audio en cockpit"

Category	Cockpit audio coordination		
Sub-category	Audio channels and saturation	Pilots' cognitive availability	Team integration and prioritisation
P1	0	0	2
P2	1	2	0
P3	6	0	2
P4	0	3	2
P5	0	0	0
P6	0	0	0
P7	0	0	0
P8	6	2	3
P9	3	5	4
P10	2	0	4
Total = 47	18	12	17

Table 5. Number of occurrences in Theme 3 "Assistant communication"

Category	Visibility		Multi-modality	Oral communication		Form of the assistant
Sub-category	Lack Info	Training		Phraseology compliance	Voice naturalness	
P1	4	2	0	0	3	0
P2	2	0	0	3	2	1
P3	2	7	5	2	2	0
P4	1	0	1	1	1	0
P5	0	3	0	0	2	1
P6	0	0	0	1	4	3
P7	1	0	0	0	1	1
P8	3	1	6	2	4	3
P9	2	1	6	0	4	5
P10	2	0	1	1	0	0
Tot = 97	17	14	19	10	23	14

Table 6. Number of occurrences in Theme 4 "Role of the assistant and control exercised by the pilot"

Category	Human responsibility and authority over the assistant	Decision support	Complementing the pilot	Supervision of the pilot
P1	2	0	0	0
P2	0	3	3	0
P3	2	1	2	0
P4	0	1	3	0
P5	0	2	1	0
P6	1	0	1	0
P7	0	1	0	0
P8	7	1	2	1
P9	2	0	2	0
P10	1	1	0	1
Tot = 41	15	10	14	2

References

1. ALPA: A gamble with safety: Reduced-crew operations. white paper, ALPA (2024). https://www.alpa.org/-/media/ALPA/Files/pdfs/news-events/white-papers/white-paper-reduced-crew-operations.pdf
2. Bangor, A., Kortum, P., Miller, J.: Determining what individual sus scores mean: adding an adjective rating scale. J. Usability Stud. **4**(3), 114–123 (2009)
3. Bell, G., Schultz, M.C., Schultz, J.T.: Voice recognition in fighter aircraft. J. Aviat./Aerosp. Edu. Res. **10**(1), 9 (2000)

4. Bouzekri, E., Berton, B., Doyon-Poulin, P.: Who is Responsible? Roles of Future Pilots in Single Pilot Operations. In: Barricelli, B.R., Valtolina, S., Bouzekri, E., Locoro, A., Mentler, T. (eds.) Human Work Interaction Design. Sustainable Workplaces by Design, pp. 158–173. Springer, Cham (2026). https://doi.org/10.1007/978-3-031-95334-7_10
5. Braun, V., Clarke, V.: Can i use ta? should i use ta? should i not use ta? comparing reflexive thematic analysis and other pattern-based qualitative analytic approaches. Couns. Psychother. Res. **21**(1), 37–47 (2021)
6. Brooke, J.: SUS: A 'Quick and Dirty' Usability Scale, chap. 21, pp. 189–194. CRC Press (1996)
7. Burian, B.K., et al.: Single-pilot workload management in entry-level jets. Tech. rep., NASA Ames Research Center (2013). number: DOTFAAAM1317
8. Burt, J.L.: Empirical studies concerning aural alerts for cockpit use leading to an aural alerting signal categorization scheme, Ph.D. thesis. Virginia Polytechnic Institute and State University (1999)
9. Byblow, W.: Effects of redundancy in the comparison of speech and pictorial displays in the cockpit environment. Appl. Ergon. **21**(2), 121–128 (1990). https://doi.org/10.1016/0003-6870(90)90134-J
10. Chen, J.Y.C., Lakhmani, S.G., Stowers, K., Selkowitz, A.R., Wright, J.L., Barnes, M.: Situation awareness-based agent transparency and human-autonomy teaming effectiveness. Theor. Issues Ergon. Sci. **19**(3), 259–282 (2018). https://doi.org/10.1080/1463922X.2017.1315750
11. Cummings, M.L., Stimpson, A., Clamann, M.: Functional Requirements for Onboard Intelligent Automation in Single Pilot Operations. In: AIAA Infotech @ Aerospace. American Institute of Aeronautics and Astronautics, San Diego, California, USA (2016). https://doi.org/10.2514/6.2016-1652
12. Dragicevic, P.: Fair Statistical Communication in HCI. In: Robertson, J., Kaptein, M. (eds.) Modern Statistical Methods for HCI. HIS, pp. 291–330. Springer, Cham (2016). https://doi.org/10.1007/978-3-319-26633-6_13
13. EASA: CS-25 Amendment 28 (2023). https://www.easa.europa.eu/en/document-library/certification-specifications/cs-25-amendment-28
14. EASA: Artificial Intelligence Concept Paper Issue 2 - Guidance for Level 1 & 2 machine-learning applications | EASA. Tech. rep., EASA (2024)
15. ECA: The human and the concepts of extended minimum crew operations (emco) and single pilot operations (sipo). white paper, ECA (2021). https://safetystartswith2.com/Portals/8/Documents/emco-sipo-position-paper-eca.pdf
16. Edworthy, J., Hellier, E., Titchener, K., Naweed, A., Roels, R.: Heterogeneity in auditory alarm sets makes them easier to learn. Int. J. Ind. Ergon. **41**(2), 136–146 (2011)
17. Estes, S., Burns, K., Helleberg, J., Long, K., Stein, J., Pollack, M.: Digital copilot: Cognitive assistance for pilots. In: 2016 AAAI Fall Symposium Series (2016)
18. Estes, S., Helleberg, J., Long, K., Pollack, M., Quezada, M.: Guidelines for speech interactions between pilot and cognitive assistant. ICNS - Integr. Commun., Navig., Surveill. Conf. 3H21–3H210. Institute of Electrical and Electronics Engineers Inc. (2018). https://doi.org/10.1109/ICNSURV.2018.8384875
19. FAA: Pilot/Controller Roles and Responsibilities (2024). https://www.faa.gov/air_traffic/publications/atpubs/aim_html/chap5_section_5.html
20. Gosper, S., et al.: Understanding the utility of digital flight assistants: A preliminary analysis. In: Proceedings of the 3rd Conference on Conversational User Interfaces, pp. 1–5 (2021)

21. Gronier, G., Baudet, A.: Psychometric Evaluation of the F-SUS: Creation and Validation of the French Version of the System Usability Scale. Int. J. Human–Comput. Inter. **37**(16), 1571–1582 (2021). https://doi.org/10.1080/10447318.2021.1898828, _eprint: https://doi.org/10.1080/10447318.2021.1898828
22. Harris, D.: Single-pilot airline operations: Designing the aircraft may be the easy part. Aeronaut. J. **127**(1313), 1171–1191 (2023). https://doi.org/10.1017/aer.2022.110
23. Kilic, U., Yalin, G., Cam, O.: Digital twin for electronic centralized aircraft monitoring by machine learning algorithms. Energy **283**, 129118 (2023)
24. Klein, A.M., Hinderks, A., Schrepp, M., Thomaschewski, J.: Construction of UEQ+ scales for voice quality: measuring user experience quality of voice interaction. In: Proceedings of Mensch und Computer 2020, pp. 1–5. MuC '20, Association for Computing Machinery, New York, NY, USA (2020). https://doi.org/10.1145/3404983.3410003
25. Künzel, D., Jamakatel, P., Shillig, T., Schulte, A.: An LLM-based agentic natural language dialogue system approach for helicopter MUM-T operations. In: 2025 IEEE 5th International Conference on Human-Machine Systems (ICHMS), pp. 459–464 (2025). https://doi.org/10.1109/ICHMS65439.2025.11154241
26. Landman, A., Groen, E.L., Van Paassen, M., Bronkhorst, A.W., Mulder, M.: Dealing with unexpected events on the flight deck: a conceptual model of startle and surprise. Hum. Factors **59**(8), 1161–1172 (2017)
27. Liu, J., Gardi, A., Ramasamy, S., Lim, Y., Sabatini, R.: Cognitive pilot-aircraft interface for single-pilot operations. Knowl.-Based Syst. **112**, 37–53 (2016). https://doi.org/10.1016/j.knosys.2016.08.031
28. Miles, M.B., Huberman, A.M.: Analyse des données qualitatives, De Boeck Supérieur (2003)
29. MiraCheck: Miracheck copilot: Voice checklists (2025). https://miracheck.com/, Accessed 2 Feb 2026
30. Mosquera Benitez, D., del Corte Valiente, A., Lanzi, P.: A novel global operational concept in cockpits under peak workload situations. Safety Sci. **102**, 38–50 (2018). https://doi.org/10.1016/j.ssci.2017.09.028
31. Myers, P.L., Starr, A.W.: Single pilot operations IN commercial cockpits: background, challenges, and options. J. Intell. Robot. Syst. **102**(1), 19 (2021). https://doi.org/10.1007/s10846-021-01371-9
32. Neis, S.M., Klingauf, U., Schiefele, J.: Classification and review of conceptual frameworks for commercial single pilot operations. In: 2018 IEEE/AIAA 37th Digital Avionics Systems Conference (DASC), pp. 1–8. IEEE, London (2018). https://doi.org/10.1109/DASC.2018.8569680
33. Onken, R., Walsdorf, A.: Assistant systems for aircraft guidance: cognitive man-machine cooperation. Aerosp. Sci. Technol. **5**(8), 511–520 (2001). https://doi.org/10.1016/S1270-9638(01)01137-3
34. OpenAI: Text-to-speech guide (voices) (2024). https://platform.openai.com/docs/guides/text-to-speech, Accessed 11 Feb 2026
35. Oviatt, S.: Ten myths of multimodal interaction. Commun. ACM **42**(11), 74–81 (1999)
36. Redimec S.A.: Cockpit checklist system: Improve safety and convenience by automatically managing and presenting your checklist. https://www.redimec.com.ar/contenido/productos/pdf/1431510571_1.pdf (nd), pDF brochure; accessed February 2, 2026

37. Schutte, P.C., Trujillo, A.C.: Flight crew task management in non-normal situations. Proc. Human Factors Ergonomics Soc. Ann. Meet. **40**(4), 244–248 (1996). https://doi.org/10.1177/154193129604000422
38. Ternus, S., Nareddy, K.K.R., Niebling, J., Papenfuß, A.: Automatic speech recognition in the cockpit: a comparative study of asr models for pilot communication (2025)
39. Ulfvengren, P.: Design of natural warning sounds in human-machine systems, Ph.D. thesis, KTH (2003).
40. Ward, K.A.: Speech interfaces and pilot performance: a meta-analysis. Int. J. Aviation, Aeronaut. Aerosp. **6**(1), 7 (2019)

Fatigue and Human-Machine Teaming Performance in Regional Civil Aviation: Moderating Mechanisms Revealed by Latent Profile Analysis

Wenchao Wang and Xinyu Gu(✉)

School of Safety Science and Engineering, Civil Aviation University of China, Tianjin 300300, China
y19939356641@163.com

Abstract. As cockpit automation evolves toward deep intelligence, this study investigates the impact mechanism of regional pilot fatigue on Human-Machine Teaming Performance (HMTP). Based on data from 83 active pilots analyzed via hierarchical regression and Latent Profile Analysis (LPA), results indicate that fatigue significantly impairs HMTP ($\beta = -0.293$, $p = 0.006$). Crucially, psychological resilience and automation trust demonstrate dual moderating effects: resilience offers a "resource gain" by elevating baseline performance, while trust functions as a "buffer" that mitigates the adverse impact of fatigue. Furthermore, LPA identified three distinct phenotypes: "High Load-Normal Resource" (54.2%), "Low Load-High Adaptation" (37.3%), and "Trust Deficit" (8.5%). The findings suggest that singular fatigue management is insufficient for complex scenarios. Consequently, a "Resilience-Trust" dual-dimensional intervention strategy is proposed, advocating for data-driven, differentiated management to enhance intelligent flight safety systems.

Keywords: Human-Machine Teaming Performance · Human-Centric Human Factors Data · Regional Pilot Fatigue · Automation Trust · Psychological Resilience · Latent Profile Analysis

1 Introduction

Operational safety constitutes the fundamental cornerstone for the sustainable development of the civil aviation industry. Accompanying the steady expansion of global air transport, the complexity, task workload, and network topology of civil aviation operation systems have intensified significantly [1, 2]. Although the profound integration of advanced avionics and Safety Management Systems (SMS) has effectively suppressed incident rates, high-workload phases such as approach and landing remain critical windows prone to flight accidents and serious unsafe events. These phases impose severe challenges on pilots regarding cognitive resource allocation, manipulative precision, and human-machine teaming capabilities [3]. As a vital component of the civil aviation transport architecture, regional aviation plays a pivotal role in connecting regional economies

W. -C. Li and A. Plioutsias (Eds.): HCII 2026, LNAI 16708, pp. 300–319, 2026.
https://doi.org/10.1007/978-3-032-29459-3_20

and serving remote areas. However, the operational environment of regional aviation is characterized by distinct specificities, including lower redundancy in airport navigation facilities, highly variable meteorological conditions, and constrained resource support capabilities. Concurrently, regional flight operations are typified by short sectors, high take-off/landing frequencies, irregular schedules, and extended duty cycles. These factors significantly exacerbate the physiological and psychological workloads of pilots, rendering the cumulative effects of fatigue particularly pronounced [4]. Fatigue significantly impairs pilots' vigilance, cognitive processing efficiency, decision-making, and attentional allocation, thereby increasing susceptibility to memory biases, operational errors, and decision-making inaccuracies [5, 6]. Such cognitive deterioration not only precipitates high-risk events like "unintentional sleep" among crew members [7] but may also induce anxiety, stress, and negative emotions. Consequently, this compromises the quality of Crew Resource Management (CRM), further amplifying systemic risks. In the context of the highly automated modern flight deck, the pilot's role has transitioned from a "direct operator" to a "system manager and supervisor." Human-Machine Teaming Performance (HMTP)—defined as the comprehensive efficacy of humans and machines achieving mission goals through information interaction and functional complementarity—has emerged as a core pillar guaranteeing flight safety. Fatigue manifests a detrimental impact on this dynamic: it diminishes pilots' situational awareness regarding system status, hindering the detection of subtle automation deviations; it disrupts attentional allocation strategies, creating an imbalance between over-reliance on automation and the inability to intervene timely due to distraction; and it erodes the foundation of "appropriate trust" between human and machine, leading to disordered interaction rhythms and misinterpretation of commands. These mechanisms indicate that the impact of fatigue on HMTP possesses characteristics of systemic propagation [8]. In complex operational scenarios, such a degradation in teaming capability significantly escalates operational risks.

Pilot fatigue, functioning as a critical endogenous interference factor, compromises individual cognitive substrates and task decision logic, thereby disrupting the equilibrium of "calibrated trust" and "loop control" within the human-machine teaming architecture. This disruption ultimately precipitates a systemic debilitation of overall operational performance. Roma et al. [9] demonstrated that sleep deprivation is prevalent among aircrew during duty periods; utilizing the Psychomotor Vigilance Test (PVT), they confirmed that such physiological fatigue induces significant neurocognitive impairment and vigilance decrement. Similarly, Gartner et al. [10] observed that while pilots may exhibit apparent manipulative stability, this performance often masks substantial underlying compensatory psychological and cognitive effort. Consequently, they emphasized the necessity of integrating subjective scales with physiological metrics to comprehensively quantify the occupancy of cognitive resources by workload and fatigue. Furthermore, Ozel et al. [11] identified a strong correlation between flight crew burnout, job satisfaction, and fatigue risk, noting that emotional exhaustion further erodes the reliability of safety procedure execution by compromising crew mental well-being. Complementing these findings, Wan et al. [12] revealed that the collaborative efficacy of human-machine teams is driven non-linearly by the accumulation of individual cognitive fatigue, demonstrating that biomathematical modeling can effectively predict the adverse impacts of cognitive resource depletion on systemic task performance.

Psychological resilience is conceptualized as a critical "psychological buffer" or "restorative capacity" for pilots navigating high-pressure and high-risk environments. It plays a determinant role in modulating an individual's recovery rate and stress resistance when confronted with mental and emotional fatigue [13–15]. Human-Machine Teaming Performance (HMTP) necessitates the maintenance of efficient communication and decision-making between pilots and automated systems [16]. However, fatigue can induce irritability or emotional despondency, thereby disrupting this synergistic interaction. Ritter [17] established that fatigue jeopardizes flight safety primarily by impairing cognitive decision-making rather than deteriorating basic manipulative skills. To counteract these adverse effects, psychological resilience is posited as a pivotal moderating variable. Complementarily, Ćosić et al. [18] proposed that a multi-metric fusion approach, integrating physiological and cognitive indicators, can effectively predict individual fatigue resistance and recovery capabilities. Conversely, in the absence of effective resilience regulation, chronic fatigue is liable to evolve into job burnout. As substantiated by Demerouti et al. [19], this progression significantly diminishes the overall performance of flight crews in human-machine collaborative tasks. Thus, psychological resilience functions as a "pressure relief valve" within the pilot system. It not only attenuates pilot sensitivity to fatigue but also preserves emotional stability and cognitive clarity, ensuring sustained high-efficiency collaboration with automation under high-pressure conditions, thereby safeguarding flight safety and mission success. Given the persistent biases in human understanding of automation and the difficulty in objectively assessing its actual capabilities, trust emerges as a critical factor in bridging this cognitive gap [20]. Trust plays a central role in facilitating effective human-machine collaboration, a function widely recognized in traditional human-human cooperative relationships [21]. Automation trust, defined as the degree of individual confidence in automated systems, has been established as a significant moderating variable influencing the human-automation relationship [22], with operating mechanisms partially analogous to interpersonal trust [23]. Due to the short-haul, high-frequency nature of regional operations, pilot situational awareness is heavily reliant on automated status cues. Consequently, fatigued pilots are prone to "automation burnout"—a state characterized by a loss of trust in and the development of resistance toward automation [24]. Therefore, determining how to leverage automation trust to enhance pilot coping mechanisms against fatigue, and thereby interrupt the transmission chain of "fatigue - HMTP degradation - safety risk," has become a critical scientific imperative in civil aviation safety management.

In light of this context, grounded in Social Cognitive Theory, this study conducts an empirical analysis involving 83 civil aviation regional pilots to investigate the following dimensions from an aviation safety perspective: (1) The direct impact pathways of fatigue on Human-Machine Teaming Performance (HMTP); (2) The moderating effects of psychological resilience and automation trust within the "fatigue–HMTP" relationship; and (3) The development of targeted safety management intervention strategies based on empirical findings. Ultimately, this research aims to provide novel theoretical insights and practical references for the field of aviation psychological safety.

2 Theoretical Hypotheses and Model Construction

2.1 Hypotheses on the Direct Effects of Fatigue on Human-Machine Collaborative Performance

Pilot operational profiles are typically characterized by extended duty periods, early report times, late arrival times, and irregular scheduling. From a multidimensional perspective, the fatigue-inducing factors faced by pilots exhibit a high degree of isomorphism with those encountered by industrial shift workers [25]. Flight fatigue is defined as a pathophysiological deviation from nominal functional baselines. In this state, pilots experience degraded cognitive faculties and diminished vigilance, which subsequently attenuate their sensitivity to critical operational behaviors. In severe instances, this can induce spatial disorientation (flight illusions) and precipitate unsafe operational states, posing a direct threat to flight safety [26]. When operating in high-density airspace, pilot workload indices can exceed 70/100, thereby precipitating the accumulation of mental fatigue [27]. Furthermore, environmental stressors such as cockpit noise, hypoxic conditions, and adverse meteorology serve to accelerate the progression of fatigue. Transmeridian flights result in circadian dysrhythmia and delayed melatonin secretion cycles, triggering declines in alertness and the deterioration of cognitive functions [28]. Utilizing Structural Equation Modeling (SEM), Sun et al. [29] elucidated the direct driving effects of sleep quality and mental health on fatigue, providing theoretical scaffolding for fatigue risk early warning systems tailored to regional pilots executing frequent take-off and landing tasks. Hancock et al. [30] observed that fatigue and stress induce dysfunctions in individual dynamic attention mechanisms. This renders it difficult for operators to maintain stable mental workload thresholds during task execution, subsequently leading to a systemic collapse in performance during sustained monitoring tasks. Research by Wickens [31] indicates that pilots rely on a finite pool of cognitive resources when processing multi-dimensional tasks. Fatigue exacerbates "Resource Competition" between distinct tasks, significantly degrading multitasking coordination capabilities and workload tolerance within complex human-machine interaction environments. Regarding automation interaction, Wohleber et al. [32] demonstrated that operator "Passive Fatigue" significantly alters dependency patterns on automated systems. Fatigue states not only reduce task execution accuracy but also induce dependency biases in human-machine teaming due to misaligned trust calibration. Furthermore, Rodriguez-Bermudez et al. [33] argued that a pilot's neurophysiological state directly influences interaction efficacy with computer interfaces. Specifically, fatigue interferes with the feature extraction and command conversion of "Motor Imagery" signals, thereby reducing the real-time collaborative precision of the human-machine system at the information transmission level. Based on the aforementioned theoretical framework, the following hypothesis is proposed:

H_1: Regional pilot fatigue is negatively associated with Human-Machine Teaming Performance (HMTP).

2.2 The Moderating Effect Hypothesis of Psychological Resilience

Psychological resilience is inextricably linked to an individual's capacity to navigate occupational challenges while minimizing the deleterious effects of vocational demands. Empirical evidence suggests that individuals exhibiting elevated resilience demonstrate superior efficacy in coping with work-related fatigue and complex scenarios; furthermore, such individuals typically experience enhanced career progression and superior job performance. Consequently, psychological resilience has been substantiated as playing a pivotal role in mitigating burnout, alleviating acute fatigue, and augmenting productivity [34]. In the specific context of aviation, Zhao et al. [35] pioneered the construction of a dual-dimensional measurement framework for Chinese civil aviation pilots, establishing "Decisiveness" and "Adaptability" as core dimensions. Specifically, Decisiveness integrates the traditional resilience elements of "Tenacity" and "Self-strengthening," while Adaptability forms a synergistic enhancement mechanism with "Optimism," collectively fortifying flight safety. Research by Polat et al. [36] indicates that psychological resilience enhances employees' self-efficacy, emotional regulation capabilities, and coping strategies, thereby elevating job performance and diminishing burnout. Furthermore, Fletcher et al. [37] identified a moderating role of resilience within the nexus of organizational justice, interpersonal conflict, and Counterproductive Work Behavior (CWB). Specifically, resilience mitigates the adverse impact of perceived organizational injustice on CWB. Shi et al. [38] demonstrated that psychological resilience functions as a mediator in the relationship between stress and job demands, while also serving as a predictor for stress and emotional states. Similarly, Guo et al. [39] posited that resilience operates as a critical job resource to meet job demands, thereby reducing the risks of burnout and compassion fatigue. Moreover, investigations by Zhang et al. [40] and Li et al. [41] revealed that biofeedback training via the Quick Coherence Technique (QCT) significantly enhances pilots' psychophysiological resilience, effectively improving mental health and cognitive function under stressful environments such as the pandemic. These studies established that such interventions not only reduce perceived stress and bolster emotional stability by regulating the Autonomic Nervous System (ANS) balance but also facilitate fatigue recovery and energy mobilization during controlled cockpit rest by optimizing psychophysiological coherence. These findings align with the posited moderating utility of psychological resilience in coping with occupational stress, alleviating flight fatigue, and optimizing HMTP, providing an empirical basis for enhancing the psychophysiological adaptability of regional pilots in complex operational environments. However, literature specifically examining the moderating mechanism of psychological resilience between fatigue and HMTP remains sparse, particularly within the demographic of regional aviation. Consequently, the following hypothesis is proposed:

H_2: Psychological resilience plays a moderating role in the impact of fatigue on Human-Machine Teaming Performance (HMTP).

2.3 The Moderating Effect Hypothesis of Automated Trust

In the civil aviation industry, safety and intelligence necessitate synergistic development. As a novel kinetic driver propelling the sector, intelligence has emerged as an inevitable trend in industrial evolution. As the quintessential representative cohort, pilots possess a direct perceptual understanding of this intelligent transformation. The increasing integration of intelligent systems and equipment has rendered modern flight deck automation characterized by complexity, digitization, and computerization. Given the inherent disparity between human cognition of automation and its actual capabilities, trust serves as a critical mechanism to bridge the deficit caused by the inability to assess automation performance objectively [42]. Automation trust—defined as the human trust in automated systems—is recognized as a determinant factor governing the human-automation relationship. Pilots are required to maintain an optimal level of trust in onboard automated equipment to realize operational safety objectives. Parasuraman et al. [43] posited that automation trust is central to the quality of human-machine interaction; inappropriate trust can directly precipitate decision-making biases in operators under conditions of cognitive load or fatigue, thereby impairing systemic collaborative performance. Recent neuroscientific investigations by Pushparaj et al. [44] revealed the dynamic conflict nature of trust states under conditions of uncertainty. Soo et al. [45] demonstrated significant cognitive load fluctuations among civil aviation pilots during the mastery of complex automation. Furthermore, Pazouki et al. [46] substantiated the destructive impact of over-trust on monitoring performance. However, within regional civil aviation, pilots confront severe fatigue stress induced by frequent take-offs and landings, extended operational segments, and night flights. Currently, there is a paucity of research systematically verifying whether fatigue in regional pilots exacerbates the imbalance of this "trust calibration" state, thereby compromising the overall safety of human-machine teaming through impaired monitoring performance. Based on this theoretical premise, the present study proposes the following hypothesis:

H_3: Automation trust plays a moderating role in the impact of fatigue on Human-Machine Teaming Performance (HMTP).

Based on the aforementioned hypotheses (H_1, H_2, and H_3), a conceptual model characterizing the "Fatigue – Psychological Resilience and Automation Trust – Human-Machine Teaming Performance" dynamic is constructed, as illustrated in Fig. 1.

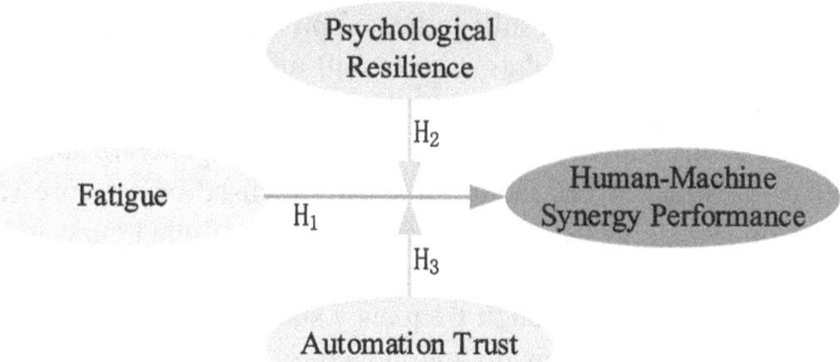

Fig. 1. Hypothesis model of fatigue–psychological resilience and trust in automation–human-machine collaborative performance.

3 Research Methodology

3.1 Research Subjects and Data Collection Methods

This study employed a cross-sectional survey design. The sampling frame comprised the entire roster of active pilots from a representative regional airline. Data collection was conducted through scientific sampling and standardized protocols, centering on the core investigation of "the impact of regional pilot fatigue on Human-Machine Teaming Performance (HMTP) and the moderating roles of psychological resilience and automation trust." To ensure the sample effectively captured the critical occupational characteristics of the target population, a stratified random sampling strategy was adopted. The population was first stratified by flight rank (Instructor Captain, Captain, First Officer, and Cadet Pilot). Subsequently, systematic random sampling based on employee identification numbers was implemented within each stratum. Ultimately, a total of 100 pilots were invited to participate in the survey.

The research protocol strictly adhered to the ethical principles outlined in the Declaration of Helsinki. Before data collection, briefing sessions were conducted to explicitly elucidate the study's objectives, data utility, confidentiality protocols, and the principle of voluntary participation to all invitees. Participants were informed that the collected data would be utilized exclusively to investigate the mechanistic associations among fatigue, psychological resilience, automation trust, and Human-Machine Teaming Performance (HMTP). Formal data collection commenced only after obtaining signed informed consent from all participants. To mitigate the potential impact of missing data on the analysis of variable relationships, all questionnaire items were configured as mandatory fields. Ultimately, 83 valid questionnaires were retrieved, yielding an effective response rate of 83%. This sample size represents approximately 20% of the regional pilot population within the subject airline.

To verify the structural consistency between the sample and the target population, a comparative distribution analysis was conducted on core demographic variables (gender, age) and critical occupational characteristics (civil aviation tenure, cumulative flight hours, and current flight rank). Results indicated no statistically significant differences between the sample and the population across all major characteristic variables (Chi-square test and Kolmogorov-Smirnov test, all $p > 0.10$). This demonstrates that the sample possesses strong statistical representativeness and generalizability. Functioning as a descriptive statistical investigation, this study focused on six core variables: gender, age, education level, civil aviation tenure, cumulative flight hours, and current flight rank. Standardized data collection was executed via structured questionnaires. A foundational dataset was established through frequency statistics and categorical aggregation (details provided in Table 1). This data architecture, encompassing both fundamental demographic features and key professional development indicators, constructs a multi-dimensional analytical framework for subsequent correlational research on regional pilot fatigue and Human-Machine Teaming Performance (HMTP).

Table 1. Survey classification.

Research categories	Classification	Frequency	Percentage/%
Gender	Male	83	100
	Female	0	0
Age	25~<31 year	40	48.19
	31~<36 year	15	18.07
	36~<41 year	12	14.46
	41~<46 year	7	8.43
	46~<51 year	5	6.02
	51~<56 year	4	4.83
Educational attainment	Undergraduate	82	98.80
	Postgraduate	1	1.20
Years of service in civil aviation	0~<11 a	52	62.65
	11~<21 a	20	24.10
	21~<31 a	8	9.64
	31~<41 a	3	3.61
Cumulative flight hours	0~<5 001 h	54	65.06
	5 001~<10 001 h	19	22.89
	10 001~<15 001 h	6	7.23
	15 001~<20 001 h	4	4.82
Current flight level	Instructor captain	10	12.05
	Captain	19	22.89
	First officer	53	63.86
	Cadet pilot	1	1.20

3.2 Measuring Tools

This study utilized internationally established scales that were subjected to localized adaptation to address the specific occupational characteristics of regional civil aviation pilots. To ensure applicability, the revised instruments underwent a rigorous validation process, including expert review and pilot testing. These procedures ensured that the psychometric properties (reliability and validity) of the scales were strictly aligned with the psychological profiles and operational scenarios unique to the regional pilot cohort.

Regional Pilot Fatigue Scale. Fatigue was assessed using the Regional Pilot Fatigue Scale developed by Sun et al. [47], which is specifically tailored to the operational scenarios of regional flight missions. The instrument comprises 12 items rated on a 5-point Likert scale, ranging from 1 ("strongly disagree" / "very inconsistent") to 5 ("strongly agree" / "very consistent"). The scale evaluates pilot fatigue across three distinct dimensions: Task Load Fatigue, Training and Development Fatigue, and Job Burnout Fatigue. In the present study, the scale demonstrated high internal consistency, yielding a Cronbach's α coefficient of 0.924. Furthermore, Confirmatory Factor Analysis (CFA) indicated that the questionnaire possesses robust construct validity.

Human-Machine Teaming Performance (HMTP) Scale. To assess the comprehensive collaborative performance of regional pilots within human-machine teaming contexts, the HMTP Scale was constructed by synthesizing guidelines from the ICAO Pilot Monitoring Manual [48], the NASA Human Factors Engineering framework [49], and Endsley's Theory of Situation Awareness [50]. Integrating the operational characteristics of automated cockpits with prior empirical research [43, 51], this study operationalized HMTP into three core dimensions: Situation Awareness, Task Management, and Decision Making & Intervention. In the present study, the scale demonstrated exceptional internal consistency, yielding a Cronbach's α coefficient of 0.941. Furthermore, Confirmatory Factor Analysis (CFA) confirmed that the instrument possesses robust construct validity.

Psychological Resilience Scale. Psychological resilience was measured using a revised version of the Connor-Davidson Resilience Scale (CD-RISC), adapted by Xiao et al. [52]. This instrument is designed to assess positive psychological traits that facilitate individual adaptation to adversity. The scale consists of 25 items distributed across three dimensions: Tenacity, Strength, and Optimism. Responses are recorded on a 5-point Likert scale ranging from 1 ("never") to 5 ("almost always"). In the current study, the scale demonstrated satisfactory internal consistency, with a Cronbach's α coefficient of 0.832. Confirmatory Factor Analysis (CFA) further indicated that the questionnaire possesses robust construct validity.

Automation Trust Scale. To assess pilots' levels of trust in cockpit automation systems, this study developed a revised instrument grounded in the automation trust theoretical framework of Lee et al. [53] and the Trust in Automation Scale developed by Jian et al. [54]. Automation trust was conceptualized as comprising three fundamental dimensions: Capability, Reliability, and Intentionality. The original items were adapted to align with the specific operational environment of civil aviation automation. Responses were recorded on a 5-point Likert scale ranging from 1 ("strongly disagree") to 5 ("strongly agree"). Analysis of the sample data yielded an overall Cronbach's α coefficient of 0.847. Furthermore, Confirmatory Factor Analysis (CFA) demonstrated that the questionnaire possesses robust construct validity.

3.3 Common Method Bias Test

Given that data regarding regional pilot fatigue, HMTP, psychological resilience, and automation trust were all obtained via self-report measures from the same respondents, the potential for Common Method Bias (CMB) was considered. Consequently, Harman's single-factor test was employed to assess the magnitude of this bias. All measurement items were subjected to an unrotated Exploratory Factor Analysis (EFA). The results revealed that the first factor accounted for only 21.30% of the total variance, which is well below the critical threshold of 40%. This indicates that no single factor emerged as the dominant determinant of variance, suggesting that Common Method Bias does not pose a significant threat to the validity of the data in this study.

4 Results

4.1 Descriptive Statistics and Correlation Analysis

The means, standard deviations, and correlation matrix of the study variables are presented in Table 2. Job tenure was significantly and positively correlated with flight hours ($r = 0.829$, $p < 0.01$), reflecting consistency between pilots' seniority and their accumulated flight experience. Additionally, job tenure exhibited a significant positive correlation with trust in automation ($r = 0.273$, $p < 0.05$), indicating that more experienced pilots demonstrate higher levels of trust in automated systems. Regarding the core variables, fatigue among regional pilots was significantly and negatively correlated with human-machine teaming performance ($r = -0.317, p < 0.01$), implying that elevated fatigue levels are associated with inferior overall collaborative performance. Although fatigue showed negative correlations with psychological resilience ($r = -0.153$) and trust in automation ($r = -0.162$), these associations did not reach statistical significance. Psychological resilience was significantly and positively correlated with trust in automation ($r = 0.545$, $p < 0.01$), and both variables demonstrated significant positive correlations with human-machine teaming performance ($r = 0.511, p < 0.01$; $r = 0.656, p < 0.01$, respectively). These findings suggest that both trust in automation and psychological resilience are critical resources for enhancing pilots' human-machine collaborative performance. Overall, the correlation analysis provides preliminary support for the research hypotheses: pilot fatigue impairs human-machine teaming performance, whereas psychological resilience and trust in automation significantly facilitate it, establishing a theoretical foundation for their roles as potential moderators.

Table 2. Descriptive statistics and correlation analysis of each variable (n = 83).

Study variables	Job tenure	Flight hours	Regional pilot fatigue	Psychological resilience	Trust in automation	Human-machine teaming performance
Job tenure	1	0.829**	−0.129	0.078	0.273*	0.186
Flight hours	0.829**	1	−0.075	0.124	0.258*	0.153
Regional pilot fatigue	−0.129	−0.075	1	−0.153	−0.162	−0.317**
Psycho-logical resilience	0.078	0.124	−0.153	1	0.545**	0.511**
Trust in automation	0.273*	0.258*	−0.162	0.545**	1	0.656**
Human-machine teaming performance	0.186	0.153	−0.317**	0.511**	0.656**	1
M	10.24	4514.28	3.35	2.54	2.83	2.72

(continued)

Table 2. *(continued)*

Study variables	Job tenure	Flight hours	Regional pilot fatigue	Psychological resilience	Trust in automation	Human-machine teaming performance
SD	8.176	4714.811	1.204	1.039	1.198	1.182

Note: M = Mean; SD = Standard Deviation. ** $p < 0.01$; * $p < 0.05$.

4.2 Main Effect Analysis

To examine the effect of regional pilot fatigue on human-machine teaming performance, a regression model was established with job tenure and flight hours as control variables, regional pilot fatigue as the independent variable, and human-machine teaming performance as the dependent variable. The regression results are presented in Table 3. The results indicated that the control variables did not significantly influence human-machine teaming performance; specifically, neither job tenure ($\beta = 0.018$, $p > 0.05$) nor flight hours ($\beta = 0$, $p > 0.05$) was significant. Regarding the core variable, regional pilot fatigue exerted a significant negative effect on human-machine teaming performance ($\beta = -0.293$, $t = -2.803$, $p = 0.006$), indicating that higher levels of pilot fatigue are associated with poorer operational performance within the human-machine teaming environment. These findings support H1. The overall model was significant ($F = 3.658$, $p = 0.016$), demonstrating that the model possesses explanatory power ($R^2 = 0.122$).

Table 3. Regression analysis results (Main effects).

Study variables	β	SE	t	p
Control variables	3.488	0.422	8.265	<0.001
Job tenure	0.018	0.027	0.665	0.508
Flight hours	0	0	0.137	0.891
Regional pilot fatigue	−0.293	0.105	−2.803	0.006

Note: β represents the standardized regression coefficient; SE represents the standard error; t represents the t-statistic; p indicates the level of significance.

4.3 Moderating Effect Analysis

Psychological Resilience. To further examine the moderating effect of psychological resilience, a simple slope analysis was conducted (see Fig. 2). The results indicated that the interaction term between regional pilot fatigue and psychological resilience was significant ($\beta = 0.143$, $p > 0.01$). As illustrated in the figure, regional pilot fatigue exerted an inhibitory effect on human-machine teaming performance under both low and high psychological resilience conditions; however, significant differences in baseline performance were observed between the two groups. Individuals with high psychological resilience ($M + 1SD$) demonstrated significantly superior human-machine teaming performance compared to those with low psychological resilience ($M - 1SD$) across all levels of regional pilot fatigue. Specifically, the mean performance for the high-resilience group was maintained within a high range (4.23–4.71), whereas the low-resilience group's performance was distributed within a lower range (3.59–3.78). This suggests that psychological resilience exerts a significant "Resource Enhancement" function within human-machine teaming. High psychological resilience provides pilots with greater psychological energy reserves. Although it did not eliminate the negative marginal effect of fatigue, it significantly elevated the performance intercept. Consequently, even under high-fatigue conditions, the collaborative performance of high-resilience pilots remained superior to that of low-resilience individuals under low-fatigue conditions. These findings support Hypothesis H_2.

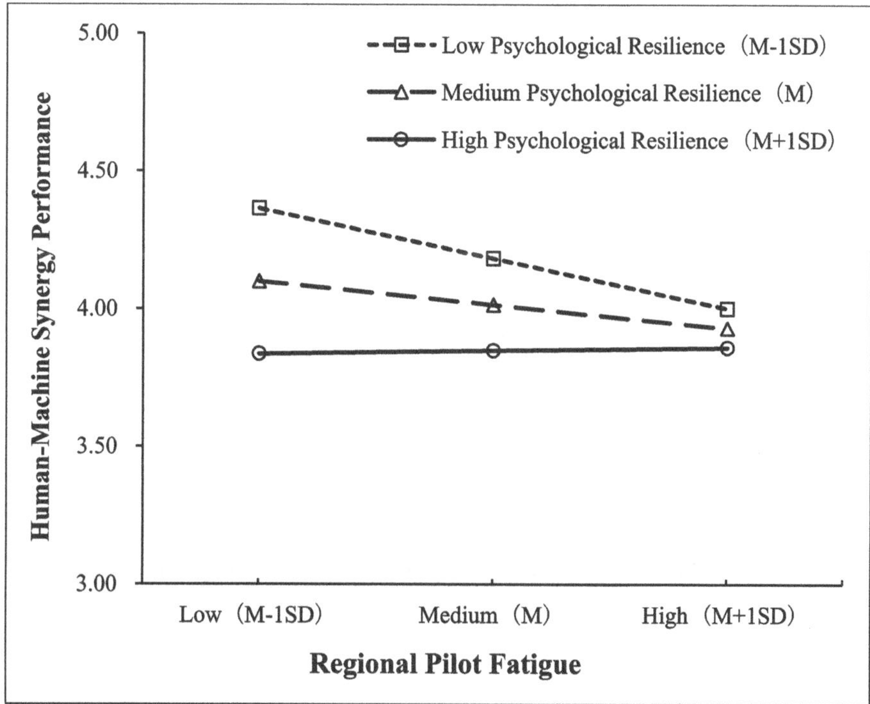

Fig. 2. The moderating role of psychological resilience on the relationship between regional pilot fatigue and human-machine teaming performance.

Trust in Automation. To elucidate the specific moderating mechanism of trust in automation on the relationship between regional pilot fatigue and human-machine teaming performance, a simple slope test was conducted (see Fig. 3). The analysis indicated that trust in automation significantly altered the effect of regional pilot fatigue on human-machine teaming performance ($\beta = 0.261, p > 0.001$). Specifically, at low levels of trust in automation ($M - 1SD$), regional pilot fatigue exerted a significant negative predictive effect on human-machine teaming performance. As fatigue increased, performance declined substantially from 4.36 to 4.00, exhibiting a steep downward trend. However, at high levels of trust in automation ($M + 1SD$), this negative effect was buffered; the regression slope of teaming performance relative to regional pilot fatigue flattened (varying only from 3.84 to 3.86), demonstrating high stability. These findings suggest that high trust in automation functions as a crucial compensatory resource, effectively mitigating the erosion of human-machine teaming capabilities caused by fatigue. It enables pilots to maintain stable performance outputs even when fatigued, thereby verifying the "protective umbrella" effect of trust in automation in fatigue contexts. These findings support Hypothesis H3.

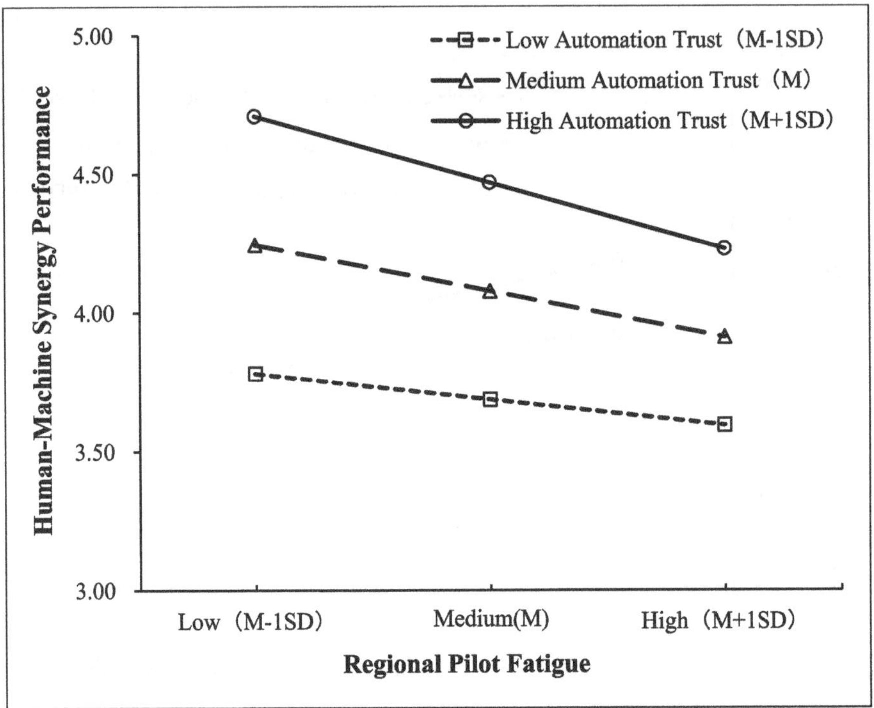

Fig. 3. The moderating role of trust in automation on the relationship between regional pilot fatigue and human-machine teaming performance.

4.4 Analysis of Pilot Typologies Based on Latent Features

To further investigate the configurational characteristics of regional pilots regarding fatigue, psychological resilience, and trust in automation, and to move beyond the limitations of single-variable linear associations, this study adopted a person-centered approach. Given the sample size ($N = 83$), the core variables (regional pilot fatigue, psychological resilience, and trust in automation) were first standardized using Z-scores.

Subsequently, the K-means clustering algorithm was employed to identify distinct categories. By integrating theoretical interpretability with fit indices (specifically, the Within-Cluster Sum of Squares and Silhouette Coefficient) to determine the optimal number of clusters, three distinct latent categories of pilots were ultimately identified (see Fig. 4).

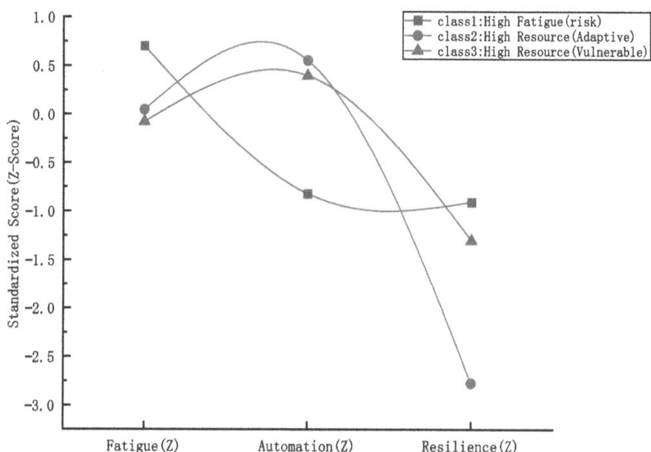

Fig. 4. Latent profile plot of regional pilot fatigue and psychological resources.

Cluster Characteristics. Through K-means cluster analysis, this study identified three distinct subgroups of regional pilots with significantly differentiated psychological characteristics: The first cluster, labeled High Load-Normal Resources ($n = 45$, 54.2%), exhibited fatigue levels significantly above the sample mean ($Z = 0.70$), while trust in automation ($Z = 0.05$) and psychological resilience ($Z = -0.07$) remained at average levels. This group failed to form a resource advantage, indicating that over half of the pilots operate under high fatigue loads without additional psychological buffering resources. Consequently, they constitute a risk-susceptible group requiring prioritized attention in flight safety management. The second cluster, labeled Low Load-High Adaptation ($n = 31$, 37.3%), presented a positive combination of "low fatigue, high trust, and high resilience." Their fatigue levels were significantly below the mean ($Z = -0.82$), whereas trust in automation ($Z = 0.56$) and psychological resilience ($Z = 0.40$) were the highest among the three groups. Capable of efficiently completing human-machine teaming tasks by leveraging abundant psychological resources and trust in automation, this group represents the ideal professional psychological state for regional pilots. The third cluster, labeled Trust Deficit ($n = 7$, 8.5%), showed fatigue levels significantly below the mean ($Z = -0.90$); however, both trust in automation ($Z = -2.77$) and psychological resilience ($Z = -1.30$) were far below the sample averages. This group exhibited a severe deficit in trust in automation. These characteristics may be associated with insufficient flight experience, doubts regarding system reliability, or psychological resistance to operation, classifying them as a marginalized group in terms of human-machine teaming adaptation.

Differences in Human-Machine Teaming Performance Across Categories. To examine the predictive validity of the latent categories regarding human-machine teaming performance, a one-way analysis of covariance (ANCOVA) was conducted with job tenure and accumulated flight hours as control variables. The results are presented in Table 4. The analysis revealed that, after controlling for the relevant variables, significant differences in human-machine teaming performance persisted among the distinct pilot categories ($F = 5.10, p = 0.008, \eta^2 = 0.11$). The effect size was moderate, indicating that the classification possesses strong explanatory power regarding performance. Post-hoc Tukey HSD multiple comparisons indicated that the mean human-machine teaming performance of the Low Load-High Adaptation group ($M = 4.31$) was significantly higher than that of the High Load-Normal Resources group ($M = 3.94, p < 0.01$). Although the mean performance of the Trust Deficit group ($M = 4.02$) was slightly higher than that of the High Load-Normal Resources group, the difference was not statistically significant ($p > 0.05$).

These results further corroborate the core conclusion of this study: individual-level psychological resources (psychological resilience and trust in automation) are crucial determinants for ensuring high-level human-machine teaming. The Low Load-High Adaptation group achieved optimal performance through a "low fatigue + high resources" combination. Conversely, although the Trust Deficit group exhibited low fatigue levels, their performance was not significantly superior to that of the high fatigue load group due to a deficiency in core psychological resources. This strongly demonstrates that mitigating fatigue alone is insufficient to guarantee human-machine teaming effectiveness; rather, it is necessary to synchronously strengthen pilots' trust in automation and psychological resilience.

Table 4. Means and tests of differences in main variables across latent categories.

Latent categories	n	Percentage	Regional pilot fatigue M(Z)	Trust in automation M(Z)	Psycho-logical resilience M(Z)	Human-machine teaming performance M(Z)
High load-normal resources	45	54.2%	2.91(0.70)	3.31(−0.07)	4.05(0.05)	3.94(0.52)
Low load-high adaptation	31	37.3%	1.78(−0.82)	3.56(0.40)	4.52(0.56)	4.31(0.48)
Trust deficit	7	8.5%	1.72(−0.90)	2.68(−1.30)	1.49(−2.77)	4.02(0.69)
F-value	-	-	-	-	-	5.10**

Note: M = Mean; Z = Z-score. ** p < 0.01.

5 Discussion

The results of this study confirm that the fatigue state of regional pilots significantly impairs human-machine teaming performance (H_1), while psychological resilience (H_2) and trust in automation (H_3) play critical moderating roles in this process. Furthermore, latent profile analysis revealed significant heterogeneity in the configuration of psychological resources among the regional pilot population, providing a basis for precision safety management.

5.1 Mechanism of Fatigue-Induced Impairment on Human-Machine Teaming Performance and Risk Quantification Analysis

The regression analysis in this study indicated that fatigue exerts a significant negative predictive effect on the human-machine teaming performance of regional pilots ($\beta = -0.428$, $p < 0.001$). This finding provides robust evidence that physiological and psychological fatigue are primary drivers of the degradation in regional flight quality. Consistent with the descriptive statistics showing high mean fatigue levels, this result aligns closely with the operational characteristics of regional aviation, which is defined by frequent takeoffs and landings, numerous short-haul round trips, and rapid ground turnarounds. The data further reveal that fatigue not only directly impairs pilot reaction speed but also compromises the quality of information interaction at the human-machine interface by degrading Situation Awareness (SA). Within the context of domestic civil aviation, these findings highlight the severe challenges associated with crew fatigue risk management under CCAR-121 regulations. Although regulatory authorities strictly limit duty periods, the cognitive load experienced by regional pilots during missions far exceeds that of mainline operations, largely due to complex meteorological conditions and relatively rudimentary support infrastructure at regional airports. Therefore, it is recommended that civil aviation authorities and airlines look beyond the "hard caps" of duty time limits. Instead, they should integrate Bio-Mathematical Models (e.g., BAM or SAFTE) within the Fatigue Risk Management System (FRMS) framework to conduct quantitative assessments of fatigue intensity on regional routes. Furthermore, drawing on the experiences of the FAA and EASA, the promotion of Standard Operating Procedures (SOPs) for "Controlled Rest on the Flight Deck" is advised. This would provide policy-level legitimacy for regional pilots to mitigate acute fatigue during non-critical flight phases.

5.2 The Psychological Buffering Value of Resilience and the Construction of Core Competencies

The simple slope test conducted in this study revealed that pilots with high psychological resilience exhibited significantly superior performance stability compared to the low-resilience group when facing high-intensity fatigue (moderating effect coefficient = 0.156). This suggests that psychological resilience functions as an internal psychological resource that provides a "secondary line of defense" upon the onset of central fatigue, assisting pilots in maintaining emotional stability and rapidly reconstructing cognitive strategies. In the high-pressure environment of regional aviation, psychological resilience constitutes the "soft power" of operational safety. Currently, China's civil aviation industry is in a critical transition period, shifting from a focus on "Technical Competency" to "Core Competency." Consequently, Pilot Mental Health and Competency Management (PLM) has been elevated to the level of a national civil aviation safety strategy. Based on the findings of this study, it is recommended that airlines introduce resilience scales (such as the CD-RISC) during the pilot selection phase for baseline assessment and incorporate Stress Exposure Training (SET) into routine recurrent training. Furthermore, in accordance with the Standards for Mental Health Evaluation of Pilots in Civil Aviation Contexts, civil aviation hospitals and airline medical departments should establish dynamic psychological profiles, paying particular attention to the state of psychological exhaustion among regional captains following long duty cycles. Through policy guidance, a non-punitive reporting mechanism for fatigue and psychological status should be established. This would encourage pilots to perform "self-declaration of unfitness" based on their resilience status, thereby facilitating an institutional shift from "compelled safety" ("I am made to be safe") to "proactive safety" ("I want to be safe").

5.3 The Moderating Effect of Trust in Automation and "Trust Calibration" Intervention Strategies

Research data indicates that trust in automation exerts a significant positive moderating effect on the relationship between fatigue and performance ($p < 0.05$). As observed in the interaction plot, the trajectory of performance decline among pilots with high trust levels was significantly more gradual than that of the low-trust group as fatigue intensified. This demonstrates that appropriate reliance on automation can effectively compensate for impaired cognitive functions. However, Latent Profile Analysis (LPA) identified a non-negligible subgroup—the "Trust Deficit" pilots (accounting for approximately 8.5%). This group exhibits a "low trust, moderate fatigue, low performance" profile, characterized by an inability to efficiently utilize automated equipment even when fully rested. Such "under-trust" leads to persistent high-intensity manual control under fatigued conditions, thereby inducing cognitive overload. In conjunction with the Evidence-Based Training (EBT) currently promoted by the Civil Aviation Administration of China (CAAC), it is recommended that "Automation Trust Calibration" be integrated into the flight simulator training syllabus. Interventions must not only address monitoring failures caused by "over-trust" but also target the 8.5% "Trust Deficit" group with "logic transparency" training. By deconstructing the decision-making logic of the Flight Management System (FMS), training should enhance pilots' willingness to delegate control and their proficiency in monitoring during fatigue. Furthermore, policymakers should reference ICAO Doc 10170 to incorporate human-machine teaming effectiveness into the assessment framework of Crew Resource Management (CRM), ensuring that automation truly functions as the pilot's "shadow co-pilot."

Acknowledgments. The authors would like to express their sincere gratitude to Chengdu Airlines for their support and assistance throughout the research process. This study was funded by the 2025 Tianjin Transportation Science and Technology Development Plan Project (General Project) (grant number: 2025-79).

Disclosure of Interests. The authors have no competing interests to declare that are relevant to the content of this article.

References

1. Luis, R.E.C., et al.: Dynamics of air transport networks: A review from a complex systems perspective. Chin. J. Aeronaut. 02 **30**(137), 7–160 (2017)
2. Zhang, J., Du, F.: Relational complexity network and air traffic controllers' workload and performance. Springer International Publishing (2015)
3. ICAO: Global Aviation Safety Report 2025[R] 11 Aug 2025
4. Lin, W.J., Ren, H., Peng, Q.Y.: A general analysis model of economical efficiency for regional aircraft operation. Civil Aircr. Des. Res. **4**, 21–30 (2019)
5. Wingelaar-Jagt, Y.Q., Wingelaar, T.T., Riedel, W.J., et al.: Fatigue in aviation: safety risks, preventive strategies and pharmacological interventions. Front. Physiol. **12**, 1399 (2021)
6. Choi, J.K.: The improvement of pilot fatigue management. Korean J. Aerosp. Environ. Med. The/Hukpang, Kwa Kisul **33**(1), 5 (2023)
7. Petrie, K.J., Dawson, A.G.: Symptoms of fatigue and coping strategies in international pilots. Int. J. Aviat. Psychol. **7**(3), 251–258 (1997)
8. Seraj, R., Ny, J.L., Mahajan, A.: Fatigue and task load dependent decision referrals for joint binary classification in human-automation teams. IEEE Control Syst. Lett. **9** (2025)
9. Roma, P.G., Mallis, M.M., Hursh, S.R., et al.: Flight attendant fatigue recommendation 2: flight attendant work/rest patterns, alertness, and performance assessment (2010)
10. Gartner, W.B., Murphy, M.R.: Pilot workload and fatigue: a critical survey of concepts and assessment techniques. Nat. Aeronaut. Space Adm. (1976)
11. Ozel, E., Hacioglu, U.: Examining the relationship between burnout and job satisfaction of flight crew: an analysis on the critical fatigue risk factors in the aviation industry. Int. J. Bus. Ecosyst. Strategy (2687–2293) (2021)
12. Wan, Y., Zhou, C.: Predicting human-robot team performance based on cognitive fatigue. In: 2023 28th International Conference on Automation and Computing (ICAC), Birmingham, United Kingdom, pp. 1–6 (2023)
13. Zhang, M., Liao, J.Q., Peng, K.P., et al.: Effects of psychological strain and resilience on pilots' work performance: a case study of general aviation pilots. J. Shanghai Univ. (Soc. Sci. Edn.) **34**(2), 134–140 (2017)
14. Li, G.R., He, S.Z., Tian, P.F.: On the emotional organization safety culture effect on the employees' safety risk under the psychological development contract: the given paper is done based on a survey from the stateowned coal enterprises. J. Saf. Environ. **19**(1), 78–87 (2019)
15. Lázaro, F.L., Nogueira, R.P.R., Melicio, R., et al.: Human factors as predictor of fatalities in aviation accidents: a neural network analysis. Appl. Sci. (2076–3417) **14**(2) (2024)
16. Hartzler, B.M.: Fatigue on the flight deck: the consequences of sleep loss and the benefits of napping. Accid. Anal. Prev. **62**, 309–318 (2014)
17. Ritter, R.D.: And we were tired': fatigue and aircrew errors. Aerosp. Electron. Syst. Mag IEEE **8**(3), 21–26 (1993)
18. Ćosić, K., Popović, S., Šarlija, M., et al.: An approach to prediction of mental resilience in fighter pilot selection. In: Proceedings of the 1st International Conference on Cognitive Aircraft Systems (2022)
19. Demerouti, E., Veldhuis, W., Coombes, C., et al.: Burnout among pilots: psychosocial factors related to happiness and performance at simulator training. Ergonomics **62**(2), 233–245 (2019)
20. Blomqvist, K.: The many faces of trust. Scand. J. Manag. **13**(3), 271–286 (1997)
21. Rotter, J.B.: A new scale for the measurement of interpersonal trust 1. J. Pers. **35**(4), 651–665 (1967)

22. Muir, B.M.: Trust in automation: Part I. theoretical issues in the study of trust and humanintervention in automated systems. Ergonomics **37**(11), 1905–1922 (1994)
23. Lewandowsky, S., Mundy, M., Tan, G.: The dynamics of trust: comparing humans to automation. J. Exp. Psychol. Appl. **6**(2), 104 (2000)
24. Polishchuk, V., Kelemen, M., Polishchuk, I., et al.: Hybrid technology for assessing the fatigue level of air traffic controllers using video surveillance. In: 2024 New Trends in Aviation Development (NTAD), pp. 122–127 (2024)
25. Tvaryanas, A.P., MacPherson, G.D.: Fatigue in pilots of remotely piloted aircraft before and after shift work adjustment. Aviat. Space Environ. Med. **80**, 454–461 (2009)
26. Ge, C.: Research on influencing factors and countermeasures of flight fatigue for flight instructors . Civil Aviation Flight University of China (2016)
27. Carrieri, M., Petracca, A., Lancia, S., et al.: Prefrontal cortex activation upon a demanding virtual hand-controlled task: a new frontier for neuroergonomics. Front HumNeurosci **10**, 53 (2016)
28. Federal Aviation Administration. Advisory Circular 61-65K: Certification: Pilots and Flight and Ground Instructors. U.S. Department of Transportation. https://www.faa.gov/regulations_policies/advisory_circulars. Accessed 14 Nov 2025
29. Sun, R., Wang, P.: Research on influencing factors of pilot fatigue based on structural equation modeling. J. Saf. Environ. **22**(6), 3252–3258 (2022)
30. Hancock, P.A., Warm, J.S.: A dynamic model of stress and sustained attention. Hum. Fact. **31**(5), 519 (2003)
31. Wickens, C.D.: Multiple resources and mental workload. Hum. Fact. **50**(3), 449 (2008)
32. Wohleber, R.W., et al.: The impact of automation reliability and operator fatigue on performance and reliance. In: Proceedings of the Human Factors and Ergonomics Society Annual Meeting, vol. 60, no. 1, pp. 211–215 (2016)
33. Rodriguez-Bermudez, G., Lopez-Belchi, A., Girault, A.: Testing brain–computer interfaces with airplane pilots under new motor imagery tasks. Int. J. Comput. Intell. Syst. (2019)
34. Shatte, A., Perlman, A., Smith, B., et al.: The positive effect of resilience on stress and business outcomes in difficult work environments. J. Occup. Environ. Med. **59**(2), 135–140 (2017)
35. Zhao, Y.Z., Zhu, K.Y., Zhang, J., et al.: Exploring the measurement of psychological resilience in Chinese civil aviation pilots based on generalizability theory and item response theory. Sci. Rep. **14**(1), 1856 (2024)
36. Polat, H., Karakose, T., Ozdemir, T.Y., et al.: An examination of the relationships between psychological resilience, organizational ostracism, and burnout in K–12 teachers through structural equation modelling. Behav. Sci. **13**(2), 164 (2023)
37. Fletcher, D., Sarkar, M.: Psychological resilience: a review and critique of definitions, concepts, and theory. Eur. Psychol. **18**(1), 12–23 (2013)
38. Shi, L., Xin, S., Li, D.N., et al.: The mediating role of resilience in job satisfaction and burnout among Chinese plateau military personnel. Sci. Rep. **15**(1), 13785 (2025)
39. Guo, Y.F., Luo, Y.H., Louisa, L., et al.: Burnout and its association with resilience in nurses: a cross-sectional study. J. Clin. Nurs. **27**(2), 441–449 (2018)
40. Zhang, J., Li, W.C., Andrews, G.: Applying psychophysiological coherence training based on HRV-biofeedback to enhance pilots' resilience and wellbeing. Transp. Res. Procedia **66**, 49–56 (2022)
41. Li, W.C., Zhang, J., Braithwaite, G., et al.: Quick coherence technique facilitating commercial pilots' psychophysiological resilience to the impact of COVID-19. Ergonomics **66**(8), 1176–1189 (2023)
42. Wang, X., Li, Y., Chang, M., et al.: The hazards of trust in and reliance on automation to aviation safety and their improvements. Adv. Psychol. Sci. **25**(9), 1614–1622 (2017)
43. Parasuraman, R., Riley, V.: Humans and automation: use, misuse, disuse, abuse. Hum. Fact. **39**(2), 230–253 (1997)

44. Pushparaj, K., Ky, G., Ayeni, A.J., et al.: A quantum-inspired model for human-automation trust in air traffic controllers derived from functional Magnetic Resonance Imaging and correlated with behavioural indicators. J. Air Transp. Manag. **97**, 102143 (2021)
45. Soo, K.K.Y., Mavin, T.J., Kikkawa, Y.: Mastering automation: new airline pilots' perspective. Int. J. Hum.-Comput. Interact. **37**(7), 717–727 (2021)
46. Pazouki, K., Forbes, N., Norman, R.A., et al.: Investigation on the impact of human-automation interaction in maritime operations. Ocean Eng. **153**, 297–304 (2018)
47. Jun-Ya, S., Rui-Shan, S.: Pilot fatigue survey: a study of the mutual influence among fatigue factors in the "work" dimension. Front. Public Health **11**, 1014503 (2023)
48. International Civil Aviation Organization: Crew Resource Management (CRM) Training Manual: Monitoring and Interventions: Doc 10170, AN 597. ICAO, Montreal (2022)
49. National Aeronautics and Space Administration: NASA Space Flight Human-System Standard: Volume 2, Human Factors, Habitability, and Environmental Health: NASA-STD-3001, Volume 2. NASA, Washington, D.C. (2022)
50. Endsley, M.R.: Toward a theory of situation awareness in dynamic systems. In: Situational Awareness, pp. 9–42. Routledge (2017)
51. Xu, W., Chen, Y., Dong, W., et al.: Human factors engineering research on single pilot operations for large commercial aircraft: status and prospect. arXiv preprint arXiv:2110.07770 (2021)
52. Yu, X.N., Zhang, J.X.: A comparison between the Chinese version of ego-resiliency scale and Connor-Davidson resilience scale. J. Psychol. Sci. **30**(5), 1169–1171 (2007)
53. Lee, J.D., See, K.A.: Trust in automation: designing for appropriate reliance. Hum. Fact. **46**(1), 50–80 (2004)
54. Jian, J.Y., Bisantz, A.M., Drury, C.G.: Foundations for an empirically determined scale of trust in automated systems. Int. J. Cogn. Ergon. **4**(1), 53–71 (2000)

Insights from a Simulator Study: How the Intelligent Pilot Advisory System (IPAS) Could Impact Decision-Making in Flight Operations

Jakob Würfel[1,2](✉) and Ramón Lenting[3]

[1] German Aerospace Center (DLR e.V.), Lilienthalplatz 7, 38108 Braunschweig, Germany
[2] RWTH Aachen University, Aachen, Germany
jakob.wuerfel@dlr.de
[3] European Air Transport GmbH (EAT), August-Euler-Straße 1, 04435 Leipzig, Germany

Abstract. The Intelligent Pilot Advisory System (IPAS), developed by the German Aerospace Center (Deutsches Zentrum für Luft- und Raumfahrt (DLR)), is an AI-based cockpit assistance system that supports decision-making in normal, abnormal, and emergency flight situations. Previous work on IPAS has mainly addressed conceptual, technical, or explainability aspects and has not examined its operational impact. It is still unknown how automating parts of the pilots' decision-making process affects the decision-making structure, crew collaboration, information usage, and how the crews perceive the assistance in terms of usefulness and operational AI explainability. This exploratory study looked at six flight crews performing simulator flights involving technical malfunctions requiring diversions, both with and without the IPAS. The IPAS assists the crew by automatically identifying, assessing and selecting alternative airports based on technical, operational and environmental criteria. The crews' decision-making processes were evaluated through analysis of decision-making duration, expert reviews conducted by an experienced pilot, and questionnaires on system usefulness and explainability. The results indicated improvements in decision-making and collaboration within the crew when using the IPAS. Expert reviews revealed a slight tendency towards uncritical acceptance of the system's recommendations, suggesting a potential risk of automation bias. This study provides the first operational insights into the integration of the IPAS into the flight deck and its effect on decision-making. Further research with detailed and objective metrics is needed to comprehensively assess the effect of the IPAS on decision-making.

Keywords: AI-Based Cockpit Assistance · Operational AI Explainability · Flight Crew Decision-Making

W. -C. Li and A. Plioutsias (Eds.): HCII 2026, LNAI 16708, pp. 320–339, 2026.
https://doi.org/10.1007/978-3-032-29459-3_21

1 Introduction

The integration of Artificial Intelligence (AI)-based decision-support systems into the flight deck environment offers significant potential for supporting flight crews in complex and time-critical situations. Recent advances in machine learning and data-driven methods have enabled the development of AI systems that can process large amounts of operational data and provide recommendations to human operators. In aviation, such systems are increasingly discussed not only as automation tools, but as operational assistants that support human decision-making while keeping the human in the loop (e.g. [13,26,38]). Recognising AI's opportunities and risks in safety-critical domains, the European Union Aviation Safety Agency (EASA)'s AI-Roadmap 2.0 guides the integration of AI into aviation, highlighting human-centred integration, Human-AI teaming and operational explainability to secure trust, situation awareness, usability and safety [15].

The Intelligent Pilot Advisory System (IPAS) is being developed to investigate and demonstrate the introduction, operation, and human interaction with AI-based systems in the flight deck. The IPAS is an AI-based cockpit assistance system that supports flight crews during in-flight decision-making, particularly in abnormal and emergency situations. One functionality of the IPAS is its alternate airport support function, which generates, assesses, and presents potential alternate airport options based on operational constraints, aircraft state, environmental conditions, and company requirements. Previous work on the IPAS has focused on its conceptual design [32,34], technical architecture [4,5], and operational explainability [36].

Previous studies focusing on identifying explainability requirements involved only individual pilots. While the IPAS automates key elements of the decision-making process, its effect on flight-crew decision-making, perceived usefulness, and the operational explainability of the AI has not yet been evaluated with more realistic two-person cockpit crews. The aim of this exploratory study is to gain initial insights and identify potential risks, such as automation bias, before specific hypotheses are formulated and tested. Consequently, the study investigates how the IPAS influences two-person crew decision-making in abnormal scenarios, focusing on decision-making behaviour, information usage, and temporal structure, as well as perceived explainability and usefulness, to uncover possible advantages, effects, and risks associated with the system. As an exploratory investigation, no causal claims are made.

2 Motivation

On 15 November 2025, an Air Canada Rouge aircraft was on a flight from Antigua to Toronto. Forty-five minutes into the flight, the pilots detected a strong odour of fumes on board the Airbus A319 and decided to abort the flight for technical reasons, diverting to Punta Cana. One hour later the aircraft landed safely [25]. According to EUROCONTROL, approximately 30000 flights (0.32%

of all flights in Europe) landed at a different airport than originally planned in 2024 [12]. Diversions are required for a variety of reasons: weather, technical problems, medical emergencies, air-traffic constraints, or airport-related issues [29]. For each of these events a decision must be made, requiring good crew collaboration and communication, most likely using a structured decision-making model such as FORDEC (Facts, Options, Risks & Benefits, Decision, Execution, Check).

2.1 Decision-Making Processes in Airline Operations

The responsibility for the decision whether to divert and which alternate airport to select lies with the flight crew [16]. The application of Crew Resource Management (CRM) and structured decision-making processes are important elements in handling such scenarios safely and efficiently. CRM originated in the late 1970s as a response to crew-related accident causal factors, with the aim of reducing flight crew errors by improving non-technical skills such as communication, teamwork, leadership, and workload management [22]. Today, CRM training is widely implemented across airlines and is a standard safety component of aviation training programs (e.g., [14,19]). A central aspect within CRM is collaborative decision-making among flight crew members. One of the structured approaches to support this process is the FORDEC model [24,30]. Following to this model, crews systematically go through the FORDEC phases to gather facts, identify possible options, assess the associated risks and benefits, and come to an informed decision.

2.2 Challenges of Operational AI in Aviation

Since the 1980s the growing automation of commercial aircraft cockpits has turned the pilot from a manual operator into a system manager [2], exposing the "irony of automation" [1]. While automation raises efficiency and safety, it also creates human-factors risks such as out-of-the-loop loss of situation awareness, skill degradation, and automation bias [9,14,33]. Billings therefore advocated a human-centred automation approach that tailors automated functions to operators' capabilities [2].

The introduction of AI-based systems introduces additional challenges. Most AI algorithms behave as "black boxes" for humans, making their inner workings difficult or impossible to comprehend [18,21]. This opacity can result in poor situation awareness and increase out-of-the-loop effects [10]. Consequently, human-centred AI and Human-AI teaming demand explainable outputs that reveal the reasoning behind recommendations [8,11,21]. Another important aspect is calibrated trust. Users should neither distrust the system, which reduces acceptance, nor place too much trust in it, which can cause complacency, automation bias and unsafe overreliance [7,8,18,28].

The EASA published the AI Roadmap 2.0 as guidance for the introduction of AI in aviation [15]. In this roadmap, AI-based systems are classified according to their level of automation. The spectrum ranges from Level 1A systems, which provide automation support for information acquisition while full authority and responsibility remain with the end user, to Level 2B human-AI teaming systems. The latter involve the supervision of automatic decision-making and action implementation, with authority being shared between the human operator and the AI system. Beyond these levels, the roadmap also outlines the longer-term objective of Level 3A systems, characterised by safeguarded automatic decision and action implementation with limited authority remaining with the end user. To enable this, the roadmap defines so-called building blocks. One of these building blocks addresses human factors, identifying operational AI explainability as a central objective. Operational explainability refers to the explainability provided to the end user during system operation. This enables the user to understand the reasoning behind the system's output and interact with the AI system appropriately. EASA explicitly states that operational explainability is a key requirement for AI-based systems at all EASA AI levels [15,17].

3 Methodology

The aim of the study is to explore how the IPAS influences crew decision-making in a two-person cockpit and how pilots perceive its usefulness and explainability.

3.1 Description of the Intelligent Pilot Advisory System (IPAS)

The IPAS is an example of how AI-based decision support could be integrated into the flight deck. It covers use cases in normal operations [31,32] as well as use cases in abnormal and emergency situations [6,34]. Figure 1 provides an overview of the structure and functions of the IPAS. The IPAS consists of the AI Core Module (AICOM) and the AI-Crew Interaction System (AICIS) The present study focuses on the *Alternate Airport Support* function, which supports the Facts, Options, Risks & Benefits (FOR) phases of the FORDEC model, helping crews identify and evaluate suitable alternate airports in case of a diversion.

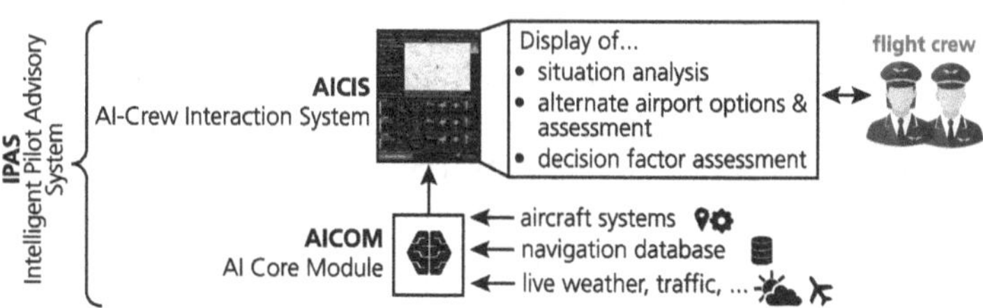

Fig. 1. Overview of the IPAS and its subsystems (Figure created by authors).

The AICOM collects information from the aircraft systems (position, technical status), accesses the navigation database (route, way-points, airports) and uses dynamic information such as current weather and traffic. The AICOM analyses the situation and, in the case of a required diversion, processes suitable alternate airport options by assessing nearby airports based on the detected situation and relevant decision factors. These airport options and their detailed assessments based on individual decision factors are presented to the pilots via the AICIS. The AICIS was developed with a focus on operational AI explainability, enabling crews to understand the rationale behind AI-based selections and assessments [36]. It was developed through a user-centred, iterative human-system exploration design process involving pilots from the start via interviews and mock-up studies [35], ensuring that the explanations and interface structure, a crucial element of the explainability concept, match the information and functionality required by the flight crew. Based on its current state of development, the IPAS can be classified as a Level 1B system according to the categorization of the EASA Roadmap 2.0 [15]: the IPAS is a cognitive assistance system that supports the crew in decision-making and selection tasks. In contrast, a Level 2 or 3 system would take over the selection and execution of the chosen alternate airport autonomously, leaving only supervisory oversight to the pilots. By remaining at Level 1B, the IPAS preserves full authority and responsibility with the crew.

A detailed description of the functionalities, the system structure and internal mechanisms of the IPAS is provided in [6].

The IPAS Used in the Conducted Study. For each FOR phase, the IPAS provides the information required and AI-based information for the respective step of the decision-making process. In the Facts phase, the system presents a situation analysis, the operational consequences of the situation, and the requirements for the search for a suitable airport. In the Options phase, suitable options are displayed with a preliminary assessment. For the Risks & Benefits phase, the crew can inspect assessed decision factors for each proposed option in order to support and justify the decision. The display used in the study is shown as follows: The *Alternate Airport Page* for the two scenarios used in the study, namely Spain and Italy, is shown in Fig. 2 and an excerpt from the *Detailed Airport View* of Rome is shown in Fig. 3.

On the *Alternate Airport Page* (representing Options), the current aircraft position is highlighted on a map and the proposed alternate airports are marked ①. The *Alternate Airport List* presents the available options (② shows the Spain scenario) in a ranked order according to the AI-based assessment result. A coloured bar visualizes the overall AI score for each option. In addition, the list provides the most relevant decision factors grouped into six categories (Position/Distance, Runway, Wind, Weather, Visibility, and Airport Operations) together with their respective assessments. The colours green, amber, and red indicate the influence of these factors on the airport assessment ③. ④ shows the *Alternate Airport List* for the Italy scenario. By selecting Rome, the *Detailed Airport View* (representing Risks & Benefits), shown in Fig. 3, opens, in which all

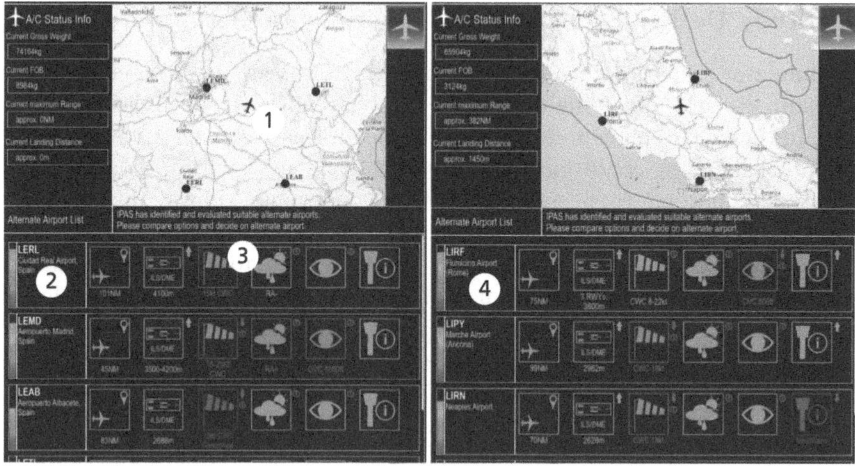

Fig. 2. *Alternate Airport Page* in the Spain and Italy scenario (Figure created by authors). ① Map, ② Alternate Airports Spain Scenario, ③ Factors, ④ Alternate Airports Italy Scenario.

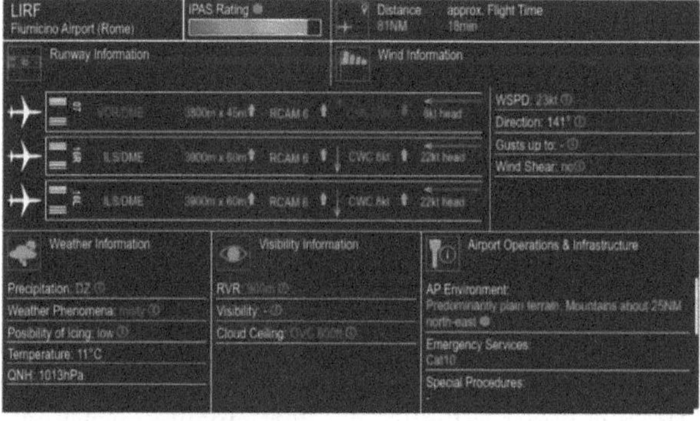

Fig. 3. *Detailed Airport View* for Rome Airport in the Italy scenario (Figure created by authors).

six categories are listed and a detailed overview of all decision factors influencing the airport assessment is provided.

For the purposes of this study, the information and assessments shown on the interface were generated with a Wizard-of-Oz paradigm [3], using simulated and predefined AI-Core outputs. As the two subsystems (AICOM and AICIS) had not yet been integrated and were still being developed separately, the mission effects, airport requirements, airport ratings and decision-factor assessments were all generated using the same multi-criteria decision-making approach underlying AICOM. None of these originated from a machine-learning model.

3.2 Study Design: Scenarios and Experimental Setup

Two simulator scenarios with technical malfunctions were used: an engine-fire in the Spain scenario and a fuel-leak in the Italy scenario. In both cases the crew had to initiate a diversion and select a suitable alternate airport under time pressure and challenging conditions (heavy rain, strong cross-winds, reduced visibility, limited maintenance, passenger-handling constraints, runway infrastructure, and approach procedures). Two different scenarios were selected to enable more flights to be carried out and evaluated with the available crews. The scenarios differ in terms of their environmental characteristics, such as geography and weather, but the chosen technical failures also require different responses, as fuel leaks are significantly more time-critical than (extinguished) engine fires. An experienced airline pilot simulated Air Traffic Control (ATC), providing realistic clearances and weather information. The flight deck environment was provided by the iSim flat-panel simulator of the Institute of Flight Guidance (DLR, Braunschweig), which was configured as an Airbus A321 cockpit (see [35] for details). The IPAS was mounted on the centre console.

Figure 4 shows the procedure of the study. Each crew flew both scenarios twice. These repetitions were chosen to establish comparability between the "with-IPAS" and "without-IPAS" settings. It was acknowledged that this may introduce training effects, but these were accepted given the exploratory nature of the study. At the beginning of the study, the participants received an initial briefing in which the purpose and procedure of the study were explained. As the participants were already familiar with the simulator from a previous study, no training session was necessary. Before each flight, the crew additionally received a short scenario briefing covering the planned route and basic flight parameters in order to facilitate immersion into the scenario. In the first two flights, the crews operated the scenarios without the IPAS under conventional settings (CONV) and had to solve the scenarios using their standard tools, ATC and procedures only. In the third and fourth flights, the crews operated the same scenarios with IPAS support. Finally, the participants answered questionnaires on the usefulness and explainability of the IPAS.

Fig. 4. Study procedure (Figure created by authors).

The study was approved by the DLR Ethics Committee on 30 January 2024. All participants signed an informed-consent form together with a GDPR-compliant data-protection declaration before the first briefing. The experiment reported here was one of several that were carried out consecutively on the same day. The whole test day lasted approx. 8h, during which participants moved from one study to the next. The present study required 1–1.5h. Each participant received a monetary compensation.

3.3 Pilot Sample

The study involved six flight crews, twelve commercial airline pilots in total. All participants held a valid Airbus type rating covering the A300, A320, A330, and A350 aircraft families. Age and number of flight hours were captured in categories: Age categories: < 30 years; 30–39 years; 40–49 years; 50–59 years; >59 years; Total flight-hour categories: 0–1500 h; 1501–3000 h; 3001–5000 h; 5001–10000 h; $>$10,000 h. Three participants were younger than 30 years, seven were between 30 and 39 years old, and two were older than 40 years. Three participants had less than 3000 total flight hours, while nine participants had more than 3000 flight hours. The sample included four captains or senior first officers and eight first officers.

3.4 Evaluation Measures

The evaluation combined qualitative observations of crew decision-making, quantitative decision-making parameters, and questionnaires on explainability and system usefulness. An experienced airline pilot and flight instructor (more than 3500 flight hours on various aircraft types) observed the crews providing free text notes focusing on decision-making behaviour, information usage and crew interaction, and provided qualitative comments on decision-making quality. Two quantitative measures complemented the qualitative analysis: (i) the time required for the FOR phases and the total decision time, and (ii) the number of alternate airports mentioned and the subset that were considered in detail. To assess perceived explainability, the Explanation Satisfaction Scale (ESS) [23] was used. Additionally the IPAS were assessed by the participants using a tailor-made questionnaire addressing perceived usefulness, ease of use, stress, and perceived safety impact. The metrics and scales used can be found in the results Sect. 4.4.

4 Results

In total, 24 simulator flights were analysed. Twelve flights were conducted under conventional setting (CONV), and twelve flights were conducted with IPAS support, with six flights per scenario and setting. The scenarios are analysed and compared separately, as they are not comparable with each other.

4.1 Quantitative Decision Process Analysis

Table 1 presents the time required each FOR phase and the total decision time for the Italy and Spain scenarios, comparing the conventional and IPAS settings. The times shown are the means across the six crews in decimal minutes (standard

Table 1. Mean decision-making time (in minutes) for the FOR-phases in the Italy and Spain scenarios, averaged across all crews and compared between the CONV and IPAS settings.

Scenario	Setting		Facts	Options	Risks & Benefits	Total
Italy	CONV	min (SD) perc.	0.29 (0.22) 6.35%	3.23 (0.36) 70.30%	1.07 (0.64) 23.35%	4.59 (0.94)
	IPAS	min (SD) perc.	1.39 (0.67) 33.42%	1.22 (1.02) 29.47%	1.54 (0.97) 37.11%	4.15 (1.80)
		Δ (rounded)	+27%	-41%	+14%	-0.44
Spain	CONV	min (SD) perc.	0.90 (0.86) 10.01%	4.49 (0.99) 50.11%	3.58 (1.80) 39.88%	8.96 (2.68)
	IPAS	min (SD)	1.26 (0.72) 23.06%	1.27 (0.47) 23.21%	2.94 (1.48) 53.73%	5.47 (1.96)
		Δ (rounded)	+13%	-27%	+14%	-3.49

deviations are given in brackets). The Δ-row shows the rounded percentage change from CONV to IPAS for every phase and for the overall decision time.

For both scenarios the IPAS reduced the relative share of the Options phase (-41% in Italy, -27% in Spain) and increased the share of the Facts and Risks & Benefits phases. Mean total decision time dropped slightly from 4.59 min (CONV) to 4.15 min (IPAS) in Italy and from 8.96 min to 5.47 min in Spain. The standard-deviation values reveal that the decision times under the IPAS condition in the Italy scenario are considerably more variable (SD = 1.80 min) than under the conventional setting (SD = 0.94 min).

Table 2 shows the number of airports mentioned, as well as the number of airports in closer consideration per crew in the different settings in the Italy scenario. Table 4 shows the crews' final decision in the Italy scenario. Table 3 and Table 5 show the airport-related statistics for the Spain scenario.

4.2 Qualitative Observations on Decision-Making and Collaboration

Across both scenarios, qualitative expert observation revealed differences between the conventional and the IPAS-supported settings in decision-making structure, information usage, and crew interaction. To summarize the free text notes delivered by the flight instructor, they were post-hoc grouped into thematic clusters by the authors.

Structure: In the conventional setting, the decision-making process was frequently unstructured or incomplete. Several crews consulted the FOR phases in the wrong order, and some phases were skipped completely or addressed only briefly. When the IPAS was used, all crews followed a more structured process, consistently applying the FORDEC model. **Airports assessed:** In both settings some crews showed a tendency to lock onto the nearest or largest airport. In the IPAS setting, some crews considered only the first IPAS-recommended option. **Detail of assessment:** In the conventional setting, decision factors such as passenger handling, technical ground support, and company preference were often

Table 2. Airport statistics in the Italy scenario for each setting and crew.

Crew	Setting	Airports mentioned	Airports on closer consideration
1	CONV	4	2
	IPAS	4	1
2	CONV	3	2
	IPAS	3	1
3	CONV	3	3
	IPAS	4	3
4	CONV	5	1
	IPAS	4	2
5	CONV	2	2
	IPAS	4	2
6	CONV	6	2
	IPAS	4	2
Total Mean	CONV	3.83	2.00
	IPAS	3.83	1.83

Table 3. Airport statistic in the Spain scenario.

Crew	Setting	Airports mentioned	Airports on closer consideration
1	CONV	7	3
	IPAS	4	2
2	CONV	5	1
	IPAS	3	2
3	CONV	4	3
	IPAS	4	3
4	CONV	3	1
	IPAS	4	2
5	CONV	3	3
	IPAS	4	2
6	CONV	6	2
	IPAS	3	2
Total Mean	CONV	4.67	2.17
	IPAS	3.67	2.17

Table 4. Airports selection in the Italy scenario.

Airports	CONV	IPAS
Rome (LIRF)	4	5
Ancona (LIPY)	1	1
Naples (LIRN)	1	0
Pescara (LIBP)	0	0

Table 5. Airports selection in the Spain scenario.

Airports	CONV	IPAS
Ciudad (LERL)	0	1
Madrid (LEMD)	6	5
Albacete (LEAB)	0	0
Teruel (LETL)	0	0

omitted. With the IPAS, most crews evaluated a broader set of decision factors (weather, runway length, terrain, visibility, wind, passenger handling, technical support, and company preference) and assessed them in greater detail. **CRM:** Under the conventional setting, CRM issues were observed for one crew, including directive communication and unilateral decisions without a joint airport assessment in both scenarios. In the IPAS setting, the same crew showed a more structured and communicative interaction, exchanging preferences and conducting a joint assessment of options. **Overall**, the qualitative observations suggest that the IPAS was associated with more structured decision-making processes, more comprehensive use of available information, and more coordinated crew interaction. Notably, various decision-making patterns were observed: sequential option review, pairwise comparisons, comparing several alternatives against a favored candidate, generating additional options after an initial set, or producing the full set of alternatives initially.

Because the experiment employed a fixed order (CONV always before IPAS) and a within-subject design, the observed differences may be influences by order, practice, or training effects.

4.3 Explanation Satisfaction Scale

Table 6 shows the ESS results. The table shows the mean scores on the original 1–5 Likert scale (Strongly disagree (1) to Strongly agree (5)) as well as the Standard Deviation.

Table 6. Explanation Satisfaction Scale (ESS) results. (N=12)

Item	Mean (SD)
From the explanation, I know how the IPAS works.	3.83 (0.94)
The explanation of how the IPAS works is satisfying.	3.50 (0.80)
The explanation of how the IPAS works has sufficient detail.	3.25 (1.06)
The explanation of how the IPAS works seems complete.	3.08 (0.79)
The explanation of how the IPAS works tells me how to use it.	3.67 (0.98)
The explanation of how the IPAS works is useful to my goals.	4.08 (0.79)
The explanation of the IPAS shows me how accurate the IPAS is.	3.31 (1.00)
Total mean	3.53

The ESS results ratings with mean scores ranging from 3.08 to 4.08. The highest scores were observed for perceived usefulness of the explanations and for understanding how the system works, whereas lower scores were obtained for perceived completeness and level of detail.

4.4 Tailor Made Questionnaire

The results of the tailor-made questionnaire are presented in two tables. Table 7 summarizes the crew's overall attitude toward the IPAS concept on a seven-point Likert scale.

Table 7. Rating of tailor-made questionnaire. 7-point Likert scale (1 = Totaly dislike, 7 = Totaly like). Additionally total mean and standard deviation.

Item	1	2	3	4	5	6	7	Total mean (SD)
How much do you like the concept of the IPAS?	0	0	0	1	1	4	6	6.25 (0.97)

The concept of the IPAS was rated positively, with 11 out of 12 participants indicating that they liked the concept. The overall attitude toward the IPAS was very homogeneous: the total mean of 6.25 on the 7-point scale is accompanied by a low standard deviation (SD = 0.97), indicating that almost all participants rated the concept positively.

Table 8. Ratings of tailor-made questionnaire. 5-point Likert scale (1 = Strongly disagree, 5 = Strongly agree). Additionally Total mean and standard deviation.

Item	1	2	3	4	5	Total mean (SD)
Was it easy to use the IPAS considering it was only shortly introduced to you?	0	0	0	8	4	4.33 (0.49)
Does the use of the IPAS make your job more comfortable?	0	0	2	6	4	4.17 (0.72)
Does the IPAS provide you with a better overview of the options compared to when you collect the data conventionally?	0	0	3	6	3	4.00 (0.74)
Did you perceive a lower stress level when using the IPAS?	0	0	0	3	9	4,25 (0,45)
Do you think the use of an AI tool like the IPAS improves safety?	0	0	3	6	3	4.00 (0.74)

Table 8 reports more detailed statements about the usefulness of the IPAS on a five-point Likert scale. For each item the numbers in the table indicate the count of participants who selected the corresponding Likert point.

All participants reported that the system was easy to use despite only a brief introduction. Regarding perceived usefulness, 10 out of 12 participants indicated that a system like the IPAS could make their job more comfortable. 9 out of 12 participants indicated that the IPAS provides a better overview of the available options compared with conventional data collection, while 3 out of 12 responded neutrally. All participants reported a reduction in perceived stress when using the IPAS. With respect to safety, 9 out of 12 participants indicated that the use of an AI tool such as the IPAS could improve safety, while 3 out of 12 responded neutrally.

In total, the detailed statements yielded total means between 4.00 and 4.33 on the 5-point scale, with standard deviations ranging from 0.45 to 0.74, which reflects a consistently narrow spread of responses across the crew.

5 Discussion

This study provides exploratory insights into the impact of the IPAS on flight-crew decision-making, pilots' perceived usefulness of the system, and the explainability of its AI-based outputs. Potential implications for flight safety and operational efficiency are also discussed, followed by a brief outline of the study's limitations.

5.1 Effects on Flight Crew Decision-Making

The Use of the IPAS Seems to Primarily Affects the Temporal Structure of Decision-Making Rather than the Overall Time Needed. Due to the study design, this observation may be attributable to the study design, which means that no clear statement can be made. Also, a reduction in decision time does not imply higher decision quality, so no direct conclusions about decision quality can be drawn from timing alone. Across both scenarios, a consistent pattern emerges in which the relative time allocation shifts from the Options phase toward the Risks & Benefits phases when using the IPAS (-41% Options to +27% Facts and +14% Risks & Benefits in Italy scenario, -27% Options to +13% Facts and +14% Risks & Benefits in Spain scenario). This shift can be explained by the fact that the IPAS takes over the generation and rating of suitable options, as well as information gathering and assessment of relevant decision factors, thereby freeing cognitive and temporal resources for a more detailed assessment of the recommended option. The qualitative observations confirm this interpretation: crews examined each option in greater detail and evaluated a broader set of decision factors. A similar timely shift is observed towards the Facts phase. Qualitative observations confirm, that this phase was either skipped or only briefly addressed, whereas the dedicated Facts page of the IPAS encourages crews to explicitly review the situation, constraints, and requirements for potential airports, as can be confirmed by the observation.

The IPAS Does Not Change the Size of the Option Space, But it Could Influences How Options are Generated. With respect to the number of airports mentioned or taken into closer consideration, no effect of the IPAS was observed. In some cases, only a single option was examined in more detail when using the IPAS, which may indicate a risk of premature narrowing of the option space and neglected consideration of lower-ranked alternatives. This may indicate a tendency toward overtrust in the system. On the other hand, this could also be due to learning effects in the repetition of the scenario, whereby the pilots already had their preferred option in mind. In other cases, crews that considered only a single option under conventional settings compared multiple alternatives when using the IPAS, suggesting that the system can also support broader option consideration. Notably, in the Spanish scenario, most crews chose a different airport to the top-ranked IPAS recommendation, instead selecting the second-ranked option, which was also chosen by all crews under conventional settings. This suggests that crews do not follow the AI ranking blindly but actively assess and, where appropriate, overrule the recommendations based on their own operational judgement. At the same time, the experience from the first flight without IPAS may also have influenced the choice here. Taken together, risks such as overtrust, premature narrowing of the option space, and loss of critical thinking, known as automation bias, should be considered both in the design of AI-based systems and in related training and operational procedures. However, the study design does not permit the distinction between a narrowing of the option space caused by the system and a narrowing that occurs after participants have explored the scenario once.

It Seems that the IPAS is Contributing to a More Structured and Informed Decision-Making Process. The qualitative observations, supported by the qualitative analysis, indicate that the IPAS supports a more consistent application of the FOR phases. In several conventional runs, the Facts phase was incomplete or omitted, whereas with the IPAS the phases tend to be applied more consistently. The interface structure mirrors the FOR process, which appears to support both procedural guidance and flexible movement between phases, for example by allowing crews to return from detailed airport. Observations suggest that option assessments were often superficial and omitted relevant decision factors under conventional settings. In contrast, using the IPAS crews evaluated a broader set of decision factors, resulting in a more detailed airport assessment. This can be explained by the reduced effort required for collecting and analysing information, as well as by the overview of important factors and their colour-coded assessment provided by the IPAS. Even in scenarios where time savings are marginal, decisions made with IPAS support appear to be more informed. Standard practices primarily focused on checking the weather conditions at the next major airport (e.g., Madrid or Rome) and occasionally one additional option. However, other critical parameters, such as runway condition, technical support availability, passenger handling capabilities, and company preferences, were often neglected. This can be attributed to IPAS's detailed analysis of all relevant factors and alternatives, encompassing a wider range of decision factors than typically considered in conventional decision-making processes.

The IPAS May Influence Decision Strategies and Recurring Decision Patterns. Across crews, the observation revealed recurring decision-making patterns, such as sequential option generation after an initial assessment, early fixation on a single option, or systematic one-by-one comparison of alternatives. The IPAS may influence not only decision-making structure and information use but also decision strategy. This points to a promising direction for future research, for example along the lines of decision pattern analyses such as those reported by [37].

Observation Suggests that the IPAS May have a Positive Impact on CRM. Finally, a remarkable but anecdotal observation was that the CRM issues previously observed in one crew under conventional settings did not occur when the IPAS was used. The IPAS may serve as an third neutral agent in the cockpit hierarchy, providing an objective baseline that mitigates interpersonal friction and appears to facilitate coordinated discussion, flatten hierarchies, and support joint decision-making. This interpretation remains speculative and would require a detailed investigation. However, it is very difficult to reproduce CRM problems specifically for a study.

5.2 Explainability and Perceived Usefulness

The Explainability of the IPAS is Rated Positively and as Helpful for Decision-Making. The explainability of the IPAS received an overall ESS mean of 3.55, indicating that participants generally agreed that the explanations were useful and helped them understand how the system works, while still leaving room for improvement. In particular, the explanations provided by the IPAS, such as the presentation of relevant decision factors influencing airport ratings, the use of color coding to indicate individual factor assessments and the indication of factor weightings [36], supported pilots in understanding the justification behind alternate airport assessments. These explanations were also perceived as useful for decision-making, indicating that they supported the operational task.

There Could be a Tension Field Between Depth of Explanation and Operational Applicability. At the same time, the perceived level of detail and completeness of the explanations received lower ratings. Taken together, this suggests a trade-off between the amount and depth of explanatory information on the one hand and the need for explanations at an appropriate level of detail that allows pilots to focus on operational decision-making on the other, as also discussed in the literature (e.g., [7,21]). In this tension field, the IPAS appears to provide fewer but operationally relevant explanations, which were sufficient to support decision-making without overloading the crew, while at the same time possibly providing slightly too little detail. This tension field should be carefully balanced when designing explainable and operational AI-based systems.

The IPAS is Perceived as a Useful and Supportive Decision-Support Tool. The results of the tailor-made questionnaire further indicate that the IPAS was perceived as useful and supportive for the decision-making process. The concept was positively received, the system was considered easy to use, and its use was associated with increased perceived comfort and reduced perceived stress. In addition, a majority of pilots indicated that the IPAS provides a better overview of available options compared to conventional data collection.

5.3 Potential Implications for Flight Safety and Operational Efficiency

When evaluating socio-technical systems, consideration should be given not only to the system qualities discussed in this study, but also to their overall impact on organisation, society and the environment [20]. While the present study was not designed to assess safety outcomes or operational performance metrics directly, the observed changes in flight crew decision-making processes suggest potential implications for flight safety, operational efficiency and sustainability. From a flight safety perspective, the IPAS was associated with a more structured and explicit application of the FORDEC model. Research in human factors and CRM has repeatedly shown that incomplete situation assessment, premature fixation on a single option, and unstructured trade-offs are recurrent contributors to inadequate operational decisions [22,27,30]. These patterns were frequently observed under conventional settings, whereas the IPAS-supported setting was characterized by more systematic consideration of operational constraints, explicit articulation of consequences, and more coordinated crew interaction. Although no causal claims can be made, these mechanisms are widely regarded as supporting factors for safe flight operations and align with established principles of structured aeronautical decision-making [24]. In addition to safety-related considerations, the findings indicate possible implications for operational efficiency. Diversion decisions affect flight-path length, holding time, airport suitability and secondary-diversion risk. The observed shift in time allocation from option generation toward information assessment and comparison suggests that the IPAS may reduce the effort required for ad hoc information gathering and processing while enabling more informed assessments of available alternatives. From an airline operations and management perspective, more informed and timely diversion decisions may contribute to reduced downstream effects such as extended fuel burn, additional ground handling complexity, and passenger disruption. Reduced fuel burn and emissions are a likely indirect benefit. These potential effects should be quantified by integrating decision-making analyses with operational, economic and environmental performance models.

5.4 Limitations and Future Research Directions

This study has several limitations that need to be considered when interpreting the results. First, the study followed a non-randomized within-subject design with a fixed order of settings and scenarios. This limits the ability to attribute observed effects unambiguously to the use of the IPAS and does not allow for strong causal claims. Future studies should employ randomized and counterbalanced designs to control for learning and order effects. Second, the qualitative evaluation of decision-making was conducted by a single expert observer. While this provided rich domain-specific insights, it also introduces subjectivity and potential bias. If qualitative observations are used as a metric in future work, multiple domain experts should be consulted to increase the objectivity of qualitative observations. The present study included quantitative performance measures (e.g., the duration of the FOR phases). The qualitative observations were used to complement these metrics by assessing how crews used information, interacted, and by revealing decision-making patterns. Information that is not evident from timing data alone. A promising direction for future research is to quantify the qualitative findings, for example by analysing phase-transitions and information-usage, to obtain a deeper and more objective insight into the decision-making structure. As previously mentioned, the impact of the IPAS could also be evaluated through an analysis of decision-making patterns and strategies that differ between conventional and IPAS-supported settings (e.g., [37]).

With respect to further development of the IPAS, future work should focus on the tension between explainability and information load, for example by enabling adaptive levels of explanation detail depending on the operational context and user needs. In addition, training concepts and procedural guidance should be developed to support critical reflection when working with AI-based systems and to mitigate risks of automation bias. Future research could investigate how implementing IPAS translates into measurable outcomes relating to safety, efficiency, costs and emissions, for example by combining simulator studies with operational data, fuel burn models and airline performance metrics.

6 Conclusion

This paper presented an exploratory simulator study on the effects of the IPAS on flight-crew decision-making and on pilots' perceptions of its explainability and usefulness. The results suggest that the IPAS primarily supports a more structured and more detailed consideration of facts, possible options, and their risks and benefits. The study revealed a shift from time spent on searching for options towards time spent on the detailed assessment of the decision factors and available options when using the IPAS, potentially leading to more informed decisions. Pilots perceived the IPAS as useful and supportive, and they rated its explanations as helpful for understanding and justifying system outputs. At the same time, the findings point to a potential tension between the depth of explanations and the cognitive and temporal resources required to process them, indicating that the level of explanatory detail can directly influence operational applicability. Importantly, CRM-related issues observed in the conventional condition disappeared when the IPAS was used, suggesting that the system can act as a neutral third-party that facilitates coordinated crew interaction. At the same time, the risk of premature narrowing of the option space and over-trust (related to automation bias) was noted.

Overall, the results highlight the potential of user-centred, explainable AI systems such as the IPAS to support flight-crew decision-making in complex operational contexts, while underlining the importance of careful system design, appropriate explainability, and training to mitigate known risks of operational AI: premature narrowing of the option space, automation bias, and overreliance on AI-generated rankings. The findings suggest that AI-based decision-support systems such as the IPAS can influence decision-making structure, information usage and CRM, with possible impacts on flight safety, operational efficiency and sustainability.

Acknowledgments. JARVIS has received funding from the SESAR Joint Undertaking under the European Union's Horizon Europe research and innovation program under grant agreement No 101114692. Views and opinions expressed are however those of the authors only and do not necessarily reflect those of the European Union or SESAR 3 Joint Undertaking. Neither the European Union nor SESAR 3 Joint Undertaking can be held responsible for them.

References

1. Bainbridge, L.: Ironies of automation. Automatica **19**(6), 775–779 (1983). https://doi.org/10.1016/0005-1098(83)90046-8
2. Billings, C.E.: Human-centered aviation automation: Principles and guidelines. Technical Memorandum NASA-TM-110381. NASA Ames Research Center, Moffett Field, CA, USA (1996)
3. Dahlbäck, N., Jönsson, A., Ahrenberg, L.: Wizard of oz studies - why and how. Knowl.-Based Syst. **6**(4), 258–266 (1993). https://doi.org/10.1016/0950-7051(93)90017-N

4. Djartov, B., Mostaghim, S., Papenfuß, A., Wies, M.: Description and first evaluation of an approach for a pilot decision support system based on multi-attribute decision making. In: IEEE Symposium Series on Computational Intelligence, pp. 141–147 (2022). https://doi.org/10.1109/SSCI51031.2022.10022076
5. Djartov, B., Mostaghim, S., Papenfuß, A., Wies, M.: A learning classifier system approach to time-critical decision-making in dynamic alternate airport selection. In: IEEE Congress on Evolutionary Computation (CEC), pp. 1–8 (2024). https://doi.org/10.1109/CEC60901.2024.10612016
6. Djartov, B., Würfel, J.: Navigating Decisions in the Cockpit: The Intelligent Pilot Advisory System, pp. 305–325. Springer, Cham (2025). https://doi.org/10.1007/978-3-031-83512-4_18
7. Droogenbroeck, C., Rankova, E., Papenfuss, A., Bos, T., Zon, R.: Human-ai teaming - challenges from a practitioner's perspective. In: Harris, D., Li, WC. (eds.) Engineering Psychology and Cognitive Ergonomics, pp. 337–354. Springer, Cham (2025). https://doi.org/10.1007/978-3-031-93718-7_22
8. Dubey, A., Abhinav, K., Jain, S., Arora, V., Puttaveerana, A.: Haco: A framework for developing human-ai teaming. In: Proceedings of the 13th Innovations in Software Engineering Conference (Formerly Known as India Software Engineering Conference). ISEC '20 (2020). https://doi.org/10.1145/3385032.3385044
9. Endsley, M.R.: Automation and situation awareness. In: Proceedings of the 1996 International Conference on Human-Computer Interaction (1996). https://api.semanticscholar.org/CorpusID:261054213
10. Endsley, M.R.: Autonomous horizons: System autonomy in the air force – a path to the future. volume i: Human-autonomyteaming (2015). https://doi.org/10.13140/RG.2.1.1164.2003
11. Endsley, M.R.: Supporting human-ai teams:transparency, explainability, and situation awareness. Comput. Hum. Behav. **140**, 107574 (2023). https://doi.org/10.1016/j.chb.2022.107574
12. EUROCONTROL: Cost of diversion (2025). https://ansperformance.eu/economics/cba/standard-inputs/latest/chapters/cost_of_diversion.html
13. Commission, E.: Just a rather very intelligent system (Jarvis) (2026). https://doi.org/10.3030/101114692
14. European Union Aviation Safety Agency: Crm training implementation (2017). https://www.easa.europa.eu/en/document-library/general-publications/crm-training-implementation
15. European Union Aviation Safety Agency: Easa-ai-roadmap 2.0: A human-centric approach to ai in aviation (2023). https://www.easa.europa.eu/en/domains/research-innovation/ai
16. European Union Aviation Safety Agency: Easy access rules for air operations – nco.gen.105 pilot-in-command responsibilities and authority (2023). https://www.easa.europa.eu/en/document-library/easy-access-rules/online-publications/easy-access-rules-air-operations?kw=Journey&page=4
17. European Union Aviation Safety Agency: Easa concept paper: Guidance for levelâĂŕ1 &âĂŕ2 machine-learning applications (2024). https://www.easa.europa.eu/en/domains/research-innovation/ai
18. Ezer, N., Bruni, S., Cai, Y., Hepenstal, S.J., Miller, C.A., Schmorrow, D.D.: Trust engineering for human-ai teams. Proc. Human Factors Ergonomics Soc. Ann. Meet. **63**(1), 322–326 (2019). https://doi.org/10.1177/1071181319631264
19. Federal Aviation Administration: Advisory circular 120-51d: Crew resource management training (2001). https://www.faa.gov/documentLibrary/media/Advisory_Circular/AC_120-51D.pdf

20. Flemisch, F., Preutenborbeck, M., Herzberger, N., et al.: Vom Teufelsquadrat zum nachhaltigen Engelsdiamanten und holistischen Bow-Tie-Modell: Methodenentwicklung für die ganzheitliche Analyse, Gestaltung und Entwicklung von nachhaltigen Arbeitssystemen. Zeitschrift für Arbeitswissenschaft **78**, 146–159 (2024). https://doi.org/10.1007/s41449-024-00418-5, https://doi.org/10.1007/s41449-024-00418-5
21. Gunning, D., Vorm, E., Wang, J.Y., Turek, M.: Darpa's explainable ai (xai) program: A retrospective. Appl. AI Lett. **2**(4), (2021). https://doi.org/10.1002/ail2.61
22. Helmreich, R.L., Foushee, H.C.: ChapterâĂŕ1 – why crm? empirical and theoretical bases of human-factors training. In: Kanki, B.G., Helmreich, R.L., Anca, J. (eds.) Crew Resource Management (Second Edition), pp. 3–57. Academic Press, San Diego, second edn. (2010). https://doi.org/10.1016/B978-0-12-374946-8.10001-9
23. Hoffmann, R.R., Mueller, S.T., Klein, G., Litman, J.: Measures for explainable ai: Explanation goodness, user satisfaction, mental models, curiosity, trust, and human-ai performance. Front. Comput. Sci. **5** (2023). https://doi.org/10.3389/fcomp.2023.1096257
24. Hörmann, H.J.: For-dec - a prescriptive model for aeronautical decision making. In: 21st WEAAP Conference, Dublin (1994). https://elib.dlr.de/27044/
25. Hradecky, S.: Accident: Canada rouge a319 near punta cana on nov 15th 2025, fumes on board (2025). https://avherald.com/h?article=5307c73e
26. Miller, M., Holley, S., Halawi, L.: The evolution of ai on the commercial flight deck: Finding balance between efficiency and safety while maintaining the integrity of operator trust. In: Proceedings of the AHFE 2023 (2023). https://doi.org/10.54941/ahfe1004175
27. Orasanu, J., Martin, L., Davison, J.: Errors in aviation decision making: Bad decisions or bad luck? In: Fourth Conference on Naturalistic Decision Making. NASA-Ames Research Center, Warrenton, VA (1998). https://ntrs.nasa.gov/citations/20020063485
28. Parasuraman, R., Manzey, D.: Complacency and bias in human use of automation: An attentional integration. Human factors **52**, 381–410 (2010). https://doi.org/10.1177/0018720810376055
29. SKYbrary: Diversion (2025). https://skybrary.aero/articles/diversion
30. Soll, H., Proske, S., Hofinger, G., Steinhardt, G.: Decision-making tools for aeronautical teams: For-dec and beyond (2016). https://doi.org/10.1027/2192-0923/a000099
31. Ternus, S.: User-Centered Design of an Intelligent Pilot Advisory System for Non-Emergency Scenarios: A Case Study. Master's thesis, Hochschule Trier (2024). https://elib.dlr.de/206128/
32. Ternus, S., Würfel, J., Papenfuß, A., Wies, M., Rumpler, M.: Exploring functionalities for an intelligent pilot advisory system in normal operation. In: Engineering Psychology and Cognitive Ergonomics: 21st International Conference, EPCE 2024 (HCII 2024), pp. 235–247. Washington, DC, USA. Springer, Cham (2024). https://doi.org/10.1007/978-3-031-60728-8_19
33. Wiener, E.L., Curry, R.E.: Flight-deck automation: promises and problems. Ergonomics **23**(10), 995–1011 (1980). https://doi.org/10.1080/00140138008924809
34. Würfel, J., Djartov, B., Papenfuß, A., Wies, M.: Intelligent pilot advisory system: The journey from ideation to an early system design of an ai-based decision support system for airline flight decks. In: AHFE 2023 (2023). https://doi.org/10.54941/ahfe1003844

35. Würfel, J., Flemisch, F.O.: Human system exploration for the ai-based flight deck decision support system ipas. In: de Waard, D., et al. (eds.) Proceedings of the Human Factors and Ergonomics Society Europe Chapter 2024 Annual Conference. Avail (2024) https://doi.org/10.60575/31n5-2a06
36. Würfel, J., Papenfuß, A., Wies, M.: Operationalizing ai explainability using interpretability cues in the cockpit: Insights from user-centered development of the intelligent pilot advisory system (ipas). In: Degen, H., Ntoa, S. (eds.) Artificial Intelligence in HCI, pp. 297–315. Springer, Cham (2024). https://doi.org/10.1007/978-3-031-60606-9_17
37. Zhang, Z.T., et al.: Beyond recommendations: From backward to forward ai support of pilots' decision-making process. Proc. ACM Human-Comput. Inter. **8**(CSCW2), 1–32 (2024). https://doi.org/10.1145/3687024
38. Zhang, Z.T., Liu, Y., Husmann, H.: Pilot attitudes toward ai in the cockpit: Implications for design. In: Nürnberger, A. (ed.) Proceedings of the 2021 IEEE International Conference on Human-Machine Systems, pp. 1–6. IEEE (2021). https://doi.org/10.1109/ICHMS53169.2021.9582448

Analysis of the Pilots' Physiological Arousal Level in Simulated Single Pilot Operations Tasks

Xinrui Xiao(✉), Ruiyuan Hong, and Lei Wang

College of Safety Science and Engineering, Civil Aviation University of China, Tianjin 300300, China

Xiao15035113824@163.com, leiwang@cauc.edu.cn

Abstract. To investigate the impact of simulated single pilot operations (SPO) flight tasks on pilots' physiological arousal levels, a task scenario experiment under SPO mode was designed and implemented. Firstly, the scenarios were designed as normal climb without faults and climb with fire alarm tasks, based on a full-flight simulator to construct the independent variables for different SPO operation modes: the SPO single-pilot group (pilot only) and the SPO-RIA responsive intelligent assistant group (pilot and simulated intelligent assistant role). Secondly, 48 airline pilot subjects were recruited to conduct corresponding simulated flight experiments. The heart rate, skin conductance, and eye movement signal indicators were recorded. Finally, by combining objective data, the impact of different SPO modes on pilots' physiological states was analyzed. The research results indicate that simulated SPO flight tasks have significant differences in their impact on pilots' physiological arousal levels (e.g. heart rate variability and skin conductance level) under different modes. The physiological arousal level of pilots in the SPO group was significantly higher than that in the SPO-RIA group, with increased autonomic nervous load and a state of high alertness. Pilots in the SPO-RIA group had better autonomic nervous regulation functions, with improved stability and adaptability in physiological regulation. Therefore, the introduction of an intelligent assistant role in the cockpit significantly changed the pilots' physiological states, helping to alleviate high arousal levels. The research results can provide a theoretical basis for the future design of SPO intelligent cockpit systems.

Keywords: Single pilot operations · Arousal · Physiological Signals · Eye Movement · Electrodermal Activity

1 Introduction

With the development of communication and navigation technologies and the improvement of automation systems, the cockpit crew configuration has successfully transitioned from the early five-person system to the currently prevalent Double Pilot Operations (DPO) mode [1], where the captain, acting as the pilot flying (PF), and the co-pilot, serving as the pilot monitoring (PM), collaborate to execute flight tasks. According to relevant data [2–5], the time cycle and economic cost required to train a mature pilot are gradually increasing. To reduce airlines' input costs and enhance economic efficiency, driven by

W. -C. Li and A. Plioutsias (Eds.): HCII 2026, LNAI 16708, pp. 340–351, 2026.
https://doi.org/10.1007/978-3-032-29459-3_22

both technological innovation and market demand, Single pilot operations (SPO) has emerged as a key direction for the development of next-generation commercial aircraft [6]. The SPO mode lacks a clear and unified conceptual framework; it generally refers to a scenario where a single pilot completes flight tasks smoothly with the enhanced assistance of on-board intelligent systems, remote ground stations, or a combination of both. Its direct manifestation lies in the reduction of crew size and the shrinkage of cockpit space, while the intrinsic transformation involves the strengthening of automation, autonomy, and intelligent collaborative control technologies. To explore the feasibility of the next-generation SPO mode, institutions such as the National Aeronautics and Space Administration (NASA) and the European Aviation Safety Agency (EASA) have invested substantial resources in research. NASA [7] took the lead in organizing an aviation technology conference to systematically describe SPO, initially proposing five SPO mode concepts and discussing issues including cockpit workload management, human-machine interaction task allocation, and pilots' mental workload levels, thus laying the foundation for the design and application of the SPO mode. Through multi-party verification, it is theoretically concluded that the "cockpit + ground station" SPO air-ground collaborative operation architecture holds relatively high value [8, 9].

The "human factor" during flight has long been the primary cause of civil aviation accidents or unsafe incidents [10]. To achieve a safety level no lower than that of the DPO mode, the framework design concept of the SPO mode has gradually focused on the field of human factors engineering. Harris [11] was the first to explicitly point out that the "Human-Centered Design (HCD)" principle will effectively guide the in-depth development and iterative optimization of SPO mode cockpit technologies. In this context, the aviation field has initiated further research on the dynamic allocation of human-machine functions in the cockpit and the construction of a ground-based distributed conceptual framework [12–14]. However, while the SPO mode reduces the human factor, it places higher demands on pilots' cognitive processing capabilities and psychological adaptation, potentially leading to an increase in pilots' mental workload [15]. Based on the core requirement of achieving safety redundancy for SPO, the NASA Langley Research Center [16] has built a cockpit automation integration system specifically designed to support the SPO mode; EASA [17] has developed the "Advanced Cockpit for Reduced Stress and Workload" program, aiming to ensure a balance between pilots' psychological stress and workload. COMAC (Commercial Aircraft Corporation of China) [18] leads the development of intelligent cockpits, designing machines with human-machine collaborative driving functions. Existing studies indicate that approximately 60% to 90% of human factor errors occur during periods of high mental workload among pilots [19]. Therefore, it is imperative to simulate and verify the impact of SPO cockpit design on pilots' mental workload.

In the latest revision of the Safety Information Classification System by the International Air Transport Association (IATA) in 2025 [20], three major human factors have been incorporated into the aviation safety management framework, emphasizing the importance of pilots' psychological and physiological states in the dimension of risk identification. In 1989, Odink et al. [21] found that mental workload is related to individual capabilities, emotions, and states, laying the foundation for the measurement and evaluation system of mental workload. In recent years, a basic consensus has been reached on methods for assessing pilots' mental workload, which mainly include subjective scale evaluation, objective physiological measurement, and task performance assessment [22]. Among these, indicators such as heart rate (HR), heart rate variability (HRV), and skin conductance are widely used to characterize fatigue, stress, and mental workload due to their practicality and reliability. Given the positive correlation between mental workload and task complexity [23], the dynamic diversity of the SPO mode has prompted relevant research to focus on analyzing pilots' mental workload in abnormal scenarios from aspects such as physiological indicators and task performance, and to preliminarily explore issues such as cognitive overload, human-machine interaction decision conflicts, and improper dynamic function allocation using various methods and models [24].

Pilots' mental workload during flight operations is closely related to the physiological arousal level of their individual emotions. Arousal level refers to the degree of excitement of the human body in response to external stimuli and serves as an objective physiological externalization of mental workload [25]. Emotions are accompanied by changes in the activities of the autonomic nervous system, including the sympathetic nervous system (SNS) and the parasympathetic nervous system (PNS), which is known as the physiological arousal of emotions. The SNS dominates stress responses, mobilizing the body's resources to cope with emergencies; the PNS promotes relaxation responses, responsible for calming arousal, conserving energy, and restoring internal homeostasis. They typically function in an antagonistic manner but also collaborate to maintain the stability and adaptability of the body's internal environment. HR, HRV, skin conductance, and pupil dilation are commonly used to measure the activation of the autonomic nervous system and thus assess an individual's physiological arousal level [26–28]. When pilots are in a state of high tension or stress, their SNS may become more active. Pupil diameter is influenced by the balance between SNS and PNS activities [29, 30] and has been validated as a useful indicator for measuring physiological arousal levels [31]. Kinney et al. [32] found that pilots' HR and pupil diameter increase significantly during single-engine failure. Due to the increasingly prominent contradictions between SPO cockpit intelligent assistance devices and pilots' psychological, physiological, conditional constraints, and task allocation, research on arousal level intensity is crucial for optimizing human-machine function allocation and maintaining pilots' task performance.

However, there is currently no unified operational framework for the SPO mode, and there is a lack of direct experimental research based on physiological indicators to explore how it affects pilots' physiological arousal states, particularly whether the introduction of intelligent assistance helps regulate the autonomic nervous system and alleviate sustained high alert states. With the high cognitive demands of the SPO mode on pilots, intelligent flight assistance systems driven by physiological states are expected to become the core development direction of future SPO, and their research value and practical significance urgently need to be emphasized [33]. In view of this, the study designs a simulated SPO task scenario to investigate the impact of introducing cockpit intelligent assistant role on the physiological arousal levels of SPO pilots and the degree of physiological arousal during different flight phases. The aim is to promote the application of the SPO mode and the design of cockpit human-machine interaction, scientifically reduce pilots' mental workload, and thus hold significant implications for reducing flight accidents and improving the safety level of flight operations.

2 Method

2.1 Participants

A total of 48 male airline pilots from a domestic airline were recruited as participants. All participants were in good health, with no color vision deficiencies, normal or corrected-to-normal visual acuity, and normal hearing. To ensure the accuracy of experimental data, participants were required to have adequate rest prior to the experiment, refrain from consuming stimulant beverages, and avoid taking any medication.

2.2 Experimental Equipment

Experimental Platform. Given the current lack of a truly SPO-capable cockpit, a high-fidelity single-pilot platform was established utilizing a Boeing 737–800 full-flight simulator and a one-way vision panel. This experimental setup was designed to simulate two distinct single-pilot operational conditions.

Operation without intelligent assistance: The PM role in the DPO mode was entirely removed. The PF performed all flight tasks independently without any intelligent assistance (see Fig. 1 (a)).

Operation with simulated intelligent assistance: A one-way vision panel blocked the PF's view of the right-side instrument panel and controls. A pilot in the copilot's seat acted as a simulated intelligent assistant with limited functionality. This assistant only responded to one-way voice commands from the PF, performing voice recognition, semantic understanding, and task responses. It possessed no capability for autonomous communication or collaborative decision-making, ensuring the absolute disposal dominance of the PF throughout the experiment (see Fig. 1(b)).

(a) Full-flight simulator

(b) Full-flight simulator with one-way vision panel

Fig. 1. Experimental platform.

Physiological Data Collection. The experiment uses the following three physiological measurement devices: Photoplethysmograph (PPG) sensor, Electrodermal Activity (EDA) sensor, and Tobii Pro Glasses 2 head-mounted eye tracker [34–36] (see Fig. 2).

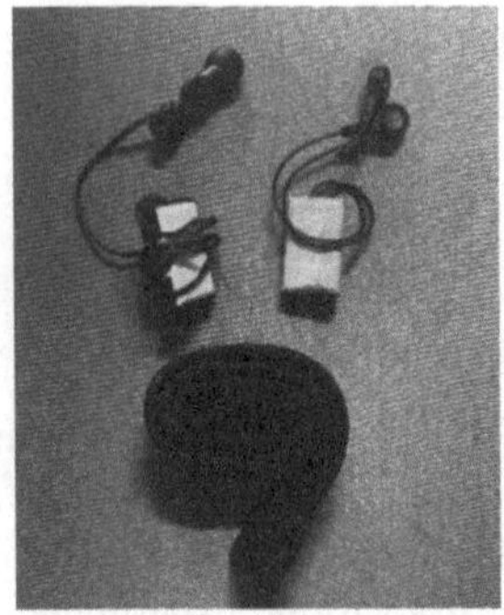

(a) PPG (left) and EDA (right) sensors

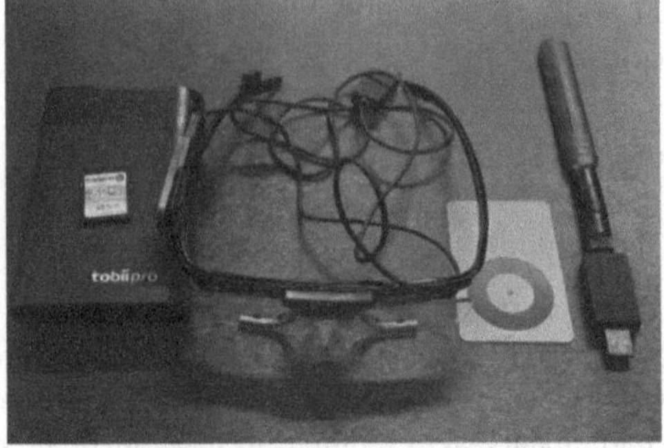

(b) Tobii head-mounted eye-tracker

Fig. 2. Experimental measuring equipment.

The PPG sensor collects HR and HRV related data through sensor devices clipped to the earlobe, fingers, arms, etc. It mainly uses the principle of light beam transmission and reflection to calculate the changes in light signals and blood flow, converting light signals into electrical signals to obtain average indicators, including mean heart rate (Mean HR), mean inter-beat intervals (Mean IBI), standard deviation of N-N intervals (SDNN), and root mean square of N-N intervals difference (RMSSD).

The EDA sensor collects skin conductance data between two points through electrode patches attached to the fingers and wrists, including two important physiological indicators: skin conductance level (SCL) and skin conductance response (SCR). The size of the above two physiological measurement sensors is 43 $\times$ 25 $\times$ 12 mm, with a 24-bit resolution and a 64 Hz sampling frequency. They both transmit physiological data wirelessly at a 2.4 GHz frequency and a rate of 2 Mbps.

The Tobii Pro Glasses 2 head-mounted eye tracker has four eye movement cameras and can track the eye movement data of the subject within a horizontal range of 85° and a vertical range of 52°, used to collect average pupil diameter and average blink rate, etc.

2.3 Experimental Design

Scenarios Design. Based on the full-flight simulator, the simulated flight segment was set as taking off from Jinan Yaoqiang (TNA) and performing a standard climb route to Shanghai Hongqiao (SHA). Each subject conducted the experiment separately. The focus of the experiment was the climb phase after takeoff, starting at an altitude of 3900 ft, with a climb rate of approximately 1000 ft/min, and a target altitude of 8900 ft. The meteorological conditions were set as daytime, light turbulence, calm wind and normal visibility.

Scenario 1: Normal climb without faults. The aircraft started climbing from 3900 ft and followed the standard operating procedures under light turbulence for about 2 min. There were no abnormal alerts or system failures during this period. The crew maintained the heading and climb rate according to their normal task division and completed the routine flight communication and parameter monitoring before ending the scenario.

Scenario 2: Climb with fire alarm fault. The aircraft climbed along the same route and under the same initial conditions as in Scenario 1. About 1 min into the climb, a single-engine fire alarm fault was set, triggering a sudden warning. The subjects needed to identify, diagnose and handle this emergency in a light turbulence environment, including executing the Quick Reference Handbook (QRH), communicating and coordinating, and deciding whether to return. The emergency lasted until the crew completed the initial handling or the situation stabilized (about 3–4 min), and then the scenario ended.

Variable Design. Independent variable design. The experiment adopted a 2 × 2 mixed factor design for the independent variables, namely the existence of the intelligent assistant role and the flight phase. The existence of the intelligent assistant role was a between-subjects variable, and the flight phase was a within-subjects variable.

The 48 subjects were randomly divided into 2 groups based on whether the intelligent assistant role was introduced: the single pilot operations (SPO) group and the single pilot operations responsive intelligent assistance (SPO-RIA) group. The flight phases were divided into 2: normal climb without faults and climb fire alarm fault. The SPO group conducted the flight tasks without intelligent assistance, while the SPO-RIA group operated with a simulated intelligent assistant (see Table 1).

Table 1. Experimental conditions of each variable group.

Independent Variable	Abbreviation	Experimental Platform
Single pilot operations	SPO Group	Without intelligent assistance
Responsive Intelligent Assistance	SPO-RIA Group	With simulated intelligent assistance

Dependent variable design. The experiment selected physiological arousal level as the dependent variable. The evaluation indicators of physiological arousal level included heart rate signal (e.g. HRV), skin conductance signal (e.g. EDA) and eye movement signal. According to existing research [36], the heart rate signal included Mean HR, Mean IBI and HRV time domain indicators SDNN, RMSSD, SDSD (standard deviation of successive differences), PNN50 (percentage of the number of successive N-N interval pairs that differ by more than 50 ms), PNN20 (percentage of the number of successive N-N interval pairs that differ by more than 20 ms). The enhancement of physiological arousal level is mainly manifested as an increase in Mean HR and a shortening of Mean IBI, accompanied by a decrease in HRV time domain indicators, at which point the PNS activation decreased [28]. The skin conductance signal selected SCL and SCR, which could reflect the degree of emotional arousal, and skin conductance was linearly correlated with the arousal level. When a person experienced emotions such as tension and anxiety, SCL increased [37, 38]. The eye movement signal selected average pupil diameter, saccade frequency and blink frequency. The higher the arousal level, the larger the pupil diameter.

2.4 Experimental Procedure

The experiment was divided into two stages: the preparation stage and the flight stage (see Fig. 3).

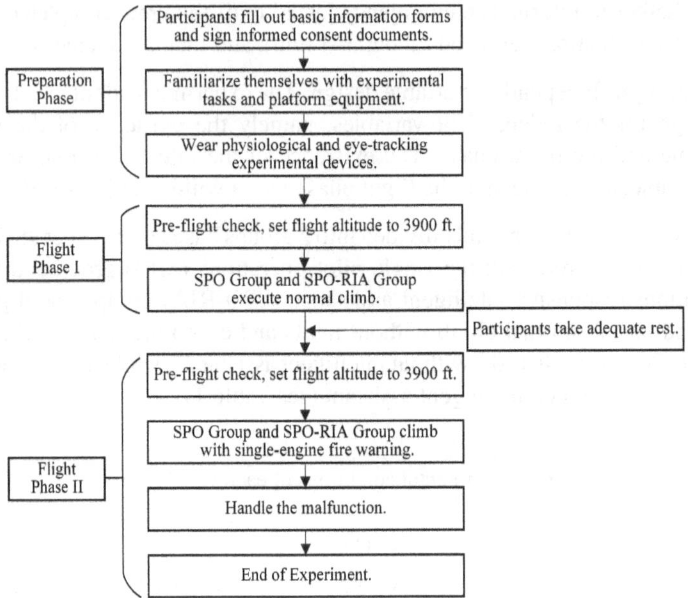

Fig. 3. Experimental procedure.

2.5 Data Processing

The physiological analysis and eye movement analysis modules of the Ergo-Lab software were used for data preprocessing. The preprocessed experimental data were statistically analyzed using SPSS 27.0 software. The normality of the data was analyzed by the Shapiro-Wilk test ($p > 0.05$ indicating normal distribution), and then a significance test was conducted ($p < 0.05$ indicating a significant difference).

Between-subjects data processing: For the data of the two groups that were normally distributed in the first flight phase, an independent t-test was conducted. If one group didn't meet the normal distribution, the Mann-Whitney U non-parametric test method was used. The differences between the SPO group and the SPO-RIA group in the normal climb without faults scenario were judged and analyzed after the test.

Within-subject data processing: For the SPO-RIA group, paired t-tests were conducted on the data with differences that conformed to a normal distribution in different flight phases, while the Wilcoxon signed-rank test was used for non-parametric analysis otherwise. The differences between the normal climb without fault phase and the climb fire alarm fault phase within the SPO-RIA group were evaluated and analyzed.

3 Results

The statistical analysis results indicated that the existence of the simulated intelligent assistant role had significant differences ($p < 0.05$) only on the HRV time-domain indicators SDNN, RMSSD, and SDSD of the heart rate signal. Specifically, in the normal climb without fault scenario, the HRV time-domain indicators of the SPO group were significantly lower than those of the SPO-RIA group (see Fig. 4).

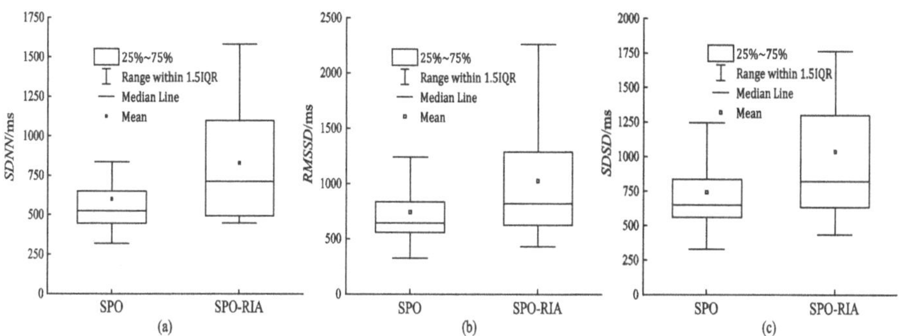

Fig. 4. Measurement values of HRV indicators.

In addition, the existence of the simulated intelligent assistant role had a significant difference ($p < 0.05$) in the SCL. Specifically, in the normal climb without fault scenario, the SCL of the SPO group was significantly higher than that of the SPO-RIA group (see Fig. 5(a)). The presence or absence of the simulated intelligent assistant role had no significant effect ($p > 0.05$) in the SCR (see Fig. 5(b)).

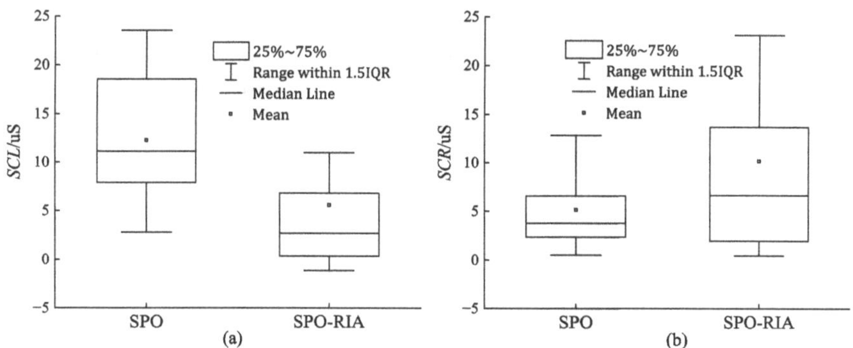

Fig. 5. Measurement values of SCL and SCR indicators.

However, the existence of the simulated intelligent assistant role had no significant effect ($p > 0.05$) on the eye movement signal indicators of average pupil diameter, saccade frequency, and blink frequency.

4 Discussion

This study aimed to explore the impact of the cockpit intelligent assistant role in the SPO mode on the physiological arousal level of pilots and to compare the differences in physiological arousal levels in different flight phases.

The experimental results showed that in the normal climb without fault scenario, the SDNN, RMSSD, and SDSD of the SPO group were significantly lower than those of the SPO-RIA group. The HRV time-domain indicators positively reflect the activation level of the PNS [28], and a decrease in PNS activation indicates an increase in arousal. At this time, the pilot may be in a highly concentrated or tense state [39]. Without intelligent assistance, SPO pilots need to independently complete the full process of manipulation, monitoring, and cross-checking, continuously occupying cognitive resources and reducing the ability of autonomic nerve regulation [40]. The introduction of an intelligent assistant role has a positive impact on the pilot's operation and can reduce the pilot's cross-checking steps, to a certain extent, performing the function of the PM, thereby reducing the pilot's continuous cognitive load and psychological stress. This result confirms from a physiological perspective that the cockpit intelligent assistant role can alleviate the high arousal state of pilots in the normal climb without fault scenario.

At the same time, the SCL of the SPO group pilots was significantly higher than that of the SPO-RIA group, with no significant effect on the SCR ($p > 0.05$). When a person is in a highly concentrated or tense state, an increase in SCL is considered a phenomenon of SNS excitation [41]. The inter-group difference in SCL during normal climb without fault further verifies that pilots without intelligent assistance are in a higher sympathetic arousal and stress level for a long time; while no difference was found in SCR, which might be due to the normal climb without fault being a routine task and not triggering a strong event-related stress response. The changes in HRV time-domain indicators and SCL physiological indices jointly indicate that cockpit intelligent assistance can reduce the physiological arousal level of pilots in SPO mode.

In addition, there was no significant difference in the average pupil diameter between the two groups of pilots ($p > 0.05$). As the workload decreases, the average blink time shows an upward trend, while the average pupil diameter shows a decreasing trend [42]. Pupil diameter changes are simultaneously regulated by cognitive demand and physiological arousal [32]: in the normal climb without fault flight task set in this study, pilots are always in a certain level of cognitive processing and attention load state, and the contribution of cognitive activity to pupil regulation is relatively prominent, to a certain extent masking or weakening the external manifestation of differences in physiological arousal levels in pupil indices.

However, the flight phase had no significant impact on the heart rate signal, skin conductance signal and eye movement signal indicators of the SPO-RIA group pilots ($p > 0.05$). Generally speaking, unexpected emergencies would increase HRV and pupil diameter [32, 43]. The reasons for this result might be that the selected scenarios were common items in pilot training, and the pilots were quite familiar with the handling procedures, thus not showing the expected arousal level; in the simulated cockpit, the pilots could not exhibit the real flight state; the experimental environment and individual differences affected the pilots' trust in the intelligent assistant role. Subjective evaluation is an important supplementary dimension of physiological arousal. In the future, the "calmness-excitement" dimension in the NASA-TLX scale can be combined to achieve a joint assessment of subjective and objective physiology, and further explore the impact of the flight phase on the pilots' arousal level under intelligent assistance.

5 Conclusion

By designing a simulated SPO task scenario and using physiological data, it was confirmed that the introduction of a cockpit intelligent assistant role can to some extent reduce the physiological arousal level of SPO pilots, thereby reducing their psychological load. However, after the intervention of the intelligent assistant, the physiological arousal level of pilots based on different flight phases is easily affected by other factors, and further verification is still needed.

The study of the physiological arousal level of pilots under different SPO operation frameworks can provide index references for the functional distribution of the SPO mode and future cockpit design, and offer a certain theoretical support for the future implementation of SPO.

Since the simulated cockpit scenarios in the experiment did not reach the real situation of the SPO cockpit, it needs to be further improved. In addition, more experimental scenarios and subjects should be added in subsequent studies to reduce the impact of experimental scenarios and individual differences on the experimental results.

Acknowledgments. We appreciate the support this work received from the Fundamental Research Funds for the Central Universities (grant no. XJ2024002702).

Disclosure of Interests. The authors have no competing interests to declare that are relevant to the content of this article.

References

1. Harris, D.: Single-pilot airline operations: designing the aircraft may be the easy part. Aeronaut. J. **127**(1313), 1171–1191 (2023)
2. Boeing. Commercial market outlook 2022–2041. https://www.boeing.com/content/dam/boeing/boeingdotcom/market/assets/downloads/CMO_2022_Report_FINAL_v02.pdf. 20 Jan 2026
3. Lutte, R.: An investigation of the United States airline pilot labour supply. J. Air Transp. Stud. **5**(2), 53–83 (2014)
4. Duggar, J.W., Smith, B.J., Harrison, J.: International supply and demand for US trained commercial airline pilots. J. Aviat. Manag. Educ. **1**(1), 16 (2011)
5. International Civil Aviation Organization. Global and regional 20-year forecasts: pilots, maintenance personnel, and air traffic controllers. ICAO, Montreal Canada (2011)
6. Xu, W., Chen, Y., Dong, W.J., Dong, W.Y., Ge, L.Z.: Progress and prospect of human factor engineering research on single pilot piloting of large commercial aircraft. Aeronaut. Eng. Progress **13**(1), 1–18 (2022). (in Chinese)
7. Comerford, D., et al.: Nasa's single-pilot operations technical interchange meeting: proceedings and findings. NASA, Moffett field (2013)

8. Bilimoria, K.D., Johnson, W.W., Schutte, P.C.: Conceptual framework for single pilot operations. In: Proceedings of the International Conference on Human-Computer Interaction in Aerospace, New York, USA, pp. 1–8 (2014)
9. Neis, S.M., Klingauf, U., Schiefele, J.: Classification and review of conceptual frameworks for commercial single pilot operations. In: 2018 IEEE/AIAA 37th Digital Avionics Systems Conference (DASC), London, UK, pp. 1–8 (2018)
10. De Sant, D., De Hilal, A.: The impact of human factors on pilots' safety behavior in offshore aviation companies: a Brazilian case. Saf. Sci. **140**, 105272 (2021)
11. Harris, D.: A human-centred design agenda for the development of single crew operated commercial aircraft. Aircr. Eng. Aerosp. Technol. **79**(5), 518–526 (2007)
12. Brandt, S.L., Lachter, J., Battiste, V., Johnson, W.: Pilot situation awareness and its implications for single pilot operations: analysis of a human-in-the-loop study. Procedia Manufact. **3**, 3017–3024 (2015)
13. Matessa, M., Strybel, T., Vu, K., Battiste, V., Schnell, T.: Concept of operations for RCO SPO. NASA, Washington DC, USA (2017)
14. Xu, W.: User centered design (VII): from automated to intelligent flight deck. Chin. J. Appl. Psychol. **28**(4), 291–313 (2022)
15. Lean, Y., Fu, S.: Brief review on physiological and biochemical evaluations of human mental workload. Hum. Fact. Ergon. Manuf. Serv. Ind. **22**(3), 177–187 (2012)
16. Schutte, P.C., et al.: The naturalistic flight deck system: an integrated system concept for improved single-pilot operations. NASA/TM-2007-215090. NASA Langley Research Center, NTRS, US (2007)
17. European Commission: Advanced cockpit for reduction of stress and work-load. https://trimis.ec.europa.eu/project/advanced-cockpit-reduction-stress-and-workload. 20 Jan 2026
18. Zhang, X.M., Yu, Z.W., Yang, Y.Q.: Application and consideration to Boeing 787 influenced by artificial intelligence. Ind. Eng. Manag. **22**(6), 169–174 (2017)
19. Duan, L.: Cockpit human-machine interface evolution and development trend. Civil Aircr. Des. Res. **1**, 7–11 (2017)
20. International Air Transport Association: IATA annual safety report addendum and appendices first half year 2024. International Air Transport Association, Montreal, Canada (2025)
21. Odink, J., Wientjes, C.J.E., Thissen, J.T.N.M., Van Der Beek, E.J., Kramer, F.M.: Type a behaviour, borderline hyperventilation and psychological, psychosomatic and neuroendocrine responses to mental task load. Biol. Psychol. **25**(2), 107–118 (1987)
22. Charles, R.L., Nixon, J.: Measuring mental workload using physiological measures: a systematic review. Appl. Ergon. **74**, 221–232 (2019)
23. Wang, L., Wang, S., Zou, Y., Zhang, M.X., Wu, J.J., Li, S.: A study on airline pilots' mental workload characteristics based on task situation. J. Saf. Environ. **23**(4), 1202–1208 (2023)
24. Wang, L., Gao, S.: Study on eye movement and physiological characteristics of flying risk-taking behaviors. China Saf. Sci. J. **30**(9), 22–28 (2020)
25. Kerr, N.H., Tacon, P.: Psychological responses to different types of locations and activities. J. Environ. Psychol. **19**(3), 287–294 (1999)
26. Bradley, M.M., Miccoli, L., Escrig, M.A., Lang, P.J.: The pupil as a measure of emotional arousal and autonomic activation. Psychophysiology **45**(4), 602–607 (2008)
27. Mathôt, S.: Pupillometry: psychology, physiology, and function. J. Cogn. **1**(1), 16 (2018)
28. Weissman, D.G., Guyer, A.E., Ferrer, E., Robins, R.W., Hastings, P.D.: Adolescents' brain-autonomic coupling during emotion processing. Neuro Image **183**, 818–827 (2018)
29. Jerčić, P., Sennersten, C., Lindley, C.: Modeling cognitive load and physiological arousal through pupil diameter and heart rate. Multimedia Tools Appl. **79**(5), 3145–3159 (2020)
30. He, X., Wang, L., Gao, X., Chen, Y.: The eye activity measurement of mental workload based on basic flight task. In: Proceedings of IEEE 10th International Conference on Industrial Informatics, Piscataway, NJ, pp. 502–507 (2012)

31. Laeng, B., Sirois, S., Gredebäck, G.: Pupillometry: a window to the preconscious? Perspect. Psychol. Sci. **7**(1), 18–27 (2012)
32. Kinney, L., O'Hare, D.: Responding to an unexpected in-flight event: physiological arousal, information processing, and performance. Hum. Fact. J. Hum. Fact. Ergon. Soc. **62**(5), 737–750 (2020)
33. Davidoff, A., Vonderhaar, L., Caldwell, A., Procko, T., Ochoa, O.: Role, needs, and state of cognitive assistants in single-pilot operations. J. Aerosp. Inf. Syst. **21**(12), 1014–1024 (2024)
34. Park, J., Seok, H.S., Kim, S.S., Shin, H.: Photoplethysmogram analysis and applications: an integrative review. Front. Physiol. **12**, 808451 (2022)
35. Lim, C.L., et al.: Decomposing skin conductance into tonic and phasic components. Int. J. Psychophysiol. **25**(2), 97–109 (1997)
36. Heine, T., Lenis, G., Reichensperger, P., Beran, T., Doessel, O., Deml, B.: Electrocardiographic features for the measurement of drivers' mental workload. Appl. Ergon. **61**, 31–43 (2017)
37. Wang, G.H., Stein, P., Brown, V.W.: Brainstem reticular system and galvanic skin reflex in acute decerebrate cats. J. Neurophysiol. **19**(4), 350 (1956)
38. Lowe, D.G.: Distinctive image features from scale-invariant keypoints. Int. J. Comput. Vision **60**(2), 91–110 (2004)
39. Bellato, A., Arora, I., Hollis, C., Groom, M.J.: Is autonomic nervous system function atypical in attention deficit hyperactivity disorder (ADHD)? A systematic review of the evidence. Neurosci. Biobehav. Rev. **108**, 182–206 (2020)
40. Zou, D., Li, H., Wang, F.S.: An investigation into the definition of arousal and its cognitive neurophysiological basis. Adv. Psychol. Sci. **30**(9), 2020–2033 (2022)
41. Braithwaite, J.J., Watson, D.G., Jones, R., Rowe, M.: A guide for analyzing electrodermal activity (EDA) & skin conductance responses (SCR) for psychological experiments. Psychophysiology **49**, 1017–1034 (2013)
42. Feng, C.Y., Wanyan, X.R., Yang, K., Zhuang, D.M., Wu, X.: A comprehensive prediction and evaluation method of pilot workload. Technol. Health Care **26**(S1), 65–78 (2018)
43. Canales-Johnson, A., et al.: Decreased alertness reconfigures cognitive control networks. J. Neurosci. **40**, 7142–7154 (2020)

Exploring Commercial Pilots' Need for Transparency in Aircraft Cockpit with AI-Integration

Lanyun Zhang[1](✉), Yihong Liu[1], Qiuyuan Jing[1], Lin Zhang[2], Zhenxing Qi[3], and Xuchen Wang[4]

[1] Nanjing University of Aeronautics and Astronautics, 29 Yudao Street, Nanjing 210016, People's Republic of China
lanyunzhang@nuaa.edu.cn
[2] Civil Aviation Shanghai Hospital, 1448 Hongqiao Street, Shanghai 200336, People's Republic of China
[3] Xiamen Airlines, 321 Donghuang Street, Xiamen 361006, People's Republic of China
[4] Xi'an Jiaotong-Liverpool University, 111 Ren'ai Road, Suzhou 215123, People's Republic of China

Abstract. With the wide application of automation technology and heated discussion about artificial intelligence (AI) in aviation, the execution of flight mission is shifting from human-centered mode to human-machine collaboration. It is important to investigate how AI can be effectively integrated into the flight decision-making process without diminishing pilots' situational awareness or proactive decision-making capabilities. This study aimed to focus on exploring the need for transparency in AI-integrated aviation from commercial pilots' perspective. This study employed semi-structured interviews with fourteen experienced pilots. A thematic analysis of the interview recordings was conducted using NVivo. Five needs for transparency were found: system and state monitoring, information presentation and communication, decision-making and prediction, information integration and task planning, and human-computer collaboration and adaption. Further, three types of need for transparency were summarized: comprehensive and transparent information feedback, real-time and predictive feedback, and personalized and adaptive feedback. This study also revealed limitations in the applicability of existing transparency frameworks: IEEE 7001 and SAT, to explore how the two well-established frameworks can explain the need for transparency found in this study.

Keywords: Transparency · Aviation Cockpit · AI-integration · Commercial Pilot

1 Introduction

With the wide application of automation technology and heated discussion about artificial intelligence (AI) in aviation, the execution of flight mission is shifting from human-centered mode to human-machine collaboration. The automation systems are gradually

W. -C. Li and A. Plioutsias (Eds.): HCII 2026, LNAI 16708, pp. 352–366, 2026.
https://doi.org/10.1007/978-3-032-29459-3_23

evolving from passive monitors to proactive teammates in the cockpit [1]. Although this significantly improves operational efficiency and safety, it also brings concerns such as information mismatch and cognitive differences between pilots and the system [2].

Information transparency is essential in human-computer interaction and the key to connecting human pilots and machines [3]. Its suitable configuration under different levels of automation directly affects pilot's situational awareness, trust, and decision-making quality. Insufficient transparency may prevent pilots from accurately understanding the system's intentions, thereby causing them to miss critical opportunities for intervention. Conversely, excessive transparency can result in information overload and reduced decision-making efficiency [3]. Consequently, achieving an appropriate balance between automation level and transparency level has become a key research focus in aircraft cockpit design, especially with the increase of AI in aviation. Therefore, this study aims to investigate pilots' requirements for transparency under increasing levels of automation such as AI-integration.

Currently, the most widely used frameworks that describe the transparency in human-computer interaction are the IEEE 7001 standard [4] and the situational awareness transparency (SAT) framework [5]. The IEEE 7001 standard emphasizes information requirements and compliance across a system's entire life cycle, whereas the SAT framework is grounded in situational awareness theory. They provide theoretical foundations for research, yet they are not proposed in the context of aviation. Therefore, they may not be fully applicable to the human-machine systems in modern aviation. Accordingly, the second objective of this study is to examine the applicability of the two transparency frameworks in the context of aircraft cockpit.

The bigger picture of this study is to investigate how AI can be effectively integrated into the flight decision-making process without diminishing pilots' situational awareness or proactive decision-making capabilities. This study aims to focus on exploring the need for transparency in aviation from commercial pilots' perspective. There are two objectives:

- To explore pilots' need for transparency in AI-integrated automated systems, an area that has received limited attention in existing research.
- To examine the applicability of two well-established transparency frameworks, e.g. IEEE 7001 and Situation Awareness Transparency (SAT), in describing the transparency needs identified in this study within the aviation context.

2 Background and Related Work

This section introduces related work in three parts: AI-integration in aircraft cockpit, need for transparency in aviation, and aim of this research.

2.1 AI-Integration in Aircraft Cockpit

Automation with AI-integration does not simply imply the replacement of human operators by machines; rather, it represents a functional allocation and coordination between humans and automated systems. Such systems are often viewed as extensions of human cognitive capabilities, with the primary objective of supporting operators in maintaining and enhancing situation awareness (SA), rather than diminishing human understanding or control of system states [6]. Situational awareness (SA) refers to knowing what's going on, understanding the meanings, and anticipating what will happen next, especially in dynamic, high-risk environments like aviation, healthcare, driving, or military operations [7]. It is commonly conceptualized as comprising three levels: the perception of elements in the environment, the comprehension of their meaning, and the projection of their future status [8].

In recent years, AI-assisted decision-making has been widely studied in fields such as medicine and autonomous driving. In the medical domain, AI is primarily implemented through Clinical Decision Support Systems (CDSS) to assist clinicians with diagnosis, risk assessment, and treatment selection [9]. Studies have shown that AI can enhance diagnostic efficiency and accuracy by analyzing medical images and patient cases in real time [10]. More recently, research has increasingly focused on Explainable Artificial Intelligence (XAI), which aims to improve system transparency and user trust by providing clear explanations of AI decision-making processes [11].

AI-Integration in Related Domains. In the field of autonomous driving, AI is extensively used for environmental perception, path planning, and decision support [12]. AI enables vehicles to perceive the environment and make real-time decisions through computer vision, sensor fusion, and predictive algorithms. For example, companies such as Tesla and Waymo have made substantial progress by leveraging AI to perform lane keeping, collision avoidance, pedestrian detection, and adaptive cruise control [13]. However, despite these technological advances, higher levels of automation do not necessarily guarantee safety; they may reduce driver attention and situational awareness [14, 15]. Consequently, research has increasingly emphasized shared control and human-centered AI design, including explainable AI, which focuses on communicating system intent, risk assessment, and predictions of future behavior to drivers via the interface to maintain user understanding and trust [16]. For instance, Morra et al. demonstrated that presenting shared paths on visual displays and providing explanations for system decisions can enhance drivers' trust in autonomous vehicles [17].

AI-Integration in Aviation. In the aircraft cockpit, AI is expected to be applied to fields such as flight decision support, system status monitoring, and risk prediction. With advances in onboard sensors and data acquisition capabilities, AI is increasingly used to analyze the operational status of aircraft systems. For example, AI can integrate multi-source flight data to detect anomalies and trigger alerts [19]. These applications enhance both the perceptibility and safety of system operations.

Specifically, AI as a decision-support tool has been explored in many studies in aviation. Compared with traditional decision support tools, AI systems emphasize comprehensive analysis of complex flight situations. Studies have proposed the concept of an intelligent co-pilot to provide decision support in high-demand scenarios. For example, in emergencies such as engine failure, the Xavion system combines factors including aircraft altitude, estimated arrival time, and remaining fuel to recommend runways that enable safer landings, thereby assisting pilots in making rapid decisions [20].

Beyond single-instance decision-making, research has also examined AI's ability to integrate information and compare alternatives in complex flight situations. Angela et al.

investigated AI-assisted systems for in-flight diversion and alternate airport selection through interviews and prototype evaluation. Their system supports pilots in comparing multiple alternate landing options, and the results demonstrated its effectiveness under high workload conditions [21]. Similarly, Würfel et al. proposed the concept of an intelligent pilot consultation system, emphasizing that AI should present analysis results and recommendations in an interpretable manner to support decision-making during emergencies [22]. These studies highlight the growing emphasis on transparency and interpretability in aviation human factors research. Additionally, Zhang et al. compared two AI decision-support approaches in flight operations: a traditional recommendation-centered method and a continuous support method. The continuous support approach provides pilots with decision-relevant information throughout normal flight phases rather than delivering final recommendations only during emergencies, thereby enhancing situational awareness and decision-making [23].

Overall, existing research on AI-integrated systems has mainly focused on recommendation-centered decision support, in which the system generates decision suggestions or candidate solutions and the pilot evaluates and selects among them. Such systems primarily support decision outcomes while often omitting the decision-making process that leads to those outcomes [18, 24]. Consequently, how to effectively integrate AI into the flight decision-making process without diminishing pilots' situational awareness or proactive decision-making capabilities remains an open question that warrants further investigation.

2.2 Need for Transparency in Aircraft Cockpit

Frameworks of Transparency. In the field of the transparency of automated systems, theoretical frameworks generally fall into two categories: information hierarchy-based transparency frameworks (e.g., IEEE 7001) and situation awareness-based transparency frameworks (SAT). IEEE 7001 [4] starts from the hierarchical structure of information presented by the system to the user, classifying information content across different levels of transparency. SAT [5], grounded in situation awareness theory, links system transparency to the user's understanding of a system's state, intentions, and future behavior. Building on these two frameworks, we tried to extend the definitions and applications of IEEE 7001 and SAT to aviation domain, see details in Tables 1 for IEEE 7001 and Table 2 for SAT.

Exploration of Transparency in General. Beyond the aviation sector, transparency has been widely studied and applied in domains with safety requirements, uncertainties, and risk factors, such as autonomous driving, medical decision support, smart manufacturing, and financial risk control. Prior research indicates that, in high-risk automated systems, appropriate levels of information transparency help users develop calibrated trust, thereby avoiding both over-reliance on and unwarranted avoidance of automation. For example, in the field of autonomous driving, researchers have explored the idea of explaining decision-making logics to users to support drivers' understanding of system behavior and to further facilitate takeovers when necessary. Such explanatory designs not only improve drivers' comprehension of automation but also enhance their perceived system reliability. In the medical domain, transparency research emphasizes the

Table 1. IEEE 7001 framework and its adaptation in aviation.

level	IEEE 7001 Definition	Adaptation in aviation
0 (lowest)	No transparency	No transparency
1	The user shall be provided with accessible information	Pilots can obtain key information from the cockpit automation system in a clear, timely, and intuitive manner
2	The user shall be provided with interactive training material	Transparency is practiced through pilots' routine simulator training
3	Produces a brief and immediate explanation of the system's most recent activity under requests	Pilots can quickly access explanations for current alarms or commands generated by the automation system, with requests
4	Produces a brief and immediate explanation of what the system does under requests	The automation system can predict future states and provide operators with advance information under requests
5 (highest)	The user shall be provided with a continuous explanation of behavior without requesting	The automation system continuously provides information about current states and future predictions, dynamically adapting both the content and presentation of information to pilot needs and the flight environment

Table 2. SAT framework and its adaptation in aviation.

level	SAT Definition	Adaptation in aviation
1 (lowest)	Automation's goals/status/actions/plans	Present the pilot with information about the automation system's goals, status, actions, and environmental perceptions
2	Automation's reasoning process/explanations	Present the automation system's decision-making process, environmental constraints, and underlying logic
3 (highest)	Automation's projections/predictions; uncertainty	Provide information on predicted future actions, risk assessments, and uncertainties

explanation of diagnostic criteria, data sources, and associated uncertainties to support clinicians' final decision-making, which reflects the concept of explainable AI.

In summary, these studies collectively demonstrate that transparency is not merely a matter of increasing information quantity; rather, it involves *selective information presentation* constrained by factors such as task demands, time pressure, and users' cognitive load. Therefore, transparency should be designed to meet specific requirements under certain situation.

Related Work of Transparency in Aircraft Cockpit. In the aviation industry, information transparency refers to the clarity and explainability of operational information, system states, and the underlying basis for system decisions as presented to pilots by flight control systems. As such, information transparency is critical to pilots' decision-making, emergency response, and trust in the system.

Highly transparent aviation interfaces can effectively enhance pilots' trust in automated systems and reduce operational errors. In highly automated environments, pilots who understand the decision-making processes of automated systems are more likely to intervene better during emergencies. Moreover, transparent information enables pilots to quickly identify the root causes of problems and take timely corrective actions.

Clear system status displays and operational feedback can significantly improve pilots' emergency response performance. During normal flight operations, effective collaboration among pilots, co-pilots, air traffic controllers, and other operators also depends on transparent information sharing. By communicating aircraft status, route selections, and other relevant data, flight crews can achieve more efficient coordination and teamwork.

While transparency is essential for ensuring aviation safety, careful attention must be paid to the potential risks and challenges associated with excessive transparency. Presenting too much information simultaneously can lead to cognitive overload. Moreover, excessive transparency may encourage over-reliance on automation, potentially reducing pilots' situational awareness and leading to insufficient intervention at critical moments. Therefore, a key challenge in system design is achieving an appropriate balance between transparency and automation.

2.3 Aim of Research

While information transparency has become an important topic in human-computer interaction, existing studies are still largely grounded in general systems. Little has focused on aviation. Specifically, the civil aviation cockpit constitutes a highly complex operational environment characterized by stringent safety requirements, severe time constraints, and teamwork. Pilots' interactions with automated systems exhibit domain-specific characteristics. There is a lack of research on pilots' perceptions of the need for transparency in automative cockpits, especially with the AI integration. Further, it remains unknown whether mainstream transparency frameworks (e.g., IEEE 7001 and SAT) can effectively describe the need. Overall, limited research has focused on exploring the insights of pilots' need for transparency under AI-integrated automation, such as *what* information should be presented, *how* it should be presented, and *at which stages* of decision-making. To address the research gap, this paper draws on semi-structured interviews with 14 in-service commercial pilots to collect their needs for transparency of cockpit automation systems.

3 Method

3.1 Study Design

This study employs a semi-structured interview design to investigate pilots' needs for transparency in AI-integrated automated cockpits and to further examine the applicability of IEEE 7001 and SAT frameworks in aviation contexts. To ensure question clarity and the authenticity of participants' responses, a progressive inquiry approach is adopted, guiding participants to recall and describe flight scenarios and their interactions with automated systems. Then, questions about needs for transparency were asked.

Based on the interview data, the study synthesizes pilots' requirements for transparency across different levels of automation and how pilots understand and process system feedback in AI-integrated automated environments. In parallel, the study evaluates the compatibility and limitations of existing transparency frameworks, particularly IEEE 7001 and SAT, in this context.

3.2 Participants

This study interviewed 14 experienced pilots (all male), with a mean age of 37.3 years and an average total flight time of 8,732.8 h. All participants were currently employed by Xiamen Airlines, including 11 captains (seven of whom were captain instructors) and three first officers. The aircraft types operated by the participants included the Boeing 737 series (700, 800, and MAX variants), Boeing 787, and Airbus A320 and A321, thereby ensuring a diverse and representative sample. Ethical approval was obtained prior to the commencement of the study, and all participants provided written informed consent after receiving relevant study information. The research procedures were reviewed and approved by the ethics committee, ensuring compliance with ethical standards and the protection of participants' rights. Detailed participant information is presented in Table 3.

Table 3. Participant information.

No	Age	Total flying hours	Models of aircraft flying	Rank
01	38	11000	B737	Captain and instructor
02	35	5100	B737	Captain
03	31	3000	B737	First officer
04	34	3500	B737-700/800/max	First officer
05	42	14000	A321	Captain and instructor
06	46	17000	B737, A321	Captain and instructor
07	41	11000	A321	First officer
08	40	11000	A321	Captain
09	40	11000	B737, A320	Captain and instructor
10	33	7500	A320	Captain

(continued)

Table 3. (*continued*)

No	Age	Total flying hours	Models of aircraft flying	Rank
11	37	7200	A320	Captain and instructor
12	37	9000	B737, A320	Captain and instructor
13	36	8300	B737, A321, B787	Captain and instructor
14	33	6000	A321	Captain

3.3 Study Procedure

After signing the consent form, the study's purpose and background were explained to each participant, emphasizing that the research aimed to investigate pilots' decision-making processes, cognitive responses, and transparency needs in AI-integrated automated flight environments. Participants were instructed to answer questions related to decision-making, cognitive activities, and need for transparency during flight based on their real-world operational experience and flight scenarios.

The interview procedure was structured as follows. First, participants were asked to recall and describe memorable aircraft automation functions and their application in actual flight operations, with a particular focus on the current design of transparency. Subsequently, a semi-structured interview format was employed to explore these topics in greater depth. The detailed interview outline is presented in Table 4.

Table 4. Interview structure.

No	Topic	Question
1	Functions and levels of automation	The assistance provided by the current cockpit automation system
2		Call-out assistance among crew members
3		What types of assistance does the intelligent system provide?
4	Task allocation and human-computer interaction	Tasks accomplished in collaboration with automation
5		The role allocation between the intelligent system and the pilot
6		Compared to automated systems, what are the strengths and weaknesses of pilots?
7	Changes in trust levels	Level of trust in the automation system
8		The level of trust in the intelligent system
9	Transparency and interaction modes	Interaction with the automation system
10		Are new interaction methods emerging?

(*continued*)

Table 4. (*continued*)

No	Topic	Question
11	Information presentation and decision support	Will the introduction of the intelligent system bring new challenges?
12		Amount of information provided by the automation system
13		Will these strengths and weaknesses change with increased information volume?
14	How transparency influences situational awareness	The purpose of inter-crew communication
15		Will standard communication between flight crews be affected by the assistance of the intelligent system?

3.4 Data Collection and Analysis

All interviews were audio-recorded, with key points noted during the sessions. After transcription, NVivo software was used for systematic data organization and analysis. First, the interview transcripts were imported into an NVivo project, and separate nodes were created for each participant to facilitate data management and subsequent analysis. The transcripts were then reviewed in detail, and key information was extracted from each segment to generate initial codes. These codes were developed around themes such as the support provided by automation, pilots' concerns regarding automated systems, changes in trust in automation, factors contributing to increased workload during flight, the respective advantages and limitations of human pilots and automated systems, the current use of cockpit automation, and anticipated future developments. The initial codes, derived from the topics in the interview structure, provided a foundation for subsequent analysis and categorization.

4 Results

Overall, 22 comments regarding the requirements for transparency were collected. This study extracted five needs for transparency: system and state monitoring, information presentation and communication, decision-making and prediction, information integration and task planning, and human-computer collaboration and adaption.

1. System and state monitoring. Automated systems should possess robust monitoring capabilities in terms of system and aircraft state, particularly for assessing the status of various aircraft subsystems. For example, pilots expressed a desire for the system to proactively predict low fuel conditions and issue timely warnings to support appropriate action (e.g., "*The aircraft's fuel level is low. Can you provide a warning immediately*?"). In addition, five participants indicated that the system should be able to accurately identify faulty components to enable rapid intervention (e.g., "*precisely determining which component is malfunct*ioning").

When confronted with conflicting checklist recommendations, pilots also expected the system to assist in diagnosing the source of the discrepancy (e.g., "If the checklist offers conflicting recommendations, could the computer help us pinpoint the error?"). For common abnormal situations, such as engine failures, pilots further expressed the need for standardized handling guidance (e.g., "The system should provide standardized handling for specific recurring malfunctions, such as engine failure"). Finally, pilots highlighted the importance of clear alerts for abnormal conditions, including exceedances of thrust limits, deviations from expected parameters, or the presentation of salient visual cues to attract attention (e.g., "exceeding thrust limits, deviating from expected values, or displaying a new line of information to draw attention").

2. Information presentation and communication. The information presentation and communication adopted by automated systems should align as closely as possible with their natural communication among flight crews. In other words, large language models should be effectively integrated into the information communication. One interviewee noted that the system should be able to "*directly tell me what the current status is and what I need to do in the language of our daily communication,*" enabling pilots to quickly grasp critical information and take appropriate action under high workload conditions.

In addition, three participants suggested that automated systems should integrate external information sources more, such as by transmitting air traffic control instructions into the cockpit in a structured form. As one pilot explained, "the controller's instructions, or rather, through some codes, can be sent directly to the aircraft", which could lower the risk of misunderstanding or delays in information transmission by pilots.

3. Decision-making and prediction. Automated systems should possess strong predictive assistance and decision-support features to help manage complex and uncertain flight scenarios. Five pilots expressed the expectation that the system could proactively identify potential weather-related changes during flight, such as by "*judging the weather outside to see if there's a risk of lightning strikes.*"

Some participants further noted that when facing uncertain weather conditions, the system should be able to comprehensively assess multiple attributes, such as destination weather changes, feasibility of alternate airports, and remaining fuel. So, the system can provide with integrated decision support (e.g., "*Will the weather be good when I arrive? If not, where should I alternate? And will I have enough fuel?*"). Some participants emphasized that automated systems should not only present current weather conditions but also predict future weather to support more informed decision-making, such as "*accurately telling me the weather prediction about my destination around my arrival time and suggesting that, if the weather conditions do not improve, I can or cannot continue flying.*"

In addition, several pilots indicated that under complex weather conditions, the integration of real-time radar data with intelligent analysis to generate recommended diversion routes would significantly reduce their mental workload (e.g., "I would really like the system to provide me with real-time radar scanning, weather image comparison, and then AI can intervene to analyze and tell me the best detour route").

4. Information integration and task planning. Automation systems should be able to integrate information from different sources and mission-planning for pilots to provide more comprehensive and accurate decision support. For instance, six participants expressed a desire for systems to present all critical information holistically, to avoid the omission of critical factors that could influence decision-making.

In addition, pilots expected automated systems to demonstrate robust analytical capabilities by generating multiple optional solutions based on the current circumstance (e.g., "*I need the system to be able to analyze information from all its sources and generate multiple solutions to me. Maybe it can finally calculate a best solution for me*"). Two participants further noted that systems should be able to filter out irrelevant information to help pilots focus on the most critical elements (e.g., "*I need the system to directly filter out useless information for me, so I won't lose focus*"). Finally, pilots emphasized the importance of real-time information delivery to support timely adjustments to decisions.

5. Human-computer collaboration and adaption. Effective human-machine collaboration and adaptive information support were required. Pilots indicated a strong expectation for systems to adapt to individual needs and provide personalized information displays. For example, one participant noted that for less experienced pilots, automated systems should provide a broader range of suggestions to facilitate safer decision-making, which may not be necessary for experienced pilots.

Three participants expressed their desires for more detailed information in uncertain situations, stating that they should be able to select the level of detail provided by the system (e.g., "*I can choose the level of detail in the information it provides. My confidence level may change and I might need more details if I'm less confident about a problem.*").

Overall, based on the interview, pilots' requirements for transparency in automated systems primarily centered on the following themes: status monitoring and recognition, information presentation and communication, predictive assistance and decision support, information integration and mission planning, as well as human-machine collaboration and adaptive information provision. These findings provide in-depth insights into current commercial pilots' views on transparency and provide valuable guidance for the development of automated cockpit systems in the future.

5 Discussion

This section discusses the types of pilots' need for transparency and applicability of well-established transparency models in this context.

5.1 Pilot's Need for Transparency

In this study, three types of needs for transparency are summarized among commercial pilots. The three categories of needs are: comprehensive and transparent information feedback, real-time and predictive feedback, and personalized and adaptive feedback.

1. The need for comprehensive and transparent information feedback. With the increasing integration of intelligent and automated systems, pilots seek more than basic flight status information (e.g. speed, altitude, and fuel level) to include more advanced feedback, such as systems being able to explain their decision-making processes and underlying logic. Pilots require automated systems to clearly articulate why specific actions or decisions are taken and to provide sufficient contextual information to support pilots' understanding of system behavior.

For example, when flight paths are adjusted automatically, pilots expect the system to explain the rationale for the adjustment and the anticipated outcomes (e.g., "They can judge whether there is a risk of lightning strikes based on the weather conditions outside."). This expectation underscores that pilots value not only operational feedback, but also transparency in decision-making logic and risk assessment.

2. The need for real-time and predictive feedback. AI-integrated automated systems lead pilots to rely more on decision-support functions during tasks and emergency situations. Pilots expect automated systems to provide real-time and predictive feedback, particularly when responding to unforeseen events. This need is to provide pilots with continuous information updates, which are related to predicting a future situation. For example, pilots expect the systems to predict weather changes and the business of landing-site for when the aircraft is planning to land in about 1 h. So, the pilots can assess the appropriate diversion options.
3. The need for personalized and adaptive feedback. Pilots' levels of experience significantly influence their needs for transparency. More experienced pilots tend to prefer concise, high-level information, whereas less experienced pilots require greater detail and guidance. Accordingly, pilots expect automated systems to tailor information presentation to individual needs by providing adjustable levels of details. This demand for personalization reflects pilots' expectations for transparency in AI-integrated automated environments, in other words, to maintain clarity and conciseness while ensuring sufficient detailed information support at critical moments.

5.2 Applicability of Two Transparency Frameworks

In this study, two transparency frameworks were explored in terms of their applicability to describe the pilots' needs for transparency found in this study. This section elaborates the limitations of IEEE 7001 and SAT frameworks in this context.

1. IEEE 7001 cannot fully cover the requirements of pilots. According to the IEEE 7001 standard, the five levels of transparency (TL1-TL5) are intended to represent a progression from basic information presentation to intelligent and adaptive feedback. However, none of the pilots interviewed expressed a need to actively query system information. In other words, all information, regardless of the level of transparency, should be shown to pilots without waiting for pilots to activate. Therefore, the description of TL3 and TL4 in IEEE 7001 are not fully applicable to this scenario.

Moreover, TL1 and TL2 primarily emphasize reading documentation and training-related requirements. Such content is largely irrelevant to pilots' real-time operational needs during flight tasks. In terms of TL5, although some interview findings align with some aspects of TL5 (e.g. the system proactively and continuously providing explanations), TL5 requires the fulfilment of transparency levels TL1-TL4 as formal preconditions.

Consequently, the IEEE 7001 framework appears insufficient to fully capture or accommodate the transparency needs identified in this study, particularly given pilots' reliance on proactive rather than user-initiated information provision. In addition, while TL5 emphasizes on-demand and adaptive feedback, pilots consistently described a preference for continuous and automatic system feedback during operations, which stands in contrast to the on-demand feature of TL5.

SAT is more applicable compared to IEEE 7001 in this context. The situation awareness-based transparency (SAT) framework is more suitable to describe pilots' needs for transparency found in this study. However, it also exhibits challenges, particularly with respect to uncertainty prediction and the presentation of future-oriented information. Specifically, SAT Level 1 requires systems to share the goals with the human to make sure that both systems and humans are on the same page. However, the participants in this study did not mention this need, presumably by the fact that the goals are centered on flight safety. SAT Level 3 requires systems to provide projections of future states and associated uncertainties. The description of this level is mostly aligned with the findings of this study. Yet the participants also expressed the need for real-time reflection of futuristic information, that is omitted by Level 3.

6 Conclusions, Limitations, and Future Work

6.1 Conclusions

Through a semi-structured interview approach, this study identified pilots' core needs for transparency in automated cockpits with AI-integration in the future. Five needs for transparency include: system and state monitoring, information presentation and communication, decision-making and prediction, information integration and task planning, and human-computer collaboration and adaption. Further, three types of need for transparency were summarized: comprehensive and transparent information feedback, real-time and predictive feedback, and personalized and adaptive feedback.

Then, the study revealed limitations in the applicability of existing transparency frameworks: IEEE 7001 and SAT, to explore how the two well-established frameworks can explain the need for transparency found in this study. Specifically, TL1 and TL2 in IEEE 7001 model focus on reading documentations and training-oriented transparency, which are less relevant to the context of real-time aircraft operation. TL3 and TL4 describe closer to the findings of this work, but more focus on providing information after human proactively request it. Overall, IEEE 7001 illustrates poor applicability to describe the needs for transparency in aircraft cockpit. On the contrary, SAT model is more suitable in this context.

The main contributions of this study are summarized in two aspects:

1. This study explored the commercial pilots' needs for transparency in AI-integrated cockpit, in terms of five needs and three types of needs. This work provides fundamental evidence for how transparency is viewed by pilots and can potentially guide the design of AI-integrated cockpits in the future.

2. This study explored the applicability of two well-established frameworks of transparency theory, i.e. IEEE 7001 and SAT, to describe the needs for transparency found in this work, in the context of aviation. This work examined and challenged the theories and models of transparency in aviation, which expanded the research of transparency in practice.

6.2 Limitations and Future Work

This study has several limitations. First, the participant sample consisted solely of male pilots from a single airline. Although multiple aircraft types were represented, the sample cannot fully capture the diversity of civil aviation operations. Second, the interview-based methodology may be subjective to personal memory. Future research could address these limitations by expanding the sample size, incorporating flight simulation experiments and employing multi-source data triangulation.

Acknowledgements. This work is supported in part by China Aeronautical Science Foundation (2024Z050052003), in part by Philosophy and Social Sciences Research of Jiangsu Universities (2024SJYB0017), in part by Humanity and Social Science Foundation of Ministry of Education (22YJEZH002), in part by Jiangsu Key Laboratory of Bionic Materials and Equipment, and in part by Safety Capacity Project of China Civil Aviation Administration (2024-121).

References

1. Sellen, A., Horvitz, E.: The rise of the AI co-pilot: lessons for design from aviation and beyond. Commun. ACM **67**(7), 18–23 (2024)
2. Mohan, A., Simonovic, B., Vione, C.K., Stupple, E.: Examining flight time, cognitive reflection, workload, stress and metacognition on decision making performance for pilots during flight simulation. Ergonomics **68**(8), 1335–1347 (2025)
3. Bhaskara, A., Skinner, M., Loft, S.: Agent transparency: a review of current theory and evidence. IEEE Trans. Hum.-Mach. Syst. **50**(3), 215–224 (2020)
4. IEEE Standards Association: IEEE standard for transparency of autonomous systems. IEEE Std 7001, 1–49 (2022)
5. Chen, J.Y., Lakhmani, S.G., Stowers, K., Selkowitz, A.R., Wright, J.L., Barnes, M.: Situation awareness-based agent transparency and human-autonomy teaming effectiveness. Theor. Issues Ergon. Sci. **19**(3), 259–282 (2018)
6. Endsley, M.R.: Automation and Situation Awareness. Automation and Human Performance, pp. 163–181. CRC Press (2018)
7. Endsley, M.R.: Design and evaluation for situation awareness enhancement. Proc. Hum. Fact. Soc. Ann. Meet. **32**(2), 97–101 (1988)
8. Endsley, M.R.: A taxonomy of situation awareness errors. Hum. Fact. Aviat. Oper. **3**(2), 287–292 (1995)
9. Ahmed, Z., Mohamed, K., Zeeshan, S., Dong, X.: Artificial intelligence with multi-functional machine learning platform development for better healthcare and precision medicine. Database **2020**, baaa010 (2020)
10. Bertsimas, D., Margonis, G.A.: Explainable vs. interpretable artificial intelligence frameworks in oncology. Transl. Cancer Res. **12**(2), 217 (2023)

11. Abbas, Q., Jeong, W., Lee, S.W.: Explainable AI in clinical decision support systems: a meta-analysis of methods, applications, and usability challenges. Healthcare **13**(17), 2154 (2025)
12. Gaul, S., Gade, D., Deshmukh, M., Jorwekar, K., Jamdar, A., Dhumase, S.: A comprehensive study of AI integration in perception and decision-making for autonomous vehicles (2025)
13. Pandey, K.: Artificial intelligence (AI) in electric vehicle ecosystems: challenges, opportunities, and models for accelerated adoption. Int. J. Appl. Sci. Eng. Rev. **5**, 1–19 (2024)
14. Merat, N., et al.: The "Out-of-the-Loop" concept in automated driving: proposed definition, measures and implications. Cogn. Technol. Work **21**(1), 87–98 (2019)
15. Marti, P., Jallais, C., Koustanaï, A., Guillaume, A., Mars, F.: Impact of the driver's visual engagement on situation awareness and takeover quality. Transport. Res. F Traffic Psychol. Behav. **87**, 391–402 (2022)
16. Swain, R., Kaye, S.A., Rakotonirainy, A.: Shared intention and shared awareness for conditional automated driving: an online, randomized video experiment. Traffic Inj. Prev. **26**(4), 398–406 (2025)
17. Morra, L., Lamberti, F., Prattichó, F.G., La Rosa, S., Montuschi, P.: Building trust in autonomous vehicles: role of virtual reality driving simulators in HMI design. IEEE Trans. Veh. Technol. **68**(10), 9438–9450 (2019)
18. Ferreira, J.J., Monteiro, M.S.: What are people doing about XAI user experience? A survey on AI explainability research and practice. Int. Conf. Hum.-Comput. Interact., 56–73 (2020)
19. Korentsides, J., Merwin, E.R., Berger, L., Laskey, L., Winter, S.R., Sobel, B., Keebler, J.R.: The use of artificial intelligence (AI) in the flight deck: enhancing human-AI teamwork in aviation. J. Air Transp. Res. Soc., 100099 (2025)
20. Xavion. Extracted from https://xavion.com/. 27 Jan 2026
21. Menig, A., Becker, N., Kleudgen, J.P.: Investigating the role of an AI-based assistance system for the decision-making process of pilots–an interview study. Transp. Res. Procedia **88**, 167–175 (2025)
22. Würfel, J., Djartov, B., Papenfuß, A., Wies, M.: Intelligent pilot advisory system: the journey from ideation to an early system design of an AI-based decision support system for airline flight decks. In: AHFE (2023)
23. Zhang, Z.T., et al.: Beyond recommendations: from backward to forward AI support of pilots' decision-making process. Proc. ACM Hum.-Comput. Interact. **8**(CSCW2), 1–32 (2024)
24. Orasanu, J., Calderwood, R., Zsambok, C.E.: Decision making in action: models and methods. In: Klein, G.A. (ed.) vol. 3, p. 1. Ablex, Norwood, NJ (1993)

Author Index

W. -C. Li and A. Plioutsias (Eds.): HCII 2026, LNAI 16708, pp. 367–368, 2026.
https://doi.org/10.1007/978-3-032-29459-3

Zeitfracht Medien GmbH
Ferdinand-Jühlke-Straße 7
99095 Erfurt, Deutschland
produktsicherheit@kolibri360.de